Urban America
A History

Urban America
A History
SECOND EDITION

David R.
Goldfield

*University of North Carolina,
Charlotte*

Blaine A.
Brownell

*University of Alabama,
Birmingham*

Houghton Mifflin Company   Boston

Dallas   **Geneva, Illinois**   **Palo Alto**
Princeton, New Jersey

For our parents

Printed in the U.S.A.

Library of Congress Catalog Card Number: 89-80937

ISBN: 0-395-46501-X

ABCDEFGHIJ-A-9543210/89

Text credits

Quotes from Bayrd Still, ed., *Urban America: A History
with Documents* (Boston: Little, Brown and Company,
1974). Reprinted with permission.

Quotes from Jon C. Teaford, *The Twentieth-Century
American City: Problem, Promise, and Reality* (Baltimore: Johns Hopkins University Press, 1986). Reprinted with permission.

Claude McKay, "If We Must Die," from *Selected Poems
of Claude McKay.* Copyright 1981 and reprinted with
the permission of Twayne Publishers, a division of
G. K. Hall & Co., Boston.

Photo credits

Chapter 1: **Page 15:** From *America 1585: The Complete Drawings of John White,* edited by Paul Hulton.
© 1984, The University of North Carolina Press.

Copyright page continues on page 493.

CONTENTS

Preface   xi

Introduction   1

Patterns of Growth: Central Places and Urban Networks   2
Urban Ecology   4
Characteristic Aspects of American Urbanization   4
Predominant Urban Forms in American History   6

PART 1   Seedtime for Urban America: The Colonial Town   10

Chapter 1 First Settlements   13

The First Urban America   13
Spanish and French Settlements: Urbane Outposts   18
Jamestown and Virginia: The First English Settlements   20
New England: Cities on the Hill   25
New York and Philadelphia: The Gridiron Emerges   28
The Carolinas: Rice Planters and English Nostalgia   30
Savannah: A Four-Part Vision   32

Chapter 2 On the Waterfront: Economy and Society in Eighteenth-Century English Colonies   38

    The Atlantic Trade   40
    New Crops and New Markets   41
    Social Classes, Old and New   47
    Precarious Lives   51
    Supporting Institutions: Family, Church, Tavern   53
    Urbanity   56

Chapter 3 Governing the Colonial Town   62

    The Varieties of Disorder   64
    The Response of Local Government   65
    Popular Politics   68
    Towns in the Revolution   70
    External Relationships and Internal Structure   72

PART 2 The Market Place, 1790–1870   76

Chapter 4 Creating a National Urban Economy   81

    Urbanmania in the West   81
    Eastern Cities and Western Clones   84
    Foundations: The Northeastern Regional Economy   86
    Factories in the Fields   87
    Urban Industry and the Changing Nature of Work   91
    Canals and Railroads: New Arteries   95
    Forging a Western Urban Region   97
    New York Takes Charge   102
    Wallflower at the Ball: The Urban South   104
    Political Implications of a National Urban Economy   109

Chapter 5 Different Spaces, Separate Lives   113

    A New Place Called Downtown   114
    The Residential City: Where to Live and How to Get There   118
    Far from the Madding Crowd: The Suburban Ideal   123
    The Home as Sanctuary   128
    Space and Class   131
    Immigrant Cities   134
    Blacks: A Separate Urban Nation   137
    The Drawing Apart of Classes and Cultures   142

Chapter 6 The Burgeoning of Middle-Class Urban Reform

149

The Ideals of Reform	150
City Government and the Business of Reform	151
Public Health: A New Urban Concept	152
The Professionalization of Fire and Police Protection	157
Poverty as a Moral Issue	161
The Search for Open Space: Cemeteries and Parks	166
The City as a Way of Life	172

PART 3   The Radial Center, 1870–1920

178

Chapter 7 Yearning to Breathe Free: Urban Society and the Great Migration

185

Twilight's First Gleaming: Steel-Driving Cities	185
Working Is Not a Living: Labor in the Industrial City	191
A Woman's Work . . .	196
The Web of Poverty	200
The Workers' Response	204
The Foreigners Arrive	207
Ethnic Space: The Neighborhood	212
Making It	215
Blacks: The Forgotten Ethnic Group	221
Racial Space: The Ghetto	226

Chapter 8 The Age of Urban Reform

236

Ward Heelers and Mornin' Glories: Urban Politics in a Diverse Society	236
The Service City: A Progressive Ideal	243
The Technocrat: A New Force in the Cities	245
Helping the Other Half: Housing the Urban Poor	248
Radial Suburbs	259
Radiant Centers	266
The Columbian Exposition and the City Beautiful	274
Urban Planning and the City Efficient	277
The Garden City: Starting from Scratch	279

PART **4** The Vital Fringe, 1920–1970   284

Chapter 9 The First Suburban Decade   289

The Nuclear Home   290
Automobility and the New Metropolis   292
The Urban Economy Decentralizes   296
Shaping the Twentieth-Century Metropolis   302
Los Angeles: The Present as Future   306
Creating a National Urban Culture   309
Organized Crime Incorporates   317
Ethnic Mobility: The Jewish Example   320

**Chapter 10 The Federal Connection: Urban America
in Depression and War**   323

The Great Depression and the American City   323
Putting the Cities Back to Work   327
The New Deal Legacy   334
Cities at War   336

**Chapter 11 Divided Metropolis: City and Suburb
in the Postwar Era, 1945–1970**   342

The Apotheosis of the Suburban Dream   343
Urban Renewal: Towers and Tombs   348
Springtime for Urban America: Images from the Fifties and Sixties   357
The Long, Hot Summers: The Inner City Explodes   360
Federal Urban Initiatives: From Renewal to Conservation 363
The Widening Gap: The City Splits in Two   368

PART **5** The Multicentered Metropolis:
1970 to the Present   374

Chapter 12 Frostbelt and Sunbelt: The Regional Shift 379

The High Costs of Urban Decline   380
The New Federalism: Revenue Sharing and Its Consequences 388
The Rise of the Sunbelt   394
The Newest Immigrants: Hispanics and Asians   400
Shadows on the Sunbelt   405

Chapter 13 Central City and Out-Town: The Metropolitan Shift 410

Urban Recovery: The Story of Two Cities   412
Downtowns: The New Hub of the Knowledge Economy   414
Renovating the Central Cities   416
Neighborhood Preservation   419
The Second City: Separate and Unequal   424
Urban Administration: The Management Metaphor   429
Reagan and the Federal Retreat from Urban Assistance   433
The Multicentered Urban Chain: Out-Towns, Mall-Towns,
    and Conurbations   435
Precedents and Prefigurations   438
Controlling the Leviathan   440
Social Implications of the Multicentered Metropolis   443

Appendix 1 Population and Rank of Largest U.S. Cities, 1790–1986   447

Appendix 2 Suggestions for Further Reading   453

Index   473

P R E F A C E

A simple description of an American city at any particular point in time is usually misleading. The city is a complex and energetic subject. The best and the worst of American life have congregated in the city, and the history of urban America is not merely a history of cities, but a reflection of national history as well.

The Second Edition of *Urban America,* like the First Edition, is distinguished by its emphasis on the spatial relationships within and between cities. This emphasis, a study of the geographical patterns of residential, commercial, political, and cultural development, allows a balanced, flexible examination of the varied aspects of urban life. It permits a comprehensive look at the social, economic, political, and cultural history of the city. At the same time, this edition minimizes its review of spatial theory; many students and instructors told us the theoretical material tended to encumber rather than enlighten.

Once again, our book examines all of the United States. Although most of the major trends in American urban history have been centered in the large cities of the Northeast and the Midwest, we also chart the development of western and southern cities. We pay particular attention to regional differences. Mobile and Milwaukee may have gone through similar stages of development, but their differences are more striking than their similarities. If the variability of the American urban experience makes the formulation of state and national urban policy difficult, it makes writing about American cities almost as treacherous.

The new edition of *Urban America* maintains the organization of the first edition, except that we now cover five, not four, time periods that correspond to the predominance of a certain spatial form: the *cluster,* or the colonial town (pre-1790); the *market place* (1790–1870); the *radial center* (1870–1920); the *vital fringe* (1920–1970); and, the new form this edition discusses, the *multi-centered metropolis* (1970 to the present). This new form is characterized by a vital, though not necessarily dominant, central city and self-contained communities that include a variety of commercial, employment, entertainment, and residential functions.

And we continue to offer a thorough examination of each of the various time periods. For instance, we present more than a cursory discussion of the colonial era, which we view as a crucial period in American urbanization.

Readers will find that this edition contains some notable differences from the first edition. Approximately two-thirds of the book consists of new material. Urban history has been a vibrant and exciting field of inquiry over the past decade, and we have attempted to synthesize much new information and many new trends. For instance, we have broadened and reinterpreted our approach to urban politics and policy, believing that social and economic relationships are better explicated within the context of power and government. We view this as an integrated approach to urban history.

We have also given more attention to the concepts of class and culture. Historians have known about the pluralism of American cities for a long time; the distinctive cultures of different ethnic and racial groups shape and are shaped by the urban experience. More recently, we have discovered that identifiable groups of people we call "classes"—the working class, the middle class, and the elite— also have distinctive cultures. The formation of these cultures is a new theme of the second edition.

Textbook authors rely heavily on what other scholars have written, and we are no exception. Our gratitude and dependence are acknowledged in the section "Suggestions for Further Reading." We are especially thankful for the thoughtful and helpful suggestions provided by our reviewers:

John Bauman, California University of Pennsylvania

Roger Biles, Oklahoma State University

J. William Harris, University of New Hampshire

Anthony J. Kuzniewski, College of the Holy Cross

Marc Levine, University of Wisconsin—Milwaukee

Roger Lotchin, University of North Carolina at Chapel Hill

Eric Monkkonen, University of California, Los Angeles

Seth Scheiner, Rutgers University

Neil Larry Shumsky, Virginia Polytechnic Institute and State University

Jon Teaford, Purdue University

Ray Frankle and his staff at the library of the University of North Carolina at Charlotte were very helpful in securing some recent works, and we appreciate their allowing us to monopolize the library's urban history collection for so long.

Our families provided support and displayed a great deal of patience. We can assure them that the fine meals we had in cities across the country were not exercises in gluttony, but part of the process of creativity. We are grateful to our children for allowing us to rediscover the city yet again. And we dedicate this book to our parents because without them this effort would not have been possible, and because they were our first guides to the city.

D.R.G.

B.A.B.

Urban America
A History

INTRODUCTION

City building in America was often an act of faith. Sometimes, as in colonial New England, the object of that faith was God. More often, the object was economic gain. Whatever motivation prompted each new beginning, the history of American cities is a history of the men and women who molded their cities' destinies and were in turn shaped by their creations.

This book discusses what one scholar phrased "the process of city building over time."[1] To illuminate the process, we examine the physical layout of the city; changes in that layout, or the *spatial order,* have a major impact on the lives of the city's residents. We also examine the city's relationships with other cities and with the nation as a whole. This discussion charts a process of growth and development, decay and transformation.

Geographers and sociologists have been grappling with the subject of American urban development since the early twentieth century, searching for theories that explain the city's internal structure and external relations. No one theory fully explains how cities grow, and some theories have themselves become historical artifacts, firmly rooted in a particular place and time. But the basic questions theories raise and attempt to answer are at the heart of any examination of urbanization: Why are particular businesses and industries located in certain places? Why do the social interactions of entire neighborhoods change during the span of one or two generations? Why do once-thriving commercial areas fall to ruin? Why do successful office parks and shopping malls develop on vacant land on the urban periphery? Why do cities that seem to have every economic advantage lose their dominant positions in their region? And, perhaps most important, why do some cities prosper and others fail?

"The process of city building over time" is not some abstract concept; it is a reality that surrounds you every day. Where do you go to have fun with friends? Where do you prefer to shop? Which areas of your community do you know best—and why? Which areas do you not know well, and which do you avoid? Do you still live in the same house, neighborhood, or city where you were born; if not, why not? When you return to your old neighborhood, what changes do you notice? Do you think of your community as a city? Regardless of whether you have actually visited them, how would you describe certain cities—say, New York, Los Angeles, Chicago, Toledo, El Paso, Salt Lake City? Your answers to these questions form your personal understanding of the city-building process.

The reasons for and consequences of each change in the urban landscape are unique and complex. The new shopping mall along the interstate did not happen by accident, and it was not solely a product of the developers' speculation. A host of factors contributed to its construction: the invention and widespread use of the automobile; federal highway policies that established an interstate system and encouraged new residential construction on the city's outskirts; the specific direction of the flow of population from the core of the city; the attractiveness of real estate investment, which has been prevalent in American urban communities since the eighteenth century; and various shifting patterns of social and consumer behavior.

Likewise, the consequences of the mall's construction will not be limited to the people who use it or the goods sold. The mall will increase land values in its vicinity, create reduced prospects for nearby areas that do not receive similar investments, pose greater difficulties for the mall employees who have to travel longer distances to go to work, and decrease tax revenues for the city's core.

Behind the complexities of individual expressions of the urban experience, however, there are some basic, shared characteristics of the urbanization process. In a broad sense, we can chart how cities evolve.

Patterns of Growth: Central Places and Urban Networks

A fundamental relationship exists between an urban place and the surrounding rural area. Anthropologists refer to this relationship as the *urban-rural continuum:* Small towns reflect distinctly rural characteristics; even the largest cities bear some similarities to surrounding rural areas since raw materials and new populations are drawn from the countryside. The broad context and environment of the city always include the countryside. This is especially true today; urban sprawl and electronic media have forged even closer ties between the countryside and the city.

Our own observations tell us that cities did not spring up at random places in the rural landscape. Early American cities were often located on rivers, railroad lines, or the coast, or in the midst of a rich agricultural area. Their attachment to the lifeblood of trade allowed them to grow and prosper.

A theory constructed in 1933 by Walter Christaller, a German geographer, elaborated on the pattern of urban development. Christaller noted that cities exist as central points for the territory surrounding them. Cities depend on the surrounding territory, or *hinterland,* for food and raw materials. In turn, cities supply processed goods, markets, and a variety of economic, social, administrative, and transportation services to the surrounding area. Christaller's *central place theory* postulates that if population is equally distributed throughout a rural area, a pattern of equally spaced cities will result, each city serving as the heart of a trade area or a hinterland.

Of course, not all cities are central places. But one aspect of Christaller's theory is especially interesting: his notion that the location, size, and functions of a city are directly related to the assets, size, and needs of the area it serves.

Another pattern of urban relationships also exists. Within a country or a large region—the Midwest, for example—cities are connected in various ways to one another. These connections, which most often take the form of transportation or trade, create *urban networks,* or *systems.* Within a network, each city has a specific role or function that can, and usually does, change over time.

Various theories describe these relationships, but the essential points of some are all that need concern us here. For instance, the cities that become larger and more dominant in a network usually enjoy some distinct advantages in economic competition—faster and more numerous sources of information, lower prices, or better and more frequent transportation. Also, the area of a city's economic dominance is partly defined by the distance over which it maintains a price advantage in products or services. In basic terms, if you can buy something cheaper from Chicago than from Kansas City, Chicago gets your business.

American urban history reflects the practical consequences of the price-distance relationship. Cities in the forefront of urban development were almost invariably located close to the best transportation routes, which provided access to markets and raw materials and accommodated shifts in population. The fate of towns bypassed by the railroad is well known. Of course, some market towns that served a limited territory had long lives. But successful cities generally had an edge in transportation, information transmission, and the production and sale of goods and services.

Today, economic advantages are expressed in very different terms than they were in the nineteenth century. We live in a truly national and international marketplace. Information is almost instantly available whether you live in New York, Des Moines, or a suburb of Jackson, Mississippi. The same consumer goods are readily available everywhere at similar prices. Although price-distance factors are less important today, factors such as bank location, city size and economic complexity, the concentration of technological and educational expertise, and the extent of transportation and communication networks remain important. We will have to wait to evaluate the impact of these new economic conditions on the patterns of urbanization in the United States.

Urban Ecology

Just as relationships between cities change, relationships within a city change as well. The study of *urban ecology*—the system of spatial relationships in an urban environment—provides valuable information about a city's stage of development and the lives of its residents.

The city is a complex mechanism—a web of social activities, economic functions, population patterns, and lifestyles arrayed in space. If we imagine the city to be like a biological ecosystem, composed of a complex variety of interrelated elements, we can study the function of these elements and identify the regular patterns involved. Of particular importance are the patterns of social interaction. Where do people meet and exchange information? Which groups cooperate and which compete? Where do certain groups live in relation to other groups?

We quickly realize that the spatial organization of the city reflects its social order. Once we know this, the simplest spatial element can illuminate basic social forms, and the physical outlines of the city become a map of its social and economic landscape. According to one of the best-known American urban analysts, "most if not all cultural changes in society will be correlated with changes in its territorial organization, and every change in the territorial and occupational distribution of the population will effect changes in the existing culture."[2]

As the city grows, the areas within it change, and their relationships shift. An increase in physical distance often means an increase in social separation, and urban dwellers come to function not within the city as a whole but within various distinct parts of it. Thus, social patterns are given form in space.

Early urban analysts described a basic pattern of change: A business and industrial district grows at the city's core, the quality of the residential districts that border the core declines steadily, and higher-class residential districts are built on the city's periphery. Some analysts even suggested that this was the inevitable dynamic of urbanization. But, as we shall see, urban growth was immensely more complex than this.

Characteristic Aspects of American Urbanization

Although cities in the United States are similar to cities everywhere, certain patterns render the American urbanization process distinctive. For example, the consistent tendency in America has been toward urban expansion. In fact, *ur-banization* and *growth* are virtually synonymous in the American consciousness. The abundance of land in the New World, the lure that first attracted settlers, eroded all attempts to build tightly-knit, highly disciplined, and strictly delimited communities. Desire for a homestead and a plot of land, no less an urban phenomenon than a rural one, was a fundamental impetus to the urbanization and suburbanization of the countryside. Technology fueled the process: Americans were usually the first to take maximum advantage of new forms of mobility; the railroad and the automobile are the most obvious examples.

American cities were not created by administrative fiat or royal command, but usually by economic forces and geographical imperatives. Their development was likewise not carefully controlled; it was driven by the desire for land and by the hunger of the huge markets that arose in that quest. Land speculation was a major factor behind the location and development of cities, the creation of urban wealth, the development of new transportation technologies, and the provision of city services (the value of land rose dramatically with the extension of water and sewer lines, paved streets, and police and fire protection). American cities are, perhaps to a greater extent than anywhere else in the world, the products of unrestrained capitalism.

The contrast between the domains of the rich and the poor in many large American cities has often been as vivid as that described by Charles Dickens. One of the most persistent aspects of American urbanization is the appearance of wealth and poverty, progress and deterioration within the same city boundaries. American urbanization is in some respects a "tale of two cities"—or multiple cities—within a city, each reflecting a very different form of urban reality. The mansions along New York's Fifth Avenue cast only the palest light on the nearby slums; resplendent shopping malls provide little comfort for those living in decaying inner-city housing projects. Although various economic theories attempt to explain this dichotomy, perhaps the best explanation is that American urbanization is fundamentally paradoxical, exhibiting the best and worst of American life along with every gradation in between.

One of the most important reasons for the persistence of urban poverty in America is the division among races and classes that has fragmented cities almost from their beginnings. Foreign immigrants have usually found themselves in the bleakest and most crowded sections of the city. African-Americans have suffered a similar fate throughout this country's history. The cultural geography of any American city reveals palpable divisions along ethnic, racial, and economic lines. Even though these barriers have been scaled by many immigrant groups (particularly the ones who are not dark-skinned) and have been reduced by recent government policies and judicial action, they are still formidable obstacles.

Finally, the development of American cities has included various efforts to correct urban ills, foster security and justice, and protect individual interests. Although these efforts are not unique, they can be seen as peculiarly American in that they often result from some perception of a failure of the "American dream." Over time, city governments have become larger and more sophisticated in their attempts to solve problems. And state and federal governments have begun to help with various reform efforts. Once America became an urban nation, its problems became mostly urban in nature.

Predominant Urban Forms in American History

No two cities are alike. Each varies along an endless number of dimensions: rates of development, terrain, population size and composition, problems, challenges, and resources, to name a few. It is dangerous to think of cities as slightly different forms of one phenomenon. If we know one city, we do not know them all.

Cities also change over time, sometimes with great rapidity. The distance between our lives and the lives of the settlers who clustered in small bands in the New World is not just measured by centuries but by an awesome leap in social experience.

Cities do, however, share a number of characteristics and develop in similar ways. We find that certain patterns of urban growth and arrangement are more characteristic of some periods than others, just as certain tools and processes characterize particular technological epochs. The identification of those shared characteristics and broad patterns of change will help us appreciate and comprehend the varieties of the urban experience.

The five parts of this book are organized around five basic urban forms. Although the dates associated with the forms serve as reference points rather than definitive boundaries, each form was predominant at a different stage in U.S. history. You should remember, however, that the processes of change always prevail, and the characteristics of a city are in constant flux. One configuration always contains remnants of the past and seeds for the future.

The five urban forms we focus on are:

1. The *cluster* (from the European settlement of North America to 1790). Early towns in America were to a large extent European towns. Some, like Plymouth and Jamestown, were surrounded by walls according to the European pattern. Others, like Mobile, Jacksonville, New Amsterdam (later New York), and St. Louis were built around fortresses to provide protection and sites for trade. This was another European form, drawn principally from towns in France and Ireland. Residents of these early communities clustered together for secu-

rity, commerce, and social intercourse. In modern terms, the city center (or downtown) *was* the city.

Merchants developed a transatlantic pattern of trade. As they became more established, they began to venture into their hinterlands as well. Merchants not only built an urban economy, they also played a major role in ordering the life of the city, from making fire regulations to influencing public opinion. Geography may have dictated the urban form in the early years of settlement, but the merchant was responsible for the growth and style of the colonial town.

2. The *market place* (1790–1870). Building on a commercial economic base, the merchants took the colonial town into a period of rapid population growth. The steam engine enabled cities to expand their economic spheres, and cities on navigable waterways took maximum advantage of the new technology. Coastal cities continued to dominate, but interior ports like Cincinnati, Richmond, and Pittsburgh also achieved prominence. In addition, the development of industrial technology accounted for the rise of several New England cities. The major shift within the urban system was the formation of a national economy centered at New York.

Within the city, economic growth caused the expansion of downtown, the sorting out of some economic activities by location, and the development of distinctive residential districts that reflected social stratification. The city was still quite small (1½ to 2 miles square, usually), even though transportation technologies continued to develop.

Despite the relatively small space, a great deal of movement occurred within and to and from the city. Transience and geographic mobility were common themes of mid-nineteenth-century urban life. Ethnic and racial diversity increased and created additional tensions. More than ever, merchants attempted to order this volatile situation through the use of local government.

3. The *radial center* (1870–1920). The regionalization of the American urban system began during this period. Cities such as Chicago, St. Louis, and eventually San Francisco achieved regional economic supremacy and, on the national level, a growing parity with New York. A degree of urban specialization developed, with particular cities serving particular functions. Industrial cities, dominant early in this period, began to fare more poorly than cities that emphasized insurance, finance, or commerce.

The internal structure of the city was characterized by significant expansion, typically along transportation routes radiating from the city center (hence the name of this configuration). A growing affluence, the tremendous influx of racial and ethnic groups into the city center, and improved transportation technology spurred the movement outward. As the city expanded, it became segregated. Downtown areas became primarily retail, wholesale, or financial. Some small industries clung to the edges of downtown, but larger industries moved to the periphery for more and cheaper space. Residential neighborhoods became more clearly defined along economic, racial, and ethnic lines. Residential mobility continued, and some social mobility occurred, though it was much rarer. Reformers sought to alleviate economic and social problems without disturbing the existing social order.

4. The *vital fringe* (1920–1970).   The regionalization that began in the previous period continued, though New York and Chicago maintained a shaky dominance in the national economy. The most significant development in the national urban system was the emergence of southern and western cities as centers of regional dominance.

Specialization accelerated as industrial cities continued their decline and cities whose economy was based on service activities—finance, real estate, insurance, and administration—increased in importance or held their ground. Natural advantages such as climate and topography were also spurs for urban growth, much as geographic location had influenced urbanization during the first wave of settlement.

The physical expansion of the city was so pronounced that the suburbs frequently had more political power and a larger population than the city center. Ever-increasing affluence, the larger presence of racial and ethnic groups, and advances in transportation technology continued to hasten the outward movement. A new featured player, the federal government, encouraged settlement on the fringe of the city through an array of post–World War II policies that stimulated the national economy. Commercial centers multiplied throughout the suburbs, weakening the traditional economic dominance of downtown. The majority of metropolitan jobs were located in the suburbs by 1970. Spatial segregation solidified, as black and Hispanic ghettos expanded toward the urban periphery.

By the end of the period, urban settlements were spread over much of the country. Figures from the 1970 census revealed that for the first time since the nineteenth century, non-metropolitan areas were growing more rapidly than metropolitan areas. Although these figures were a sign of the decline of the traditional core-and-periphery arrangement, urban culture and influence were being spread through the communications and transportation revolution. The traditional configuration was being replaced by a new urban form.

5. The *multicentered metropolis* (1970 to the present).   The most recent urban form is characterized by a transformed core, more specialized in terms of function, and the emergence of specialized clusters of businesses, industries, and residences throughout a larger urban area. The core remains important but is less dominant and inclusive. Its significance is related primarily to the realms of

finance, legal services, government, and culture, though it also contains a disproportionate number of the area's minorities and poor.

The city center has two faces. One is a mass of deteriorating neighborhoods, dingy commercial strips, and overcrowded projects. The other is a group of shiny glass skyscrapers, decorated plazas, multi-purpose civic centers, and, frequently, stations for rapid transit lines that serve outlying commercial districts. The city center is no longer the only center, but one of several *nodes,* or clusters of activities, that define the metropolis. Other nodes include residential suburbs (with their own commercial districts), industrial parks, and offices and hotels surrounding a large shopping mall.

Some of these nodes were at one time "mini-cities" or "out-towns," different from traditional suburbs in that they contained housing, workplaces, retail shops, entertainment centers, and most other elements of urban life. These mini-cities were not swallowed up by a growing metropolitan region. Instead, they developed and flourished to meet the particular needs of certain economic groups.

The multicentered metropolis is more fragmented than any earlier urban form. Greater distances separate ethnic and economic groups. An inclusive public policy can no longer address all the metropolis's needs. Federal government policies and funds are still critically important to beleaguered mayors and city councils, but such help is increasingly focused on specific purposes—like encouraging business development in inner-city neighborhoods—rather than the revivification of the metropolitan area as a whole. Some cities have plunged into bankruptcy; others are hovering at the brink. The split between the wealthy and impoverished segments of urban life worsens by degrees.

Within the framework of the five urban forms, this book describes the social, economic, demographic, and political forces that affected and continue to affect the city-building process. The impact of these forces varies from period to period, so our coverage of particular forces will vary as well. We will not try to define the American city. Our goal is to show how and why settlements in America have changed over time, to trace a rich source of American history.

Notes

1. Roy Lubove, "The Urbanization Process: An Approach to Historical Research," *Journal of the American Institute of Planners* 33 (January 1967): 33.
2. Robert E. Park, *Human Communities* (New York: Free Press, 1952), p. 14.

PART 1

Seedtime for Urban America:

The Colonial Town

The making of urban America was the continuation of a process, not a new beginning. The Europeans came from country farms, modest villages, and great cities. The settlements they established in the New World were not so much innovations as they were adaptations of what they left behind them and what they found already built in North America. They did not create, in one historian's unfortunate metaphor, "cities in the wilderness."[1] The Indian villages that dotted the landscape informed the structure of the early colonial towns, which were also a blend of Old World urban and rural forms. Most urban residents cultivated the land, especially in the first decades of settlement. Later, farms sustained the towns and the growing linkages between city and countryside helped to build a thriving colonial economy that grew to international dimensions.

The colonial towns of America were constantly in the process of becoming something else, evolving into different forms, functions, and societies. Three themes dominated this process of change: First, the towns took their shape from the land. The key feature that distinguished them from their European counterparts was the abundance of, and access to, land—acres of it. Second, by the eighteenth century a social structure emerged in the seaport towns that was stratified but mobile; individuals moved up and down the social ladder and into and out of towns with relative ease. Finally, new institutions emerged to order the urban fragments and reduce the friction between them. Local government was probably the most prominent of these institutions.

By the time of the American Revolution, the outlines of nineteenth-century urban America were becoming clear—the development of an urban core region in the Northeast, the ordering of urban space into distinctive land and social uses, and the emergence of social classes. The colonial towns were not miniature modern cities, however. The largest, New York and Philadelphia, probably had no more than 25,000 residents by 1775, compared with London's population of 800,000 at the same time. Nor did the smaller interior settlements experience all the internal and external changes that took place in the colonial seaports, though they were influenced by these changes. Finally, the colonial era did not fix the boundaries of American cities and regions for all time. Urbanization is a dynamic process that builds on the past but is not permanently bound to it. Tracing this complex interplay of tradition and change not only demonstrates the value of urban history, it tells the story of urban America. Part 1, the "beginning" of this story, puts us squarely in the middle of the process.

Notes

1. Carl Bridenbaugh, *Cities in the Wilderness: Urban Life in America, 1625–1742* (New York: The Ronald Press, 1938).

First Settlements

Europeans stepping onto American soil for the first time encountered a new land and a new people. The newcomers—explorers, adventurers, missionaries, and colonists—arrived with certain ideas about how life should be lived. These ideas had been shaped by the world they left behind, a world of finite resources, limited opportunities, and little tolerance for ethnic, religious, racial, and social differences. But as Europeans soon learned, sometimes the hard way, America was different, and early European settlements reflected the tensions between Old World ideals and New World realities.

The First Urban America

America's first urban dwellers were the thousands of ethnically, culturally, and linguistically diverse groups that the Europeans dubbed "Indians." For centuries before the Spaniards first crossed the Atlantic, these peoples scattered over the face of the North American continent had typically lived in small agricultural villages. In the most sedentary of these settlements, located in the southern portion of today's United States, the numbers of inhabitants ranged from fifty to several thousand. Residents tended garden plots behind their houses while waiting for their crops of corn, beans, and squash to ripen in the main fields on the outskirts of town. Their dwellings were round or rectangular wooden structures with thatched roofs. Most villages had a central square with three or four buildings in which residents conducted the community's business or welcomed visiting dignitaries. If the village was especially large or important, a circular town hall dominated the square with room for as many as several hundred people. Close by, a 50-foot pole used for ball games or displaying enemy scalps rose above the village.

Because the early inhabitants of North America were nonliterate, much of our knowledge about these communities has reached us through the filter of the first white observers, writers and artists, as well as from archaeological evidence unearthed centuries later. In 1585, Sir Walter Raleigh led an expedition to the New World at the request of Queen Elizabeth I. The settlement he founded on the coast of North Carolina, Roanoke Island, was short lived. But a visual chronicle of the Carolina Algonquians survives from the pen of the artist John White, who accompanied Raleigh. White's drawings indicate that the Algonquians lived in two distinct kinds of urban settlements. One was an open village, the other a village enclosed by a palisade. Both types of villages contained between 100 and 200 inhabitants who lived in rectangular wooden houses. The houses were large—72 feet by 36 feet—and residents slept on benches arranged around the walls. The longhouses faced common open areas where religious ceremonies and athletic competitions took place. In Secoton, one of the villages White sketched, agriculture was an especially dominant activity. The Indians cultivated at least three varieties of corn next to their dwellings, and they grew tobacco. There is some fragmentary evidence that larger towns existed—such as the capital, Chawanoac, with more than 1,000 inhabitants—but we have no visual record of them.

When the English established their first permanent settlement at Jamestown (just north of Roanoke Island in the colony of Virginia) in 1607, Captain John Smith reported that a powerful Indian chief, Powhatan, had consolidated at least two dozen of these villages into a large, centralized chiefdom. The broader Chesapeake region held more than 200 Indian villages tied loosely together by the numerous streams and rivers that penetrated the interior. According to Smith, the dwellings were similar to those John White encountered two decades earlier. Rather than opening on squares or other areas of general activity, however, these houses were placed in the midst·of fields ranging from 20 to 200 acres. The houses were situated close together. A village consisted of as few as two, up to as many as 100, of these dwellings. Occasionally, a small grove of trees separated individual houses. Formal religious ceremonies were conducted in separate communities inhabited only by priests.

Although the importance of agriculture implied a settled existence, southern Indians were considerably more mobile than John White's placid scenes implied. They altered their residence patterns frequently for political, economic, and seasonal reasons. During periodic tribal wars, they built their houses fairly close together. Other times, they preferred a more dispersed settlement pattern that allowed space for grazing livestock as well as outbuildings for their crops. The

Secoton

An Indian village on the Pamlico River in present-day North Carolina, as drawn by John White in July 1585. Note the typical lightweight pole-and-mat construction of the houses, the ceremonial dance around a circle of posts, the fire labeled "the place of solemne prayer," and the three fields of corn in different stages of cultivation.

search for new lands and richer hunting and fishing grounds led to new village locations as well. Indians preferred open areas for summer settlements, but some groups repaired to the woods in the winter.

Further north, where the climate inhibited the cultivation of a variety of garden crops, the native peoples of North America led even more mobile lives. As John Josselyn, an Englishman exploring Maine in 1674, commented, "Towns they have none, being always removing from one place to another for conveniency of food." Accustomed to more sedentary patterns back home, the English found this mobility disconcerting and were shocked to find Indian women "troubled like snails to carry their houses on their backs."[1]

Comments by white observers on the easy mobility of the Indians may have derived from other motives as well. The English justified their land claims by noting that Indians only used the land temporarily. As Massachusetts Bay founder John Winthrop reasoned even before he had ever set foot on American soil, "They [the Indians] inclose noe Land, neither have any setled habytation, nor any tame Cattle to improve the Land by . . . soe as if we leave them sufficient for their use we may lawfully take the rest, there being more than enough for them and us."[2] Not content with usurping land rights, the Massachusetts Bay authorities eventually established "praying towns" to convert the Indians to Christian civilization and end their peripatetic lifestyle.

In the Southwest, Spanish explorers encountered Indians who resided in communities that they dubbed *pueblos*. In these agricultural settlements that doubled as religious centers, dwellings rose to five stories; the floors were connected by ladders projecting from individual apartments. After they established Santa Fe, New Mexico, as a headquarters in 1610, Roman Catholic priests fanned out into the pueblo communities to conduct missionary work. In the meantime, Spanish lay authorities found the pueblos a convenient source of labor and taxation.

We can only guess at the size of most Indian towns in North America. A few, such as Cofitachiqui and Mabila in the Southeast, probably had populations of several thousand people or more. Cahokia, located across the Mississippi River from modern-day St. Louis, covered 6 square miles and featured more than 100 mounds of different sizes and shapes. The mounds apparently had two uses. Priests conducted their ceremonies in temples erected on top; leading families also lived on the mound tops, a fact that indicates that native peoples in areas beyond the Appalachian mountains possessed hierarchical social organizations.

The Cahokia mounds and the southwestern pueblos imply a more settled existence than was apparent among native peoples in the East. But the evidence presented by white observers on the temporary nature of eastern Indian settlements should not obscure the important fact that the cultural roots of these sites ran deep even if their specific locations were variable. Portable longhouses were the structural foundations of native culture. The presence of several generations of an extended family within these longhouses ensured the transmission of native culture. It is possible to imagine how this might have occurred among, say, the Iroquois of upstate New York some 500 years ago. On a cold winter night in the longhouse, eight to ten children wrapped in animal skin robes are seated on lower bunks around a blazing fire as an elderly storyteller begins to speak. The children listen in rapt attention. The story is entertaining and, at the same time, it delivers a cultural lesson. This scene is repeated throughout the winter—the storytelling season—because during these months the serpents and monsters who are often the villains of these tales are fast asleep and cannot take offense at what is said about them.

Space and structure have functional and cultural dimensions. What a people build and how they arrange it, internally and externally, reflects what and who they are. As the basic structural component of many eastern Indian villages, the longhouse had its utilitarian advantages—it could house members of an extended family under one roof and its wooden pole construction made it highly portable—but it played an important cultural role as well. For some Indian groups, cultural heritage was one of the few permanent features of their lives.

Decimated by disease after contact with the Spanish and their European successors and pulled apart by intertribal warfare, most of the Indian settlements of North America were gone by the end of the seventeenth century. But their presence is nonetheless important because these villages and their inhabitants were often the first points of contact for European settlers. When the newcomers built their communities, they sought advice and borrowed ideas from the locals, and consequently found themselves doing things they had never done in the Old World: using soft wood for house construction, building palisaded fortifications (rows of wooden posts sharpened at the top); and cultivating crops such as corn and tobacco. All these practices reflected Indian influence. In a subtler way, Indian settlements presaged a major fact of American urbanization—the abundance of open land. The Indians' easy mobility would not have been possible in Europe, where land was a scarce resource and owned by a relative few. Abundance encouraged transience and a proliferation of towns—two characteristics that would sharply distinguish them from European settlements. The ready access to land also modified the stark demarcation between city and countryside that existed in Western Europe, where town walls defined the separation. Even in the palisaded Indian towns, the movement between town and farm was easy. The town provided social, religious, and political sustenance, while the soil offered livelihood. The Indian village, then, was not only a precursor of European urban settlement in the New World, but its prototype as well. It offered Europeans, especially the English, the kind of balanced environment that was disappearing in the rapidly urbanizing Old World. Europeans did not, of course, set out consciously to recreate Indian settlements, but the abundance of land and the wealth it yielded worked the same influence on the new arrivals that it had on those who came before.

Spanish and French Settlements: Urbane Outposts

The Spanish were inveterate city dwellers. Their New World holdings made up an "empire of towns."[3] By the first decade of the seventeenth century, this urban empire had reached what is now the southern border of the United States, stretching from Santa Fe to St. Augustine. Though the Spanish distinguished three types of settlements—*missiones,* or religious outposts; *presidios,* military garrisons; and *pueblos,* civil settlements for trade and colonization—the functions of these settlements were often mixed. Their forms merged as well: a Spanish soldier, citizen, or missionary felt quite at home walking the straight streets of these villages and gathering with colleagues in the large central plaza in the shadow of the church. The town boundaries frequently included an adjacent rural area with lands held privately by townsmen and perhaps an Indian agricultural settlement. Beyond lay what the Spanish called *confusión,* the wilderness, the land beyond the order and civilization of town life.

Some of these borderlands communities became key outposts in the vast Spanish American empire. St. Augustine, established in 1565 by Pedro Menéndez de Avilés, became an important base for Spanish expansion up the Atlantic coast and, not incidentally, to thwart French colonial intentions in the area. The first settlers Menéndez brought with him were an emblem of the variety of activities conducted in a Spanish town: there were soldiers, farmers, artisans, and their wives, and black slaves. St. Augustine served as a base for founding settlements as far north as the Chesapeake, including a prosperous trading community, Santa Elena, in what would become South Carolina. Between Santa Elena and St. Augustine, the Spanish established mission towns, walled communities that resembled to a remarkable degree the configuration and aspect of the Indian agricultural villages. Sometimes the Spanish merely adapted existing Indian settlements for their own purposes. A wooden cross now challenged the game pole for dominance, and a church joined the council house in the town square. At least in the physical components, it was not difficult for the Spanish to adjust to the Indian way of urban life, and vice versa.

The barren Atlantic Coast beaches yielded Spain little except a temporary strategic advantage that the French and the English eventually managed to erode with the establishment of their own settlements and through successful military forays. The decimation of the Indian population destroyed the workforce necessary to support Spanish settlements, and French and English privateers plucked lucrative cargoes from the Spanish almost at will. A weakened Spanish empire withdrew from "la Florida" (the name Spain gave to the territory from St. Augustine north to the Chesapeake) to concentrate on protecting the borderlands area from the Gulf Coast to California, especially from the French.

Santa Fe, in present-day New Mexico, was one such defensive outpost in the western borderlands. Founded in 1610, this town reflected the importance of land in attracting settlers to the outermost reaches of the Spanish empire. Each resident received two 1-acre lots for a house and garden, as well as a separate vegetable garden and land for vineyards and olive groves on the town periphery. Residents also received four 106-acre land grants for general farming. In return, the settler agreed to remain in Santa Fe for ten years. Life in Santa Fe reflected a deliberate balance between the public and the private. Residences were clustered closely together. Behind the three-foot-thick adobe brick walls (a climate-adapted feature borrowed from the pueblo-dwelling Indians), however, privacy reigned, and life focused on the interior patio where a citizen could relax unobserved by his neighbors or passersby. Public life centered on the plaza, which served as the community meeting place, market, refuge for livestock should Indians attack, and site of religious observances and fiestas. Together, house and plaza framed and defined the lives of the Spanish colonists, representing order and civilization amid the "sterile chaos" of the arid high desert surrounding them.[4]

In contrast to the Spanish, the French focused their attention on North America, founding the cities of Quebec and Montreal and sending traders and missionaries deep into the Mississippi Valley. The fortified outpost of Detroit, established in 1701, closely resembled the *bastide* towns of southern France with their gridiron street patterns and elaborate fortress walls. The original town burned to the ground, however, and was later rebuilt by the Americans. Fort Duquesne, constructed on the present site of Pittsburgh, and St. Louis were also fortified French settlements that did not significantly expand until after the Revolutionary War.

By the early eighteenth century, French settlers were moving into the area that comprises present-day Illinois. They established Kaskaskia (named after a local tribe) as an Indian mission settlement on the Mississippi River in 1703. By the 1740s, the French residents of Kaskaskia, requiring more arable land, moved across the river and founded Sainte Geneviève. The new town reflected the close-knit nature of New France urban settlements; at the same time it also borrowed features of the Spanish borderlands settlements. Both tradition and the need for security dictated the clustering of houses at the center of town. The dwellings were one-story log houses. The house lot usually included a barn, a poultry house, a slave cabin, and other outbuildings. There was enough space for a modest garden, an orchard, and a flower garden. A palisade enclosed the lot, providing the resident with privacy. The church also stood at the center of town. Beyond the village lay common agricultural lands; beyond that, common woodlots. The community generated its livelihood from shipping wheat to the new French community located at New Orleans.

The French decision to establish towns in the lower Mississippi region resulted from a developing imperial plan to extend their control from the Gulf of St. Lawrence to the Gulf of Mexico and monopolize the rich fur trade in the lands between. The Spanish were active again in the Gulf of Mexico, and the English were probing the interior from their position along the Atlantic coast. In response to these threats, within a twenty-year period the French founded three towns with access to the Gulf—Biloxi, Mobile, and, in 1718, New Orleans.

New Orleans became the administrative center of France's lower Mississippi empire, which they called Louisiana. The town lay in the crescent of the Mississippi River with access to the Gulf. The plan of New Orleans reflected its role as both a military outpost and an administrative center. In its early years, at least, the town's commercial functions were secondary. A wall girdled part of the town, enclosing a rather monotonous forty-four-block gridiron street system broken primarily by the Place d'Armes (now Jackson Square), which functioned much as the plaza in Spanish settlements. St. Louis Cathedral dominated the Place with its imposing white presence, flanked by government buildings and, along the riverfront, commercial establishments. This ensemble of structures, grouped around the modest square, has been called the "most important architectural plaza in the United States" because of its style and coherence.[5] Behind the Place d'Armes lay the residential areas dotted with homes raised on pillars with verandas wrapped around them, features adapted to the hot and humid climate of the Mississippi delta.

The French, like the Spanish, were town dwellers, and sought to make their New World outpost as urbane as possible. And, indeed, if you had visited New Orleans, say, in 1740, you would have encountered an abundance of cafés and ballrooms as well as a crowded calendar of social and religious events. For all its liveliness, however, the town remained an artificial creation that was never able to sustain itself, dependent on frequent transfusions of supplies and funds from the Caribbean settlement of Saint Domingue. Only after the Americans took over in 1803 would New Orleans realize its full economic potential as the gateway to some of the richest land in the nation.

Jamestown and Virginia: The First English Settlements

Ironically, the French and the Spanish, Europe's great town builders, ultimately failed to establish thriving, self-sustaining cities in the present-day United

States, yet the English, who glorified country life, succeeded in planting an urban civilization in the New World. The irony, in fact, has a double edge. Though the English were successful in establishing towns, the communities eventually bore little resemblance to the models of urban life the colonists brought with them. The abundance of land and the means to obtain it reshaped both English perceptions and the towns they built.

After some halting and unfortunate experiences at colony planting along the North Carolina coast in the 1580s, the Virginia Company of London established Jamestown in 1607. As a private venture, Jamestown was a commercial enterprise from the beginning, though its blessing from the Crown indicated a strategic element as well, for Spain had claimed the area. Though Jamestown may have had a good location for military defense, its swampy surroundings did not provide a sound agricultural base and the colony struggled in its early years. Within a decade, however, tobacco cultivation began to support the settlers, though the town itself remained a tiny outpost. As the countryside gradually came to be the wealth of Virginia, even after a century of settlement Jamestown had not grown "beyond a disheveled village."[6]

Tobacco enabled Jamestown to survive—barely—but the town's continued existence owed more to its administrative functions. After Williamsburg became colony capital in the 1690s, the swamp slowly reclaimed Jamestown. Jamestown's unfavorable location combined with the many deep rivers penetrating into the colony's interior meant that the potentially lucrative tobacco trade could bypass the town altogether. Because tobacco required no lengthy storage or processing but could simply be cut, cured, packed, and shipped directly from the plantation, a central collection point was unnecessary. Jamestown's fate seemed to herald a colony without towns.

Contemporaries thought as much and regretted the absence of urban civilization in Virginia. In 1705, Robert Beverley, a first-generation Virginian, lamented that his compatriots "have not any one Place of Cohabitation among them that may reasonably bear the Name of a Town." The results of this unfortunate circumstance were a lapse in both crafts and manners, a reversion to a "natural" state that may have been fine for Indians, but would not do for Englishmen. Beverley attributed this settlement pattern to "the Advantage of the many Rivers, which afforded a commodious Road for Shipping at every Man's Door." Two decades later, an English-born minister living in the colony described the scene in much the same manner, but without Beverley's judgmental rhetoric. The Reverend Hugh Jones noted that Virginians had "neither the interest nor inclinations . . . to cohabit in towns . . . every plantation affording the owner the provision of a little market."[7]

English authorities were also unhappy with the settlement patterns of their Virginian subjects and from time to time issued directives to force the colonials to establish towns. The English were less concerned about the absence of urbanity in their New World colony than they were about the loss of revenue from a commerce scattered over hundreds of miles of inland rivers and plantations. It was easier to monitor trade in centralized collection points—towns.

Despite these expressions of discomfort from observers and Crown alike, Virginians themselves were not opposed to town life. Their attitude on the subject was simply different from that of other Englishmen. Virginia towns reflected the economic and geographic realities of the new environment, both in form and function. Colonial Virginians appreciated the efficacy of towns; they recognized that urbanization could generate a diverse economy by promoting crafts and making possible the marketing of a variety of crops, thus stimulating the agricultural sector. By the late seventeenth century, planters were well aware of the fickle nature of international markets and the dangers of becoming too dependent on one crop. Also, some of the more productive tobacco planters favored the establishment of a few central collection points for the inspection and shipping of tobacco. This move would introduce a measure of quality control and enhance their product overseas.

In 1680 and again in 1705, Virginians passed their own legislation to encourage town development for these purposes. Despite their oft-stated wish for town settlement in Virginia, however, the English suspended these measures. Queen Anne explained that the statutes were "detrimental by drawing the inhabitants off from their planting tobacco in the country to the cohabiting and setting up handicraft trades."[8] The Queen's reasoning indicates why England's attempts to enforce its Parliament's town acts were never very serious. Colonial manufactured products would compete with English goods, and any diversification by Virginia planters would jeopardize a vast mercantile and financial network in England constructed from the tobacco trade.

The case of Williamsburg underscores these points. Although settlers had been present in the area as early as 1633, it was not until the chartering of the College of William and Mary in 1693 that interest in a formal urban settlement grew. Virginia planters, anticipating English objections in chartering a town that could promote mercantile and manufacturing pursuits, carefully framed their petition to state that the new town would be strictly a political and cultural center. Williamsburg would become the new capital of the colony, and the College would be its cultural centerpiece. The town plan reflected these purposes. It was a rectilinear plan centered on a broad avenue (Duke of Gloucester Street) that would give focus to the two major institutions of the town. At the western end of the avenue, two diagonal roads converged on the College, creating either the letter "W" or "M" (depending on perspective). At the eastern end of the avenue stood the capitol building. A century later, twin focal points connected by a broad avenue would reappear in Pierre L'Enfant's plan for another new capital—Washington, D.C.

The plan embodied a "celebration of authority—secular, spiritual, and cultural," and the structures that sprang from these ideals were mathematically precise, balanced, and symmetrical. The buildings reflected both an internal and an external harmony. The governor's mansion or "Palace," completed in 1720, was a fine example of the symmetry of Georgian design. A formal garden and elaborate wrought iron gates complemented this portrait of order and authority. This was no "disheveled" Jamestown; it was the capital and ceremonial center of a confident colony within a secure empire.

Yet despite its grand pretensions Williamsburg became an early example, often repeated in ensuing decades, of a town that never quite lived up to its plan. An elastic settlement bubbling with energy and life when the colonial legislature—the House of Burgesses—met in quarterly sessions, Williamsburg was as languid as a steamy summer afternoon during the rest of the year. The colonials' promise that the town would function only as a political and cultural center proved too accurate, as Tidewater planters ignored it as a potential market or shipping center. As early as the 1740s, Virginians began to agitate for the removal of the capital to a more propitious interior location, preferably Richmond. Demographic trends favored a capital further inland as well as a site that would be more conducive to economic enterprise. As William Gooch, a supporter of the Richmond location, put it: "Williamsburg was in so bad a situation for Trade, that it had not hitherto flourished, and there was no Likelihood it ever would, to the Advantage of the colony."[9] Gooch's analysis served notice that politics and culture were fine, but city making meant profit taking in America. It also did not hurt Richmond's cause that William Byrd II, planter and gentleman, had a strong financial interest in the project. His rather unimaginative grid plan for the town did not measure up to the innovative style of Williamsburg, but Byrd's aim was to sell town lots, not to frame an ideal.

Byrd's interest in urban development was not unique among Virginia's leading planters. In fact, his colleagues had managed to landscape the colony with quite a number of towns, despite the sometimes open displeasure of the Crown. Though England had struck down both the 1680 and 1705 Town Acts, the interim between passage and rejection enabled Virginians to begin the process of town building, an activity they allegedly avoided. These were hardly metropolises, of course, but they compared favorably to urban settlements in other parts of the colonies. Urbanna, in Middlesex County, a beneficiary of the 1680 act, encompassed at its highest point of growth "no more than thirty houses, a hundred-odd buildings if all its kitchens, warehouses, stores, and sundry outbuildings were counted."[10] As with many similar and even larger settlements throughout the colonies, the town was "an extension of the countryside." And the edges between urban and rural, town and country, remained undefined.

The 1680 Town Act also led to what became the colony's largest city, Norfolk, which grew to over 1,000 inhabitants by the time of the Revolution. Norfolk owed its growth to the fact that it had become an outlet for the export of wheat and corn, commodities that, unlike tobacco, needed storage and processing facilities.

Besides the town acts, the Warehouse Act of 1730 was another major legislative boost to town building. The purpose of this legislation, passed by the Burgesses, was to regulate the quality of tobacco in such a way that the wild price fluctuations that characterized the international market could be moderated. At forty designated locations (chosen by leading local planters), inspectors would place their imprimatur on each grower's crop. The act introduced quality control and at the same time funneled vast quantities of tobacco into central locations where merchants gathered the crop and shipped it to Britain. Stores, houses, and various services grew up around the warehouses. Small and middling planters stopped patronizing larger planters for seed, tools, and dry goods and began to visit these warehouse towns, sustaining them if not actually adding to their development.

The colonial government fostered the growth of towns in Virginia in other ways. Parish churches and county courts, the basic institutions of English town settlement, had sprung up at country crossroads and were soon joined by taverns and a scattering of shops and houses. Each time the legislature created a county, the basic unit of government in Virginia, it automatically established a new town as the county seat. Though local proprietors (who frequently lived in the older areas of the colony) invariably decided the location of these county seats, they were usually in or near the center of the county, equally accessible from all areas (or, considering the poor condition of the roads, equally inaccessible). Because the large planters usually served as county court justices, they also planned the roads, which meant that the location of the courthouse would be chosen for its convenience to their plantations. Like Williamsburg, the county seats were elastic communities, bustling with activity on court days and Sundays, blending into the quiet countryside at other times. Because they rarely doubled as warehouse towns, these settlements had few economic activities to combine with their essentially religious and administrative functions.

By the 1750s, settlers moved west into the Piedmont and Valley regions of Virginia, establishing county courthouse towns as they went; along the rivers, warehouse towns served the interior farmlands, and towns further east, such as Falmouth, Dumfries, and Alexandria, supplied the major needs of the new settlers. With the exception of Norfolk, all types of towns in colonial Virginia were roughly the same size, containing scarcely more than a few hundred inhabitants. That contemporary observers could overlook them is not surprising. But these small settlements carried on the governmental and commercial functions associated with urban centers and played an important role in the colony's political and economic life.

Early Virginians sought to extract resources from the land, and they established their base at Jamestown to further that end. Towns became distinctly subsidiary to plantations, which were self-contained communities in their own right. Technically, any farm was a "plantation," but the term eventually referred only to larger units with slaves, outbuildings, and a main house. Plantations produced most of the crafts and goods a small town could offer. Gunston Hall, George Mason's estate, for example, included carpenters, coopers, blacksmiths, shoemakers, spinners, weavers, and even a distiller. Virginia's towns derived from the plantation: as a speculative venture carried on by planter-capitalists, as a place to pursue the policies deemed beneficial to planter interests, or as a center to market and inspect the source of the planter's livelihood — tobacco. As tobacco moved westward through the colony, so did the towns. (And Richmond would later emerge as the new capital during the Revolution precisely because the voracious land appetite of tobacco cultivation required a more convenient place to do the business of government.)

Towns everywhere owed their existence to the farm. But it seldom happened that *all* urban places within a given jurisdiction could trace their origins back to the countryside. That was true in Virginia. Another unusual feature was that the colony's elite rarely if ever resided in town but preferred their country estates, something an Englishman of similar means would find difficult to comprehend. The hospitality for which Virginians became famous occurred almost exclusively on the plantations. Towns were dull by comparison. The bright lights of Virginia burned in the countryside, not in town. Civilization and culture, long associated with urban life, now had a rural locus. In effect, the Virginians had turned the need for cities on its head—as other colonists, before they were through, would also turn traditional conceptions of urbanization topsy-turvy.

New England: Cities on the Hill

To an Old World eye, there was little traditional about New England urban design, either. In Plymouth in 1620 and especially in Massachusetts Bay a decade later, colonists sought to establish cities of God that would enable them to live Christian lives. Town planning was crucial to this religious purpose because a community of saints had to have both its physical as well as spiritual manifestation. Accordingly, the casual dispersion of the population into the countryside that characterized the settlement of Virginia would not do for the Puritans. The devout colonists did not, however, abandon the countryside. Many early settlers came from agricultural villages in England, and the communities they built in Massachusetts and in other parts of what became New England reflected their rural origins. The town's layout also reflected the necessity of providing food.

Each family received a garden plot in town as well as at least one parcel of farmland in adjacent fields. Households shared common pastures and woodlands. The New England town common was, in a sense, a very scaled-down version of the plaza or place. It was typically a grassy area set aside for common grazing. The meeting house, a simple structure, stood near the common and contained the town's religious and political functions; homes and shops framed the common. The compactness of the New England town did not diminish the fact that it was primarily agricultural. The household, the basic social unit of English country life, performed that function here as well. Visitors in the early years of settlement (1630s) often commented on the easy juxtaposition of "faire houses" and "fruitful gardens" in these "fair and handsome Country-Towne[s]."[11]

John Winthrop, the leader of the expedition to Massachusetts Bay in 1630, had promised that "Wee shall be as a Citty upon a Hill."[12] He also believed that God and Mammon could be reconciled in this holy community—that colonists living in the light of the Lord would use their property and wealth in godly ways. In this expectation Winthrop was as unrealistic as those early Virginia colonists who had hoped to extract gold from the marshes around Jamestown, and his disillusionment was swift. Within two months of his arrival in Boston, he complained that Satan was bending "his forces against us . . . so that I thinke heere are some persons who never shewed so much wickednesse in England as they have doone heer."[13] Rather than settling in one town, his colonists dispersed into many. The abundance of land that made this mobility possible soon proved the general undoing of the communal spirit. Within Boston, the city on a hill, the profits from real estate and the press of population led in fact to a literal leveling of all hills save Beacon, and that was considerably reduced. Land meant wealth, and wealth meant status, and soon Boston and the surrounding communities evinced wide variations in wealth and status that further undermined the interconnectedness of settlers.

By the mid-1630s, Boston was becoming the economic hub of a growing New England region and attracted a diversity of newcomers, many of whom had not the faintest notions of Winthrop's original intent. Initially, church and community were one; government and religious functions took place in the same building. But as Boston's population grew, the identity of church and community was split apart. By 1635, the colony passed a mandatory church attendance law that clearly reflected the decline in Sunday worship. By 1650, the church established by Winthrop and his companions, the First Church of Boston, contained only a fraction of the town's population—and Boston had acquired in the meantime at least one house of prostitution.

In a sense, Boston's success doomed Winthrop's dream. By 1650, the city was not only thriving but sustained a rich hinterland of towns and farms, quite different from the settlement pattern in Virginia. Boston's position as a colonial capital generated income, but Jamestown and later Williamsburg held similar advantages. The crucial difference was that by the mid-1630s the towns surrounding Boston were producing a surplus of foodstuffs—crops that demanded marketing, storage, and distribution. The surplus was not sufficient to generate the kind of wealth that Virginia planters received from tobacco, but it was enough to feed the growing demand of the city. Boston, with its strategic position and harbor, marketed the surplus and thereby attracted merchants, who in turn drew artisans, shipbuilders, attorneys, physicians, butchers, tanners, and draymen. The newcomers expanded the market for hinterland commodities, and the outlying towns obliged with increased productivity. By the late 1640s, when the limited fertility of the New England soil gave out and the influx of newcomers had slackened, Boston launched a new career as a center of the Atlantic trade. Though Winthrop had fled to the New World to isolate his community from the corruptions of the Old, the sons and daughters of the original settlers eagerly sought to reestablish connections.

The towns surrounding Boston had been founded on similar ideals and experienced a similar transformation, though not as dramatic or as quick as that Boston had undergone. Land was also a major factor in undoing the smaller towns. Towns had fixed boundaries and distributed land to citizens until no more land was available and it became necessary to subdivide what had already been given out. By the second or third generations, inheritance of land was likely to be meager. Furthermore, because the finite nature of each town's land resources made no provision for newcomers, the population remained static or grew slowly, for births did not significantly outstrip deaths. Moving on relieved the population pressure, and new towns sprang up everywhere. As colonists moved westward in Massachusetts and fanned out through the river valleys of New England, by the late seventeenth century some did not bother to settle in towns at all but established farms straightaway. Religious and political dissent also fractured the early towns, producing still more new communities.

Most important, however, was the fact that no New England town could remain isolated. Roads, rivers, and streams led from these more or less contiguous communities to other towns and to Boston. The "coyne and commodities" of Boston, wrote a contemporary, lured town dwellers into taking "many a long walk" with their farm produce.[14] Economic exchange cemented other bonds of social interaction—such as marriage and kinship—that transcended individual communities. This process began within the first five or six years of settlement. Residents of the newer interior towns such as Springfield were decidedly more interested in making money than in building the kingdom of God, and settlers in the newer coastal communities such as Gloucester and Marblehead likewise eschewed communal ideals at least until they attained some economic affluence and stability. But the community these residents created was based more on political consensus than religious purpose.

By the middle of the seventeenth century, the masts of sailing ships in Boston harbor challenged the church spires for physical and cultural dominance. The new vista reflected Boston's role in connecting the surrounding small communities to the larger Atlantic world. William Bradford, a contemporary, compared Boston to a giant tree spreading its roots out to all other New England towns so that "all trade and commerce fell in her way." Bradford believed that the spiritual loss accompanying this pattern far surpassed its economic benefits and issued this warning in a poem: "The trade is all in your own hand,/ Take heed ye doe not wrong the land,/ Lest he that hath lift you on high . . . throw you downe from your high state,/ And make you low and desolate."[15]

Bradford's warning was prescient. It would be less a curse from God that limited Boston's potential, however, than the fact that powerful rivals emerged to the south, possessing more fertile hinterlands and an equally voracious appetite for land and trade.

New York and Philadelphia: The Gridiron Emerges

The first permanent settlement on Manhattan Island, New Amsterdam, was established around 1625 by the Dutch. Within a generation, a four-cornered fort overlooked the harbor and a fortress wall isolated this community from the rest of the island to the north. By 1660, the city was closely settled in variously shaped blocks reminiscent of the meandering medieval patterns of the Old World except for a single broad avenue that led to the fort from the main town gate. The wharf was the focus for this outpost of one of the most highly developed commercial societies in the Old World. In 1664, the city fell without a struggle into the hands of the British, who renamed it New York, and the Dutch dream of New Amsterdam as the center for a North American commercial empire expired.

A century later, the character and appearance of the Dutch town had changed considerably. The wall had come down, but the broad avenue to the wharf, Wall Street, remained a permanent feature of the city's structure. Houses and farms spread north beyond the confines of the original settlement, already assuming the relentless gridiron pattern that became the official municipal policy of land division in the early nineteenth century. "This populous and well built Town," as one observer described it in 1753, was the second largest city in the colonies by the end of the colonial period and was superbly situated to outstrip all competitors in later years.[16] A fertile surrounding countryside and a fine natural harbor would be the building blocks for its future economic prominence.

In the meantime, however, New York played a secondary role to a precocious competitor to the south that was founded on a religious vision and, like Boston, quickly transformed into a thriving commercial center. William Penn, hoping to plant a "greene Country Towne" where every household would have "room enough for House, Garden and small Orchard," had established Philadelphia as the capital of the Quaker haven that bore his name. Penn's ideal was similar in many respects to the designs of other planned European urban settlements in the New World.[17] But by this time—1681—Europeans were aware that the vast expanses of land in the New World required new concepts of urbanization, and the "room" Penn had in mind consisted of 100-acre lots with houses set in the middle of the lot. Unfortunately, this was a vision that neither the site—a narrow, 2-mile neck of land between the Schuylkill and Delaware rivers—nor the exigencies of the city's commercial role could sustain. Thomas Holme, Penn's on-site planner, adjusted the design by laying out a grid street system featuring two major crossing thoroughfares, Broad Street and High (later Market) Street, that divided the city into four quadrants and intersected at a 10-acre square in the city center set aside for public buildings. Four small parks, the first dedicated public parks in America, relieved the grid pattern in each of the quadrants. The smallest lots measured no more than one-half acre.

It was a plan calculated to sell town lots. The easily surveyed, rectangular plats were uniform, a feature that speculator and resident alike would appreciate. Esthetics retreated before economy, and the success of the town soon overran Holme's modest provisions for open spaces. But parts of the Philadelphia plan lived on as settlers in new areas often repeated the grid and quadrant design. Even the tree-inspired street names such as Chestnut, Pine, and Cherry appeared in rude frontier outposts whose founders were determined to extend the nomenclature of civilization, if not its fact.

The Philadelphia plan highlighted another important feature of future town planning: the importance of private land sales in the process of urbanization. The early New England settlements owned collectively a good deal of common land; when the community distributed land in the initial phase of settlement, households, not individuals, received the plots. Though this pattern soon broke down, the idea of public or community interest and responsibility in land persisted. In Philadelphia, however, land was a commodity. The proprietor, William Penn, made the initial sales, of course, but after that, as in Boston and Virginia, the speculative whims of the owners became the dominant theme of land use. This would become a characteristic American urban reality as much as the grid became the typical planning design.

Although we hardly think of the grid as an innovative device today, it was a brand new idea in the late seventeenth century. Just a half-century earlier, Boston began as a typical medieval town criss-crossed with narrow, winding streets

Plan of Philadelphia, 1682
This design would serve as the prototype for most American towns. Note the gridiron
street plan, the square for public buildings at the intersection of Broad and High
streets, and the four small parks.

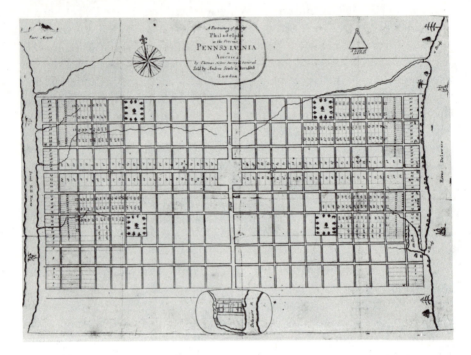

framed by half-timbered houses. Philadelphia, in contrast, was an open city,
reflecting not only the confidence of nearly a century of English settlement in
the New World but changing concepts of Old World urban design as well. The
cramped walled cities of Europe gave way to open broad avenues with limitless
vistas and monumental structures. Sharp boundaries between city and countryside, as we saw earlier, softened. And Philadelphia was the American expression
of this new direction in urban planning. Visitors admired the city's straight
streets, the handsome brick and stone buildings, and the flagstone sidewalks that
exuded a sense of order and prosperity. Not incidentally, the straight streets also
helped such varied civic functions as tax assessments and traffic flow. Esthetics
and economics had at last been joined.

The Carolinas: Rice Planters and English Nostalgia

The same combination of esthetics and economics was also evident in the two
towns that emerged on the South Atlantic coast, Charles Town and Savannah.

English emigres from Barbados founded Charleston (or "Charles Town," as colonials called it) in 1670. This "colony of a colony" grew dramatically over the
next century as its coastal location gave the town access to Atlantic shipping
lanes and, more immediately, to the adjacent low country that produced the
crop rice in great abundance. South Carolina and rice differed in two important
respects from Virginia and tobacco. Ocean-going vessels could not negotiate the
river and creek systems that comprised the Carolina rice districts, and the marketing and processing of this crop required centrally located facilities. For these
reasons, Charles Town soon emerged as the metropolis of the southern colonies.
Buoyed by rice and the West Indies trade, its population grew between 1700
and 1740 to 6,000 inhabitants—an increase of more than 500 percent—and the
port took its place among the five leading towns in colonial America.

At that latter date, Charles Town was the one settlement in colonial America
perhaps most English in appearance. Steadfastly ignoring climate and prevailing
North American urban patterns, its Barbadan transplants built houses in the
English style—solid, square, one-and-a-half-story wooden buildings that exuded middle-class respectability in this rising port. The town's leaders also
erected imposing public buildings in the English style. St. Michael's Church was
a copy of a famous English church, and the Exchange Building not only duplicated English style but was made of building materials from the Mother Country. Charles Town reminded most of its visitors of a miniature London. As elsewhere, however, the spatial realities of the New World had modified European
urban traditions. The medieval-looking town wall came down in 1718, and
narrow paths gave way to long blocks and broad streets. Residents began planting the now-famous gardens and nearby bogs and swamps were filled. The
edges between city and countryside began to erode.

By the 1750s, building styles had been adapted to the climate and location,
further modifying the city's English accent. The so-called "single house" made
its appearance, a structure whose narrow end faced the street, with the entrance
on the long side that extended back into the lot, away from the increasingly
congested streets. A door fronting the street led not to the interior of the house
but to the outdoor gallery (or veranda). The single house came in one-, two-,
and three-story versions, constructed of brick or wood depending on its owner's
affluence.

Despite its imposing architecture, heterogeneous population (the town was
host to a variety of ethnic and religious groups), and advancing economy and
population, Charles Town was in some respects more like Virginia's towns than
northern urban settlements because the Carolina port was essentially an extension of the low country rice plantations. The rice planters were the city's elite
and they resided in Charles Town only part of the year, escaping their country
estates to avoid both fever and boredom. In the city their lives revolved around
each other, with dinner parties and various other social events occupying a good

deal of their time. Theirs was a social group that did not relate to the larger community of the town. Whatever public institutions existed in Charles Town—the library and local government primarily—emerged from the efforts of small groups of merchants and physicians who were handicapped by the lack of participation from the town's monied elements. Inadequate support of public institutions would be a persisting problem for Charles Town well into the nineteenth century.

The planters and merchants of Charles Town were responsible, in their separate ways, for settling a good deal of the colony's interior. The planters carried low country culture along the larger streams that penetrated the upcountry. The merchants established trading outposts to service the growing agricultural economy. Camden, South Carolina, was a typical inland trading town that initially served the needs of the local farming community. As wheat became a profitable crop in the 1750s, the town's merchants, with a financial boost from mercantile houses in Charles Town (and personnel as well), established milling enterprises and shipped the flour to their colleagues on the coast who, in turn, sent it across the Atlantic. In less than a generation, Camden had transformed itself from a small frontier trading post to a participant in the vast trans-Atlantic trade.

Besides the migration and influence from the low country, the interior portions of the South Carolina colony benefited from a totally different population movement. Beginning in the early years of the eighteenth century, a steadily increasing flow of German and Scotch-Irish settlers left Pennsylvania and followed the wagon road from Lancaster down the Valley of Virginia and into the Carolina upcountry. They established towns along the way, such as the Moravian community of Salem in the North Carolina colony and a number of German settlements in South Carolina including Ebenezer, Orangeburg, and Saxe Gotha. The town names York, Chester, and Lancaster in the South Carolina upcountry reflected the Pennsylvania origins of the settlers. These were primarily farm communities, producing and sometimes processing grains for export. Their number grew so substantially that by the 1770s more than half the population of North and South Carolina resided in the interior districts.

Savannah: A Four-Part Vision

Further south, German settlers were to play an important role in the settling of a new colony, Georgia, in 1733. Along the coast south of Charles Town the English philanthropist James Oglethorpe brought together a group of German religious dissenters and English ne'er-do-wells to erect a model community and colony. The plan for Savannah reflected the by-then familiar strategy of blending rural and urban influences, an approach dictated by both the availability of land

and the necessity for urban dwellers to be self-supporting. The Georgia Trustees, the group of Englishmen that governed the colony, sought a close-knit community of farm households and discrete neighborhoods.

The Savannah plan called for a city without a central focus. Emphasis was placed instead on the four neighborhoods or wards flanking the main street. Each of these wards contained forty houselots oriented to a central square. Besides the 60- by 90-foot town lot, a household would receive one 5-acre garden lot and a 44-four acre farm lot. The combined rural-urban land grant was not unique to Savannah; New England towns issued this type of land allotment and William Penn experimented with the practice in Philadelphia. The Savannah grants differed, however, because they were part of a regional plan that resembled the Spanish design of Santa Fe. Beyond the four rectangular neighborhoods were the garden plots; surrounding these 5-acre parcels were the larger farm lots. Still larger tracts of one square mile each lay beyond the farm areas. A common or greenbelt surrounded the town to provide for orderly expansion in the future.

This remarkable plan, which combined traditional English elements such as residential squares and neighborhoods with more innovative regional land use design, provided for a self-sufficient community able to feed itself and market its produce. By the 1730s, English settlement had accumulated enough of a track record to remind Oglethorpe that the ideal must be tied to an economic reality and, in fact, the siting of Savannah emphasized the new town's strategic location for trade. The plan itself outlived the ideal, however, as Old World conceptions once again gave way before New World realities. Proximity to the abundance of fertile land in South Carolina proved Savannah's undoing as slavery and individual farmsteads became the rule by the time of the Revolution. The neat juxtaposition between town and country occupations and land use faded. But the squares and the neighborhoods survive to the present day, less from conscious efforts to preserve them than from the relative absence of the severe development pressures that engulfed towns to the north.

Oglethorpe's utopian vision culminated a century-long English colonial planning tradition by combining two objectives into one town design: the ideal of a just community working in concert for the general welfare, and the practical necessity of feeding and sustaining a population in a new and sometimes hostile environment. For the most part, only the latter objective survived. The abundance of land to plant and build on and the proximity of navigable waterways quickly diverted attention from the founding ideals. Space changed as well as priorities. Virginia's dispersed settlement patterns, which had been fostered by easy access to rich land and the demanding qualities of the tobacco plant, established the plantation and the planter as prime arbiters of urban location and function. In New England, the deliberate arrangement of buildings and homes

Plan of Savannah, 1757

Much of James Oglethorpe's original 1733 plan remains intact here, including the four
neighborhoods and the spacious squares that relieve the monotony of the gridiron.

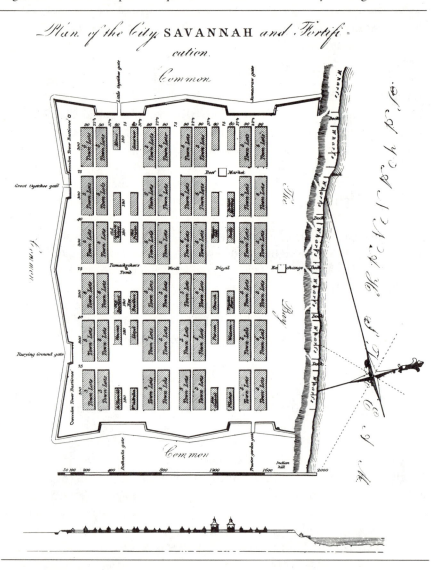

around the town common gave way to more individualistic designs, though the common itself persisted as a physical entity. William Penn's spacious town quickly became crowded, and Charles Town and Savannah were able to maintain neither English traditions nor philanthropic visions, respectively. The Carolina port eventually shed its spatial and architectural Englishness, and Savannah residents soon abandoned the balance between farm and city by choosing one or the other.

Settlement did not proceed evenly and consistently from east to west. The major cities were found along the Atlantic coast and usually spawned a number of smaller outlying communities that were the nation's first suburbs. To the west and in the more sparsely populated areas along the coast, small market centers developed, serving the immediately surrounding agricultural territory. Then there were the smallest settlements, scattered in the backcountry or on the edges of the hinterlands of other towns. Colonial urban places could, in fact, be arranged on a scale from the smallest to the largest and from the simplest to the most complex, and the colonies themselves could be pictured as composed of the various hinterlands carved out by towns and cities. The smallest places were often no more than mere villages with a meetinghouse or an inn, perhaps, but little else. At most, they served as collectors for nearby agricultural products. The intermediate-sized towns usually provided markets for a limited trading territory and boasted at least some skilled artisans and perhaps some professional services. But the largest institutions, the most influential leaders, and the most highly skilled craftsmen were to be found in the major cities.

Judged by where most people lived, the American colonies could not be called primarily urban. But colonization itself would have been virtually impossible without urban places. Boston, Philadelphia, and New York were truly dominant centers in this era, with Charleston playing a similar role in the South. Dozens of other cities cropped up in response to commercial opportunities or new population flows westward. By 1690 Boston contained more than 7,000 persons, and the five major seaboard cities (Boston, Newport, New York, Philadelphia, and Charleston) accounted for a combined population of roughly 18,000. On the eve of the American Revolution, Philadelphia and New York had surpassed Boston in size, and the total number of inhabitants in these five cities was approaching 104,000 (see Table 1.1). According to some modern estimates, Philadelphia ranked as the largest English city outside of London.

North American cities were small compared with the great agglomerations to the south: Mexico City had some 70,000 inhabitants by 1750, and Lima, Peru, about 60,000. But these Spanish cities stood aloof from their surrounding regions. They were, more than anything else, symbols of Old World power and domination and administrative centers for colonial control. Boston, New York,

Table 1.1

Population Growth in the Major Colonial Cities, 1690–1775

	1690	1720	1742	1760	1775	
Boston	7,000	12,000	16,382	15,631	16,000	
Charleston	1,100	3,500	6,800	8,000	12,000	
New York	3,900	7,000	11,000	18,000	25,000	
Newport	2,600	3,800	6,200	7,500	11,000	
Philadelphia	4,000	10,000	13,000	23,750	40,000	(23,750)ᵃ

ᵃThe first figure is Bridenbaugh's; the second, Warner's. Philadelphia's population of roughly 28,500 in 1790 suggests that Warner's more conservative figure is closer to the actual population total in 1775.

Sources: Carl Bridenbaugh, *Cities in the Wilderness: The First Century of Urban Life in America, 1625–1742,* 2nd ed. (New York: Putnam, 1964), pp. 6, 143, 303, and *Cities in Revolt: Urban Life in America: 1743–1776* (New York: Knopf, 1955), p. 216; and Sam Bass Warner, Jr., *The Private City: Philadelphia in Three Periods of Its Growth* (Philadelphia: University of Pennsylvania Press, 1968), p. 12.

Philadelphia, and other towns to the north, by contrast, grew in conjunction with their hinterlands and gradually evolved from fortified clusters into market places.

By the late seventeenth century, urban America reflected both the realities of the New World environment and the century-long development of a prosperous agriculture and commerce. Colonial towns and their residents were turning outward, forging economic links with the countryside, with other towns, and with the great cities of Europe. Increasingly fragmented as their economies grew more complex, the towns of America were no longer held together by the ideals of their founders and had already diversified in religion, ethnicity, social class, and land use.

Notes

1. Quoted in James Axtell, *The Invasion Within: The Contest of Cultures in Colonial North America* (New York: Oxford University Press, 1985), p. 138.
2. *Ibid.*, p. 137.
3. D. W. Meinig, *The Shaping of America: A Geographical Perspective on 500 Years of History, vol. 1: Atlantic America, 1492–1800* (New Haven: Yale University Press, 1986), p. 14.
4. John R. Stilgoe, *Common Landscape of America, 1580 to 1845* (New Haven: Yale University Press, 1982), p. 42.
5. Christopher Tunnard and Henry Hope Reed, *American Skyline: The Growth and Form of Our Cities and Towns* (New York: New American Library, 1953), p. 89.
6. Meinig, *Atlantic America,* p. 148.
7. Quoted in Rhys Isaac, *The Transformation of Virginia, 1740–1790* (Chapel Hill: University of North Carolina Press, 1982), pp. 15, 16.

8. Quoted in Sylvia Doughty Fries, *The Urban Idea in Colonial America* (Philadelphia: Temple University Press, 1977), pp. 111–112.
9. Quoted in James O'Mara, *An Historical Geography of Urban System Development: Tidewater Virginia in the Eighteenth Century,* York University Geographical Monographs, no. 13, 1983, p. 191.
10. Darrett B. Rutman and Anita H. Rutman, *A Place in Time: Middlesex County, Virginia, 1650–1750* (New York: W. W. Norton, 1984), p. 226.
11. Quoted in Fries, *Urban Idea,* pp. 49–50.
12. Quoted in Darrett B. Rutman, *Winthrop's Boston: Portrait of a Puritan Town, 1630–1649* (New York: W. W. Norton, 1965), p. 4.
13. Quoted in *ibid.,* p. 22.
14. Quoted in Darrett B. Rutman, "Assessing the Little Communities of Early America," *William and Mary Quarterly* 43 (April 1986), p. 175.
15. Quoted in Fries, *Urban Idea,* pp. 56–57.
16. Quoted in Carl Bridenbaugh, *Cities in Revolt: Urban Life in America, 1743–1776* (New York: Capricorn, 1955), p. 3.
17. Quoted in Fries, *Urban Idea,* p. 90.

CHAPTER 2

On the Waterfront: Economy and Society in Eighteenth-Century English Colonies

They gathered at the river, or the bay, or the ocean. People, produce, and structures clustered at the North American waterfront, drawn by the magnet of commerce. And commerce meant profits. The great towns of English colonial America were great because of their participation in the mercantile system. These towns—Boston, Newport, New York, Philadelphia, Charles Town, and later Baltimore and Savannah—were strung out along the Atlantic coast like pearls threaded on a watery chain, a source of seemingly inexhaustible wealth to the London and Bristol merchants who sat in their countinghouses scarcely believing the profits emerging from the Atlantic ports. England's power, the wealth of her merchants, and the success of her colonies and subjects all were bound to the waterfront. There lay the heartbeat of empire.

Farm and city met at the water's edge in the form of the urban market, the most visible indicator of the close interrelationship of the two environments. This array of wares and food, usually situated along a city's major thoroughfare, provided exciting variety for the urban shopper, who doubtless marveled at the fertility of the countryside and the skills of local artisans on display.

The waterfront's preeminence fixed the shape of the colonial city. William

Penn located Philadelphia with a sharp commercial eye. The Delaware River afforded a protected yet accessible highway to the markets of Europe. Ships of the heaviest tonnage were able to reach the port in all seasons, because the salty water of the Delaware rarely froze. Market Street, the city's main artery, began at the waterfront as Penn had designed it, but his plans had failed to account for the force of the river's attraction on his city's inhabitants. Philadelphia positively hugged its waterfront, with warehouses and wharves extending more than a mile along the shore. Philadelphia became a linear city simply because settlement in the eighteenth century rarely wandered more than half a mile from the river.

The affinity of Philadelphians for their river destroyed Penn's plans for a spacious, almost pastoral urban environment. A mix of businesses and residences crowded along the river. The marine trades and merchants spawned retail activities and artisans' workshops, all of which were packed into a narrow area. Noise, air pollution, and congestion forced those who could afford to leave to move to the suburbs, where the original ideal of spaciousness could be temporarily revived. Benjamin Franklin, one of the city's more notable citizens, captured the essence of turbulent waterfront life when he complained: "The din of the Market increases upon me; and that, with frequent interruptions, has, I find, made me say something twice over."[1]

Franklin soon moved away from the river. By the 1740s, he and many other established Philadelphians had discovered Germantown, a village 5 miles north of the city and noted for its salubrious climate. Philadelphians quickly transformed the town into a resort suburb, and eventually some citizens established permanent residences there. The exodus to Germantown, temporary or permanent, portended the suburban trend of the nineteenth century.

Back in Philadelphia, Penn's spacious blocks were divided and subdivided. Alleys and small houses sprang up like weeds as the value of land came to be measured by the square foot rather than by the acre. People and produce still mingled near the wharves, but by 1750 the lure of the waterfront finally forced city officials to sort out land uses. A commercial district was formed, pushing private homes away from the Delaware as riverfront property became too expensive and undesirable for residential purposes.

The other Atlantic cities experienced a similar concentration of settlement at the waterfront, though the degree of differentiation and crowding was not as great as in Philadelphia, the most active colonial port by the time of the Revolution. In seventeenth-century Boston, for example, the homes of the leading merchants overlooked the wharves and warehouses of the harbor; by 1775, however, many wealthy citizens had moved to the suburban towns of Roxbury and Cambridge.

The major source of this waterfront activity was, of course, the Atlantic trade.

The extent of each city's participation and success in the trade depended on the ability of local merchants to market commodities desired by the Atlantic nations. The English mercantile system imposed relentless pressure on colonial merchants to find, process, and ship farm produce and goods in order to pay for the manufactured commodities sent to colonial ports. Failure to keep up produced, for the city in question, an imbalance of trade, a strain on credit, and a blow to growth and prosperity. Waterfront activity was the gauge of a city's success or failure in the world of international commerce.

The Atlantic Trade

International commerce was a nerve-racking business. Merchants and their employees periodically paced the wharves checking the wind, chatting with customs officials, and hoping that their store of flour and grain warehoused nearby would not burn, rot, or be stolen before it could be loaded on their overdue vessel. They shared their woes and traded rumors. Suddenly declining or rising prices, new statutes, and messages bearing ill or good tidings were typical topics of conversation. Usually the outcome of these gatherings was good. Sometimes it was not, and the result could be personal or even general ruin. Uncertainty always lurked beneath the hubbub of activity on the waterfront. From the dock laborer to the sailmaker to the merchant, their future and entire livelihood were utterly dependent on the Atlantic trade.

Sometimes cities simply failed. Urbanization is not like fermentation; cities do not necessarily keep on improving until they reach a state of perfection. In fact, at almost any moment a city can sour. The men and women down at the waterfront were optimistic by nature, or they or their parents would never have left Europe. They were well aware, however, of the capriciousness of fate. They could not make the wind blow gently, replenish the soil, or alter a coastline. They knew their own and their city's fallibility. Failure had happened before.

There was New Haven, Connecticut. A medium-sized city today, in its past it had held greater hopes. Settled as an outpost in the New England fur trade during the 1630s, New Haven's location at the mouth of the Quinnipiac River seemed critically important. The young settlement was to be the largest port between Boston and New Amsterdam. Local merchants readying the first great cargo of furs to be shipped directly to England hoped to inaugurate an era of unequaled growth and prosperity. The ship, however, never reached its destination. As a consequence of one lost vessel and its cargo, New Haven's merchants suffered severe financial misfortune, direct trade was never established with England, and the town sank back into a semirural condition. A visitor to the once-hopeful settlement in 1660 tersely recorded the scene: "the land very barren, the Merchants either dead or come away, the rest gotten to their Farmes, The Towne is not so glorious as once it was."[2] New Haven revived in the nineteenth century as industrialization created new urban growth, but by then the city's pretensions to commercial preeminence had evaporated and it was merely one more river town on the way from Boston to New York.

New Haven's redemption after a long period of dormancy indicates the often cyclical nature of the urbanization process. To its citizens at the time, however, the decline seemed very real and permanent. Nearly a century later, another protometropolis was launched further south. Unlike New Haven, however, this town experienced a few moments in the limelight and then quickly expired, a victim of geography and the insatiable appetite of the mercantile system.

London Town, Maryland, as the name implied, was an ambitious upstart of a settlement. Tobacco, that inestimable commodity for merchants on both sides of the Atlantic, was responsible for the initial dream and temporary realization of London Town's presumptions of glory. The intricate river system of the Chesapeake region produced many sites like London Town, often as little as 5 miles apart but separated by water. A traveler from Williamsburg to Annapolis, for example, had to take at least twelve ferries to negotiate 120 miles. A 5-mile journey from London Town to Annapolis lasted more than an hour. The isolation of each settlement from the others enabled the towns to market the produce from their own backcountry without significant danger of competition from neighboring communities.

London Town was especially blessed with fertile soil that produced high-quality and high-priced tobacco. A fine product plus increasing European demand for the weed attracted capital and merchants to the small community, and by 1720 a flourishing trade with England had developed. In late October, luffing sails and stately masts bobbed gracefully at the town's harbor as ships unloaded manufactured goods, luxury items, and wine in exchange for the precious tobacco. Unfortunately, however, all this waterfront activity suddenly came to a halt. The decline in tobacco prices during the 1740s induced the Maryland assembly to pass an inspection law to ensure that the colony's tobacco would compete favorably in the tight market with crops from the other colonies. To this end, the colony established government warehouses at designated inspection stations. The assembly overlooked London Town, and within a generation the community shriveled and disappeared.

New Crops and New Markets

There were no end of New Havens and London Towns, and no certainties, in the Atlantic trading world. The search for marketable commodities and markets was neverending for the waterfront denizens. Their ingenuity in seeking out these necessities in a mercantile world created, in large part, the success stories of colonial urban America. Some of these stories will be told in the pages that follow, but their blueprint appears in Figure 2.1.

The merchants in each American seaport were subject to the strict demands of colonial trade. According to English mercantile law, the English colonies were to trade directly only with England. The objective of the Atlantic trade, from the English as well as the colonial viewpoint, was for colonials to secure a marketable commodity to exchange for England's manufactured goods. Without such a commodity, colonial merchants would be perpetually in debt to their English counterparts. The catch, though, was that none of the colonial cities along the Atlantic seaboard could disgorge enough produce to pay for the articles shipped on the return voyage from England. It made sense, therefore, to seek out other markets where more favorable balances could be struck to pay for English cargoes. Rationalizing that the alternative to illicit trade was penury, the ingenious merchants scoured the Atlantic world for legal and illegal trading partners. The presence of French and Dutch translators in urban counting-houses of the English colonies indicates how formalized the illegal trade had become by 1740. The extent of these connections and the diversity of commod-

Figure 2.1 *Colonial Trading Patterns*

(From *Cities and Immigrants: A Geography of Change in Nineteenth-Century America* by David Ward. Copyright © 1971 by Oxford University Press, Inc. Reprinted by permission.)

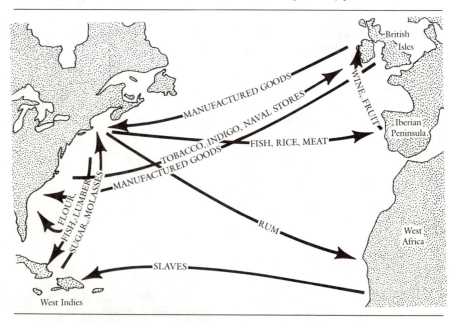

ities traded by colonial merchants comes through in the comments of Philadelphia merchant John Reynall in 1741:

> We make our Remittances [for British manufactures] in a great many different ways, sometimes to the West Indies in Bread, flour, Pork, Indian Corn, and hogshead Staves, sometimes to Carrolina and Newfoundland in Bread and Flour sometimes to Portugall in Wheat, Flour and Pipe Staves sometimes to Ireland in Flax Seed Flour, Oak and Walnut Planks and Barrel Staves and to England in Skinns, Tobacco, Beeswax, staves of all Kinds, Oak and Walnut Planks, Boat Boards, Pigg Iron, Tarr, Pitch, Turpentine, Ships, and Bills of Exchange.[3]

(The stops in the West Indies and Portugal, we may note, were probably illegal.)

Philadelphia, in fact, provides a good example of the relationship between urbanization and international trade in colonial America. This city's merchants began their Atlantic commerce modestly in 1690 by establishing a trade in horses and provisions with various Caribbean ports. In return, the merchants received rum, molasses, and sugar, which could either be shipped to England to settle the trade imbalance or distributed at other colonial ports for a profit that could be used, in part, to redress that same imbalance. The West Indies trade demonstrated a number of good commercial maxims. First, for a port with marginal commodities like horses and provisions (few English merchants yearned for these items), it was essential to seek out markets with more attractive products. Second, despite the modest level of initial trade, when Philadelphia's fertile countryside began to produce wheat in the eighteenth century, the trade contacts made in the seventeenth century provided immediate entrees for wheat and its products. Finally, opening up new trade areas often led to further interesting discoveries. It seems that early Quaker captains got "lost" in the maze of islands and wandered onto Dutch and French West Indian shores—forbidden harbors, according to English mercantile statutes. The Quaker captains no doubt felt at home in these foreign ports, however, because they were joined by officers and crews from New York, Boston, and Charles Town vessels who had similarly lost their way. By the 1740s, the Dutch and French island ports of call were commonplace itineraries on sailing orders: "My order to you," wrote a Boston merchant to one of his captains in 1743, "is that you take the first wind and weather for sailing and proceed to the West Indies. You have Liberty to go to any of the English Islands, and if you think it Safe to any of the french Islands."[4]

By this time, Philadelphia had expanded her trade across the Atlantic. Wheat was the commercial catapult. Palatine (German) and Scotch-Irish immigrants sailed across the Atlantic highway to settle in the tolerant woods and fields of William Penn's plantation. Their diligent cultivation of wheat enabled Philadelphia merchants to feed a hungry Atlantic world whose appetite for wheat products had been sharpened by the incessant European warfare. Philadelphia merchants loaded Quaker ships with flour and bread bound for old trading partners in the Caribbean—and by 1775, the city exported more flour to these ports than did all the other colonies combined. The ships loaded with flour and bread sailed on to southern Europe and the Wine Islands off the Iberian coast, where the precious grain was exchanged for salt and wine—two more marketable commodities. The extent of Philadelphia's trade with southern Europe outdistanced that of all other colonial ports. Then the ships sailed on to England for the dry goods, woolens, and other manufactured products from the dismal factories of that country's crowded cities. To the end of the colonial period, Philadelphia merchants could not find a significant commodity to interest their English counterparts. But the colonials' resourcefulness in seeking out new markets produced profits for themselves and growth for their city.

It was obvious that wheat had played an important role in the Philadelphia success story, and this was another lesson for the rising Atlantic ports. Finding a marketable commodity became such a pressing need that urban merchants probed deep into the interior, braved icy waters, and invested in processing industries. In early Boston, for example, the fur trade was a lucrative business. Because animals were a finite commodity and security on the fur frontier was generally absent, Boston merchants soon turned to another of God's creatures—fish—to make their way in the Atlantic world. The merchants disposed of the fish in Spain and the Wine Islands, where profits were sufficient either in bills of exchange (the equivalent of cash) or in produce to pay for English manufactured products. As fishing proved an arduous and marginal activity, Boston merchants turned first to shipbuilding and the carrying trade, and finally to widespread illicit trade, to keep generating profits.

The odyssey of Boston merchant Thomas Hancock's ships in the 1740s proves that Philadelphia's John Reynall had company as he roamed the Caribbean and Atlantic. Hancock's vessels took fish to the West Indies, calling at British and at forbidden French ports to load molasses, headed back to Boston to unload a portion of the cargo, and then proceeded to Holland—another prohibited port—to pick up European manufactured products. For Boston merchants, who had an unproductive hinterland at their backs and rival colonial ports snipping at their carrying trade, the illegal cargo was one way to scratch profits out of the Atlantic trade. Though most of their commerce was conducted within the bounds of mercantile propriety, that portion of their trade carried on outside the British Empire provided essential profits for a seaport that had seen commercial leadership in the colonies pass to Philadelphia.

Farther south, Charles Town merchants enjoyed a less difficult situation. The gentle breezes that blew along the wide waterfront promenade lent a leisurely, esthetic quality to this city that contrasted with the frenetic and crowded ports in the northern colonies. Closer inspection, however, revealed the same graceful ships, the same concerned merchants, and the same collection of trades and people associated with maritime endeavors. If less strain was visible on the faces of Charles Town's merchants, it was probably thanks to two commodities: rice and indigo.

In the industrial cities of northern Europe, rice had become almost a household necessity. From the 1720s until the Revolution, rice accounted for one-half to two-thirds of the total value of Charles Town's exports. The value of rice and the volume of the trade allowed the city's merchants to trade directly with England. The crystal chandeliers and broadlooms that graced the interiors of spacious Charles Town homes were purchased with rice.

The city's merchants were not about to rest on the laurels of their comfortable rice trade, however. The proximity of the Caribbean gave rise to a flourishing West Indian trade, not only in rice but also in naval stores, with molasses, rum, and slaves (from Jamaica and Barbados) as the return cargo. Equally important, ships from other colonial ports returning from the West Indies found the South Carolina port a convenient point to unload a portion of their cargos for distribution throughout the Carolinas and Georgia.

Meanwhile, the New York merchants, released from the constraints of the Dutch West India Company that had monopolized trade at the port, moved to secure trade connections with illegal ports and even with pirates in the early years of the eighteenth century. It was not until 1730, however, that New Yorkers were able to mount a local fleet to prevent Bostonians from carrying away the city's hinterland produce. By then, the fertile lands of the Hudson River Valley were producing wheat and livestock in sufficient quantities for New York merchants to sail the trade circuit of the Caribbean, southern Europe, and England. It would be another half century before New Yorkers assumed the leadership in North American trade. For the present, that role still belonged to Philadelphia.

By 1775, the urban merchants of colonial America held a sophisticated if somewhat cynical world view. Gone were the days when the major concern was catching a few animals in the forest or harvesting the backyard crop. These businessmen and their cities played an important role in the great Atlantic mercantile world—a challenging world that was mined with any number of obstacles to success. Whether surveying the waterfront from his countinghouse or ruminating in the study of his comfortable town house removed from the din of the docks, the merchant was likely to be mulling over complex credit arrangements or dreaming up new markets and commodities and new opportunities for investments. His ships criss-crossed the entire Atlantic: up and down the colonial coast and to Newfoundland, the West Indies, the Wine Islands, the European continent, and the British Isles.

Commerce was the cornerstone of urban growth. The capital generated by mercantile enterprises found its way into numerous other economic activities, especially in northern towns. In the South, agricultural land and slaves absorbed profits and the few notable urban settlements—Charles Town and Savannah— grew more slowly than their northern counterparts. By the 1750s, colonial merchants were channeling a portion of their capital into modest manufacturing enterprises. Boston began to manufacture and export furniture and shoes. Shipbuilding continued to expand as an investment outlet for merchants. Merchants in several towns formed organizations designed to develop manufacturing as a way of diversifying the urban economy and improving the balance of trade with England. A group of New York merchants, for example, founded the Society for the Promotion of Arts, Agriculture, and Economy in 1765; on the eve of the Revolution, leading merchants in Philadelphia organized the United Company of Philadelphia for Promoting American Manufactures.

Urban merchants reinvested part of their fortunes in themselves. By the middle of the eighteenth century, elegant homes and mansions decorated select districts of the growing seaports. Some Charles Town planters even built two grand houses, one in the city on Meeting Street or along the Battery, and the other in the rice fields of the low country. These homes were furnished with the finest imported goods and maintained with a retinue of slaves. Philadelphia's wealthiest merchants, though not as affluent as the southern planters, began nevertheless to live in a style reminiscent of the English urban gentry. They resided in high-ceilinged, ornate three-story town houses in the center of town and, like the rice planters, repaired occasionally to country estates. They traveled to and from these places in fine four-wheeled carriages imported from London and patronized the best wigmakers and silk dyers. They took music and dancing lessons to improve their cultural cachet. When they died, they were buried in the heaviest mahogany coffins.

Before leaving this world, however, the colonial elite bequeathed other monuments to their cities besides their residences. Public buildings became more massive and imposing than ever, reflecting urban economic prosperity. The classical style of architecture that had dominated the reconstruction of London after the 1666 fire flowered in eighteenth-century colonial cities. Columns and domes imparted a sense of authority and permanence to the public buildings they adorned. Peter Harrison, an English architect of considerable fame, left his substantial mark on the seacoast towns. Newport's Sephardic Jewish synagogue and the Redwood Library, a miniature Doric temple, are two of the finest examples of Harrison's simple yet impressive architectural style.

The colonial economy that generated this wealth also produced significant social disparities. Such distinctions were not new to colonial towns. But the second century of colonial life in America witnessed a marked sharpening of

The Old State House in Boston
Built in 1713, this handsome structure was an early example of the impressive public buildings that appeared in major seaport towns during the colonial period.

existing stratification. The new social classes, coupled with the growing diversity and spatial expansion of the towns, resulted in some important changes.

Social Classes, Old and New

Europeans came to this country from highly organized and socially stratified societies in which each person had a place that was more often than not handed down from generation to generation. Some doubtless emigrated to escape oppression and persecution in their homelands, but an organized society was considered a prerequisite for civilized life. For the average European, a social system without lines of order and authority was a frightening, not a liberating, prospect. The emphasis was on *order*—in social life and town building alike. The goal of colonization was not innovation or invention, but the establishment of traditional and comfortable customs and forms in a new environment.

A major characteristic of colonial urban society was the presence of an elite wealthy class that controlled a disproportionate amount of the community's resources. Generally speaking, the larger the town, the more disproportionate the concentration of wealth and the larger the numbers of citizens without real property.

At the top of urban society were the professional class and more successful merchants (and planters in Charles Town). Physicians varied widely in their skills, social prestige, and earnings, but lawyers generally held the most wealth in towns and cities. The merchants who dominated the waterfronts and imported goods at wholesale did very well as a group. Classified in contemporary parlance as the "better sort," these people had the financial resources to expand their own economic interests, dominate the councils of municipal government, and indulge their tastes in books, art, music, and the finer things of life. The "middling sort," or middle-ranking groups, included shopkeepers, skilled artisans who had their own businesses, mechanics who benefited from the chronic shortage of skilled and semiskilled labor in colonial towns, and those professionals and merchants who could not be truly considered among the elite. Those who belonged to the middle group were usually able to acquire some property and lead relatively comfortable lives, though their fortunes were more likely to fluctuate depending on the shifts in the general economic pattern. At the bottom of the social and economic scale, among the "inferior sort," were unskilled laborers (many of whom were frequently without regular employment), indentured servants, and slaves. These people were likely to own no property and their lives were often given over to the struggle for survival. There were exceptions to this general scheme, such as schoolteachers, who were miserably paid and thus relegated to the lower economic ranks despite their education and skills.

As the coastal cities grew and commerce became the dominant feature of urban economic life, the gap between rich and poor tended to widen. James Henretta's comparison of tax lists in colonial Boston reveals that in 1687 the top 15 percent of the city's property owners controlled 52 percent of the taxable assets of the town, whereas the top 5 percent held more than a quarter of the wealth. At the same time, around 14 percent of the adult males of Boston neither owned property nor were dependent on parents or others for sustenance. These people, often young men seeking better opportunities in the urban setting, were dependent on wages, rather than property or investments, to make their way in the world. By 1771, Boston's taxable wealth was even more concentrated: 15 percent of the property owners accounted for almost 66 percent of the wealth, with the top 5 percent controlling more than 44 percent of the city's taxable wealth. And the nondependent, propertyless wage earners had increased from 14 percent of the adult male population in 1687 to 29 percent in 1771.[5] The trends toward a greater concentration of wealth at the top of the social and economic scale, an increase in the numbers of propertyless wage earners, and the relatively declining position of the middle-ranking economic groups (artisans, shopkeepers, and traders) over this 85-year period in Boston were reflected in virtually all the major colonial cities, despite the general prosperity of these groups.

In 1770, the top 10 percent of the population with taxable assets accounted for about half the wealth in Portsmouth, 40 percent in Newburyport, 44 percent in Albany, New York, 57 percent in Boston, and about 62 percent in Charles Town. About a tenth of the households with taxable assets in Philadelphia controlled almost 90 percent of the taxable property, reflecting "a pyramid of wealth in which about 500 men guided the town's economic life."[6] The proportion of propertyless workers was considerably higher in the towns and cities—reaching about 65 percent of the population in Charles Town if black slaves are included in the figures—than it was in the rural areas or small villages.

There is nothing especially unusual about this inequality in the distribution of wealth when it is compared with European patterns. But the possibility that New World opportunities would be limited to only a few disturbed a number of colonists and was perhaps one of the main reasons for the conviction shared by Thomas Jefferson and others that only a rural society could foster and preserve a roughly equal balance of economic resources and political power among the general population.

In America, however, the concentrated wealth of the cities was not—as it was in Europe—confined largely to a permanent and closed aristocracy. Social stratification did not mean social immobility. There was movement within and among the various social categories, even if the gaps between the segments increased over time. The availability of credit and the relative ease of breaking into international trade enabled ambitious town dwellers to move into (and out of) the mercantile class with great frequency. The growth of that city also provided work for artisans and unskilled laborers. Although the wealth of these workers did not grow as fast as the wealth of groups higher on the status ladder, they were able to increase their standards of living as measured by the variety of consumer goods they possessed and the homes they purchased. Finally, the geographic mobility of the colonial urban population mitigated the growing social inequality by providing a safety valve for younger individuals.

Room at the top existed for the lucky or especially enterprising, and people who could learn a trade stood a good chance of making a comfortable living.

Whereas family status was the key in most of Europe, wealth opened virtually all doors in colonial America. As a disapproving English observer of Newport society noted in 1748, "A Man who had Money here, no matter how he came by it, he is Every thing, and wanting that he's a meer Nothing, let his Conduct be ever so ereproachable. Money is here the true Fuller's Earth for Reputation, there is not a Spot or Stain but it will take out."[7] It was possible for artisans to become merchants, or even for modest farmers to become lawyers. Perhaps as many as one-third to two-fifths of the merchants in late colonial New York City were "self-made men" who rose to their positions from lower rungs on the social and economic ladder. Henry Laurens, one of Charles Town's leading merchants, was the son of a saddler; Newport's Samuel Vernon moved into commercial ventures from his silversmith's shop; and Thomas Hancock of Boston, who began his career as a bookseller's apprentice, had amassed a fortune of over £100,000 by the time of his death in 1764.

Social distinctions grew more obvious in the later colonial years. Those persons and groups with the greatest financial resources were able to take advantage of new opportunities and thus consolidate their positions in the social hierarchy. The members of the "better sort" also tended to dominate the policy-making process, especially in the larger cities. As Henretta observed of Boston, "All of the important offices of the town government . . . were lodged firmly in the hands of a broad elite, entry into which was conditioned by commercial achievement and family background."[8] In New York, too, where the highest tenth of the taxpayers in the early eighteenth century controlled 47 percent of the assessed wealth, political power was heavily concentrated, with the rich holding all offices and the wealthiest among them holding the most important positions.

As smaller towns grew into cities, family association gave way to wealth as the bridge to success and power and property became more concentrated in the hands of a relatively small percentage of the total urban population. These trends first became visible in the larger northeastern ports, but they would be repeated in the developing cities of the urban frontier and among the rising commercial towns of the interior and were, in fact, dominant features in the North American urbanization process. What distinguished American from European society was not the absence of a class structure but the greater prospect that those lower on the socioeconomic scale could rise.

At the same time, the social structure developed a self-reinforcing quality. The leading families in each town sealed their positions with intermarriage, membership in social clubs, and numerous visits with their counterparts in other colonies. The Allens, Shippens, and Francises of Philadelphia, for example, were related to each other as well as to leading citizens in other towns. William Allen's wife was sister to Governor James Hamilton of Pennsylvania; one of their sons, James, married Elizabeth, daughter of Philadelphia's Mayor John Lawrence;

another son, Andrew, wedded Sally Coxe, whose mother was a Francis; and son John married Mary Johnston, daughter of a prominent New York City family. Daughter Ann Allen became the wife of Pennsylvania's Lieutenant Governor, John Penn, and daughter Margaret married one of New York's leading figures, James De Lancey. When not appearing at each other's weddings, the colonial urban gentry enjoyed lengthy mutual visits, a remarkable fact considering the hazards and difficulties of traveling in those days. Ralph and Susannah De Lancey Izard regularly sailed back and forth from New York to Charles Town. Thomas Mifflin and his family journeyed from Philadelphia to Boston on occasion, and many of the elite enjoyed winter sojourns in the West Indies or grand tours of Europe.

The lifestyles and connections of the colonial urban elite set them apart from even the "middling sort," but especially from the poor. In the seventeenth century, the prevailing notion was that the poor were merely unfortunate members of the corporate body to which all town residents belonged. By the eighteenth century, urban society—more diverse, more stratified, and larger—perceived the poor as a separate class.

Precarious Lives

Chronic poverty emerged in the seaport towns early in the eighteenth century and became particularly evident by the 1750s. Ironically, poverty surfaced as an issue in colonial towns just as the public perception of poverty began to change. Before 1700, colonists generally distinguished between the worthy and the unworthy poor, the former held as not responsible for their reduced circumstances and therefore eligible for public aid and comfort. This view began to change in the new century. In New England, the clergy instigated the new perception as a means of stimulating the faltering public-mindedness of the urban elite and publicizing the creeping vices of idleness, extravagance, and irreligion. Poverty was the punishment of vice, wealth was the product of piety. "'Tis the Lord who has Taken away from you," New England divine Cotton Mather advised Boston's poor in 1712, "what He has Given to Others."[9]

The downgrading of the poor in public perception gave rise to institutions such as public almshouses to warehouse the poor, workhouses to put the poor to work (usually turning out cloth), and prisons to catch the overflow. By the 1760s, visitors to the colonial seaports noted that the newest and most impressive structures were the workhouses, almshouses, and prisons.

An even greater irony relating to the new perception of poverty was that the majority of those on public relief were in fact quite helpless. They were women and children. Thirty percent of Boston's women were widows in 1750, many of them victims of the periodic colonial wars during the 1740s. Not all or even most of these women were poor, of course, but considering the status of women in colonial towns, they were likely candidates for public relief and accounted for most of the poverty in Boston. Even in the small towns of Middlesex County, Virginia, women dominated the relief rolls. In Charles Town, more than 80 percent of relief recipients were women and children between 1751 and 1774.

The frequent appearance of women on poverty lists reflected their low status. Though some widows (nuptiality was high in colonial towns, so the number of spinsters was relatively small) picked up the reins of the family business, most did not; and most, moreover, had not had husbands who maintained businesses. Widows were often bereft because their role in society centered on the household and childrearing, with their only "marketable" skills confined to sewing. Some resourceful widows opened boarding houses or taught school, but again their numbers were small. Less than 10 percent of colonial urban women worked outside the home. Colonial husbands controlled and managed family finances, placing widows at the mercy of relatives or children in the management of the estate. The high geographic mobility into and out of colonial towns complicated the widow's lot, making the support of extended family less likely.

Woman's primary role in the colonies, regardless of location, was childbearing. Colonial promoters recognized the importance of women as "breeders" to stabilize mobile males and to increase population, and promotional pamphlets touted various colonial sites as particularly conducive to fertility. The typical colonial wife could expect to bear a child every two years. Consequently, when housework was not occupying her time, she had to attend to the duties of childrearing. Not until the Revolutionary era did women's status and self-image improve, even though they and their offspring continued to dominate the ranks of the poor.

By the 1740s, most of the larger urban centers had settled on institutional solutions to the poverty problem. The almshouses, workhouses, and prisons reflected the increasing impersonality of urban life as well as the economic dependence of increasing numbers of urban dwellers.

The poor were not the only group in colonial towns to live marginal lives. Except in Charles Town, which had emerged by the 1750s as the leading slave market in the colonies, wage labor had come to dominate work systems in the towns. The colonial urban engagement with international markets cut two ways. On one hand, towns participated in the profits of a vast imperial network; on the other, they were susceptible to the usual cyclical nature of such markets. Accordingly, employers discovered that wage labor hired on a short-term basis—not with year-long contracts, as was customary before the 1750s—was more suitable to the prevailing economic conditions. They also recognized, for the same reason, that slave labor was less attractive than periodic wage labor. In

New York City, slave labor had accounted for 23.5 percent of the adult male workforce in the 1730s. By 1771, that share had fallen to 15 percent. In effect, employers passed along the uncertainties of the international economy to their workers.

The increasing housing shortage compounded the workers' precarious situation. After 1750, population grew much faster than the housing stock. Construction laborers were in short supply, and because most people worked in and about the waterfront in the seaports, proximity to that area was important. Carters and their wagons provided the only internal transportation system in the city, and these wagons were hardly mass transit vehicles. Thus, people's place of work had to be within reasonable walking distance of their place of residence.

Housing shortages and severe crowding were the inevitable results. In Philadelphia, small houses were constructed in the once-ample backyards of older homesites. A typical dwelling in that location was no more than 17 feet wide and 25 feet deep, with no more than 800 square feet of floor space and a story and a half of height. Space for housing was a premium commodity. English traveler Andrew Burnaby, touring Philadelphia in 1760, marveled that "Houses are so dear, that they will let for £100 currency per annum; and lots, not above thirty feet in breadth and a hundred in length, in advantageous situations, will sell for £1000 sterling."[10] When a family could not afford even the tiniest dwelling on a back lot, doubling-up and tripling-up took place. This practice lent an air of crowded squalor to the prosperous seaport.

Boston presented a similar appearance of urban disarray. The tortuous streets of the North End near the waterfront held a jumble of people and houses. By 1750, a typical house in this area contained nine or ten people, whereas a few decades earlier it was extremely rare to find more than seven persons in the same dwelling. At the same time, handsome mansions and massive public buildings were going up at strategic locations. Real estate had become an important urban commodity, and the ordering of space—or absence of order—within the city was coming to play a crucial role in the quality of life.

Supporting Institutions: Family, Church, Tavern

Despite the rising insecurities of work and housing, the colonial town offered institutional sustenance for some of its beleaguered residents. The family, the church, and the tavern provided spiritual, psychological, and in some cases financial support for their members. These venerable institutions helped to make urban life more manageable by offering a social network and interaction that affirmed identity and self-esteem.

Families in colonial America were basically *nuclear.* That is, they consisted of a married couple and their children, and perhaps a grandparent or other relative. Kinship ties were important, but extended kin groups were rarely assembled under one roof in a single household. The family was a center for discipline and for the inculcation of social norms and religious values—and, in an age when residence and workplace were often one and the same, it was also an institution for vocational training. Families served a broad range of social purposes, from nurturing young apprentices who were learning a trade with a family member to housing and caring for indentured servants and keeping the elderly and indigent at public expense.

The church was perhaps second only to the family as an important social institution, even if its religious function was weak, as in numerous Southern communities. Although various forms of Protestantism dominated colonial America, Roman Catholics (especially in Maryland) and Jews (in Charles Town and Newport) added considerably to the pattern of religious diversity. The church building was either the centerpiece of a city or its dominant architectural feature. The spires of the colonial churches framed the skylines of most towns and cities as the institutions themselves seemed to frame the lives of the inhabitants.

The religious impulse in colonial America rose and fell from time to time and from place to place, and often existed outside the established churches. In the 1730s and 1740s, the colonies were swept up in a Great Awakening. A number of itinerant ministers—as, for example, the English revivalist George Whitefield, who first arrived in America in 1739—offered salvation in exchange for repentance and fired an outpouring of religious enthusiasm across the colonies. Speaking in towns and cities as well as in rural hamlets, the preachers sometimes threatened the religious establishment, deemphasizing the importance of denominational lines. Whitefield conducted revival campaigns in towns from Savannah to Boston. His oratory was powerful enough to sway even the cosmopolitan and urbane Benjamin Franklin to contribute a few coins to the cause: "And he finish'd so admirably," Franklin recalled, "that I empty'd my pockets wholly into the collector's dish, gold and all."[11]

Whitefield created considerable agitation in the towns, especially among the established clergy. When Anglican minister Timothy Cutler encountered Whitefield on a Boston street, he greeted him with, "I am sorry to see you here." "So is the Devil," Whitefield replied.[12] In 1747, the English evangelist preached before 20,000 Bostonians in one outdoor service, haranguing his audience on sin and the evils of the Catholic church (a favorite theme among some colonial Protestants). The Awakening brought new people into the Protestant fold, divided existing churches, prompted the founding of a variety of colleges and schools to serve the various sects, and offered perhaps the most significant shared experience in the colonies—embracing rich and poor, rural and urban—

before the Revolution. In the towns, the Awakening added to the already fragmented character of society by fracturing established congregations. For all their
comparative sophistication and worldliness, towns were perennially susceptible
to the call of "pure" religion, and the revivalists constantly frequented the cities
for the simple reason that they could reach the greatest number of people there.

Even the Great Awakening did not alter one important fact, however: most
colonists were not affiliated with any church. As New York's governor wrote in
1687, "of all sorts of opinions there are some and the most part none at all."[13]
Church membership was declining in New England by the last half of the seventeenth century, and many people in the middle colonies and the South had
seemingly never been touched with religious piety. The church remained a
prominent, even essential, social institution, but it was not the only one. And
for many urban colonists, certainly as the colonial era unfolded, the tavern became a much more central part of their lives than any organized church.

Taverns, inns, and coffeehouses were usually places of great activity where
people gathered to exchange information, read and discuss the latest news from
abroad, do business, find employment, hold auctions, celebrate special occasions, and generally enjoy social intercourse with their fellows. The taverns
served a varied clientele, from rough sailors and vagabonds to ships' captains
and leading merchants. Identified by the colorful names inscribed on shingles
or plaques at the door, they were indisputably the major social institutions along
the waterfront. The characteristic smells of wharves from Boston to Savannah
were aromas of rope, canvas, tar, pitch, a salt sea, and the grog and ale served
in the taverns. The arrival of a ship fresh from Liverpool with newspapers and
mail aboard was always a big event, drawing residents and newcomers alike to
"The Wild Boar," the "Black Horse," or "The Green Dragon."

Some taverns and inns appealed especially to the colonial urban elite, offering
sumptuous banquets and entertainment. Tavern shows of a less sophisticated
sort—and the inevitable cockfights, ninepins, and billiards—attracted the
rougher elements of the port cities; meanwhile the coffeehouses swarmed with
assemblymen and politicians in Philadelphia, Williamsburg, and other government centers. Even at this early date, New York boasted a fairly sophisticated
social life that revolved around the taverns. One New Yorker complained in
1734 of the "Luxury and Profuseness" characteristic of these places: "We strive
who shall have the most Dishes of Meat at his Table, and in the best Order;
who shall drink the richest Wine, who shall wear the most costly apparell."[14]
Two Philadelphia establishments, the London Coffee House (opened in 1754)
and the City Tavern (1773), were founded by merchants, and their customary
midday gatherings soon drew the entire commercial community. Some coffeehouses developed quickly into taverns and inns, offering lodging as well as food
and drink.

Inland towns had their taverns too, serving local residents and travelers who passed through by coach. Some cities, like Boston (where the first tavern opened in 1634), took special pains to regulate these places and thereby control or prohibit gambling, prostitution, brawls, and other vices and unseemly pursuits. But maintaining order was very difficult in the larger towns as new taverns and inns kept popping up. Though not confined to towns, they were characteristic urban institutions—places of communication, entertainment, social contact, bargaining, and variety. These "public houses," which existed by the scores and even hundreds in the larger cities, remained an essential part of urban life.

Urbanity

Family, church, and tavern were especially important institutions in the maturing cities of colonial America because they were social anchors in an increasingly diverse society. Ethnic and religious diversity (in Philadelphia, street signs in some areas were lettered in English and German), growing distinctions in wealth and social status, and the continual coming and going of people combined to create a unique environment. Though the physical boundaries between city and country were unclear, the differences in lifestyle and atmosphere were evident. As one English traveler noted at the end of the colonial period, the colonists were "much alike except in the great towns, where the inhabitants are more civilized." In 1773, a resident of Baltimore summarized the importance of urban civilization:

> Liberty, science, and commerce, the great friends of man, are sister adventurers. They are intimately, indeed inseparably connected together, and always take up their chief residence in the cities. Thither the greatest geniuses of the age generally resort, and incited by emulation or fired by ambition, they stimulate each other to successful exertions of native talents; . . . a Boston, a New-York, and a Philadelphia add lustre and dignity to the colonies to which they belong.[15]

The colonial seaports possessed, in a word, "urbanity," a distinctive richness of social, economic, and cultural life. The leading colonial cultural centers were, not surprisingly, the largest towns. Boston was preeminent in theology, literature, and higher learning—the result of generations of dedicated Puritan scholars and clergymen. Among the colonial cities New York boasted the most cosmopolitan social life, and the influence of various ethnic and religious groups stimulated a lively cultural life as well. Philadelphia was a hearty commercial town, boasting some of the best newspapers in the colonies and a notable civic spirit; it soon became a center of book publishing. Charles Town's prosperous harbor supported a very wealthy elite, which included a number of educated people of refined tastes, although many spent a good part of the year on their

Charles Town Harbor, 1739
Businesses and residences clustered along the waterfront in colonial
seaports. The number and variety of sailing vessels depicted here
reflect the diversity and prosperity of Charles Town's commerce.

plantations. Whatever the level of cultural life in the North American towns, however, it was invariably more advanced and active by European norms than anything to be found in rural areas.

Though the pursuits of high culture were usually confined to a leisured upper class, the literacy rate in the colonies was quite high by European standards. Because the Puritans placed great importance on the ability to read the Scriptures directly, instruction in at least the basics of reading and writing was especially stressed in New England, along with the training of clergymen to fill established pulpits and lead new flocks. Harvard College, the first institution of higher learning in the English colonies, was founded in 1636 at Cambridge, just outside Boston, to provide educated clergy, magistrates, and scholars. A modest effort at public education at the lower levels was also made in the Bay Colony. The middle and southern colonies had a fair proportion of educated colonists, including a number of university-trained men. The College of William and Mary was founded in 1693 in Williamsburg, though most other instruction in the southern colonies was left to private academies and tutors who served generally well-to-do families.

Private libraries containing basic reference works as well as some of the latest literary and philosophical volumes from London bookshops were not uncommon among the colonial elite. John Harvard's 300-volume collection, left to the College in 1638, constituted the first library for public use in America. In 1732, Benjamin Franklin founded the first subscription library in Philadelphia, which gave members access to a much larger number of books than they could possibly amass individually. The first library building appeared in Newport, Rhode Island, fifteen years later. The New York Society Library, dating from 1754, provided a significant resource for the cultural life of the city destined to be the largest in the country by the early nineteenth century.

Literature and book collections were not, of course, confined to towns, but the largest private collections, the first public libraries, and the printing and distribution of books were distinctly urban features. Printing presses were brought to America quite early (Boston had a press a hundred years before Liverpool, for example), though until the eighteenth century large publishing projects—even those by colonial writers—were almost always done in London. By 1750, colonial publishing had grown much more prominent and active. Philadelphia emerged as the leading publishing center in North America, followed closely by Boston and New York.

The image of the city as reflected in colonial literature was, as in later periods, ambivalent and shifting. American writers were clearly preoccupied with agriculture, both because of its economic importance in a developing country and because the individual ownership of land and the discipline of husbandry seemed so important to the evolving American character. Even the urbane

Franklin insisted that agriculture was the basis of a good society, and Thomas Jefferson saw in the common yeoman both a bastion against the concentrated and abused authority of European states and an alternative to the struggling and dependent masses of Old World cities. "The mobs of great cities," he wrote in *Notes on the State of Virginia,* "add just so much to the support of pure government, as sores do to the strength of the human body."[16] The New England vision, in contrast, often looked to heaven rather than to earth. Anne Bradstreet's ideal city, for instance, was not of this world: "The City where I hope to dwell,/There's none on Earth can parallel."[17] Yet the young John Adams, after a visit to Boston in 1758, remarked on the city's elegance, learned conversation, and exciting activity as well as its tumult, noise, and dirt. Those inclined to favor industry and commerce were similarly inclined to favor cities and the high degree of economic organization and opportunity they afforded.

Painting and music were prominent features of the European cultural scene. Not surprisingly, these arts were also far less advanced in America, though educated colonists were fairly successful at keeping up with the latest developments from afar. Few could afford to collect great art, but prints, copies of great paintings, and maps were popular throughout the colonies and graced the walls of even modest houses.

The theater was also a favored diversion for the urban social elite, though theatrical productions did not appear until the eighteenth century. Puritan disapproval of all public amusements inhibited theatrical development in Boston, but a number of plays were performed in Charles Town in the 1730s and in most other large towns thereafter. The refined arts pursued by the upper classes became increasingly visible as the Revolution approached, though they were perhaps not as vital in the colonial period as the ballads, songs, lively dances, and entertainment of popular culture. At taverns, wayside inns, and around waterfronts and city markets, a variety of sports and spirited performances flourished, especially as the pious restrictions of the seventeenth century wore off.

In fact, achievements in the creative arts were difficult and infrequent in a society preoccupied with survival and growth. Science, however, was a different matter. The mysteries of the New World inspired the curiosity of learned Europeans, and colonists were superbly located for launching geographical and naturalist studies. The identification and classification of new flora and fauna began with the first settlements and continued throughout the colonial period. Colonists were also in the forefront of speculation about vast, and largely uncharted, areas of the continent west of the Appalachians, and new discoveries often accompanied the waves of settlement and commercial ventures made by the coastal cities into virgin territory in the mid- and late eighteenth century. Colonial physicians produced medical treatises on various subjects from inoculation to new drugs and potions that drew the attention of their English and

European colleagues. Their achievements in the various areas of science caused a good many colonists to be invited to membership in England's prestigious Royal Society.

Newspapers and pamphlets were the principal means of circulating ideas in the eighteenth century—and they were usually produced in towns. The first regularly appearing newspaper in the colonies was the *Boston News-Letter*, which began publication in 1704. By mid-century, newspapers existed in all the larger towns. Crossing the barriers between refined and popular culture, newspapers were crucial to all groups and classes in colonial cities. Commerce was highly dependent on information—about fluctuating prices on English markets, international conditions, commodity gluts and shortages, the latest finished goods available in London and Liverpool—and fresh news from abroad was rushed into print. Newspapers were the source of many conversations in taverns and coffeehouses; as the Revolution approached, they played a major role in disseminating political essays and diatribes against King and Parliament. Perhaps the most famous colonial newssheet was Philadelphia's *Pennsylvania Gazette*, purchased by Benjamin Franklin in 1730. Colonial printers also did a brisk business in pamphlets, handbills, and broadsides, some dealing with advertising and announcements and others with politics. These circulated through the fledgling mail system and were hawked in the streets and posted to walls, doors, and fences.

By the time of the Revolution most of the larger colonial cities had libraries, theaters, concert halls, and at least several newspapers and printing establishments. Philadelphia, Boston, and New York led in the creative arts, whereas Charles Town was perhaps foremost in the elegance of its elite social and cultural life. Colonial America had not developed a unique culture by any means; its arts and fashions were very much within the English and European tradition. But Americans were fashioning a sense of their own identity as a creative and maturing society removed from the Old World.

Like the institutions of church, family, and tavern, the developing urban culture served as a new bond in the increasingly complex colonial cities, at the same time reflecting the social divisions within them. In fact, the nature of town life was such that forces were constantly pulling the population together and apart, sorting them physically and by class. Groups in urban society were becoming defined by where and how they lived, what they read, the type of entertainment they enjoyed, who they married, how they spent their leisure time, what churches they belonged to, and how they behaved. Institutions had emerged in urban society that softened the edges of town life and provided a sense of belonging and comradeship. But few cut across group lines and some, occasionally, helped to generate friction. In consequence, by the mid-eighteenth century local governments were playing greater roles than these institutions in serving as a common focus for urban life.

Notes

1. Quoted in Carl Bridenbaugh, *Cities in Revolt: Urban Life in America, 1743–1776* (New York: Capricorn, 1955), p. 24.
2. Quoted in Bayrd Still, ed., *Urban America: A History with Documents* (Boston: Little, Brown, 1974), p. 14.
3. Quoted in John J. McCusker and Russell R. Menard, *The Economy of British America, 1607–1789* (Chapel Hill: University of North Carolina Press, 1985), p. 205.
4. Quoted in Still, ed., *Urban America,* p. 30.
5. James A. Henretta, "Economic Development and Social Structure in Colonial Boston," *William and Mary Quarterly* 22 (January 1965): 75–92.
6. Sam Bass Warner, Jr., *The Private City: Philadelphia in Three Periods of Its Growth* (Philadelphia: University of Pennsylvania Press, 1968), p. 9. Figures on Philadelphia are taken from this source; those on the other cities are taken from Jackson Turner Main, *The Social Structure of Revolutionary America* (Princeton, N.J.: Princeton University Press, 1965), pp. 35–36.
7. Quoted in Bridenbaugh, *Cities in Revolt,* p. 140.
8. Henretta, "Economic Development and Social Structure," p. 84.
9. Quoted in Gary B. Nash, *The Urban Crucible: Social Change, Political Consciousness, and the Origins of the American Revolution* (Cambridge, Mass.: Harvard University Press, 1979), p. 3.
10. Quoted in Bridenbaugh, *Cities in Revolt,* p. 15.
11. Benjamin Franklin, *Autobiography,* rev. ed. (New York: Macmillan, 1962), p. 102.
12. Quoted in Bridenbaugh, *Cities in Revolt,* p. 151.
13. Quoted in Thomas J. Archdeacon, *New York City, 1664–1710: Conquest and Change* (Ithaca, N.Y.: Cornell University Press, 1976), p. 33.
14. Quoted in Carl Bridenbaugh, *Cities in the Wilderness: Urban Life in America, 1625–1724* (New York: The Ronald Press, 1938), p. 427.
15. Quoted in Bridenbaugh, *Cities in Revolt,* p. 215.
16. Quoted in Thomas Bender, *Toward an Urban Vision: Ideas and Institutions in Nineteenth-Century America* (Lexington, Ky.: University Press of Kentucky, 1975), p. 4.
17. From Bradstreet's poem, "The Flesh and the Spirit." For further reading, see Jeannine Hensley, ed., *The Works of Anne Bradstreet* (Cambridge, Mass.: Harvard University Press, 1967), p. 217.

3

Governing the Colonial Town

Before 1700, local government served an essentially economic role, busying itself with regulating the urban economy. Public services such as road building and maintenance, fire and police protection, and public health regulation were generally unknown. The fledgling town of Albany, which had neither paved roads nor the means to protect its buildings and citizens from fire or crime, built numerous fur trading depots and drafted intricate ordinances regulating trade with the Iroquois. New Yorkers did not seem to mind trudging through open sewers or drinking tainted water while their government spent considerable sums on constructing wharves and public market houses. Local government was highly specific on who could trade what and where. This emphasis was not surprising, given the fact that most cities initially limited citizenship to those who engaged in commerce and, later in the seventeenth century, to property holders. In Albany, for example, a man voted in the district where he worked, not where he lived.

The exceptions to this rule were the town governments in New England, which also concerned themselves with matters of public conduct, moral behavior, and public health and safety. New England towns enjoyed a large measure of political autonomy and did not have formal charters of incorporation as did their counterparts in England. In contrast, most other colonial towns were much more concerned with economic than with social regulations. Even though they defended their rights and prerogatives jealously, many had never been free of outside influence and control.

The English model of municipal incorporation was especially prominent in the middle colonies. Of fourteen municipal corporations in America in 1750, for example, ten were in Pennsylvania, New Jersey, and New York. Two basic forms prevailed: the closed corporation and the open corporation. In the closed corporation, the principal municipal officials—usually a mayor, a recorder, and aldermen—exercised a wide range of powers and could keep themselves in office indefinitely by means of long terms and their right to appoint successors. Open corporations often held similar powers, but officials were periodically elected by "freemen" (property owners). New York City was governed by an open corporation, and annual elections were held for aldermen and councilmen. Philadelphia, on the other hand, maintained a closed corporate government, the members of which guarded their prerogatives closely and resisted pressures to hold popular elections. The Pennsylvania assembly made several efforts to modify this often unresponsive and inefficient arrangement by establishing special-purpose boards with elected members and by creating additional elected positions (such as tax assessor and commissioner) outside the corporation. By the time of the Revolution, the Philadelphia corporation had lost many of its original powers and its jurisdiction had been curtailed.

The British encouraged the exercise of broad powers by local colonial governments. Presumably, localities would thus be in a better position to promote settlement and control trade. But local autonomy barely existed for some cities, and this autonomy was in any event difficult to maintain as provincial governments grew stronger. In Charles Town, for example, the board of commissioners was appointed by the South Carolina legislature and was responsible to that body. As a result, one of the largest cities in the colonies was virtually without local authority or initiative for much of the colonial period. One consequence of this situation was a comparatively low level of municipal services in Charles Town. Other cities, like New York, were underrepresented in colonial assemblies.

Both the nature and functions of local government began to change by the early 1700s. Political power broadened to include all adult male property holders, and officials became more attentive to the community's service needs. Several factors were responsible for these changes. First, the traditional role of local government as an economic regulator was grounded in the European concept of scarcity: with limited resources in food and goods, government must regulate quantity and price as well as ensuring the honesty of those engaging in the trade of these scarce commodities. In New World cities, as the initial planners of urban settlements discovered, scarcity was not a problem. In addition, thanks to new intellectual trends in Europe, more optimistic views on man's nature were current by the early 1700s. Regulations to prevent price gouging, ensure standard weights and measures, and limit competition were not necessary if man was basically good. Finally, and most obvious, the towns themselves had been transformed from their small, homogeneous beginnings. They were now diverse, fragmented, and disorderly.

The Varieties of Disorder

By the 1740s, the level of violence had increased in the port communities, or that at least was the perception of most civic leaders. Brawls became more frequent, especially along the waterfront, as the volume of trade rose and immigration swelled colonial urban populations. Drunkenness was also made almost inevitable by the proliferation of taverns and grog shops and the rising number of sailors. Crimes ranging from theft to assault and even murder were on the increase as well, creating the need for some official action. Colonial cities had nothing resembling uniformed professional police forces; a night watch and a few constables were the general rule. Charles Town authorities were more attentive to the maintenance of social order than other colonial city officials because of the perceived threat of slave revolt, but even here law enforcement was informal and inefficient by twentieth-century standards. The problems colonial cities faced were often less severe than those in the larger European ports and capitals, where an established "criminal element" flourished in fetid slums, but they were nevertheless troubling and growing more prevalent. .

Certainly by Puritan standards, moral depravity was rampant by the eighteenth century. Reality had afflicted John Winthrop's dream of a godly commonwealth from the beginning, but by 1650 the spirit of commerce and worldly pursuits prevailed in Boston. A century later, the city on the hill was only slightly less noted than New York for its bawdyhouses and some women even solicited on the streets. Madams usually presided over their flocks near the swirling waterfront, catering to sailors, tradesmen, soldiers, and on occasion members of the gentry. Groups of angry citizens sometimes reacted violently against these blights on civic virtue—and the prospect of supporting illegitimate children with public funds—by burning the infamous houses or sending the prostitutes out of town. In 1734, a band of reformers demolished one of Boston's "houses of ill fame," and three years later a brothel "for harbouring lewd and dissolute Persons, was beset by a mob which broke all the windows, stove in the doors, and did so much damage to the place that the Woman who kept the same . . . [was] obliged to quit it."[1] But this was a losing effort. In the eighteenth century, especially as the transient populations of colonial cities mounted, prostitution, gaming, drunkenness, and rowdy behavior became all too familiar.

The presence of relatively large numbers of blacks fed public concern over disorder. When conspiracies among blacks were suspected, the reaction could be swift and brutal. A presumed "Negro conspiracy" in New York City led to harsh repression in 1741: thirteen blacks were burned at the stake, eight were hanged, and seventy-one were sent from the colony.

Aside from contending with social upheaval, urban residents also experienced the disorder arising from fire and epidemic disease. No danger was more frightening in colonial cities than fire. An errant spark from a lantern, a fireplace, or a spent match was all it took to build a blaze that could grow out of control almost as it began, quickly consuming buildings and, if carried on a strong wind, whole blocks of buildings. Severe fires struck Boston in 1676, 1679, and 1711, and the city experienced the worst conflagration of the entire colonial era in 1760. The very core of the town—some 400 structures—was destroyed. The wooden buildings of Charles Town were also ripe for disaster. Much of that city was devastated by fire in 1731, and again in 1740 when more than 300 dwellings and a number of other buildings were consumed.

The sudden outbreak of fire was feared perhaps only slightly more than the convulsive and fatal effects of epidemic disease. Cities were especially susceptible to waves of illness because their high concentrations of population allowed the easy spread of germs from one person to another. Larger seaports were also in the mainstream of international and intercolonial commerce, which carried, along with trading goods, dangerous organisms from far-off places. Smallpox, cholera, and yellow fever were especially deadly, striking quickly and claiming victims seemingly at random from among the population. A smallpox epidemic in Boston in 1721 infected nearly 6,000 residents, more than 800 of whom died despite the availability of a preventive vaccine. Smallpox also struck New York and Philadelphia. In 1731, commenting on an epidemic raging in New York, an observer wrote, "Many Children dye . . . as well as grown Persons, and the Country People are afraid to come to Town which makes Markets thin, Provisions dear, and deadens all Trade, and it goes very hard with the Poor."[2] Roughly 6 percent of the city's population succumbed to the disease that year. Charles Town suffered doubly from yellow fever outbreaks and smallpox. Almost every urban family was victimized at some time by the major scourges while being exposed at the same time to the threat posed by the high incidence of other maladies such as tuberculosis, influenza, and dysentery. The mortality rate among infants and young children was high, and any infectious illness was extremely difficult to contain in urban places.

The Response of Local Government

Civic leaders—primarily merchants—responded to these various natural and social disorders by attempting to manage the urban environment in much the same manner as they controlled the urban economy: by regulation. To finance the expanded scope of local government, leaders slowly abandoned their dependence on license fees and fines and turned to property taxes. The result was an urban economy freed of financial and regulatory constraints and protected by a new level of public services. In the case of fire, town leaders realized that they could do only so much once a blaze got out of control. Water was often in short supply, and local governments acted to dig new wells and even import water from nearby sources. Adequate urban water supplies were, in fact, demanded as much for fire control as for use in drinking and washing. Some of the larger cities purchased modern firefighting equipment, sometimes more advanced than that of major European cities. And the volunteer fire company was an American urban innovation, tracing its origins to the Union Fire Company of Philadelphia, organized by Benjamin Franklin in 1736. In 1700, Boston was the only colonial town with a fire brigade. Their primary weapon for fighting fires was a water bucket. By 1775, most towns possessed an organized battalion of firemen who employed at least one modern pumping engine.

The most effective measures were preventive in nature. Fire regulations in Boston were especially stringent. Laws passed in 1638 and 1646 by the Mas-

A Blaze in New York, 1730
Firefighting methods were still very primitive in 1730; note the efforts of the bucket brigade. Despite subsequent increases in building regulations and the emergence of volunteer fire companies, colonial towns remained vulnerable to fire.

sachusetts Bay government prohibited smoking outdoors to reduce the fire hazard, and curfew laws were adopted for the same purpose. Night watches were
established primarily to alert the townspeople in case of fire, though they were
also supposed to serve a limited law enforcement function. Defective and dirty
chimneys were the major cause of fire, and some cities required periodic chim-
ney cleaning. To the extent possible, localities encouraged construction in brick
and stone rather than in wood, though the high cost of these alternative materials precluded their consistent use. Tile and slate began to replace wood roofing
on Philadelphia residences at least by 1740, and a building boom in the decade
before the Revolution inaugurated the city's first urban renewal effort by replacing tinder-box wooden homes with three-story brick structures. New York
City prohibited wooden structures altogether after 1776 and required tile and
slate on all roofs. But brick was expensive, and wood remained the only realistic
building material for most people. Circumventing the law was thus common
practice in New York. Even among the affluent of Charles Town and Newport,
brick was a relatively uncommon building material. Generally, fire prevention
regulations were widely violated and were enforced most strictly just after serious fires had occurred, as towns were periodically reminded of their importance.

The collective battle against disease was even more difficult. European towns
and cities were not known for their cleanliness, and this situation generally held
true in colonial cities also. Household garbage was routinely dumped out of
windows into the streets, where pigs and dogs consumed some of it. Human
wastes were put directly into the ground, occasionally entering drinking water
sources. Boston, New York, and Philadelphia, among other cities, outlawed garbage disposal in the public streets by the beginning of the eighteenth century.
And municipalities attempted to provide sufficient clear water for drinking and
washing. Philadelphia's system of public wells distributed throughout the city
was a notable achievement, whereas New York's water was notoriously noxious.

The greatest breakthrough in managing communicable diseases during the
colonial era was the introduction of inoculation against smallpox in the Boston
epidemic of 1721. Even though inoculation proponents did not fully understand how the process worked and many people who were understandably
afraid of the strange procedure refused to be inoculated, it did show results.
Inoculation grew more and more popular and became an accepted way of com-
bating smallpox in the fifteen years before the Revolution.

Nothing resembling an organized police force appeared during the colonial
period. New England towns typically had at least one constable, but law enforcement in the modern sense was not really a part of his role. When more-or-
less organized night watches did appear, their primary job was to provide early
warning of fires and disturbances. Consistent with the idea of the consensual
and compact community, citizens were expected to rely upon one another in

maintaining public order. As towns grew, however, and the close ties among neighbors and coreligionists gave way to the more impersonal connections that exist among strangers and different social groups, this was not a sufficient remedy.

Municipal ordinances did ban certain kinds of activities—such as working on the Sabbath and public drunkenness—in addition to obvious criminal offenses. Other than a general reliance on public pressure, however, rarely was a system established to deal with transgressors. A major exception was Charles Town, where the presence of a large number of black slaves induced whites to provide not only a strict slave code but also special patrols and enforcement measures. Though frequently lax in its actual operation, this system did exist in the event of emergency. Likewise, Boston passed a strict code in 1724 curtailing the rights of blacks and Indians. Generally, though, towns and cities failed to develop effective and consistent means of dealing with crime and disorder. And as the Revolution approached, the deep-seated colonial resistance to established armies and uniformed police forces (symbols of "foreign" domination) postponed innovations in law enforcement until the nineteenth century.

Most towns, however, accepted their responsibilities, at least as they were perceived at the time in the light of English experience and tradition. Regulating trade, maintaining order, and responding to natural disasters like fire and disease were established and accepted roles for municipal authority. Poverty had to be dealt with, though generally in a moralistic and condescending fashion. Building streets and providing adequate water supplies were perceived as both public and private responsiblities, with different cities emphasizing one approach or the other. Housing, however, was not considered a matter of public policy, except to the extent that poor housing might endanger other people's property if it caught fire.

Popular Politics

Civic leaders did not, of course, operate in a vacuum. The expanding role of local government resulted not only from the obvious problems that accompanied development, but also from the pressure applied by residents. Perhaps the main difference in local politics between England and America was the wider political participation that prevailed in the colonies. Although only tradesmen and certain taxpayers voted in the English municipal corporation, the franchise was generally extended throughout the colonies to all freeholders by the early eighteenth century. Because land was readily available in the New World (indeed, land ownership was sometimes a condition of residency in some New

England towns), the majority of adult males could qualify to vote, even in closed corporation cities like Philadelphia, Williamsburg, and Annapolis.

Adult male property owners, however, constituted only a fifth of the total urban population. And exercise of the franchise was neither an automatic solution for all ills nor a guarantee of social or political change. In New York City, entrenched local officials encouraged a liberal use of the franchise to demonstrate their broad popular support and thus retain their positions. As in our own day, voting was often a means of organizing political support and even of social control. In general, the larger the town, the smaller the proportion of the population was eligible to vote or hold public office and the more likely it was that wealthy individuals would occupy leadership positions.

Politics in the seaport towns was not a closed affair, however. By the 1750s, if not earlier, the combination of economic dislocation and social distress among a broad spectrum of the urban population contributed to a considerable political volatility. Discontented groups within urban society expressed themselves strongly and often. The channels for such expression grew, in fact, during the eighteenth century. Outdoor political rallies, newspapers (the first urban newspaper did not appear until 1704), incendiary campaign literature, petition campaigns, club activities, and even targeted bursts of violence against wealthy leaders and their property had become commonplace by the 1750s. The diversity of urban populations, fluctuations in the urban economy, and the broadening of the electorate encouraged the development of factions or parties. In Philadelphia during the 1720s, a populist party emerged under the unlikely leadership of Scottish nobleman Sir William Keith, who organized opposition against wealthy leaders. The Keithians formed party tickets, recruited immigrant German and Scots-Irish voters, published pamphlets touting their cause, and held outdoor rallies. In 1726, Keith successfully secured a seat in the colonial Assembly and led a celebration that featured "Mobs, Bonfires, Bunns, Huzzas" and the torching of the pillory and stocks, the symbols of authority.[3] A bloodier election-day confrontation occurred in that city in 1742, when a group of seventy sailors, to prevent the voting of unnaturalized German immigrants, stormed Philadelphia's courthouse where civic leaders had retreated.

Urban leaders did not as a rule cower before dangerous mobs. Deference to the "better sort" remained part of the political process in the mid-eighteenth century. Much of provincial politics acted out in the seaports involved power struggles between small numbers of elites. Because political alliances tended to be vertical, with leadership and direction issuing from the top down, politics represented much less a clash of classes than a contest among the elites for the votes of the masses. And the "masses" of course were a diverse lot. All this, combined with the heterogeneity of urban populations and the frequent movement into and out of the towns, tended to deflect social discontent and class feeling—though urban crowds, artisan groups, and various laborers were able to influence provincial policies through their various channels of protest.

Towns in the Revolution

The evolving political traditions and agencies of protest in colonial towns enabled these communities to play a major role in the coming of the American Revolution. As economic centers, the towns, especially the seaports, would also be the focus of imperial legislation designed to rationalize a now far-flung and costly empire. Though most colonial Americans still lived in the countryside by the 1770s, the influence of the larger communities ran considerably ahead of their share of the total population because of these economic and political circumstances.

The change in the nature of the British Empire after the conclusion of the Seven Years' War in 1763 prompted Parliament to tighten restrictions on currency and trade. Unfortunately for the British, such restrictions coincided with an economic downturn in colonial seaports immediately after the war's end. The depression, which affected working classes most heavily, revived popular discontent. Urban leaders perceived this discontent as a means of securing their authority and they led or encouraged urban crowds through the traditional channels of protest, particularly during the Stamp Act crisis in 1765. Economic distress was greatest in Boston, where leaders such as James Otis and Samuel Adams used the presence of British troops and unpopular legislation to rally the workers to their standard. In Charles Town, leaders such as Henry Laurens and William Henry Drayton, fearing that British policies would create a situation "pregnant with horrible uproar and wild confusion" attempted to organize and take control of the sentiment against the Crown.[4]

The merger of local issues and fears with the economic and legislative crisis generated by British policies was characteristic of not only the seaports but of interior settlements as well. In the numerous county seats of the Virginia colony, for example, leaders gathered citizens to petition and protest policies. The growing Revolutionary crisis enabled county leaders to reassert their authority, an authority that, according to historian Rhys Isaacs, had been weakened by evangelical insurgency (as it had in Boston) and by the mounting debt and credit problems affecting the larger planters.

This is not to say that town leaders used the Revolutionary crisis cynically or that sentiment against the British was unanimous. Loyalist feeling was strong, especially in the seaport towns where merchants had enjoyed the benefits and protection of the British Empire. In fact, some merchants became involved in

Street Politics Before the Revolution

During the Stamp Act crisis of 1765, a mob attacked Massachusetts Royal Governor Thomas Hutchinson and destroyed his house. Urban leaders could effectively mobilize workers against the British, especially in Boston, which was suffering economically. Demonstrations were an accepted means of expressing public opinion in colonial towns, although the violence that sometimes resulted was more controversial.

FLIGHT OF HUTCHINSON BEFORE THE RIOTERS.

anti-British activities for the express purpose of muting dissent and reaction against the Crown. This was especially the case in Charles Town, a Loyalist stronghold. There were also genuine patriots among the urban leadership who believed for economic and political reasons that a break from the Mother Country was essential to advance both interests. These sentiments were most evident in struggling Boston, where British policy weighed most heavily.

The British recognized the strategic and economic importance of the seaport towns. They were, first of all, centers of communication. By the 1770s, the colonial elite had built up a web of economic and familial connections that transcended urban boundaries; news traveled as fast as the wind drove the ships up and down the coast. In the years immediately preceding the Revolution, the British sought to direct policies to bring these coastal populations to heel. The attempt failed; decades of political activism and rising social discontent found a ready target in British policies and functionaries. Once the war began, British tacticians felt that by occupying cities such as New York, Philadelphia, Charles

Town, and Savannah, they could encourage Loyalist sentiment and cripple the economy of the rebellious colonies. The British could not hold these towns for long, however; more important, the self-sufficency of the colonists, even in the towns where garden plots and farm animals were fixtures of the urban landscape, undermined such strategies.

By the time the first armed conflicts of the Revolution began, most of the major colonial cities were over a century old. No longer clusters of new settlers dedicated to survival and the maintenance of an organic community, they had become market places with active mercantile elites, interest groups, a variety of cultural, religious, and political institutions, dynamic commerce, and a new spirit of entrepreneurism and individualism. The emphasis of public policy had shifted from maintaining the good of the larger community to providing maximum opportunities for individuals and families. The voluntary associations formed to achieve various civic purposes were cooperative endeavors, to be sure, but they were nevertheless designed to fulfill the new spirit of private interests and individual fulfillment. More and more, the shape and life of American cities were determined by competition among individuals, families, and private interest groups. The Revolution also highlighted the new relationships among and between cities, connections that would have regional and national implications in the coming decades.

External Relationships and Internal Structure

By the 1770s, an "incipient urban core" was emerging in North America that included Boston, New York, and Philadelphia. Each city "drew daily upon the trade and talent of three states in its immediate hinterland."[5] Merchants in these cities corresponded with each other, conducted business together, and socialized; their offspring married each other. Southern ports drifted outside the core and became dependent on it. By the middle of the eighteenth century, Philadelphia merchants, for example, had established a lucrative carrying trade with Norfolk, Charles Town, and later Savannah, shipping tobacco, naval stores, indigo, and rice from these places in exchange for manufactured products (domestic and foreign), as well as meat, rum, and flour. But Philadelphia's merchants played a more intrusive role in the Southern economy than they did with their trading partners in the Northeast: they owned more than half the shipping plying the Southern coastal trade and they provided an array of financial services. By the 1770s, the Chesapeake tobacco region could already be considered part of Philadelphia's hinterland.

The South's subsidiary trade position seems odd in the face of its success in cultivating marketable staple crops. The opulent mansions of the Virginia planters were legendary even as early as the 1730s, and the low country South Carolina rice planters were the wealthiest individuals in colonial America. Yet the Southerners were dependent—on Scottish merchants and on merchants from Philadelphia and New York—by the time of the Revolution.

Perhaps the southern colonists had too much of a good thing. Land was colonial America's greatest resource, and no one exploited it better than Southerners, particularly Virginians. Though northern lands were fertile enough to provide cities like Philadelphia with a lucrative trade, the cash crop—grains—could never command a sufficiently high price in Europe because of competition from other parts of the continent. Not so tobacco or rice or, later, cotton. Southerners could rely on agriculture almost exclusively without needing to experiment with different economic activities; northerners could not. Their spirit of enterprise thus dulled, southerners, almost by default, ceded much of their trade to the Scots and to northern urban merchants. Their leadership lacked the flexibility, turnover, and diversity of urban societies in the North that encouraged innovation. In fact, there were precious few places a diverse population could congregate. Alexandria, Virginia, for example, had no more than twenty merchants in 1775. Southern urbanization was dispersed; where more than modest concentrations existed, such as in Charles Town, rural elites dominated and overshadowed the mercantile communities. Thus, in many respects, the regional specialization and imbalances that would characterize urban development during the nineteenth century were already outlined in the colonial era.

Virginians, at least, were aware of the relationship between urbanization and regional imbalances. In 1784, James Madison sponsored a bill in the state legislature designed to confine maritime trade to one or two ports (Norfolk and Alexandria), explaining that he was "sensible of the utility of establishing a Philadelphia or a Baltimore among ourselves." Though Madison was successful in securing passage of his scheme, the legislature eventually repealed the act. Fifty years later, a Norfolk newspaper complained bitterly that "without foreign commerce Norfolk must dwindle to a village, and Virginia sink to the lowest scale in the Union, while New York, vampire-like, is sucking her blood to the last drop."[6] The origins of that frustration were apparent in the 1780s.

Madison appreciated the importance of commercial port towns not only for Virginia, but for the new nation as well. A strong urban commercial economy was an essential prop for national well-being. His draft for the federal Constitution attempted, among other things, to create a national support system for mercantile activities. The provisions giving the federal government the power to tax, regulate commerce, issue patents, and put down insurrections reflected Madison's belief in the close connection between political and economic stability. As one historian noted, "Federalist merchants . . . had gotten what they wanted: a stable constitutional framework within which they could prosper."[7]

Much as the external relationships of colonial towns provided a preview of the next century's patterns, their internal structure was also a harbinger of the future. The rapid rise in land values as a result of prosperity and speculation instituted a form of social zoning, moving those unable to pay increased costs from choice locations and even out of the city boundaries altogether. Though land use differentiation was obviously not a major theme in these geographically small towns, the average "man on the street" could tell you where the "better sort" lived, as well as those areas you would do well to avoid, particularly at night. The beginnings of separation of work from residence not only had a spatial impact on the evolving city but significantly affected the lives of men and women, which in turn resulted in various architectural and spatial accommodations. In terms of architecture, at least, it is good to recall Louis Sullivan's dictum that "what the people are within, the buildings express without; and inversely what the buildings are objectively is a sure index of what the people are subjectively."[8] Already in the colonial period, architecture was one means of marking distinctions between people and spaces, trends that would become more pronounced in the nineteenth century.

Decisions on the use and appropriation of urban space were invariably private by the eighteenth century. Though local government provided some framework by means of fire regulations and the suppression of noxious activities, urban land became as much an economic venture as international trade, and often more remunerative. The consequences of this privatization of urban land would become more apparent in the nineteenth-century city.

Finally, the colonial town reflected the ambivalence of the English and then the Americans toward urban civilization. Both early (New England) and late (Savannah) town plans attempted to create middle landscapes. Invariably, most of these schemes failed; Penn's "greene Country Towne" soon became a dense and dirty city. Repeated failures did not dampen the compromise spirit of the planners or prospective urban dwellers, however. The abundance of land and building materials and, in the not-too-distant future, the assist of technology and capital, fired their vision beyond the Revolution and into the nineteenth century. Although we did not become a suburban nation until the twentieth century, both the attempt and the perspective were already visible three hundred years earlier.

Political scientist Clinton Rossiter has dubbed the decades before the American Revolution the "seedtime of the Republic": in institutions, beliefs, and values, the colonists were, in many ways, already Americans by the time of the Revolution.[9] It is equally appropriate to designate the colonial era the "seedtime of the American city." Urban settlements continued to evolve, of course, in ways scarcely discernible in the eighteenth century. In both its internal and external relationships, however, the American city of the nineteenth and twentieth centuries was a direct descendant of the modest towns and villages that dotted the Atlantic coast, and had barely penetrated the Appalachian foothills, by the time of the American Revolution.

Notes

1. Quoted in Carl Bridenbaugh, *Cities in the Wilderness: Urban Life in America, 1625–1742* (New York: The Ronald Press, 1938), p. 389.
2. Quoted in *ibid.*, p. 400.
3. *Ibid.*, p. 383.
4. Quoted in Walter J. Fraser, Jr., "The City Elite, 'Disorder,' and the Poor Children of Pre-Revolutionary Charleston," *South Carolina Historical Magazine* 84 (July 1983): 176.
5. D. W. Meinig, *The Shaping of America: A Geographical Perspective on 500 Years of History*, vol. 1, *Atlantic America, 1492–1800* (New Haven, Conn.: Yale University Press, 1986), pp. 400–401.
6. Both quotes from Thomas Doerflinger, *A Vigorous Spirit of Enterprise: Merchants and Economic Development in Revolutionary Philadelphia* (Chapel Hill: University of North Carolina Press, 1986), pp. 361, 362–363.
7. Quoted in *ibid.*, p. 280.
8. Quoted in Peter A. Coclanis, "The Sociology of Architecture in Colonial Charleston: Pattern and Process in an Eighteenth-Century Southern City," *Journal of Social History* 18 (Summer 1985): 613.
9. Clinton Rossiter, *Seedtime of the Republic* (New York: Harcourt, Brace, 1953).

PART 2

The
Market
Place

1790–1870

The basic outlines of the modern American city, barely visible by the end of the colonial era, became clearer between 1790 and 1870. Cities had experienced different fates during the American Revolution. The British had occupied New York, retreated from Boston, and moved into and out of Philadelphia several times. Although the colonials had held Norfolk, they burned much of it to the ground to prevent its falling to the British. On the other hand, the occupation of New York proved to be a blessing. The British soldiers circulated hard money, not paper issues of dubious value, through the city's economy. The presence of the British forces attracted a large number of loyalists, whose properties were promptly confiscated and sold at bargain prices after the war. And a relative abundance of investment capital helped New York merchants get a running start on their urban competitors—a situation they used to good advantage during the following decades. In general, the net effect of the war on American urbanization was to accelerate the trends that had begun during the colonial period.

Perhaps the most dramatic change that occurred during the period of 1790 to 1870 was an increase in urban growth. In 1790, roughly 5 percent of the new nation's population resided in cities. Thirty years later, the figure had slowly risen to 7 percent. But every decade between 1820 and 1870 saw urban population grow three times as fast as national population, so that by 1870 more than one out of four Americans lived in cities. In 1820, there were only twelve cities with a population larger then 10,000; by 1860, 101 cities had at least that many people, and eight of those had more than 100,000 inhabitants. Though the Northeast, particularly New York, led the nation in urban population, the distribution of city dwellers was widespread. In 1840, the five largest cities accounted for 49 percent of the urban population. In 1860, that figure had declined to 38 percent.

What accounted for this growth, and how did it affect the lives of urban residents? A look at three major developments—

the development of a national urban economy, the spatial and cultural separation of individuals and groups in urban society, and the appearance of middle-class urban reform—provide some answers.

The national urban economy rested on the foundation of intraregional trade. Commercial connections among the cities of the Northeast generated profits that entrepreneurs invested in manufacturing enterprises, transportation systems, and business services. Expanding economic opportunities attracted newcomers from the countryside and abroad, further fueling demand and investment. In the meantime, western cities were developing along similar lines. After 1840 both the supply of and demand for goods and services had reached proportions that made linking the Northeast and the West a profitable undertaking. Technology, especially the railroad, made that connection possible. One important result of the connection was an urban core that extended in a broad crescent from New England down through the Middle Atlantic states, growing wider to encompass the Great Lakes cities and the Ohio River valley before narrowing at St. Louis on the Mississippi. This linking of cities carried political implications as well. The South's peculiar agricultural and labor systems limited southern cities to a subsidiary role within the national economy. Combined with the region's declining political fortunes during the 1850s, these factors exacerbated sectional tensions.

As the city expanded economically, it grew geographically. A downtown emerged, and so did residential neighborhoods within and outside the city. The new apportionment of space reflected the growing separation of different groups in urban society. New occupations and new ways of organizing work expanded both the middle and working classes, and the lifestyles of these two classes revolved around domestic ideals, associational contacts, and leisure activities that differed markedly. Racial and ethnic distinctions further fractured the physical space and social organization of the larger cities.

These growing social and economic distinctions in urban society were disturbing to middle-class men and women. Despite their growing estrangement from those less fortunate, the city was still sufficiently compact to offer visual confirmation of the contrasts of poverty and plenty. These contrasts not only touched the conscience of these religious people but awakened their fear as well. The result was the emergence of a middle-class urban reform movement that infused public policy with a strong dose of morality.

Social reforms were part of a larger effort to impose order on an increasingly diverse and fragmented city. A similar motivation had moved reformers in the colonial era, but by the nineteenth century the ordering of the American city required the organized, systematic efforts of private groups and the continued expansion of local government. Middle-class urban reform came to encompass the public provision of such vital services as health, fire, and police protection. Although efforts in these areas fell short of expectations, they laid the groundwork for the emergence of a trained urban bureaucracy later in the nineteenth century. As in the colonial era, one period of urbanization led into the next.

We call this era of urbanization from 1790 to 1870 the "Market Place." The term has two meanings. First, commerce was the engine that drove the urban economy. The growing diversity of that economy—manufacturing and business services in particular—was based on the profits derived from commerce. The market place is thus an appropriate metaphor for the importance of commerce in directing the development of cities and regions in the nineteenth century. Second, the term implies buying and selling. Real estate, stocks and bonds, goods and services, and, in the urban South, people were all fair game in the unregulated market place. The preoccupation with buying and selling accelerated the spatial expansion of cities, the application of new technologies, and the development of new functions to facilitate more buying and selling. The abundance of land had become the abundance of everything, and—so the popular wisdom went—everyone could try

for everything. This prevailing attitude provided the context
within which social reforms, public services, and individual decisions on where and how to live were made.

We are not implying that economic calculations governed all
decision making or that greed made its first appearance in the
nineteenth-century American city. We are suggesting that the
social disparities that emerged and the difficulties urban dwellers had in understanding and effectively dealing with those disparities resulted from the city's primary function as a commercial market place.

CHAPTER 4

Creating a National Urban Economy

Of all the territories of continental North America, the real prize was the West. Fertile soil and deep, swift-flowing rivers awaited those who ventured beyond the Appalachian Mountains after the Revolution. Merchants along the Atlantic coast calculated not only the wealth these pioneers would generate for eastern markets but the profits derived from the buying and selling of the land itself. The motives for planting colonial settlements were varied, but by the nineteenth century, with very few exceptions, town planting had become strictly a business enterprise. Besides lining the pockets of eastern entrepreneurs, western urbanization helped to forge a new urban core extending from the Northeast to the lake and river states of the West. The development of this core region and the accompanying political implications involved more than western promise and eastern enterprise. Winning the West, however, was a key element and the obvious first step.

Urbanmania in the West

"GAIN! GAIN! GAIN! is the beginning, the middle and the end, the alpha and omega of the founders of American towns."[1] Western town building as a speculative venture followed a general pattern, but the process produced widely varied results. The speculator, typically an agent for an eastern-based real-estate company, purchased 200 acres from the government. The next step was the survey and the division of the land into lots and streets in a gridiron pattern, marked by stakes in the ground, to make it easy to sell. Finally, the agent had a map prepared that showed not only the street and lot plan but buildings as well—the latter often existing solely in the town builder's imagination or marked out by a few rude log structures.

The map was merely the first step in a strenuous and extravagant promotional campaign designed to lure easterners to the western promised land. Few if any of these prospective urban residents would have the opportunity to make on-site inspections. For this reason, as well as because the competition for the real-estate dollar was intense, truth in advertising was irrelevant. Town building was strictly a matter of selling lots, and selling lots depended on promotion. As towns sprang up all over the western landscape, the promotional literature became the nation's greatest fictional resource.

A riverside site was deemed essential for a town's success. The metropolis of New Athens at the juncture of the Mississippi and Missouri rivers seemed singled out for glory, according to its promoters. It was, after all, "the most desirable spot in the known world." The speculators were evidently so touched by the location that they expressed their rapture in verse:

Again shall Athens bid her columns rise,
Again her lofty turrets reach the skies,
Science again shall find a safe retreat,
And commerce here as in a centre meet.[2]

Unfortunately for those who purchased lots in New Athens and other "paper cities," the grandiose futures predicted by sanguine promoters never materialized. Disappointed purchasers penned laments about scores of these paper cities in the West. The account of one gullible buyer probably reflected the typical scene that confronted hundreds of these would-be town dwellers:

There are no churches in the place, instead of four, as was represented to me. No respectable residences; no society; no women except a few woebegone, desolate-looking old creatures . . . no schools, no children; nothing but the total reverse of the picture which was presented to me. On the engraved romance [map] a "college" was imagined, of which no person here has even so much as heard the idea advanced.[3]

Such swindles capitalized on the enthusiasm that greeted the prospect of western urbanization. Americans seemed to be caught up in the mania of town building, and owning a city lot became a national fad. A trip down the Ohio or the Mississippi River in the 1820s offered a traveler a preview of what awaited him on dry land. According to one such voyager, all the passengers "were discussing the flattering prospects of the 'Great West'. . . great cities and towns were named of whose existence I had no previous knowledge." It seemed to this traveler that along the river route there was a hopeful village "on either bank, every six or seven miles."[4]

The frenzy of town-lot speculation in the West continued unabated through the first half of the nineteenth century. When the urban veins in the Ohio and the Mississippi River valleys had been exhaustively worked, the scene shifted to Kansas and later to Denver and San Francisco. The speculative mania gripped travelers to such an extent that rapid inflation fueled by easy credit inevitably followed in the wake of a successful promotional venture. The Panic of 1837 was probably the first major depression in the country where urbanization and its consequences played a significant role. In Chicago, where land values had inflated to an unrealistic $10 million, they plummeted to $1,250,000 almost overnight. The fact that speculation in town lots bore little relation to reality provided satirists with some excellent material. One Augusta, Georgia, newspaper, for example, described for its readers the "City of Skunksburgh," which lay hard by a "noble stream" that included "delicate minnows, a variety of terrapins, and . . . frogs which, in size, voice, and movement, are inferior to none." The elevation of the site was especially impressive to the writer. "A noble bluff of eighteen inches commands the harbor, and affords a most advantageous situation for military works." Awaiting the lucky visitor on arrival or shortly thereafter were an "Exchange and City Hall, a church, one Gymnastic and one Polytechnic foundation, one Olympic and two Dramatic theatres, an Equestrian circus, an observatory, two marine and two Foundling Hospitals . . . seventeen banks, to each of which may be attached a lunatic hospital." This visionary scheme was signed by "Andrew Aircastle, Theory M' Vision, and L. Moonlight, Jr. & Co."[5]

Skunksburgh was only slightly more outrageous than some of the flagrant specimens of western urban promotion. The attraction of these fraudulent sites lay in the fact that the great cities of the Ohio and the Mississippi River Valley had also been promotional schemes at one time. The success of Chicago, Cincinnati, Louisville, Pittsburgh, St. Louis, and New Orleans—all river cities—kept hopes and gullibility alive. Each city had been the scene of speculative activity, but there the similarity with the paper cities ended: the mere fact of location on a body of water was no guarantee of urban success.

The growth of successful cities resulted, in fact, from a break in the transportation of produce and manufactured goods (a transportation break was a point at which a natural obstacle—mountains, rapids, or deep water, for instance—stopped the flow of commerce). In 1778, George Rogers Clark had the foresight to establish Louisville as an interior military base. The new town offered the only major break in transportation between Pittsburgh and New Orleans, a distance of 2,000 miles by water. The falls of the Ohio River provided the fortunate obstruction, and a sheltered harbor allowed Louisville to take advantage of it. Cincinnati's first settlers in 1788 were impressed by the fact that the Licking River, which flowed into the Ohio, reached into the fertile bluegrass country of Kentucky. It was not difficult to conjure up a vision of Cincinnati "serving as the market center for this lush region."[6]

Not all the new major urban centers enjoyed a felicitous river view. Some cities grew in spite of their geography. Denver, founded in 1858, was strictly a Gold Rush community. Hard by the precipitous cliffs of the Rocky Mountains, Denver was 200 miles to the south, and 500 miles to the east and to the west, of the nearest urban settlements and possessed few redeeming geographic advantages other than its proximity to Pike's Peak. Brigham Young's Mormon community at Salt Lake City was another settlement whose location was not an advantage, except for its isolation from white civilization. Perhaps the most curious new community in post-Revolutionary America, however, was Washington, D.C. Its location amid the swampy lowlands of the Potomac River, hardly a stroke of planning genius, reflected a Congressional compromise, not a strategic coup.

Whether created by gold, God, or Congress, the instant cities, devoid of much geographic advantage, eventually lent themselves to speculative enterprise as much as did their more favorably situated counterparts. Both types of cities reflected the efforts of their planners to impart a sense of order and stability that would not only attract lot buyers but also serve as a foundation for future growth. The vehicle for establishing order in the new cities was the town plan, a blueprint that reveals to us a good deal about the planners and their urban vision.

Eastern Cities and Western Clones

Had William Penn lived long enough to wander the urban West, he would have felt very much at home. And that was the point of the new towns. Because eastern cities were still "home" to most of the western urban dwellers, like the Puritans before them they sought to surround themselves with much that was familiar. As one of the most populous and prosperous eastern metropolises—as well as one of the best planned cities—Philadelphia seemed a worthy model. As a result, William Penn's neat street gridiron became the predominant urban form in the West. The pattern was familiar, simple and, above all, facilitated the survey and sale of town lots.

Cincinnati, for example, reproduced Philadelphia's plan faithfully, even down to the same street widths. The familiar plan, however, was superimposed on unfamiliar terrain. Topography had divided Cincinnati into two communities:

the "bottom," only 7 feet above the river, and the "hill," which climbed quickly to form a mile-wide table. From the river the tiered city "looked like a green and open theater carved out of the hills."[7] The symmetrical grid and the irregular terrain clashed, but the economy and orderliness of the town plan ultimately prevailed.

The legacy of Philadelphia went beyond the spatial layout to touch other aspects of the street system. In Cincinnati and even in St. Louis, which was modeled after New Orleans, the streets running parallel to the river were numbered as they were in Philadelphia. The names of the cross-streets—Sycamore, Vine, Cherry, Walnut, Chestnut, and Pine in the Quaker City—stayed the same in their new cities over the mountains: most streets in Nashville and half the streets in Cincinnati bore Philadelphia names. Even more remarkable was the fact that the occasional alleys that broke the gridiron in Philadelphia were reproduced in name, if not in space, in some western cities. When one western traveler observed that "no daughter is more like her mother than St. Louis is like Philadelphia," he might equally have noted Louisville, Cincinnati, and Pittsburgh as other offspring of the eastern metropolis.[8]

River cities were not the only gridiron imitators. The all-pervasive pattern invaded the prairie in northern Illinois as Chicago began to expand from its Lake Michigan shore. In the Far West, San Francisco presented the spectacle of a slightly drunken gridiron staggering up colossal inclines and hurtling down precipitous declines. Here the superimposition of the grid on steep hills created hardships for pedestrian and animal alike and forever confined the business district to the base of the hills around Market Street (another good Philadelphia name). The redeeming feature of this plan, hurriedly implemented to accommodate the first wave of Gold Rushers, was the measure of instant order it provided the city, along with a great many permanent spectacular vistas, which make San Francisco one of the most lovely and inspiring American cities today. The city's characteristic exhausting climbs up steep hills and the breathtaking panoramas awaiting at the top both come courtesy of William Penn's grid.

The grid did not bring about such striking results in other cities. Momentous it was not; monotonous it was. The grid produced endless bland vistas uninterrupted by squares or buildings. The pedestrian had no relief from this monotony, nor from the chill winds that whipped down these corridors. A visitor to Cincinnati complained about the "dull monotony" of the street system, and a disappointed traveler in St. Louis hoped for "a conflagration" that would "burn it [the city] to the ground" so that planners could start anew.[9] Besides its visual poverty, the relentless grid seemed to forestall any variety in the urban landscape in the form of occasional parks, squares, and recreational spaces. Few promoters took advantage of their cities' river locations and relentlessly plotted their grids right up to the waterfront. One critic regretted that Louisville had "turned its back upon the varied and interesting prospect presented by the Ohio and its Falls." Dwellings, warehouses, and stores usurped the rightful domain of trees and grass.

The grid marched across the West and conquered most of America by 1860. Cities by this time were so closely associated with grids that one resident could state flatly: "Curved lines, you know, symbolize the country, straight lines the city."[10] From the perspective of the eastern entrepreneur, the singular advantage of the grid was that it ordered the western cities quickly. Organizing for commerce would follow organizing for settlement. Two conditions had to be met, however, before easterners could reap the benefits from western urbanization. First, an efficient means of transportation was necessary to lower the costs and ensure the reliability of moving agricultural produce from west to east. Second, easterners had to have something to exchange for western foodstuffs. Unless eastern merchants were content with being middlemen for European (mainly English) manufactured goods, they would need to develop industrial enterprises.

The development and application of transportation technology and industry occurred simultaneously in the young United States. Ironically, neither enterprise initially had much relationship with western commerce, though they became prerequisites for that trade. The early impact of both was to enhance the commerce between the towns and cities of the Northeast. By the 1840s, however, both the demand from growing western cities and the produce they could ship from the fertile farmlands of the Ohio and Mississippi River valleys slowly shifted the commercial emphasis of the northeastern economy from its own region to the West. The result was a national urban economy.

Foundations: The Northeastern Regional Economy

That the Northeast would play such a major role in winning the West was not surprising. The economic advantages of the Northeast were clearly visible by the time of the Revolution: a geography that placed several large urban centers in relatively close proximity; a diverse economy; entrepreneurs who were willing and encouraged to take risks; and a pool of cheap labor. These elements primed the cities of the Northeast to make money, and the fastest way they could accumulate capital was by trading with each other and by investing the profits in new enterprises and technologies.

The cities of the Northeast, in fact, were their own best trading partners. A major reason for this state of affairs was demand. As urban populations in the region grew at unprecedented rates, so did demand for food and manufactured goods. Demand outpaced population growth because urban residents generally had more disposable income than those living on farms. City households generally spent three times as much as rural households. Also, home manufactures—from butter to clothes—were much less common in the larger cities than in the countryside. This circumstance further increased demand. Because the farms and cities of the Northeast produced food and goods in sufficient quantity to satisfy the demand well into the 1840s, trade linkages between the cities of the region remained more important than commercial ties with the West or the South. Sixty-three percent of Philadelphia's exports were to other cities in the Northeast during the 1840s; a decade earlier, the figure had been 35 percent. The rise resulted from numerous factors—the growing efficiency of trade, reduced freight costs, and easier credit—but most important was the large-scale migration from the farms to the cities and from Europe to the urban Northeast during the 1840s. As late as 1860, in fact, northeastern cities derived only 15 percent of their trade income from other regions.

The growing domestic demand for food and goods generated profits and encouraged new investments. Also, some ports (Philadelphia is a prime example) declined as international trade centers after 1800 as New York engrossed the import trade. The trend forced merchants to seek new sources of income. Finally, merchants considered noncommercial investments such as manufacturing to be less risky than trade ventures. As merchants cast about for alternatives and complements to their commercial enterprises, they initiated the processes that led to the Industrial Revolution and the age of great cities in the late nineteenth century.

Factories in the Fields

The Industrial Revolution was already well under way in England when America's first textile mill opened in Pawtucket, Rhode Island in 1790. The English, extremely protective of their textile technology, had prohibited the export of machines or descriptions of them and restricted the rights of skilled mechanics to emigrate. One mechanic, however, foiled the English by committing to memory the design of a new textile machine. Samuel Slater completed his mental piracy by migrating to Pawtucket, where he recreated the machine and, together with partner Moses Brown, set nine children to work turning out cotton yarn.

The fact that Pawtucket never rivaled the great industrial cities of England is a measure of the tenuous connection between industrialization and urbanization during the early decades of the nineteenth century, when the United States was still an overwhelmingly rural nation. Negative images of the besooted, overcrowded, and squalid manufacturing cities of England were common in the popular mythology of the day. The countryside, on the other hand, was thought

by many serious thinkers to offer a wholesome environment, free from the dis-
tractions of urban life. Aesthetics aside, it would also be easier for employers to
control and cajole their workers in the more isolated countryside. And, for a
further practical matter, textile milling was dependent on water power. It was
easier and cheaper to harness rapids and waterfalls in the country than rivers
and bays near major cities. As a writer for the American Society for the Encouragement of Domestic Manufacturers asserted in 1817,

> Our factories will not require to be situated near mines of coal, to be worked by fire
> or steam, but rather on chosen sites, by the fall of waters and the running stream, the
> seats of health and cheerfulness, where good instruction will secure the morals of the
> young, and good regulations will promote in all, order, cleanliness, and the exercise
> of the civil duties.[11]

A frail Boston merchant named Francis Cabot Lowell believed in this dream
of factories nestled among the lovely New England hills, and in 1813 he realized
his vision of industrial America at Waltham, Massachusetts, at the falls of the
Charles River. Lowell's financial backers, a group of merchants organized into
the Boston Manufacturing Company, sank the considerable resources they had
gained from commerce into erecting not only the textile mill but the workers'
dormitories, churches, and schools. Using a power loom perfected by Lowell
himself, the Waltham mill proved an immediate success and spawned another
rural factory town—Lowell—four years later.

The towns themselves looked more like New England college campuses than
industrial complexes. This effect was to the credit of the Boston Manufacturing
Company, which had intended the factories to be indistinguishable from the
buildings at Harvard University and included a belfry on each building and a
grassy common nearby. The dormitories overlooked the rural countryside, and
the very fact they were called "dormitories" underscored the connection between Waltham, Lowell, and the college campus. Perhaps the most striking feature of these rural workshops, however, was the workforce itself. The grim and
downcast faces of European laborers were nowhere to be seen. Instead, the
cheery, wholesome faces of New England schoolgirls peered out from behind
the looms.

These factory girls were not the downtrodden proletariat many middle-class
Americans had come to fear. They earned relatively high wages, were given clean
and decent accommodations, and attended school and church regularly. Working 70 hours a week, they still found time, energy, and inclination to publish
their own literary magazine. They did not form a permanent laboring class,
either. After two or three years, the young women returned to their communities and usually married, bringing the savings of several years of factory work
to grateful grooms.

The practice of employing young farm girls who sang at their looms while composing poetry lasted for only a decade or two as Waltham and Lowell became victims of their own successes. With profits nearing 20 percent annually, the pastoral villages, especially Lowell, grew rapidly. Within twenty years, Lowell had developed from a small farm hamlet of 200 persons to the fourteenth largest city in the United States with a population of over 20,000. As one observer marveled: "The change seems more the work of enchantment than the regular process of human agency."[12] As if by magic also, the rural landscape receded into the past. One young woman looked out from her dormitory window and saw her view of nature slowly but surely obliterated by another factory building as it rose story by story:

> Then I began to measure . . . and to calculate how long I would retain this or that beauty. I hoped that the brow of the hill would remain when the structure was complete. But no! I had not calculated wisely. It began to recede from me . . . for the building rose still higher and higher. One hope after another is gone . . . one image after another, that has been beautiful to our eye, and dear to our heart has forever disappeared.[13]

Soon the young woman herself would also become a relic of the past.

Lowell's managers discovered that Irish immigrants worked more cheaply and

Lowell, Massachusetts, 1834
Although this industrial city had outgrown its "college campus" look by 1834, its surroundings were still pastoral. The multi-storied buildings shown here were typical of mill communities during this time.

just as well as its former employees, for newer technology no longer required the comparatively small, nimble hands of the farm girls. The once-comfortable dormitories filled to overflowing as a permanent workforce settled in. Lowell had become a city, with all of a city's attendant problems. The ideal of industry and countryside coexisting side by side was quietly laid to rest. Other, less pretentious industrial communities began to dot the New England landscape. For their founders, anxious to leave their rural past far behind as quickly as possible in order to realize greater profits, urban growth became a major objective. The armory at Springfield, the textile mills at Holyoke, and Charles Goodyear's rubber factory at Naugatuck—to name only a few examples of industrial and urban growth in New England—were gritty communities that foreshadowed the future urban industrial giants of the late nineteenth century. The glimpse into the future they offered was not very pleasant.

Soon other areas in the Northeast were vying to imitate the success of these industrial communities. The Rockdale manufacturing district was a series of seven rural hamlets in the Philadelphia region that drew sustenance from the swiftly flowing streams that provided water power for more than a dozen textile enterprises during the 1820s. The rocky, hilly terrain sought by entrepreneurs (steeper grades meant greater water power) was generally unsuited for farming, so mill entrepreneurs purchased the properties cheaply. A description of Rockdale in 1841 reflects the close relationship and compatibility between countryside and factory:

> The quality of life in Rockdale, day by day, had a naturalness that appealed to romantic sensibility, rocky hillsides and beech woods, farms and mills, combined wildness with cultivation in a pastoral landscape. . . . There was as yet no jarring sound of locomotive engines and shrieking whistles. . . . The mills themselves, powered only by water, whispered and grunted softly; the looms clattered behind windows closed to keep moisture in the air; even when the workers were summoned, it was by the bell in the cupola and not by a steam whistle. The machine was in the garden, to be sure, but it was a machine that had grown almost organically in its niche, like a mutant flower that was finding a congenial place among the rocks, displacing no one else and in fact contributing to the welfare of the whole.[14]

The factory soon outgrew its pastoral surroundings, however. Machine shops dotted the Rockdale district—dark, small workplaces where a sole proprietor, and perhaps a few family members, designed, hammered, tempered, cut, and designed again. The innovations that occurred in the textile industry in Rockdale and other rural districts during and after this time did not result from vast leaps of inventive genius. The process of invention was incremental. Machinists—or "mechanicians," as they came to be called—worked constantly to improve on their last innovation. Textile entrepreneurs grumbled that this planned obsolescence was expensive for them, that they could not afford to bypass the latest model or else they would lose their competitive edge. Machines became more complex, heavier, and more productive, straining to keep up with demand.

Urban Industry and the Changing Nature of Work

Part of urban America's industrial destiny was visible in the larger cities as early as the 1820s. Advantages in strategic location, an abundance of cheap labor fueled by migration from the countryside and Europe (New York's population, for example, grew 750 percent between 1800 and 1850, one of the highest rates in the world), rapidly increasing demand for manufactured products, and capital generated by expanding trade opportunities smoothed the way for the growth of industrial enterprises in the cities. This is not to say that an industrial revolution had taken place in America by this date; most of the "factories" were actually glorified workshops employing less than twenty workers, and many "industries" relied on "outside" work—individuals scattered in dwellings across the city. But these activities were significant in diversifying the urban economy and enhancing the economic power of the port cities.

Much as the status and conditions of workers deteriorated in the industrializing countryside, so the nature of work changed in the port cities. The rapid increase in demand placed a premium on mass-produced goods. The high-quality workmanship of the artisan became less prized than the number of units of a product he could turn out. Master craftsmen saw the opportunities in the urban market place and expanded production by adding machines, dividing tasks, and employing cheap labor to limit costs. By 1850, in cities such as New York and Philadelphia, the typical workshop held very few craftsmen. The apprenticeship system that trained skilled artisans was disappearing; the new workers were semiskilled laborers tending machines. At the same time, the capital costs required by mechanization shut out journeymen (those who eventually hoped to attain craftsman status) from rising through the ranks. By the 1840s, for example, journeymen in the printing industry worked out of unmechanized shops, "Lilliputian garret offices, whose type, press, &c., would not bring more than fifty dollars at auction."[15] In the meantime, master printers were employing boys at low wages to run powerful presses with greater productive capacity and efficiency. In 1845, the New York *Tribune* estimated that not more than one in twenty journeymen eventually opened his own print shop. Even then, the enterprises were marginal and susceptible to a high rate of failure.

A decline in wages, a reduction in the quality of work, and the proliferation of "outwork" were among the immediate consequences of diluted skills and divided labor. Wages in the major trades fell between 1830 and 1850. When the *New York Times* reported in 1853 that the minimum budget for a family of four was $600, the average annual salary for a trade worker was $300. It was not surprising that by the 1850s a majority of trade workers were women and immigrants, the groups with the fewest employment options and, historically, the lowest paid. As skill levels and wages declined, so did quality. The overriding goal was quantity of production. As early as the 1820s, observers noted the worsening quality of workmanship in the building trades, where the division of labor had reduced skill levels significantly. In 1825, a New York editor reported the consequences of slipshod construction: "It is astonishing how carelessly buildings are erected in this city—six houses which were nearly finished in Reed-street, fell to the ground and broke three ribs of one of the workmen— this is the second time these houses have fallen . . . we understand that the thickness of the walls was only that of *one brick!*"[16]

The division of labor into separate tasks—for example, one craftsman would no longer make a shoe or a table, but the task would be divided into numerous subtasks to speed production and take advantage of the abundance of cheap labor—enabled an employer to farm out the work and then assemble the finished product with a small number of skilled workers in the workshop or factory. This was especially so in the "Southern trade cutting" industry, where workers stitched together cheap ready-made clothing, much of which found its way to southern plantations. Women and children sat in their cramped quarters stitching garments for a subcontractor, who returned them to a master tailor, who then sent them to a merchant. If the clothes were destined for a higher-class market (such as department stores), the master tailor often employed skilled workers to finish the garments. The master tailor for Brooks Brothers, for example, employed seventy workers inside and 3,000 outside, typically in dwellings, in 1860.

Most operations were considerably smaller, but the result for outside workers—mainly women—was the same. Their top annual salary at this time was $91; tradesmen's wages were more than three times that sum. Consequently, outwork was often a family activity with daughters, sons, husbands, and relatives or boarders helping out. But in probably a majority of cases, women in the needle trades supported households without employed men. Even then, income was uncertain. A soiled garment, a poorly aligned buttonhole, or a frayed sleeve would cost a seamstress her $1 deposit as well as her wage for work completed. The chance for chicanery in this system was great because profit margins were narrow and subcontractors did not get paid until they returned the completed garment. The system worked best for the master tailors, who benefited from the low overhead and the high volume of production. By 1860, 25,000 women, or one quarter of New York's female labor force, worked in the outside system.

These workers toiled in unlighted tenements in lower Manhattan, four- and five-story structures that were thrown up following the minimum standards of materials, space, and light. The rooms were dark during the day; candles were an expense that eroded meager budgets. It was easy to spot seamstresses on the street; their stooped posture and sallow complexions gave them away. Even the sewing machine, which came into use during the 1850s, only quickened the pace of work and ensured a certain regularity. It did nothing to relieve the physical discomfort of workers.

Mothers hoped that their daughters would do better. But there were few options to the needle trades for young women, especially immigrant women. In an effort to escape the harsh existence in the textile industry, many gave up their seamstress work and entered domestic service. The pay was less, but they received decent food and shelter. Because their only expense would be clothes, they could help out their families and perhaps set some money aside for a dowry. Despite the dramatic changes in the urban economy during the first half of the nineteenth century, domestic service remained the largest paid occupation for women, especially if they were immigrants. By 1855, nearly three out of every four domestic servants were Irish.

By that time, a new employment alternative was emerging for women in the larger cities—factory work. The sewing machine enabled employers to centralize activities under one roof, and similar installations of light machinery in other industries also made indoor work more feasible than before. Wages were typically higher than for outside work, and jobs were more secure. The new breed of factory girls were generally single and between the ages of 16 and 25, but they were a far cry from the sedate country girls that initially populated the New England manufacturing villages. As one historian noted, "The factory girl was, in her own way, an emblem of female self-assertion: impudent rather than timid, sociable rather than retiring, robust rather than thin and pale."[17] She was the precursor of the urban industrial working woman and a growing cause for alarm among middle-class men and women, who had different notions of acceptable working-class demeanor. A sense of independence and higher wages led young working women to prefer the factory, for all its dull routine and unhealthful working conditions, to domestic service.

The expansion of the manufacturing sector, both in the countryside and in the cities, benefited the urban merchants who bankrolled and initially managed these enterprises. Industrial towns in the hinterlands not only carried on a flourishing trade with the major port cities, but also helped to stimulate commerce between those cities. The boot and shoe industry in several Massachusetts towns supported commerce in hide and leather in Boston. The boots and shoes themselves wound up in Boston, where merchants exported nearly half of them to

New York, Baltimore, and Philadelphia, and another quarter to smaller cities in the northeastern region. The intraregional trade in boots and shoes alone was worth $43 million to Boston merchants.

The northeastern ports also became centers for generating and dispersing technological innovations and information. Philadelphia's Franklin Institute, a technological clearinghouse founded in 1824, maintained information on patents and inventions in Great Britain and France, published a journal, and, most important of all, provided a meeting place for mechanicians, scientists, and engineers from throughout the Philadelphia region and as far away as New York and Europe. New York industry was not highly mechanized, but the concentration of artisans, the city's excellent communications, and a freewheeling spirit of enterprise provided an ideal environment for technological experimentation. Also, as in Philadelphia, New York offered several forums for the formal and informal exchange of ideas.

The introduction of new technologies tended to concentrate industries in larger towns, close to labor pools, new inventions, credit, and transportation facilities. The steam engine, for example, eliminated reliance on water power sources for textiles. This also meant an end to the seasonal frustration caused by low water in the summer, frozen water in the winter, and periodic freshets in between. Skilled water wheelmen were no longer needed to repair the wheel and control the water flow. Now all a textile manufacturer needed was someone to mind the boiler so that neither the workers nor the building would be blown to smithereens.

There was also the matter of time. The vagaries of water flow, no matter how skilled the man in the wheelhouse, meant periodic shutdowns. Theoretically, a steam engine kept a steady pace indefinitely and did not wear out like a wooden water wheel. Time, to quote a popular proverb of the day, was money, and the steam engine saved both. This meant that manufacturers could produce more goods. The best location now was not near water, but near the railroad, which connected the production line both to far-flung markets and to sources of raw materials. And the major rail junctions were in the great cities.

By the 1850s, Philadelphia had emerged as the leading textile manufacturer in the nation, though New York was the foremost manufacturing city. Overall, by 1860, the United States, though still an agricultural nation, was the second-ranking industrial nation in the world. Manufacturing accounted for 32 percent of the nation's gross national product that year, compared with 17 percent twenty years earlier. The concentration of skills, innovation, and capital in the city led to a diversity of industrial activities. Aside from textiles, Philadelphia also manufactured textile machinery to supply its own plants as well as those in textile areas such as the Rockdale district. The city also became a center for the production of medicines, paints, and dyes. By 1840, Philadelphia's economy derived as much profit from industry as it did from commerce.

Boston manufactured very little of what the industrial towns in its region produced—shoes, boots, and textiles. But the city came to specialize in industries that required high degrees of skill and initial capital investment. After 1830, Boston established itself as the premier publishing center of the nation; the city's entrepreneurs also produced fine instruments used in a wide variety of activities from navigation to textiles. An industrial pattern was evolving in the northeastern region: the major cities were specializing in finishing goods (as in Philadelphia's textile industry) or in activities that required the concentration of expertise, capital, and transportation facilities.

The profits generated from industrial enterprises spurred yet other investments in the port cities. Foremost among new investment opportunities after the 1820s were internal improvements—canals, roads, and railroads. These projects were essential to lowering the cost of shipping to and from the cities and from the cities to the surrounding smaller towns. Lower costs meant higher profits, which encouraged more production of both food and manufactured products, which in turn generated more capital for investment in new enterprises, technologies, or increased production. Improved transportation also meant the expansion of urban markets beyond the immediate hinterland.

Canals and Railroads: New Arteries

A major technological breakthrough occurred in 1825 with the completion of the Erie Canal, which joined the Great Lakes and the Atlantic Ocean at New York City. With much pomp and ceremony, a crowd of notables that included Governor DeWitt Clinton of New York, who once resigned his seat in the U.S. Senate to run for mayor of New York City and whom some people considered mentally unstable (for attempting to construct the canal, not for resigning from the Senate), dumped some Lake Erie water into the Atlantic. Clinton, whose urban vision included making a majestic metropolis of New York City, almost singlehandedly pursued and engineered the canal, with great success.

Observers heralded the Erie Canal both as the dawn of a new commercial era and as the making of New York City. Actually, little of the traffic on the canal came from beyond New York State until the mid-1830s, when the first shipments of wheat from Ohio arrived via the canal. Moreover, the canal did not "make" New York; it merely enhanced the city's already strong commercial position. The canal, however, generated significant urban growth in upstate New

York and helped to establish Buffalo, the canal terminus, as the fastest-growing city in the state.

The Erie Canal reoriented the economy of upstate New York toward those communities fortunate enough to be located along it. The town of Salina, for example, as its name implies, was a center for the marketing of salt. Syracuse, however, had a superior location on the canal and usurped Salina's trade in addition to becoming a market for the area's agricultural produce. The improved connections with New York City enabled Syracuse to ship produce down the canal and to receive and then distribute to the upstate region manufactured products from the Atlantic port. Improved access to New York also meant receiving the latest price and credit information. This news gave the town's merchants an edge in serving the farmers in the surrounding countryside.

The Erie Canal demonstrated, as later transportation developments would reconfirm, that new technologies produced different results in different places. The small processing industries of the countryside, especially flour milling, disappeared as much larger, heavily capitalized plants emerged in and near the larger towns such as Syracuse. The home manufacture of textiles ceased, overcome by the relatively quick access to finished textiles provided by New York City. The canal, in other words, advanced the position of Syracuse as an important economic force in the upstate region while reducing the nonagricultural role of smaller communities away from the canal.

Leaders in both Philadelphia and Baltimore reacted to the Erie Canal in varying ways. Philadelphian promoters hoped to construct a canal from their city to Pittsburgh that would connect there with the Ohio River, but they soon discovered that the mountains running through the central portion of Pennsylvania formed an impenetrable barrier to a canal. Technology could conquer space, but water could not flow uphill. In the meantime, Philadelphia concentrated on building canals north and south that would link the city with New York and Baltimore as well as securing the intervening hinterland of small towns and farms.

By the early 1830s, the Delaware & Raritan and Chesapeake & Delaware canals reduced the shipping time to New York from three days to 24 or 30 hours. One result was to cut coal shipping charges sharply. The Lehigh Canal lowered freight charges between Reading (located in the coal fields), and Philadelphia from 40 to 12.5 cents per hundredweight. Canals also opened up the fertile agricultural areas of southeastern and southcentral Pennsylvania to the Philadelphia market.

Baltimore merchants were more daring. Perhaps the greater proximity of Philadelphia, New York, and Boston to the Atlantic shipping lanes spurred the city's merchants to look for alternatives to water travel. Baltimore was also the new city on the block. Rising from obscurity to become the nation's third largest city by 1820 probably convinced its leaders that virtually anything was possible. In 1826, one of those leaders, merchant Evan Thomas, went to England on a business trip and observed firsthand a new invention, the steam railroad. After he reported back to his colleagues the news of this amazing machine, the railroad era in America began on February 28, 1827, with the chartering of the Baltimore and Ohio Railroad. Using their own capital gained primarily from the wheat trade, Baltimore merchants began construction of what was still an untested technology in July 1828. Although they did not reach the western terminus of the railroad at Wheeling, Virginia, until 1853, the completion of sections long before that date provided conclusive evidence that the railroad was a profitable enterprise.

Before 1850, the major impact of the railroad, as with the canal, was to accelerate intraregional trade and further the economic prospects of the eastern termini. Baltimore began to cut into the agricultural and processing trade of Philadelphia. By 1835, Boston merchants had constructed rail lines to Lowell, Providence, and Worcester. These cities, in turn, built branches to smaller localities, tying the entire system to Boston and, therefore, to other Atlantic ports and to international commerce as well. The railroad did not so much alter the pattern of trade as it reinforced existing trade relationships within the northeast region.

By 1840, a network of canals and railroads crisscrossed the northeast region, sustaining the major ports and smaller cities and towns along the way. The strong intraregional trade patterns and the capital generated from it were crucial to the next phase of urban economic growth—the joining of the cities of the West and the South to the urban Northeast.

Forging a Western Urban Region

Northeastern entrepreneurs dreamed of passages to the West in much the same manner as the explorers of old envisioned the Northwest Passage to the Orient. The ultimate destinations of canals and railroads, whatever their local benefits, was the West. The West became more attractive after 1840 for three reasons. First, the rapid growth of the urban Northeast was outstripping the agricultural supply of the region. In the meantime, the fertile farms of the West were producing bumper crops of wheat, corn, and cattle. Second, the cities of the West were passing from their initial settlement phases and entering a period of rapid growth. Cincinnati's population was five times greater in 1840 than in 1820. By the former date, that Ohio River city had 46,000 inhabitants. Louisville experienced a fivefold increase as well to 21,000 people by 1840. Cleveland, which barely existed in 1820, had grown to 6,000 inhabitants by 1840. St.

Louis was a frontier outpost of several hundred residents in 1820; by 1840, the city claimed 16,500 inhabitants. And Chicago, the future metropolis of the region, did not exist in 1820. By 1840, the new town had 4,000 people. A decade later it boasted a population of 30,000, the fourth largest western city behind Cincinnati, St. Louis, and Louisville. In other words, the West was becoming a vast market for northeastern manufactures.

The growth of western cities was remarkably similar to the growth of the urban Northeast. Intraregional trade formed the foundation of economic prosperity and development. Canals linked fledgling western towns to the Great Lakes, creating boom times in Cleveland, Toledo, and Chicago during the 1830s. Later, railroads helped strengthen the commercial bonds among western towns. Even before the canal and railroad era, the fledgling towns of the West engaged in profitable trade with each other. The main agency was the steamboat, which could buck the swift upstream currents of the Ohio and Mississippi rivers. Before the 1820s, when the steamboat became a common sight on the western waters, the inefficient transportation technologies then available limited the size of western cities and their hinterlands. The mark-up on manufactured goods in the urban West was sometimes 100 percent above the prices in eastern cities. The rivers that gave life to western towns also restricted their growth. Both the Ohio and Mississippi flowed south. The rafts that plied the trade along these rivers during the first two decades of the nineteenth century—keelboats and flatboats—could not run against the swift current, and the pattern of trade reflected this awkward situation. Western urban merchants gathered up the agricultural produce in their immediate hinterland, floated it downriver to New Orleans, broke up the boat and sold it for lumber; then they shipped the crops to an eastern port and bought manufactured goods from eastern firms, which sent the goods on an arduous overland journey to the West.

The system frustrated everyone. The western farmer saw his profits eroded in transportation costs and inflated prices for supplies and manufactured articles. Small profits inhibited agricultural expansion and thereby reduced the trade of the western urban merchant. The lengthy trade network victimized the western merchant by limiting the number of exchanges. The greater the volume of turnovers—buying and selling—the greater profits. Eastern entrepreneurs were similarly vexed by the slow pace of commerce. In addition, they were unable to sell as many manufactured goods as they would have liked because the exorbitant transportation costs reduced the attractiveness of these articles in the West. Even more alarming for eastern businessmen, cities like Cincinnati and Pittsburgh began to develop industries of their own. The mountains formed an effective trade barrier against eastern manufactures.

Although the steamboat could not climb mountains or churn up the delicate canals, it could and did run against the currents of the western waters. A colorful era began in the 1820s as steamboat whistles shattered the forested silence along the riverbanks. The steamboat trade helped to found new cities and made old ones grow. Louisville to Cairo, Cairo to St. Louis, St. Louis to Memphis, Memphis to Natchez, and Natchez to New Orleans and back up again, the side-wheelers and sternwheelers churned up the muddy waters bringing produce and people to towns and cities along the shore. As the steamboat conquered the long distances and shortened travel time on the river, it brought a piece of urban civilization wherever it went. A bit of New Orleans, a bit of Cincinnati, showboats, livestock boats, and passenger boats all steamed up and down the river as the Mississippi became the nation's major commercial highway. For a time during the 1830s, New Orleans surpassed New York City as the nation's leading export center. But the Crescent City's leadership was short lived. While railroads in the Northeast were reinforcing existing commercial relationships, railroads in the West forged new trade connections.

The reorientation of trade occurred within the context of intraregional commerce. Western cities evolved their own patterns of trade before establishing connections with northeastern entrepôts. Once again, intraregional trade formed the basis of wider commercial contacts.

The example of Keokuk, Iowa, located on the west bank of the Mississippi River, reflects both the importance of intraregional trade and the shifting character of that trade once the railroad appeared in the West. The presence of rapids just above Keokuk provided a crucial break in transportation that made the town an important station for Mississippi River traffic. The break frustrated upriver merchants who sought to ship their goods past Keokuk to St. Louis, the nearest major commercial center on the river. The expense of carrying goods around the rapids left upriver merchants at a competitive disadvantage with merchants in towns below Keokuk. One obvious solution was to eliminate the rapids. But upriver merchants could not afford the heavy capital outlay for such a project, and St. Louis entrepreneurs were more interested in cultivating the increasingly lucrative cotton trade of the lower Mississippi valley. Northeastern entrepreneurs proposed a second alternative: construct a railroad bypassing the rapids and then link up with a line coming west from Chicago. Rebuffed by St. Louis, upriver merchants were amenable to the railroad plan and completed the project in the mid-1850s.

Upriver merchants had now outflanked both Keokuk and St. Louis, altering the pattern of trade from a north-south direction to a west-east direction. Keokuk's fortunes declined dramatically between 1854 and 1856 when the railroad began service to Chicago. Small upriver communities that had lost trade because of the rapids near Keokuk, like Davenport and Dubuque, replaced it as centers for the upriver trade. And St. Louis, which had been the focal point for the upriver trade, saw part of its empire slip away to Chicago.

This scenario was played out in a number of Mississippi River towns during the 1850s—whether to hook up with Chicago via the railroad or persist in the steamboat trade with St. Louis. In hindsight, the decision to go with the railroad was the most appropriate, but contemporary merchants did not have that perspective. The amount of available investment capital, the extent of personal and commercial ties to St. Louis, the assessment of which city could fulfill credit and marketing needs best, and the nature of the crop or goods to be shipped were all factors that entered into their decision. Natural resources and locational advantages were important, of course, in determining the success of certain towns. But, as this episode illustrates, decisions by individuals could play an important role in determining a given town's future.

The importance of entrepreneurial decision making is even more evident in the case of the two protagonists in this commercial drama—St. Louis and Chicago. Chicago's initial growth in the 1830s resulted from a planned canal that would link Lake Michigan to the Illinois River and ultimately to the Mississippi. Although the canal did not materialize until the following decade, the mere promise of one touched off a flurry of speculation in town lots and a resultant increase in population.

Chicago's business leaders, led by upstate New Yorker William B. Ogden, were more interested in the potential of the railroad, which they correctly viewed as the ultimate transportation weapon for their city. If they could attract eastern railroads and build railroads of their own across the broad prairie, the thinking went, the parade of commerce that now floated down the Mississippi River might be diverted eastward. In this scheme Chicago's rival for western commercial supremacy, St. Louis, was the main target.

St. Louis leaders recognized the threat from Chicago but placed their faith in the magnetic Mississippi to keep attracting agricultural produce as farmers and merchants shunned the new-fangled rattling hunk of metal from out East. It was a mistake. By 1870, Chicago was a major rail terminus whose iron tentacles reached into the prairie to draw river trade away from St. Louis. During the 1860s, Chicago tripled its population while St. Louis's increased less than twofold.

Another lesson from this episode is the crucial importance of the railroad in determining the character of western urbanization. Riding the crest of its success, the steam railroad became a legend in its own time. Railroads could attract population and promote "human enjoyment"; they would "reorient society." In the 1850s, Senator Charles Sumner of Massachusetts asserted that "where railroads are not, civilization cannot be. . . . Under God, the railroad and the schoolmaster are the two chief agents of human improvement." A Presbyterian minister from New York went even further. He saw railroads as "the evolution of divine purposes, infinite, eternal—connecting social revolutions with the progress of Christianity and the coming reign of Christ." Small wonder that communities all across America enthusiastically embraced this Iron Messiah.[18]

Though the spiritual benefits of the railroad may be doubted, its impact on cities extended far beyond the reorientation of trade. Financing these projects was a unique experience for urban America. Railroads required such large capital outlays that financing efforts typically involved individuals, local government, and the state legislature. Pennsylvania came close to insolvency in its railroad-building efforts. In Virginia, three-fifths of the capitalization for railroads and canals came from the state treasury. This system of mixed enterprise was common throughout the country.

The financial initiatives, however, came through the urban leadership and their local governments. Between 1830 and 1860, for example, Savannah invested $2.7 million in railroads. Business people in the city invested at least that much, for the private subscription for the Georgia Central Railroad alone was nearly $2 million. Funding for northern railroads was less localized than this. Chicago's network, for example, was constructed largely with eastern money. European investments also accounted for significant financial support for northern railroad projects. Railroads, therefore, provided one of the first major outlets for excess capital accumulated largely through commercial pursuits.

Railroads, finally, gave the urban elite their first opportunity at corporate management. At times, the results were chastening. Mismanagement of funds, labor disputes, inadequate technical skill, and poor decisions about routes and timing plagued most railroads from time to time. Urban leaders often managed their railroads as weapons in commercial competition. The varying gauges of the tracks throughout the country bore witness to the desire of local entrepreneurs to keep the break in transportation advantage for their communities. Rate wars sometimes flared as rival railroads sought competitive benefits for passengers and freight. Eventually, management became more sophisticated and scaled their fares according to distance, with longer hauls receiving a lower per mile rate. The railroad provided a convenient if sometimes rocky training ground for these urban leaders' future endeavors in corporate management.

And the railroad was the crucial link in forging a national economy. As railroads helped to increase both supplies and demand within the Northeast and West, the next logical step was to join the two regional systems. Eventually, the advantage of Plains communities connecting with Chicago was not only the marketing and credit that city could offer, but also the connections with northeastern centers and, by implication, with the international trade. By the mid-1850s, the railroad had effectively reoriented the continental trade pattern from a north-south to a west-east direction. In 1850, for example, Cincinnati's prime trading partner was New Orleans. The steamboat commerce along the Ohio and Mississippi rivers to the Crescent City accounted for well over half of

Cincinnati's exports. As Cincinnati constructed rail lines heading west and east, and as these lines tapped into the growing Chicago rail system, the New Orleans connection not only diminished but virtually disappeared. In the early 1850s, New Orleans received up to 35 percent of its flour from Cincinnati; by 1857, this figure had declined to 4 percent. In contrast, in 1851, 1 percent of Cincinnati's flour exports ended up in one of the northeastern entrepôts; by 1855, 62 percent of the city's flour exports was destined for the Northeast. In 1860, a U.S. Census Bureau official noted that "as an outlet to the ocean for the grain trade of the West, the Mississippi River has almost ceased to be depended upon by merchants."[19]

New York Takes Charge

The Northeast was the dominant region in the new national urban economy, and New York occupied the central position. By dint of luck, hard work, and geography, this city had become the major beneficiary of the Northeast's monopoly on credit, marketing, industrial production, and communications and transportation. The first commercial coup occurred during and after the American Revolution. New York merchants courted English manufacturers when other cities still felt more protective toward their own industry. When trade resumed following the War of 1812, the British dumped their manufactured surpluses with their New York merchants and the city quickly became the national center for European manufactured goods. This meant that merchants from Boston to St. Louis shopped at New York to satisfy their customers' renewed demand for British manufactured articles.

Once the surpluses had been exhausted, other cities could potentially have established closer ties with British manufacturers and reaped similar benefits. New York merchants, however, headed off this possibility in 1818 by inaugurating the Black Ball Line, the first regularly scheduled packet service to Liverpool. The Black Ball Line revolutionized the Atlantic trade. Now cotton farmers in Georgia, factors in Charleston, and merchants in Boston could plan the shipment and delivery of their goods with some precision. Produce no longer rotted on Atlantic docks; manufactured goods no longer waited for ships on the other side of the ocean—these delays in the flow of commerce were no longer necessary. As every American businessman and farmer knew, time was money. The packet service saved both.

At about the same time, New York established yet another commercial innovation: the auction sale of merchandise. In the typical trade sequence, a British manufacturer would sell his wares to a British exporter, who would in turn sell the goods to an American importer. Under the auction system, the manufacturer consigned his shipment to an auctioneer in New York, who disposed of the wares at favorable prices. Because the auction system cut out two middlemen, New York became an even more attractive port for the buying and selling of foreign manufactured products.

With their Atlantic trade flourishing, New York merchants turned their international advantages into domestic success. The Erie Canal was one of the early fruits of this policy. Less spectacularly, but perhaps more significantly, New Yorkers inaugurated steamship services to coastal and Gulf ports to take advantage of the fact that New York, located directly on the ocean, had readier access to these ports than either Baltimore or Philadelphia, her two closest rivals, did. New York merchants, therefore, insinuated themselves into the commercial life of dozens of coastal cities. Vessels from New York not only engaged in coastwise commerce but brought resident agents to coastal cities to help local merchants market rural produce and arrange for the sale and distribution of domestic and foreign manufactured goods.

South Street, New York City, 1828
The activity shown in this small view of the New York harbor hints at the city's commercial dominance. The row of buildings on the right indicates how eagerly merchants and businesspeople capitalized on that success.

When the agents established relationships with local merchants, a quick ship and low-priced manufactured products in return were not the only inducements offered. The cumulative effects of aggressive decision making had made New York a financial center as well: the tremendous volume of business generated huge sums of capital that facilitated loans and other credit arrangements. Whether financing a Chicago railroad or extending credit to a Richmond tobacco merchant, New York money had a greater impact on local economies than the New York agents who arranged these deals.

New York's position as a trade center enhanced its reputation as an informational center. Merchants, manufacturers, and farmers did business in the Empire City with the knowledge that their transactions would receive the benefit of the latest and most sophisticated market information. The best lawyers, the wealthiest financiers, the sharpest accountants, and the best-informed merchants resided in New York and streamlined methods of doing business. Scarcely any new commercial development occurred without New York merchants and financiers knowing about and, more important, taking advantage of it. "Every new mine opened, every town built up, comes into relations with New York; and every railroad, no matter how short, has one terminus here," noted one New Yorker in 1865 with equal cockiness and accuracy.[20]

The path of the nation's commerce led straight to New York. The diversion of trade from its accustomed routes to new avenues altered the commercial geography of the United States. It also had major political repercussions.

Wallflower at the Ball: The Urban South

After the Revolution, southerners reestablished their plantations and slaves in the territories below the Ohio River. A new staple crop—cotton—emerged. In 1793, Eli Whitney invented a device that separated seed from cotton, a process previously done by hand; the cotton gin drastically reduced the time required to prepare cotton for market. Combined with the fertile black soil of the lower Mississippi valley, the gin created a cotton kingdom. Its capital was the port city of New Orleans.

But the urban South fared poorly in the new national commercial order. New Orleans merchants suffered from the same delusion that afflicted their colleagues in St. Louis: they believed the Misssissippi River bounty would roll in forever. But entrepreneurial shortcomings were only a part of the urban South's problems. Civic leaders in other southern cities knew about the importance of railroads and setting up commercial connections within and outside the South. Between 1850 and 1860, southern railroad mileage quadrupled whereas northern mileage tripled. Most of the capital came from within the South as local and state governments, planters, and merchants pooled their financial resources. Though several cities flirted with bankruptcy, the urban South generally profited from railroad investments. Savannah, an economic backwater for most of the early nineteenth century, raised nearly $3 million in private and public subscriptions to four railroad companies during the 1850s. The sum led Mayor Richard Arnold to boast that "in the ratio of her population, [Savannah] can challenge most cities to a comparison of the capital contributed."[21] The heavy subscriptions resulted in record cotton receipts and the city's greatest expansion since the eighteenth century. In one decade, Savannah's cotton exports jumped from 300,000 to 500,000 bales, and the value of total exports more than doubled. By 1860, Savannah was the third largest exporting center in the South.

As impressive as these figures are, they do not reflect the total relative decline of the urban South after 1840. Southerners built railroads but not railroad systems. State legislatures were so overwhelmed by chartering and appropriations requests that they did the politically expedient thing and funded virtually every scheme that came before them. When New Orleans entrepreneurs finally sought to build a railroad in the 1850s, they received a charter from the state legislature but only a paltry appropriation. The legislature simply divided the money between New Orleans and the dozens of other localities that had requested railroad appropriations. Fierce urban rivalry scuttled long-distance rail lines in other states because competing cities could not agree on routes.

Even when railroads received enough financial support to operate, poor management and a dearth of technical skill limited their efficiency. Southern railroads typically hired northern engineers, but there were simply not enough to go around in the railroad-building boom of the 1850s. Few southern railroads achieved financial stability. The absence of reciprocal trade—crops went to the city, but few manufactured goods went back into the countryside—undermined the limited capital reserves of many railroad companies.

Railroads in the South were not primarily city-to-city conveyances as they were in the Northeast and West. They served instead as transportation links between staple regions and port cities. The railroads expedited export because that was the customary commercial fate of staples. The Georgia Central Railroad brought record cotton shipments to Savannah in the 1850s, but the bales were quickly loaded on northern vessels bound for northern ports. Commercial steamship service from Savannah to New York began in 1848, and by 1856 no less than nine lines carried cotton to New York. Southern railroads were, in effect, expensive (for the South) ferries for northern merchants. As one southern urban entrepreneur sadly observed in 1858: "We are mere way stations to Philadelphia, New York, and Boston."[22] The dependence of the South on the urban Northeast, evident as early as the late colonial era, had become the established pattern by the time of the Civil War.

The development of the "cotton triangle" provides a good example of the nature of this dependence and its commercial impact. Northeastern and especially New York merchants sent their agents into southern ports during the 1820s to purchase cotton from either the planter or his urban merchant. In addition, the agent extended credit to the local merchant, who, in turn, could then make credit arrangements with his rural customers. The agent then provided vessels to sail to New York, where they would rendezvous with larger ocean-going ships for the trip to Liverpool. Thus New York merchants provided a market, shipping, and credit to southern merchants—an irresistible package.

The triangle was institutionalized over the years through the working of several commercial mechanisms. First, as the cotton culture spread throughout the South and as commercial services centered in the Northeast, regional economic specialization occurred. Both on the farms and in the cities, the southern economy revolved around the cultivation, marketing, and processing of a staple crop for its eventual delivery to a northern port like New York. Northeastern cities, especially New York, tailored their economies on the exchange and shipping of these commodities coastwise and overseas. By the 1840s, this pattern had solidified.

Second, southern growth strengthened the pattern of trade. When Savannah's railroad connections increased the city's commerce, for example, New York merchants promptly dispatched a fleet of vessels to inaugurate regular service between New York and the Georgia port. Southern cities traded relatively little with each other. Their economic existence depended, rather, on the interregional trade with the North. In extracting raw materials from the South, New York also drained capital. Fees for shipping, commissions, and interest on loans limited the profits from commerce, which in turn limited the capital available for investment in southern cities.

Ironically, the major problem confronting the urban South was the South itself. The South's soil and climate were particularly conducive to the cultivation of its two major staples, cotton and tobacco. Since the colonial period, these crops had generated few urban activities because of their simple marketing requirements. The steps involved in the marketing of grains, as one historian noted, do not apply to either cotton or tobacco: "Grain has to be marketed, milled and packed or baked into biscuits, then stored, and finally loaded into wagons. . . . All this calls for . . . mills and bakers, storage space, public houses and agencies to establish links between producer and purchaser."[23] The intimate relationship that evolved between countryside and city in the North was much looser in the South. And with the large labor force required to cultivate tobacco and cotton, plantation owners found it expedient to develop numerous urban activities on their property, further short-circuiting the connection with real cities.

Loading Cotton in Alabama, 1862

With the exception of New Orleans and Mobile, the cotton economy did not build great cities, largely because the crop was so easy to handle. It could be loaded onto steamboats from most river banks and required no additional storage or processing during its trip to market.

The lucrative intercity trade that built the towns of the Northeast and the West into urban regions was insignificant in the South. Richmond and Charleston, despite their geographic proximity, had no regularly scheduled shipping operating between them in the 1850s. Savannah and Charleston, even closer, also had very little commercial interaction. What could these cities offer each other? Very little, because all southern cities served, more or less, as collection points for cotton or tobacco.

The nature of southern agriculture also limited the value of the hinterland to the urban South. The hinterland was sparsely settled; plantation acreage was extensive, not only because of crop and labor characteristics, but because of the soil-depleting nature of those crops. Vast areas of the rural South were either abandoned or held for future cultivation. So when southern cities built their railroads, the tracks did not penetrate into fertile farms and villages as did those of the Baltimore & Ohio Railroad or the Pennsylvania Railroad. In the 1830s,

Charlestonians built the longest railroad in the world and nothing happened. As one embittered investor explained, it was a railroad "which ran into uninhabited wilderness in the absurd and chimerical expectation that [it] would create commerce and build New Yorks in a day."[24]

Southern cities also suffered from chronic labor shortages. Local railroad companies sometimes searched months for an engineer, delaying vital rail links with other parts of the South. The influx of immigrants during the 1850s helped ease the shortage to some extent. By 1850, more than a fifth of Charleston's residents and more than a third of Mobile's were foreign born. Because the majority of immigrants were young men and women, their share of the free workforce was even larger. In Richmond, foreign born comprised 40 percent of the free workingmen, nearly 50 percent in Charleston, and 60 percent in Mobile.

But as immigrant workers moved in, slaves were moving out of the urban South during the 1850s, when a boom in cotton and tobacco cultivation reclaimed many urban slaves, further underscoring the role of southern cities as adjuncts to the agricultural economy. The abundance of cheap labor that freed capital and encouraged investments in machinery and other enterprises in northern cities was not available to the urban South.

Southern cities were, in fact, simply cotton or tobacco towns. Investments, labor, occupational structure, local government—indeed, all the elements that go into the formula for urbanization—depended on and were limited by the southern countryside. Visitors to the major cities of the South noted how much these places were extensions of that countryside. As a British visitor described Mobile in 1858:

> Mobile—a pleasant cotton city of some thirty thousand inhabitants—where the people live in cotton houses and ride in cotton carriages. They buy cotton, sell cotton, think cotton, eat cotton, drink cotton and dream cotton. They marry cotton wives, and unto them are born cotton children. In enumerating the charms of a fair widow, they begin by saying she makes so many bales of cotton. It is the great staple—the sum and substance of Alabama. It has made Mobile, and all its citizens.[25]

The cities of the urban South consequently functioned by the seasons much as the rural South did. Social seasons ran from October to April; so did processing industries. Depending on the latitude, anytime after April a wholesale abandonment of the city took place. A northern visitor in 1840 noted the impact of these cycles on Mobile:

> Mobile might be made a delightful place in Winter and a pleasant one in Summer, but unfortunately, like too many of the Southern Towns & Cities but little attention is paid to it by the authorities. . . . [s]o too many of the inhabitants leave there in the Summers, that their erratic life forbids them making improvements or paying much

attention to these little conveniences & Comforts without which any life & especially a city one is unpleasant.[26]

The South's idiosyncratic agricultural economy presented a vicious circle for southern cities. Because cities in the Old South were so similar, they did not need to trade with each other. This, in turn, inhibited the development of a diverse economy and the concentration of population—for the presence of more people would have generated demand for local industries, which would have stimulated intraregional trade.

By 1860, a national urban economy had emerged, an economy that had been orchestrated by the northeastern cities. Western cities, by virtue of their vigorous intraregional trade and their fertile hinterlands, were almost equal partners in the national economic coalition. Chicago was emerging as the western anchor of an urban core that stretched from New England to the Mississippi River at St. Louis. The South was part of the national urban economy as well, but as a decidedly junior partner. Southern cities served more as adjuncts of the northeastern regional economy than as cogs in an independent regional urban system.

Political Implications of a National Urban Economy

The reorientation of commerce had national political ramifications, especially for the most dependent partner in the regional coalition, the South. The emergence of a national urban economy coincided with the increased involvement of the federal government in that economy. Of course, the Congress has always influenced economic development with tariff and banking legislation. With the passage of the Rivers and Harbors Act in 1826, cities obtained the assistance of the Army Corps of Engineers in dredging rivers and harbors. On occasion, the federal government had also entered into joint internal improvement ventures with states and cities. Norfolk benefited from the construction of the Dismal Swamp Canal in the 1820s, and Alexandria profited from a federal partnership in the Chesapeake and Ohio Canal. Before the 1830s, the Bank of the United States had established a uniform currency that promoted interstate trade. And various Supreme Court decisions facilitated competition and incorporation and protected contractual arrangements.

But even as our national domain expanded significantly in the 1840s and 1850s, so did the federal government. The federal patronage power increased, as did its role as a western land developer and internal improvement promoter. Federal initiatives had always generated vigorous national debate, especially over tariffs and banks. As the South's political power declined in the 1850s with the admission of additional free states and as its relative economic position suffered, southern concern over federal economic policy mounted.

As long as the Democratic Party remained in power, the South felt secure that its economic interests would be protected. After 1854, however, the emergence and rise of the Republican Party increased fears that every economic activity from the lucrative domestic slave trade to southern efforts to build a transcontinental railroad would be jeopardized. In 1860, the Republicans announced a broad array of economic initiatives, including a protective tariff that would benefit northern industries, a northern route for a transcontinental railroad built with federal land subsidies, and a homestead act designed to secure the West for the free states. Also, because the Republican Party was almost exclusively a northern party, such traditional federal responsibilities as river and harbor improvement and appointments to ports and post office installations would favor the North and northerners to the detriment of the South.

Urban southerners weighed the difficult choices after Lincoln's election in November 1860. Some believed that northern cities would not sacrifice their intimate economic connections to the South by forcefully challenging secession, and certain New York leaders had implied as much. At a large Union rally in New York City, Mayor Fernando Wood reminded the crowd that the issue of slavery was unimportant beside the crucial issue—"our continued commercial prosperity." Leaving the Union, the South could still trade with the North but would also be free to develop its economy independently. John Forsyth, editor of the Mobile *Register,* argued that "the effect of separation would be to transfer the energies of industry, population, commerce, and wealth, from the North to the South. . . . [I]t is to . . . us, the wealth-producing States, that the North owes its great progress in material prosperity. . . . The Union broken, we should have what has been so long the dream of the South—direct trade and commercial independence."[27]

On the other hand, some southern urban leaders believed that without northern credit, market connections, and distribution network, the South's economy would founder. In the view of New Orleans businessman James Robb and South Carolina industrialist William Gregg, two of the South's most prominent entrepreneurs, the region would merely be trading dependency on the North for dependency on some European country. Moreover, whatever industry the South nurtured would be overcome by British industrial might. In the cities of the Upper South, there were concerns that obsessions with free trade in the Lower South would ruin industry. Though dependence on the North was indeed uncomfortable, the alternative would be worse and could ultimately threaten the institution of slavery.

The situation was perplexing for the South's urban leaders. Looking at the spring of 1861 from the perspective of one city, Richmond, highlights the difficulties of all southern cities at that time. Like many of their counterparts in cities across the country, Richmond's urban leaders participated in almost every phase of urban life—serving on the city council and the board of trade, running successful mercantile enterprises, investing in industrial and transportation projects, and participating in philanthropic endeavors. Their days were filled with rounds of meetings and attention to their varied business affairs. They were keenly aware of the realities of competition: all cities, they knew, could not share equally in the commercial bounty. There were no ties in the race for commercial empire, only victories and losses.

Was Richmond losing? It seemed odd that the city could be doing just that. Bridges and roads were overcoming the deep ravines and steep terrain in the city. The James River and Kanawha Canal docks seemed busier now than they had ever been. The railroad depots, and anything resembling a business district, did not exist in the 1830s. Now there were not only fine rows of stores and offices, but a fire department to protect them and pavement to walk on without sinking in a mire of mud, or choking from the dust. Local officials had adopted a health policy, though it was indifferently enforced; they had numbered houses; they had supported agricultural fairs and constructed produce markets to lure and accommodate farmers to trade in the city; and they had spent millions to bring railroads into the city.

Richmond offered many more cultural attractions by 1860. There were concert performances by such international luminaries as Jenny Lind, the "Swedish Nightingale"; there were public lectures at the Atheneum; traveling troupes came to the city to perform anything from Shakespeare to low comedies. A number of new hotels had opened in recent years. The Ballard House could be compared to the finest hotels in the nation. And the city's leaders were well read and well traveled.

Yet Richmond's business leaders believed that Virginia's persistent preoccupation with its brilliant past as the "mother of presidents" threatened to overcome the momentum they had generated to expand the city's economy. The constant pull between tradition and progress was exhausting. New Yorkers, on the other hand, seemed rarely to worry about tradition. Profit, not the past, drove them on, and their memories rarely extended beyond the term of a bank note. Such men, with no anchor or roots, would as soon make war as make trade if there was profit in it.

The development of a national urban economy provided both the framework and the impetus for urban growth in the years before the Civil War. The bloody conflict that followed closely on the cementing of interregional commercial relationships would, among many other things, ratify the status and power of a new urban core. Though a minority of Americans were urban residents, cities were already playing crucial roles in American life, defining and determining a national destiny.

The creation of a national urban economy did more than reorient and expand the patterns of trade. As we will see in the next chapter, it also recast the cities and helped to establish new relationships between urban spaces and the people who coveted them, and among the people themselves.

Notes

1. Quoted in John W. Reps, *The Making of Urban America: A History of City Planning in the United States* (Princeton, N.J.: Princeton University Press, 1965), p. 349.
2. Quoted in Richard C. Wade, *The Urban Frontier: Pioneer Life in Early Pittsburgh, Cincinnati, Lexington, Louisville, and St. Louis* (Chicago: University of Chicago Press, 1964), p. 51.
3. Quoted in Reps, *Making of Urban America,* p. 371.
4. Quoted in Charles N. Glaab, ed., *The American City: A Documentary History* (Homewood, Ill.: Dorsey Press, 1963), p. 157.
5. Quoted in Wade, *Urban Frontier,* p. 33.
6. Quoted in *ibid.,* pp. 22–23.
7. *Ibid.,* p. 24.
8. Quoted in Bayrd Still, ed., *Urban America: A History with Documents* (Boston: Little, Brown, 1974), p. 101.
9. Quoted in Wade, *Urban Frontier,* p. 28.
10. Quoted in *ibid.,* p. 16, p. 28.
11. Quoted in Thomas Bender, *Toward an Urban Vision: Ideas and Institutions in Nineteenth-Century America* (Lexington, Ky.: University Press of Kentucky, 1975), p. 29.
12. Quoted in *ibid.,* p. 40.
13. Quoted in *ibid.,* pp. 78–79.
14. Anthony F. C. Wallace, *Rockdale: The Growth of an American Village in the Early Industrial Revolution* (New York: Alfred A. Knopf, 1978), p. 4.
15. Quoted in Sean Wilentz, *Chants Democratic: New York City & and the Rise of the American Working Class, 1788–1850* (New York: Oxford University Press, 1984), p. 130.
16. Quoted in *ibid.,* pp. 132–133n.
17. Christine Stansell, *City of Women: Sex and Class in New York, 1789–1860* (New York: Alfred A. Knopf, 1986), p. 125.
18. Quoted in David R. Goldfield, "Pursuing the American Urban Dream: Cities in the Old South," in Blaine A. Brownell and David R. Goldfield, eds., *The City in Southern History: The Growth of Urban Civilization in the South* (Port Washington, N.Y.: Kennikat Press, 1977), pp. 53–54.
19. Quoted in David R. Goldfield, *Cotton Fields and Skyscrapers: Southern City and Region, 1607–1980* (Baton Rouge: Louisiana State University Press, 1982), p. 61.
20. Quoted in *ibid.,* p. 60.
21. Quoted in *ibid.,* p. 63.
22. Quoted in *ibid.,* p. 65.
23. Frederick F. Siegel, *The Roots of Southern Distinctiveness: Tobacco and Society in Danville, Virginia, 1780–1865* (Chapel Hill: University of North Carolina Press, 1987), p. 66.
24. Quoted in William H. Pease and Jane H. Pease, *The Web of Progress: Private Values and Public Styles in Boston and Charleston, 1828–1843* (New York: Oxford University Press, 1985), p. 219.
25. Quoted in Harriet E. Amos, *Cotton City: Urban Development in Antebellum Mobile* (University, Ala.: University of Alabama Press, 1985), xiii.
26. Quoted in *ibid.,* p. 78.
27. Quoted in Goldfield, *Cotton Fields and Skyscrapers,* p. 77.

CHAPTER 5

Different Spaces, Separate Lives

"An orgasm of locomotion," was the succinct appraisal of New York City streets offered by native son George Templeton Strong in 1856. The impetus for the city's far-flung commercial empire began on the streets, where one could observe thousands of citizens striding purposefully to and fro. Their energy was notable, and so was their diversity; "innumerable varieties of figure, dress, air, gait, visage and expression of countenance," wrote Edgar Allan Poe.[1] A babble of different languages and accents, the sounds made by vehicles clattering over the pavement, the cries of vendors hawking hot corn or newspapers, and the bells from churches and horsecars provided the noisy soundtrack to this visual feast.

To the casual observer, the city street was a metaphor of American democracy. Here men and women, boys and girls, black and white, rich and poor, German, Irish, and native born mingled peacefully. These main thoroughfares coursed through a new urban entity—downtown—a district lined with shops, offices, and entertainment where the demand that generated a national urban economy merged with the profits and goods derived from that economy. By the 1850s, though some residences remained, especially in smaller cities, the downtown had replaced the waterfront as the economic center of the city. It was a center dedicated to satisfying the demands of the consumer and servicing the national urban economy.

A New Place Called Downtown

The national urban economy had increased the volume and complexity of trade. Merchants could no longer wear several hats—wholesaler, retailer, and financier. The activities and requirements of each role were becoming well defined, and participation in more than one meant an inadequate mastery of both or of all three. In smaller cities and towns one merchant could conceivably perform all three tasks. In the larger cities urbanization and specialization went hand in hand.

Wholesalers usually occupied the waterfront edges of the new downtown. As a rule, they owned the warehouses and even some of the docks, and their capital helped to establish industry in the warehouses. Besides performing this new role, the wholesalers received European goods and played the role of commission merchant as they forwarded agricultural produce to other cities and abroad. The retailers, whose livelihood depended on close association and cooperation with the wholesalers, were located nearby. Because their customers were usually individual citizens and occasional visitors, however, they did not open their stores along the crowded, often filthy, and sometimes unsafe waterfront. They sought more comfortable accommodations where they could display their wares in relative spaciousness and cleanliness. It was much easier to attract and keep customers if the retailer showed his goods to advantage and made his shop distinctive. This was not possible on the shabby waterfront.

By the 1830s, the city markets, which had been a fixture since the colonial period, were being upstaged by these merchant-showmen who had usurped many of the market's functions. Retail butchers, grocers, and fruiterers provided their customers with convenient personal service. These establishments were generally in the better parts of town, whereas the old market houses were sometimes located in crowded and unsanitary quarters. Finally, in the antimonopoly spirit that characterized Jacksonian America (1828–1845), it did not seem appropriate for one agency—the market house—to control the provisioning of the city. If free enterprise entrepreneurs were to be trusted to build commercial empires, they certainly should be allowed to provide their neighbors with fresh food.

Besides the provisioners, an entire array of retailing activity began to appear in the expanding downtown. Dry-goods stores, readymade clothing shops, and jewelry stores were some of the specialized establishments that departed from the general store concept of an earlier era. For the shopper, the proliferation of these retail outlets must have been dizzying. No "one-stop shopping" here: It was one store for an overcoat, another for some cigars, a third for a harness, and finally the shoe store or the tavern so the shopper could be fortified one way or another to continue the shopping trip. Increased consumer demand and affluence generated by the expansion of trade encouraged retail specialization. By the same token, common sense indicated that the shopper, especially in inclement weather, would be inconvenienced by these shopping rounds. It would be much more worthwhile—that is, profitable—if all the retail activities were brought under one roof. This idea did not necessarily result in a step backward to the general store, but rather in a giant stride into the future: the department store, replete with extensive inventories, items for every budget, sumptuous surroundings, and efficient, trained personnel to cater to the public's buying whims.

By the 1850s, consumers' appetites had been sufficiently whetted to create the demand for these emporia and merchants had accumulated sufficient capital in the larger cities to finance the undertaking. Boston's Jordan Marsh, Philadelphia's Wanamaker and Brown, New York's Lord & Taylor, and Chicago's Marshall Field were the marvels of their day as residents and tourists alike gaped at their first sight of the latest wrinkle in retail establishments. Guidebooks and newspapers devoted considerable space to these commercial edifices, which, much like the cathedrals of medieval Europe, not only dominated the urban landscape but reflected the spirit of the age. The usually staid *New York Times* observed that Lord & Taylor, opened in 1859, was "more like an Italian palace than a place for the sale of broadcloth."

Writers, at least if they were from Philadelphia, reserved the most lavish praise for Philadelphia's department store, Wanamaker and Brown. It would be difficult to find a building in the city that received more publicity during the 1860s than the Wanamaker and Brown building. A shopper encountering this edifice for the first time must have felt awed. Walking up Market Street several blocks removed from the waterfront, the shopper entered the store through a grand arch. The ground floor included men's and boy's furnishings, with sufficient inventory to keep a modest retail operation in stock for quite a while. Although Wanamaker and Brown did not have escalators—moving stairways had not yet been invented—their substitute, a massive walnut staircase, seemed to meet with the approval of customers, who compared it with "the grand staircase at the Capitol at Washington." This association evidently placed shoppers in the proper frame of mind for spending money. Climbing the stairs, the shopper encountered the Custom Clothes Department on the second floor; on the third floor the customer could choose from a vast array of overcoats and dress coats. For the shopper who had not wearied or become insolvent, there were two more floors with assorted dry goods to wander through. If the shopper decided to purchase an article, the store was arranged like a mechanized factory to make the transaction. One clerk wrote out a ticket while another packed and delivered the article. If the shopper had made purchases on several floors, speaking tubes and a dumbwaiter system coordinated these sales.[2]

Lord & Taylor Department Store, c. 1859
As shown in this wood engraving from a merchants directory, the Lord & Taylor building reflected the new emphasis on middle-class consumerism in urban America. Its architecture was palatial, inviting the shopper to participate in a kind of luxury that was previously unattainable. Note how the large street-level windows facilitated window shopping.

The department store was the newest and most significant tenant of the new downtown. Aside from its innovations in retail marketing, the institution also reflected a change in the role of women in the city. A store like Wanamaker's employed hundreds of salespeople, managers, floor walkers, buyers, and cashiers. A. T. Stewart's new store, opening in New York in 1861, employed more than 2,000 workers. Women occupied many of these positions, especially dominating the sales force. The attraction of working for a department store was not the salary, which was comparable to domestic service, but rather the atmosphere and prestige associated with the finest emporia in the nation. Although standing on one's feet for ten hours six days a week was tiring, the job offered opportunities to meet different people and see the latest fashions. It was an entrée into the comfortable middle-class world. It was also a chance to experience the new urban milieu—the city of women shopping, spending money, and crowding the sidewalks in and around the store. As downtown became a retail center, it also became a woman's place for the first time, and women of all classes shared in this new experience. Mr. Stewart, for example, always schooled his department heads to make certain their clerks treated every customer alike. As reported in a popular book of etiquette at the time, "the rule of 'first come, first served,' is rigidly observed."[3]

At first, most of the customers were middle-class married women. The evolving downtown of offices, shops, and leisure activities generated new positions such as office clerks, insurance agents, bank tellers, legal assistants, and shop managers—what we would call today "white-collar" employees. Their wives, according to the propriety of the era, did not work outside the home. The basic role of a married middle-class woman was to attend to children and home. With disposable income and more flexible schedules than women who worked outside the home, these women had the means and time to wander in the marble retail palaces. The department stores catered directly to their tastes by stocking such items as prefabricated household furnishings, ready-made clothing, toys, stationery, and dime novels, all of which appealed to the current emphasis on home and domesticity as well as to the decline in home production that freed middle-class women to pursue other domestic interests both inside and outside the home.

The spectacle and merchandise of the department store drew women from all status levels, not just the middle class. Though many of the seamstresses and domestic servants merely "window-shopped" (a new expression occasioned by the large plate glass display windows retailers installed in their stores to attract customers), some spent their earnings on the merchandise arrayed before them. The salespeople they encountered were usually from similar working-class backgrounds. By 1860, major department store owners, motivated less by altruism than by the increasing presence of Irish women among their customers, began to hire Irish girls to clerk in their establishments.

The department store, like the street out front, was a democratic place. The diverse city came together at that point. No longer did visitors repair to the waterfront to take the pulse of urban life; they went to The Street—the block or group of blocks that included the city's retail trade. Canal Street in New Orleans, Market Street in Philadelphia, or King Street in Charleston—all these thoroughfares became the showcases for downtown and the city alike.

The emergence of downtown as a primarily nonresidential area had a significant impact on where and how people lived. As the uses of downtown—wholesale, industrial, retail, and financial—expanded, these uses required new space. Owners of private homes and town houses located in the path of economic development soon found themselves sitting on valuable real estate—too valuable not to be cashed in and perhaps too valuable for the owners to be able to afford to pay rising property taxes that were assessed on the value of the land. Every time a home changed hands or a newcomer sought housing downtown, the same story repeated itself. Commercial, financial, and industrial users of spaces easily outbid the single-family homeowner for downtown property.

Downtown was also getting crowded and noisy. Entrepreneurs in the colonial era had sought out residences near the waterfront. Prestige, proximity to economic interests, and maintaining close ties with Europe made other choices unthinkable. But now the waterfront was more cluttered. It was the oldest section of the city, and even in the newer cities of the West it did not age gracefully. Downtown, finally, was in a constant uproar. The pressure on local entrepreneurs experimenting with new policies, taking new risks with borrowed capital, and fretting about urban rivals made them want a respite from the scene of their worries. Staying downtown after business hours was no longer a convenience; for some, it was a burden.

The Residential City: Where to Live and How to Get There

As merchants, clerks, artisans, and some laborers were forced from downtown, a new phenomenon evolved in the city: the residential neighborhood. Like downtown space, residential space came to be specialized. Even though all segments of urban society lived in close proximity to each other and mingled together, a clearly defined residential pattern based on economic status was emerging. Urban leaders and their colleagues who left the mélange of downtown settled in relatively homogeneous neighborhoods. Their residences were usually near enough to their downtown offices so that they could walk to and from work, for these American cities were still very much geared to pedestrians through the 1860s. Probably the most desirable residential location was an area in close proximity to the financial district. The financial district exercised the greatest influence over the city's economy, it was relatively quiet, and leading financiers tended to live near it, adding status to the area.

By the 1860s, the desire of the well-to-do to live close to downtown was receding. In New York, for example, the middle class and the wealthy had left lower Manhattan, pushing the boundaries of the city farther north at an incredible pace. Between 1820 and 1860, New York's border moved more than a mile and a half from City Hall in lower Manhattan to 42nd Street. "How this city marches northward!" George Templeton Strong exclaimed after a walk in 1850.[4] Downtown itself was constantly expanding and shifting so that living near this volatile area one year might mean living in it the next. Construction and destruction were ongoing dynamic processes in the expanding commercial city. In 1856, a writer in *Harper's Monthly* remarked that New York "is never the same city for a dozen years altogether." A forty-year resident would "find nothing, absolutely nothing of the New York he knew."[5] Newcomers from the countryside and from abroad were also flooding into the city, seeking residences as close to downtown (and, therefore, to jobs) as possible. Congestion reached epic proportions in New York City, at this time probably the most crowded metropolis in the world with an average density of 135 persons per acre or 86,400 persons per square mile. By today's occupancy standards, a density this great is likely to be found in blocks of apartments of a minimum of twelve stories. In nineteenth-century New York, tenements ranged from two to five stories.

Advances in transportation technology coincided with the real estate market and personal preferences to move residences from downtown. The omnibus, an import from Paris, served as the basis of the first major transportation system to appear in American cities. It was in New York, not surprisingly, that omnibus service in the United States was inaugurated in the late 1820s. The omnibus, a covered vehicle drawn by two horses, carried about twelve passengers. It operated along fixed routes and made frequent stops to pick up and discharge passengers. The "city stages," as they were called, proved immensely popular with business people and white-collar employees. By 1837, ridership in the city had increased to 25,000 per day. Few members of the working class were included in that group. One-way fares averaged 12½ cents. The growing numbers of semiskilled and unskilled workers earned less than a dollar a day, and the dwindling numbers of craftsmen rarely earned more than two dollars. Because it was the custom to go home for lunch, riding the omnibus would have eroded half to a quarter of the worker's daily salary. The omnibus made feasible the relocation of a number of white-collar workers and their families. For the urban worker, however, the fare structure and the price of housing precluded residence in "the upper part of the city."[6]

The omnibus helped to begin a modest movement to the suburbs. Traditionally, the urban periphery was the home of vagabonds and destitute immigrants. The crowding of urban space, though, and the reduction of commuting time brought about by the omnibus and other public and private conveyances, made the suburbs with their rural quietude potentially attractive residences. Although only a few omnibus lines in New York traveled as far as suburbs like Harlem, in Boston the omnibus stopped regularly in suburban Dorchester and Roxbury. A new type of American, the suburban commuter, was born: "They reach their stores and offices in the morning and at night, sleep with their wives and children in the suburbs."[7]

The omnibus had drawbacks, however, that citizens initially overlooked because of its novelty. According to Mark Twain, a very disgruntled passenger, the omnibus "labors, and plunges, and struggles along at the rate of three miles in four hours and a half, always getting left behind by fast walkers, and always apparently hopelessly tangled up with vehicles that are trying to get to some place or other and can't."[8] The omnibus was too slow, it sometimes overturned, spilling its occupants onto the hard cobblestone or into the soft mud, and it was uncomfortable. By the 1850s, the time had arrived for an improved system.

The basis for that improved system was the horse-drawn railway, which urban residents hailed as "the improvement of the age." The street railways, as they were also called, were simply railroad cars pulled by horses. Operating on tracks, the street railway generated less friction than the omnibus. A two-horse team, therefore, was capable of pulling a larger vehicle. The horse-cars usually accommodated forty riders in relative comfort without the jostle that accompanied a ride over the city streets on an omnibus. They were also not as accident prone as the omnibus because they were confined to rails. Most important, whereas the omnibus rarely exceeded 4 miles per hour, the street railway whizzed along at 6 miles per hour. The necessity for living at or near work receded further for white-collar workers. For example, in Philadelphia between 1829 and 1862, the proportion of merchants who resided some distance away from their businesses doubled, as did their average commuting length (measured in space rather than in time). A comparison of Figures 5.1 and 5.2 will illustrate this point. For lawyers working in New York City during a similar period (1835 to 1865), the average journey to work tripled. In other words, the residential areas around downtown were losing the economic and occupational mixture they had once possessed and were becoming increasingly a working-class neighborhood.

The greater capacity of the horse-car and the relative speed at which one car could complete a run resulted in a lowering of public transit fares by half. Despite this reduction, the street railway was still beyond the means of most work-

Figure 5.1 *Journey to Work of Philadelphia Merchants, 1829*

(Figures 5.1 and 5.2 are Figures 3-3 and 3-4 from Kenneth T. Jackson, "Urban Deconcentration in the Nineteenth Century: A Statistical Inquiry," in *The New Urban History: Quantitative Explorations by American Historians,* ed. Leo F. Schnore with a Foreword by Erich E. Lampard [copyright © 1975 by the Center for Advanced Study in the Behavioral Sciences, Stanford, CA]. Princeton, N.J.: Princeton University Press, 1975.)

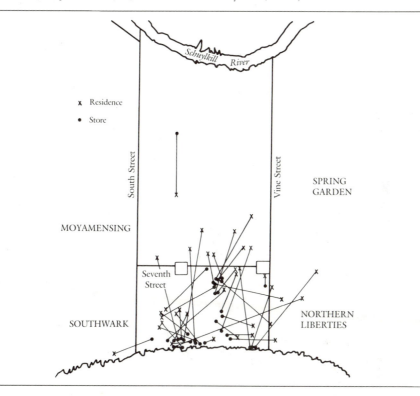

ers. Again, public transit failed to loosen the tightly packed tenement districts. By 1860, more than half of New York City's residents still crowded into dwellings below 14th Street, an area one-tenth the size of the entire city. For these New Yorkers, the city was still very much a pedestrian place.

Other transportation systems had their urban debuts during the 1840s and 1850s, though they were even more exclusive than the popular omnibus or horse-car systems. The steam-driven commuter railroad was effective in cities like Boston, where suburbs were close together yet separated by inlets and marshlands that made traditional overland communication difficult. The commuter railroad, which raced along at 30 miles per hour maximum speed, made possible settlement far beyond the city line. Assuming that 30 minutes is the maximum time an individual would want to spend commuting and figuring an

Figure 5.2 *Journey to Work of Philadelphia Merchants, 1862*
Transportation technology, downtown crowding, and personal preference increasingly
separated work place and residence for those who could afford to live in outlying
residential districts. Workers generally remained near downtown.

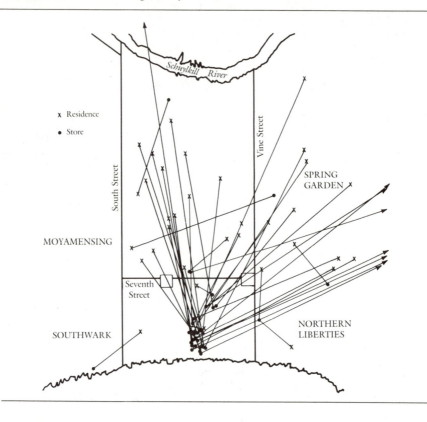

average speed of 15 miles per hour, we see that the 2-square-mile area of habi-
tation could be at least tripled.

In extending into the rural countryside, the commuter lines performed another equally valuable service. They allowed city residents, for the first time, to
receive fresh produce, especially milk, from the farms surrounding the city.
Farmers in these areas began to specialize in highly perishable commodities that
had found only a localized market before the railroad, when the wagon road
was the only transportation link to the city. By the time milk and milk products,
fruits, and vegetables arrived at city markets, considerable spoilage would have
occurred, particularly on warm days. As the city expanded and pushed farms
further out, deliveries became less frequent until the appearance of the commuter railroad. A New Yorker noted the marked improvement in the milk supply in 1850 over the "deleterious fluid" from "swill-fed cows, diseased through

constant confinement and unnatural food," that passed for milk in the days before the railroad: "The railroads now bring fresh milk every morning from a distance of 60 miles in time for use, and consequently the proportion of healthy milk used has much increased, while the price at which it is afforded to citizens has been proportionally reduced."[9]

Although most Americans were ecstatic about the railroad, some city residents disapproved of them. The noise, pollution, danger of fire from sparks, and disruption of traffic led urban residents to ban the locomotive from the city. Commuter railroads as a result never entered downtown. At best, the commuter would have a half-hour walk from the terminal to his office downtown or to adjacent areas. Some railroad companies merely detached the locomotive at the terminal and hitched up a team of horses in a version of the horse-car. The delay and inconvenience associated with this procedure kept suburbanization at a relatively low level.

For cities like New York and Boston, where bodies of water blocked the approach to the city, the steam ferry provided an additional system to serve suburban commuters. In the 1840s, regular and reliable steam ferry service was inaugurated from Long Island and New Jersey to New York. The most popular run, the Fulton Street ferry to Brooklyn, dispatched boats every 5 minutes. With a one-way fare of 1 cent, the ferry was well within the means of everyone, though most workers rode the ferry for pleasure because the rapidly rising land values in Brooklyn precluded residence there. Some businessmen rode commuter railroads from rural Queens to the ferry slip. The rapid growth of suburban Brooklyn reflected the improved commuting facilities. From a sleepy suburb of 21,000 in 1820, it became the nation's third largest city by 1860, with a population of 279,000.

The growing intraurban transportation network played a significant role in the city's spatial expansion. Although its benefits touched a minority of urban residents, this network relieved areas of potential tension and crowding. Development followed the omnibus and particularly the street-railway lines. The private transportation companies encouraged development by dealing in adjacent real estate as a lucrative sideline to their transit activities. The uneven distribution of built-up areas in some cities attests to transit's influence on space. In St. Louis, for example, horse-car lines stretched northwest from downtown. The northwest section of the city settled rapidly, whereas the southwest remained sparsely populated for years.

Far from the Madding Crowd: The Suburban Ideal

For some of those who could afford to leave the congested areas of the city, merely moving uptown was not enough. The pressures of land use on

Manhattan were such that today's frontier could be on the edge of commercial development or immigrant housing tomorrow. Indeed, tenement house construction had leaped to 14th Street by the 1840s. Perhaps only a natural setting, sufficiently buffered from the city, could fulfill the ideal of domesticity that was emerging by the mid-nineteenth century. But those people who were looking beyond the city did not do so merely to escape the congestion and contagion they associated with urban life. Many urban Americans during the first half of the nineteenth century shared a fondness for the natural landscape. Even as thousands left the countryside for the opportunities of the city, urban residents waxed nostalgic about the rural life. Such nostalgia had little to do with the reality of life in the country, a rigorous and generally unrewarding existence in nineteenth-century America. It had everything to do, however, with the changes going on in the city: rising population densities, land use pressures, and the influx of foreigners. Residents of European cities attempted to deal with some of these issues by remaking their cities; Americans responded by leaving.

Leaving resulted from many factors, including the complicated and costly land use patterns in built-up portions of the city, the availability and abundance of cheap land on the periphery, transit accessibility, an affluent and growing middle class, and the desire to own land and a detached house. Leaving did not necessarily imply abandonment, as it would in the twentieth century. Urban Americans of a hundred and fifty years ago believed that they were not so much escaping as recreating a more humane urban form. This movement did not scorn the city as an entity, for it provided economic sustenance and cultural attractions such as concerts, theater, lecture series, libraries, and schools. The city had failed simply as a residential environment. In the mid-nineteenth-century perception, the city was a difficult (though not impossible) place to create a home and nurture a family.

The split between work and residence was an early manifestation of the desire to separate from the harmful aspects of the urban environment, given the financial means and the transportation access to do so. A few urban residents began to go farther than others to make the separation more definitive. Brooklyn was an early example of this decentralizing tendency. At first, mere distance was the major distinguishing characteristic of the flight from the city. The early-nineteenth-century residents of Brooklyn had merely transferred their traditional urban row house across the river. Brooklyn was no agrarian idyll even at this early date; in fact, the inhabitants would have rejected such an environment. An advertisement for lots in Brooklyn Heights in 1823 aimed to capture buyers' objectives by combining "all the advantages of the country with most of the conveniences of the city."[10]

The suburb was no rival to the city; it harmonized with its urban partner, a balance between rural and urban. Frederick Law Olmsted, landscape architect, planner, farmer, journalist, believed that he could combine the positive aspects of both urban and rural environments. His suburb would not be a rejection of the city but "a higher rise of the same flood"; it would be "not a sacrifice of urban conveniences but their combination with the special charms and substantial advantages of rural conditions of life." The suburb, he concluded in a letter to a friend, meant "elbow room about a house without going into the country, without sacrifice of butchers, bakers, & theaters."[11]

Olmsted did not test his theory until 1868. His opportunity came on a flat 1,600-acre farm nine miles west of Chicago. The Chicago, Burlington, and Quincy Railroad would erect its first suburban station and provide convenient access to the city. Olmsted's plan stressed privacy and spaciousness. Village greens, ball fields, and playgrounds as well as facilities for boating and ice skating emphasized leisure. Fashionable villas hidden behind trees and fences offered the domestic intimacy that suburban dwellers increasingly sought. As Olmsted noted in his written comments accompanying the plan, "the essential qualification of a suburb is domesticity."[12] Riverside was a lovely community designed to imitate nature, with winding roads and lush landscaping complementing the residential and recreational features. Except for the railroad station, no hint of urbanity was betrayed. Riverside was an enclave whose common denominator was the family in a rural-like setting.

Olmsted was not being hypocritical; he was, after all, in the midst of a long career to enhance the livability of American cities. For him, "urban" meant a village in perfect harmony with nature, blending into the natural landscape, with no hard edges to mark where rural ended and urban began. In 1868, a good many—perhaps most—urban communities exhibited these characteristics. But this idyllic topography had long since passed from the major cities such as New York and Chicago. When Olmsted noted to a colleague that he hoped to eliminate all the "undesirable" elements of urban life in his Riverside plan, he was reflecting his clients' wishes to have none of the density, diversity, congestion, disease, disorder, and pollution associated with urban environments. They had no objection to—and, in fact, demanded—frequent contact with the city; the railroad station was a major selling point of the community. But they wanted to ensure the integrity of their suburb from the predations of the metropolis. Urban residents seeking a better life had overrun Brooklyn; such would not be the fate of Riverside. The homes and lot sizes would ensure a particular clientele, as would the expensive connections with the city of Chicago.

Olmsted's use of fences is a telling example of how important isolation and privacy had become by that time. In 1857, what is generally recognized as the nation's first planned suburban community took shape 12 miles west of New York City on the eastern slope of Orange Mountain. Llewellyn Haskell, a New York drug importer, had retired to the New Jersey countryside to regain his

Plan of Riverside, Illinois, 1868
Frederick Law Olmsted and his partner Calvert Vaux designed a community that, with
its winding streets, ample lots, and open spaces, provided the privacy and the aesthetic
qualities the city lacked.

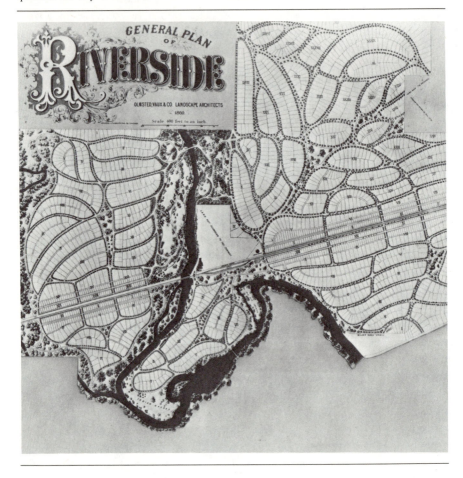

health. The prescription was successful and Haskell concluded that others might
benefit from the change as well. Along with architect Alexander Jackson Davis,
Haskell designed a community on a 350-acre site that would provide "country
homes for city people." A 50-acre park, called the "Ramble," lay at the center
of the plan. Residents would jointly own the park, which would abut all the
individual house lots. No fences or other man-made boundaries would mark
property lines. Haskell explained that he wanted to give "the appearance of a
single very large landscaped estate." The plan would enable a "family occupying
a small place in the country, costing only a few thousands of dollars, to enjoy

all the advantages of an extensive country-seat, without the expense or trouble attending the latter."[13] Haskell criss-crossed the community with winding roads and footpaths and spent $100,000 on landscaping, an enormous sum at that time.

Haskell's notions of collectively owned parks were idiosyncratic. Olmsted understood that those few who could afford such spatial indulgence desired privacy. The city more than filled their needs for social intercourse. The home was a refuge, an island, and a family looking out on its own domain was not anxious to share this view with others. Olmsted's fences were simple but crucial elements in giving these ideals a spatial dimension.

Very few urban residents could afford to reside in either Riverside or Llewellyn Park. The principles that guided the planning of both suburbs, however, were apparent in less extravagant surroundings. As early as 1815, the modern suburb—"the systematic growth of fringe areas at a pace more rapid than that of core cities," where residents "daily commute to jobs in the center," as one defined it—began appearing outside the major cities.[14] In an era when walking was the primary means of getting about a city, the limits of transportation technology imposed similar limits on suburban development. Nonetheless, suburbs began to emerge in the era of the walking city. Those who could afford a personal carriage and who did not mind the indifferent roads also moved out to the periphery. And some were not daunted by walking. A Boston resident noted in 1838, "A number of our merchants have found that it is not absolutely necessary that their dwellings should be within five minutes' walk of their counting houses. Nay, they have even discovered that a daily walk from a cottage in an adjacent town is not a very frightful task."[15]

Until the 1840s, however, the suburb was primarily a preserve of those who could afford the time and money to live there—the urban well-to-do. At that time, and up through the Civil War, improvements in public transit smoothed the way for that outward movement. Even at this early decade, the areas outside New York began to grow at a faster rate than the burgeoning city itself. In 1847, the New York *Tribune* expressed alarm over this trend:

> Property is continually tending from our city to escape the oppressiveness of our taxation; many who have made fortunes here are carrying them away to be expended and enjoyed, while thousands who continue to do business here, reside, and are taxed elsewhere on the same amount. Thus, while every suburb of New York is rapidly growing, and villages twenty and thirty miles distant are sustained by incomes earned here and expended there, our City has no equivalent rapidity of growth, and unimproved property here is often unsalable at a nominal price.[16]

The horse-car accelerated this trend during the 1850s. In 1859, Sidney George Fisher, a wealthy Philadelphian, predicted the effect of recent horse-car connections beyond the borders of his city. "A beneficial effect of this will be to enable everyone to have a suburban . . . or country home, to spread the city over a vast space, with all the advantages of compactness and the advantages, moreover, of pure air, gardens, and rural pleasures. Before long, town life, life in close streets and alleys, will be confined to a few occupations, and cities will be mere collections of shops, warehouses, factories, and places of business."[17] Though he was at least a century too early in his prognosis, Fisher accurately juxtaposed the elements that persuaded people (families above all) to leave the city: the possibility for a detached home with sufficient space and privacy; a healthful environment; and the inspiration of a natural setting. These elements were not only spatial manifestations of the suburban ideal, but they had become, by 1859, ideological principles as well, lending powerful support to the process of urban decentralization.

The Home as Sanctuary

During the 1840s and 1850s, the American urban middle class heard and read countless homilies on the sanctity and centrality of the home and family. In 1853, for example, the Rev. William G. Eliot, Jr., lectured a female audience: "The foundation of our free institutions is in our love, as a people, for our homes. . . . The corner-stone of our republic is the hearthstone." Poet and journalist Walt Whitman had corresponding advice for the men: "A man is not a whole and complete man unless he owns a house and the ground it stands on."[18] Among the most influential books in the decades immediately preceding the Civil War was Catherine Beecher's *Treatise on Domestic Economy* (1841). Beecher was part of a prominent New York family whose members included her father, Lyman Beecher, the nation's most influential evangelist, and sister Harriet Beecher Stowe. One historian has called the volume "the definitive handbook of the American home."[19] It included instructions on furnishings, child care, design, gardening, and etiquette. Beecher presented the home as a complete environment explicitly separate from the world of work. Above all, the home was the wellspring of Christian morality. The evangelical reform spirit focused on the home as the paragon institution for the reordering of urban society. Though Beecher did not specifically link the home with the suburb, her emphasis on carefully segregated space, gardens, and landscaping made the suburb the ideal environment for attaining Christian objectives.

Andrew Jackson Downing was representative of a group of young architect-designers who adapted Beecher's domestic philosophy into three-dimensional form. Downing believed that "above all things under heaven is the power and influence of the *individual home*."[20] Downing stressed the individuality of a dwelling, both in terms of its design as an expression of the occupants and its free-standing prospect, removed from artificial influences and close to nature. In his travels throughout America in the 1830s, French writer Alexis de Tocqueville had used the word "individualism" to describe the American character. That character blended well with post-Enlightenment intellectual currents such as transcendentalism, which argued for the importance of contact with nature as a function of the inherent perfectability of humankind. Henry David Thoreau's Walden experience and Emerson's essay on "Nature" (1836) are two of the more important literary products of this early-nineteenth-century American world view.

The natural world outside cities served at least two important higher purposes—renewal and inspiration. Nineteenth-century reformers were beginning to make the connection between conditions in working-class districts and the behavior of their occupants. But the dangers of urban life affected more than the working classes. Other residents of the city, shut off from beauty, immersed in a cash economy, thrown together with other ethnic groups, and subject to the physical dangers of congestion, also risked their spiritual and physical well-being. Frederick Law Olmsted noted the "peculiarly hard sort of selfishness," spawned by urban living, that "compel[s] us to walk circumspectly, watchfully, jealously," and to "look closely upon others without sympathy."[21] The growing emphasis on the importance of leisure, the home environment as a refuge, and the healthful benefits of light and fresh air that found expression in everything from A. T. Stewart's huge display windows to parks and recreation areas reflected the attempt to mitigate the *un*natural characteristics of urban life for all residents. The retreat to nature, however fleeting and temporary, at least offered an opportunity to renew oneself, to return to natural rhythms, and to contemplate life in peaceful tranquility.

Besides offering the opportunity for renewal, nature was inspirational. Its beauty and symmetry taught harmony and peace; cleared the mind and enabled it to function better; invigorated the soul and restored optimism. Frederick Law Olmsted recalled his own moment of revelation about the powers of nature. As a boy, he had lived in Hartford, where his father John would periodically take him on rambles to discover nature. "On a Sunday evening," the son wrote years later, "we were crossing the meadows alone. I was tired and he had taken me in his arms. I soon noticed that he was inattentive to my prattle and looking into his face saw in it something unusual. Following the direction of his eyes, I said: 'Oh! there's a star.' Then he said something of Infinite Love with a tone and manner which really moved me, chick that I was, so much that it has ever since remained in my heart."[22]

So urban Americans of the early nineteenth century began to cross the meadows and search for the stars, convinced that a home closer to nature would endow them with the qualities they were losing in the city. But the movement to the meadows and stars was not simply the fulfillment of an intellectual or cultural propensity. Several practical considerations were at work to make the countryside yet more attractive than the urban alternative. We have talked about the innovations in public transit. Equally important was the lack of progress in the field of public health. Promoters of the suburb and the home usually emphasized the healthfulness of these environments. The very isolation of the suburban home as a discrete, detached unit limited the opportunity for contagion. If bad air was indeed the cause of epidemic disease, then the countryside offered limitless supplies of fresh air. The suburb, in contrast to the city, was open and clean.

In addition, advances in building technology aided in the construction and design of suburban homes. Until the 1840s, much of suburban residential architecture was similar to urban design. The row house dominated. But as the benefits of the free-standing home impressed themselves on the urban consciousness along with a corresponding appreciation for isolation and for contact with nature, detached homes began to appear on the urban periphery. Within the home a new ordering of space continued to lay emphasis on privacy. Each room became associated with a specific function and even a particular person. The parlor was set apart to entertain outsiders; a nursery provided a child-oriented environment; each member of the family had a separate bedroom; and the kitchen, the traditional center of family work and socializing, became strictly a place for the preparation of meals.

The external structure of the home also changed. In 1833, a new construction technique called the balloon frame appeared in the frontier town of Chicago. It resembled a bird cage in that the weight of the structure was distributed evenly across a large number of light 2-by-4 boards nailed together (the iron nail, mass produced, was another innovation). Although it looked frail, the balloon frame was actually sounder than the heavy-timber frame construction that had characterized building up to that time. More important, the balloon frame required less skill and strength to assemble than the old method, which meant that home construction no longer demanded large numbers of people and at least someone skilled in master carpentry. A project that took twenty grown men could be handled now by a small family. As one advocate of the balloon frame explained: "The heavy beams, the laborious framing, the use of mortises and tenons, have all been replaced by lightness and constructive skill, so that a single man and a boy can put up a house, such as formerly, for its 'raising,' required the combined force of a village."[23] The balloon frame was flexible enough to allow for variations in design. Prospective home owners could now flip through carpenters' drawings or building supply catalogues, choose a style, have the timber delivered, and begin construction.

Individual designers such as Andrew Jackson Downing and Frederick Law Olmsted promoted the detached, single-family home in their plans. Both Downing and Olmsted had visited England in 1850 and were especially impressed with both the parklike nature of London's suburbs and the villas grouped around a large common area. Llewellyn Park, in fact, was an American idealization of the English suburb. Downing wrote about and popularized the various styles of English villa architecture. Olmsted, though impressed with the natural aspect of the London suburb, was equally taken with the many parks in the city. It was obvious, however, that suburban living in both England and the United States was still an option for the few. Though the ideals that attained their expression in the suburban lifestyle were those of the middle class, usually only the most affluent portions of that group could afford the land, building materials, construction costs, commuting time and money, and appropriate landscaping for a suburban environment. Suburban living was clearly out of the reach of even skilled workers, though again a few skilled craftsmen in the shipping or printing trades, for example, might qualify for a suburban residence by 1860. In any event, the vast majority of the population in New York, other American cities, and London were likely to remain there for the foreseeable future.

Space and Class

Residential distinctions developed within these expanded urban boundaries. New York's Fifth Avenue, for example, was among the most fashionable residential streets in the nation. Newer cities in the West also experienced a similar concentration of wealthy residences beyond downtown. Even Chicago, among the newest of the western cities, carved out an attractive residential area. This location, known to Chicagoans as the "Garden City," was an oasis of loveliness to residents fresh from the battles of downtown.

These streets and areas were not merely wealthy residential locations, they were extensions of the individuals who lived in them. Usually more ornate and ostentatious than the homes of the colonial elite, the homes of the wealthy, like the retail palaces downtown, were the physical symbols of growth and prosperity. The wealth of the commercial city had grown exponentially in the half-century after the American Revolution and the residential architecture of the well-to-do mushroomed in size and form as well. Spacious brownstones, Greek Revival mansions, Italian villas, and French stucco town houses were merely some of the styles preferred by urban leaders. Although visitors could not wander through these homes in the way they toured department stores, they would have undoubtedly been just as impressed if they could have done so. The villa constructed by Cleveland industrialist Amasa Stone, Jr. on Euclid Avenue during the 1850s embodied both the beauty and the overuse of Old World copies in the urban West. Stone's builders used over 700,000 bricks in the structure. The ceilings were recessed, with intricate cornice work that made looking up just as much of a visual feast as looking straight ahead. Mahogany, rosewood, and oak were the materials of choice for stairs and floors. The villa even boasted central heating and hot and cold running water—a luxury at that time—in nearly every room.

Other residential districts, less impressive but equally well defined, evolved in the city. The simple row house, that functional innovation of the colonial era, housed the growing numbers of clerks, civil servants, and other white-collar employees. These middling groups could not afford sumptious residences on Euclid Avenue but wanted the benefits of a single-family home. At the same time, they hoped to remain near downtown, where they worked and hoped to rise. The row houses, slapped together side by side, conserved space and, therefore, money. They could be built at the edge of downtown and still be priced within the means of the clerks and civil servants. Philadelphia and Baltimore continued to be the major centers of row house architecture. Several welcome improvements, however, had taken place since the colonial period. The houses were usually larger—four to six rooms, instead of three—which allowed the family more living space and privacy, major deficiencies of the earlier structures. In addition, the front of the house, historically reserved for an office or shop, was now converted into a parlor as work and home became separated, thus giving the family even more space. Finally, the rising urban prosperity enabled these groups to spruce up their dwellings with carpeting, wallpaper, and furniture—many items that had been luxuries during colonial days.

These row houses were generally located near the retail district of downtown. Few of their occupants were well-heeled enough to live in the neighborhood adjacent to the financial district, yet they could afford to escape the increasingly undesirable areas along the waterfront. They were not far removed from the affluent, however; often the great residences of the wealthy were merely a block or two away. Occasionally, an expensive home interrupted the monotony of the row houses. These mansions, so near and yet so far, doubtless provided inspiration for some and perhaps frustration for others as symbols of what economic success could buy in an expanding commercial economy.

Other groups in urban society had smaller dreams and fewer residential options. Shut out of downtown and priced out of home ownership, these less privileged city dwellers found lodging to be a major problem. Part of the difficulty stemmed from an ongoing housing shortage. Boarding houses and rental units converted from private homes attested to the shortage. These structures were either adjacent to the older wholesale section of downtown or were located in that district itself. Thus arose the anomaly of the city's poorest people living on the most expensive residential land in the city. To support these structures on the high-priced real estate, landlords subdivided the buildings and charged inflated rents. These crowded one- or two-room apartments, often renting for as much as three dollars a week, placed a great strain on working-class families, few of whom earned more than one dollar a day.

The sublandlord system made the housing situation even worse, not only by inflating rents but also by contributing to the deterioration of the building as well. The sublandlord rented a group of houses in or near downtown from owners who had left for better residential neighborhoods. These leases were usually short term, lasting only two or three years. During that time, the sublandlord desired to extract as much profit as possible from the dwellings. This meant high rents and few, if any, repairs. If the tenants complained, eviction or the threat of eviction was sufficient to mute most renters. A place to live was a valuable commodity in a city whose economy was expanding much faster than the housing supply. The irony of the situation was that the very same commercial expansion that had generated economic growth and wealth was daily removing structures from the pool of available housing, as houses were torn down to make way for warehouses and retail establishments or were merely converted into these enterprises. By destruction or conversion, some cities actually began to lose housing at the very time housing was an extremely scarce commodity.

The spread of the commercial area generated further deterioration and subsequent loss of housing by encouraging the removal of residential structures in the name of commercial expansion. Why improve a building that would, within a year or two, give way to a retail store or a bank? Invariably, this reasoning allowed some housing to stand unattended and ultimately uninhabited for decades. Finally, the expansion of downtown meant that many more jobs became available but fewer people could live there. The result was extensive overcrowding of workers' quarters in adjacent areas, which, in turn, led to property deterioration and eventually to loss of housing stock.

The occupational needs of working-class men and women further restricted their living quarters to the areas around downtown. Even if some secured work in a factory on the urban periphery, they often maintained their central city residence. A Massachusetts state official surveying housing in Boston during the 1860s told of a downtown resident who woke before 5 A.M. and left home at 5:30 to make the 7 A.M. whistle at the peripheral factory. Explaining this seemingly inconvenient arrangement, the surveyor noted: "By living in town, chance work, when out of steady work, is more readily obtained. This is quite customary with workmen."[24]

The glittering retail emporia and stately banks contrasted sharply with the seamier side of downtown and its adjacent area. The competition for lodging in what was becoming a full-fledged tenement or slum district belied the poor conditions that existed inside these hovels. We have visited the commercial and residential palaces as well as the more modest structures of the middle class. A visit to the other half brings with it awe and amazement as well—but of a different kind. In 1845, Dr. John Griscom, a New York biologist, made the first comprehensive survey of slum housing in the city's history. His revelations shocked many, but it was not until several decades later that city officials undertook effective housing reform. The conditions he described were not peculiar to New York but were common to cities in all regions experiencing the pangs of rapid economic expansion.

In a typical apartment that Griscom visited, he recorded that the walls and ceilings of the dwelling were "smeared with the blood of unmentionable insects and dirt of all indescribable colors." Because most sublandlords preferred short-term leases for their tenants, the apartments turned over every month or so, sometimes at higher rents, so few tenants bothered to clean the premises. The result was, according to Griscom, broken windows, chimneys "filled with soot, the whole premises populated thickly with vermin; the stairways, the common passage of several families, the receptacle for all things noxious, [and] whatever self-respect the family might have had . . . crushed under the pressure of the degrading circumstances by which they are surrounded."[25]

Some urban residents, especially newcomers from Europe and the country-side, could not afford even these wretched accommodations. They settled on the urban periphery, on semirural land that today we would call suburbia. There the poor set up shanties just adequate to keep out inclement weather. Because they were some distance from the nearest employment centers, they maintained a footloose life living off the land, drinking and brawling, often meeting premature death. These urban outskirts developed notorious reputations as districts of vice and corruption. Eventually the expanding city reached out and engulfed these ring areas. The districts, however, maintained their degenerate character, though with significantly more crowding.

These were the darker sides of the city as dwelling place by the 1840s. These were the people for whom choice of living space and technological advances had little relevance and for whom the ideals of suburbia and of the home, if known, were distant dreams. The reflection from the tenement's broken pane showed a city becoming more spatially divided by economic status every day. Never was urban prosperity greater or the burdens of poverty more miserable.

Immigrant Cities

The commercial city was divided not only along class and occupational lines, but by ethnicity as well. As immigrants began to make up a more substantial element in the urban population, there was a tendency toward ethnic concentration that was often superimposed on existing patterns of economic stratification. Before 1870, the great majority of immigrants were of German or Irish ancestry. From the 1830s to the Civil War, severe economic distress in Ireland and political upheaval in the German states generated an unprecedented exodus to American cities. The opportunities derived from a developing national economy in the United States played an important role as well in attracting large numbers of immigrants. By 1850, one-half of New York City's population was foreign born. At that same date, the Irish alone composed more than one-quarter of Boston's population. Cities in the West also received an important share of immigrants: more than one-half of the population of Milwaukee and Chicago was foreign born.

These antebellum immigrants were frequently scattered about the city. It was very rare, for example, to find the overwhelming majority of the Irish or Germans concentrated in a single city ward. Yet wherever they landed, immigrants settled in groups rather than as individuals. The common bonds of culture, the forces of discrimination, the size of the immigrant group, and their economic and occupational status ensured that some concentration would occur. German immigrants usually settled in kin groups in various parts of a city. The Irish were more footloose. In Milwaukee, for example, which possessed a relatively high percentage of foreign born, 83 percent of the German households lived in German neighborhoods in 1860, whereas only 47 percent of the Irish lived in Irish neighborhoods. This concentration was actually less than the residential concentration of the native born (53 percent). Factors of culture and occupation—the Irish were mostly unskilled and nomadic in terms of jobs and residences—accounted for this difference. In cities where the immigrant influx was proportionately less, there was less concentration.

The best evidence of residential clustering among Germans in many cities was the development of ethnic institutions that served both to solidify the German community and lend increasing importance to its residential space. For many native-born families, their residential neighborhoods were merely places to live and sometimes—depending on the quality of housing—to despise. For immigrants, the neighborhood became an extension of their homeland and, regardless of the decay, a part of their personal identity. In Milwaukee, a German theater, German schools, newspaper, relief societies, fire companies, and even a baseball team developed alongside, but separate from, similar native institutions. The ethnic community comprising not only residential but commercial, recreational, and religious structures as well foreshadowed the formation of the late-nineteenth-century ethnic ghettos that existed as separate entities in urban society. But it is also misleading to talk of "*the* ethnic community." Despite some institutional and cultural bonds, various national groups transferred their class and lifestyle differences from the Old World to the New—German club life and fraternal organizations, for example, divided along class and religious lines.

Kin networks, on the other hand, were important for all German immigrants in determining both living and working arrangements. The financial and advisory support of relatives was crucial in enabling German newcomers to pursue their retail expertise in antebellum American cities. In Richmond during the 1850s, for example, many of the small shops that dotted the city's evolving business district on Main Street were owned by German Jews who offered services and goods ranging from jewelry to livery. William Thalhimer, who arrived in the city early in the decade, opened a small dry-goods establishment in 1853 with the help of relatives that eventually became the urban South's first department store. In larger cities like New York, German Jews such as the Guggenheims, the Wertheims, and the Baches established their own banks, often receiving resources from Jewish bankers in Europe. After the Civil War, the assistance of such financial institutions enabled Julius Rosenwald to purchase Sears, Roebuck and Company, which eventually became the nation's premier retail mail-order establishment. The notion of mail order also came from Germany, incidentally.

Most immigrants, however, especially the Irish, joined the labor force at low occupational levels. These immigrants were most likely to find work in warehouse and terminal facilities down by the waterfront. Even skilled German and Jewish tailors and seamstresses worked in the warehouse district, where the early garment industry made its home. Proximity to the warehouses was an important concern, so the foreign born tended to reinforce the pattern of downtown and its environs as a residential location of low economic status. Some German immigrants opened grocery stores, ice cream parlors, or small restaurants and were able to be more selective in their residential locations because their businesses usually bordered on the more fashionable retail district.

Employers developed their own stereotypes about immigrant workers, and often the upward mobility of an ethnic group depended as much on the perceptions of those employers as on their Old World skills. Managers of the Boston and Lowell Railroad, for example, hired only Irishmen as brakemen during the 1850s. They believed that Irish workers were generally more contented than native-born employees and would not press for promotions or improved working conditions. In Milwaukee, employers apparently developed an ethnic work quality rating system, with the Germans considered most "thrifty, frugal, and industrious," followed by the Poles, Italians, and the Greeks.[26] In most cities, prospective employers perceived the Irish along with blacks as best for the most menial occupations. By the mid-1850s, more than 50 percent of New York's day laborers were Irish males. And nearly 25 percent of all domestic servants in the city were Irish girls.

As the ethnic work stereotyping implies, nativism became an important urban force after 1830. There are few better examples of how the commercial city was evolving into a realm of separate territories than the often-violent turf battles between ethnic and native-born young men during the late antebellum era. The sporadic skirmishes along the Bowery in New York and more serious battles in other cities punctuated election campaigns and holiday celebrations. In 1834, a mob of native-born Bostonians burned and looted an Ursuline convent. A clash between Protestants and Irish Catholics in Philadelphia in 1844 left thirteen dead. Though much of the nativist violence was directed at Irish Catholics, German Jews and Protestants occasionally became embroiled in mob actions. In 1855, an election-day riot in Louisville between Germans and nativists resulted in twenty dead.

Of course, not all nativist sentiment was expressed through violence. More subtle forms of discrimination in jobs, restrictive legislation on office holding (attempted unsuccessfully in New York in 1835), and adverse credit reports by such rating agencies as Dun & Co. limited immigrants' economic opportunity and restricted their residential mobility. During the mid-1850s, a nativist political party, the Know Nothings, attained brief ascendancy in several cities, blending a concern about government efficiency with virulent anti-immigrant rhetoric. The Know Nothings charged local Democratic party organizations with recruiting and bribing large numbers of illiterate Irish immigrants to maintain political power, but little came of their efforts to reform the urban political system in their own image.

Even as immigrants strove to "make it" in urban America during the 1840s and 1850s, the rising nativist fervor reminded them of their separateness. One wonders what went through a young Irishman's mind when he saw a "Help Wanted" sign in a shop window beneath which was the addendum: "No Irish Need Apply." Or the religious slurs he occasionally experienced, or the condescension shown his sister who worked in domestic service. Urban America had attracted a diverse mix of people since the colonial era, of course. But never had the differences of religion or national origin seemed to take on such importance and mirror so well the larger social divisions in urban society.

To the matrix of ethnic and social distinctions in antebellum urban America can be added the significant division of race. Though blacks had been a society apart almost from their first appearance, the spatial and social distance between black and white grew and hardened during the nineteenth century.

Blacks: A Separate Urban Nation

Urban blacks tended to reside in more concentrated residential patterns than immigrants, though generalizations are difficult because of sectional and status differences. Wherever they were or whatever they were doing, urban blacks were invariably better off than their comrades in the countryside.

"Better off," of course, in relative terms. Some historians have used the word "caste" to describe the black experience in the urban North before 1870. Regardless of state constitutional provisions, black men and women possessed few civil rights that could be exercised with unequivocal freedom. Black suffrage was

A Whites-Only Car, Philadelphia, c. 1850

This free black man is being expelled from a segregated railroad car. The urban North, no less than the urban South, was dominated and controlled by white men. The abolition movement in the North, however, provided some encouragement for challenges to racial segregation and discrimination.

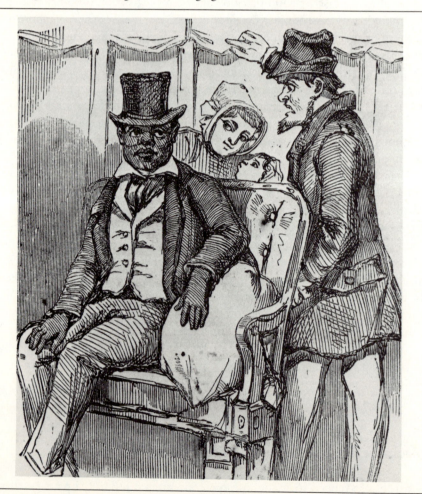

maintained only in New England, and in New York State suffrage was granted only to blacks who possessed more than $250 in property. Should blacks attempt to seek redress through the judicial process, chances of relief were slim, given white judges and all-white juries. When Worcester, Massachusetts broke tradition and allowed the town's blacks to serve on juries, an Indiana congressman predicted that this precedent

> would allow a white man to be accused of crime by a negro; to be arrested on the affidavit of a negro, by a negro officer; to be prosecuted by a negro lawyer; testified against by a negro witness; tried before a negro judge, convicted before a negro jury; and executed by a negro executioner; and either one of these negroes might become the husband of his widow or his daughter![27]

White authorities in Cincinnati, evidently concerned by this projected sequence of events, decided to rid the city of blacks in 1829. Cincinnati, on the Ohio River, was a haven for runaway slaves, and whites in the city feared their increasing presence. Local officials invoked a little-used state statute and gave their black citizens thirty days to leave town. Impatient for their removal, a white mob destroyed most of the black neighborhood in the city, prompting roughly half of the city's black population to leave for Canada. After losing a good deal of their labor force, officials lifted the eviction decree. As Cincinnatians acted out their racial fantasies, numerous cities in the West and Northeast harbored similar fears and hatreds. There were, according to one foreign observer, "two nations—one white and another black—growing up together within the same political circle, but never mingling on a principle of equality."[28] More than a century later a federal commission investigating the riots of the 1960s would reach the same conclusion.

In addition to suffering from inferior social and political status, blacks in the urban North had few opportunities for economic advancement. Like the immigrant, the black filled primarily menial occupational roles. In antebellum Detroit, for example, where the black experience was not particularly frightening, the small black workforce (140) worked at twenty-six different occupations in 1850. This seeming occupational variety obscured the fact that every one of these jobs was in the unskilled and semiskilled category.

The lowly, isolated social position of the urban blacks was mirrored in their residential location: lowly and isolated. Blacks were the most residentially concentrated group in urban society. In Philadelphia, where both Irish and German immigrants were scattered throughout the city in small enclaves, blacks were concentrated near downtown. In Boston, blacks were confined to two areas: "New Guinea" along the wharves and the infamous "Nigger Hill" near downtown. More than one-half of the city's black population resided in the latter neighborhood, which one historian has described as a mixture of "combustible houses, bars, sailor dance halls, and low boarding houses," or, in the words of a contemporary, a "horrid sink of pollution."[29]

In southern cities, which rarely had such concentrations, blacks resided in virtually every section. If a tendency toward concentration existed, it was more along economic and occupational lines than by the racial distinction characteristic of northern cities. Blacks tended to live near their place of work. Because free blacks were employed in a greater variety of occupations than northern blacks, it was not surprising that they showed a wider variety of residential locations. The use of residential space by blacks in antebellum Charleston is typical of this pattern. Though Charleston's blacks tended to be overrepresented in the poorer neighborhoods in and about downtown, they lived in all sections of the city; an all-black block did not exist. The degree of racial and ethnic segregation in Charleston was much less than segregation by status. Free blacks and poor whites were often neighbors, though this was becoming less true as the Civil War approached. Even so, the patterns of segregation conformed to economic rather than to racial divisions.

Blacks in the urban North took advantage of their residential segregation by developing institutions much like the immigrants. In the South, with its dispersed residential pattern, the divisions between slaves and freemen, the occupational distinctions, and above all the fear among whites of any associational activity among blacks reduced the incidence of this process of institution formation. One great advantage possessed by their northern brethren living in a more open society was the freedom not only to form social or religious groups, but also to develop organizations that furthered the civil rights of blacks. This means of agitation was closed to southern urban blacks regardless of their economic status.

In northern cities, as in the urban South, churches were the focal points of black associational activity. Churches extended their influence into mutual aid societies and into politics as well. The 1840s throughout the urban North saw a great deal of participation in the national Negro Convention Movement, which was designed to advance the civil rights of blacks in the region. Literary societies and black newspapers—rare in the urban South—shifted their efforts from more prosaic concerns to a strong advocacy of black rights. The black schools that flourished in northern cities were also helpful in instructing black children that their role in society need not be second class. Though most of these efforts were unavailing, they helped to prepare numerous blacks for leadership positions and imparted a sense of identity and pride to group members. In a segregated society, self-help was perhaps the most realistic option.

The possibility of developing institutions apart from direct white control and the relative diversity of occupational opportunities made the urban South especially attractive to slaves. On a few occasions, slaves could accumulate sufficient savings in bonuses to purchase their own freedom and that of their family. Failing that, they could embark on a hazardous journey on the Underground Railroad and steal away to freedom. The career of Fields Cook highlights the possibilities for slaves and free blacks in Richmond.

Cook was born and raised a slave outside of Richmond. As a young man, Cook asked his master for permission to hire himself out in the city. His master agreed and Cook eventually became a barber as well as a leech doctor (drawing blood remained a common medical practice throughout the antebellum era). At some time before 1850, Cook had saved enough money to purchase his freedom. He worked successfully to purchase his wife, Mary, and his son, Fields. During the next decade, Cook invested in Richmond real estate and lived in a white middle-class neighborhood. His life revolved around the First African Baptist Church, one of four black Baptist churches in the city, and at one point he became a lay preacher.

Cook's career in Richmond was hardly typical of southern urban blacks, slave or free. But his life would never have taken the course it did had he remained on the farm. It also reflected the strengths of the city's black community in the face of considerable adversity—the opportunity to perform skilled labor and the rich institutional life revolving around the black church, which was relatively free of white control.

Cook's experiences also imply additional distinctions between black life in northern and southern cities. In northern cities, most blacks occupied the lowest rungs of the urban social ladder. In some southern cities, especially in the deep South—Mobile, Natchez, and New Orleans—the "free people of color," as they were called, enjoyed some wealth, freedom, and status. Free blacks filtered into skilled occupations and monopolized several. In Charleston, South Carolina, three-quarters of the free black workforce in 1860 was found in skilled trades, especially barbering, carpentry, and catering. This was in marked contrast to the low occupational status of black workers in Detroit at the same time.

In terms of personal rights, however, slaves were constantly under surveillance in southern cities, and free blacks experienced frequent harassment. The laws circumscribing the freedom of the free black were extensive in the urban South, but their enforcement was spotty. Laws requiring employers to determine whether their free black employees were in fact free were openly ignored, as were laws requiring recently manumitted slaves to leave the state within a certain time period. As long as black labor performed an essential function in the urban South, a limited degree of choice and mobility was available for blacks, slave or free. The introduction of large numbers of immigrants into the workforce of the urban North depressed the occupational status of blacks. Southern cities experienced a lesser degree of immigration, especially for unskilled positions, so the competition was less keen there.

The Drawing Apart of Classes and Cultures

The increasingly diverse groups in urban society sought their identities in separate spaces, even as space defined their isolation and, in some cases, their in-
feriority. This quest for identity was a sorting-out process. As work became
separate from residence and residents separate from each other, the spatial sep-
arations implied divisions of status, behavior, and perception. Urban America
was not becoming a society bound by a rigid class structure, but it was becoming a milieu where, more and more, class mattered.

Urban society had maintained roughly a three-tiered social structure, with
merchants and professionals comprising the upper tier; the so-called respectable
workingmen, including the fading craftsmen as well as clerks and shopkeepers,
occupying the middle rung; and unskilled and semiskilled laborers, the unemployed, and transients making up the lower tier. The major feature of this traditional hierarchy was the growing separation of the three tiers. As downtown
expanded and residential areas became differentiated, social classes in urban society grew apart from each other.

The most obvious social separation occurred between the elite and the rest of
urban society. Just as wealthy cities with extensive commercial contacts continued to grow at an almost geometrical pace, so, too, wealthy individuals accumulated greater wealth at rates considerably faster than their fellow citizens were
able to. Just as there was a hierarchy of cities, with New York pulling farther
away from the other cities with each passing decade, there was a hierarchy of
people, with similar results.

The ascendancy of New York as a symbol of the ascendancy of the American
elite is especially appropriate because it was in that city that the greatest gap
between social groups occurred. According to one popular New York newspaper, "the classes are so distinctly marked, that they exist, as it were, in different
worlds. . . . No city in the world offers greater inducements to the rich than
New York, or less to the poor."[30] In other large cities, similar though less distinct
patterns were visible. Boston's leaders were accumulating wealth at such an impressive rate that between 1830 and 1860 their wealth quadrupled as the proportion of propertyless individuals in the city's population rose from 44.6 percent to 57.3 percent. Figures for western cities provided slightly less contrast,
and in southern cities the difference was even less. The largest and wealthiest
cities manifested the greatest social inequality.

Statistics are merely general representations of the growing social chasm. In
day-to-day urban life the disparities in the social structure gave rise to separate
cultures—different patterns of living, working, playing, and thinking. Residence, both location and type, was an increasing manifestation of division.
Where one lived and the type of dwelling one lived in reflected not only class

distinctions but differing perceptions about the street, privacy, home, children, and morality. The associational activities of the various social groups drew them farther apart as well. Fraternal organizations, literary societies, and churches tended to divide along class lines. Urban society, in fact, seemed in danger of becoming overly stratified and segregated. As early as 1815, Cincinnati, barely removed from the frontier, seemed to be undergoing the associational mania: "Twenty sermons a week—Sunday evening Discourses on Theology—Private assemblies—State Cotillion Parties—Saturday Night Clubs, and chemical lectures . . . like the ague, return every day with distressing regularity."[31] On the more serious side, the proliferation of associations tended to decrease communication across class lines. Individuals moved in tighter and tighter social circles.

Businessmen formed boards of trade and exchanges because they shared the same objectives and assumptions about economic growth. Workers also organized into economic associations through which they expressed their common interests in the level of their wages. Though most of these associations were short lived, while they existed they provided workers, collectively, with their first formal opportunities to express the new facts about working-class life.

These workers' associations were common in the larger cities where class divisions were sharpest. The old, almost filial, relations between masters, journeymen, and apprentices had broken down earliest in their cities. Cut adrift in a society where associations were becoming the major vehicles of advancement, workers sought out each other. The earliest groups were divided into masters, journeymen, and apprentices, reflecting the growing estrangement of these craftsworkers from each other. With the decline of the artisan class as a whole, broader organizations emerged to protect their eroding status. In 1828, Philadelphia's craftsmen formed the Working Men's Party. The group espoused a number of wide-ranging reforms designed to overhaul society: free universal public education, abolition of compulsory militia training and of imprisonment for debt, and close regulations on the sale of liquor. Although the artisans continued their decline, the Pennsylvania legislature passed all these reform measures during the next two decades.

Of more immediate use to artisans was the growing union movement, which organized artisans and unskilled workers together, thus demonstrating the artisans' new identification with the employed rather than with the employer. Between the spring of 1835 and the fall of 1836, 6,000 craftsworkers and unskilled union members won the 10-hour day and higher wages in a succession of strikes. Almost a century would pass before trade unionism would compile such a glittering record.

Leisure and recreational habits provided additional evidence of separate cultures. The leisure-time activities of the wealthy became increasingly removed from the rest of urban life. A glimpse of this lifestyle underscores the inbred and exclusive nature of the elite. New York again represented the ultimate in high life. A mansion on Fifth Avenue, carriages and horses for transportation, a pony for the younger children, a saddle horse for the older ones, and a yacht were prerequisites to enjoying the good life.

> Then there is the opera and the theatre, unless, as one New York millionaire has chosen to do, he chooses to build a theatre of his own. There are balls, costumes, and otherwise . . . and last, though not least, there is shopping at . . . Lord & Taylor's and such other economical places, where really a lady could not expect to get anything to wear short of a morning's bill of two or three thousand dollars. Ah! money may be the root of all evil, but it is a mighty pleasant esculent for the New York market.[32]

This is not to say that the rest of urban society did without recreation entirely. The most common working-class leisure activity was drinking. The tavern, as in the colonial era, was a male preserve. It was race course, ballroom, salon, and resort combined. The social aspect of taverns was at least as important as the alcohol. Nevertheless, because most bars offered free lunches, drinking usually began in the early afternoon. Unfortunately, alcoholism became a severe problem in cities, especially, though not exclusively, among male workers.

Much like residence and work, recreation had its own well-defined spaces. While the "better sort" cavorted on Broadway, for example, workers flooded the Bowery. Among the widest streets in a city of narrow thoroughfares, the Bowery ran along the eastern edge of the island in close proximity to the crowded tenements of the Lower East Side. Where Broadway was refined, the Bowery was raucous, especially on a Saturday night. There, amid the tangle of oyster houses, taverns ("groggeries," they were called), dance halls, brothels, and gambling dens, working-class youth spent their energy and wages. Inevitably, fights broke out (often over ethnic slurs), and occasionally a full-scale battle erupted. Young men and women attended lively stage performances at the Bowery Theatre.

The working-class culture that flourished on the Bowery generated identity and pride. Here young men could be seen on the streets in the evenings, with their swagger and distinctive dress, exhibiting what one observer called in obvious disgust, "Boweriness."[33] Perhaps the most famous of these groups were the Bowery B'Hoys, celebrated in the dime novels of the day, a loose association of mainly native-born youths who dressed in outlandish styles and hairdos. Sometimes the gangs would provide a convenient organization for Tammany Hall, the Democratic Party political machine. On election day, party workers would come by the Bowery and see to it that the "boys" voted often, or, if the results appeared to be going against the Tammany ticket, ballot boxes might mysteriously disappear. These gangs also provided protection for their neighborhoods. Most of the time the gangs functioned as social clubs, promenading on the Bowery, meeting girls, and visiting groggeries and beer gardens.

Popular novelist George G. Foster brought these fellows to public attention as well as their female counterparts, the Bowery Girls. Foster's characterizations of the Bowery Girls as lusty, pleasure-seeking, almost masculine types shocked conventional middle-class morality (and doubtless accounted for the popularity of his works). Yet readers also found much that was admirable in the Bowery Girls. Like the city they lived in, the girls alternately outraged and pleased their followers. Lize, a recurring character in his stories, is one such "girl" who "never feels herself at home but at the theater or the dance. . . . She is perfectly willing to work for a living, works hard and cheerfully, as any day laborer or journeyman mechanic of the other sex." Lize is not a housewife, Foster informs his readers, but an independent working woman: "She rises before the sun . . . swallows her frugal breakfast in a hurry, puts a still more frugal dinner in her little tin kettle . . . and starts off to her daily labor. . . . From six to six o'clock she works steadily, with little gossip and no interruption save the hour from twelve to one, devoted to dinner."[34] This rigorous schedule does not dull Lize's demeanor or disposition. "Her very walk has a swing of mischief and defiance in it, and the tones of her voice are loud, hearty, and free. Her dress is 'high' and its various ingredients are gotten together in utter defiance of those conventional laws of harmony and taste."[35]

In the dynamic commercial city, conventional morality, courting patterns, and traditions of women living in family situations had turned topsy turvy by 1870. Indeed, much of the concern expressed about working-class women related to this street culture that seemed so different from, and threatening to, concepts of home and domesticity and the morality those concepts implied.

The street, in fact, became a dividing line expressing distinctions in class and culture. Although it was appropriate for a "respectable" woman to shop unescorted on Broadway, it was improper for her to seek pleasure, whether in a theater or a café, without the company of a man. Women who used the street for a living—food vendors, rag pickers, and scavengers—were beyond the pale of respectability. The young men of the Bowery also did not escape the disdain of middle-class moralists. Drink was at the center of their culture and it was plentiful along that thoroughfare. Drinking fraternities evolved into street gangs, initially divided by craft and later by ethnic background or neighborhood residence.

Religion was another activity that widened the cultural disparity between classes. Religion was an important force in cities at this time. Religious institutions launched charity drives, operated schools, provided recreational space, and imparted important values in a changing society. Like cities, however, religious denominations engaged in rivalries of their own. In an era when large church membership signified success, the number of members in a given church became increasingly important. Many denominations guarded their domains protectively while seeking converts at the same time. Through it all, however, the Episcopal, Congregational, and Presbyterian churches tended to remain the religious home of the elite, whereas those who were not members of the urban leadership tended to practice the more evangelical Protestant faiths, Catholicism, and Judaism. An individual's position in society could virtually be fixed by the church he or she belonged to.

Residence, associational activity, leisure, and religion confirmed the growing differences in urban society. Further, it did not appear that the mobility between the different groups was sufficient to ameliorate class and cultural differences. Historians conducting social mobility studies of cities in a variety of types and sizes have generally agreed that the rags-to-riches stories were few. For the most part, the elite tended to be a self-perpetuating group. They intermarried and rarely conducted business or social affairs with anyone outside their class. They also attended the "right" schools, preferably Harvard or a comparable university. By 1870, social mobility between the tiers was generally less than it had been a generation earlier. As the contacts of the elite contracted, so did opportunities to enter this privileged class.

This does not mean that decade by decade individuals and families below the leadership group failed to enhance their position. They did—and frequently. If success is measured by the accumulation of property, during any given decade roughly one-third to one-half the members of the second and third social tiers were successful. A purchase of a store, a horse, some new furniture, and the ultimate in urban advancement, a home, were within reach of some urban workers. By 1859, Irish residents of San Francisco, for example, had deposited more than $10 million in the Hibernia Savings and Loan bank, most of which went into home mortgages. For the Irish, a home was more a measure of "success" than an upgrade in job status.

Mobility, of course, varied from city to city. In older cities like New York and Boston, the social structure was more stable. In newer cities like Cincinnati and Chicago, where economic growth was more rapid and an entrenched leadership did not exist, movement up and down the social ladder was easier. In these western cities, however, economic growth and maturity resulted in decreased social mobility.

The decline in mobility solidified certain roles in urban society, a fact that spatial patterns such as the Bowery, the tenement, and the home had already demonstrated. The various groups in the city began to identify themselves as permanent members of their social strata. Though many members of the working class hoped for and achieved improvement in their economic condition, few realistically pursued the objective of entering the entrepreneurial ranks. Business leaders, for their part, more than likely grew up in the sheltered confines of an elite family and had virtually no contact and little in common with the working-class lifestyle.

America's cities grew up in the first half of the nineteenth century. Pressures applied by economic prosperity and population growth fueled the early phases of expansion; transportation systems and personal preference extended the city line farther. One city, San Francisco, hemmed in by water and hills, filled in part of its bay to accommodate expansion. Another, Philadelphia, gathered up its suburban neighborhoods and increased in size on a single day in 1854 from 2 square miles to 129 square miles. Though few other cities could boast expansion on this scale, urban space in all parts of the continent fanned rapidly outward from downtown. Citizens were acting on their desires for more space, quiet, and beauty—a vision that would continue to expand the boundaries of American cities. Growing pains accompanied this vision. The working class remained trapped in the city center, burdened by lack of mobility and a deteriorating housing situation. Public transit and the availability of new residential space did not relieve their burdens. And they were not the only group to feel the adverse effects of rapid growth. Residents clamored for better streets, protection from disease and fire, and a general improvement in the quality of life. As urban leaders had formerly reached out to organize the hinterland and streamline the processes of trade, so they now turned to their immediate surroundings and worked to make their cities worthy showplaces of their new commercial empire.

Notes

1. Both quotes in Gunther Barth, *City People: The Rise of Modern City Culture in Nineteenth-Century America* (New York: Oxford University Press, 1980), pp. 10, 11.
2. Quotations and other details of this description of department stores are from Bayrd Still, ed., *Urban America: A History with Documents* (Boston: Little, Brown, 1974), pp. 148–149.
3. Quoted in Barth, *City People*, p. 123.
4. Quoted in Christine Stansell, *City of Women: Sex and Class in New York, 1789–1860* (New York: Alfred A. Knopf, 1986), p. 43.
5. Quoted in Barth, *City People*, p. 31.
6. Quoted in Still, ed., *Urban America*, p. 86.
7. Quoted in Elizabeth Dougherty, "Nineteenth Century Transportation Modes and Their Influence on Urban Spatial Forms," unpublished paper, Virginia Polytechnic Institute and State University, March 1976.
8. Quoted in Still, *Urban America*, p. 197.
9. Quoted in *ibid.*, p. 86.
10. Quoted in David Schuyler, *The New Urban Landscape: The Redefinition of City Form in Nineteenth-Century America* (Baltimore: Johns Hopkins University Press, 1986), p. 36.
11. Quoted in Robert Fishman, *Bourgeois Utopias: The Rise and Fall of Suburbia* (New York: Basic Books, 1987), p. 128.
12. Quoted in Schuyler, *New Urban Landscape*, p. 162.
13. Quoted in *ibid.*, p. 159.
14. Kenneth T. Jackson, *Crabgrass Frontier: The Suburbanization of the United States* (New York: Oxford University Press, 1985), p. 13.
15. Quoted in Schuyler, *New Urban Landscape*, p. 150.
16. Quoted in Jackson, *Crabgrass Frontier*, pp. 29–30.

17. Quoted in *ibid.*, pp. 41–42.
18. Both quotes in *ibid.*, p. 50.
19. Fishman, *Bourgeois Utopias,* p. 122.
20. Quoted in *ibid.*, p. 123.
21. Quoted in *ibid.*, p. 127.
22. Quoted in Schuyler, *New Urban Landscape,* p. 28.
23. Horace Greeley (1872), quoted in John R. Stilgoe, *Common Landscape of America, 1580–1845* (New Haven: Yale University Press, 1982), p. 321.
24. Quoted in Still, ed., *Urban America,* p. 121.
25. Quoted in Charles N. Glaab, ed., *The American City: A Documentary History* (Homewood, Ill.: Dorsey Press, 1963), pp. 121–122.
26. John Bodnar, *The Transplanted: A History of Immigrants in America* (Bloomington, Ind.: Indiana University Press, 1985), p. 69.
27. Quoted in Leon F. Litwack, *North of Slavery: The Negro in the Free States, 1790–1860* (Chicago: University of Chicago Press, 1961), p. 93.
28. Quoted in *ibid.*, p. 102.
29. Quoted in Oscar Handlin, *Boston's Immigrants: A Study in Acculturation* (Cambridge, Mass.: Harvard University Press, 1941), p. 96.
30. Quoted in Still, ed., *Urban America,* p. 155.
31. Quoted in Richard C. Wade, *The Urban Frontier: Pioneer Life in Early Pittsburgh, Cincinnati, Lexington, Louisville, and St. Louis* (Chicago: University of Chicago Press, 1964), p. 157.
32. Quoted in Still, ed., *Urban America,* p. 155.
33. Quoted in Sean Wilentz, *Chants Democratic: New York City and the Rise of the American Working Class, 1788–1850* (New York: Oxford University Press, 1984), p. 263.
34. Quoted in Still, ed., *Urban America,* pp. 141–142.
35. Quoted in Stansell, *City of Women,* p. 93.

CHAPTER 6

The Burgeoning of Middle-Class Urban Reform

The separation of work from residence, of different ethnic, racial, and social groups from each other, did not imply isolation. Urban residents came together and mingled in downtown; disease did not honor neighborhood boundaries; and tenements could not always contain social and political passions. The various groups in urban society were aware of each other, sometimes fearfully so, sometimes with attitudes of self-righteousness and disdain, and sometimes with the concern born of deep religious conviction. The economic diversification and specialization of the early-nineteenth-century city expanded the middle-class population. In their flight from downtown, their search for security in the home, and their consumer behavior, the middle class established urban trends. Some of their aspirations and behaviors derived from the elite, but their sheer numbers ensured middle-class residents of being a force in their own right.

The neat department store shelves, the well-appointed home, and the efficient workplace were key emblems of the regulated lives of the middle class. They sought the same order for their cities. What they saw in their daily travels on the horse-car or omnibus, and in the streets of downtown, as well as what they read about in the growing literature on the urban condition, was something far different. Reform was necessary. Urban residents had been concerned about ordering their society since the colonial era, but only in the nineteenth century did a systematic, institutionalized effort for social improvement emerge that engaged public and private resources.

The Ideals of Reform

By the 1850s, the contrasts of urban life were becoming too great to ignore: opulent five-story town houses and dark, crowded tenements; fabulous fortunes and crushing poverty; women in ragged clothes walking the streets carrying starving babies and begging for food while fashionable ladies stepped from elegant carriages to enter posh emporia of retail splendor; and the children, some of whom wandered the streets while others sat in comfortable homes, reading or playing with their parents. The contrasts touched the sentimental and religious sensibilities of the "better sort." As evangelical fervor swept through American cities in the decades before the Civil War, the responsibility of Christians became clear. Though the religious enthusiasm was lost on Roman Catholic immigrants, who were alternately amused and alarmed at the efforts made to save them in both a religious and social sense, the tenets of evangelical theology made a deep impression on the conscience-plagued Protestant middle class.

Memories also lingered from an earlier time before the immigrants, before congestion, before unseemly poverty and vice (or so it seemed)—a time when the city was a village, a compact, contractual society, where workers were craftsmen and the commodities that entrepreneurs dealt with were goods and services, not men. It had also been a time when women and children were sheltered from the moil of the city, safe at home, however modest that dwelling had been. Whether such an idyllic place ever existed is beside the point; reformers in the middle decades of the nineteenth century referred to it, believed in it, and sought to recreate it for themselves in their private homes.

A more practical motivation for reform efforts was the danger associated with the chaos of the tenement districts. Middle-class reformers read the penny presses, those cheaply printed newspapers that made their appearance in cities up and down the East Coast in the 1830s. Editors, freed of the ties to political parties that had subsidized the traditional press, carved out a living on circulation and advertisements. The fierce competition among these tabloids produced sensational stories, avid readerships, and a general decline in the quality if not veracity of American journalism. Whether urban America was less safe than previously was beside the point. Violence and crime—the more lurid and heinous the better—were now favorite topics in the press.

Urban reform would, therefore, be both practical and moral in its effects.

Reformers would order the city by moving against disease, violence, and poverty, at the same time ensuring that those who were responsible for the disorder, knowingly or otherwise, would be trained in the tenets of middle-class respectability. In the process, reformers would develop two mechanisms for dealing with the problems they attributed to urban life: the private, voluntary association and local government.

City Government and the Business of Reform

Since late in the colonial era, city government had reduced its responsibility for regulating the economy while increasing its role as a provider of services. The scale of this role increased significantly after 1830 as middle-class reformers looked to local government as an agency both for enhancing the city's economic development and providing services. City governments invested heavily in a variety of development projects, including canals, railroads, and port facilities, and they also supported public health, police and fire departments, and social services. Civic leaders often justified the last category by asserting that social services secured and enhanced their investment in the other services. This justification was necessary because once state-granted charters were amended to approve revenue-raising powers, the burden of supporting new programs fell on property holders—in other words, the leaders themselves and their middle-class constituents. The property tax became the greatest source of public revenue. And as the economic and service appetites of cities outpaced revenues, local leaders found themselves plunging into deficit financing by issuing municipal bonds to satisfy these needs.

Because major property holders became the prime supporters of local government, it is not surprising that civic priorities reflected their wishes. Though the economic leadership of the larger cities had become too diverse by the 1840s to agree unanimously on all policies, a general understanding equated the common welfare with the priorities of the leadership. Those priorities emphasized economic development. Accordingly, government and business became partners. "The interests of commerce," declared one Philadelphian, "as connected with politics, are so striking, that it is difficult to separate one from the other."[1]

This should not imply that moral, altruistic, or other motives were absent. Evangelical fervor gripped cities periodically in the 1840s and fifties, infusing major reform movements such as abolitionism and temperance. But religious sentiment did not build or maintain the national urban economy, nor did it direct the fierce competition that accompanied commercial growth. If moral considerations coincided with cost-benefit calculations, so much the better. If not, consciences could be accommodated accordingly.

Although new and expanded revenue sources provided local government with more flexibility in providing services and funding economic development projects, the administrative structure of government was an obstacle to decision making. The city council, composed either of two bodies or of one, was the dominant urban political institution. In the early nineteenth century, this body legislated for the city, executed its laws, and served as the lower court system. Before 1830, the lack of separation of powers was innocuous given local government's minor role in urban affairs; the expansion of activities after that date highlighted its cumbersome structure. Until the 1820s, the mayor had been primarily a ceremonial figure with duties restricted to minor judicial matters. Gradually, in a process lasting most of the century, mayors came to assume more substantive powers of initiating, approving, and vetoing council measures.

The city council governed by committee. The trend toward bicameral councils usually meant that it took twice as long to push legislation through the council. Under the ward system, each member of the council represented only a portion of the city, so only large projects that benefited all wards or projects that benefited the business district enjoyed smooth passage through the council. Council members generally subscribed to the "psychology of scarcity"—a doctrine that, in the words of one historian, "elevated thrift, minimal consumption, and avoidance of debt to moral imperatives."[2] In other words, the council saw to it that local government played a limited role in community life. But the buoyant economy that had evolved by the 1820s and the common perception of mounting urban problems convinced elected officials that the "psychology of scarcity" was ill suited to the realities of the modern commercial city.

Public Health: A New Urban Concept

Few realities were more frightening to city dwellers than epidemic disease. Once a disease began, its course seemed relentless. Before the acceptance of the germ theory of disease in the late nineteenth century, physicians were powerless to deal with epidemics. The only proven remedy was flight. Epidemic disease had been a scourge of the colonial city, but the growth and congestion of the nineteenth-century commercial city resulted in shockingly high death tolls. A yellow fever epidemic in Philadelphia in 1793 took the lives of 5,000 people, nearly one out of every ten people residing in the city; St. Louis lost one-tenth of its population in an 1849 cholera epidemic; in 1853, yellow fever ravaged New Orleans, killing 11,000 people; and in 1855, Norfolk was decimated by a yellow fever epidemic that carried off nearly one-sixth of its population.

In the face of this onslaught physicians attempted futile remedies. Calomel, a white mercury compound, was a popular prescription for cholera. Large doses induced mercury poisoning, if the patient had not died from the cholera first. A common remedy for disease was bleeding, which weakened already dehydrated patients and probably hastened their death. To check diarrhea, a prevalent symptom of cholera, the president of the New York State Medical Society suggested plugging the rectum with beeswax. Strychnine, electric shocks, and tobacco smoke enemas were also popular cures. Little wonder that one survivor quipped: "Cholera kills, and doctors slay, and every foe will have its way!"[3]

Most of the time, fatalities were confined to the poorer classes. The 1832 cholera epidemic in New York, however, along with a similar major outbreak in 1849 overstepped class boundaries. The new appetite of epidemic disease for middle-class victims had also become a growing problem in European cities at the time. The one variable that distinguished contemporary outbreaks from previous plagues was the extent and nature of urbanization. Migrations to the great cities of Europe (occasioned as much by the trauma of agricultural transformation as by the opportunities available in the cities) and industrialization had created intolerable living conditions. In an effort to document this new city and the new scale of its problems, as well as to stem the ravaging and costly epidemics, French social scientists early in the nineteenth century began to take systematic surveys of Parisian working class life. By 1840, the Paris Health Council had published nearly 10,000 reports detailing the relationship between environment and health.

The Paris reports stimulated English researchers to conduct similar scientific surveys. Edwin Chadwick, an attorney with a keen interest in social service reform, undertook an extensive study of England's congested urban working class districts that had become festering breeding grounds for disease, blight, and crime. His findings, *Report on the Sanitary Condition of the Labouring Population and on the Means for Its Improvement* (1842), quickly became a classic reference work in both the medical and social science communities. The American biologist Dr. John C. Griscom was among Chadwick's numerous international correspondents. Since the 1820s, Griscom had shared the concerns of his French and English colleagues on the implications of congested urban life. Inspired by Chadwick's work, Griscom published *The Sanitary Condition of the Laboring Population of New York* (1845), a volume that exhibited the same painstaking collection of data, detailed description of living conditions, and comparisons with cities in other countries.

The widespread circulation of this and similar reports, as well as the mounting toll from epidemic disease, convinced local officials of the wisdom of public health policies as a long-term investment. The concept of public health seemed to fulfill both the economic and moral imperatives of the commercial city. Disease was bad for business: no farmer wanted to trade his crops for yellow fever, and no investor wished to see his capital sunk into a sickly city. Epidemics were expensive: commerce stopped, prominent leaders were carried off, and cities' reputations were damaged. One physician estimated that New Orleans lost $45,000,000 in commerce during its yellow fever epidemics of the late 1840s. In addition, rival cities' newspaper editors were quick in attempting to dissuade farmers, tourists, and investors from traveling to a competing city by publishing reports of that city's inherent unhealthfulness. It took some communities years to recover from the shock of a severe epidemic.

Despite this depressing litany, local government's response was partial and selective. There was general agreement that cleanliness and quarantine were the two most effective policies against disease. Attempts by local governments to maintain cleanliness were haphazard and inefficient, however. Most efforts focused on streets, which were, after all, arteries of commerce and communication essential to business. It was thus not unusual for cities to devote one-fourth of their budgets to street cleaning and paving.

A good street, though, was hard to find. Muddy when it rained, dusty when it did not, and easily passable only occasionally, urban streets resembled steeple-chase courses rather than pedestrian and wheeled-vehicle thoroughfares. A popular story of the era told of a citizen who rushed into the street to help a man buried up to his neck in mud. "No need to worry," the trapped victim replied, "I have a horse underneath me."[4]

The need for improving the condition of the streets, and especially for paving them, was there, to be sure. Few urban streets were paved, however, despite the time and money expended by the city for this purpose. City funds were applied only toward paving the major thoroughfares—the business arteries of the city. Elsewhere the city required petitions and financial subsidies from property holders to perform this service. Civic leaders justified public support for main streets as a function of the government's role to promote the general welfare, which they equated with business interests.

Besides being generally unpaved, city streets were usually extremely filthy. New York by all accounts possessed the dirtiest streets in urban America. "With the exception of a very few thoroughfares, all the streets are one mass of reeking, disgusting filth, which in some places is piled to such a height as to render them almost impassable by vehicles." But New York had a great deal of company: places "too foul to serve as the sties for the hogs" and "filthy in the extreme," streets where a pedestrian might "literally go entangled in pigs' tails and jaw bones" and "me[e]t with the putrefying carcass of a dead dog," were some of the descriptions evoked by various American cities.[5] Evidently the gentleman up to his neck in the mud was encased in a more exotic substance than he probably realized.

The problem of street cleaning, seemingly insoluble, was nevertheless ex-premely pressing. Dirty streets pointed to a disorderly community and possibly an unhealthy one, and both implications were bad for business. "It is of vast importance to the trade and prosperity of Norfolk," an editor warned, "to say nothing of the lives of the people, that the standing pools in our streets should be removed by the . . . councils instantly."[6]

Local government mobilized on several fronts. Several cities assigned the bulk of the street-cleaning chores to animals. Pigs were the most popular, scavenging streets in New York, St. Louis, and Cincinnati. For cities that were serious about their street-cleaning efforts, this zoo parade could only be a temporary expedient because the cure often became worse than the disease. By the 1860s, a new sense of public dignity and an overpopulation of greedy porkers led to a discontin-uation of pigs as street scavengers, and city councils henceforth contracted with private companies or with individuals to clean—or scavenge, as it was called—city streets. Unfortunately, these contracts were often political rewards rather than genuine performance agreements. In New York, according to the popular wisdom of the time, the only way to have the streets cleaned was to bribe the city councilmen.

This is not to say that local government expended little effort and money on street cleaning. As the Norfolk editor stated, there were good business and health reasons to be concerned about clean streets—but only certain streets. The major business streets were generally clean regardless of the condition of the rest of the city's streets. Predictably, the streets that were most neglected—those in the poorest sections of the city—were the dirtiest and most likely to foster the spread of disease. They were also the least visible streets, and business leaders, always keen to present a good image at the least cost, felt justified in directing local government's street-cleaning efforts, meager as they were, toward the few main business arteries. The inequity did not go unnoticed, and some leaders themselves pointed this out to their colleagues: "It has been too much the prac-tice to cause the large thoroughfares to be scrupulously cleaned," New York's Mayor Ambrose Kingsland warned councilmen, "while scarcely any attention is paid to the smaller and less frequented, but most densely populated streets in the city."[7]

John Griscom was successful in persuading city officials to commit public funds to at least one sanitary policy. Waste disposal was a particular problem in tightly packed tenements on congested streets. Privies overflowed periodically. Everything from fecal matter to dead cats coagulated in surface water drains. The fetid air from these open cesspools, medical experts theorized, contributed to contagion. In 1842, Edwin Chadwick had devised an enclosed egg-shaped sewer through which water could be forced, thereby freeing the sewer from human and animal wastes. Through the proper grading of streets, rainwater would wash debris into the self-cleansing sewers and, ultimately, out of the city and into the nearest river or ocean. By 1855, more than a dozen cities in the United States, including New York, had built water carriage sewers in at least some portions of their communities. The popularity of sewers related, in great part, to their enhancement of property values. Though such measures produced noticeable improvements in mortality rates related to typhoid and cholera, the poorest and most congested districts in these cities continued to project discouraging statistics on disease and death. On the eve of the Civil War, New York's mortality rate was one in twenty-seven, compared with one in thirty-seven for Paris and one in forty for London. Conditions seemed to be deteriorating. In 1820, 38 percent of children under the age of five in New York died; by 1850, that figure had climbed to 52 percent and remained there for the rest of the decade.

The record of local government on the other prevailing policy against epidemic disease—quarantine—was also spotty. Quarantine involved the detention of vessels, crew, and cargo that had originated from a port where epidemic disease was raging. The period of detention usually lasted for twelve days, after which time, if no case of the disease had appeared on board, the ship was free to proceed to the dock and unload its cargo. Quarantine, of course, slowed the flow of commerce; it created delays and threw off schedules. Most merchants viewed quarantine as a restraint of trade.

The ineffectuality of local government institutions in the area of public health was purposeful. Cronies at the port and on the board of health would ensure that business interests were faithfully protected. In other words, quarantine would not be invoked, and physicians would not carp about the city's poor health—a situation that urban rivals were certain to pick up. Moreover, as a means of protecting the city's image, the news of an epidemic would not be divulged until the very last moment. When an independent group of physicians broke the silence about a cholera epidemic in New York, a prominent banker asked whether the "eager physicians had any idea of the disaster which such an announcement would bring to the city's business."[8] Well might one disgusted Cincinnatian remark: "Every consideration of health . . . yields to the views of mercantile convenience."[9]

To the business leaders, their poor performance on health matters was the result of a simple and justifiable cost-benefit analysis. The benefits to be gained by comprehensive public health planning did not offset the costs to the taxpayers. Although this may seem a mechanistic and insensitive way of looking at something as vital as the city's health, from the leaders' perspective and, given their knowledge of the course of disease, it may be construed as a reasonable position. First, it was not clear that maintaining a clean city did prevent disease.

Epidemics visited cities that were considered clean by the standards of the time. Savannah had expended $200,000 to drain the lands around the city and place them under dry cultivation, but without noticeable effect on the rate of epidemic disease. Second, because physicians were virtually unanimous in avowing the noncontagion of the epidemic diseases, it seemed useless to expend funds on implementing a quarantine policy.

By the mid-1860s, volumes of reports detailing the destructive course of epidemic disease and the failure of public authorities to act expeditiously and vigorously sat on shelves in physicians' offices. However, Griscom and his colleagues were successful at least in persuading New York state legislators of the efficacy of public health policy. In 1866, the state imposed a board of health on the city of New York.

The Professionalization of Fire and Police Protection

By the 1840s, business leaders no longer perceived local government in narrow terms. Because they equated business interests with the general welfare, the policy realm of local government was theoretically vast. But the review of public health policy indicates the narrow track on which this broad ideal rested. When cities began to provide other services, particularly fire and police protection along with relief for the poor, the level of those services reflected the same selectivity that characterized government response to public health issues.

As property values skyrocketed, business inventories boomed, and investments diversified, the city became an increasingly valuable commodity. And as different groups crowded in unhealthy, unsafe, and ungodly environments, the city became increasingly vulnerable. Local governments came to see the virtue of supporting professional, public firefighting and police forces.

The switch from bucket brigades to hydrants in the early nineteenth century was a major advance, but the continued prevalence of volunteer companies was not. Depending on their size, cities possessed anywhere from a half-dozen to thirty volunteer fire companies. These companies were clubs of men who met periodically for social purposes and occasionally to fight fires. They were essentially fraternal organizations, primarily working class, whose hobby was firefighting. Fierce competition between the companies often erupted at the scene of the fire into a full-fledged melee. It was not uncommon for members of fire companies, who habitually fortified themselves with alcohol to generate sufficient bravery to fight conflagrations, to turn their hoses on each other while the fire burned merrily away.

Urban government gradually brought order to the chaos of firefighting by first bringing all volunteer companies under the supervision of one appointed public official, screening membership, and, beginning with Cincinnati in 1829, paying a modest salary. These regulations evolved to produce professional, independent fire departments in most cities by the 1860s. Firefighting, like disease prevention, required a systematic and professional solution.

As American cities were organizing to fight fires, they were also developing the means to fight crime. Popular perception held that cities were becoming unsafe. Considering the growing diversity and increasing social and spatial separation of urban society, this perception seemed reasonable. In reality, however, crimes of personal violence had been declining steadily since the late eighteenth century. The perception of crime had more to do with a general image of urban society than with the incidence of crime itself. The appearance of sensational sagas of urban depravity in the penny presses and in the popular pulp novels and sketches confirmed suspicions that the disorderly city was also a violent city. The diversity of the urban population and the divergence from middle-class morals evident in neighborhoods such as the Bowery and the grim residential streets of lower Manhattan made it easy to conclude that the city required a strong dose of authority.

This is not to say that crime was a fantasy of the anxious middle class. In the newer settlements of the West, violent crime was commonplace. Periodic shootings and drunken brawls occurred during the formative years of western cities like Houston, Denver, and San Francisco. In the older cities, such disorderly behavior was less frequent, though the form it took threatened the fabric of urban society much more. Mob violence or riots increased in eastern cities after the 1830s. Philadelphia, the staid city of brotherly love, averaged one major riot a year between 1834 and 1842, a frequency that would be scandalous today. Cities like Boston, Baltimore, Louisville, New York, and Washington, D.C., were also victimized by mob outbursts, though with less frequency.

The origins, nature, and participants of the urban riots reflected both the growing divisions in urban society and the inadequacy of law enforcement. The animosity between Catholics and Protestants accounted for a good portion of mob violence in the nineteenth-century cities. The competition for employment and the fact that the Irish always seemed willing to work for lower wages fueled Protestant prejudices. Equally important, among Protestants there existed a deep distrust of the Catholic religion. The separate schools, the hierarchical organization of the church, and the anti-Protestant traditions among Catholics roused fears in American cities. A riot erupted in Philadelphia in the spring of 1844 that stemmed from a controversy over the use of the King James version of the Bible in public schools, a practice Catholics had objected to. A group of

Protestants foolishly held an anti-Catholic rally in an Irish neighborhood, and in the inevitable battle that occurred a Protestant teenager was shot and killed. The incident touched off three days of uncontrolled rioting that left six people dead, a score injured, and $250,000 worth of property damaged, including two Catholic churches, which were destroyed. The local police were totally ineffective, and the militia, almost all of whom were Protestant, made only half-hearted attempts at controlling the mobs.

Catholics were not the only victims of the sharpening divisions in urban society. Blacks and their white abolitionist associates were frequent targets of mobs. There were disturbances in Cincinnati, Detroit, Philadelphia, and Boston. On three separate occasions between 1834 and 1844, blacks and abolitionists were victimized by mob violence in Philadelphia. The most serious riot in 1838 involved the destruction of a meeting hall used by abolitionists. In 1835, a bumper year for riots—thirty-seven throughout urban America—racial conflict erupted in Washington, D.C. A drunken mob of whites, provoked by the discovery of a huge stockpile of abolitionist literature, went on a two-night rampage in the black community, burning several buildings but fortunately killing no one. The unchecked manner in which these mobs were able to proceed about their business reflected the inadequacy of the meager police forces of the affected cities.

Violence was an accepted means of settling disputes in American cities because it was deemed desirable to use force to achieve great social ends. The antiabolitionist mob in Philadelphia believed they were preserving order by striking at a group that openly acknowledged its position above the law. The poor Protestant working people believed they were saving the city and perhaps the nation from what they considered the insidious doctrines of the Roman Catholic church. The spirit of the times encouraged these beliefs. Andrew Jackson, the national hero of the period, was himself a man of action and, at times, of violence—but always for the cause of good. To riot, therefore, was to be "a kind of apotheosis for democratic man," to be a kind of John Wayne "en masse."[10]

Despite the romance of collective violence and its deep roots in American urban tradition, civic leaders began to have second thoughts about these mass expressions of ill will toward the city's outcasts. A number of their own employees had participated in the affairs, and there was a deep-seated fear that violence against blacks and the Irish would lose its edge after a while and the hunters would seek bigger game. After all, the issue of employment figured prominently in a number of the urban riots. Entrepreneurs were also fearful that the increasing violence would injure the city's reputation. A lawless community was not an especially safe place for investment. A St. Louis editor summarized

the feelings of the business leaders of his city when he advised that "the prosperity of our city, its increase in business, the enhancement in the value of its
property . . . depend upon the preservation of order."[11]

Though civic leaders realized that public demonstrations of unhappiness
could not and should not be curtailed, controlling such groups before they
reached the violent stage was an important preventive step. A visible, substantial, and professional police force was necessary to achieve the goal of an orderly
city. Though most cities possessed a group of individuals called a night watch,
this "force" was inadequate and, for the most part, ineffective. The members of
the night watch often held jobs during the day and used this tour of duty to
catch up on their sleep. Some watch members were more of a menace than the
criminals they reputedly sought. When they were not perpetrating crimes themselves, they could usually be found at the local tavern. In particular, the New
Orleans and New York night watch vied for the title of the most corrupt and
disorderly watch in the nation during the first half of the nineteenth century.
To build up urban defenses, some cities hired a day patrol to complement the
night watch. The day constables were not much of an improvement, primarily
because there were so few of them. St. Louis was typical, employing fifty constables to protect a citizenry of 100,000 in the 1850s.

During the 1840s and 1850s, the cities most affected by mass violence—
Philadelphia, Boston, and New York—consolidated their separate day and night
police into one uniformed force supervised by an appointed, salaried official.
Though politics would continue to predominate in the choice of personnel for
several decades, the "cop on the beat" soon became a familiar sight in cities
across the country.

The police service was a further indication of the growing divisions—both
spatial and economic—within urban society. Police protection continued to be
inadequate in the crowded working-class districts of the city. Because visitors
rarely ventured there and because the retail district and the residential districts
of the more affluent were physically separated from the working-class districts,
violence in this quarter could be tolerated. Some crime, vice in particular, was
not only tolerated but actually protected. Criminal activity thus took on a spatial
character, too. The necessity of a uniformed professional police force also demonstrated the depth of division that now split the American city: Protestant
versus Catholic, white workers versus black workers, antiabolitionists versus abolitionists, employee versus employer. The consensual social order that had once
been sufficient to control the colonial city no longer existed. The policeman was
now the only buffer between society's hostile groups.

The policeman also took on other public responsibilities as local government
expanded its authority into areas previously reserved for private initiative. The

police became health and boiler inspectors and finders of lost children as well as protectors of abused youngsters. Later in the nineteenth century, local governments established separate agencies to assume these functions, creating the specialized administrative bureaucracies common in cities today.

Poverty as a Moral Issue

It seemed anomolous that, along with the wealth generated by the creation of a national urban economy, an increase in urban poverty also took place. In some of its aspects this situation was more troubling to the urban middle class than the perceived rise in violent crime. At least they could find evidence in what they read and what they saw to support their view of the unsafe city. But poverty amid plenty was a more difficult concept to grasp. If scarcity no longer informed public policy or thought, then how was poverty to be accounted for?

The obvious answer was that in a prosperous urban society the poor were responsible for their predicament. Poor work and moral habits along with dependence on public and private handouts were the causes of poverty. As early as 1821, the New York–based Society for the Prevention of Pauperism concluded "that a great portion of the pauperism in this country arises from a reluctance to labor and dependence on the public bounty." The morality issue was especially prominent among middle-class women and their organizations. Take the case of Maria Burley, for example. The admissions committee of the Asylum for Lying-In Women, a shelter for poor pregnant women, turned Burley away in 1827 on the grounds that she lacked letters testifying to her good moral character. This despite the fact that she was nine months pregnant and had no place to go in New York's cold winter. Subsequently,

> it is painful to relate that after a walk of two miles in this extreme cold she was obliged to seek refuge for the night in an open garret with only one quilt for covering and before morning and alone she was delivered of a female infant, which when she was found by two men was frozen to her clothing and with great difficulty restored to life.

The committee quickly made some inquiries and finally admitted Mrs. Burley, justifying their earlier action by citing "the difficulties of meeting at the same time the demands of justice and charity."[12]

By the 1850s, the emphasis on the moral shortcomings of the poor had produced even less charitable sentiments. When Dr. Griscom and others had written about poverty during the 1840s, they had managed to evoke some sympathy for their subjects. A decade later, the poor were less to be pitied than feared. A state report on the condition of the poor in New York City referred to the "pariah inhabitants" of poor neighborhoods and went on to suggest that "if they be disregarded, the heart and limbs of the city will sooner or later suffer, as surely as the vitals of the human system must suffer by the poisoning or disease of the smallest vehicle."[13] These views did not result in the abandonment of public and private poor relief; if anything, the role of private organizations and local government expanded during the 1840s and 1850s. The attitudes expressed in these comments, however, lent a heavy moral overtone to reforming the poor in the mid-nineteenth-century city. If it were possible to infuse the poor with middle-class morals, then poverty could be eradicated. This objective was especially evident in three social programs: home visiting, children's aid, and temperance. There was only occasional understanding that the changing nature of work, the abundance of cheap labor, and the inherent burdens of being a woman (especially a widow) or a child were more imminent causes of poverty than a lack of morality.

The institution of the home visit grew out of the middle-class emphasis on the home as the nurturer of morality. The middle-class men and women who

Five Points, New York City, c. 1850
The Five Points neighborhood was New York's most congested residential district. In the view of middle-class reformers, the poverty, vice, and unhealthfulness of the area corrupted children and destroyed family life.

went out to battle the "growing moral desolations of the city" carried the evangelical fervor of missionaries to the poor.[14] The missionaries entered dwellings that were not homes at all, or at least not by middle-class standards. The housing of poor people blended into the street, and vice versa. As one observer noted in 1846, "At the Five Points [a notoriously poor district in New York], nobody goes in doors except to eat and sleep. The streets swarm with men, women, and children. . . . They are all out in the sun, idling, jesting, quarrelling, everything but weeping, or sighing, or complaining. . . . A viler place than Five Points by any light you could not find. Yet to a superficial eye, it is the merriest quarter of New York."[15] What bothered the visitors most was that the poor were neither contrite nor constrained in their poverty. Though the home visit provided some middle-class women with an outlet for their energies outside their own homes, it was not a productive device for moderating the effects of poverty, for actually improving the lives of the poor.

The home visits they performed had convinced middle-class men and women that their ministrations alone were not enough to counteract the vile surroundings of these districts. They were especially concerned by their discovery of street children—youngsters who had no permanent home (and, therefore, no possibility to experience its nurturing qualities) and who roamed the streets engaging in petty crime (and, therefore, did not possess the work ethic). One reformer, Charles Loring Brace, organized the Children's Aid Society in 1853 for two purposes. One was to publicize the plight of street children and the other was to rescue them from adults in their neighborhoods who would "transmit a progeny of crime."[16] Brace's solution was to place these children in foster homes in the countryside where they could learn the work ethic and restore their health.

Though Brace's plan hardly solved the problem of street children, it represented a growing awareness among some reformers that the environment as well as the poor themselves contributed to poverty and its attendant evils. Though it was far from representing a true understanding of the economic roots of poverty, this perspective allowed some of the causal burden to be taken off the victim. The realization that environment played a part would assume more prominence later in the century.

In the meantime, however, the general focus of reform was on the poor themselves. This was especially true of the temperance movement. In the prevailing assumption, poverty and alcohol were connected; drink was a simpler target to eradicate than the tenement environment. Of all the causes of poverty, one reformer asserted in 1834, "there is none more prominently conspicuous than that of alcohol."[17] During the 1840s, one of the most prominent temperance groups, the Washingtonians, was not a middle-class group at all. Four craftsmen formed the first chapter in Baltimore in 1840 and, within six months, the group claimed 20,000 members and over 50 chapters across the country. Their methods of encouraging abstinence included holding weekly "experience" meetings featuring confessions of reformed alcoholics and songs. The religious influence was evident as members talked of "conversion" to sobriety. Auxiliary Martha Washington Societies emerged to attract female alcoholics. By the middle of the decade, however, the workers' temperance societies had disbanded. Workers had formed these groups during the depths of a depression and once prosperity returned, the compulsion for reform declined. Middle-class temperance organizations soon filled the vacuum with more sedate and equally ineffective methods.

But the temperance movement is important less for its moral accomplishments than for the fact that it represented for many middle-class urban dwellers their first foray into organized urban reform. Eventually the temperance societies of northern cities swelled the ranks of the nascent abolition movement with many new members. And the evangelical fervor of the overwhelmingly Protestant and often condescending temperance advocates carried over into the abolition societies. It was not surprising that these groups supported nativist movements such as the Know Nothings, or that immigrants, especially the Irish, had little use for the moralizing abolitionists.

In addition to emphasizing morality, middle-class reformers sought to bring efficiency to their relief efforts. The Norfolk Association for the Improvement of the Condition of the Poor, organized by young entrepreneurs in the 1840s, was a typical example of the new systematic private charity efforts. The founders of the association viewed poor relief in much the same manner as they approached other services: organized aid to the poverty stricken was another means of ordering urban growth.

The group divided the city into districts, and its members made visitations to the homes of the poor. These reformers were the forerunners of modern social workers; although they were not professionals, their methods served as guideposts for professionals during the late nineteenth century. The task of these visitors was narrow. They were to root out "artful mendicants" and "give to none who will not exhibit evidence of improvement from the aid afforded."[18] This was the familiar distinction, though practiced more scientifically, of "undeserving" versus "deserving" poor of an earlier era.

If the members of these private organizations agreed on anything, it was that they alone could not cope with the problem of poverty. As with disease, fire, and crime, local government attempted to bridge the gap between private efforts and public problems and, following the lead of private citizens, devised two responses to the problem of urban poverty. These responses reflected the business leadership's perception of the proper role of government in social policy. The first type of relief was seasonal. During the winter months, the city council budgeted a small amount for wood, clothing, and some food. In New York, nearly one-tenth of the city's residents received winter aid. Despite this large proportion, cities rarely appropriated more than 2 percent of their annual expenditures for relief efforts, of which the outdoor charity program was only a small part.

The second form of charitable activity was the heart of government's contribution toward relieving the condition of the poor. Because the seasonal ministrations merely provided stopgap measures to arrest poverty, it was obvious that more elaborate mechanisms were needed to deal with this increasingly troublesome problem. Local leaders relied on institutions to mitigate urban poverty. The almshouse, or poorhouse, was the major local government relief effort. The idea was to isolate the poor from their immoral environment outside, provide religious instruction in certain instances, and above all inculcate a belief in the benefits of hard work. This was local government's contribution to the evangelical reform efforts of the urban middle class. It was another way to order the city and make it safe, segregated, and productive. Poor relief thus complemented local government's other service provisions during the last decades of the antebellum period.

It is doubtful whether public poor relief efforts had any more success than public health policies. Tenement rooms were as dark as ever; the streets were crowded; the air was foul; employment was sporadic and wages low. Disease, crime, and poverty were all related in the public mind. Congestion bred crime and disease, and the most criminal and disease prone were the poor because they lived in the most congested circumstances. Public policies and private efforts could moralize and isolate various parts of this vicious cycle, but they could not break it.

And these facts troubled reformers, city officials among them. The modest advances in health and public safety as well as the institutionalization of charity had primarily served to reinforce spatial and social trends without improving the condition of the working classes. It stood to reason that if the home and a natural setting were necessary accompaniments to civilized living for the middle class, then its benefits were even more obvious for lesser privileged groups in urban society. Yet it was neither feasible nor desirable to uproot these groups (except for the innocent children). A plebeian environment near to or within the city might be created to relieve congestion, however temporarily, to which *all* urban residents could repair periodically for inspiration and renewal. In other words, it could be possible to re-form the city *and* reform its less fortunate citizens by bringing the benefits of nature and domesticity within everyone's reach. This was an environmental solution to an economic problem.

The Search for Open Space: Cemeteries and Parks

The provision of any kind of open space, any sliver of nature, was notoriously rare in early-nineteenth-century American cities. Cities were engines of commerce, as the expansion of local government underscored. Whatever enhanced the urban economy was a worthwhile endeavor. There were exceptions to this line of thought, of course—most notably the city of Charleston, South Carolina, which prided itself on a certain contrariness in any case. In that port city, blood lines, quiet neighborhoods, race, and cotton and rice cultivation counted most. Anything else was unimportant, if not vulgar.

There was a certain charm to this mentality that placed esthetics above profits. It also provided residents with a comfortable accommodation to the reality that, regardless of what policies the city might implement, a barren hinterland and a tributary economic role in both region and nation restricted development in any case. So why not sit back and enjoy life? And visitors to Charleston happily adjusted to the slower rhythms, enjoyed a promenade along the Battery, and strolled the tree-lined streets. The city was suburbia, magnolia style. Savannah shared some of Charleston's style; its economic aspirations were greater, even if the results were not appreciably better. But Savannah, like Charleston, was an exception. Thanks to James Oglethorpe's original plan, the city included enough park space for its residents—the only American city to do so by 1850. Savannah stood out, however, only because the record of other American cities on providing open spaces was abysmal. Also, the preservation of the city's parklike squares owed less to the work of civic leaders than to Savannah's slow growth that relieved speculative pressures on these areas.

But as public wisdom began to point to the urban environment as a volatile element in the republican compound, opinions on the expendability of open spaces began to shift. The policy of developing rural cemeteries on the urban periphery had a great deal to recommend it as a way of ameliorating the impact of congestion and contagion. Dead people had to be buried. In the colonial period, churchyards performed this function. But as the major cities of the Northeast grew and as religion and nonreligion proliferated, the churchyard was no longer a feasible venue for burials, especially as epidemics produced thousands of deaths within a week's time. The difficulty, from the perspective of the city as a commercial engine, was that land given over to cemeteries meant land taken out of the development cycle. But if these institutions could be located far enough away from the development path for the foreseeable future, then they could be tolerated. The stress was on "far" because several cities before the nineteenth century had made the mistake of locating cemeteries too near built-up areas, primarily on the assumption that relatives and friends would want to visit their departed colleagues on occasion. Rather than building around these precious grounds, however, developers simply hauled up the bodies and threw them in trenches some distance away. The practice resulted in at least one pitched battle between grieving relatives and laborers in Philadelphia early in the nineteenth century.

Peripheral locations ensured that whatever contagion resulted from corpses (especially during epidemics) would be minimized. Also, as long as potentially good (i.e., developable) land was wasted, it might as well serve as a recreational area for the living, thus having the virtue of performing two functions for the price of none.

America's first rural cemetery, Mount Auburn, opened in the town of Cambridge outside Boston in 1831. The cemetery fulfilled the dream of Harvard Medical School professor Jacob Bigelow, who was also a botanist. The design of the cemetery reflected Bigelow's horticultural interests as well as his desire to create an environment that differed considerably from the grid-dominated, nature-poor city beyond the cemetery gates. At least one visitor fell in love with the place on first sight:

> The avenues are winding in their course and exceedingly beautiful in their gentle circuits, adapted picturesquely to the inequalities of the surface of the ground, and producing charming landscape effects from this natural arrangement, such as could never be had from straightness or regularity. Various small lakes, or ponds of different size and shape embellish the grounds. . . . The gates of the enclosure are opened at sunrise and closed at sunset, and thither crowds go up to meditate, and to wander in a field of peace.[19]

In 1835, Laurel Hill Cemetery opened outside Philadelphia, and the largest rural cemetery up to that time, Green-Wood in Brooklyn, covering a 200-acre site overlooking New York harbor, began burying New York's dead in 1838.

But as Mount Auburn's chronicler implied, it was as a haven for the living that the rural cemetery attained its greatest notice in antebellum America. Initially, the cemeteries were too far from the developed portions of the city to serve as recreational spaces. With improvements in transportation and the expansion of the city, however, access became easier. Between April and December, 1848, nearly 30,000 people visited Philadelphia's lovely Laurel Hill Cemetery, with "most of the visitors . . . simply out for a good time."[20] Soon these spots of rural quietude became landmarks and main attractions in a visitor's

Plan of Mount Auburn Cemetery, Cambridge, Massachusetts, 1831
The success of this plan initiated a trend of designing cemeteries for the living as much
as for the dead. Its rural setting, meandering avenues, and landscaped shrubs and
ponds offered a pleasing contrast to the congested gridiron of the city.

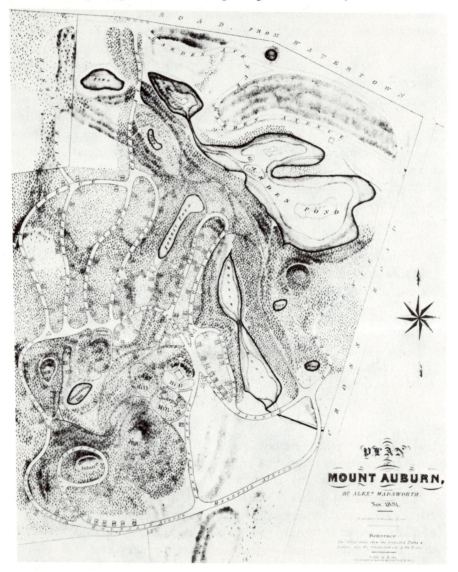

itinerary. By the late 1840s, rural cemeteries had appeared on the outskirts of all the major cities and several smaller ones as well. Andrew Jackson Downing, a leading publicist for rural cemeteries, declared in 1849 "there is scarcely a city of note in the whole country that has not its rural cemetery."[21] But there were growing concerns that the inspirational attributes of these areas were receding as they became popular picnic and recreational sites. Solitude and contemplation were becoming more difficult, not to mention the interference with mourners. Access also remained a problem, especially for the working classes.

The urban park solved the need for open spaces exclusively for the living, though it did not become common until after the Civil War. But in the decade before that conflict, New York took the lead in urban park design. That city was a likely candidate for this experiment primarily because it had failed so miserably to provide any open space whatsoever for its burgeoning population. Officials had long held that the two rivers embracing the island were sufficient nature for the city's residents.

As reformers produced evidence linking congestion with contagion and social disorder, however, the pressure increased to rectify the omission. William Cullen Bryant, poet and editor of the New York *Post,* and Walt Whitman, poet and editor of the Brooklyn *Eagle,* were among the leading publicists for the development of parkland in the city. In 1847, Whitman was successful in promoting the creation of Fort Greene Park in Brooklyn, in the heart of a working-class district. The park, however, was less an inspiration for future endeavors than an example of the limitations of urban parks. The site was very hilly, totally unsuited for any form of development, and its area was small, scarcely sufficient to accommodate its neighborhood, much less the residents of the entire city of Brooklyn.

A more ambitious effort took shape across the river in New York nearly a decade later. In 1856, city officials, prodded at last into providing some open space on their congested island, held a competition for the design of an urban park. Frederick Law Olmsted and the Englishman Calvert Vaux, who had worked with Andrew Jackson Downing, teamed up to win the competition and, a year later, set to the task of creating a park. The project, on a site extending from 59th Street to 110th Street, resembled Fort Greene Park in that the costs of land preparation for development would have been significant, assuming the technological means were at hand to alter the area in a major way. It was a desolate expanse, alternately swampy and rocky, dotted with jagged outcroppings of granite. Olmsted had hoped that his park would serve as the "lungs of the city" and that it would inspire all classes in the city, especially the poor who would be "educat[ed] to refinement and taste and the mental & moral capital of gentlemen."[22] But the site was neither especially healthful nor attractive enough to be inspirational to anyone except a geologist.

Central Park, 1872

Although Frederick Law Olmsted sought to create a "natural" haven within New York City, he was clearly influenced by mid-nineteenth-century notions about recreating nature. To modern eyes, the park in this engraving looks formal and highly structured.

So Olmsted improvised. He hired thousands of laborers who blasted tons of rock, moved acres of dirt, and transformed swamps into lakes and ponds. Olmsted installed an underground drainage system and planted grass, trees, and shrubs. As he would do at Riverside, Illinois, Olmsted isolated the park from urban influences through boundary plantings, the separation of through traffic, and a winding pathway system that broke free of the city's relentless grid. The irony of the enterprise was that Olmsted and Vaux had created a natural environment that was as man-made as the city from which it differed so drastically. The result underscored the fact that when reformers offered nature as a cure for urban pathology, what they really meant was a refined and molded nature—molded by humans—rather than the wilderness or the open and unimproved countryside. In reality, the latter could prove just as disorderly and destructive of civilized impulses as the most crowded tenement districts.

Central Park was not central, however. It would be quite a journey for those who lived on the southern end of the island. Development and the horse-car lines did not extend past 42nd Street in the 1860s. Not until the last decades of the nineteenth century would the park be truly accessible.

Olmsted believed that his urban park would be only one element in a planned series of open spaces extending outward from it, including not just parkland, but parkways, too—as Olmsted put it, "a series of ways designed with express reference to the pleasure with which they may be used for walking, riding, and driving of carriages; for rest, recreation, refreshment, and social intercourse."[23] In this manner, Olmsted would address the difficulty of access; parkways would bring the park to the people. During the 1860s, Olmsted and Vaux tried out their notions in Brooklyn, first creating Prospect Park and then two parkways—Ocean and Eastern—radiating from the park into residential areas. The parkways were extremely wide—260 feet (compared with Broadway, for example, at 120 feet)—and included a central roadway, service roads, and pedestrian paths, each separated by plantings and trees. These broad, tree-lined avenues bore a strong resemblance to the Parisian designs Baron Haussmann was creating at that time.

But again, as successful as these efforts were from an esthetic standpoint, they scarcely answered the needs of the city's working classes, at whom, presumably, much of this reform sentiment was directed. Eastern and Ocean Parkways would not become working-class residential areas. And Central Park would not, for some time, become a working-class playground. As much as Haussmann's reconstruction of Paris, these reforms of urban space primarily benefited the middle class on up. Although that was a meritorious result, it left out the other half of the urban population. Persistent concerns about this other half would make urban reform a major American industry over the next century. And, as always, demand would outpace the supply.

The City as a Way of Life

The movement to naturalize the urban environment was another indication that reformers shared an uneasiness about the city as a way of life. This concern was most evident in Charles Loring Brace's efforts to rescue street children, but it was also present in the attempts to reform the poor through morality or isolation. By 1870 fewer than one in four Americans lived in cities, so the danger that whatever ailed urban America would soon be characteristic of the nation at large was not so imminent. Nevertheless, the growing economic importance of the city extended its influence far beyond the numbers of its citizens. Its dynamism and wealth thrilled many even as an equal number felt disturbed. Few writers captured the essential attraction of the mid-nineteenth-century city better than Walt Whitman:

> The splendor, picturesqueness, and oceanic amplitude and rush of these great cities, the . . . lofty new buildings, facades of marble and iron, of original grandeur and elegance of design, with the masses of gay color, the preponderance of white and blue, the flags flying, the endless ships, the tumultuous streets, Broadway, the heavy, low, musical roar, hardly ever intermitted, even at night . . . the assemblages of the citizens in their groups, conversations, trades, evening amusements . . . these, I say, and the like of these, completely satisfy my senses of power, fullness, motion, etc., and give me, through such senses . . . a continued exaltation and absolute fulfillment.[24]

If the city brought Whitman "absolute fulfillment," to others the increasing urbanization of America engendered deep concern, alarm, and disgust. America had always been an agricultural nation. It had been the place where, in Emerson's words, "the embattled farmers stood,/And fired the shot heard 'round the world"; it had been the place where brave yeomen tamed a wilderness and turned it into productive farms; and it had been a place where the virtues of rural life were the subject of everyday homilies to most people.[25] In a nation of common people, the city seemed like an alien form. It was un-American. And, in a nation where democracy was still an experiment, it represented an alarming specter.

As cities began to intrude into the national consciousness in the late eighteenth and early nineteenth centuries, national leaders sounded warnings. Historian David Ramsey predicted in 1793: "Your towns will probably e're long be engulphed in luxury and effeminacy. If your liberties and future prospects depended on them, your career of liberty would be short." George Washington, in his usual succinct manner, warned that "the tumultuous populace of large cities are ever to be dreaded."[26] As cities grew and became the homes for diverse populations and ideas (the same features that had attracted the other writers), the perceived threat to liberty remained severe. "In the formation of a nation's education," wrote one woman at mid-century, "as of a national character, the country more than the city must control. The city becomes cosmopolitan; its people, blending all nationalities, lose distinctive national characteristics, and . . . love of country as well."[27]

It was only a small step from viewing the city as un-American to depicting it as ungodly. This view informed a good deal of the reform efforts after 1820. A certain amount of self-righteousness crept into the religious movements that periodically affected cities, and critics mixed genuine concern for the souls of the unfortunate city dwellers with a bit of condescension and revulsion. The remedy for urban sin seemed simple to a Brooklyn divine: "We must preach Him IN THE CITIES; for nowhere else is the need of this greater, and nowhere else are the opportunities for doing it more numerous and inviting."[28]

In addition to the usual catalog of sensual sins, there was growing concern about whose God really reigned in the cities. Was it the God of Abraham or the God of Mammon? To critics, everyone seemed engrossed in the "eternal hunger and thirst after money, to the exclusion of almost every other pursuit." The pursuit began at an early age. "As soon as a boy can read, write, and cast up a bill, he is withdrawn from school and placed at a desk, there to be initiated into the mysteries of buying and selling."[29]

The headlong rush of city dwellers toward economic gain lent an air of impersonality to the city, as critics perceived it. The only relationship that seemed to count was the one between man and money. Personal interaction was typically a means to that end, rather than an end in itself. The cities that visibly displayed civility were few, and the most obvious were in the South—Charleston and Savannah, among others. But their relatively small size and their growing economic and political weakness and dependency indicated that nice cities finished last.

Life in the lonely crowd of the cities was an unnatural human condition that had slowly become natural. Mark Twain, whose keen perceptions of western life would earn him a national reputation, visited New York early in his career and referred to it as "a splendid desert—a domed and steepled solitude, where a stranger is lonely in the midst of a million of his race."[30] A mechanical regimen seemed to characterize city living as the routine of business and factory dominated the life cycle. Those who were not able to relate to their money interacted with their machines. In the words of Henry David Thoreau, a writer who witnessed the grim realities of New England industrial life first hand, "men have become the tools of their tools."[31]

These allegations against their environment distressed civic leaders. They were aware of the city's shortcomings, and they worked hard to improve the situation.

The inauguration of social and environmental services were examples of this awareness of the need to seek a remedy for urban problems. It was also unfair, they believed, to generalize from a few unfortunate urban experiences to all of the cities in the nation. Moreover, it was naive to throw garlands of praise over rural America. One urban champion found country life "instead of a bed of roses to be one of thorns."[32] As to charges that cities are the natural repositories of sin, a Richmond resident agreed that "there is a great amount of vice in cities," but only, he argued, "because there is a great amount of humanity. The country is not without vice. There is probably more scandal and gossiping in a small town in twenty-four hours than there has been in London or New York for the last one-hundred years."[33]

Generalizations about urban life belied the distinct character of individual cities. One well-traveled gentleman summarized these differences as follows: "New York is the most bustling; Philadelphia the most symmetrical; Baltimore the most picturesque; and Washington the most bewildering."[34] Visitors remarked about the distinctive French influence in New Orleans, the homes of Natchez, perpetually shrouded in Spanish moss, and the frantic pace of San Francisco, which led one resident to boast: "We are a fast people here. There is no stopping or halting—no time to breathe a full breath—no time to eat or sleep—and scarcely time to drink or gamble. You have heard of our fires. They throw light on our character; we burn down our city in a night and build it in a day."[35]

So while cities borrowed each other's innovations—from street names to technology—they maintained their own unique characters. Visitors could know at once whether they were in Chicago or Mobile, though both metropolises had gridiron streets, new urban parks, and a dozen other characteristics in common. This uniqueness was all the more remarkable considering that city leaders generally strove for the same goals and set similar priorities in building their communities. For those who charged that the city fostered impersonality and anonymity, the unique identity of each city indicated that at least some individuality flourished. It also demonstrated that only a city could support such a variety of architecture, peoples, shops, gardens, or whatever it was that lent a special character to that city.

That such variety should elicit such a confusing stream of support and detraction for the city, then, was probably only fitting. A poet like Walt Whitman found his romantic yearning tugging in two directions at the same time, as he trumpeted the city in one breath and implied in his *Leaves of Grass* that democracy and the pastoral life are synonymous. Such contradictions were common, even within the same individual. Anyone who has ever lived in a city for any length of time knows that it is an environment that can be wonderfully exciting yet extremely frustrating, for this is the urban condition. Civic leaders helped to erect ugly warehouse districts and allowed working-class housing to fester while they built expensive parks and squandered millions on railroads. Though the contradictions in such behavior were apparent from the outside, to the leaders such practices were merely good business and were in keeping with their own sense of the general welfare, two ideas that were difficult for them to separate.

The city represented the best in American society and, at times, the worst. Pursuit of profit permeated urban life, determining space, social structure, and government policy. Yet there was still room for humanitarian concern. During this period when the market place dominated urban activity, providing for charity, public health and safety, pure water, and a better natural environment became important elements of public policy. Though these humanitarian movements were carried out within the framework of economic growth, they nonetheless improved urban life. That the great reform movements of the period bore urban origins is not coincidental. The city was the environment where it was all possible.

If cities offered marked contrasts within their borders and elicited diverse reactions from both within and without, few doubted their growing influence. A national economy had developed with cities at the focal points; the nation's literary and artistic talents found the city a receptive environment for their creative efforts, regardless of how severely they criticized that environment; and the major technological advances of the day—from developing water supply systems and sewers to gas lighting—took place in the city. Civilization, in short, was located in the city, even if it was a bit rough around the edges.

By 1870, the city was grudgingly accepted as an integral part of American life, in contrast to its stepchild status of a half-century earlier. The city's inescapable influence led to its incorporation into the American consciousness. This is not to say that Americans loved their cities now; far from it. For at least a half-century, though, the city had been the subject of magazine articles, newspaper features, books, sermons, conversations, and thought. The American city was no longer a mere curiosity; it was an established fact of life. The city had not only expanded spatially into rural land and bound the farms inextricably to itself, it had also expanded into the rural mind, for better or for worse. The next decades would be exciting. As the national spotlight shone on the city, it would expose serious ailments that in turn spurred great activity to heal the urban sores. Few would disagree with Frederick Law Olmsted's view of the urban and national futures in 1868: "Our country has entered upon a stage of progress in which its welfare is to depend on the convenience, safety, order and economy of life in its great cities. It cannot prosper independently of them; cannot gain in virtue, wisdom, comfort, except as they also advance."[36] That is the kind of place the city had become—in success the best, and in failure the worst, of American life.

Notes

1. Quoted in Edward Pessen, "Who Governed the Nation's Cities in the 'Era of the Common Man,'" *Political Science Quarterly* 87 (December 1972): 610.
2. Michael H. Frisch, *Town into City: Springfield, Massachusetts, and the Meaning of Community, 1840–1880* (Cambridge, Mass.: Harvard University Press, 1972), p. 44.
3. Quoted in Charles E. Rosenberg, *The Cholera Years: The United States in 1832, 1849, and 1866* (Chicago: University of Chicago Press, 1968), p. 68.
4. Quoted in Charles N. Glaab, ed., *The American City: A Documentary History* (Homewood, Ill.: Dorsey Press, 1963), p. 115.
5. Quoted in Lawrence H. Larsen, "Nineteenth-Century Street Sanitation: A Study of Filth and Frustration," *Wisconsin Magazine of History* 72 (Spring 1969): 239, 240.
6. Quoted in David R. Goldfield, "Pursuing the American Urban Dream: Cities in the Old South," in Blaine A. Brownell and David R. Goldfield, eds., *The City in Southern History: The Growth of Urban Civilization in the South* (Port Washington, N.Y.: Kennikat Press, 1977), p. 70.
7. Quoted in Bayrd Still, ed., *Urban America: A History with Documents* (Boston: Little, Brown, 1974), p. 176.
8. Quoted in Rosenberg, *Cholera Years,* p. 27.
9. Henry A. Ford, *A History of Cincinnati, Ohio* (Cleveland: L. A. Williams & Co., 1881), p. 74.
10. David Grimsted, "Rioting in its Jacksonian Setting," *American Historical Review* 77 (April 1972): 393.
11. Quoted in Theodore M. Hammett, "Two Mobs of Jacksonian Boston: Ideology and Interest," *Journal of American History* 62 (March 1976): 860.
12. Quoted in Christine Stansell, *City of Women: Sex and Class in New York, 1789–1860* (New York: Alfred A. Knopf, 1986), p. 71.
13. Quoted in *ibid.,* pp. 201–202.
14. Quoted in *ibid.,* p. 65.
15. Quoted in *ibid.,* p. 74.
16. Quoted in *ibid.,* p. 209.
17. Quoted in Sean Wilentz, *Chants Democratic: New York City and the Rise of the American Working Class, 1788–1850* (New York: Oxford University Press, 1984), p. 255.
18. Quoted in Goldfield, "Cities in the Old South," p. 79.
19. Quoted in John W. Reps, *The Making of Urban America: A History of City Planning in the United States* (Princeton, N.J.: Princeton University Press, 1965), p. 326.
20. *Ibid.*
21. Quoted in David Schuyler, *The New Urban Landscape: The Redefinition of City Form in Nineteenth-Century America* (Baltimore: Johns Hopkins University Press, 1986), p. 47.
22. Quoted in *ibid.,* p. 66.
23. Quoted in *ibid.,* p. 128.
24. Quoted in Still, ed., *Urban America,* p. 198.
25. Quoted in Glaab, ed., *The American City,* p. 52.
26. Quoted in Thomas Bender, *Toward an Urban Vision: Ideas and Institutions in Nineteenth-Century America* (Lexington, Ky.: University Press of Kentucky, 1975), pp. 3, 4.
27. Quoted in Glaab, ed., *American City,* p. 62.

28. Quoted in Bender, *Toward an Urban Vision,* p. 11.

29. Quoted in Glaab, ed., *American City,* p. 50.

30. Quoted in Still, ed., *Urban America,* p. 198.

31. Quoted in Leo Marx, *The Machine in the Garden: Technology and the Pastoral Ideal in America* (New York: Oxford University Press, 1964), p. 247.

32. Quoted in Glaab, *American City,* p. 56.

33. Quoted in David R. Goldfield, *Urban Growth in the Age of Sectionalism: Virginia, 1847–1861* (Baton Rouge: Louisiana State University Press, 1977), p. 251.

34. Quoted in Raphael Semmes, *Baltimore as Seen by Visitors, 1783–1860* (Baltimore: Maryland Historical Society, 1973), p. 116.

35. Richard E. Amacher and George W. Polhemus, eds., *The Flush Times of California by Joseph Glover Baldwin* (Athens, Ga.: University of Georgia Press, 1966), p. 13.

36. Quoted in Bender, *Toward an Urban Vision,* p. 13.

PART 3

The Radial Center

1870–1920

The late-nineteenth-century city had a dynamism and a rhythm
that seemed to drive its residents at a furious pace. The factory
whistles, the trolley bells, the pounding of a thousand feet on
pavements, the wails of babies in packed tenements, the endless
clanking of coins, and the voices of a dozen different dialects:
this was the new urban symphony. The rising crescendo of activities foretold new wealth, new technology, new peoples,
new triumphs, and new miseries. Its music echoed down man-
made stone canyons and out to brand-new suburbs. One of
the great arenas for this energy and expansion was Chicago.
Devastated by a disastrous fire in 1871, the city rose from its
ashes to become an even greater metropolis than its early
boosters had ever dreamed possible. Theodore Dreiser, a
young, impoverished novelist from Terre Haute, Indiana,
walked its new streets in the 1880s and recorded his impres-
sions in *Sister Carrie*:

> Chicago was . . . a giant magnet, drawing to itself, from all quar-
> ters, the hopeful and the hopeless. . . . It was a city of over
> 500,000, with the ambition, the daring, the activity of a metropolis
> of a million. Its streets and houses were already scattered over an
> area of seventy-five square miles. . . . The entire metropolitan
> centre possessed a high and mighty air calculated to overawe and
> abash the common applicant and to make the gulf between poverty
> and success both wide and deep.[1]

Indeed, it seemed as though many American cities at the
turn of the last century were "giant magnets" attracting a numerous and diverse population. "Urbanization," as pioneer urban historian Arthur M. Schlesinger, Sr., observed of the
1880s, "for the first time became a controlling factor in national life."[2] Between the Civil War and World War I the
number of urban residents increased from 6,200,000 to
42,000,000. Though urban America had experienced its greatest spurt of growth between 1840 and 1860, the scale of urbanization changed by 1900 to much larger cities, and more
of them. In 1850, six cities had a population exceeding

100,000; by 1900, thirty-eight did. Similarly, in 1850, only 5 percent of the nation's population lived in cities of more than 100,000 inhabitants; by 1900, the figure was 19 percent. The nation's population tripled between 1860 and 1920, but the urban population increased by ninefold. The 1900 census listed more than 1,700 bona fide cities, 98 percent of which had not existed in 1800.

Unlike the trend in Europe, where Paris and Berlin, for example, absorbed most of the urban population increase, the distribution fell more evenly among cities in the United States. In 1820, New York, the largest city, contained 18 percent of the country's urban population; by 1890, its share had fallen to 7 percent. This meant that many U.S. cities were experiencing the phenomena of rapid growth, industrialization, the expanding role of government, and the problems that arose from these trends.

Despite the relative evenness of growth, a distinctive urban system had emerged by 1900, with New York and Chicago anchoring an urban-industrial core extending in a crescent from New England to the cities bordering on the Great Lakes. Nine of the nation's ten largest cities in 1920 were located in this region. Western cities such as Denver, San Francisco, and Los Angeles were becoming dominant in their respective regions but were not major rivals to the urban core. Southern cities continued to function more as colonial outliers than as equal participants with the great cities of the North. Staple crop prices, the devastation of the Civil War, and white supremacy combined to keep demand low, capital formation weak, and dependent status strong.

This is not to say that urbanization in the South was inconsequential during this era. Although the dominance of New York and Chicago was already prefigured in the antebellum era, new patterns emerged after the Civil War that altered the rank and functions of southern cities. Atlanta, an offspring of the railroad, was the symbol for a major shift in this pattern.

The city's strategic location astride a middle land known as the Southern Piedmont ensured its prominence in carrying the South's wealth into the North's coffers. As the Piedmont developed after 1870 along the route of the Southern Railway and dozens of small branch lines, Atlanta became a regional capital.

In the established cities of the urban core, changes in scale meant life changes. One of the great wonders of New York after 1909 was the Metropolitan Life Insurance Company's giant clock, visible for blocks atop the tallest tower in the world. Time, as the company's salesmen would tell you, was on their side. The clock was not just a good metaphor for the insurance industry but for the great cities generally. Earnest young men with stopwatches patrolled factory floors, calculating worker movements and production quotas. Commuter railroads and, in a few cities, new subway systems proudly posted schedules, assuring commuters that they would all converge on downtown at the same time. A new phrase, the "rush hour," captured both the pace and the split-second timing required for the new order of things. Workers, blue- and white-collar alike, learned the regimen of time—when to report to work, when to take lunch, when to leave. Time had a sound in the working-class neighborhoods that clustered around the factory: the whistle controlled the rhythm of workers' lives; days were broken into hours, hours into minutes.

The tyranny of time set the pace not only for the factory but for a new city center as well. Downtown buzzed with excitement and activity. Thousands of white-collar workers inhabited the towering hives of commerce; countless others came and went on the multiple types of rail transit available to visitors and commuters alike. But downtown, for all its diversity, reflected the growing specialization and segregation of the city. The center was also the center of wealth and power, a fact to which the new edifices loudly attested. For the first time in the city's history, the destiny of the entrepreneurs who built and inhabited the new structures were not identical with the destiny of the city. The city was a honeycomb of geography—economic geography as reflected by downtown, residential neighborhoods, and suburbs; moral geography, as indicated by the presence or absence of saloons, dance halls, and related forms of entertainment; and political geography, as reflected in the ward system, the allocation of services, and the increase in annexed territory.

Writers have often interpreted these geographies as markers of the general fragmentation of urban society in the radial center era. They contrast the period with an earlier time, when the city was more compact and residence and commerce jostled each other for space, as did different kinds of residences. But this earlier period was a temporary moment in the development of urban space. As long as such things as free trade in private property and the general means and desire to attain personal objectives existed, the city tended toward segregation. But segregation did not necessarily equal fragmentation.

The turn-of-the-century city offered numerous points of community. Department stores, professional baseball games, and vaudeville drew a broad clientele together to engage in a new mass urban culture. Museums also attracted a diverse audience. Newspapers created a common language and perception of the city. Public schools offered a uniform curriculum to moderate the diversity of urban life. Professionals joined peer organizations that sharpened their expertise and provided a sense of common purpose. Even skyscrapers eventually lost their identification with specific entrepreneurs and businesses and became city artifacts. This is not to deny that serious fissures existed in early-twentieth-century urban society, probably wider and deeper than at any other time. But it is also important to note that forces operated to draw the disparate geography of the city together, if only temporarily.

Reformers appeared who recognized the fissures and sought to bridge them. With an emphasis on professionalism, research, and efficiency, they applied their principles to local government, city infrastructure, social services, and education. These men and women were instrumental in building the service city—a city that provided a broad range of services to its citizens. Though at times motivated by condescension, fear, and a desire for control, many of the reformers displayed genuinely altruistic motives. The results, in any case, were impressive. Many urban services that we take for granted today owe their origin to these dedicated individuals. Social services such as health, dental, and optometry clinics, school hot lunch programs, and employment centers originated during the early years of the twentieth century. Such necessary regulation of urban growth as building inspections, zoning, and civil service also emerged during the progressive era, as did the commission and city manager forms of government that remain popular in small and medium-sized cities. Some reforms resulted in important changes in family life. Compulsory schooling laws and restrictions on child labor, for example, meant that children became more of an economic liability than an asset to working-class families. The birth rate declined. As historian Eric Monkkonen concluded, these reforms "made the mechanics of city living ordinary and invisible; that is their [the reformers'] true success story."[3]

The accomplishments of reform were significant, given the jump in scale from earlier times represented by the great cities. Difference in scale was a difference in kind. As Henry Adams put it: "In the essentials of life . . . the boy of 1854 stood nearer the year one than to the year 1900."[4] The new city was less easy to understand than its antebellum counterpart. The reformers' emphasis on applying new technologies reflected their attempt to unite the city by means of gas, electricity, and sewer and water systems. Even writers and painters found the new city difficult to grasp. As historian Thomas Bender concluded, "What the new metropolis made impossible, at least for the artists, was any totalizing configuration of perception, visual or otherwise."[5]

Here, then, are the three major themes of the radial center

era. First came the rise of the great cities of the urban core. Industry and the migration of millions of newcomers fueled this growth. Second, a major consequence of this growth was the segregation of urban space as symbolized by distinctive city centers, residential neighborhoods, and suburbs held together by the radial arms of rail transit. Last to arise was the response to the political and social implications of this new ordering of urban space. As with the previous era of urbanization, the era of the radial center reflected how sharply urban America differed from cities in Europe—in abundance of space, and in financial and technological access to it.

Notes

1. Theodore Dreiser, *Sister Carrie*, rev. ed. (New York: W. W. Norton, 1970), p. 11.
2. Quoted in Charles N. Glaab, ed., *The American City: A Documentary History* (Homewood, Ill.: Dorsey Press, 1963), p. 173.
3. Eric H. Monkkonen, *America Becomes Urban: The Development of U.S. Cities and Towns, 1780–1980* (Berkeley: University of California Press, 1988), p. 221.
4. Quoted in Robert Fisher, *Let the People Decide: Neighborhood Organizing in America* (Boston: Twayne, 1984), p. 1.
5. Thomas Bender, "The Culture of the Metropolis," *Journal of Urban History* 14 (August 1988): 497.

Yearning to Breathe Free: Urban Society and the Great Migrations

If you had lived in the 1880s and approached Pittsburgh at nightfall, you would be awed by the surrealistic grandeur of urban industrial might. At the city's edge, the outlines of the steel mills loomed like specters against the darkening sky. As a contemporary observer saw it, "Fiery lights stream forth, looking angrily and fiercely up toward the heavens."[1] Here was the industrial heartland of the country. The battleships at sea, the skyscrapers of great cities, and the locomotives steaming across the plains all began in Pittsburgh, yet this city represented only a fraction of the national industrial realm. Since the Civil War, dozens of cities had aspired to and achieved the joys of twilight's first gleaming: that fiery reminder that wealth and growth lay in the smoky sky. But such cities also brought forth social dislocation and human misery, crowded slums as well as industrial marvels.

Twilight's First Gleaming: Steel-Driving Cities

Chicago and Cleveland with their excellent rail connections that enabled the efficient transport of important industrial raw materials, especially coal and iron, built their own steel mills. Milwaukee, noted for its breweries, also opened its city to iron and steel plants following the Civil War. The city developed related industries, such as machinery and motor production; by 1910, only Buffalo and Detroit had a higher percentage of workers engaged in manufacturing pursuits.

The South's major industrial phenomenon was Birmingham. As late as 1869, the city did not exist. A combination of railroad connections and coal, limestone, and iron deposits transformed the north Alabama woods into a thriving industrial community. Within thirty years, 500 manufacturing establishments, most related to iron and steel production, had been established. Between 1880 and 1910, the population had increased from 3,800 to 130,000 and the city was producing more than $12 million worth of manufactured products.

The Birmingham story indicated, if it was not apparent already, that industry and the American city formed a profitable partnership, especially if the city was close to natural resources. The connection was enhanced by the concentration of labor, the accumulation of capital, large consumer demand, and the presence of the kind of supporting facilities, from railroad depots to retail stores, that only a city could provide. The technological advances of the late nineteenth century were also most effective when applied to large-scale enterprises, which, in turn, required the vast inputs of capital and labor found in the urban environment.

In the steel industry, large-scale production was impossible until the costs of mixing wrought iron and carbon could be reduced. In 1859, Englishman Henry Bessemer developed a process that significantly reduced the amount of coal necessary to make steel. Several years later, German-born William Siemens invented the open-hearth process, which produced a higher-quality steel essential for building construction and machinery manufacturing. As demand increased and production costs declined, sprawling operations became feasible and cities were the logical repositories for such plants.

Steelmaking was not the only activity to benefit from innovation and an urban location. The clothing industry achieved similar advantages. Before the Civil War, most clothing was custom-made; the tailor and perhaps several helpers were the major clothing manufacturers. The demand for Civil War uniforms, the influx of cheap immigrant labor, and above all the introduction of the electric sewing machine generated a vast ready-made clothing industry, organized along mass-production lines, with dozens of sewing machine operators working under one roof. Home industries declined, and a new industry located in warehouses and converted tenements churned out apparel for retail outlets. New York, with its large immigrant workforce and burgeoning local demand, became the national garment center, though cities like Baltimore and Boston turned clothing manufacturing into major industrial enterprises.

Elsewhere in the country the connection between industry and urbanization was less clear. The antebellum association between industry and the countryside persisted in the post–Civil War South. As the railroad crossed the Southern Piedmont, so did industry in small towns and villages along the tracks. This

Union Stock Yards, Chicago, c. 1878
This operation was so large and employed so many people that it seemed a city
in itself.

region, in fact, became the national center for textile production after 1900. But
the dozens of mill villages in the South rarely added to the population and
prosperity of cities because of chronically low wages and small operations. In
1900, Gaston County, North Carolina, was the most industrialized county in
the South; it was also an overwhelmingly rural county.

But even when the Industrial Revolution was in full force in the urban core
by the 1880s and 1890s, the identity between industry and northern urbanization was far from complete. The very size of the new consolidated industries
required new spatial arrangements. By 1910, a few large producers controlled
the steel, farm machinery, rubber, oil, and meat industries. Mergers enabled the
new larger corporations to take even greater advantage of modern technology
and expand their manufacturing operations. Plants became tightly organized
fiefdoms, occupying extensive portions of urban real estate and employing
thousands of people. The stockyards in Chicago, the center of the meat trust,
typified the sprawling, comprehensive industrial operations common by 1900.
Upton Sinclair, in his 1906 novel *The Jungle,* exposed the working conditions in the meat-packing plants. Although the plants revolted him, his minute

descriptions of the activities within the slaughterhouses indicate a fascination, if not admiration, for the application of mass-production technology in the meat industry.

The meat plants employed 30,000 people, and at least 100,000 more depended on their salaries. This constituted not only a city, but a large city at that. This mechanized community, which caused Sinclair to marvel at "the wonderful efficiency of it all," elevated butchering almost to an art form. Hogs, for example, were sent down chutes hoisted up on their hind legs and sent along an assembly line, where one man slit their throats. The half-dead hogs were then summarily dispatched into a churning cauldron of boiling water from which they passed "through a wonderful machine" that removed their bristles. The hogs, by now quite dead, were strung up by the machinery again and passed between two lines of workers, each with a specific task to perform on the carcasses, from severing the head to removing the entrails. Sinclair described this procession of men and carcasses in vivid detail: "Looking down this room, one saw, creeping slowly, a line of dangling hogs a hundred yards in length; and for every yard there was a man, working as if a demon were after him."[2]

After the carcass spent 24 hours in the chilling room, a new process was begun on another floor: cutting it up, with each man responsible for a different part of the anatomy. Finally, the bottom floor housed the pickling and packing rooms, where the various meats were prepared for shipment. Not one part of the hog was wasted in this process, as products from fertilizer to food were disgorged from the factory. Reflecting on what he had seen, Sinclair observed: "It was all so very businesslike that one watched it fascinated. It was pork-making by machinery, pork-making by applied mathematics."[3]

The immense presence of such industrial operations obviously had a considerable impact on the city and on the process of urbanization itself. Industry had generally outgrown its close association with the central business district by 1900. The demand for space, both vertical and horizontal, drove industrial uses outward. The clothing industry in Baltimore, for example, was centralized in warehouses next to downtown. The introduction of sewing machines and the consequent expansion in operations made incursions by the industry into tenement districts away from the central business area necessary. Moreover, because these districts housed the workforce (primarily immigrant labor), such a location was convenient to both employer and employee.

Some industries could not find such beneficial accommodations within the city and moved to the suburbs. Heavy industries like steel, for example, reduced their noxious influence on the environment by locating on the urban periphery. There, where land was cheap and municipal regulations were few, manufacturing could go on with sufficient room for future expansion. As communities in themselves (like the stockyards), the manufacturing plants had little need for close proximity to downtown. The workers were spared lengthy commuting

Plan of Pullman, Illinois, 1885

George Pullman oversaw every detail of the town he built for the workers in his sleeping-car factory. His attempts to control his workers' personal lives caused the town to disintegrate in 1894.

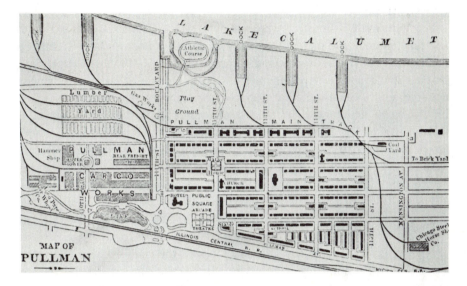

trips, for some employers constructed workers' housing adjacent to the factory site.

Some industrialists attempted to create new communities beyond the metropolitan area. George H. Pullman, proprietor of the famous sleeping-car manufactory in Chicago, constructed an elaborate town south of the city complete with brick homes for the workers, a street system that emphasized residential privacy, a hotel, schools, churches, and libraries. The satellite city was called Pullman. Pullman disintegrated in 1894 during a violent strike that resulted from the proprietor's overbearing involvement not only with his employees' working lives, but with their lives away from work as well.

A little more than a decade later, Elbert Gary, chairman of the board of a new conglomerate, the United States Steel Corporation, bought a vast tract of land east of Chicago on Lake Michigan and called the place, not surprisingly, Gary. The new industrial town was almost as comprehensive as Pullman, with the exception that the proprietor, no doubt remembering his colleague's difficulties, exercised less control over community life. Labor relations were no smoother in Gary, however, than in Pullman—there was a bloody strike in 1919—and for all its planning, the city was indistinguishable from the grimy metropolises that hugged the Great Lakes. Another opportunity for creating a positive industrial environment for both management and labor through the resources of private enterprise had been lost. More successful, though on a considerably smaller scale, was another United States Steel development, this one outside Birmingham, Alabama, which included neat homes for employees and attempted to introduce some esthetic influence into the smoky environment by means of professional landscaping.

Few industrialists, however, were willing to sink the large amounts of capital and time required to build a community from the ground up. Most contented themselves with finding appropriate locations within or near a city, depending on their spatial and labor requirements. A portion of the garment industry, for example, still hovered near downtown, especially where tenements were close by. Others, like shipping, required close connections with a natural resource, in this case, water. The dockside location remained, but shipbuilders moved farther up- or downriver to suit their specific industry. Finally, steel, rubber, and glass factories were located on the urban periphery. These three industrial rings reflected the different land use and technology requirements of each industry.

The diffusion of industrial land use inevitably meant the diffusion of residences, particularly for the large workforce required by the new technology and organization. In the preindustrial era, it was common for workers to reside next to the city center because this area encompassed the city's major employment basin. Industrialization brought the growth of residential nodes adjacent to plants. The so-called "back of the yards" neighborhood on Chicago's periphery housed the workforce for the meat plants. Birmingham's steel workers similarly clustered around the mills east of the city. Even in Greensboro, North Carolina, which hardly rivaled Chicago, industrialization meant residential dispersal. In fact, residence was so tied to the factory in Greensboro that the community failed to develop a thriving downtown because commercial uses built up around the industrial nodes.

The residential proximity of workers to their factories was further fixed in practice by the fact that workers still could not afford the daily trolley fares despite major technological advances in mass transit. With more than one member of the family working in an industrial economy and with women and children receiving meager wages, trolley or cable car rides were reserved for special occasions rather than daily commuting.

Living within a 10-minute walk to the factory, many of these workers knew with great intimacy that the impact of industry on the city went beyond mere spatial rearrangements. The natural environment of the city, never particularly chaste, began to deteriorate rapidly. Steel-driving cities might generate imposing twilights, but the stench and smoke permeated the atmosphere seven days a week. A visitor to Pittsburgh in 1884 left a vivid account of the perpetual twilight that covered the city. Of the buildings he wrote: "whatever their original material and color, [they] are smoked to a uniform, dirty drab." Of the atmosphere during the day, he observed that "a drab twilight hangs over the town, and the gas-lights which are left burning at mid-day, shine out of the murkiness with a dull, reddish glare." The sun, when it could be seen, looked "coppery through the sooty haze."[4]

Even the peaceful and pastoral Allegheny River fell victim to the industrial onslaught. An oil barge occasionally sank "and its freight, liberated, refuses to sink with it, and spreads itself out on the surface of the stream."[5] Indeed, the urban rivers in the industrial cities were becoming garbage dumps for industrial waste. The water around Baltimore in the 1880s smelled "like a billion polecats" according to one observer, and the Cuyahoga River in Cleveland was "an open sewer through the center of the city."[6]

The environmental costs of urban industrial development were great. The human costs were equally significant. Industry rearranged the city and the air and water as well, but the impact on the urban majority—the workers and their families—went considerably beyond residential location and esthetics.

Working Is Not a Living: Labor in the Industrial City

The nature of work was transformed as the city changed from primarily a commercial entrepôt to an industrial metropolis. As late as the 1880s, most manufacturing in American cities consisted of "congeries of craftsmen's shops."[7] Yet by 1906, a U.S. Department of Labor report noted the subdivision of industrial labor into minute, low-skilled operations that made craft and skill obsolete. It was a process that had been underway since earlier in the century, and the Labor Department was chronicling its triumph.

The dilution of skills coincided with a sharp increase in overseas immigration. Perhaps more important than the availability of a vast reservoir of cheap labor was the advance in technology that made the employment of unskilled workers profitable. Ninety percent of the 1 million patents registered at the U.S. Patent Office in 1910 were filed in the years after 1870. Contrary to popular assumption, technology did not reduce employment (though it eliminated some jobs). Rather, it helped to increase the workforce dramatically by creating new industries such as steelmaking, automobiles, electrical equipment, cigarettes, food canning, and machine tools. In older industries, improved technology expanded markets, further expanding workforces. In 1860, railroads employed 80,000 workers. By 1920, more than 2.2 million people worked for the railroads. At that date, the Ford and Goodyear companies—firms that had not existed two decades earlier—employed 33,000 workers alone. Four years later, Ford opened its massive River Rouge plant with new assembly line technology employing over 68,000 workers.

Workers shared little of the wealth generated by industrial expansion. Notoriously low wages, even in the efficient conglomerate industries, had created a large urban subsistence class. A family with small children "has a small chance of living properly" off the wages of a factory worker, the Massachusetts Bureau of the Statistics of Labor concluded in 1882.[8] Confirming this diagnosis were the wages of common laborers, over 14,000 of them, at the Carnegie Steel Works in Pittsburgh. Most earned less than $12.50 a week, whereas conservative state government estimates calculated that $15 a week was necessary to support a family of four. A group of Illinois investigators reported that even skilled workers—the former artisan class—"fail to make a living" in Chicago's factories.[9]

Wages fluctuated from industry to industry and from skill to skill. In Philadelphia, for example, some skilled workers in the largest plants received nearly $2.50 a day for a six-day week, whereas skilled personnel in tiny garment industry sweatshops earned only $1.65 a day, less than some unskilled workers in a nearby shoe factory. Despite these distinctions, however, it is noteworthy that only the skilled worker in a large-scale industrial operation met the minimum subsistence requirements for heads of families.

Working hours were scarcely better than the wages. Typical factory operatives worked 10 hours a day in the 1880s, six days a week. Hours, like wages, however, tended to vary widely. Canners, for example, worked a staggering total of 77 hours a week, and some workers in the construction industry had achieved the 8-hour day. In the steel industry, workers put in a 12-hour day. Because the mills operated 24 hours a day, once every two weeks when the workers changed shifts, one work group stayed on the job for 24 hours.

The obsession with efficiency that gripped many sectors of early-twentieth-century urban life influenced the nature of factory work as well. The expert became part of the shop floor scene, conducting time-and-motion studies to determine the most effective use of each employee's time. The studies represented the introduction of "scientific management" popularized by Frederick W. Taylor. The idea was to streamline and increase production, reduce the workforce and, consequently, raise wages and improve working conditions. The impact of Taylorization varied, but it usually involved the subdivision and further dilution of skills, the introduction of new technologies, and it enhanced the power of management on the shop floor.

The impact of these wages and working conditions on the workers' lives was significant. Toward the end of the work day, they were obviously very tired and apt to be careless. Employers took few precautions for their employees' safety. Between 1907 and 1910, for example, nearly 25 percent of the recent immigrants employed at one of the Carnegie steel mills in Pittsburgh were injured or killed each year. In Chicago's meat plants injuries were part of the daily routine, most caused by carelessness brought on by fatigue or long-term exposure to the intense heat or cold of working conditions. Meat cutters working rapidly with sharp knives would contract a numbness in their fingers by the end of the day, leaving them prone to slicing off part of a digit. As Sinclair wrote, "it was to be counted as a wonder that there were not more men slaughtered than cattle."[10]

Away from the factory, the impact of long hours was equally numbing. Sunday was a day most working people looked forward to. They were usually so exhausted from the work week that sitting or lying in the house was the extent of their recreational activity. During the week, of course, any activity other than eating or sleeping was out of the question. As one machinist testified with considerable poignancy before a United States Senate investigative committee in 1883:

> They were pretty well played out when they come home, and the first thing they think of is having something to eat and sitting down, and resting, and then of striking a bed. Of course when a man is dragged out in that way he is naturally cranky, and he makes all around him cranky . . . and staring starvation in the face makes him feel sad, and the head of the house being sad, of course the whole family are the same, so the house looks like a dull prison.[11]

Workers attempted to deal with the problems of long hours by living as close to the factory as possible. The environmental conditions were apt to make even this convenience detrimental in the long run, however. Once the worker was inside the factory, options were further reduced because of the rigorous discipline imposed. International Harvester, a midwestern agricultural machinery manufacturer, presented each employee at its Milwaukee plant with a lesson book composed of thirty lessons, the first of which was a primer on factory discipline:

> I hear the whistle. I must hurry.
> I hear the five minute whistle.
> It is time to go into the shop. . . .
> I change my clothes and get ready to work.
> The starting whistle blows.
> I eat my lunch.
> It is forbidden to eat until then.
> The whistle blows at five minutes of starting time.
> I get ready to go to work.
> I work until the whistle blows to quit.
> I leave my place nice and clean.
> I put all my clothes in my locker.
> I go home.[12]

This exercise was particularly effective with European immigrants and rural Americans. The shock of factory regimen on all workers was likely to be great and lasting. The routine was tedious, boring, and repetitive. Such work was so dehumanizing that, as the machinist alleged, the worker "becomes almost a part of the machinery."[13] In Chicago, Jewish glovemakers fought the subdivision of labor in their industry despite the prospect of higher wages. Though making gloves 9 hours a day was an onerous task regardless of the method of production, the workers at least achieved some satisfaction with their finished product: "You cling to the variety, the mental luxury of first, finger-sides, and then, five separate leather pieces, for relaxation, to play with! Here is a luxury worth fighting for!"[14]

When not constrained by factory discipline, workers suffered from the conditions around them. The garment industry sweatshops were exactly what their name implied. The succinct words of a Chicago investigator provide some insight into the conditions of the workers: "The father, mother, two daughters, and a cousin work together making trousers at seventy-five cents a dozen pairs. . . . They work seven days a week. . . . Their destitution is very great."[15] The entire family of eight lived and worked in a three-room tenement. The reorganization of the garment industry meant that manufacturers subcontracted the sewing and finishing of garments to contractors. The contractors were charged with gathering the labor and supplying accommodations, materials, and machines, thus relieving the manufacturers of these expenses. To maximize their profits, the contractors squeezed workers into attics, lofts, and dwellings. Barely adequate for living, these dark, damp, and badly ventilated quarters were abominable for working.

Low wages, long hours, dulling work, and loathsome working conditions were onerous enough for grown men. The prevailing wage structure, however, made it unlikely for a family to subsist on the wages of one member. Children and women were forced into the factories, too, and the consequences for them were even uglier than the impact on the men. By 1900, it was against the law in many states for children to work before they were sixteen years of age. Because children usually received a third of the pay of an adult, and because many factory positions were relatively mindless, children often found it easier to find employment than their parents; hence they were valuable as a necessary income source. Some textile mill owners in the South, in fact, employed only women and children well into the 1930s. Child labor, serving both the interests of the parents and the employer, resulted in widespread violations of these laws until the fourth decade of the twentieth century.

The results of child labor were predictable: physical and mental debility. Social workers told of children in Chicago who refused candy at Christmas. They later discovered that the youngsters worked six days a week in a candy factory

Lower East Side, New York City, 1905
An immigrant family does piecework in their tenement. The use of family labor in apartments or converted sweatshops continued to characterize the garment industry after the turn of the century.

and hated the sight of it. Then there was the seven-year-old girl, a four-year veteran of the garment industry, whose long hours of toil "day after day with little legs crossed, pulling out bastings from garments," resulted in paralyzed and contorted legs from lack of use.[16] Finally, the story that came to epitomize the miseries of child labor appeared in urban reformer Jacob A. Riis's writings in the 1890s and again in Upton Sinclair's *The Jungle* a decade later. In both versions the story told of a small boy, perhaps eight or nine years old, who was employed by a local factory to carry beer from a nearby saloon (though the law specifically forbade such sale to minors) back to the plant. Occasionally, the boy himself imbibed, until one day he had too much to drink and fell asleep in a cellar, where rats gnawed him to death.

These accounts represent the most severe consequences of child labor. Most working children did not die, nor were they irreparably damaged, physically or mentally. All, however, lost their childhood. A generation, perhaps two, of working-class children shared the adult burden of factory work, the adult recreation of the saloon, and the adult feelings of fatigue and purposelessness long before they attained chronological adulthood. Ultimately, they shared the premature death of their fellow workers.

A Woman's Work . . .

For working women, the situation was scarcely better, though motherhood offered an occasional respite from the factory routine. Young working-class women, whether married or single, had few options in the urban industrial society. More precisely, they had two. They could go to work in a factory or they could, in the words of one Chicago writer, "tread the cinder path of sin."[17] Maggie Johnson's brother in Stephen Crane's 1893 novel *Maggie: A Girl of the Streets* described the choice more colorfully: "Mag, I'll tell yeh dis! See? Yeh've eeder got t' go on d' toif er go t' work."[18] Maggie went to work.

Theoretically, a young working-class woman could look forward to marriage. It was unlikely that she could marry a prosperous man, because such a match was frowned on in late Victorian society and, more important, the opportunity for meeting young men of a higher social class was rare in the segregated spatial and lifestyle arrangements of the industrial city. Marriage to a working man offered no release from factory work, given the prevalent wage structure. Although childbirth resulted in temporary "vacations," the absence of appropriate medical care and the presence of unsanitary conditions made the process of childbearing a dangerous procedure for both mother and infant.

Living close to factories, as many workers' families did, complicated household chores for the housewife. If she was fortunate enough to have city water, the great water demands of the factory often curtailed the flow to a trickle from dawn to dusk. The alternative was to haul water or rise at five in the morning to fill up tubs and buckets. The technological advances that revolutionized housekeeping in the late nineteenth century—washing machines, central heating, toilets, iceboxes, gas, and electricity—were generally too expensive for working-class families. Even ice, at 42 cents per week for a very small block, was a luxury, so food shopping was a daily routine. Because the housewife purchased items in small quantities, she purchased in the most uneconomical fashion. Quality was another problem. Working-class districts received the poorest foodstuffs, including milk doctored with formaldehyde. Planning and preparing meals, given these constraints, were arduous chores.

The factory was worse. Six dollars a week was a typical salary. On these wages, a married working woman often pulled her family up to a subsistence level. For a single woman attempting to fend for herself in the city, such wages allowed her to eat, in short story writer O. Henry's words, little that was more nourishing "than marshmallows and tea." Lodging rarely meant more than one room, and recreation was affordable once or twice a year. Dulcie, the factory girl O. Henry wrote about, had twice been to Coney Island, a popular resort in Brooklyn. "'Tis a weary thing," he wrote, "to count your pleasures by summers instead of years."[19]

The factory stole not only recreation but also youth from the working woman. Francie Nolan, the young turn-of-the-century working-class heroine of Betty Smith's novel *A Tree Grows in Brooklyn,* captured the futility of the working woman with these observations:

> You work eight hours a day covering wires to earn money to buy food and to pay for a place to sleep so that you can keep living to come back to cover more wires. Some people are born and kept living just to come to this. Of course, some of the girls will marry; marry men who have the same kind of life. What will they gain? They'll gain someone to hold conversations with in the few hours at night between work and sleep.[20]

The temptation to break from this deadening scenario must have been great. For married women, comfort in husband and children was the only diversion possible, if fatigue allowed them that. Cheap amusements were attractions for single working girls, if they could afford to squander precious pennies on the cheapest forms of entertainment. There were few other recreational alternatives. As reformer Jane Addams noted: "Apparently the modern city sees in these girls only two possibilities, both of them commercial: first, a chance to utilize by day their labor power in its factories and shops, and then another chance in the evening to extract from them their petty wages by pandering to their love of pleasure."[21]

It was not surprising that many working-class women entered the world of prostitution. There were different types of prostitution. Frequently, white slavery merchants enticed young and bored factory girls into the business. Sometimes, in return for rent, food, and clothing, a resourceful woman attached herself to a well-to-do man. She might join one of the many brothels that flourished in all cities. The life of a lone streetwalker was the last resort for desperate women. There was never, in any case, a shortage of working girls in prostitution. "So is it any wonder," asked the Chicago Vice Commission, "that a tempted girl who receives only six dollars per week working with her hands sells her body for twenty-five dollars per week when she learns there is a demand for it and men are willing to pay the price?"[22]

Certainly the routine of the brothel was a sharp change from factory life. English writer William T. Stead commented on the daily regimen of one Chicago house of prostitution in 1894. The girls rose just before noon and were served cocktails. They dressed and "took another refresher. At breakfast they had wine. Then the day's work began." At 15-minute intervals, the girls would sit in couples at the windows and beckon at each passing man. The law was of little concern because most houses operated under police protection. "At five they dined, and then the evening's business began, with more drinking at intervals, all night through, to the accompaniment of piano-playing with occasional dancing and adjournments."[23]

The prostitute, however, was a total social outcast. In Victorian America, prevailing attitudes about women's sexual behavior took little account of the realities of urban life. Even the most trivial moral transgression earned social ostracism. And those who urged understanding for women who violated conventional morality faced ostracism as well. Kate Chopin, a St. Louis novelist of the 1890s, caused a tremendous uproar with her books describing adultery, female alcoholism, and divorce in non-condemnatory tones. Theodore Dreiser found himself the target of a boycott because his novel *Sister Carrie* did not condemn the conduct of the title character, who lived with a succession of men, including a married man. Dreiser's heartfelt explanation at the end of what he knew would be a controversial novel placed Carrie's conduct in its appropriate urban industrial context, but it fell on largely unsympathetic eyes:

> If honest labour be unremunerative and difficult to endure; if it be the long, long road which never reaches beauty, but wearies the feet and the heart; if the drag to follow beauty be such that one abandons the admired way, taking rather the despised path leading to her dream quickly, who shall cast the first stone? Not evil, but longing for that which is better, more often directs the steps of the erring.[24]

The working woman's dreams were eventually extinguished by the factory or the brothel. The industrial city rose in condemnation against sexual immorality but was generally silent on the immorality of the economic order. O. Henry, whose stories were generally apolitical, could not contain his rage in his story about Dulcie. Instead of ending the story with one of his characteristic surprise endings, he related the following dream:

> I dreamed that I was standing near a crowd of prosperous-looking angels, and a policeman took me by the wing and asked if I belonged with them.
> "Who are they?" I asked.
> "Why," said he, "they are the men who hire working girls, and paid 'em five or six dollars a week to live on. Are you one of the bunch?"
> "Not on your immortality," said I. "I'm only a fellow that set fire to an orphan asylum, and murdered a blind man for his pennies."[25]

Increasingly, however, work options became available for women, though the choices were still circumscribed by low wages and poor working conditions. Technology was especially instrumental in drawing more women into the workforce. The widespread use of the sewing machine by the 1870s resulted in more work but compartmentalized the production process. Wages were as low as 20 cents a day in 1870 at a time when the cheapest room in New York City cost one dollar a week. One advantage of the sewing machine was the elimination of the exploitative contractor by 1900, as factory production typically replaced at-home work, though working conditions were scarcely better. It was not surprising, for example, when 20,000 women walked out of New York's garment shops in protest in 1909.

The change in the nature of office work also reflected the impact of technology. In the 1870s, most clerical personnel were male. But the introduction of the typewriter and women's allegedly greater dexterity and tolerance for repetition resulted in transforming office duties into primarily a female occupation, usually at half the salary of the male employee. Parents generally perceived office work as clean and honorable employment, especially compared with factory or sales work, and allowed their daughters to apply for clerical positions. As a consequence, native-born young women entered the workforce in appreciable numbers for the first time. A top-paid office worker in the 1890s could receive as much as $900 a year, which compared well with other women's employment, such as teaching, which typically paid $500 a year.

Technology combined with the trend toward professionalism also created new opportunities for women workers. Between 1900 and 1910, for example, the number of trained nurses increased sevenfold. There were 1,000 women social workers in 1890 and nearly 30,000 by 1920. Reflecting new theories on the nurturing role of women, school boards by 1900 turned exclusively to female teachers for the elementary grades. The numbers of women in the workforce increased in all areas of the economy during the first two decades of the twentieth century. Even married women, for whom work outside the home was frowned on, began to enter the workforce in greater numbers: 3.3 percent of all married women worked in 1890, and 9 percent by 1920.

Despite these gains, women were segregated within urban employment, for better than 90 percent of all wage-earning women in 1900 worked at jobs where women were heavily represented. Protective legislation tended to reinforce this segregation by limiting hours and restricting women to "clean" occupations such as clerical work. Not all of these measures were well meaning. Some were devised to restrict women's potential for competing with men in the workforce. As contemporary economist John R. Commons explained, "the wage bargaining power of men is weakened by the competition of women and children, hence a law restricting the hours of women and children may also be looked upon as a law to protect men in their bargaining power."[26]

Women also had to confront prevailing negative images about working women. In an era when a woman's role was defined by home and family, work outside the home was considered, at best, a temporary expedient. In the minds of employers women were marginal laborers, working until they got married and paid accordingly. Unions made the same assumption. One union official noted in 1901 that he and his colleagues had "successfully adopted a new method of preventing women from working in the shop. They marry the women."[27] Male workers and employers alike were inclined to believe that some women worked for frivolous reasons and that these women were responsible for keeping wage levels low. Carroll Wright, the U.S. Commissioner of Labor, commented on Buffalo's "working girls" in 1888: "A large proportion will work for small pay, needing money only for dress or pleasure. This cause contributes with others to make wages low."[28]

Aside from their marginal position, single working women also suffered from popular stereotypes questioning their virtue. Stories abounded about loose salesgirls, flirtatious secretaries, and libidinous factory workers. The numerous newspaper and magazine exposés of working girls descending into prostitution fed the image. This stereotyping also encouraged sexual exploitation, which, in turn, fueled the image. Union organizer Benjamin Gitlow testified before the federal Commission on Industrial Relations in 1914 that "a good many girls in many department stores have got to give in to the demands in the respect of certain members, buyers, managers, and floor walkers who take advantage of girls working under them and need the jobs very badly. . . . We know of cases of girls who have got to submit to buyers if they want to hold their positions."[29]

The trade union movement offered little protection and, in fact, considerable hostility for working women. Women who worked in the garment industry, however, were successful in organizing their ranks after 1900 and participated in several significant but ultimately unsatisfying strikes over the next two decades. Working women and their allies faced a difficult dilemma. To improve their education and training, they had to frame their arguments in domestic terms, suggesting that this education would enhance their abilities to function as wives and mothers. In seeking improved wages and working conditions, women also had to support protective legislation that restricted opportunities in the workplace even if it did improve conditions in certain areas.

The Web of Poverty

Between 1873 and 1895, three economic depressions threw tens of thousands out of work and created overwhelming demands on public and private philanthropy. The depressions also triggered strikes, labor-management confrontations that occasionally erupted into violence, mass marches of the hungry and unemployed, and radical recommendations for changes in the nation's economic and political systems. In the midst of these developments, and at times contributing to them, immigrants from southern and eastern Europe began to appear in American cities in large numbers. Housing, employment, and the nascent if growing city services often could not keep up with demand.

But these were not novel events. Major economic downturns took place in 1837 and again in 1857. Violence, inspired by labor problems, ethnic differences, and ideological clashes, flared periodically after the 1830s. German and Irish immigrants became a significant presence in the major cities, especially after 1848. They crowded into dense, unsanitary neighborhoods, sparking concern, an avalanche of reports, and, ultimately, reform.

The city of the 1880s and 1890s, however, was different from the city of a half century earlier. The major differences, as noted before, lay in scale and segregation. Lives became more compartmentalized as well. Home and work grew increasingly separated. Middle-class men and women joined clubs, churches, and professional organizations that further segregated their relationships. Conventional wisdom as expressed in widely read journals and books stressed privacy and leisure as crucial to physical and mental well-being. And privacy usually meant a single-family home in an appropriately middle-class neighborhood or suburb; leisure meant activities with family and friends in and around that same environment.

The more segregated the city, the less a resident of one neighborhood knew about its other parts, and even less about the whole. Besides books and periodical literature, federal agencies, state and local bodies, and private organizations generated reams of statistics, observations, and recommendations. Though it is doubtful that few but the most avid citizens saw these reports, most urban residents did read newspapers. The ills of urban life were present in earlier decades as well, but never before had they been so well publicized.

By the 1890s an uneasy feeling was developing that two widely disparate and separate societies were emerging in America's cities. In his exposure of poverty in New York, *How the Other Half Lives* (1890), urban reformer Jacob Riis wrote that "the half that is on top cares little for the struggles, and less for the fate of those who are underneath so long as it is able to hold them there and keep its own seat."[30] That the evidence uncovered by Riis to support his conclusion seemed new and startling indicates how isolated and separated urban society had become. Knowledge of this division was a necessary first step toward attacking the city's most dangerous and pervasive problem: poverty.

Poor people constituted a large segment of the urban population. The group included workers as well as the unemployed, aged, widowed, and disabled. The poor encountered staggering obstacles simply because of the very fact that they were poor. In what became a perverse cycle, these obstacles served in turn to perpetuate their poverty. The simple matter of purchasing consumer goods serves as a good illustration of the principle. Coal kept urban residents warm during the winter. Like most other commodities, the unit price was cheaper if the quantity purchased was larger. The poor, however, were unable to afford coal in large quantities. They purchased the fuel by the basket, paying almost double what they would have paid if they had been able to afford to buy by the bin.

In buying food the poor encountered the same economic realities. Not only did they have few alternatives, their ignorance made them prey to adulterated products. Upton Sinclair cataloged the typical grocery list that confronted poor "back-of-the-yards" residents in Chicago: "pale-blue milk . . . watered and doctored with formaldehyde . . . tea and coffee, sugar and flour had been doctored . . . canned peas had been colored with copper salts, and their fruit jams with aniline dyes." But suppose they had known better? Sinclair replied: "What good would it have done them, since there was no place within miles of them where any other sort was to be had?"[31] The new spatial organization in industrial cities, with manufacturing plants located toward the periphery and workers living near them, left residents far away from more reliable and less expensive downtown establishments. The poor faced similar problems in the purchase of clothing and housing—paying more for less.

Being poor was not only expensive, it was stressful. Jacob Riis related how one day he came upon an Irish laborer with a hatchet in his pocket. As a result of a disability caused by his job, he was unemployed with seven children and a wife to provide for. So that the city would not take away his children, he decided to murder them. Fortunately, he was arrested before he could carry out his mad plan. Riis also told of a "hardworking family of man and wife . . . who took poison together . . . because they were 'tired.'"[32] It was not surprising that suicide rates were highest in the poorest districts.

The stress on family life was great even if a wage earner was in residence, as we noted earlier. Industrial accidents and higher mortality rates generally increased the likelihood of single-parent households and the accompanying hardships associated with the loss of a wage earner. Poverty had its greatest impact, though, on the children. Infant mortality among the poor usually exceeded the citywide norm by one and a half to two times. Poverty and its attendant evils hardened those children who survived very early in life. Violence and death were common accompaniments of poverty, and children learned early that alcohol was one of the few means of escape from the strains of being poor. The prevalence of prostitutes inaugurated both boys and girls precociously into the realities of sex. Reminiscing about his childhood years, one former slum resident remarked that it took "years to learn that sex can be good as well as evil; more than the thing truck drivers bought for fifty cents on my street."[33] Given this type of environment, it was not surprising that children sought refuge in street gangs as a source of protection, excitement, and identity.

Even the forms of entertainment the poor engaged in distressed reformers, who believed that these sensual and raucous pleasures not only threatened their moral and physical well-being but also kept them in their impoverished state. The saloon, of course, was an oft-mentioned and deplored institution in reformers' reports, which ignored its social functions and concentrated on its role in fostering alcoholism and thriftlessness. The so-called "dives," however, were more obnoxious to reformers than the saloons. Dives, in the words of one investigator, were "dance-halls where abandoned women congregate to try their charms on easily tempted men." Often these basement room bistros sold doctored liquor and were havens for criminals and prostitutes. The women "patrons," the investigator discovered, had typically "given up their positions in the shops and factories to earn their living in the dance-hall."[34] Because the poor had precious little money to spend even on necessities, these dives, though providing temporary and perhaps necessary diversion, merely ensnared them deeper in the web of poverty.

As distressing as the manner in which the poor lived was their place of residence. The high visibility of housing made it the indelible and most obvious badge of poverty. The term *slum,* which described the housing of the poor, was a mid-nineteenth-century coinage whose appearance coincided with the spatial isolation of the poor in distinct residential districts. With the exception of workers' residences, which coalesced around the grimy factories on the urban periphery, the slums were located in the city's oldest housing on the edge of the central business district. Slum housing was invariably filthy, overcrowded, and overpriced.

In his writings Jacob Riis introduced many Americans to the central city slum by taking them on a tour of housing in lower New York's Mulberry Bend neighborhood, where a typical apartment consisted of a parlor, which included the kitchen, and "two pitch-dark coops called bedrooms." There were a total of three beds, "if the old boxes and heaps of foul straw can be called by that name." Riis related that "the closeness and smell are appalling."[35] In July, when the temperature reached 90 degrees outside, it was at least 115 degrees inside the apartment, which housed six people. At this point, Riis's tour turned to melodrama, a favorite device he used to rouse his readers' sympathy and anger: "Here is a door. Listen! That short hacking cough, that tiny, helpless wail—what do they mean? Another child dying. With half a chance it might have lived but it had none. That dark bedroom killed it."[36] Unfortunately, Riis's melodramatic statement was probably accurate.

With or without sensationalization, the miseries of slum life were real enough. Even dry statistics told an appalling story: in New York's tenement district, for example, the density of 986.4 persons per acre in 1894 was the highest in the world. (Today, by comparison, the densest areas of our cities rarely have more than 400 people per acre.) Laws prohibiting overcrowding were simply not enforced. It was difficult to pay the rent with a legal number of residents. More-over, the effect of enforcement would be to turn people out into the streets, creating further hardships for tenants. Given the extremely short housing sup-ply, an apartment, no matter how vile, was a desirable commodity. Riis related how the tenants he interviewed insisted on retaining their anonymity for fear of arousing the landlord's wrath and facing consequent eviction. In this situation, tenants rarely forced landlords to make necessary repairs on the dwellings; overcrowding and deterioration continued in a downward spiral.

The Workers' Response

Most working men and women, if not reduced to outright poverty, led difficult lives. A new regimen, shaped by the demands of industrial production, gov-erned the lives of most urban dwellers after 1880. Conditions in the factory were often unsafe, the hours long, the wages low, and the prospects for a better future uncertain. Why, then, did workers not organize, protest, and strike to change conditions? Workers, in fact, did all these things—but certainly not in proportion to the ills that affected them. There were several reasons for the relative passivity of the urban industrial labor force. First and most important, the supply of labor constantly outstripped the demand. Although large-scale industrial enterprises required immense workforces, the urban population, swelled by migrants from rural areas, Europe, and Asia, easily filled all the avail-able jobs and left a sufficient excess to keep wages low and labor fairly docile. Unemployment and underemployment were common aspects of industrializing cities, especially for newcomers. Although unemployment figures for the period are scarce, one machinist estimated in 1883 that approximately 20 percent of that skilled craft were jobless in New York City. With competition for positions so severe, an employer had significant leverage on a protesting employee. In some industries blacklists were created that excluded "troublemakers" from work in other factories. As the machinist informed Senate investigators: "If they know that we open our mouths on the labor question . . . we are quietly told that 'business is slack' and we have got to go. Many of my trade have been on the 'black list,' and have had to leave town to find work."[37] Because many work-ers' families lived on the borderline between subsistence and starvation, the loss of one family member's wages could have tragic consequences.

In plants that employed a large number of immigrants, some of the workers viewed their factory careers as short term. They hoped to save enough money and then return to Europe. Also, because immigrants had little in the Old World experience to compare it with, factory life probably did not seem as burdensome initially as it did to natives or second-generation immigrants. Finally, some employers hired different nationalities for different tasks, precluding any factory-wide organization because of language and cultural distinctions.

The relative spatial separation of the workers' places of residence was another factor that inhibited concerted action. The presence of one or two distinct working-class districts, commonplace in many European cities, was rare in America, for workers clustered around specific industries wherever they were located: on the periphery, downtown, and in between.

Despite these obstacles, some workers organized and disruptions, sometimes violent ones, occurred. The Knights of Labor, formed following the Civil War, attempted to attract a variety of laborers and professionals into its fold. Its membership grew from 9,000 in 1879 to over 700,000 by 1886. This rapid growth resulted more from the desperation of laborers than from the organizing abilities of the leadership. Terence V. Powderly, who assumed the presidency of the organization from its founder Uriah Stephens, maintained Stephens's antistrike philosophy, thereby neutralizing the major weapon labor had at its command. The nationwide strike in 1886, which the Knights had futilely attempted to prevent, and the strike's subsequent collapse led to widespread disillusionment with the union leadership. In December of that year, a group of disaffected members formed the American Federation of Labor with Samuel Gompers, a cigar maker, as its president. This union disavowed the Knights' antistrike stand and adopted a more militant stance on wages, hours, and working conditions—issues that the leadership of the Knights had barely addressed.

Much less comprehensive in membership and considerably more structured than the Knights of Labor, the new union—known as the AF of L—was organized along craft lines and generally included only skilled workers. Using to advantage the vernacular of the time ("business unionism," he called his approach), Samuel Gompers pushed his program for a better life for workers. For forty years Gompers toiled at this task. By the time he died, the 8-hour day as well as sanitary and safe factory conditions had been established in many industries.

American workers' first groping efforts to find some vehicle through which to express their concerns was frustrating because national organizations, by their very nature, functioned slowly, if at all, and local groups, hoping for widespread membership, lacked focus and often deteriorated into social clubs. Despite many obstacles, such as differences in crafts, skill levels, language, and aspirations, and despite spatial separation, the desire for dignity and a decent living sometimes overcame these barriers and erupted onto city streets. Between 1877 and 1894, a series of strikes took place that were remarkable for their ferocity. Among these were the great railroad strike of 1877, which paralyzed most of the nation's railroads; the Homestead steel strike of 1892 in Pittsburgh, which culminated in a violent shootout between workers and hired detectives; and the Pullman strike of 1894, which shut down the railroads again.

The national rail strike of 1877 brought the desperation of workers to a national forum. Beginning as a localized disturbance in Martinsville, West Virginia, in response to a wage cut (after more than a year of wage cuts), the walkout soon spread to Baltimore and Pittsburgh. In Baltimore, workers surrounded the armory, trapping the state militia inside. The soldiers opened fire and killed ten persons. In Pittsburgh, strikers destroyed a considerable amount of railroad property including 2,000 freight cars. In a matter of days, the strike had spread to Chicago, Indianapolis, and Buffalo.

In Chicago, railroad workers were joined by factory employees in a general strike. Without any formal organization, work came to a halt in Chicago and workers demanded wage-and-hour reforms. Workers and their families massed in the streets of the city's working-class neighborhoods. In the lumber district on the city's west side, observers estimated that 25,000 people, or virtually the entire district, were out in the streets. Pitched battles with police followed, with the workers eventually routing the police. Reinforced by federal troops, the police charged into the district the following day only to discover that the lumber workers had been joined by stockyard workers wielding butcher knives. The superior fire power of the police and the U.S. Army, however, succeeded in dispersing the workers, who regrouped in small bands to carry on guerrilla warfare until exhaustion overtook both sides after four days and nights of disturbances.

The violence in Chicago in 1877 verged on class warfare, and newspaper accounts of the strike compared the scene with some of the worst upheavals in European cities. It was, as one historian has observed, "the first expression of a national working class—as an expression of collective anger over the transformation of working people's lives."[38] As middle-class Chicagoans armed themselves and journalists and officials ignored the legitimacy of the workers' grievances to dwell on the "mob mania," it seemed indeed that the social divisions of urban industrial Europe were at last manifesting themselves in American cities.

In the years that followed, working conditions remained unrelieved and, in some industries, worsened. Not surprisingly, the violence continued. In the spring of 1886, for example, another rail strike mobilized 190,000 men primarily in Chicago, Cincinnati, and New York. In addition to railroad workers, meat packers and skilled factory hands joined the walkout. The worst violence occurred, once again, in Chicago, where police shot a worker, triggering a series of events that climaxed with a bomb explosion at a Haymarket Square workers' rally that killed seven policemen and touched off a riot.

The collective expression of anger that erupted periodically and violently during these decades moved many employers to greater intransigence. Some acknowledged the miseries of their employees but attributed their condition to the workers' own failings. One employer, in public testimony, voiced a widespread feeling among his colleagues that "the chief cause of the impecunious condition of millions of the wage classes of this country is due to their own improvidence and misdirected efforts."[39] Other employers made less pretense about searching for the causes of their workers' discontent. Said one: "I regard my workpeople as I regard my machinery. So long as they can do my work for what I choose to pay them, I keep them, getting out of them all I can."[40]

Not all employers, of course, subscribed to these hostile views. A few launched programs to improve factory conditions and the workers' lot. Though motives for welfare capitalism, as it was called, varied widely, it marked the first major recognition of the legitimacy of workers' complaints. At the opening of a new plant in Milwaukee, for example, an agricultural machinery company threw a ball for its workers and once a year thereafter treated workers to a picnic. The same company, E. P. Allis, also contributed to an employee benevolent association to care for injured workers. Some of these programs, however, seem to have been suspiciously beside the point, for the important issues of wages and hours were not addressed. Historians have suggested that they contained an element of social control—that is, these programs were attempts to ensure peace and divert attention away from more substantive concerns.

Other than conscience or fear, an employer had little motivation to expend time and capital on extensive welfare programs. As class divisions widened, employers found little common ground between themselves and their employees. Aiding the industrialists' reluctance to institute reforms were the ethnic, cultural, and occupational differences among the workers. Further, during the 1880s and for a generation afterward, new population elements began to surge into the city. The renewed supply of labor maintained the intensity of labor competition and convinced few employers to initiate reforms.

The new urban residents, however, were more than factory fodder. Their presence altered and, in some instances, came to dominate the city. Their cultures and complexions lent diversity and often conflict to urban society, and their spatial arrangements added new dimensions to the urban geography. The city neither totally absorbed nor rejected these newcomers, but both were forever changed by the contact. Although American soil might at first seem inhospitable to cultural graftings, the American city, in many ways, was to become an extension of the European environment in the years of the great migrations. The immigrants' daily lives during their first years, even their first decades, would be guided as much by the Old World as by the New.

The Foreigners Arrive

The industrial engine was fueled by coal and oil and iron—and also by millions of new workers, about half drawn from the American countryside and half from other countries. The era from 1880 to 1920 witnessed, in fact, the greatest migration to the United States from abroad in this country's history. Though some immigrants came from Europe to escape religious or political persecution and a few sought a new heaven on earth, most simply wanted an opportunity to improve their condition, earn a decent income, and—as one Lithuanian newcomer in Sinclair's *The Jungle* boasts—count themselves as good as any other man.

The American city, in the midst of industrial expansion, seemed to offer that opportunity, and the "new" immigrants, as they were called to distinguish them from their northern European predecessors who had come before the Civil War, settled overwhelmingly in the cities. During the 1880s, when the migrations from southern and eastern Europe first assumed significant proportions, more than 5 million immigrants came to America, or twice as many as had come in any previous decade. Two-thirds of these newcomers were job-seeking males.

But this was merely the beginning of a series of great migrations. Between 1900 and 1910, a record number of immigrants—8¾ million—entered the United States. In the next decade 5¾ million arrived, a remarkable figure considering that Europe was at war and travel was virtually impossible for four of those years. Though roughly one-third of these immigrants eventually returned to their native countries, the net migration figure is still significant.

Given their objectives, it is not surprising that immigrants tended to settle in, or more accurately, to overwhelm the cities. In 1890, roughly one-third of the nation's population lived in cities, whereas nearly two-thirds of the foreign born resided in urban areas. By 1920 an impressive three-fourths of the foreign born lived in cities. This was especially true of medium-sized industrial cities. As early as 1900, three-quarters of the population of Buffalo was either foreign born or native born of foreign parents. By 1890, nearly nine out of ten Milwaukee residents fit this description (see Table 7.1). The "new" immigration even made inroads into the South: in industrial Birmingham, one-quarter of the white factory workers were either first- or second-generation immigrants.

Europeans not only brought themselves in great numbers, they brought their distinctive cultures as well. Although the immigrants from southern and eastern Europe may be lumped together under the heading of "new" immigrants, the timing of their arrival in this country is one of the few things they had in common. Cultural differences extended not only between various national groups but within national groups as well. In discussing the immigrant experience in urban America, it is misleading, therefore, to generalize about the "Italian" experience or the "Jewish" experience, let alone the "new immigrant" experience. To account for these distinctly separate experiences, we must return to the Old World, where the roots of the immigrant in urban America lay.

It would be impossible, of course, to review the distinctions among the

Table 7.1

Constituents of the Population of the Great Cities, 1890

| Native of Native Parents | ///// | Foreign | \\\\\ |
| Native of Foreign Parents | ░░░░ | Nonwhite | ▓▓▓ |

Percent	0	10	20	30	40	50	60	70	80	90	100

Milwaukee
New York
Chicago
Detroit
San Francisco
Buffalo
St. Paul
Cleveland
Jersey City
St. Louis
Cincinnati
Brooklyn
Pittsburgh
Boston
Rochester
New Orleans
Newark
Minneapolis
Allegheny[a]
Providence
Louisville
Philadelphia
Baltimore
Washington
Omaha
Denver
Indianapolis
Kansas City

[a]Once an independent city, Allegheny is now part of Pittsburgh.

Source: U.S. Bureau of the Census, *Eleventh Census, 1890* (Washington, D.C., 1895), I, pt. 1: plate B, p. xcii.

hundreds of different immigrant groups that came to American cities between 1880 and 1920. A few examples from the largest national groups to emigrate will suffice to demonstrate the richness and diversity of immigrant life in urban America.

Because Italy was not a unified country until 1870, it was not to be expected that the people who migrated from the new country would think of themselves as Italians; and, in fact, they did not. Loyalty centered around the province. Thus, by 1920 Chicago boasted not one "little Italy" but rather seventeen separate colonies located throughout the city. In some cities, like New York, the ordering principle was not province but town. Immigrants from Cinisi lived on one street; former residents of Palermo lived on another street perhaps a mile away; and several miles uptown clustered the migrants from Avigliano—all communities in Sicily, yet each with distinct traditions.

Provincial loyalties were not just a phenomenon of the new immigration, but were common to all immigrant groups. Germans who had migrated as early as the 1830s still thought of themselves as Bavarians, Prussians, or Saxons as late as 1900. Within those provincial divisions were religious and political distinctions as well, all of which contributed to the variance in their response to American urban life among the different groups of Germans.

The relationship between provincial background and New World urban experience was placed in sharp relief in a study of Chicago Italians from the Mezzogiorno (southern Italy and Sicily). The study also demonstrated the danger of generalizing about the culture and experience of a national group. The majority of these Chicago *contadini* (peasants) came from towns, not farms. The stereotype of rural immigrants overwhelmed by American cities and the consequent problems of adjustment to city life did not apply here, if in fact it was an accurate description of the experience of any national group. The family was the basic institution in the Mezzogiorno; family ties, nuclear and extended, were in fact so strong that voluntary associations in the towns were rare. This is probably the reason for the great difficulty experienced by the *contadini* in developing national mutual aid societies in American cities. Beyond the family, everyone was a stranger.

The Mezzogiorno was a land of violence. Violations of family pride or honor, especially of a sexual nature, were dealt with harshly by the offended family, and southern Italy possessed the highest homicide rate in Europe. Family revenge was duly transferred to the new environment of American cities, as was another southern Italian custom, extortion under threat of death. The extortionists, known collectively in Sicily as the Mafia, made their way across the Atlantic and became a vicious presence in southern Italian neighborhoods. Thus, crime and violence in Italian districts, which some historians have attributed to the frustrations and disorganization of American urban life, were in fact cultural legacies from the Old World.

Other Mezzogiorno folk customs not only survived the Atlantic crossing but also thrived in American cities. Southern Italians were Catholics but had little use for the church or the clergy, associating the hierarchy with exploitation and oppression. Accordingly, they transferred their devotion to saints. This practice gave their religion a folksy, almost pagan aspect. "Magic, not religion, pervaded their everyday existence"; the *contadini* went to church "to be christened, married, or buried and that is about all."[41] These traditions persisted in Chicago, where feast days honoring the saints became the major neighborhood events.

The study of the *contadini*'s roots in Italy underscores the importance of looking to Europe for an explanation of immigrant life in American cities. Galician Poles, for example, placed significant value on steady work and close family ties. The concept of upward mobility, so fascinating to American historians, was irrelevant to the Poles and was not part of their aspirational framework. When they came to a city like Pittsburgh, success was achieved by steady, if dulling, factory work and a rich family life. Thus, premigration attitudes influenced the type of work and hence the lifestyle of Pittsburgh's Poles.

Other more specific traditions also persisted and sometimes created strange new scenarios in American cities. Jewish immigrants, for example, had no national ties; they were literally without a country. Their loyalties were concentrated on their religion and on the customs which emanated from it. Sabbath observances, dietary customs, and dialects were assiduously maintained and reinforced through the synagogue, Sunday schools, Yiddish theater, and the press. This was particularly true of the Russian Jews, who were part of the new immigration. Their isolation and strict adherence to tradition were strengthened by the hostility between them and their German Jewish brethren, who had migrated a generation earlier and were practicing a more Americanized brand of Judaism.

Class differences, often carryovers from stratifications in the old countries, further fractured immigrant communities. Some fraternal organizations had their origins among occupational groups in the homeland. Milwaukee's German middle class, for example, reestablished their homeland beer halls and fraternal organizations.

These remnants of Old World culture, which translated into distinct urban American lifestyles, led contemporary observers to report that the new immigrants were sharply different from the rest of urban society. Social workers talked of walking into neighborhoods and finding a European community delivered intact on American soil. New York City's Lower East Side, where 150,000 Jewish immigrants crowded together in one of the world's most densely populated areas, was a favorite subject for investigators eager to describe the immigrants' unique lifestyle to their curious readers. In 1902, journalist Edward Steiner captured the special flavor of the district where "street signs are written in Hebrew letters, and the passerby is invited . . . to purchase a prayer-mantle or 'kosher' meat, to enter a beer-saloon or a synagogue. . . . Everything is for sale on the street, from pickled cucumbers to feather beds."[42] Philadelphia social worker Emily Dinwiddie's account of an Italian neighborhood in that city similarly illuminated the foreign atmosphere of the district, describing "black-eyed children, rolling and tumbling together, the gaily colored dresses of the women and the crowds of street vendors, that give the neighborhood a wholly foreign appearance."[43]

Ethnic Space: The Neighborhood

Accounts like these gave contemporary readers the impression that most immigrants resided in homogeneous communities isolated from the rest of society. *Ghettos,* as these neighborhoods were called, were believed to be the major spatial element in urban immigrant settlement. Recent studies have demonstrated, however, that few immigrant districts were homogeneous.

In fact, it is as difficult to generalize about ethnic residential habits as it is to generalize about immigrant lifestyles. Where an immigrant lived depended on many factors besides ethnicity. The size and ethnic mix of a city may have had something to do with residential decision making, but it is not certain which combinations promoted ghettos (neighborhoods where 50 percent or more of a given ethnic group resided) and which favored smaller residential clusters within neighborhoods. The rate of urban growth may have been related to ghetto formation in the fact that the absence of new housing locked immigrants into specific neighborhoods for longer periods of time, whereas a vigorous housing market increased geographic mobility. Different stages in the immigrants' life cycle, too, may have affected residence patterns, with older people tending to be less likely to move. Finally, as we noted earlier, employment opportunities rather than ethnic camaraderie may have determined residential patterns. Workers of various ethnic backgrounds clustered around a factory, and even if one provincial or national group dominated several streets the neighborhood as a whole was ethnically mixed. The employment opportunities of downtown also led a variety of ethnic groups to cluster together there. The Lower East Side of Manhattan, for example, which scholars have repeatedly singled out as the Jewish ghetto par excellence, was actually an ethnic potpourri.

The relationship of city size, ethnic mix, urban growth, and employment to ethnic residential patterns was strikingly illustrated by the residential patterns in the cities of Detroit and Omaha. Polish immigrants were Detroit's most visible ethnic group from 1890 to 1920, and they tended to dominate neighborhoods numerically, though employment opportunity vied with ethnicity as the major reason for this phenomenon. The Poles came to Detroit as unskilled laborers in the 1890s and entered the construction trades located on the city's west side. Eventually they became this area's ethnic majority, but only for a short time. By 1910, Poles were leaving their old neighborhood for the urban periphery, where the new auto industry was developing. They established dominance in that district, too. The sheer size of the Polish community and the tendency of community members to be attracted to the same type of work helped to create a ghetto neighborhood.

In Omaha, a smaller city where one-third of the population was foreign born, most foreigners were scattered fairly evenly throughout the city in 1880. In 1900, the effects of the "new" immigration began to register in terms of spatial location. Some Russian Jews clustered in neighborhoods near downtown, but most of this immigrant group lived elsewhere. Other groups such as Italians and Czechs also exhibited some clustering, but the pattern of domination common to Polish immigrants in Detroit did not develop in Omaha, at least through 1920.

Omaha's immigrants enjoyed a high degree of residential mobility that inhibited the formation of ghetto neighborhoods. This mobility in all directions toward the urban periphery tended to decrease residential clustering by 1920. Small Jewish and Italian clusters remained, but more as reference points for the majority of those groups than as expanding residential neighborhoods.

It is difficult to pinpoint a single determining reason for the relatively diffuse residential pattern exhibited by Omaha's immigrants. If we contrast the situation in Omaha with that in Detroit, however, we can see that Omaha was not dominated by large-scale heavy industry with massive labor requirements that could, in turn, create distinct ethnic neighborhoods. Equally important was the fact that Omaha had a fluid housing market that was constantly expanding in all directions to meet the population requirements. Finally, Omaha's smaller size and its relative newness inhibited the growth of distinct, isolated communities.

Whether one immigrant group dominated a neighborhood or not, all foreign born attempted to put some psychological, if not physical, distance between themselves and the rest of the urban population. Immigrant institutions—religious, charitable, and fraternal—were valuable in establishing the distinction and in enhancing the identity and solidarity of the ethnic group. Although the residential patterns of a group varied from city to city, the types of institutions on which the immigrants relied usually did not. If, in some cities, specific ethnic neighborhoods were difficult to discern, it was usually possible to locate a spatial clustering of institutions that immigrants scattered about the city resorted to from time to time. As such, the institutions, more than the number or relative strength of a given ethnic group, defined an immigrant community.

The charitable organizations were frequently connected with religious institutions. Religion had occupied an important position in the immigrants' Old World existence and did so in their new urban homes as well. The church or synagogue was a physical focal point in the community, even to the relatively aloof Italians. Much more than a place of worship, it was a school in which Old World values and language, as well as religious training, were transmitted. The church or synagogue was a recreational facility where immigrant children could come as an alternative to the streets. At times, community leaders would gather in it to discuss important matters and perhaps to seek some divine guidance. Finally, it functioned as an auxiliary institution for charitable purposes.

The numerous functions performed by the church or synagogue made its control by the local community imperative. Polish parishioners wanted Polish priests, and Russian Jewish communities wanted Russian rabbis. At times the nationality of the minister became such a heated topic that some Catholic national groups threatened to secede from the church. During the 1890s, the nationalism of various Catholic groups became so intense that a movement for administering the Catholic church in America by nationalities rather than by dioceses went all the way to Rome before it was squelched.

If religion was important to the immigrant community as a traditional link, other institutions with only tenuous ties to the Old World past were necessary because conditions in American cities required them. New arrivals were often prey for unscrupulous rooming-house proprietors or bogus employment agents, who promised to secure jobs for a fee paid in advance. Some charitable organizations devoted a portion of their funds and personnel to meeting the boats or trains carrying newly arrived immigrants. They would help the newcomers find lodging and even put them in contact with prospective employers.

The Italians, whose strong kinship ties inhibited the formation of the kinds of large-scale charitable organizations that other groups had established, developed a unique system of initiating newcomers into urban life. The Italian newcomer instead turned to the *padrone*, a townsman who had achieved some status in America and who was familiar with urban American customs. The *padrone* performed most of the functions that institutions executed for other immigrant groups: he extended credit, bought groceries, and found lodging and, most important, employment for the new arrival. For each of the functions performed, the *padrone* received a commission, usually from the immigrant. Frequently, this arrangement began in Italy, with the *padrone* paying for the steamship ticket to America. Most historians recognize that the *padrone* performed necessary functions, given the suspicion of southern Italian immigrants toward strangers, but they also believe that the prices exacted for these services were in many cases excessive. The system flourished until families and, later, labor unions were strong enough to assume the *padrone*'s functions.

Making It

Once the newcomers were settled, the dull routine of work dominated their lives. It is no exaggeration to state that an entire generation sacrificed itself so that future generations would enjoy a better life. The immigrants' dreams focused, in many instances, on their children, and the formula for success soon came to be hard work for the parents and education for the children. For immigrants, education had been a temporary and sometimes inaccessible luxury in the land of their birth. Its value had been recognized, especially in such locations as Jewish villages in Russia. But even there, religious institutions performed the educational function because few Jews were permitted to enter the secular Russian educational system. In the Old World, education was a class phenomenon, a privilege of social standing. The popular immigrant view of America, in contrast, was that it was a relatively classless society. If there was an aristocracy, it was an aristocracy of learning, not of blood. Education was the road to that aristocracy and the way out of a lifetime of toil and poverty. For these reasons, immigrants nurtured and supported educational institutions—though not necessarily public education—with an almost religious fervor.

To Francie Nolan, the heroine of Betty Smith's *A Tree Grows in Brooklyn*, education was indeed a religious experience. As Francie entered the dilapidated little library in her neighborhood, "the feeling she had about it was as good as the feeling she had about church." Later on, Francie's mother Katie, despondent over the future, suddenly had an inspiration of the way out for her children: "An answer came to Katie. It was so simple that a flash of astonishment that felt like pain shot through her head. Education! That was it! It was education that made the difference! Education would pull them out of the grime and dirt."[44]

It was not, of course, that simple. First, respect for the value of education varied widely among immigrant groups. German and Jewish immigrants placed much faith in the powers of education. Polish immigrants, on the other hand, with their emphasis on family and work, were relatively indifferent, some even seeing education as an interference with work. Another problem was the sometimes conflicting educational objectives the immigrants espoused. Katie Nolan had a vision of upward economic mobility to be gained by education. Other immigrants saw education as a means of preserving and handing down their own Old World traditions, values, and language. Urban public school systems were rarely the appropriate educational institutions for fulfilling that objective.

Public schools, in fact, were generally horrible institutions in turn-of-the-century cities. The flood of immigrants caused serious overcrowding, and both administration and curriculum were in a state of chaos. Inevitably, the worst physical facilities were located in immigrant districts. With sometimes as many as a hundred children packed into a dimly lit and poorly ventilated classroom, it was not far-fetched to look on the school as an educational extension of the factory. "Brutalizing is the only adjective for the public schools," Betty Smith wrote.[45]

Even when reformers tried to tinker with the system by installing vocational courses, this sort of curriculum merely fed the public stereotype of an immigrant as fit for nothing better than common labor. Some Catholic immigrant groups developed their own system of parochial schools. Yet even here, loyalty to these private educational institutions varied. If the local public schools included such ethnic-oriented courses as language and history, Catholic immigrant parents would not hesitate to send their children to these schools. The parochial schools, especially in Polish and Italian neighborhoods, were established more for cultural than for religious purposes. Expense was also a problem, though some dioceses arranged liberal scholarships for Catholic immigrant children. Local control was another factor in school choice. Where immigrant parents could dominate local public school policy and curricula, public school enrollment was high. Correspondingly, if clergy of a different nationality controlled the local parochial school, immigrant parents would have little incentive to send their children there.

Even Jews, whom many writers have identified as the most loyal adherents of public education, were not avid attenders of public schools before World War I. For one thing, families needed their children's work and income and, for another, the link between education and economic advance was not yet clear in cities where many of the available jobs were low-skilled positions. Better than one-half of all Jewish households in New York City in 1904, for example, were headed by manual laborers. Professionals accounted for only 3 percent of household heads. Perhaps even more important, Jewish families distrusted public education as reflected by an attempt in the early 1900s, called the Kehillah experiment, to create a separate school system for Jewish students in New York. The Kehillah's programs stressed assimilation and tradition in an even-handed manner, whereas the public schools seemed to favor the former over the latter.

Some of the immigrants' concerns about public education proved unfounded, for their large numbers assured that neighborhood public schools would respect to some degree the cultural heritage of their students. And, especially when the the wave of immigration subsided after World War I, a new generation of youngsters and parents came to perceive decided economic benefits in public education.

In the meantime, coping with the capitalist city became a major objective of life, and many immigrants molded their traditions to ease their adjustment. For the Russian immigrant hero of journalist Abraham Cahan's semiautobiographical novel *The Rise of David Levinsky* (1917), religious traditions were the first casualties: "The striking thing was that it was not a world of piety. . . . Very few of the women who passed my push-cart wore wigs, and men who did not shave were an exception. Also, I knew that many people with whom I came in daily contact openly patronized Gentile restaurants and would not hesitate even to eat pork."[46] Few immigrant neighborhoods were so self-contained as to avoid contact with the larger urban society. The young immigrant "on the make" came to know the standards of urban behavior necessary for advancement, one of which was conformity.

Conformity sometimes forced compromises. Sabbath observances, wedding ceremonies, and saints' festivals that did not conform to the unbending discipline of the factory were modified. Orthodox Jews from eastern Europe, for example, held a festival on the eighth day following the birth of a son. Because Sunday was the only day off from the factory, the parents had to plan the event for that day regardless of whether it was the right day or not. "The host and his guests," one historian noted, "know it is not the right day and they fall to mourning over the conditions that will not permit them to observe the old custom." The day becomes "one for secret sadness rather than rejoicing."[47]

Though it was small consolation for some, conformity sped the process of residential and economic mobility. David Levinsky's adoption of the urban lifestyle paid very well: "I was born and reared in the lowest depths of poverty and I arrived in America—in 1885—with four cents in my pocket. I am now worth more than two million dollars and recognized as one of the two or three leading men in the cloak-and-suit trade in the United States."[48] Few immigrants, of course, followed Levinsky's rags-to-riches path. In their own view, however, many immigrants were successful. Adhering to a philosophy of what historian Stephan Thernstrom has termed "ruthless underconsumption,"[49] some immigrants saved enough to move from their initial cramped residences to houses on the urban periphery. Owning a home and property around it, however small, was the definition of success for many immigrants. Sam Bass Warner, Jr., contended in his study of Boston's late-nineteenth-century suburbs[50] that within a generation portions of Boston's ethnic communities were suburbanized. By the 1870s, after one generation in Philadelphia, some Irish had attained what historian Dennis Clark has called "the cult of residential contentment" north of the city, where they were "flying the lace-curtain flags of domestic satisfaction."[51]

Despite the fact that work was often the usual and most frequent contact point between the immigrant and the outside world, it did not necessarily imply cultural compromises. Again, premigration skills and preferences often determined New World occupations. Italians, for example, preferred outdoor work and were therefore overrepresented in the construction industry. Jews often brought business skills with them and consequently moved into mercantile positions in American cities. In 1909, for example, 45 percent of Jewish immigrants in Boston were engaged in some form of business enterprise, compared with only 22 percent of Italians and 5 percent of the Irish. In the Old World Italians had often supplemented their farm incomes by engaging in seasonal commercial work. In Pittsburgh, therefore, Italians were much more likely to open a business than Poles, who were not accustomed to such work in Poland.

This is not to say that immigrant preferences and background were the paramount factors in the employment they obtained in the United States. In the complex interplay between Old World culture and American conditions, ethnic groups often had to adjust their objectives to the limits of a given urban environment. Greeks in Chicago, for example, found it difficult to establish businesses other than restaurants, so they concentrated on such enterprises and eventually owned restaurants, fruit distributorships, and ice cream factories throughout the city. The Japanese who came to Los Angeles during the first two decades of the twentieth century encountered even greater hostility and were forced into sectors of the economy whites had either shunned or failed to exploit. Japanese immigrants made the growing and selling of market garden crops, grown efficiently on small plots of land, a highly profitable enterprise.

Employers' stereotypes were also constraints on immigrant work preferences. Jewish textile entrepreneurs, for example, sometimes hired only Italians because they were thought to be less prone to unionization than Jewish workers. Other Jewish bosses hired only Jewish workers in the hope that ethnic ties would overcome the lure of the unions. As indicated, stereotypes could sometimes work to an ethnic group's advantage. This was especially so after 1900, when blacks began arriving in northern cities in appreciable numbers. Pittsburgh steelmakers, for example, preferred Polish to black workers, and Poles began a decades-long tradition of handing down steel mill jobs through the generations.

For some immigrants, the ethnic neighborhood itself provided the best opportunities for economic progress. The community's special character demanded special services and rewarded those who spoke the language of the old country and knew the traditional ways. For other immigrants, however—and increasingly for most—economic progress accompanied movement away from the old neighborhood.

Wealth did not necessarily mean the loss of tradition any more than a home in the suburbs marked the severing of ties to the old neighborhood downtown or by the factory. Total abandonment of ethnic culture was rare, which is the reason the old immigrant district retained a special psychological importance long after a group's initial dominance or even cluster in the area had dissipated. Institutions, friends, relatives, and food products continued to draw later generations and, more recently, people of all ethnic backgrounds. The various Chinatowns and Little Italies in cities like San Francisco, Chicago, and New

A Chicago Grocery Store, c. 1914

Small shops like this one, owned by Stanley P. Balzekas, were common enterprises for members of some immigrant groups. Immigrant-owned businesses provided important services for their neighborhoods as well as opportunities for upward mobility.

York serve today as institutional centers for scattered ethnic populations and as popular recreation areas for visitors who are neither Chinese nor Italian.

There were, of course, the "left behinds"—those immigrants who remained rooted where they had landed and were irrevocably tied to their Old World ways. Tradition was security and the city could be terribly insecure. Indeed, the accomplishments of the ethnic minorities, especially in the second generation, seem all the more significant in view of urban society's prevailing attitudes toward them.

The antagonism toward the immigrant cannot be passed off as the attitude of an occasional bigot. Leading molders of public opinion expressed not only their own but prevailing beliefs about immigrants, and no group remained unscathed. Americans "pretty well agreed," claimed the *New York Times,* that the Italian and Russian immigrant was "of a kind which we are better without."[52] A Jersey City newspaper referred to striking Irish laborers as "a mongrel mass of ignorance and crime and superstition, as utterly unfit for its duties, as they are for the common courtesies and decencies of civilized life." In 1884, the prestigious *Chicago Times* suggested a solution to what the editor felt was an alarming invasion of Slavic immigrants into Chicago: "Let us whip these slavic wolves back to the European dens from which they issue, or in some way exterminate them."[53]

Discrimination in housing and employment were concrete expressions of these attitudes, which took at least a generation to change or at least not to be broadcast publicly. After 1920, public inflammatory statements about immigrants were rare. Not coincidentally, it usually took one generation for the immigrants to achieve some residential and occupational mobility, if they achieved it at all. Regimented by factory work, concerned about their internal conflicts between tradition and conformity to American urban life, buffeted by adverse public opinion and occasionally by overt actions, and beset by the usual anxieties and doubts newcomers face in a strange environment, the immigrants ultimately came to call the city home and possessed a sometimes fond and sometimes melancholy attachment to their neighborhoods. If the present was onerous, the future, in the city at least, could be brighter. This was the hope of the American city—the hope of tomorrow. The immigrants would understand what the Detroit rabbi meant when he declared that the Jew was no longer a man without a country. "He has found his Canaan in America."[54]

The immigrant experience of the late-nineteenth- and early-twentieth-century city is best described as a process of adjustment rather than assimilation—for the latter word connotes the loss of one culture in favor of another; the former implies a modification of both cultures. Moreover, the process was dynamic: adjustment implies a strengthening, weakening, changing, and abandoning of both new and old cultures, the creation of entirely new forms. Adjustment was rarely a straight line toward or away from the culture of origin. The Japanese, for example, had not gone to Los Angeles to become truck farmers, but circumstances dictated otherwise and they used their cultural heritage of hard work and sober living to make a restricted livelihood successful. Sometimes economics and the availability of alternatives resulted in cultural modifications that maintained the initial intent of the tradition. In the old country, Portuguese held *festas* every Sunday honoring a patron saint. In New England towns, they confined the tradition to the churches instead of parading through the streets. And instead of baking bread themselves, Portuguese immigrant women were happy to buy all the bread they needed from local bakers.

In a few cases, the New World offered greater opportunities to observe the values of the culture of origin than the Old World. Young women who migrated from Italy's Abruzzi region to Rochester, New York, found that it was easier to retain their Old World moral code in late-nineteenth-century Rochester, where young men outnumbered them significantly. At the same time, the enhanced economic prospects in Rochester enabled them to marry earlier than they would have been able to in their home town. The availability of work also allowed these young women to work outside the home, something they rarely did in Abruzzi. They were thus able to obtain financial independence to construct the nuclear household that was the cultural ideal in the old country. In a similar way, Sicilians who migrated to lower Manhattan discovered that ready access to work and relatively high geographic mobility enabled them to observe the custom of living near and among extended family much better than in the more static environment of Sicily.

The millions from Europe had grasped the special meaning of urban life that John Winthrop and Brigham Young had envisioned. Yet another group of migrants believed in the city, however. The dreams of this group reflected a past filled with denials—of their ability, their intellect, even of their humanity. Like the Europeans, they came to the city to have their dreams fulfilled. Unlike the Europeans, they remain in the city and their dreams, if they still dream, are unfulfilled. They were the urban pioneers who still remain in the wilderness.

Blacks: The Forgotten Ethnic Group

At the turn of this century, 90 percent of American blacks were located in the South and only 17 percent of southern blacks lived in cities. By 1960, almost 40 percent lived outside the South and nearly three-quarters of all blacks were urban. In the course of six decades, the nation's blacks had redistributed themselves across the land until they comprised almost a fifth of the populations in the urban Northeast and Midwest. From the most rural of America's major minority groups, they became one of the most urban (for details, see Table 7.2).

Table 7.2

Number and Percentage of Blacks in Selected Central Cities, 1900, 1920, 1950, 1970

	1900		1920		1950		1970	
	No.	%	No.	%	No.	%	No.	%
New England								
Boston	11,591	2.1	16,350	2.2	40,057	5.0	104,707	16.3
Providence	4,817	2.7	5,655	2.4	8,304	3.3	15,875	8.9
New Haven	2,887	2.7	4,573	2.8	9,605	5.8	36,158	26.3
Middle Atlantic								
New York	60,666	1.8	152,467	2.7	747,610	9.5	1,688,115	21.1
Buffalo	1,698	9.5	4,511	9.9	36,645	6.3	94,329	20.4
Newark	6,694	2.7	16,997	4.1	74,965	17.1	207,458	54.2
Philadelphia	62,613	4.8	134,229	7.4	376,041	18.2	653,791	33.6
Pittsburgh	20,355	4.5	37,725	6.4	82,453	12.2	104,904	20.2
South Atlantic								
Baltimore	79,258	15.6	108,322	14.8	225,099	23.7	420,210	46.4
Washington	86,702	31.1	109,966	25.1	280,803	35.0	537,712	71.1
Richmond	32,230	37.9	54,041	31.5	72,996	31.7	104,766	42.0
Charlotte	7,151	39.5	14,641	31.6	37,481	28.0	72,972	30.3
Charleston	31,522	56.5	32,326	47.6	30,854	44.0	30,251	45.2
Savannah	28,090	51.8	39,179	47.1	48,282	40.4	53,111	44.9
Atlanta	35,727	39.8	62,796	31.3	121,285	36.6	255,051	51.3
North Central								
Cincinnati	14,482	4.4	30,079	7.5	78,196	15.5	125,000	27.6
Cleveland	5,988	1.6	34,451	4.3	147,847	16.1	287,841	38.3

Detroit	4,111	1.4	40,838	4.1	300,506	16.2	660,428	43.7
Milwaukee	862	0.3	2,229	0.5	21,772	3.4	105,088	14.7
Chicago	30,150	1.8	109,458	4.1	492,265	13.6	1,102,620	32.7
Indianapolis	15,931	9.4	34,677	11.0	63,867	15.0	134,320	18.0
Gary	—		5,299	9.6	39,253	29.3	29,695	52.8
St. Louis	35,516	6.2	69,854	9.0	153,766	17.9	254,191	40.9
Kansas City, Mo.	17,567	10.7	30,719	9.5	55,682	12.2	112,005	22.1
Minneapolis	1,548	0.8	3,927	1.0	6,807	1.3	19,005	4.4
South Central								
Birmingham	16,575	43.1	70,230	39.3	130,025	39.9	126,388	42.0
New Orleans	77,714	27.1	100,930	26.1	181,775	31.9	267,308	45.0
Memphis	49,910	48.8	61,181	37.7	147,141	37.2	242,513	38.9
Nashville	30,044	37.2	35,633	30.1	54,696	31.4	87,877	19.6
Louisville	39,139	19.1	40,087	17.1	57,657	15.6	86,040	23.8
Houston	14,608	32.7	33,960	24.6	124,766	20.9	316,551	25.7
Dallas	9,035	21.2	24,023	15.1	56,958	13.1	210,238	24.9
Mountain								
Denver	3,923	2.9	6,075	2.4	15,059	3.6	47,011	9.1
Salt Lake City	278	0.5	718	0.6	1,127	0.6	2,135	1.2
Pacific								
Los Angeles	2,131	2.1	15,579	2.7	171,209	8.7	503,606	17.9
Oakland	1,026	1.5	5,489	2.5	47,562	12.4	124,710	34.5
San Francisco	1,654	0.5	2,414	0.5	43,502	5.6	96,078	13.4
Portland	757	0.9	1,556	0.6	9,529	2.5	21,572	5.6
Seattle	406	0.5	2,894	0.9	15,666	3.3	37,868	7.1

Source: Condensed from table 4.3, pp. 406–407, in Bayrd Still, *Urban America: A History with Documents.* Copyright © 1974 by Little, Brown and Company (Inc.). Reprinted by permission.

Southern blacks drifted northward throughout the late nineteenth century at a rate of about 19,000 a year between 1890 and 1910. Black migration to southern cities rose during the first decade of the century, anticipating a much larger movement northward during the next ten years. Between 1910 and 1920, half a million southern blacks left the region, primarily for the Northeast and Midwest.

A combination of factors produced this northward and cityward movement. An agricultural malaise, created in large part by the infamous boll weevil that ate its way through the South, from Texas in 1901 to North Carolina in 1921. The weevil decimated southern cotton fields, drove a number of black and white tenants and sharecroppers off the land, or at least made their continued existence there supremely difficult. Without a major cash crop, farming came down to a question of simple survival. Further, the southern racial climate, always harsh and restrictive, was especially severe in rural areas. Blacks were disfranchised in the 1890s through changes in state constitutions that established complicated voter registration tests and procedures applied selectively to most blacks and some poor whites. Other laws systematically excluded and segregated blacks. Periodic lynchings in the late nineteenth and early twentieth centuries were particularly brutal reminders of their second-class citizenship. The North may not have seemed as much the promised land of freedom as it once had to escaping slaves on the underground railroad, but its cities did hold out the promise for a better life. The Chicago *Defender,* one of the leading black newspapers in the nation, gained wide circulation among blacks in the South and urged their brethren on: "To die from the bite of frost is far more glorious than at the hands of a mob. I beg you, my brother, to leave the benighted land."[55] The biblical imagery, tightly woven into slave lore, reappeared when the new migrants compared their exodus north to the "flight out of Egypt" and "going to Canaan." Indeed, a group of migrants speeding north on a train from Mississippi to Chicago stopped their watches, fell on their knees, and sang the hymn "I Done Come Out of the Land of Egypt with the Good News" as they crossed the Ohio River.[56]

It was not only the racial situation in the South that created this religious fervor, but the economic conditions in northern cities as well. Southern blacks were deeply tied to the soil—as were many white southerners—and available evidence indicates that lynchings did not significantly increase the numbers of local blacks who left. The advantages of the urban North were probably the most important motivating factor—especially the opportunities for jobs, higher wages, and a better life. These were, after all, the major attractions for millions of European and Asian immigrants. Significantly, as economic opportunities increased, so did black migration, especially to industrial cities like Chicago, Cleveland, Detroit, and Pittsburgh.

As the terminus of the Illinois Central Railroad, Chicago was a particularly favorite destination among blacks from Mississippi, Louisiana, and Arkansas. During World War I, when foreign immigration stopped, industries in Chicago and in other northern cities developed labor shortages. For a period of eighteen months beginning in January 1916, more than 50,000 blacks entered Chicago, most on free tickets supplied by local industries. The *Defender* took this opportunity to flood its southern readers with job listings, success stories, and editorial entreaties. The newspaper's efforts were so successful that white authorities in the labor-depleted South confiscated the paper in many areas. The word, however, continued to get through as labor recruiters, friends, and relatives passed the message of high wages, plentiful jobs, and city excitement. As one contemporary wrote of Chicago: "This city is really the land overflowing with milk and honey."[57]

True enough, blacks found work in the city as they migrated in record numbers after 1890. The World War I employment bonanza was a temporary departure from the depressingly typical pattern of black employment during the migration years, however. The range of occupational opportunities open to blacks was severely limited by discrimination and increasing competition from the other urban migrants, the foreign born. In most northern cities at the turn of the century, the typical black was employed as a common laborer or servant. Even more discouraging was the absence of any occupational mobility for decades. Low-paying unskilled jobs were not merely the first step toward better things for blacks, as they were for immigrants. A rigid job ceiling prevailed, limiting blacks to menial and manual tasks. In Cleveland between 1890 and 1910, the occupational status of blacks remained stationary while immigrants registered impressive gains.

Because the skill levels of both the southern and foreign migrants were roughly similar, they sought the same employment. In almost every case until World War I, the immigrant won the competition. Although the blacks' occupational status was always low, certain positions were recognized as their preserve in northern cities. With large-scale immigration after the 1870s, such monopolies crumbled, especially in barbering and in service occupations in hotels, restaurants, and transportation. Fannie Barrier Williams, a turn-of-the-century black activist in Chicago, complained that between 1895 and 1905, "the colored people of Chicago have lost . . . nearly every occupation of which they once had almost a monopoly."[58]

The situation was equally dismal in late-nineteenth-century Detroit, where Italians took over the barbering profession and the Poles worked on the docks, which had once been the exclusive territory of blacks. As more and more blacks found themselves unemployed, underemployed, or forced into backbreaking common labor, frustration naturally grew. Blacks, after all, had held established bases in northern cities since the antebellum period, whereas many of their foreign competitors were recent arrivals.

Only during World War I did blacks begin to participate in urban industry in appreciable numbers. Industrial employment did not change their low occupational status, however. Moreover, they faced the same problems adjusting to the factory regimen as foreigners encountered. Finally, the growing unions that promised some improvement in workers' conditions usually bypassed blacks. Unions were generally organized around skilled crafts, and few blacks were involved in those occupations. Blacks had also earned reputations as strikebreakers: during the periodic and sometimes violent labor struggles, employers imported trainloads of blacks to replace striking workers. Though only a few blacks were aware of the issues involved in these disputes, their role did not endear them to union organizers.

The lack of options confronting blacks in the search for employment matched similar frustrations in their quest for a place to live. The word *ghetto* was more appropriate in describing residential locations for them than for any foreign immigrant group. More important, even if some foreign groups dominated a residential area, that dominance was only temporary; for blacks it was a seemingly permanent condition that paralleled their lack of occupational mobility. One historian has described the black residential experience as the "enduring ghetto."[59]

Racial Space: The Ghetto

The black ghetto has persisted since the antebellum decades, when such spatial segregation was rare. New York, for example, had several black enclaves dispersed throughout the city. Each enclave, however, was a homogeneous community of blacks, emphasizing their isolation from the rest of the city. In 1860, although they represented a fraction of the population, four out of every five blacks in Detroit lived at the convergence of three wards, a concentration unique in the city at that time. Following the Civil War, as blacks completed the first stage of their migration process, southern and border cities also developed patterns of spatial segregation. In Washington, D.C., a twenty-block area in the southwest quadrant of the city was more than three-quarters black as early as 1880. In the 1890s, blacks dominated an area east of downtown Atlanta that was known as "Sweet Auburn" after the avenue that cuts through the ghetto.

As black migration to northern cities advanced rapidly after 1900, the pattern of residential isolation became more pronounced. Between 1910 and 1920, black ghettos expanded in size as ethnic concentrations began to dissolve. Blacks were confined to the least desirable and most dilapidated housing, usually situated adjacent to the central business district, and the rapid influx from the

South strained the already overcrowded dwellings. Unable to expand into commercial land-use areas, blacks sought nearby residential districts that invariably contained white residents.

In most cities this expansion generated a great deal of white hostility. The whites usually formed protective associations pledging not to sell to blacks; occasionally they resorted to violence to oust a black family or two that happened to move into the area undetected. Although these tactics were successful for a while, the availability, for whites, of homes on the urban periphery and their fear of the black population usually resulted in the expansion of the black ghetto into the previously white district. Though the neighborhood might remain integrated for a time, within a decade it was indistinguishable from the rest of the ghetto.

There were a few exceptions to this pattern, but all resulted in an "enduring ghetto," regardless of the differences in origin. In Cleveland and some smaller cities farther west, blacks clustered in but did not dominate certain late-nineteenth-century residential neighborhoods. The reasons for the relative absence of ethnic concentrations in Omaha, as discussed earlier, apply to blacks in these cities as well: the newness of the cities and the favorable housing market. By 1920, however, the word *ghetto* was appropriate for the black residential experience in these cities.

Harlem was unusual among black communities. Unlike most ghettos, Harlem had not been the least desirable residence area in the city. In 1890, the community on the northern edge of Manhattan Island was predominantly white and middle class with a hint of the countryside on its fringes. By 1920, it was a teeming black ghetto on its way to becoming one of the nation's most notorious slums.

This transformation began in the wake of a mad carnival of land speculation touched off by the extension of the subway in the late 1890s. As so often happened with speculative enterprises on the urban periphery, the area became overbuilt. As the boom collapsed, black realtors, especially Philip A. Payton, Jr.'s Afro-American Realty Company, moved in to take advantage of bargain prices in the area. Payton leased apartment houses from hard-pressed white owners and rented units to blacks at high rental rates. Although Payton eventually overextended himself, the opening of Harlem to blacks after 1905 was the first wave of a black rush into the community. The attractions of moving "uptown" to a middle-class neighborhood must have been great for blacks, who were denied access to decent residential districts in the city. Unfortunately, many blacks who moved to Harlem could not afford the rents, so doubling and tripling up occurred. The stately brownstones built to house one family now sheltered four or five. Overcrowding led to deterioration and a serious decline in the quality of life. By 1920, Harlem was a ghetto.

The blacks' occupational status and their residential isolation were distinct

badges of second-class citizenship. As blacks moved about the city, they encountered numerous other reminders of their lowly position. Segregation was a
fact of black life. In addition to occupational and residential segregation, they
faced discrimination in public facilities, education, and the legal system. Beginning in the 1870s and accelerating after 1900, segregation dominated race relations in American cities despite the presence of federal and state civil rights
legislation and the absence of local regulations enforcing segregation. Restaurants, hotels, and theaters threw up the color line, though most of these facilities
were too expensive for the average black in any case. Prohibitions against intermarriage between blacks and whites were common. Blacks were systematically
barred from recreational facilities and were usually forced to maintain separate
educational facilities. Where an integrated school system existed, as in Detroit,
separate desks for white and black children were common.

In southern cities after the Civil War, segregation was an improvement over
the antebellum policy of excluding blacks from public and educational facilities
altogether. The Republicans who ran southern cities during the Reconstruction
era had no intention of integrating southern urban society, but they did hope
to provide equal facilities for the segregated blacks. The separate-but-equal policy died with the end of Reconstruction, and blacks were relegated to inferior
educational facilities and public accommodations.

The unanimity of American cities in segregating blacks and in restricting their
choices revealed, of course, deep-seated prejudice against them. The popular
culture of the era depicted blacks in the most uncomplimentary manner. Vaudeville and minstrel shows, popular urban entertainment at the turn of the century,
included such black characters in their repertoire as "Useless Peabody" and
"Moses Abraham Highbrow." Songs of the period denigrating blacks, such as
"All Coons Look Alike to Me" and "I Wish My Color Would Fade," were common numbers at performances. The black image received little rehabilitation
with the advent of a new urban mass entertainment, the motion picture. In fact,
the rather innocuous, stupid, good-timing black of the earlier shows was replaced by a more evil caricature following David W. Griffith's pioneering 1915
film *Birth of a Nation,* which set box office records. Griffith's film was so powerful and so negative in its depiction of blacks that it touched off riots in several
cities, triggered a series of lawsuits by a new interracial organization, the National Association for the Advancement of Colored People (NAACP), and inspired the resurrection of the Ku Klux Klan.

As historian Gilbert Osofsky has observed, the black stereotype common in
the nation's cities at the time ran counter to virtually every American ideal. "The
Negro was conceived of as lazy in an ambitious culture; improvident and sen-
suous in a moralistic society . . . childlike in a country of men." In Osofsky's
words, the black "seemed more fit to be a servant, a 'half man,' than anything

else."[60] Immigrants were quick to pick up these stereotypes, too. Prejudice against blacks seemed to be the American thing to do. It also enabled immigrants to place some psychological distance between themselves and the bottom of society. A black New York school principal stated the situation more graphically: "Pat O'Flannagan does not have the least thing in the world against Jim from Dixie, but it didn't take Pat long after passing the Statue of Liberty to learn that it is popular to give Jim a whack."[61]

These popular prejudices were periodically extended into a good many "whacks" against blacks. Violent clashes between blacks and whites were inevitable, given the prevailing white attitudes. The great migration after 1900 seemed more like an invasion to white residents of adjacent neighborhoods and to those white laborers already concerned about the oversupply of labor. The year 1919 witnessed widespread and bloody violence as race riots occurred in twenty-six American cities. The timing of the riots was not surprising when we consider that by this time blacks had achieved some success in breaking into industrial employment and therefore were more threatening to their white co-workers. Also, with the cessation of European immigration, the continuing black migration became even more visible, especially to the immigrants.

Serious violence occurred in Chicago, where a record number of blacks had migrated during the two previous years. A good portion of these new migrants secured employment in the meat-packing houses on the city's South Side, already the site of Chicago's black ghetto. Expansion into adjoining white neighborhoods became inevitable and tensions built along the slowly shifting boundary lines separating black from white residential areas. After months of unprovoked attacks on blacks by white youths, a full-scale riot erupted during the summer of 1919 when several blacks attempted to test the segregation of a neighborhood beach. Thirty-eight people lost their lives, making the confrontation one of the bloodiest racial outbursts before 1965.

The Chicago riot demonstrated to whites that blacks must learn their place in urban society. Blacks, though, had learned this lesson long before the summer of 1919. In their own communities they sought to establish a separate society, a much more self-contained and isolated one than the immigrants had formed to preserve their foreign heritages. Unlike the foreigners, the blacks had no other options.

Although segregation provided blacks with the opportunity to create their own institutions, several obstacles had to be overcome before the ghetto could be called a community. First, there were divisions within the black ghetto as numerous as those within immigrant groups, but the differences among blacks were not as neatly defined spatially and culturally by provincial groups as they were for the immigrants. The ghetto included West Indian blacks (primarily in New York), southern rural blacks, southern urban blacks, and northern urban blacks. There were poor people, well-to-do people, and people of all degrees of poverty and wealth in between. Most serious of all was the division between oldtimers and newcomers. The rapid influx of blacks from the South after 1900 resulted in deteriorating race relations and the imposition of harsher restrictions on black life in the city. Further, the majority of migrants were both illiterate and ignorant of urban ways of life, thus confirming some of the prevailing white stereotypes. This annoyed the oldtimers, who had worked assiduously for decades to earn the respect of the white community. They called the newcomers "lazy," "overdemonstrative," "uncouth," and "undesirable."[62]

Because the oldtimers held leadership positions in the ghetto, their coolness toward the migrants presented another obstacle to ghetto unity. The oldtimers cherished their ties to the white community and viewed the creation of black institutions as a threat to the integrated society they still hoped for—a hope that was becoming increasingly unrealizable for them and impossible for the vast majority of blacks. Even when the oldtimers had created institutions such as the black church and black social clubs before the great migration, these had tended to divide rather than unite the black community. The religious affiliations of the newcomers, primarily Baptist or Pentecostal, added to these divisions.

As the migration from the South overwhelmed the oldtimers, their ideals eventually became engulfed as well. The integrationist philosophy was replaced by the philosophy of racial solidarity and self-help propounded by the urban followers of Booker T. Washington. The old elite, dominated by professionals and a few business people with connections to the white community, gave way to a new leadership of middle-class business people who viewed the ghetto in terms of economic opportunity for themselves and their fellow residents. The large and growing concentration of blacks ensured a local market.

The new middle-class leadership was most interested in developing black capitalist enterprise. Black business began to blossom in the ghetto after 1900. Although service enterprises predominated, there were several successful examples in other fields such as real estate and cosmetics. Robert Abbott's Chicago *Defender* became, by 1920, the largest black-owned business in the country. The newspaper was sensational and flamboyant, and sometimes concocted stories to capture reader interest. But it also played a significant role in the great migration during World War I. Ignored by the white urban press, the *Defender* was enthusiastically supported by its black readers. White discrimination also helped to launch black-owned amusements, such as dance halls, amusement parks, and a professional baseball league. Crime and vice were other forms of black business that also flourished in the ghetto.

The life spans of most black businesses were very short. Reliance on a black-only clientele was risky because of the limited resources possessed by ghetto blacks. The value of black businesses to the ghetto was also questionable. Black realtors tended to perpetuate spatial segregation. Most black businesses were so small that they employed only one or two ghetto residents. The overwhelming majority of black workers not only depended on white employers for their wages but also worked outside the ghetto. Finally, black landlords were hardly more virtuous than their white counterparts in exacting high rents and demanding prompt payment of those rents.

More lasting and ultimately more helpful to the ghetto than black business itself were the institutions founded to improve the quality of life directly. One of the major reasons why these institutions were both lasting and helpful was the presence of white financial, managerial, and moral support. In Chicago in 1891, black physician Daniel Hale Williams established Provident Hospital, the nation's first interracial hospital. Leading white Chicagoans such as industrialist Philip Armour and Florence Pullman provided the major financial support. The hospital was successful, but not as an interracial experiment. By 1915, most of the staff and physicians were black. The black doctors and nurses who came through the hospital's internship program could not find positions at white hospitals.

The organization of black branches of the Young Men's and Young Women's Christian Association was a beneficial addition to ghetto life, providing living accommodations, social facilities, and employment information for young blacks. White financial angels funded these "Y" projects. In Chicago, Julius Rosenwald of Sears, Roebuck was the white financial inspiration behind the black YMCA in that city. By 1910, black settlement houses modeled after white versions had appeared in several cities, though participation by neighborhood blacks in their educational and nutritional programs was low.

Two institutions with less immediate roots in the ghetto, the National Urban League and the NAACP, complete the list of major black self-help institutions. White sociologist Robert Park presided over the creation of the Chicago chapter of the Urban League during World War I. The League coordinated black welfare efforts, lectured in churches, and helped to organize block clubs and improvement societies; it also operated a manual-training school. Much of the League's efforts were aimed, admittedly, at counteracting white stereotypes of blacks as dirty and lazy. Further, by emphasizing improvement of the ghetto and vocational education, the League perpetuated black spatial and occupational patterns. Given the nature of white society at the time, however, it is difficult to see how other alternatives would have served blacks better or sustained white financial support.

The NAACP was, like the Urban League, a national institution with branches in most of the major cities where black ghettos existed. Mary-White Ovington, who was instrumental in the formation of the NAACP, was a wealthy heiress who dabbled in Socialist party politics. Responding to a speech given by black leader Booker T. Washington and to an article written by reformer William English Walling in 1909 on "The Race War in the North," Ovington decided that blacks' acceptance of their caste status must be changed in order for the caste itself to be broken. Calling a meeting of like-minded friends in New York, including Walling and Henry Moskowitz, a settlement-house leader, Ovington spearheaded the formation of the NAACP in 1909. The three principals in the Association's establishment were white.

The Association's early activities included attempts to broaden and enforce state civil rights legislation and a protracted and probably ill-advised legal battle to ban Griffith's film *Birth of a Nation* from theaters in major cities. With its emphasis on action combined with the growing frustrations of black urban life, the NAACP would have seemed likely to attract a wide following in its first decade. The absence of qualified black local leadership, however, hurt the organization. Blacks who had learned the necessity, if not the virtue, of self-help, found it difficult to rally around white leaders. The middle-class blacks that provided much of the ghetto leadership by World War I were more concerned with developing black businesses and advancing local institutions and political organizations. In their view, the challenge to the segregated city was apt to be a long and bitter struggle, so why not conserve energy and cultivate the resources of the black ghetto?

The average black, which meant the poor black, could not yet afford the luxury of concern over civil rights. For him and for countless other black migrants, jobs, food, and decent housing were needs the ghetto institutions could not fulfill. Yet one ghetto institution, a venerable one at that, maintained the ties to southern roots and fostered hope of another kind: the black church. Since the antebellum era, the church had espoused the self-help philosophy. With black leadership and with mostly black financial support, it was one of the few ghetto institutions that could truly call itself "black." Following the trend of white churches, black congregations offered social services to less fortunate parishioners and provided blacks with an opportunity for expression and leadership not available to them in the white-dominated city. By giving them an opportunity to come together periodically under one roof, the churches gave ghetto residents some sense of common destiny, a necessary counterbalance to the strong strain of individualism that ran through the black ghetto.

The tangible evidence of the black's misery, the ghetto, expanded and hardened its spatial boundaries between 1890 and 1920. The institutions that evolved during that time came into existence as a result of blacks' exclusion from the white urban world. Immigrant institutions, most of which had roots overseas, were organizations voluntarily formed both to ease the transition to urban America and to retain past traditions. This was not true of black institutions except for the church—a fact that probably accounted for the overwhelming support it drew from the black community. By 1920, most immigrants were beginning to make their way in the urban world in terms of occupations and residential areas. The blacks remained where they were and if they dared to challenge the status quo, frustration and physical injury would be the only certain results. Was this what southern blacks had left their homes for?

In 1908, black leader W. E. B. Du Bois wrote that the "country was peculiarly the seat of slavery, and its blight still rests . . . heavily on the land, but in the cities . . . the Negro has had his chance."[63] Although the chance was remote for blacks, the city still held out opportunities. It was possible to open a business and perhaps have some success. There was, after all, the example of Lillian Harris, who had been born in poverty in the Mississippi delta. She migrated to New York City in 1901. With five dollars she purchased a baby carriage, a boiler, and pigs' feet. With her gastronomic stock she wheeled her carriage throughout Harlem, expanding her restaurant on wheels and saving her profits carefully. By World War I, "Pig Foot Mary," as she was known, was a wealthy landlord. She eventually retired to southern California, where she died in 1929. To be sure, Lillian Harris, like David Levinsky, was unusual in her environment. It is difficult, however, to imagine such upward mobility taking place in the Mississippi delta. The city represented this opportunity, even though few blacks were able— or, more accurately, were allowed—to participate. The potential to advance remained, and, given the relative hopelessness of rural life for blacks, it is no coincidence that the blacks are the most heavily urbanized group in American society today.

If immigrants were beginning to achieve success according to their own definitions, many blacks were not. Workers of all backgrounds, however, found that the factory often robbed them of dignity, family life, and the joys of childhood. The turn-of-the-century city could be a place of great misery, with dirty streets, cold tenements, harsh schools, and few public services of any kind. But this environment also brought forth efforts to ameliorate intolerable conditions, ease the way for urban newcomers, support the destitute, and even transform the way in which cities functioned.

Notes

1. Quoted in Charles N. Glaab, ed., *The American City: A Documentary History* (Homewood, Ill.: Dorsey Press, 1964), p. 235.
2. Upton Sinclair, *The Jungle,* rev. ed. (New York: Signet, 1960), p. 41.
3. *Ibid.*
4. Quoted in Glaab, ed., *American City,* pp. 236–237.
5. Quoted in *ibid.,* p. 237.
6. Quoted in John A. Garraty, *The New Commonwealth, 1877–1890* (New York: Harper & Row, 1968), p. 192.

7. Quoted in John Bodnar, *The Transplanted: A History of Immigrants in America* (Bloomington, Ind.: Indiana University Press, 1985), p. 64.
8. Quoted in Garraty, *New Commonwealth,* p. 129.
9. *Ibid.,* p. 137.
10. Sinclair, *Jungle,* p. 84.
11. Quoted in Henry Nash Smith, ed., *Popular Culture and Industrialism, 1865–1890* (New York: Anchor, 1967), p. 279.
12. Quoted in Glaab, ed., *American City,* p. 432.
13. Quoted in Smith, ed. *Popular Culture and Industrialism,* p. 274.
14. Quoted in Herbert G. Gutman, "Work, Culture, and Society in Industrializing America," *American Historical Review* 78 (June 1973): 546.
15. Quoted in Garraty, *New Commonwealth,* p. 137.
16. Quoted in Roy Lubove, *The Progressives and the Slums: Tenement House Reform in New York City, 1890–1917* (Pittsburgh: University of Pittsburgh Press, 1962), p. 210.
17. Quoted in Glaab, ed., *American City,* p. 315.
18. Stephen Crane, *Maggie: A Girl of the Streets,* rev. ed. (Greenwich, Ct.: Fawcett, 1960), p. 29.
19. O. Henry, "An Unfinished Story," in Abe C. Ravitz, ed., *The American Disinherited: A Profile in Fiction* (Belmont, Calif.: Dickenson, 1970), p. 34.
20. Betty Smith, *A Tree Grows in Brooklyn* (New York: Harper & Row, 1943), p. 319.
21. Quoted in Glaab, ed., *American City,* p. 354.
22. Quoted in Allen F. Davis, *Spearheads for Reform: The Social Settlements and the Progressive Movement, 1890–1914* (New York: Oxford University Press, 1967), p. 137.
23. Quoted in Glaab, ed., *American City,* pp. 309–310.
24. Theodore Dreiser, *Sister Carrie,* rev. ed. (New York: W. W. Norton, 1970), p. 368.
25. O. Henry, "Unfinished Story," in Ravitz, ed., *American Disinherited,* p. 36.
26. Quoted in Alice Kessler-Harris, *Out to Work: A History of Wage-Earning Women in the United States* (New York: Oxford University Press, 1982), p. 202.
27. Quoted in *ibid.,* p. 99.
28. Quoted in *ibid.,* p. 100.
29. Quoted in *ibid.,* p. 103.
30. Quoted in James B. Lane, "Unmasking the Ghetto: Jacob A. Riis and *How the Other Half Lives,*" in David R. Goldfield and James B. Lane, eds., *The Enduring Ghetto: Sources and Readings* (Philadelphia: J. B. Lippincott, 1973), p. 156.
31. Upton Sinclair, *The Jungle,* rev. ed. (New York: Signet, 1960), p. 79.
32. Quoted in Lubove, *Progressives and the Slums,* p. 58.
33. *Ibid.,* p. 70.
34. Quoted in Glaab, ed., *American City,* pp. 289, 296.
35. Quoted in Bayrd Still, ed., *Urban America: A History with Documents* (Boston: Little, Brown, 1974), pp. 283–284.
36. Quoted in Lane, "Unmasking the Ghetto," p. 157.
37. Quoted in Smith, ed., *Popular Culture and Industrialism,* pp. 279–280.
38. Kenneth Kann, "The Big City Riot in 1877: Chicago," paper presented at American Historical Association Convention, Washington, D.C., 1976.
39. Quoted in Garraty, *New Commonwealth,* p. 144.
40. Quoted in Robert H. Bremner, "The Discovery of Poverty," in Allen M. Wakstein, ed., *The Urbanization of America: An Historical Anthology* (Boston: Houghton Mifflin, 1970), p. 243.
41. Rudolph J. Vecoli, "*Contadini* in Chicago: A Critique of *The Uprooted,*" in David R. Goldfield and James B. Lane, eds., *The Enduring Ghetto: Sources and Readings* (Philadelphia: Lippincott, 1973), p. 98.
42. Quoted in Still, ed., *Urban America,* p. 273.

43. Emily Dinwiddie, "Housing Conditions in Philadelphia's Ghettos," in Goldfield and Lane, eds., *Enduring Ghetto,* p. 74.
44. Smith, *A Tree Grows in Brooklyn,* pp. 23, 181.
45. *Ibid.,* p. 134.
46. Abraham Cahan, *The Rise of David Levinsky,* rev. ed. (New York: Harper & Row, 1966), pp. 93, 110.
47. Quoted in Gutman, "Work, Culture, and Society," p. 547.
48. Cahan, *Levinsky,* p. 3.
49. See Stephan Thernstrom, *Poverty and Progress: Social Mobility in a Nineteenth Century City* (New York: Atheneum, 1969), p. 136.
50. See Sam Bass Warner, Jr., *Streetcar Suburbs: The Process of Growth in Boston, 1870–1900* (New York: Atheneum, 1974).
51. Dennis Clark, *The Irish in Philadelphia: Ten Generations of Urban Experience* (Philadelphia: Temple University Press, 1973), p. 127.
52. Quoted in Lubove, *Progressives and the Slums,* p. 58.
53. Both newspapers quoted in Gutman, "Work, Culture, and Society," p. 584.
54. Quoted in Robert Rockaway, "Ethnic Conflict in an Urban Environment: The German and Russian Jew in Detroit, 1881–1914," *American Jewish Historical Quarterly* 40 (December 1970): 150.
55. Quoted in Gilbert Osofsky, ed., *The Burden of Race: A Documentary History of Negro-White Relations in America* (New York: Harper & Row, 1967), p. 263.
56. As told in Allan H. Spear, *Black Chicago: The Making of a Negro Ghetto, 1890–1920* (Chicago: University of Chicago Press, 1967), p. 137.
57. *Ibid.*
58. Quoted in Still, ed., *Urban America,* p. 279.
59. Gilbert Osofsky, "The Enduring Ghetto," *Journal of American History* 45 (September 1968): 243–255.
60. Gilbert Osofsky, *Harlem: The Making of a Ghetto* (New York: Harper & Row, 1963), p. 40.
61. Quoted in Osofsky, "Enduring Ghetto," p. 250.
62. Quoted in Osofsky, *Harlem,* p. 43.
63. Quoted in Zane L. Miller, "Urban Blacks in the South, 1865–1920: The Richmond, Savannah, New Orleans, Louisville, and Birmingham Experience," in Leo F. Schnore, ed., *The New Urban History: Quantitative Explorations by American Historians* (Princeton, N.J.: Princeton University Press, 1975), p. 187.

CHAPTER 8

The Age of
Urban Reform

Responses to the ills of the late-nineteenth-century industrial city took many different forms, from small acts of charity by individuals to sweeping reform movements and designs for dramatically spacious and efficient new cities. And the cast of characters was enormous, including political bosses, businessmen, middle-class women, and even a new breed of officialdom—the technocrat.

Ward Heelers and Mornin' Glories:
Urban Politics in a Diverse Society

The dynamics of urban politics were closely related to the basic patterns of city growth and development. In the eighteenth and early nineteenth centuries—the era of clusters and market places in the preindustrial city—urban politics were relatively unified, just as most city dwellers lived close together. Generally, the upper classes and the most powerful groups easily dominated these tightly knit communities. Beginning in the late nineteenth century, however, as cities began to add populations and to expand over greater territory, the various urban communities became separated. The radial center was a city of numerous distinct areas—immigrant districts, new suburbs, east side, west side, downtown. This spatial categorization was beautifully reflected in the ward system of political representation, in which each neighborhood or district elected representatives to the municipal council. Many of the conflicts in the late-nineteenth-century city were, in fact, struggles among various urban sectors for services, amenities, and influence. The political structure of the radial center was not unified but fragmented, reflecting the new spatial form the city was assuming.

The diverse urban layout was already visible in the years immediately preceding the Civil War. Service responsibilities of local government increased to meet these new spatial demands in areas such as health, roads, and public safety. But the apparatus of government as chartered by state legislatures was unequal to these new demands. In most places, an interlocking coalition of economic elites served as stewards of government, keeping taxes low and services minimal. Bosses and their machines stepped in to fill this vacuum and in effect reformed the ad hoc civic administration.

The boss and his elected cohorts were the first professional politicians—the first individuals to earn their living solely from local government. And, if we believe their reform critics, they earned a very good living from local government. If the bosses deigned to reply to this canard, they would undoubtedly point to the cities they virtually built—the sewers, bridges, parks, schools, and utility systems—and the jobs they provided. They would claim that their ward-based political system created order out of the chaos of antebellum urban administration. They would also note that their alleged peculations were fueled neither by increased property taxes nor by outlandish expenditures. The civic ledger sheets were not noticeably different during either reform or machine administrations.

Political machines varied from city to city, some drawing their energy entirely from the force of major personalities, others not at all. In fact, most cities did not have city-wide organizations that could be called machines. Some cities had political cliques, or "rings," based in a few wards. Other cities had prominent individuals who for a few years controlled various political factions. True political machines were complex organizations efficient enough to survive changing leadership and even grow over generations. Most machines maintained a chain-of-command structure that reached down into the precinct and even block levels. Some congested slums even boasted tenement captains. The lieutenants in this system were the precinct and ward bosses who were responsible for specific areas of the city.

The functional test for all, of course, was getting out the vote. Sometimes individual ward bosses hashed out compromises in city councils, and in some cities the ward bosses were themselves lieutenants for powerful citywide politicians. But virtually all machines reflected structure and organization among their major features. In fact, political machines usually cut through red tape and the confusion of innumerable boards and agencies to wrest a measure of stability and order from political chaos. As Martin Lomasny, a Boston ward leader, put it: "I think that there's got to be in every ward somebody that any bloke can come to—no matter what he's done—to get help. Help, you understand; none of your law and justice, but help."[1]

Beyond ministering to the immediate needs of their constituents, the bosses and their machines served business and financial interests by providing fire and police protection, paved streets, and low taxes and license fees—and sometimes by relaxing safety- and building-code enforcement. Many businesses sought profitable franchises for public utilities—especially streetcar lines—and public construction contracts. The relationship between business and the bosses was also based on mutual self-interest and most frequently led to bribes, inducements, promises of campaign funding, and the "boodling" that so upset the "better" classes.

Political machines also worked with illegitimate businesses—gambling and prostitution especially. These activities, deeply rooted in all major cities, in fact constituted a significant portion of the urban economy and were patronized in varying degrees by all social classes. It was the bosses' protection of this "immorality," not graft or bribery, that earned them the undying enmity of many reformers and a very high profile in American journalism. But perhaps the worst flaw of the political machine was that it made no effort to educate the electorate about complicated or serious political issues or to provide genuine political leadership. The widespread cynicism about the political process that bossism helped inspire tended to erode the rather fragile foundations of democracy. The British commentator James Bryce was so appalled by this spectacle that he declared, in 1888: "There is no denying that the government of cities is the one conspicuous failure of the United States."[2]

One fairly typical case, at least in the beginning, was the political organization in Kansas City. James Pendergast, born in a small Ohio town of Irish parents, found his way to Kansas City in 1876. From a job in a packing house, James rose to ownership of a hotel and saloon, purchased mostly with racetrack winnings. By 1891 he was quite successful, acquiring a new saloon and becoming active in local politics. Representing the citizens of the West Bottoms in the core of the city's industrial district, Alderman Pendergast worked for city parks and low utility rates while also protecting gambling and his own saloon interests and showering assistance and favors on friends and supporters. Jim Pendergast apparently did not indulge in illegal voting practices, and he hardly needed to. He was a strong representative of his constituency, and his favors were amply returned. He died a much beloved and respected community figure, at least among "his" people. In later years, when his younger brother Tom took over the organization, the Pendergast machine was expanded to include Kansas City and much of the surrounding area, with significant ties in state politics. And its tactics, which included influence peddling, graft, and bribery, made it a notorious example of malfeasance in the reformers' lexicon.

The intensively local base of the machine is also illustrated by the case of Chicago's first ward. There, "Bathhouse" John Coughlin and Michael "Hinky Dink" Kenna presided over a raucous and vital urban scene between 1890 and the mid-1920s. Like other local bosses in the city, they played crucial roles in electing and defeating candidates for mayor, but their main activity was protecting the interests of their constituents for their own survival—interests that included gambling, prostitution, and illegal liquor operations as well as legitimate businesses. Presidents, senators, and mayors came and went, but the political fortunes of Bathhouse John and Hinky Dink, and the conditions of the "Levee" district, were hardly affected.

The most famous big city political machine of the era was New York's Tammany Hall, which dominated the affairs of the nation's largest city into the twentieth century. Among Tammany's most well-known sachems was Richard "Boss" Croker, who saw the organization defeated in 1894 by a group of ardent reformers—including Theodore Roosevelt, who served in the reform administration as police commissioner—and oversaw its return to power three years later. Croker decentralized Tammany's patronage, putting more favors in the hands of the district leaders. He had no qualms about the spoils system (the practice of rewarding loyal supporters with government jobs); in fact, he regarded it as a logical and effective way of dispensing rewards and incentives for good performance. "Politics," Croker once said, "are impossible without the spoils. . . . [W]e have to deal with men as they are and with things as they are."[3]

One district leader was George Washington Plunkitt, whose exploits have been preserved in William L. Riordan's *Plunkitt of Tammany Hall* (1905). In a typical day, Plunkitt bailed a saloon keeper out of jail, assisted victims of a fire, intervened in court on behalf of six drunks, paid the rent for a poor family, secured jobs for four constituents, attended Italian and Jewish funerals, presided at a meeting of election district captains, attended a church fair, bought tickets to a church excursion and a community baseball game, and attended a Jewish wedding and dance late in the evening. In every instance, his assistance and generosity were conspicuous. Plunkitt referred contemptuously to reformers as "mornin' glories"; their appeal, he claimed, lasted only a short part of a day, while Tammany tended to voters' needs around the clock, no questions asked. Taking care of one's friends was a natural and honest act in private life, Plunkitt argued; why shouldn't he do the same in public life? And he insisted on the difference between "honest" and "dishonest" graft—a distinction many reformers would have found meaningless. According to the Tammany district leader, dishonest graft consisted of robbing the public treasury or "blackmailin' gamblers, saloonkeepers, disorderly people, etc.," but honest graft was simply taking advantage of one's position to make a living. "It's just like lookin' ahead in Wall Street or in the coffee or cotton market. It's honest graft, and I'm lookin' for it every day in the year." Plunkitt even proposed his own epitaph: "George W. Plunkitt. He Seen His Opportunities, and He Took 'Em."[4]

Reformers damned the machine for its corruption—for graft of any sort—and there was much truth in their accusations. Perhaps the most notorious instance in American politics, now raised to the level of political folklore, was the infamous "Tweed Ring" scandals in New York City during the late 1860s and early 1870s. Led by William Marcy Tweed, Tammany Hall rose from a Democratic club to a full-fledged political machine, its power stretching into every ward of the city and even into the corridors of the state legislature. A reform campaign launched in 1870 pointed to the ring's illegal voting tactics, the widespread diversion of public funds into the hands of favored supporters, and the systematic buying off of potential opponents through government contracts and bribery. Reformers managed to get inside information revealing the dimensions of the corruption and published it in highly subjective accounts of the ring's villainy. As the campaign gathered steam, Tweed was portrayed as a wicked thief, a threat to the foundations of democracy itself. Thomas Nast's famous cartoons in *Harper's Weekly* were only one weapon in the mounting attack. Eventually, in 1871, the Tweed Ring was brought down, and Tweed himself was later sent to prison.

The Tweed machine stole anywhere from $20 million to $200 million from the public treasury, and though the authorities recovered less than $1 million of it, reformers celebrated their victory as having saved New York City—and, indeed, American city government generally—from graft and corruption. Samuel Tilden was one of a number of prominent political figures who used the fight against Tammany to win national prominence, in Tilden's case a near-successful bid for the presidency of the country.

The reformers themselves were an even more varied group than their targets the bosses. The municipal reform movement of the 1890s, which led to a national reform spirit known as progressivism in the first two decades of the twentieth century, was based on firm opposition to the bosses and their machines. The progressive movement hoped to accomplish a number of suggested improvements in city government, notably fair and honest election practices, "home rule" municipal charters allowing localities greater autonomy in their own affairs, leadership by "proper" and "legitimate" representatives, and professional administration to ensure economy and efficiency in the public interest. Some reformers, like Jane Addams, Jacob Riis, and Frederic C. Howe, were genuinely committed to easing the plight of the less fortunate and to changes in the social and economic system that would accomplish these goals. Riis, especially, was drawn to the ideal of the small town, with its face-to-face contacts and human scale, as at least a conceptual answer to the complexities and confusion of the metropolis.

Other reformers, however, were not committed to real social change but rather to "purifying" the political system of disreputable elements and unwanted behavior and controlling the activities of the "lower classes." This branch of the reform movement saw foreign immigration as the source of many social ills by introducing alien customs into American culture and providing the basis—

Nast on Tweed, 1871

Cartoonist Thomas Nast was relentless in his pursuit of New York's corrupt political boss William M. Tweed. In this *Harper's Weekly* cartoon, he compared the police's attitude toward Tweed and his cronies with their treatment of a hapless thief trying to feed his starving family.

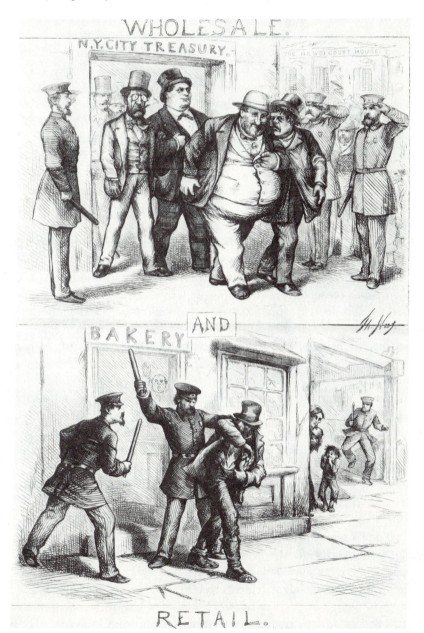

through ignorance and poverty—for the corrupt political machine. The solution, in their view, was to restrict immigration, especially from southern and eastern Europe, and to apply literacy tests, property qualifications, and stricter standards generally for voting.

Much of what we know about the bosses' activities comes from the reformers themselves and their journalist allies. Tabloid journalism, which became popular in the 1870s, delighted in the exposés of the machines, of human interest stories, of anything that would pique the interest of the public, prurient or otherwise, and sell newspapers. It is true that the bosses' performance received poor reviews. In 1867, *New York Times* editor George Jones charged that the city's government was "worse than a failure. . . . It is corrupt, inefficient, wasteful and scandalous."[5] More than a generation later, the machine's reputation had not improved. Journalist Lincoln Steffens' noted exposé of machine politics, *The Shame of the Cities* (1904), presented this unflattering profile of St. Louis municipal legislators: they were "utterly illiterate and lacking in ordinary intelligence. . . . In some, no trace of mentality or morality could be found; in others, a low order of training appeared, united with base cunning, groveling instincts, and sordid desires."[6]

The vitriol of these statements indicates something more than the usual criticism of the "ins" by the "outs." A great deal of personal dislike was involved as well. Immigrants were important cogs in big city political machines, though southern urban bosses like Edward H. Crump in Memphis and Martin Behrman in New Orleans operated successfully in cities without large foreign-born populations. Reformers were frequently, though not exclusively, white Anglo-Saxon Protestants. Immigrants were typically Jewish or Catholic. The newcomers perceived morality in individual terms, whereas Protestants tended to view morality as a standard for society. The permissive attitudes of Jews and Catholics toward alcohol, the leisurely and sometimes loud Sabbath observances by some Catholic national groups, and differing positions on child labor, education, and party politics drove a wedge between reformers and machine constituents that accounts, in part, for the relatively short life spans of most reform administrations.

Aside from the ethnic distinctions, there was the issue of behavior. Victorian Americans had a distinct understanding of propriety, especially when it was a luxury they could afford. Fashion, gestures, modes of speech, relations with women, club affiliations, occupation, and residence were all factors that went into making a gentleman. It is possible, as the city became more diverse and seemingly more chaotic, that these behavioral standards and affectations assumed even greater importance. Journalists and other commentators would often attribute outrageous statements to bosses and their colleagues and write them up in ungrammatical vernacular. The very names of machine politicians bespoke underworld rather than gentlemanly connections: Chicago ward bosses Mike "Hinky Dink" Kenna and "Bathhouse" John Coughlin, for example, as well as Tweed lieutenants Peter B. "Brains" Sweeney and Richard "Slippery Dick" Connolly did not inspire confidence in devotees of good government.

Above all, reformers perceived political machines as inefficient, out of step with both modern technology and contemporary corporate practices. Although services grew enormously during the tenure of some big city machines, the practice of letting out franchises for utilities and mass transit proved to be an open invitation to kickbacks and ineffective service. Franchise operators were more interested in turning profits to investors than in applying funds for improvements and technological innovations. They were even less interested in extending their services to poor neighborhoods. City administrators who profited from franchise decisions were not anxious to enforce or suggest regulatory measures.

In Chicago during the 1880s and 1890s, for example, railroads that received licenses to operate within the city limits ignored pleas to eliminate hazardous grade crossings. Gas companies were slow to replace worn-out pipes. The maze of overhead wires that accompanied virtually every late-nineteenth-century cityscape resulted from the refusal of utility companies to bury their lines. The numerous trolley companies did not bother to systematize and coordinate their services. City governments in the late nineteenth century were cumbersome affairs, even under the best of conditions, with limited powers, an awkward two-tier legislature laden with committees that ensured delays, and a ward-based system that made consensus difficult. Bribes were one effective means to short-circuit the contraption of government, which is one reason that franchises operated pretty much as they pleased.

The chaos at city hall stood in stark contrast to the situation at a typical corporate headquarters, where centralized management administered far-flung financial and industrial empires using the latest management techniques and technologies. The popularity of the roles of commission and city manager derived from a widespread impression that centralization and expertise would provide efficient government, especially in the delivery of services. Reformers were generally not adverse to what some referred to derisively as "sewer socialism"—municipal ownership of utilities—because a responsible government organized along modern corporate lines would be superior to the fragmented and corrupt private franchises. The wards would have to go, too, not only because they represented the growing power of ethnic neighborhoods but, even more important, because they inhibited the centralization of authority.

The Service City: A Progressive Ideal

City government, thus cleansed and turned over to the experts—so the reformers' thinking ran—would provide efficient and equitable service that would, in turn, redound to the economic benefit of the city. Progressive reformers, in fact, equated modern services and technology with high levels of civilization. A Baltimore engineer, promoting a citywide sewer system in 1905, offered Paris as an example of the benefits generated by a well-sewered city. Paris, he wrote, "is the center of all that is best in art, literature, science and architecture, and is both clean and beautiful. In the evolution of this ideal attainment, its sewers took at least a leading part."[7]

In fact, sanitary reform became a major progressive objective because it touched on so many of the reformers' themes. Advanced waste treatment facilities and clean water would reduce the incidence of epidemic disease, especially in overcrowded slum districts. These districts, whose desperate plight had been publicized by Jacob Riis, federal investigators, and novelists, frightened turn-of-the-century city dwellers. Though a bit of voyeurism was present in the public fascination with these areas, there was concern that the ailments inherent in these low environments—crime and disease, in particular—could overflow their boundaries. Sanitary reform, by improving the environment of the poor, would, according to prevailing environmentalist theory, improve the poor themselves. In turn, the rest of the city would be more secure, not to mention more pure.

Sanitary reform also represented a clear case where public intervention was absolutely necessary. The consequences of poor sewer and water systems were too grave to be left for private companies to rectify. Sanitary reform also presented the opportunity to try out new technology. Though some reformers were merely fascinated with new gadgetry of any kind in an age when technology advanced at a dizzying pace, many were genuinely interested in adapting technology for broad social ends. This was especially true of the middle-class women reformers, who viewed the sanitary city as the logical extension of the sanitary home. Historian Mary Beard expressed this connection as follows: "Woman's historic functions have been along the line of cleanliness, her instinct when she looks forth from her own clean windows is toward public cleanliness."[8]

But reformers were not the only ones clamoring for efficient and widespread services. The expanding urban middle class, bombarded by advertisements and hoping to emulate the more affluent, demanded the latest technology as well. Being old fashioned was no crime in the late-nineteenth- and early-twentieth-century city, but it *was* considered bad form. As early as the 1880s, middle-class neighborhood groups emerged, often on the poorly served urban periphery, to lobby for improved services. These groups became the shock troops of reform administrations. Baltimore mayor Ferdinand C. Latrobe noted in 1887 that "the people of a large city demand every improvement which increases the comfort of living and affords better protection of property."[9]

And, despite claims of fiscal conservatism, reformers were no less bashful than machine politicians in pledging the city's bonded indebtedness to cover current infrastructure needs. Bonds became a painless way (for the time being) to charge current expenditures against future debt. Some of these charges involved new services such as schools, waste and water treatment facilities, and bridges—items that scarcely appeared in antebellum budgets. And other services represented significant expansion of traditional urban service responsibilities, especially hard-surface streets to accommodate the insatiable desire of middle-class residents to move out from the core of the city. The extensive hard surfacing of streets that took place during the first decade of the twentieth century literally paved the way for the rapid adoption of the automobile as the preferred mode of middle-class urban transit in subsequent decades. Though it was a private vehicle par excellence, the automobile thereby received a significant start-up subsidy from local government.

The impact of the new service-oriented administrations on the urban economy in general was also significant. Cities provided a ready outlet for technology that, in turn, generated still newer technology, which created additional demand for American industrial products. Cities required iron, steel, bricks, stone, concrete, asphalt, glass, lumber, and electrical equipment. Major road and transport projects attracted huge labor forces. The 35-mile New York City subway system, completed in 1904, employed 10,000 workers and used 73,000 tons of steel and cast iron and 551,000 yards of concrete.

The Technocrat: A New Force in the Cities

The service city created a new actor in urban administration who would ultimately become more influential than either the reformer or the machine boss. This personage was the technocrat, the expert required to build and manage the new city. Technocrats were careerists who outlasted reformers and bosses alike. Their allegience was to their profession, a loyalty that crossed ethnic and public-private sector boundaries. They established procedures and guidelines, and they became the sole experts in increasingly advanced technologies beyond the comprehension as well as time and attention spans of elected officials. Some became dominant figures in their own right, bosses if you will. One observer referred to Seattle's early twentieth-century city engineer, Reginald H. Thomson, as that city's "most powerful citizen," who could "make or unmake councilmen" and "even bring the mayor of the city on his knees, begging favors."[10] Boston's health commissioner Dr. Samuel H. Durgin and San Francisco's park superintendent John McLaren wielded similar power. By the 1930s, the ultimate technocrat, New York's Robert Moses, was beginning to make his mark, literally, on that city's landscape. These were not elected officials, nor did they adhere to particular parties or philosophies apart from their zeal to build and service scientifically.

Civil engineers were probably the most important representatives of this new bureaucratic class. Their expertise was necessary for a wide range of urban services including electric and gas utilities, water and sewer facilities, and road and school building. Their training and experience enabled engineers to adopt a broad perspective on the interrelationship of services and their impact on the physical city. As early as 1877, a major engineering journal promoted this integrated viewpoint:

> If the grading, drainage, paving, cleansing, and policing of towns are worthy of careful and systematic control, so are also the general shaping of the towns, the preservation or destruction of the natural features of their sites, and the distribution of their population and residence.[11]

The writer was suggesting comprehensive city planning—that public policy should control the future expansion of the industrial city—nearly a generation before the idea attained general currency. It was not surprising that engineers were a significant part of the first professional planning association formed in 1917. They had, in effect, been planning the city for almost half a century by then.

Engineers often filled positions in newly created independent commissions or authorities such as public health boards, park planning commissions, and sewer commissions. Their work on these agencies convinced them that the city's needs had metropolitan ramifications. Engineers were among the earliest city officials to recognize the need for metropolitan cooperation. By 1890, Boston and Chicago had formed metropolitan sewage commissions in response to this need.

The broader perspective corresponded to the desire of reformers to mend the fragmentation of urban administration. Engineers perceived themselves as one of the major forces in effecting this shift, though they generally attempted to maintain a politically neutral position. At every opportunity, however, they lobbied for major public works projects, usually in the context of broader objectives. During the 1890s, for example, engineering publications stressed the importance of well-paved roads. Such thoroughfares would reduce the cost of freight handling and consequently attract new business, thereby lowering the tax rate. Engineers cultivated the belief that they knew most and best about the city, not only in physical terms but in all its increasingly complex elements. Though most city engineers belonged to the American Society of Civil Engineers, they formed a new organization in 1894, the American Society for Municipal Improvements, a progressive-sounding name that gave only a faint indication that it was a professional engineering association. In addition, most major cities had engineering clubs that included amateurs as well as professionals. These clubs published scientific reports that usually stressed the broad and indispensable perspective provided by the engineer, as in this 1894 example:

The city engineer is to the city very much what the family physician is to the family. He is constantly called upon to advise and direct in all matters pertaining to his profession. . . . He does know the character, constitution, particular needs and idiosyncracies of the city, as the family physician knows the constitutions of the family. . . . The city engineer is becoming the most important director of the material development of cities, and his office is becoming more and more a permanent one. He is thus to a certain extent responsible for holding the successive political officials to a consistent, progressive policy in all the branches of work under his charge.[12]

Engineers assured the public, especially the middle-class public, that professionals just like themselves would be running city government. Engineers were builders, and they were likely to heed the petitions of new neighborhoods on the periphery for services. Here would be another opportunity to use technology, to demonstrate expertise, to mold the future shape of the city.

Engineers were part of a general movement toward the expert and efficiency. Right or wrong, the perception that urban government was a mess led to the view that only highly trained individuals possessing the requisite technological expertise could eliminate the mess and establish an efficient administration. Not coincidentally, the appointed expert would be above the brawling politics of the ward and the saloon. The National Municipal League, formed in 1894 and dedicated to promoting the expert bureaucrat in city administration, lobbied for such reforms as at-large elections and a uniform accounting system, both of which struck directly at the decentralized political system that often supported machines.

As early as 1880, the U.S. Census Bureau began to collect data on urban services, and by 1902 it was reporting annually on municipal taxation and budget practices. The Bureau's reports enabled cities to measure their own efficiency against others. Some cities established public "think tanks" to collect data and issue reports, such as the New York Bureau of Municipal Research, founded in 1907. Numerous national publications, such as *Municipal Affairs* (1897) and *The Municipal Review* (1911), appeared to promote efficiency and technology in urban administration. One journal promised to cover for its readers "health and sanitation, street pavement, water supply, garbage and sewage disposal, public markets, municipal ownership, franchise control, city planning, charities and corrections, taxation and assessment, finance, accounting methods, home rule, and many other subjects." Another journal announced that it was "born of the need for efficiency and consecrated at the altar of information." The writer added, "We worship facts."[13]

It would be a mistake, however, to view the technocrat as another chapter in the conflict between bosses and reformers. Students of this period have overplayed that conflict to begin with. Some "bosses"—strong leaders of effective urban political organizations—worked for change. These "reform bosses" included Tom L. Johnson of Cleveland, Samuel "Golden Rule" Jones of Toledo, and Hazen Pingree of Detroit. Johnson called for public ownership of utilities while overlooking the evils of the saloon and the gaming table; much of his support came from the foreign born of Cleveland's West Side. "Golden Rule" Jones was opposed by virtually every business leader and newspaper in Toledo, but he instituted the 8-hour day in several city departments, increased public services, and favored municipal ownership of utilities. Hazen Pingree focused his fire on the corruption of big business and excessive utility rates, and—like most other urban leaders—he supported "home rule," or the independence of municipalities from the domination of state legislatures. Pingree's organization was based on a largely immigrant, lower-class constituency, and its methods included threats of economic reprisal and the use of code inspectors and city contracts as means of ensuring political loyalty.

In most smaller cities, local machines composed of "professional politicians" simply did not exist. Especially in the South and West, which did not experience substantial foreign immigration and industrialization, the big city political model was far less likely to emerge. There were exceptions—like Memphis, New Orleans, and San Francisco—but in most of the smaller towns outside the in-dustrial belt business leaders and even the local gentry were likely to hold office and have the major voice in municipal affairs. In southern mill towns and in-dustrial towns everywhere, the major political force was not a political machine but a corporation. And in the South blacks were severely limited by law and custom from any effective political participation.

Progressives wrote sensational exposés about their adversaries, and the stories make good retelling. The bosses, after all, were colorful characters. But neither bosses nor reformers occupied city hall for significant lengths of time. A more accurate, if mundane, portrayal of municipal government in the era of great cities allows greater recognition of the expert, the technocrat who persisted while bosses and reformers came and went, and who was instrumental in build-ing the service city—a city that provided a broad range of services to its citizens.

The search for order and efficiency reflected in progressive political reform had its counterpart in the social arena. There the emphasis on technical exper-tise, systematic study, and organization prevailed as well.

Helping the Other Half: Housing the Urban Poor

Tenements were among the most notorious contributors to the unwholesome living conditions of the poor, facilitating overcrowding in poor neighborhoods. Because the land in these districts was close to the central business district, it was expensive. To get the most out of the lot, a builder had to cover virtually all of it with the structure and pack as many apartments as possible within the five or six stories allowed by law.

By the 1870s, it was clear that the builder's quest for profits had to be balanced by the right of poor people to decent housing. Accordingly, a trade journal, the *Plumber and Sanitary Engineer*, announced a competition in 1878 for a tenement design on a 25 × 100 foot lot, the size of a typical lot on which builders constructed their tenements. The winning design would have to show the attributes of providing safety and comfort for the tenant as well as profit for the builder.

Architect James E. Ware won the competition with a design that came to be called the *dumbbell* tenement. The building was five or six stories high and contained fourteen rooms on a floor, seven running in a straight line on each side. There were four families to a floor. A stairwell dominated the center of the building; light came from windows overlooking an air shaft. City authorities were so impressed with the design that they required every tenement bedroom to include a window for ventilation, and thus the dumbbell, with apartment bedrooms overlooking the air shaft, was codified.

The dumbbell tenement turned out to be a very dumb idea. The coveted windows overlooked an air shaft 28 inches wide and enclosed on all sides. The air shaft provided no ventilation; instead, it was a real health and safety hazard. The shaft was a convenient duct for flames to leap from one story to the next and a garbage dump that reeked with foul odors, especially in the hot summer months. It was also an excellent echo chamber for noise. So much for the windows; the building itself occupied nearly 90 percent of its lot, so landscaping and recreation areas were impossible. Finally, the bedrooms, despite the "amenity" of the window, were tiny alcoves measuring at most 7 × 8½ feet in size. Clearly, future attempts to house the poor would have to take less account of builders' profits.

The housing reform movement really began when the failure of the dumbbell tenement became widely apparent in the 1880s. Housing held a particular fascination for reformers because they believed that many of the evils of poverty stemmed from the environment created by poor housing. The concern over housing was part of a larger trend toward viewing poverty from an environmental perspective. The early-nineteenth-century view of poverty as an inherent moral failing that was virtually insoluble had been replaced by a more professional attitude that stressed causes beyond the control of the poor. Because people could alter their environment, poverty could be solved through environmental reform. With this view in mind, an army of college-educated men and women began to probe the environment of the poor, collect data, and urge legislation based on their findings. The spatial isolation of the poor in separate residential districts was evidence in itself of the impact of environment. Housing, as the

A Dumbbell Tenement in New York City, c. 1900
The air shaft, the most attractive feature of the award-winning dumbbell design,
extended five stories and "lit" forty-five windows.

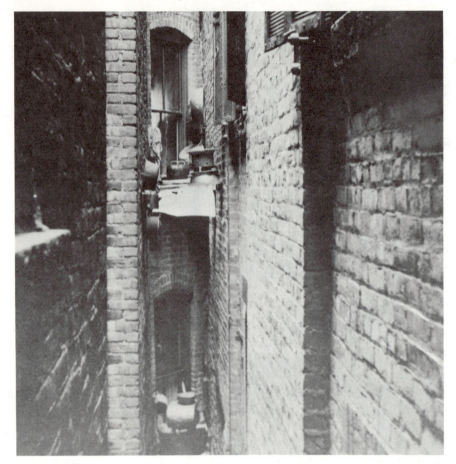

most visible feature of that spatial isolation, naturally received the greatest attention of the new professional reformer.

A chorus of reformers agreed that the environment in general, and housing
in particular, was the major cause of urban poverty. Federal investigator Carroll
Wright summarized his tour of slums in a dozen cities during the 1890s by
concluding that "bad housing is a terribly expensive thing to any community. . . . It explains much that is mysterious in relation to drunkenness, poverty,
crime, and all forms of social decline." [14] Novelist Stephen Crane explained that
his novel *Maggie: A Girl of the Streets* (1893), about a young girl who grows up
in the slums and eventually becomes a prostitute, was written "to show that

environment is a tremendous thing in this world, and often shapes lives regardlessly."[15] Crane was especially concerned about the impact of the tenement on children. Urban reformer Felix Adler probably summarized the relationship between housing and human behavior most succinctly and pointedly: "Squalid houses make squalid people."[16]

The course of action seemed clear: improve the housing of the poor, and the poor will improve. Some attempts, though well meaning, were unsuccessful. Because private enterprise built the tenements, any housing improvement scheme would have to ensure a margin of profit for builders. The so-called model tenement movement was an example of good intentions and meager results. In 1877, Brooklyn realtor Alfred T. White completed a series of model tenements built around courtyards that served as recreation space. Reading rooms and baths were some of the development's attractions. The buildings were safe, clean, and well constructed. Unfortunately, although rents were modest and White sought only a 5 percent yearly profit from his development, they were still priced beyond the reach of the poor. Most of the tenants were, at the least, skilled workers and nearly all were white and native born. Finally, though White indeed made his 5 percent return, his colleagues constructing regular tenements reaped profits of at least 10 percent. There was little incentive, outside sheer philanthropy, to construct model tenements and, in any case, few of the poor could afford to live in them.

Reformers turned instead to controlling regular tenements through legislation. New York City became the leader in the housing reform movement. The city not only had the worst housing conditions in the country but would come to have the nation's most humane housing laws. Lawrence Veiller, a product of New York's City College, was the architect and moving force behind much of this legislation. Veiller was deeply committed to restrictive legislation as the method of providing decent housing for the poor, and his philosophy was codified in the New York Tenement House Law of 1901. The triumph of that legislation was the prohibition of the notorious dumbbell tenement. The law also limited tenements to five stories, required a bathroom for each apartment, and included strict fire protection measures. Veiller had little patience with those reformers who recommended broader, more indirect solutions to the city's housing problems such as improved transit facilities to disperse the poor, new communities beyond the urban periphery, construction of model tenements, and tax reforms to redistribute wealth. As Veiller argued:

> We must get rid of our slums before we establish garden cities. We must stop people living in cellars before we concern ourselves with changes in methods of taxation. We must make it impossible for builders to build dark rooms in new houses before we urge the government to subsidize the building of houses. We must abolish privy vaults before we build model tenements.[17]

Veiller's philosophy of restrictive legislation as the major element of housing reform reached beyond New York to influence other cities. Actually, the five-story tenement was not the typical slum housing in cities across the country. Philadelphia, for example, had what housing investigator Emily Dinwiddie called "horizontal tenements." Very little of Philadelphia's housing stock was built for the express purpose of housing the poor. Instead, the poor lived in small alley and row houses. Living conditions, however, were similar to those in the worst accommodations in New York. In one three-story row house, for example, thirty-three people lived in seventeen rooms, only one-third of which were bedrooms. The alley houses were smaller and equally as bad. Dinwiddie recalled that the houses "had cellars flooded with sewage . . . the foul water standing about a foot deep in all but one of the buildings. Often the walls were overgrown with mould from the moisture, as well as tapestried with cobwebs and thick with dust and dirt."[18]

In Chicago, one- or two-story houses were common dwellings for the poor, as they were in Buffalo. Conditions were the same regardless of architectural variation. Thus, other cities were able to apply Veiller's principles on the importance of regulating conditions and hazards *within* buildings. In order to promote the passage of uniform building codes throughout the nation, Veiller founded the National Housing Association in 1910.

Many reformers, however, believed that the emphasis on building codes was too narrow a focus. Environmentalists wondered whether—because legislation changed only the interior of buildings while the slum neighborhood itself remained the same—the poor would ever be released from poverty; they could be released from bad housing, perhaps, but not necessarily from poverty. The young men and women who formulated and implemented a wide range of urban reforms from politics to poor relief were convinced that the roots of urban poverty were many and that they lay deep within urban society.

The basic premise guiding these reformers—men and women of mainly middle-class, native-born parentage, who believed that just as their country had a mission to bring democracy to the dark corners of the earth, so they had the duty to bring a decent life to the benighted sections of the city—was that the spatial isolation of the poor had created an environment, that in turn had produced a multitude of deviant effects, including poverty. Indeed, the descriptions of slum dwellers rampant through the literature of the period paint a picture of an almost subhuman race. Edward Bellamy's account of such a neighborhood in Boston in his reform novel, *Looking Backward*, was typical:

> As I passed I had glimpses within of pale babies gasping out their lives amid sultry stenches, of hopeless-faced women deformed by hardship, retaining of womanhood no trait save weakness, while from the windows leered girls with brows of brass. Like the starving bands of mongrel curs that infect the streets of Moslem towns, swarms of

Philadelphia Slum Houses, 1896

The dumbbell design was not typical of most slum housing in the country. The poor in major cities tended to live in small alley or row houses, like the three-story houses shown here.

half-clad brutalized children filled the air with shrieks and curses as they fought and tumbled among the garbage that littered the court-yards.[19]

A hint of fear is evident in Bellamy's remarks, and indeed some historians have alleged that fear of the poor was perhaps one subconscious motivation of the reformers. For a person who had spent only a generation in the city, the changes that had taken place must have seemed enormous and threatening—foreigners and blacks pouring into the city, massive industrial plants dominating the urban landscape, and neighborhoods of misery and despair developing near the urban center. In 1871, Charles Loring Brace, a pioneer in the treatment of juvenile delinquency, wrote *The Dangerous Classes of New York,* a book whose title summed up Brace's view of the poor. Brace warned that if "the civilizing influence of American life fails to reach them [the poor] . . . we should see an explosion from this class which might leave this city in ashes and blood."[20]

That some reformers may indeed have been motivated by fear should not diminish the positive remedies they sought. One reaction to fear, of course, is flight. The reformers, on the contrary, stood their ground and fought to make their city and its people better. The relationship of fear to the reform movement is important, however, in providing a major clue to why these men and women did not seek to overhaul society (though they recognized society's complicity in producing a poverty class), but rather attempted to relieve the plight of the poor by working within the system they wanted so dearly to maintain. The programs they sponsored reflect this simultaneously progressive yet conservative ideal.

Many of the ideas for the reformers' programs originated in England, indicating the reformers' own educational background. In 1869, the numerous charities of London had joined to form one large organization to systematize the business of philanthropy and bring it under the control of professional social workers. The consolidation and professionalization movement spread to the United States, and in 1878 charities in New Haven and Philadelphia formed Charity Organization Societies (COS). New York, Boston, and other cities soon followed. The consolidation of antebellum charities had proved to be only a temporary phenomenon, for by 1878 Philadelphia had nearly 800 charity groups. Unlike the antebellum consolidation, the COS did not provide relief but rather functioned as a clearing-house for the city's charities. The COS was also intended to promote "scientific" charity "with least waste and with greatest efficiency."[21] Like steel production, charity had become a business complete with its own chamber of commerce.

A significant contribution of the COS was its employment of professional case workers. Because the COS itself did not dispense charity, the case worker's primary function was investigative, in the words of social work pioneer Mary E. Richmond, to bring about "better adjustments in the social relationships of individual men, women, or children."[22] The case worker would accomplish this ideal by discovering the basic reasons for a family's or an individual's poverty and then removing those causes, with financial assistance being only one of several options. As one historian has observed, the COS believed that "the very concern shown by a benevolent community would be of more value to the worthy poor than the actual material assistance dispensed."[23]

Social workers presumed a direct connection between the slum and their clients' difficulties. Their investigations showed, not surprisingly, that environment was a major cause of poverty. One obvious solution would be to disperse the poor throughout the city. Logistically, this was impossible because the poor, including the working poor, constituted half the population of some cities. Philosophically, it contradicted the basic conservatism of the reformers, who did not seek to destroy but merely to modify the slum. They emphasized, therefore, the concept of neighborhood reconstruction.

The settlement house was the indispensable element of the new reform movement. Another concept borrowed from England, it was to be the reformers' beachhead in the slum. Whereas case workers visited slum neighborhoods occasionally, the settlement worker actually lived in them. The settlement house was designed as an all-purpose community center: a home to those who were homeless or whose home lives had disintegrated; a school for those who wished to learn subjects ranging from stenography to Shakespeare; and a clubhouse for those who sought friendship and recreational activities. In short, the settlement house was its own self-contained neighborhood environment, in, but not of, the slum environment.

Although New York's Neighborhood Guild, established in 1886, was the first settlement house in the country, Chicago's Hull House, founded in 1889 by Jane Addams, a young Rockford (Illinois) College graduate, was probably the most famous. Addams had visited settlement houses in England and was convinced that the idea would work well in American cities. Like so many young and relatively affluent women college graduates of her day, Addams was restless because the opportunities available to educated women were so limited, and she resolved to devote her energies to the newly opened field of social reform.

Hull House was a rambling old residence that had been built a generation earlier in what was then a Chicago suburb. The new settlement was adjacent to clusters of at least five immigrant groups. In the neighborhood itself, according to Addams, "the streets are inexpressibly dirty, the number of schools inadequate, factory legislation unenforced, the street-lighting bad, the paving miserable . . . and the stables defy all laws of sanitation." The area, in short, seemed to be the perfect place for a settlement. Addams set as her goal "to preserve and keep for them [the poor immigrants] whatever of value their past life contained and to bring them into contact with a better type of American."[24] Thus, the settlement house appreciated the immigrants' cultural heritage and at the same time sought to balance it by introducing them to a better environment than the one in which they lived.

Hull House was a great success and quickly became a neighborhood institution. On Saturday evenings, for example, Italians and their families were guests of the house, where they came to settle legal disputes and employ Addams as an arbiter in their frequent wars of vendetta. Hull House also catered to native-born Americans, who formed a house club, the Young Citizens' Club, that discussed municipal issues. A few years after opening Hull House, Addams renovated an adjacent saloon and transformed it into a gym. She began a day nursery as well. Eventually, she even arbitrated a strike at a nearby knitting factory. Addams was careful to point out that the house's activities were not philanthropy but were meant rather to recognize the aspirations of the poor and provide them with the means of attaining those aspirations. Indeed, only in emergency cases did the settlement house dispense charity. Addams felt that the settlement worked at its best for people at the subsistence level—the working poor—rather than with the more hard-core cases of poverty. This distinction set the settlement apart from the COS, which dealt with all types of poverty, especially the most serious cases.

The settlement idea soon spread throughout the country. By 1900, there were more than a hundred settlement houses in poor neighborhoods in all of the major cities. Settlements became active participants in neighborhood life. Besides providing an array of services and facilities, settlement workers pressed for legislation to ameliorate the slum environment. They were often valuable consultants to legislative bodies and some became founders of national reform organizations like the NAACP. In 1908, Jacob Riis paid this tribute to the settlement house:

> The settlement . . . cleaned the streets. It brought the mortality among the tenements' babies down to the lowest mark, and . . . it made odious the very name of slum. . . . When today we have to fight for the things that make for the city's good . . . we fight no longer for but with the people. And this is the settlement's doing.[25]

Despite their successes, the settlements were still an external force to the poor community, especially in immigrant neighborhoods. As one immigrant declared: "No outside agency can undertake to tell my people what to do."[26] Immigrant men particularly distrusted settlement workers. Also, whether foreigner or native born, the poor stood on the other side of a social gap that proved difficult to bridge. The wife of a young settlement worker became friends with a woman who lived nearby. They shared the common experience of having both given birth on the same day, so they exchanged anecdotes daily on the progress of each baby. It soon became apparent, though, that the baby of the poor mother was not as healthy as his more well-to-do counterpart. When the settlement worker's wife suggested a particular brand of milk to improve the sick baby's health, her friend replied sadly, "Yes, but that costs too much." As the settlement worker recalled this incident, he noted with a certain amount of despair that "here at one blow was cut away all common ground between them. How could they pretend to help the family . . . when the conditions under which they were living were so different, when they were not on the same economic basis at all."[27]

As reformers realized the shortcomings of settlements, they used the houses in conjunction with other programs that would improve the neighborhood environment more directly in the short run. Recreational facilities became a concern for neighborhood reconstructionists when investigations revealed the high densities prevalent in slum districts. Settlements and religious institutions attempted to fill this void but could not provide the necessary outdoor activities. Reformers hoped that appropriate recreational facilities would lure the poor from the "unsavory" entertainment environment that existed in slum neighborhoods. The great parks, however, located on the urban periphery, were generally beyond the access of the poor. With space at a premium in the slums, reformers pushed successfully for the attachment of a park-playground to the neighborhood public schools.

The emphasis on recreation revealed the reformers' desires to protect children from the negative impact of the slum environment. This concern led to a major educational reform effort that would transform public education from an essentially educational institution to a tool for environmental reform. The broad outlines of the reformers' hopes were summarized by Jacob Riis. "When the fathers and mothers meet under the school roof as in their neighborhood house, and the children have their games, their clubs, and their dances there . . . that day the slum is beaten." The neighborhood public school would thus be something like the medieval church—"the visible symbol of the community's solidarity, the transmitter of its ideals and values."[28]

To this end, reformers were responsible for inaugurating a series of programs in the public schools. Public education of some form or other had been available in most cities before the Civil War. But the rapid influx of immigrants and newcomers from the countryside, as well as the demands of the new corporate workplace, generated a considerable amount of interest in education as a means both for advancement and for shaping the character and attitudes of future citizens and workers. As with moral reform, the school attracted the attention especially of middle-class women, who viewed it as an extension of the home. In 1900, for example, women's clubs in North Carolina cities launched a statewide program to improve the esthetics of school buildings, upgrade teacher salaries, and provide a broader curriculum. They also lobbied against child labor. These efforts were performed mostly on behalf of white students, but elsewhere different races and ethnic groups were very much on the minds of school reformers.

The modern urban public school system emerged between 1880 and 1920. Kindergartens, age-graded elementary schools, junior highs, a range of curricula including vocational education, parent-teacher associations, school lunch programs, and school nurses were some of the innovations that became standard elements in American education. Though few today would question their value, the motivations behind many of these programs indicate that sound pedagogy was sometimes a subsidiary objective. The kindergarten, for example, another

European innovation that fared well in American cities, was a turn-of-the-
century "head-start" program designed to remove the child from the tenement
environment as early as possible. The purposes of the kindergarten were thus
primarily moral rather than educative. As Jacob Riis contended, the kindergarten would "rediscover . . . the natural feelings that the tenement had smoth-
ered."[29] Besides the kindergarten, slum schools received an array of vocational
courses meant both to discipline poor students and prepare them for productive
adult lives. For the first time, women, both immigrant and native born, received
systematic vocational education in areas such as domestic service, cooking,
dressmaking, and millinery work that reinforced their segregation in the workforce. Both the kindergarten and vocational curricula were conservative measures, the former designed to inculcate society's values at the earliest possible
age and the latter to point slum children toward careers in the manual trades.
Despite this conservatism, many of the reformers' accomplishments in public
education benefited students in the long run. The evolution of public education
during the early twentieth century was, in fact, a series of compromises forged
among Protestant reformers, professional educators, working-class and ethnic
parents, and students.

Most of these educational innovations took place in the great cities of the
Northeast and Midwest. Public education lagged in southern cities for several
reasons. First, there was not enough money. Reforms were expensive and the
South remained a poor region well into the 1940s. Also, what little money was
available went to support two school systems, one black and one white, with
the result that both races, but particularly blacks, were shortchanged. Southerners also held ambivalent views about education. Free thought was not a prized
commodity in a region that believed in the sanctity and immutability of white
supremacy. In this view education, especially northern innovations, was more
likely to confuse than enlighten. Also, child labor was an essential commodity
in the numerous small textile communities. Though many mill towns provided
schools, not many children went beyond the sixth grade, and few working-class
families saw the utility in losing income in favor of continued education.

Black children probably suffered the most under these circumstances, often
passing by decent white schools on their way to dilapidated black schools. In
turn-of-the-century Atlanta, for example, appropriations for white schools outstripped black school appropriations by more than eight to one. In small communities, blacks had to provide school buildings themselves, and black teachers
rarely had more than an eighth-grade education. In Atlanta in 1900, five
schools, the newest of which had been built in 1880, served 40,000 black
children.

Blacks and immigrants were part of a larger flow of citizens into and out of
urban America. Geographic mobility had been a part of urban life since the

colonial era. But again, the scale of this movement by the late nineteenth century was unprecedented. During the 1880s, for example, almost 800,000 people moved in and out of Boston to produce a net increase of 65,000. This wholesale mobility doubtless contributed to a widespread perception of chaos, but the moves were as purposeful as always and resulted in a metropolitan sorting of class, race, and ethnicity. A major consequence of this sorting out was the development of distinctive city centers and radial suburbs.

Radial Suburbs

The expansion or decentralization of the urban population accelerated during the late nineteenth century. The rapid population growth of suburbs—in simplest terms, new or smaller communities close to the city but beyond the city limits—attested to their popularity. As early as 1873, Chicago boasted nearly a hundred suburbs with a combined population of more than 50,000. Boston's suburbs grew dramatically from 1870 to 1900, from a total population of 60,000 to 227,000. And smaller cities like Cleveland, Richmond, Memphis, Omaha, and San Francisco also sprouted large populations in outlying communities.

Though some historians have attributed this process to advances in transportation technology, especially during the 1890s, the patterns of decentralization had already been well established by that time. Without discounting the impact of the electric trolley, several other factors contributed to the radial movement to the urban periphery. First, as commercial and institutional uses crowded into an expanding downtown, the movement outward for residential uses was inevitable. Because the newest homes with the most land were available on the periphery, these locations became popular, especially as businesses moved out toward the periphery as well. Manhattan, for example, registered 1,300 single-family housing starts in 1886 and 40 in 1904. Almost all new residential construction in the city by the latter date occurred in apartment housing. Second, as blacks and immigrants spilled over into residential districts near downtown, the central part of the city became a much less desirable area in which to live. The ideals that had promoted suburban growth earlier in the century—privacy, esthetics, and home ownership—were even more relevant in the diverse city of the late nineteenth century. Finally, the growing power of government, the increase in the size of financial and insurance institutions, and the growing professionalization in fields like education and social work produced a substantial new middle class possessing modest affluence. The movement outward, heretofore primarily made up of executives, now was swelled by civil servants, teachers, and insurance agents. These new arrivals sought to legitimize their positions in society with a home, a traditional hallmark of urban success.

The new middle class also wanted to enjoy the latest service technologies and architectural innovations. They demanded hot water heaters, central heating, flush water closets, paved roadways, and the latest drainage systems—especially after 1890, when water carriage sewers became popular. Perhaps most important, they sought environments conducive to family life, environments that offered the protection and privacy necessary to nurture that life. The city, in their view, did not offer this possibility. As one suburbanite advised his city friends, "if you want to bring up a family, to prolong your days, to cultivate the neighborly feeling . . . leave your city block and become like me. It may be a little more difficult for us to attend the opera, but the robin in my elm tree struck a higher note and a sweeter one yesterday than any prima donna ever reached."[30]

Certainly the Russells of Short Hills, New Jersey, would endorse this sentiment. Short Hills was a railroad suburb 18 miles from New York City, founded in 1877. William Russell and his wife, Ella Gibson Russell, were typical of the early residents. They moved from Brooklyn to Short Hills with their six children, seeking a "pleasant, cultured people whose society we could enjoy" and a cure for Mr. Russell's rheumatism. Russell, who owned and managed a small metal brokerage in New York, described himself as a "clean liver" who enjoyed gardening, reading, and socializing with his new neighbors. Ella Russell cared for the six children with the help of a servant, but also found the time to belong to several clubs and charities, including a settlement house in a nearby community. Apparently, the country atmosphere proved helpful both for Mr. Russell's health and his family's happiness.

The basic design principles of the Russells' home followed the advice that sisters Catherine Beecher and Harriet Beecher Stowe presented in their suburban home Bible, *American Woman's Home* (1869). Mrs. Russell was transformed from a housewife to a "domestic scientist," ensuring the cleanliness of her home as well as selecting the appropriate furnishings to impart a warm, cozy atmosphere. Beecher and Stowe organized their kitchen for expedient and hygienic work. Built-in cupboards, drop-leaf tables, metal work surfaces, cement or tiled floors, and ample lighting and ventilation fulfilled these objectives.

Beecher and Stowe, through numerous editions of their book, applied the latest technologies, such as central heating, to rearrange household space. They located the utility hardware in a central core, freeing wall areas for other functions. Also, because the new technology had removed the necessity of designing small, compact rooms, each with a fireplace or stove, they opened up the first floor and reduced the number of rooms to encourage the family to pursue their individual activities in a common space. Gone were parlors and reception rooms. The rigid spatial segregation of the sexes disappeared as well. Such standards as the children's wing, the male "smoking room," and the female parlor were not included in the new allocation of space. The single-family suburban home would eventually, during the early years of the twentieth century, receive its ultimate expression of domestic togetherness in the designs of Frank Lloyd Wright.

The Russells especially enjoyed the Athletic Club grounds, where the entire family and not just the male head of household (another innovation) could play tennis, swim, or skate. Because the community bordered on undeveloped woodland traversed by trails, by the 1890s, "wheel clubs" appeared to organize families for bicycle outings.

The emphasis on family togetherness also reflected the changing role of men in late-nineteenth-century society. Stowe, especially in her late novels, ridiculed the patriarchal ideal and praised those fathers who took active roles in childrearing and participated fully in the family's leisure activities. Women's roles also broadened, as in the club activities that Mrs. Russell enjoyed. Husbands and wives were now more companions than rivals or separate units in the family setting, and the suburban home and community were the spatial reflections of these roles.[31]

Increasing numbers of suburbs like Short Hills appeared along commuter rail lines in the decades after the 1870s. The expense of commuting restricted the social composition of these communities. Some, like Chestnut Hill, on the outskirts of Philadelphia along the Pennsylvania Railroad, were elegant recreations of English country estates. In fact, in the names of streets, clubs (the first American golf club, founded in suburban Yonkers, New York in 1880, was called St. Andrews), in landscaping, and in the use of Tudor façades, British themes dominated many of these railroad suburbs. Aside from the esthetic connections, these elements helped to distinguish the new communities from the ethnic enclaves of the city.

Though ties to the city remained close—these were after all *radial* rail lines— hostility to urban life was evident in both the design and composition of these railroad suburbs. The attention to privacy, as indicated by extensive lawns that were more barriers than recreation areas; the homes, often hidden, devoted internally to family togetherness; and the ethnic and occupational homogeneity of these communities mirrored the growing class segregation of metropolitan life—a process begun earlier in the century but accelerating by its end. In some areas, such as among Chicago's North Shore suburbs, regional suburban consciousness and cooperation emerged to protect against imperialist designs of nearby cities; electoral procedures were devised to avoid consolidation with the city, and restrictive covenants filtered out "undesirable" racial and religious elements.

But if suburbs were increasingly segregated from the city, it was also true that they were sharply distinct from each other. With the advent of less expensive forms of commuter travel such as the electric trolley and elevated rail lines, suburbs became accessible to more of the middle class. The social structure, architecture, and amenities of suburbs differed depending on the rail service and distance from the city, with the commuter railroad remaining the favorite of those who could afford both the time to be far (15 miles or more) from the city center, and the expense of commuting. The trolley and elevated railroads generated middle-class neighborhoods and suburbs, with densities decreasing and income increasing toward the end of the lines.

The streetcar suburbs differed markedly from the environment inhabited by the Russells and their neighbors. They were dull and predictable, reflecting the spatial shortcomings of their cities: the faithful gridiron dominated these suburbs as it had the downtown because it made subdivision much easier. Because the typical suburban landowner was middle class, he could not afford to lavish money on the preparation of his lot, especially in view of the fact that he had to bear the cost of running utilities to the lot. It was cheapest to reduce the footage of curbs, pipes, and paving. A subdivision, therefore, was likely to contain the maximum number of lots fronting on the street, which meant that the more cross streets the subdivision had, the more frontage lots it would contain and the lower the lot preparation costs would be. Esthetically, the streetcar suburb was monotonous, if not ugly. The proliferation of streets in this situation promoted one historian to remark that "there was nothing in the process of late nineteenth-century suburbanization that built . . . neighborhoods: it built streets."[32]

Sam Bass Warner, Jr.'s study of Boston suburbs demonstrated that the uninspiring spatial patterns extended to the lifestyle of suburban residents as well. Suburbs were the logical spatial extension of the segmentation that was occurring in the city. Homogeneity met the eye at every turn in a walk through one of Boston's suburbs. With 9,000 decision makers, this would seem to be an unlikely turn of events, but in what probably was their first experience with real estate conformity spelled safety and difference was risk.

The unimaginative housing styles of Boston suburbs were directly related to the cost of land rather than to the owner's esthetic sense. On the most expensive lots in the inner suburbs, multiple dwellings on small lots were common. The three-decker, a narrow, three-story detached wooden structure with one apartment on each floor, was a popular residential choice for those who sought suburbia but were able to afford only an apartment on a narrow lot with little of the pastoral beauty synonymous with the suburban ideal. Lot owners sought to protect their investments by building what was already present in an area, so that one or two architectural styles usually predominated in a given suburb.

For those who could afford larger lots and bigger homes as well as the expense of high transportation costs, living in the less dense, more distant suburbs approached the suburban ideal to a greater extent. Here the more prosperous members of the middle class built "shingle-style" houses—large, rambling houses on relatively small lots—that imitated, in style at least, the grander city mansions of the urban elite. Exterior and interior finishing work was variable, thus imparting a greater individuality to these suburban residential streets, though the decision to build a large house rather than to spend the money on a larger lot was more in keeping with an urban, not a rural, ideal.

The suburban migration impulse sorted out and segregated the dispersing urban residents, but it was also an amazingly democratic movement. The suburbs were open to virtually half of the urban population, regardless of ethnic or religious background. Thus movement outward became the culmination of a dream, especially for immigrants. The inner suburbs were known as "zones of emergence" and rightfully so, as immigrants "began to take their place in the general life of the American middle class."[33]

Transportation technology played a significant role in the evolution of these "zones of emergence" because frequent, relatively inexpensive, and reliable service directly to downtown was a prerequisite before immigrants could move out to the suburbs. Although the late nineteenth century was a fertile period for transportation innovations such as the cable car and the subway, the electric trolley had the greatest impact on urban and suburban space and lifestyle. The trolley was similar to a horse-drawn railway, except that it had no horse. The application of electricity to such a transportation mode, however, was a great deal more complicated than its description. The electric trolley or streetcar was perfected by Frank Sprague, a young electrical engineer, who employed a four-wheeled device pulled along an overhead wire to transmit the electricity to the car. He called the device a *troller*; hence the derivation of the popular name *trolley*. Sprague tried out his experiment on the streets of Richmond, Virginia, in 1888. By 1900, only 2 percent of the nation's cities had not converted their horse railway lines to electricity.

This transportation breakthrough accelerated various spatial developments in the city (see Figure 8.1). The attractions of the trolley, which was cleaner, faster, and cheaper than the horse railway, made location near its tracks a prime asset for businesses. As the trolley tracks radiated outward from downtown, commercial land uses radiated outward with it. As property values along the streetcar routes increased considerably, residential use declined, but it sometimes merged with commercial uses to form a combination store and residence, with the business located below and the residence above. This pattern extended out into the suburbs.

The appearance of commercial land uses far away from downtown was part of a larger movement encouraged by the trolley: the decentralization of busi-

An Electric Trolley in Washington, D.C., c. 1895
Trolleys provided improved access to suburban neighborhoods and recreational
facilities; their passengers were mostly middle-class.

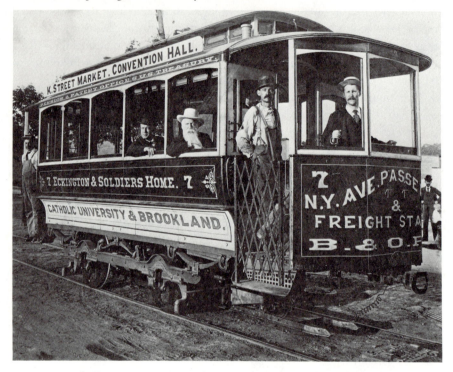

ness. As people moved outward, businesses moved also to service the peripheral
residents. Commercial districts developed along the streetcar line at the intersection of a major avenue. Outlying residents usually relied on neighborhood
stores for their daily needs, even though they still traveled to the downtown
area—only a quick and inexpensive trolley ride away—for clothes, entertainment, and the good bargains at department stores.

The streetcar companies were privately owned, often by converted horsecar
entrepreneurs who exhibited the same proclivity to speculate in real estate that
they had previously shown in the transportation business. The rapidly growing
suburbs presented lucrative opportunities, and companies extended their tracks
directly into virgin countryside to take advantage of the land uses that developed
along trolley routes. Occasionally, some trolley companies would overextend
their lines in the suburbs, hoping for rapid development that did not materialize.

Although no trolley operator would admit it publicly, his major concern was

Figure 8.1 *Spatial Expansion Along Radial Transportation Routes*
(From *Cities and Immigrants: A Geography of Change in Nineteenth-Century America* by David
Ward. Copyright © 1971 by Oxford University Press, Inc. Reprinted by permission.)

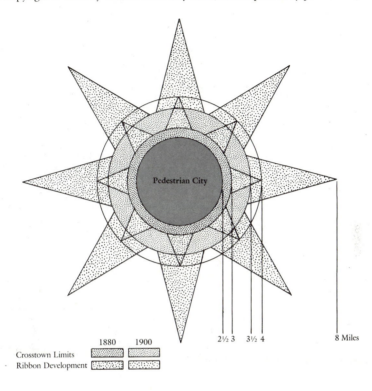

real-estate profits, not providing an efficient mass transportation system. Reformers, however, greeted the advent of the streetcar with great enthusiasm and
hailed it as the first truly *mass* transportation system the American city had ever
had. Federal investigator Carroll Wright developed an entire scenario of the
transportation of urban space in which the streetcar would enable skilled workers to move to the urban periphery, thereby relieving congestion in the central
city, reducing the demand for housing, and thus lowering rents to improve the
standard of living of the poor.

Wright's vision never materialized. Adna F. Weber, who wrote perceptively
on urban social and population trends around 1900, explained why: "Even to
the highly-paid skilled workman the five-cent fare is unduly burdensome, especially if he has a large family; to the lowly-paid laborer or sweatshop worker
the prevailing rates are actually oppressive."[34] The streetcar was the transportation system of the middle class. Its use resulted in middle-class residential de-

velopment out into the suburbs, but the residential districts of the inner city remained as congested and poor as ever. The trolley's services to the growing middle class were reflected in record patronage of mass transit. In Pittsburgh, for example, ridership increased from 46,299,227 passengers in 1890 (before electrification) to 168,632,339 in 1902, despite only a 50 percent increase in the city's population. For the inner city resident, however, a ride on the trolley was a luxury reserved only for an occasional weekend excursion out into the country, where the new amusement park offered a brief respite from life in the slums.

Although the streetcar proved irrelevant for central city residents, it was an essential component of central city business life. The radiation of the trolley lines from the downtown area attested to the continued importance of that urban space. In the early 1900s, Rich's Department Store in Atlanta boasted that no fewer than five trolley lines terminated at or near its doors. It made good economic sense for the trolley entrepreneurs to pay this homage to downtown. As the city expanded outward, exciting things were going on in its interior.

Radiant Centers

The entrepreneurial spirit that had played a crucial role in the process of urbanization since colonial times continued to direct urban affairs as the city expanded and developed an industrial economic base. Because the industrialists usually had built their fortunes from commerce, there was no drastic change in urban economic leadership. Downtown remained the focus of the city's major institutions and retained its importance as a local, if not a regional, showcase. The motto of the day remained "men and not natural advantages made great and prosperous cities."[35]

By the 1890s, however, most of the competitive economic battles matching transportation technology against natural advantages had been fought. The urban leaders and their boards of trade now sought advantage in appearance and innovation within their own community. The days of flinging railroads across the countryside were behind them. Downtown became a renewed focal point for booster activity. This did not mean, however, that the days of town building and fierce urban rivalry were gone. On the western and southern urban frontiers, scenes similar to those that had taken place during the competition for growth a generation earlier were still being played out. These city-building activities merit some mention because they demonstrate vividly that the process of urbanization was constantly being renewed. The only new feature was geography.

The catalog of new winners and losers ran westward from Kansas and Oklahoma. In Kansas during the 1870s and 1880s, boosters in towns like Abilene, Dodge City, and Ellsworth sent agents to Texas, provided a range of services, from women to credit, for cattle owners, and enticed railroads in order to get a share of the Texas cattle trade in much the same way as easterners had coveted the western wheat fields. In 1889, the greatest town promotion scheme in U.S. history, the Oklahoma land rush, began with visions of Chicago and New York dancing in the heads of prospective boosters. Rushing to make up for lost time, towns on the Oklahoma prairie sprouted waterworks, electricity, and even mass transportation within months of being raised from prairie grass.

Farther west, the railroad excited promoters as it had once tantalized eastern boosters. The extension of railroads to southern California touched off a frenzy of town promotion. As usual, frauds abounded, with one promoter successfully marketing 4,000 lots in the Mojave Desert. The area became so crowded with towns that Los Angeles County averaged one town for each mile and a half of railroad track. Los Angeles, the terminus of two major railroads, became the location of the most vigorous town promotion activities. Among the items churned out by boosters in the early years of the twentieth century were "several crimson and gold booklets . . . twenty newspapers, three volumes of scenery, two city guide books, a 200-page volume having to do with climate, twenty-seven letters from real estate firms, six motor-car catalogs, two volumes of California verse, a song book and a photograph of a citron-tree."[36]

The railroads, which had given easterners accessibility to Los Angeles and to its promoters, figured prominently in other promotion schemes for western towns. Railroad corporations that had traditionally been involved in real-estate enterprises became involved in town promotion enterprises. Railroad entrepreneur George Francis Train (his real name) dreamed of creating, as he put it, "a chain of great towns across the continent, connecting Boston with San Francisco by a magnificent highway of cities."[37] Train promoted Tacoma, Washington, terminus of his Union Pacific Railroad, as the first great metropolis in this chain. His grandiose scheme never materialized, of course, and Tacoma became indistinguishable from hundreds of other towns that owed their existence to the railroad.

Railroads were also a major force in boosting the prospects of the urban South, though their role here was less of creation than of re-creation by attracting investments from the urban core. The railroad- and industry-rich Piedmont was the focus of such efforts. Southern cities evolved an entire philosophy—the New South Creed—to pull in Yankee dollars without letting go of southern traditions. Small towns with big ambitions demonstrated their seriousness by changing names. Harmony Grove, Georgia became Commerce; Big Lick, Virginia became Roanoke. Impressed by the value of national advertising, civic leaders launched promotional schemes to enhance their city's image. The exposition became a common enterprise in the larger cities, building on a theme and showing off new buildings (such as the Parthenon in Nashville's centennial exposition of 1897) or new technology (such as Atlanta's 1909 fair featuring the automobile).

The hyperbole generated in the cities of the Old South grew into a virtual art form in the decades after 1900, the major difference being that latter-day civic leaders acted on their rhetoric, often with ludicrous results. The skyscrapers erected in the early 1900s by the civic leaders of Greensboro and Charlotte were notable less for their architectural merit than for the fact that, as Charlotte journalist W. J. Cash noted, these cities had as much need for such structures "as a hog has for a morning coat."[38]

Occasionally, the promotions paid off. In Nashville, the appropriately named Joel O. Cheek founded the Nashville Coffee and Manufacturing Company and, beginning in 1892, experimented with blending various high-quality coffee beans. The results were successful, but the blend was expensive. To promote his upscale product, Cheek persuaded the elegant Maxwell House Hotel in Nashville to serve his coffee and he used the hotel's name on his label. In 1907, President Teddy Roosevelt visited Nashville and stayed at the Maxwell House. Cheek served the coffee to the president. As he drained his cup, Roosevelt declared that the coffee was "good to the last drop," thus coining the company's famous slogan.[39]

Leaders in established cities of the urban core were thinking less of selling town lots and shilling for outside investment than in extending their national and international economic empires. As urban southerners built ersatz Greek temples and skyscrapers in an awkward attempt to attain cosmopolitan status, and as the new middle class embodied their dreams in the suburb, downtown in the urban core reflected the grandeur and power of another new group—the transurban elite.

In the era of great cities, the physical, economic, and political prowess of the city center reached its peak. In this efflorescence, the metropolitan centers rapidly overshadowed the smaller urban centers, drawing from them people, profit, and power. The centers of the great cities changed in two basic ways that sharply distinguished them from the centers of small communities: in scale and in function. The new downtown expanded out and up, pushing lingering residential uses out of the center and creating a skyline of tall monuments to business and finance. And the center included different districts—retail, corporate, and entertainment—each appealing to different segments of the urban population.

The age of the great cities was also the age of the great corporations. By 1900, consolidation in steel, rail, oil, and utilities was well underway. Entrepreneurs administered their empires from downtown, even if the factories that generated fortunes were located on the periphery or even in other cities. The major industries had transcended local operations and regional markets. As the United

States became an international power after the Spanish-American War, so did
big business. Executives became less concerned with the day-to-day operations
of cities—hence the decline in identity between economic and political elites—
and more concerned with national and international affairs that affected their
profits considerably more than whether or not the trolley franchise provided
efficient service. Eventually, the entrepreneurs' stake in urban life would be even
less as their firms increasingly joined the exodus to the suburbs after 1920, a
time when the theme of metropolitan development would shift from the radial
center to the vital fringe.

In the meantime, the wealth and power, as well as the vanity, of these business
moguls transformed downtown into a distinctive central business district with
a diversity of activities the city center would not see again. Downtown proclaimed its importance in a riotous display of light. New York's Broadway—
"the Great White Way"—glistened with electric lights so powerful that it
seemed modern technology had accomplished the impossible by turning night
into day. The hearts of other cities were similarly transformed by the coming of
electricity. In 1880 Wabash, Indiana, became the first city in the country to be
entirely lighted by electricity. Downtown businesses especially profited from the
introduction of electricity, for now their show windows could present brilliant
displays to prospective shoppers in the evening as well as the daytime.

The rapid expansion of the urban consumer market as well as the mass production of consumer goods demanded new marketing procedures. With the aid
of electricity and a good dose of the booster spirit, mass outdoor advertising on
the tops, sides, and fronts of downtown buildings as well as on billboards radiating from the central business district reminded potential customers about a
wide variety of products. The pitches were remarkably familiar: "Is your wife
pale?" a billboard inquired. "Is she discouraged, does she drag herself about the
house and find fault with everything? Why do you not tell her to try Dr.
Lanahan's Life Preservers?" Another advertisement exclaimed, "Don't be a
chump! Go and get the Goliath Bunion Cure."[40]

The introduction of electricity and popular advertising dramatized the changing profile of downtown. The central business district was continuing the process of differentiating space within its own area that had begun in the antebellum
period (see Figure 8.2). As the city itself was expanding, so was downtown,
pushing residential uses farther out toward the periphery. The financial district—banks and insurance companies in particular—experienced rapid spatial
growth during this period, reflecting its importance to the urban economy. For
regional financial centers, the clustering of financial institutions became an impressive sight in the downtown. In Atlanta, for example, the prime downtown
location, called Five Points, included no fewer than thirteen banks and insurance
companies.

Figure 8.2 *Expansion of Boston's Central Business District, 1850–1900*
Note especially the recent and extensive growth of retail land use and the expansion of
the warehouse district, which reflects the city's importance as a wholesale center.
(From *Cities and Immigrants: A Geography of Change in Nineteenth-Century America* by David
Ward. Copyright © 1971 by Oxford University Press, Inc. Reprinted by permission.)

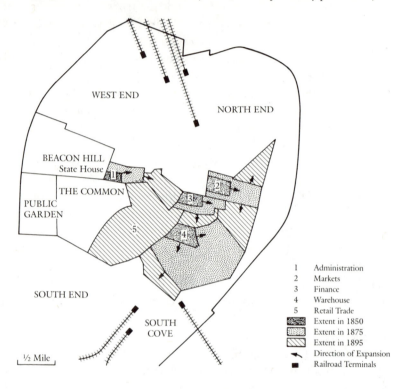

The retail district was another distinct spatial entity within the expanding
downtown. By 1900, department stores were dominating retail activity; and
when urban residents talked about going "downtown," this is the area to which
they were usually referring. The department stores typically occupied strategic
locations along the trolley tracks. Specialty shops, which displayed luxury
goods, were generally a distinct cluster, located within the retail district but
definitely separate from the department stores and their mass clientele. New
York's Fifth Avenue was probably the most prominent specialty district in the
country.

The department store had made its downtown debut earlier in the century. By the 1890s, the stores not only gave prompt, equitable service but initiated such modern lures as short-term credit, discounts, and sales. And
when Wanamaker's introduced a "Bargain Room" in 1888, other retail stores—

including Filene's famous "Automatic Bargain Basement" in Boston—followed suit.

The department store remained primarily, though not exclusively, a woman's preserve. Most of the sales personnel and customers were women, as evidenced by Marshall Field's advertising slogan, "Give the Lady What She Wants."[41] Also, as more women entered the workforce, fashion became important. Since the colonial era, a person's mode of dress reflected class and status; fine handmade clothes were available to only a small segment of the population. Despite the leveling of fashion that occurred with the introduction of ready-made garments during the mid-nineteenth century, clothing still reflected much about the wearer, men and women alike. It was one reason that many working women spent a good deal of their income on clothes. As settlement house pioneer Jane Addams explained, "Her clothes are her background and from them she is largely judged."[42] Styles changed often, and dressing in the latest versions became a reflection of status and taste as well. Department stores, as the nation's first major advertisers, encouraged these shifts, of course, and introduced them seasonally.

The department store made downtown the metropolitan focus. In the increasingly segregated American city, the department store was a democratic institution where working-class women and the wives of banking and insurance executives mingled. The big plate-glass windows and the fine interior appointments allowed everyone—from passersby to more serious shoppers—to participate in the luxury of the industrial metropolis, if only for a little while. When Marshall Field's opened its new Chicago store in 1907, it included 35 acres of selling space and a six-story rotunda topped with a 6,000-square foot Tiffany glass dome. In probably one of the few art reviews of a department store, a writer commented that the rotunda was "in a class with the nave of St. Peter's in Rome."[43]

The excitement generated by the architecture and gilt trimmings of the department store carried over to other downtown functions. Even the railroad, that smokey, noisy machine whose tracks obstructed traffic and whose warehouses and terminals took up much valuable and potentially esthetic downtown real estate, secured a new domicile that added considerably to the profile of downtown. The railroad, like other corporations, had experienced numerous mergers during the 1890s and early 1900s. Also, as both passenger and freight traffic increased, railroads and their depots clashed with other urban land uses and traffic. Major rail companies, seeking appropriate monuments and advertisements for their firms, joined forces with city governments hoping to consolidate the maze of tracks and depots. The result was giant terminal facilities that not only cleared up some of the maze, but added to the physical splendor of downtown as well. Penn Station, erected by the Pennsylvania Railroad between 1906 and 1910 on a prime chunk of Manhattan real estate, was modeled after the famous Roman baths of Caracalla. Passengers entering the 800-foot-long waiting room adorned with giant Corinthian columns supporting a high vaulted ceiling were forcibly reminded that they were entering a special world of privilege and luxury.

Outside the terminal more splendor awaited. Sumptious hotels such as New York's Waldorf Astoria, which opened in 1897, and Cleveland's Hotel Euclid, which boasted a "long distance phone in every room" and charged only $2.00 a night, compared with the exhorbitant rate of $8.00 a night at New York's luxurious St. Regis Hotel.[44] Chicago possessed the world's tallest hotel at the turn of the century, the LaSalle, twenty-two stories high with 1,172 rooms. These and similar hotels placed guests in the atmosphere of the Italian Renaissance or Louis XIV, where they could temporarily live as royalty.

Downtown also pulsed with entertainment. There were thirty-eight theaters between 30th Street and 47th Street in midtown Manhattan, where the visitor could sample everything from musical comedies to Shakespeare. Florenz Ziegfeld was presenting his famous "Follies." According to a *New York Times* review, the 1911 edition included "girls, glitter, music and rapid action," and a production number set amid "a California poppy field, with animated wheat shocks, and some extremely human-looking bumble bees."[45]

The entertainment district was a growing and increasingly important part of downtown and often tended to be its leading edge. Thus, as the theater district in New York moved northward toward Times Square and beyond, retail activities moved in this direction, too. In the 1890s, New York's principal hotels, restaurants, and theaters were clustered on Broadway between 14th Street and 34th Street. As residential land uses moved northward on the narrow island, downtown followed, led by the entertainment district. By 1900, a new theater district had emerged at 42nd Street, and new hotels and restaurants rallied around the opulent Plaza Hotel far up on 59th Street, which had been rural countryside just a half-century earlier.

As downtown was segregated into specific uses and those uses, in turn, became even more highly specialized, a new physical force was making its presence felt: the skyscraper. Skyscrapers were both a practical response to the spatial exigencies of downtown and a social comment on the nature of urban life. By the 1890s, the office building had emerged as a major type of land use in downtown. Corporate administrations needed huge staffs to keep track of their regional and national operations and downtown, as the communications and prestige center, was the logical location for corporate offices. As downtown gained in importance, however, real-estate prices rose. So precious had a downtown location become that space in most central business districts, was measured by the number of feet fronting the street. The average front-foot value in downtown Chicago, for example, rose from $500 in 1877 to $4,000 in 1891, an increase of 700 percent. With downtown real estate so expensive, it was not surprising that industries seeking to expand left the area altogether. The only alternative was to build up; this was impractical for a factory but ideal for an office building, provided that the appropriate technology was available to accomplish it.

The major technological breakthrough occurred when Chicagoan William L. Jenney constructed a steel skeleton that could support a tall building's roof and walls (previously, the use of heavy masonry had limited building heights to ten to twelve stories). Erected in 1885, Jenney's building, the Home Insurance Company, became the prototype for skyscrapers constructed in downtowns between 1890 and 1920. By eliminating the supporting masonry walls, Jenney reduced the weight of the building, drastically increased its height, and permitted greater admission of light as well as the expansion of interior space, now free of the ponderous masonry walls. At just about the same time electric elevators were perfected, and thus the skyscraper became convenient as well as practical.

The skyscraper marked the changing economy of the American city. Merchants had given way to corporation men and an economy that depended much more on mergers and capital transfers than on ships sailing the world's oceans. As the corporation and the factory dwarfed individual activity, so the skyscraper dwarfed both people and other structures. A New Yorker looking down a heretofore quiet residential Park Avenue in 1920 saw "a strange thing—an enormous office building against the back of which outlines itself the spire of a church. A big office and a little church; what a change since the Middle Ages!"[46] And, he might have added, the structures reflected a significant change in values as well.

Above all, the skyscraper was practical. It incorporated all the latest technologies and materials while saving corporations staggering land costs. Its lithe but sturdy frame provided abundant quantities of air, light, and space. The skyscraper was a cultivation of "the service to Mammon . . . with an effort to attain . . . higher artistic ideals." Practicality was the guiding principle of the Chicago School of architecture, a group of Chicago-based architects of skyscrapers and smaller office buildings. As one member of the school lectured, "Be as artistic as you can, but do not for a moment forget that you are not pictorial artists, but architects, and that your art is of little value unless you are practical."[47]

It was inevitable, however, that the architectural expression of urban values was eventually taken out of the hands of the architects by the people who really counted, the entrepreneurs. If their downtown was to be distinctive, architecture would provide the necessary panache. Ornamentation and lavishness replaced utility, with classical and Gothic façades eclipsing the simplicity of earlier skyscraper forms. The 52-story Woolworth Building, built in 1913, was probably the ultimate in the new entrepreneurial, attention-grabbing style. Louis J. Horowitz, the building's general contractor, attempted to dissuade Frank Woolworth from erecting the building, claiming it would be an economic fiasco because the expense of preparing the façade alone would never be recouped by office rents. Woolworth was unimpressed by the argument, and although he acknowledged that his building would never pay its own way, he correctly believed that it would be a giant advertisement for his five-and-ten-cent stores.

The concern with showmanship revealed itself similarly in the residential architecture of the downtown entrepreneurs. As their wealthy predecessors had erected urban mansions as physical symbols of their success, so turn-of-the-century entrepreneurs also indulged in extravagant display. This time, however, they viewed a fine home as a matter of civic duty rather than simply an expression of achievement. A Springfield, Massachusetts, journalist put the matter as a public imperative: "The rich man has no moral right to deny the community that graceful expression of his prosperity which a beautiful home conveys. . . . An ugly or mean house becomes a crime against the public."[48] Unfortunately, some leaders took their public responsibilities rather too seriously and constructed mansions large enough to house a good portion of the public, featuring such a potpourri of architectural style that any citizen could locate his or her favorite period somewhere on or in the house. The homes constructed by railroad and silver-mining tycoons in western cities reflected their additional desire to demonstrate that the wealth of the West could enable its possessors to outdo some of the most outrageous structures of the East. Such ostentation would affirm the region's urbanity despite its recent removal from the sagebrush.

It seemed evident that physical display had been elevated (or lowered) to a public art form to further the reputation of cities as well as of individual entrepreneurs. Against the backdrop of cluttered, dirty, confusing districts of one- to five-story buildings, it was but a small step from viewing a downtown skyscraper or a sparkling new residence as an important physical attribute to envisioning an entire downtown, and even an entire city, constructed in the latest and most arresting styles and ordered according to a single deliberate design. The radiant-center mystique became the guiding plan for a new vision of the city itself, befitting its economic grandeur. In its own way this new vision was as much a response to the realities of the industrial city as the settlement house or labor union. Embodied in the City Beautiful movement, the vision received its ultimate inspiration from the Chicago World's Fair of 1893.

The Columbian Exposition and the City Beautiful

The Columbian Exposition, as it was formally known, was called to celebrate the 400th anniversary of America's discovery. The idea presented itself too late for its backers to make the appropriate 1892 opening, but timing was the only aspect of the Chicago World's Fair that was not a smashing success. In contrast to the sprawling, ugly industrial cities that were becoming common at that time, the neoclassical buildings rising from blue lagoons, with their white plaster-of-Paris façades gleaming in the sun, embodied a vision of a lost utopia. Dubbed the White City, the exposition epitomized cleanliness, grandeur, beauty, and order in its architecture; the lush green lawns and groupings of Greek statuary also helped impart a classical flavor. A writer for *Harper's New Monthly Magazine* could scarcely conceal his ecstasy: "The fair! The fair! Never had the name such significance before. Fairest of all the World's present sights it is. A city of palaces set in spaces of emerald, reflected in shining lengths of water which stretch in undulating lines under flat arches of marble bridges and along banks planted with consummate skill."[49]

The fair lingered in the American imagination long after it was physically gone. Its greatest impact lay in the new perspective it gave urban leaders of the city's potential for physical beauty and the impact of that beauty on the public consciousness. Chicago architect Daniel H. Burnham, who played a leading role in implementing the physical ideals represented by the Columbian Exposition, recalled the fair's legacy nearly two decades later: "The beauty of its arrangement and of its building made a profound impression not merely upon the highly educated part of the community, but still more perhaps upon the masses, and this impression has been a lasting one."[50] No longer did the city need to be perceived as an ugly, ungainly giant; it was, rather, a beautiful, graceful physical creation of human beings. An entire city could be, in effect, one magnificent downtown.

One of the earliest manifestations of the City Beautiful effort was the municipal art movement. After the fair had demonstrated the beauty of sculptural and pictorial decorations for public buildings and parks, the Municipal Art Society of New York, a leader in the field, espoused even broader programs. They admired the broad boulevards, plazas, and monuments of European cities but could do little to impose such drastic alterations of space on New York. The society fought pollution with a similar lack of success. But the growth of local improvement societies, especially in smaller cities, heralded greater achievements in beautification. Beginning in Springfield, Ohio, in 1899, improvement societies became so numerous that the National League of Improvement Associations was formed a year later to preach "the gospel of Beauty and the cult of the god sanitation."[51]

Although these organizations stimulated numerous beautification projects, the real culmination of the City Beautiful movement was represented by two grandiose urban redevelopment plans designed to enshrine "the gospel of Beauty" on a citywide scale. The first plan began modestly enough as a proposal to improve the park system of Washington, D.C., in commemoration of its

centennial as the nation's capital in 1900. With the help of local architects, politicians, and national figures like Daniel H. Burnham and landscape architect
Frederick Law Olmsted, Jr., the modest proposal blossomed into a full-fledged
scheme to redevelop the city along the lines originally suggested by Pierre
L'Enfant in 1790.

Employing the major principles of the City Beautiful movement, the architects developed the mall as a formal open space terminating near the Capitol in
front of a plaza containing equestrian statues of three Civil War generals. The
mall would accentuate three major physical focal points: the Capitol, the White
House, and the Washington Monument. Directly west of the monument was
the Lincoln Memorial, and continuing west across the Potomac, the Custis-Lee
Mansion in Arlington National Cemetery. Borrowing ideas from both the palace at Versailles and the White City, the planners projected a long reflecting
pool with a formal park on either side connecting the memorial and the monument. With support and funding from Senator James McMillan and his Senate
Park Commission, the city of Washington today faithfully reflects the City Beautiful ideals of the 1901 plan.

Daniel H. Burnham, a leading participant in the Washington redevelopment
plan, devised an equally grand scheme for Chicago in 1909. Because it seemed
only appropriate that the site of the White City should be recast in its image,
the Commercial Club, a prestigious group of prominent business leaders, com-
missioned Burnham to develop such a plan for Chicago. With both the White
City and Paris once again serving as models, Burnham hoped to direct the attention of Chicago toward its lakefront heritage. He planned for a system of
beaches and harbors along the lake, dominated by a huge civic center. As in
Paris and in Washington, broad boulevards would radiate from this new focal
point. To relieve congestion and liberate traffic circulation in the downtown
area, Burnham included a beltway around the central business district, thereby
demonstrating that a beautiful city could be an efficient city as well: efficient
"transportation for persons and goods," especially in downtown, was a major
objective of his plan.[52] The Chicago plan was too bold, however, and although
some of its suggestions on lakefront land use were followed, most of its traffic
circulation system stayed on the drawing board.

Burnham's vision represented an important transition in the ordering of urban space. More than a city beautification plan, it included provisions for subdivision regulations on the urban periphery, requirements for railroad terminal
relocation, and farsighted statements discussing the regional impact of the reordering of urban space. In sophistication, scope, and philosophy, it was markedly
different from the beautification plans that had preceded it. The Chicago plan
ushered in a new era in the ordering of urban space and was, in essence, the
herald of the city planning movement.

Plan of Washington, D.C., 1901
This plan resurrected Pierre L'Enfant's 1790 design and recast it in modern City
Beautiful terms. Today's city still reflects the design shown here.

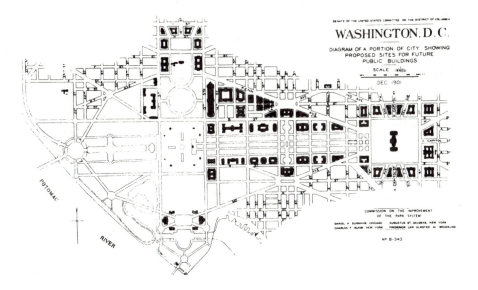

Urban Planning and the City Efficient

Business leaders, of course, had made a profession of planning for generations.
Their organizations had typically encouraged efficiency in economic affairs, the
corporation being the latest invention of business technology. Efficiency plans,
common in the new giant industries, were applied to corporate managements
and workforces alike. It was thus only a small step from orchestrating the urban
economy to ordering urban space, the physical extension of that economy. The
City Beautiful campaigns had proved that civic leaders could alter urban space
for the good, but much remained to be accomplished. The late-nineteenth-
century city was radiating outward toward suburbs that were filling up almost
as soon as land was subdivided. Some of this rapid growth had not been orderly.
Street systems, in the words of one critic, "follow the individual judgment and
advantage of the land owner, giving no heed to the advantage of the best interests of the community." The critic also deplored the rapid advance of sprawl:
"Residences go up in the remote parts of the city . . . in order to escape the
erratic tendency of shops . . . to fasten themselves upon a colony of houses . . .
only, however, to draw other small shops." The result of this leapfrogging "is a

large sprawling combination of city and village. A sharp division of localities, or even streets, according to use does not exist." The basic problem with this situation was that it created uncertainty, which, in turn, "is a direct hindrance to improvements."[53] Ultimately, property values would decline.

The expanding city required land use controls, and the City Beautiful movement was simply too narrow and its connections with enhancing economic development too tenuous to have significant impact on the ordering of urban space. By 1909, the City Efficient was replacing the City Beautiful as the guiding philosophy for those who wished to improve the urban environment through spatial policies. John C. Nolen, a Massachusetts landscape architect and planner, was a leading figure in the City Efficient movement. As one historian noted of Nolen, "the absence of beauty troubled him less than the faulty street arrangement, the condition of the waterfronts, the uncoordinated transportation, and the unsanitary and demoralizing influences of slums." In short, "urban growth . . . was too important to continue unplanned and uncoordinated, the product of countless shortsighted and selfish private decisions."[54]

The control and ordering of urban land use was a major goal of the City Efficient movement. There were few precedents for the implementation of such a program in American cities. European cities, once again, provided models for American cities groping to maintain an orderly process of growth. Since the last quarter of the nineteenth century, German cities had divided their land area into specific use districts: residential, industrial, commercial, institutional, and mixed. In the 1880s, Modesto, California, had experimented with a similar land classification or zoning scheme, dividing the city into two districts: one district prohibiting Chinese laundries and the other district permitting them. A thinly veiled attempt to confine the Chinese population to a certain area of the city, this ordinance actually had little to do with the broader purposes inherent in the German plan. For the next two decades, cities such as Baltimore, Boston, and Indianapolis passed laws limiting tall buildings to certain streets, but these too were narrower than the German classification system.

New York became the first city to enact a comprehensive zoning ordinance comparable to the German plan. The concern for orderly growth and maintenance of property values so essential to the City Efficient philosophy played a major role in developing a land-use classification for the city. The specific problem was the rapid growth of the garment industry, which had expanded out of its cramped Lower East Side location northward to other residential and commercial districts. The expansion was coming perilously close to Fifth Avenue, where the city's luxury shopping district was located. The Fifth Avenue Association, composed of the avenue's shopowners, demanded that the city prevent the incursion of the garment industry, with its towering buildings, Jewish immigrant workers, and the inevitable refuse left by industry. Because the city leaders had heard similar complaints about the potential conflict in land uses in other parts of the city, they decided that the time was ripe for a comprehensive solution to the problem. Under the leadership of Edward M. Bassett, a Brooklyn lawyer, the city drafted a comprehensive zoning ordinance that became the prototype for similar plans in 591 cities throughout the country during the next decade.

As with most reforms of the period, zoning was, essentially, a conservative land-use tool that aimed to protect property values by projecting present land use into the future. Zoning reinforced and made more rigid the highly segregated spatial patterns then emerging in American cities. Not only by segregating different classifications of land use such as commercial from residential, but also by differentiating types of residential structures such as single-family and apartment dwellings, zoning determined who was going to live where. As one historian has noted, "just as zoning had given wealthy retailers of Fifth Avenue a means of defense against the encroaching garment factories, so subsequent zoning gave suburbanites a defense against 'undesirable' activities and people."[55]

Zoning, the key concept of the City Efficient movement, was no more successful than the City Beautiful programs at solving basic urban problems. By 1917, when John Nolen and his fellow land-use reformers founded the American City Planning Institute, the forerunner of the American Planning Association, planning had come to be synonymous with spatial controls, order, and the maintenance of property values. A genuine opportunity had been missed. "Zoning could not clean slums, nor provide adequate housing for those elements of the population whom the commercial builder could not profitably accommodate, nor establish criteria for satisfactory residential environments."[56]

Some planners believed that, given the political and especially the economic realities of urban life, significant manipulation of space to provide a better environment was impossible. The creation of entire new communities where planners could apply their theories from "scratch" was an attractive alternative to tinkering with an urban environment where spatial and social problems were so complex. This was not necessarily an abandonment of the city as the site for spatial experimentation, but rather a more indirect method of relieving some of the city's problems. The new communities could serve both as testing models for methods that might be used on a larger scale in cities and as receptacles for the relief of urban congestion, which planners viewed as a serious social problem.

The Garden City: Starting from Scratch

An English social reformer, Ebenezer Howard, drew up the basic outline for these communities. Howard believed that there were natural limits to the spatial and population growth of communities and that by 1900 most of the major cities had exceeded those limits. Howard's planned "garden city," as he called it, would include the essential features of urban life, such as business, industry, and education, as well as some of the attributes of the countryside, such as public parks and private gardens. Maintaining a balance between city and country in this way would serve to control density.

Though this description sounds suspiciously like an idealized suburb, the garden city differed from a suburb in at least one major feature. Howard's community would be self-contained. Unlike the suburb, the garden community would depend only minimally on the city. Residents would work in the community, go to school there, play there, and patronize its entertainment facilities. This self-containment would relieve the burdens placed on the city not only by decreasing traffic congestion, but also by loosening the crowded living conditions in working-class districts. These garden cities would be constructed specifically to attract workers and their families. In this manner the large cities would be aired and life there would improve. Howard hoped, in short, that "the success of the new garden city would give back to the overpopulated center the fresh air, sunlight, and beauty that its own inordinate growth had largely robbed it of."[57] Thus, the garden city was as much a scheme to save the large city as it was to create a new, attractive "middle landscape" environment. In 1904, Howard and several colleagues began construction of Letchworth, outside London, as the prototype garden city. Though it was not as self-contained as Howard had hoped, Letchworth was an imaginative, attractive, and successful working-class community that still reflects its original plan today.

The idea of the garden city struck a responsive chord among some American urban reformers, who relished the opportunity to create miniature White Cities and also save the old ones. Further, it was, in a sense, an opportunity to renew the faith in city building—that great optimism that had spurred men and women to cross the ocean or the desert in search of the perfect urban environment. The first garden city constructed along Howard's outline in this country was Forest Hills Gardens, in Queens, New York, sponsored by the Russell Sage Foundation in 1909.

Forest Hills was a successful example of the benefits derived from comprehensive planning. The community was an orderly, attractive environment that included neat Tudor-style homes on spacious lots; winding roads that offered a refreshing escape from the thralldom of the gridiron; a shopping center rather than the commercial strip characteristic of many suburbs; public schools; and small parks scattered throughout the development so that families could have easy access to open spaces. Unfortunately, the planners allocated little space for industry and other employment opportunities to encourage self-containment— a major attribute of the garden city. More important, despite the rhetoric of the planners, few workers could afford the homes and lots devised for the community. As a means of decongesting New York City, Forest Hills was useless. As historian Roy Lubove summarized the experience, Forest Hills "proved nothing except the obvious—that attractive suburban communities could be created for those able to afford them."[58]

Despite continued interest in the concept of the garden city, it would be almost two decades before another serious effort was launched to create one. It did not seem feasible to construct garden cities with all their amenities and expect workers to afford to live there. In America, the emphasis was on the garden portion of the garden city and Howard's more subtle social objectives did not receive sufficient attention.

It was abundantly clear by 1920, if not before, that the city was at the cutting edge of American civilization. A "giant magnet" for people and ideas, a generator and user of the latest technologies, the city was America's future. By 1920, more people lived in cities than in the countryside. From its initial role as an unwanted intruder into America's pastoral democracy, the city had come to represent America itself. Still anchored by a vigorous downtown, it had radiated its culture, institutions, spatial patterns, and even many of its problems into the suburbs. This movement seemed at first to provide a perfect equilibrium: as the city's heart grew stronger, so did its extremities. But there were deep rents in the urban fabric that threatened to unravel the delicate balances of the radial center: poverty, the status of blacks, the conditions endured by working men and women, and the spatial segregation that seemed to create enclaves instead of community. After 1920, these trends and pressures would accelerate along a path paved by even newer technologies, as the relatively orderly patterns of the radial center gave way to those of the twentieth-century metropolis.

Notes

1. Quoted in Lincoln Steffens, *The Autobiography of Lincoln Steffens* (New York: Harcourt, Brace and Company, 1931), p. 618.
2. Quoted in Jon C. Teaford, *The Unheralded Triumph: City Government in America, 1870–1900* (Baltimore: Johns Hopkins University Press, 1984), p. 1.
3. Quoted in Blaine A. Brownell and Warren E. Stickle, eds., *Bosses and Reformers: Urban Politics in America, 1880–1920* (Boston: Houghton Mifflin, 1973), p. 25.
4. Quoted in *ibid.*, pp. 33, 35.
5. Quoted in Raymond A. Mohl, *The New City: Urban America in the Industrial Age, 1860–1920* (Arlington Heights, Ill.: Harlan Davidson, 1985), p. 85.
6. Quoted in Jon C. Teaford, *The Twentieth-Century American City: Problem, Promise, and Reality* (Baltimore: Johns Hopkins University Press, 1986), p. 15.
7. Quoted in Stanley K. Schultz and Clay McShane, "To Engineer the Metropolis: Sewers, Sanitation, and City Planning in Late-Nineteenth-Century America," *Journal of American History* 65 (September 1978): 389.
8. Quoted in Marlene Stein Wortman, "Domesticating the Nineteenth-Century American City," *Prospects* 3 (1977): 531.
9. Quoted in Joseph L. Arnold, "The Neighborhood and City Hall: The Origin of Neighbor-

hood Associations in Baltimore, 1800–1911," *Journal of Urban History* 6 (November 1979): 10.

10. Quoted in Teaford, *Twentieth-Century American City,* p. 16.
11. Quoted in Schultz and McShane, "To Engineer the Metropolis," p. 397.
12. Quoted in *ibid.,* p. 403.
13. Both quotes from Eric H. Monkkonen, *America Becomes Urban: The Development of U. S. Cities and Towns, 1780–1980* (Berkeley: University of California Press, 1988), p. 221.
14. Carroll D. Wright, "Housing of the Working People," in David R. Goldfield and James B. Lane, eds., *The Enduring Ghetto: Sources and Readings* (Philadelphia: Lippincott, 1973), p. 150.
15. Quoted in Bayrd Still, ed., *Urban America: A History with Documents* (Boston: Little, Brown, 1974), p. 284.
16. Quoted in Gordon Atkins, "Health, Housing, and Poverty in New York City, 1865–1898" (Ph.D. dissertation, Columbia University, 1947), p. 230.
17. Quoted in Still, ed., *Urban America,* p. 292.
18. Emily Dinwiddie, "Housing Conditions in Philadelphia's Ghettos," in Goldfield and Lane, eds., *Enduring Ghetto,* p. 77.
19. Edward Bellamy, *Looking Backward* (New York: Amsco, 1888), p. 198.
20. Quoted in Henry Nash Smith, ed., *Popular Culture and Industrialism, 1865–1890* (New York: Anchor, 1967), p. 200.
21. Quoted in Walter Trattner, *From Poor Law to Welfare State* (New York: Free Press, 1974), p. 98.
22. Quoted in Roy Lubove, *The Progressives and the Slums: Tenement House Reform in New York City, 1890–1917* (Pittsburgh: University of Pittsburgh Press, 1962), p. 200.
23. Michael H. Frisch, *Town into City: Springfield, Massachusetts, and the Meaning of Community, 1840–1880* (Cambridge, Mass.: Harvard University Press, 1972), p. 227.
24. Quoted in Still, ed., *Urban America,* p. 294.
25. Quoted in *ibid.,* p. 296.
26. Quoted in Allen F. Davis, *Spearheads for Reform: The Social Settlements and the Progressive Movement, 1890–1914* (New York: Oxford University Press, 1967), p. 87.
27. Quoted in *ibid.*
28. Quoted in Lubove, *Progressives and the Slums,* p. 73.
29. Quoted in *ibid.,* p. 74.
30. Quoted in Still, ed., *Urban America,* p. 259.
31. For the discussion of the Russells' suburban life, see Mary Corbin Sies, "The City Transformed: Nature, Technology, and the Suburban Ideal, 1877–1917," *Journal of Urban History* 14 (November 1987): 81–111.
32. Sam Bass Warner, Jr., *Streetcar Suburbs: The Process of Growth in Boston, 1870–1900,* rev. ed. (New York: Atheneum, 1974), p. 158.
33. *Ibid.,* p. 66.
34. Quoted in Still, ed., *Urban America,* p. 256.
35. Quoted in Carol E. Hoffecker, *Wilmington, Delaware: Portrait of an Industrial City, 1830–1910* (Charlottesville, Va.: University Press of Virginia, 1974), p. 39.
36. Quoted in Still, ed., *Urban America,* p. 227.
37. Quoted in John W. Reps, *The Making of Urban America: A History of City Planning in the United States* (Princeton, N.J.: Princeton University Press, 1965), p. 402.
38. Quoted in David R. Goldfield, *Cotton Fields and Skyscrapers: Southern City and Region, 1607–1980* (Baton Rouge: Louisiana State University Press, 1982), p. 130.
39. Joel O. Cheek's story is told in Don H. Doyle, *Nashville and the New South, 1880–1930* (Knoxville: University of Tennessee Press, 1982), p. 43.
40. Upton Sinclair, *The Jungle,* rev. ed. (New York: Signet, 1960), p. 58.
41. Quoted in Teaford, *Twentieth-Century American City,* p. 13.
42. Quoted in Gunther Barth, *City People: The Rise of Modern City Culture in Nineteenth-Century America* (New York: Oxford University Press, 1980), p. 141.

43. Quoted in Teaford, *Twentieth-Century American City,* p. 13.
44. *Ibid.,* p. 11.
45. *Ibid.,* p. 13.
46. Quoted in Still, *Urban America,* p. 253.
47. Quoted in Frank A. Randall, *A History of the Development of Building Construction in Chicago* (Urbana, Ill.: University of Illinois Press, 1949), pp. 12–13.
48. Quoted in Frisch, *Town into City,* p. 154.
49. Quoted in John W. Reps, *The Making of Urban America: A History of City Planning in the United States* (Princeton, N.J.: Princeton University Press, 1965), p. 501.
50. Quoted in *ibid.,* p. 497.
51. Quoted in Jon A. Peterson, "The City Beautiful Movement: Forgotten Origins and Lost Meaning," *Journal of Urban History* 2 (August 1976): 425.
52. Quoted in Joseph L. Arnold, "City Planning in America," in Raymond A. Mohl and James R. Richardson, eds., *The Urban Experience: Themes in American History* (Belmont, Calif.: Wadsworth, 1973), p. 25.
53. Quoted in Charles N. Glaab, ed., *The American City: A Documentary History* (Homewood, Ill.: Dorsey Press, 1963), p. 261.
54. Lubove, *Progressives and the Slums,* p. 220.
55. Sam Bass Warner, Jr., *The Urban Wilderness: A History of the American City* (New York: Harper & Row, 1972), p. 31.
56. Lubove, *Progressives and the Slums,* p. 245.
57. Lewis Mumford, *The City in History* (New York: Harcourt, Brace & World, 1961), p. 517.
58. Lubove, *Progressives and the Slums,* p. 227.

PART 4

The
Vital
Fringe

1920–1970

The history of urban America is in many respects the history of expanding cities: the transformation of space into settlement, social networks, and political institutions. In 1920, a majority (51.4 percent) of Americans lived in urban areas. Some of these locations were mere villages of 2,500 or so people, to be sure, but the statistics supplied further evidence of a trend that had been gaining momentum for over a century and was reflected in major population movements and a consistent decline in agricultural employment. By 1950, the American city was so large and spread out and overwhelming that some observers wondered whether it was a city at all by the traditional definition. By 1970, more than 75 percent of all Americans lived in urban areas, but the urban population density was less than it had ever been and more people lived in suburbs than in central cities. The metropolis had grown from a center to a region.

We call the era from 1920 to 1970 the "vital fringe." Since the colonial era, the American city had acted as a giant magnet attracting population and economic base. After 1920, the areas outside the city—the suburbs—became the most dynamic areas of growth in the nation. The balance between city and suburb, precariously sustained during the era of the radial center, broke down in the twentieth century. The collapse of this tenuous equilibrium resulted from the same basic forces that had influenced urbanization in earlier periods: technology, new patterns of economic organization and activity, and migrations of population. Technology supplied much of the impetus and means for the formation of the twentieth-century metropolitan area, not only in terms of new transportation modes like the automobile and the airplane, but also in manufacturing, construction, and more efficient means of communication and marketing like the telephone, the radio, and television. Economic organization in the United States gained a new sophistication with the rise of corporations that commanded untold resources and stretched worldwide. The industrial city evolved into the

285

corporate city. The emphasis of the economy shifted increasingly, especially after World War II, from heavy manufacturing to new light industries and the delivery of professional and personal services to a growing consumer market.

The breakdown in metropolitan balance did not imply decline, though some contemporary observers believed it did. It did, however, imply change, as the city assumed new economic and cultural roles after 1920. The city became a center for activities that serviced the corporate economy—banking, insurance, accounting, education, and legal services; its industrial and retail functions were reduced. The cultural prominence of the city increased, in terms of mass culture—popular music, films, and sports—and high culture—museums, symphony orchestras, and libraries. Cultural institutions drew the city together, even as its changing economic roles created deeper divisions.

During the 1930s a new force emerged as a factor in shaping the metropolis: the federal government. Though federal policies, from tariffs to land grants, had affected cities in the nineteenth century, federal-city relations were at best indirect. This situation changed during the New Deal era, when massive government expenditures played a significant role in metropolitan expansion. Washington did not act so much as an innovator as a catalyst, reinforcing the movement to the vital fringe and the consequent transformation of the central city.

These two themes—the rapid growth of the suburbs and the change in central city fortunes and functions—became especially evident after World War II. As cities grew beyond the political boundaries of the central core, the metropolitan area became fragmented into scores of politically independent communities. The loss of population and economic base in the central cities and the consequent decline in revenues coincided with the influx of low-income, poorly educated people who demanded additional social services. The riots that engulfed inner city neighborhoods during the 1960s symbolized this urban dilemma.

But the city has always offered ample cause for both pessimism and optimism about its future. Good and bad are not sequential dimensions of urbanization, they occur together. When Frederic C. Howe, one of the most prolific writers on the early-twentieth-century city, reflected on the complexities of urban life and death in *The City: The Hope of Democracy* (1905), his remarks would prove to apply equally to the metropolis of 1970: "The modern city marks an epoch in our civilization," a revolution "in industry, politics, society, and life itself." The city was "El Dorado, the promised land which fires the imagination," a place where "there is the chance, and life, movement, and recreation even in failure." But the city also had a dark side. "The city has replaced simplicity, industrial freedom, and equality of fortune," Howe wrote, "with complexity, dependence, poverty, and misery close beside a barbaric luxury like unto that of ancient Rome. . . . The city exacts an awful price for the gain it has given us, a price that is being paid in human life, suffering, and the decay of virtue and the family."[1]

By 1970, most of these problems could no longer be attributed to "the city" as a specific entity. Indeed, they are endemic to American life. Through most of the twentieth century the problems of growth and decay, fragmented decision making, new technology and environmental disaster, progress and poverty were not confined to cities. The cities had become, in a very real sense, the harbingers of social patterns for the nation.

Note

1. Frederic C. Howe, *The City: The Hope of Democracy* (New York: Scribner, 1905), pp. 9, 25, 32.

CHAPTER 9

The First
Suburban Decade

The 1920s were America's first suburban decade. During those years, for the first time in the nation's history the areas beyond the city grew faster than the city itself. This was not an unexpected phenomenon. Since early in the nineteenth century, urban Americans had moved to suburban residences to fulfill their dreams and flee the nightmare of city decay. The modest row houses in Brooklyn and the equally unpretentious triple-deckers outside Boston did not seem dramatically different from the city their inhabitants left behind. But congestion was less, home ownership was a considerably greater opportunity, and the uncomfortable and unpredictable range of people and experiences the city offered was often absent. The affluent suburbs, ranging from railroad communities (such as Lake Forest outside Chicago) to planned streetcar developments (such as Atlanta's Druid Hills), showed sharper contrasts to the city than the plebeian suburbs, but the motivations of their residents were similar.

In 1910, the suburb was granted official recognition when the census bureau reported on "metropolitan districts"—areas including central cities of more than 100,000 inhabitants and surrounding jurisdictions within a 10-mile radius. The bureau presented 44 districts that year, justifying the new concept by noting that

> all of our great urban communities have suburban districts with a comparatively dense population adjacent to the boundary and so closely connected with the business center of the city . . . as to be practically a part of the city. . . . The wage earners residing in

these suburbs are employed in the city, but through the restrictions of the city boundary are not counted by the Census as part of its population.[1]

The metropolitan concept, given the imprimatur of an official government agency, became a valuable industrial and investment recruitment tool. City officials began to think in regional terms not only for marketing purposes, but also as a spur to urban imperialism through annexation. The Merchants Association of San Francisco, for example, employed the census designation to promote the "Great San Francisco" concept as a vehicle to secure the annexation of Oakland across the bay. Oakland merchants had their own ideas and soon countered with a "Greater Oakland" plan whereby the city and its suburbs jointly would outdistance San Francisco.[2]

By 1920, the cumulative effect of a century of migration from the city was now documented in significant statistics. In the 1920s, though, the suburb was both more accessible and affordable for the expanding urban middle class than ever before. White-collar occupations including advertising, banking, insurance, and the various levels of corporate management had expanded rapidly after the 1890s, fueled by the active participation of the United States in an international economy, the development of corporate giants, and the growing concentration of people in the great cities. In addition, by the 1920s, second-generation immigrants were becoming school teachers and civil servants as education and government bureaucracies expanded to service the urban nation. The parents and grandparents of the new middle class typically could afford neither a suburban residence nor the time and expense of commuting unless they were willing to compromise on housing type, lot size, and services. As the streetcar suburbs of the 1880s and 1890s indicated, some urban residents accepted these limitations just to get out of the city center. A generation later, compromises were less necessary as salaries moved up, white-collar opportunities expanded, and automobile prices plummeted. The radial pattern of settlement that characterized the age of the great cities became less dependent on the rigid spatial layout of railroad and trolley lines, as settlement spread out in the interstices of the radial spokes and into the countryside beyond. By mid-decade, the movement outward had become commonplace enough for a sociologist to title a book *The Suburban Trend* (1925) and conclude that "a crowded world must be either suburban or savage."[3]

The Nuclear Home

The locus of that civilized world, in the new twentieth century, remained the single-family home. As home ownership became a wider opportunity, the government and private agencies sought to encourage the trend. The U.S. Department of Commerce launched an "Own Your Home" campaign in 1920. Commerce Secretary Herbert Hoover encouraged developers to standardize building codes and materials grades. The YMCA offered do-it-yourself courses for prospective home owners. And a new organization, Better Homes in America, churned out literature on home buying and home building and sponsored thousands of local committees that organized "Better Homes Week" activities during April. One result of these organized efforts was an increase of 3.5 million nonfarm home-owning households during the 1920s. Most of these new households were located from 2 to 6 miles from central city neighborhoods and had considerably lower densities than the streetcar suburbs of a generation earlier. The average building lot in the automobile suburbs of the 1920s, for example, was 5,000 square feet, compared with an average lot size of 3,000 square feet for the streetcar communities.

The homes were different as well. The so-called "small California house" or bungalow became a standard middle-class suburban dwelling in the 1920s, including anywhere from three to eight rooms all on one floor. An obligatory garage was more often than not attached to the house rather than separate from it, for the car had become a virtual member of the family. The house interior also underwent redesign. The parlor, servants' quarters, and the separation of public from private space were gone in the new suburban homes. Kitchen, living, dining, and recreation areas merged into a largely undifferentiated space with the bedrooms positioned at a right angle to the main space. Domestic experts of the late nineteenth century considered such a mixture of uses dangerously promiscuous, but for a new generation of suburban dwellers it was a functional and inexpensive solution to fulfilling the dream of home ownership and suburban living. The style also suited the mobility of the new urban generation, who might change residences several times during their adult lives. The smaller, functional homes also involved less maintenance, which meant some relief for women, especially for the minority of middle-class women (roughly one out of six in the 1920s) who joined the growing masses of white-collar employees in civil service and teaching positions in the city.

The homes were ideally suited to experimentation with new technologies. Consumers demanded "all-electric" homes and the wiring to support an array of new appliances such as electric vacuum cleaners, irons, refrigerators, fans, and toasters. The coal furnace soon went the way of the ice man as suburban homes included oil or natural gas furnaces that reduced home maintenance costs and labor as well. Though these appliances hardly freed women from their traditional roles as housekeepers (in fact, it can be argued that the household inventions only freed men because they no longer had to chop wood or feed coal furnaces), but it lightened the physical exertion of some of their tasks. In less than two decades electricity had moved from a rare and luxurious technology to a necessity.

Automobility and the New Metropolis

The automobile, like electricity, became a fixture in the suburbs of the 1920s. F. Scott Fitzgerald's *The Great Gatsby* (1925), arguably America's first suburban novel, focuses on Jay Gatsby's rise from golf course caddy to twenties-style millionaire entrepreneur. Gatsby's quest for love and social respectability takes him to a posh suburb on Long Island, outside New York City. Gatsby's dreams end in disaster, but both he and the other major characters in the novel glide easily between city and suburb in motor cars, a fact reviewers took little note of simply because the automobile and suburban life were already synonymous in the minds of Americans by this relatively early date. The motor vehicle did not, of course, create suburbia, but it played a major role in shaping the modern metropolitan area. The vitality of the fringe depended in great part on its accessibility, and the automobile provided that access more quickly and efficiently than its predecessors, the electric trolley and the commuter railroad. Unlike earlier transit systems, the automobile offered door-to-door service, departing and arriving on the driver's own schedule, not that of the trolley or railroad company. What better way, also, to express individualism and self-reliance—two character traits in high currency during the 1920s? The car was a portable living room that promoted family togetherness; there was no need to share a compartment or a crowded streetcar with strangers if you had a home on wheels. Not surprisingly, the mobile home or trailer also became a popular item during the twenties.

By 1927, more than one out of every two families in urban America owned an automobile, compared with less than one out of six in 1920. This was also the first year that sales for replacement or second cars exceeded sales to first-time owners. Henry Ford had opened his vast River Rouge complex outside Detroit in 1919. Five years later, employing the latest assembly-line technology, Ford was able to drop the price of the popular Model T from $950 in 1910 to $290. At the same time, average wages increased. In addition, federal and state governments subsidized the auto through various measures including the Federal Road Act of 1916, which offered grants to states that organized highway departments, and the Federal Road Act of 1921, which designated 200,000 roads as "primary" and thus eligible for matching federal funds. The 1921 act also created a Bureau of Public Roads to plan a highway network designed to connect cities of more than 50,000 residents. States picked up the federal initiative, and by 1929 every state had enacted a gasoline tax to pay for road construction and maintenance. Cities participated in the road-building bonanza as well. Chicago, for example, spent $340 million between 1910 and 1940 on street widening alone.

Together with private sources, government subsidies helped to create a na-

The Road to Forest Park, St. Louis, c. 1925
Despite the traffic jams it created, the automobile quickly became the recreational vehicle of choice for middle-class urban residents, and the Sunday afternoon drive to the park became part of American culture.

tional system of interstate highways by 1930. Much as the automobile helped to create a new metropolitan form, so it began to alter (along with the motor truck) the patterns of communication between urban regions. Specifically, the South reemerged as an important transportation center. Increased leisure time and expendable income attracted tourists and vacationers to the sunny, inexpensive South. The Dixie Highway from Detroit and Chicago to Miami Beach played a major role in developing urban real estate in Florida. The Atlantic Coastal Highway stretched from New England to Miami, and the Bankhead Highway went from Washington, D.C. to Atlanta, then west through Alabama, Mississippi, and Louisiana, and, ultimately, to San Diego—the nation's first transcontinental highway. Atlanta's strategic position in the growing national road network enabled the city to become a major distributing center for automobiles. The number of auto dealers in Atlanta rose from four in 1908 to eighty in 1920, and auto-related businesses numbered 236. One estimate for 1917 put the total Atlanta bank clearings attributable to automobile retailing at $50 million. Measured in building rentals, new construction, and new jobs, the dimensions of the transportation revolution became even larger.

In the long run the new roads helped the South reduce its economic isolation. What economists call the "multiplier effect"—in this case, the number of activities spawned by and dependent on the automobile—was a significant factor in generating prosperity not only in Atlanta but all across urban America in the 1920s. As with the highway system, these activities were not centralized in a few locations but scattered throughout the nation. Few major cities lacked some portion of the automobile industry. Mass production of automobiles not only provided jobs and economic benefits in areas with vehicle plants, but also generated huge demands for raw and processed materials—steel and other metals, wood, canvas, and rubber—that boosted urban economies from Maine to California. Automobile dealers proliferated, adding scores of new retail businesses to local economies. Related businesses, both wholesale and retail, sprang up: garages, filling stations, repair shops, tire stores, parts establishments, and even "automobile laundries" appeared all over the city—many of them located along "automobile rows" in and around the urban core.

The indirect economic consequences of the motor vehicle were equally impressive and far reaching. Roadhouses, highway campgrounds, and the earliest "auto hotels" depended largely on the motor vehicle trade. Perhaps even more important, the new territory that the automobile opened for development stimulated real-estate sales, construction and insurance businesses, and led to new public outlays for utilities, streets, and other facilities.

The motor vehicle became the chief competitor of urban mass transit systems, especially in smaller cities that did not have elaborate streetcar networks in the 1920s. Ridership on public transit declined for the first time during that decade. A combination of the auto, expenditures for roads, management problems, aging equipment, the sale and development of real-estate holdings, and changes in preferences and residential locations spelled doom for the electric trolley. Sinclair Lewis's George Babbitt, the epitome of the 1920s booster businessman, took particular glee in driving by the trolley stop and shouting "Have a lift?" to a colleague waiting in the hot sun or in the bitter cold winter weather.[4]

The impact of the automobile's popularity on social patterns and lifestyles was also significant, though less easily measured. In the 1920s, the motor vehicle seemed to some a license for immoral behavior, drawing families away from church and out into the country on Sunday drives and young couples into the rumble seat on unchaperoned dates. Along with the motion picture, the motorcar was an invitation to recreation outside the home that fit nicely into the racy new world of flappers and hip flasks. And the auto had a reputation for fast getaways for those who needed to make them.

Increasing reliance on auto travel led to the development of new lifestyles, symbolized by the two-car garage, limited-access highways, and drive-in facilities of all descriptions—banks, restaurants, movies, and even mortuaries. But it did not necessarily follow that the new road and auto-related facilities made commuting for shopping or work any easier in the 1920s. In 1923, *Motor* magazine asked, "Will Passenger Cars Be Barred from City Streets?" because of the growing congestion.[5] City governments and planners rushed to solve the problem. Downtown survival, they fretted, depended on accommodating the craze for cars to the technological and spatial limitations of the city center. Cities experimented with automatic traffic signals, wooden policemen, parking meters, road designs, and banning curbside parking downtown. The dilemma of "automobility" gave the new city planning profession the opportunity to demonstrate its indispensability to urban policy making. By 1920, city planners had zeroed in on zoning and transportation circulation as their special fields of expertise.

Among the experiments to alleviate downtown congestion was Chicago's Wacker Drive, a double-decked roadway with one lane underground. Wacker carried twice the traffic of conventional roads. Some planners, however, got carried away by the challenge of ordering the new urban traffic flow. One Chicago planner, for example, suggested paving over the Chicago River; a New York planner proposed a tri-level parkway along the Hudson River. There were even plans for four- and six-layer road systems. Among the more practical ideas, parking garages strategically located on the edge of downtown seemed to offer some relief to the chronic congestion. The most elaborate garage was the twenty-two-story Pure Oil Garage in Chicago complete with three elevators that transported cars from the entrance of the lower level of Wacker Drive to the floors above. At the floor designated by a switchboard operator, the car rolled out onto a conveyer belt that deposited it in the appropriate parking place. There was no report, however, on what happened at 5 o'clock, when all the car owners arrived at the same time to retrieve their machines from day care.

Most of these remedies failed to relieve traffic congestion. The real culprit was the famous pigeon effect: the more peanuts you throw on the ground, the more pigeons show up. As the roads of America widened and grew more numerous, as parking decks added more levels, the automobile proliferated. In 1923, the *Literary Digest* noted that "the American public is thinking more about where to park its cars than about the League of Nations."[6] The situation had not improved by 1930, when an Atlanta editor summarized the general frustration: "When Mr. Henry Ford . . . put some kind of automobile within easy reach of almost everybody, [he] inadvertently created a monster that has caused more trouble in the larger cities than bootleggers, speakeasies, and alley bandits."[7]

By the mid-1920s, it was evident that the "monster" was wreaking havoc on the central business district. Aside from the frustration to motorists (George Babbitt's passengers did not improve their commuting times by riding in his automobile), merchants expressed alarm at the difficulty in receiving deliveries and customers, and residents complained about the deteriorating quality of life brought about by the auto and its accompanying roads, filling stations, and parking facilities. Given this state of affairs, it made even more sense to hop into the car and join the move to suburbia.

The Urban Economy Decentralizes

More than just people and automobiles was being drawn to suburbia. In an era when central cities were growing at faster rates than suburban areas, businesses and industries had few incentives to locate or move to outlying districts. On the other hand, they had several good reasons for remaining in central locations. For factories, access to railroad sidings and labor was a major concern; for businesses, all roads literally led to downtown. But by the 1920s, the suburbs had absorbed a critical population mass that overshadowed the growth of central cities. The congestion downtown, the increasing reliance on technology as opposed to cheap, unskilled labor, and the growth of motor truck freight transport lessened the attraction of a central location and enhanced the value of suburban commercial and industrial properties.

A few industrialists had eyed suburban sites long before the 1920s. Company towns such as Pullman and Gary as well as the countless mill villages in the southern Piedmont attested to the efficacy of locations outside cities. Aside from their relatively inexpensive land, these sites ensured that workers could be isolated from outside influences, especially labor unions. Sometimes, suburban locations were advantageous because they were close to natural resources. The discovery of vast amounts of oil in and near Orange County, California in the mid-1890s led to a thriving suburban oil industry in the Los Angeles metropolitan area and stimulated the growth of that area's ubiquitous suburbs long before the automobile came on the scene. Unlike the older cities of the Northeast and Midwest, Los Angeles never developed an industrial urban core but rather an administrative-residential core surrounded by industrial suburbs. Though that configuration was an anomaly in urban America during the 1920s, it prefigured the trend of metropolitan land use by the 1970s.

By the 1920s, several developments combined to make suburban locations desirable for other industries besides the extractive and textile firms. The introduction of high-voltage electrical systems late in the nineteenth century reduced the cost of power transmission to outlying areas. In addition, efficiency experts in the early decades of the twentieth century had concluded that production was more efficiently run on a single level rather than on several floors. The four- and five-story concrete factories that concentrated at rail and waterfront depots were now obsolete. These factories occupied, on average, 1,040 square feet per worker. The new, more efficient plants covered at least 2,000 square feet per worker. Even in those cities where land was available to satisfy the needs of efficiency-minded industrialists, the expense was prohibitive. This restriction, combined with the growing importance of trucking, motivated entrepreneurs to seek out suburban locations. And if public transit did not or could not service city-dwelling workers who wished to work in the suburbs (the automobile did not filter down to the working class in appreciable numbers until after World War II), then why not build a suburb just for them? This idea took shape in such massive suburban facilities as Henry Ford's River Rouge plant and U.S. Steel's Fairfield works outside Birmingham.

Slowly and inevitably, the central city was losing some of the functions it had accrued during its heyday in the late nineteenth century. Retailers followed the factories and the families to the suburbs in the 1920s. In fact, the first shopping center in America appeared on what was then the outskirts of Kansas City. In 1923, developer J. C. Nichols opened Country Club Plaza, a series of shops designed in a Spanish motif, including red-tile roofs and arcaded walkways. Perhaps the most attractive element as far as shoppers were concerned was the provision of ample parking spaces in front of the stores, away from the flow of traffic on the street. Though most businesses that came to the suburbs did not enjoy such well-appointed surroundings, merchants understood that providing service for the customer now meant providing for their customers' cars as well.

The impact of suburban residential and commercial growth on central city dwellers and merchants was clearly visible by the middle of the 1920s. Richmond novelist Ellen Glasgow lived in a house on once-fashionable West Main Street. By 1925, the quiet charm of the Victorian era had passed and she found herself "increasingly adrift in a sea of rooming houses and filling stations." Her street and similar residential streets, once extensions of the home and almost an open space, were now thoroughfares for traffic, separated from the life behind the window. The front porch disappeared from standard residential architecture as the new function of the road emerged.

"Everywhere," Glasgow noted sadly, "people were pushing one another into the slums or the country."[8] Businesses left, too. In 1926, a Nashville businessman complained that "lack of parking space causes purchasers to patronize suburban rather than downtown stores." In Atlanta that same year, Thomas H. Pitts closed his "drugs and sundries store" for good at Five Points in the heart of downtown, explaining that "traffic got so congested that the only hope was to keep going. Hundreds used to stop; now thousands pass. Five Points has become a thoroughfare, instead of a center." Some businessmen weathered the rapid geographic expansion by opening branches in peripheral or suburban areas. A Memphis merchant placed the following revealing advertisement in a local newspaper in 1929: "To relieve its customers of the inconvenience of parking in the Downtown congested area, the House-Bond Hardware Co. is opening neighborhood stores throughout the city. The locations . . . are selected with the plan of offering the present day shopper a convenient spot to park her car without violating traffic regulations."[9] Here it is interesting to note that, aside from the obvious decentralization of retail establishments, shopping—even for hardware—was still primarily a woman's activity.

The suburban trend was also evident in the location of the newest transportation technology: the airplane. The wharves and later the railroad depots of major cities occupied locations in or near the city center. All visitors and new residents to urban life made their entrance to the city through the gates of the port or rail terminal. Although this was still the case in the 1920s, the connection between transportation and the city center had begun to weaken.

Planners, architects, and city officials were aware of the potential of commercial air transport in the years following World War I. They believed that a modern metropolis could and should adapt to the new technology. In 1919, architect Thomas Mitchell demonstrated how airports could coexist with skyscrapers in a reconstructed city center. Mitchell proposed the erection of several sixty-story skyscrapers that would support 3,000-foot landing strips with glass surfaces to allow sunlight to penetrate to the street below. As airplanes increased in size and became more numerous, however, such schemes became impractical, not to mention the disruption they posed to the already troubled city center.

In 1928, planner John C. Nolen recommended that developers locate airports on the urban periphery. Airports, Nolen reasoned, would attract numerous other functions much like the railroad termini generated hotels, shops, and offices. The congested city center could not support such additional uses. Because most airports were private ventures through the early 1930s, it was unlikely that entrepreneurs could afford to expand operations and provide subsidiary activities (some airport owners sought to attract patrons with swimming pools, rooftop dance floors, and miniature golf courses) on valuable city center land. By the 1930s, airports began their suburban relocations, a process that accelerated after World War II with the construction of such massive facilities as Chicago's O'Hare Airport and New York's John F. Kennedy (then called Idlewild) terminal. The predictions proved correct as the major new airports drew a wide variety of uses around them to become, in effect, minicities on the urban periphery.

Those concerned about the continued vitality of the city center were not necessarily upset by some of these decentralizing trends. Centers, they agreed, were too congested. Since at least the Chicago World's Fair of 1893, planners and officials had sought to move industry and railroads out of the center for both esthetic and practical reasons. But there would come a point, some feared, when the city center would lose too many of its activities and residents to suburban locations. This draining of resources would threaten property values.

Banks as well as corporate headquarters had significant financial stakes in the central business districts. But the constituency that cared about downtown vitality was dwindling. Aside from middle-class residents who focused energies and income on their new suburban residences, the civic elite increasingly had divided loyalties. In 1910, for example, 1,800 of Detroit's 2,000 leading families lived in the city; by 1930, that figure had declined to 1,000. In their posh suburban communities such as Grosse Pointe, protected by racial and religious convenants that excluded blacks and immigrants (the U.S. Supreme Court did not declare such covenants unconstitutional until 1948), the civic elite came to view the city and its center as a good place to do business but a lousy place to live, a place to be exploited rather than nurtured. Their abiding affection and exclusivity they reserved for their suburban communities.

The changing nature of the corporation, from a local or regional entity to a national and international organization, meant simultaneously that local markets were less important but that central city locations were more important than ever. As residential ties between city and executive weakened, the connection between corporate administration and the city became stronger, countering the outward movement of other economic activities. As corporations grew, they required more sophisticated services, including banking, advertising, accounting, and legal assistance, which often meant locating in the largest cities such as New York, Chicago, or Los Angeles. By 1920, more than one-quarter of the nation's 300 largest firms were located in New York City. And trends pointed toward increased concentration in the future. Though the conglomerate—a corporation composed of numerous enterprises in a variety of areas ranging, for example, from textiles to spark plugs to medical instruments—and the multinational corporation—which conducted operations in many countries, shifting capital reserves to achieve the best tax advantage, extracting raw materials from one area, processing them with cheap labor in another, and selling them in a world market—would not become prominent until after World War II, the trend was evident in the 1920s, especially in the field of energy. The larger and more complex the corporate organization, the more important it became to maintain close touch with supporting services that were concentrated in the city center.

Corporations also found it necessary to demonstrate high visibility. More people, in other words, were likely to see a corporate headquarters downtown than at a low-cost suburban site. The corporate building became part of the

advertising campaign for numerous large firms. Frank W. Woolworth demonstrated the efficacy of this strategy in 1913, and the skyscraper boom continued
into the 1920s. The Chrysler Building, financed by auto tycoon Walter Chrysler
and completed in 1929, was perhaps the most graceful of the gargantuan structures, a slender Art Deco cathedral of commerce rising seventy-seven stories
above New York. The structure was capped by six stories of stainless steel featuring a frieze of abstract automobiles circling the tower. Gargoyles modeled
after radiator cap ornaments guarded the tower. By this time, Standard Oil magnate John D. Rockefeller had broken ground for what chic planners in the 1980s
would call a "multiuse development," a complex of offices and retail buildings
known as Rockefeller Center. The nation's major communications giant, the
Radio Corporation of America, became the Center's primary tenant.

The skyscraper, which had made its first appearance in the late nineteenth
century, became the prime symbol for the twentieth-century city. Sleek, built of
the latest materials, furnished with a fleet of fast elevators, ornamented with
icons from the new technology, and creating a brand-new urban landscape and
climate, the skyscraper fascinated tourists and residents alike, inspiring a generation of artists and photographers who sought to capture the excitement of
the modern metropolis by focusing on its most evident symbol. Photographers
such as Alfred Stieglitz, Edward Steichen, and Louis Hine took the skyscraper
as their frequent subject, often resorting to impressionistic effects to soften and
humanize the buildings.

The city, especially New York, had fascinated artists since early in the century.
The so-called "Ash Can School" depicted the ordinary yet heroic urban life in
works such as George Bellows' *Cliff Dwellers* or John Sloan's glimpses of New
York from rooftops and elevated trains. By the 1920s, futurists, cubists, and
surrealists had replaced the realistic art of the Ash Can School, though the subjects remained similar. Georgia O'Keeffe, known mainly for her paintings of the
Southwest, painted *The Radiator Building* in honor of her husband Alfred
Stieglitz. The building, one critic noted, resembles a "jewel in the neon-lit
night."[10] Joseph Stella, an Italian immigrant to New York, captured the city's
life in a five-panel work completed in 1922 entitled *New York Interpreted*. The
central panel, "Skyscrapers," links these structures with the Old World Gothic
cathedral, as Stella evoked Italian religious art in his frequent use of stained
glass.

Because it was both inspirational and functional, the skyscraper represented
the marriage of art and economy. It was as much a cultural symbol as an example
of capitalist success. And it underscored the preeminence of the central city even
as suburbia outpaced this district in population growth. But the skyscraper was
also a symbol of increasing concentration, both of people and of power in the
city center. To some, it was an individualistic and selfish flaunting of wealth

The Chrysler Building, New York City

For sheer grace and style, this skyscraper had few peers among the tall structures built during the post–World War I era. It served as a monumental advertisement for auto magnate Walter Chrysler.

without concern for the general welfare. This kind of self-interest, however, was not limited to the city but had spread to the suburb along with the automobile and the single-family home. The home, the car, and the factory gobbled up suburban space willy-nilly. To some, the suburb was becoming the horizontal equivalent of the vertical chaos that threatened to engulf the city.

Shaping the Twentieth-Century Metropolis

In 1922, a group of young planning activists led by Lewis Mumford formed the Regional Planning Association of America (RPAA). The group assumed that the corporate city was a hopeless environment, poisoned by inequality and ugliness. The suburb was only a temporary refuge that the city would soon overcome physically and culturally. As Mumford wrote in the *New Republic* in 1921: "Suburbia . . . demonstrates the incapacity of our civilization to foster concrete ways and means for living well. Having failed to create a common life in our modern cities, we have builded suburbia, which is a common refuge from life, and the remedy is an aggravation of the disease." For Mumford, the suburb was not an alternative to the city but an environment created uneasily in its image. "The suburb," Mumford argued five years later, "is not a solution. It is merely a halting place. So long as the big city continues to grow, the suburb cannot remain suburban."[11]

Mumford's alternative, borrowing an ecological metaphor from his RPAA colleague Benton MacKaye, was "community aforestation." Simply put, this concept meant the "building up of new communities in the hinterland, which will hold back the flood . . . [and] drain off some of the surplus from existing centers [cities]."[12] These communities would be located far enough away from "existing centers" so that imminent contamination would not be a problem. To ensure their immunity, an agricultural greenbelt would surround them that would serve both as productive farmland and inspirational open space. As self-contained urban settlements of up to 50,000 inhabitants, these communities would include employment and educational opportunities, with residential land safely and imaginatively sequestered from other uses.

The RPAA represented a formal acknowledgment that a new urban form was emerging—the metropolitan area, consisting of city, suburbs, and open spaces, interdependent though with the city as the dominant partner. The RPAA sought to change that dominance and restore the metropolitan balance of the radiant center era by building communities on the urban periphery according to the precepts advanced by their founding members. In 1927, RPAA leaders put their regional theories into practice by developing a community, Radburn, New Jersey, 17 miles from New York City. The close proximity of Radburn to the city (literally 45 minutes from Broadway via commuter train) precluded the type of self-contained settlement that Mumford had proposed. In addition, the cost of land in the New York metropolitan area ruled out a settlement that could accommodate more than 50,000 inhabitants. Whatever Radburn lacked in size and land use diversity, however, it made up for in its focus on the family and the neighborhood, two of the major casualties of the new mobile metropolis.

The primary planning unit of Radburn was the 40- to 60-acre superblock that would contain residential, educational, recreational, and convenience shopping facilities. The neighborhood unit plan, as Clarence Perry, an RPAA founder, called it, utilized the school as the organizing point for a "superblock," a unit he defined by the distance a child could walk to school. The separation of pedestrian from vehicular traffic was a major feature of the unit plan. Technology, especially the automobile, Perry reasoned, "has been . . . a destroyer of neighborhood life . . . [by] cutting up residential areas into small islands separated from each other by raging streams of traffic."[13]

But Perry and his colleagues were realistic enough to recognize that they could not ignore the automobile. Their compromise was a series of peripheral roads terminating in cul-de-sacs that would give residents access to their neighborhoods without impeding pedestrian flows in the interior of the superblock. Perry believed that these neighborhood units would become the building blocks for a new, decentralized region. A promotional film for the project showed a child bouncing a ball from the door of his modest home to his school without once having to stop because of traffic or other obstructions. The superblock, according to Perry, provided the nurturing environment, space, and order that were lacking in all sectors, urban and suburban, of the metropolitan area.

The Radburn plan drew international attention. Unfortunately, however, the RPAA completed the project at the onset of the Depression, and even at the height of its settlement, no more than 3,000 people lived in the community before suburban New Jersey engulfed it by the time of World War II. Though the RPAA had hoped to demonstrate the efficacy of such communities for urban working-class families, the Depression and construction costs limited the population to the middle class.

By the time Radburn was underway, another major metropolitan milepost appeared—the publication of the *Regional Plan of New York and Its Environs* in 1929. A ten-volume document that had taken nearly nine years to complete, the plan represented official acknowledgment by the nation's largest city that the metropolitan era had arrived. Charles Dyer Norton, a banker with the House of Morgan, and Frederic A. Delano, an engineer, convinced the Russell Sage Foundation to donate $1.2 million to undertake a regional survey of the New York metropolitan area and draw conclusions and policy recommendations based on collection and analysis of the survey data. Thomas Adams, a Scotsman who had assisted with the planning of Ebenezer Howard's garden cities of Letchworth and Welwyn, directed the planning staff, which included the nation's leading urban planners.

Sharing the concern of the RPAA over the negative impact of the city's growth on the surrounding suburbs and countryside, these planners crafted a document that addressed both the problems of congestion in the center and uncontrolled development on the periphery. The plan projected that the population of the New York metropolitan area would grow from the 1929 figure of 8.9 million people to 21 million people by 1965 (the actual 1965 population was 17.3 million). Despite the planners' concerns about congestion, they predicted that 4 million of these residents would be residing in the central city or in the older cities within the metropolitan area. This fact alone indicated that New York's regional planners had a very different perspective on the problem than the RPAA, even if their diagnoses were similar.

Simply put, the plan's purpose was to devise strategies to save the urban core of New York City, especially its economic vitality. For these planners, the esthetic and moral concerns of the RPAA were beside the point, and the New York Regional Plan scarcely mentioned garden cities as possible solutions to the urban congestion problem. The plan did address the "diffused recentralization of industry" by suggesting new industrial centers on the periphery with adjacent workers' residences.[14] The planners sought to decongest New York, in short, just enough for the city to function in a more efficient manner. Transportation, especially roads and rail, dominated the plan, including a proposal to construct 630 miles of circumferential highways. Considering that both Norton and Delano hailed from Chicago, the similarity of their vision with the 1909 Burnham Plan and the City Efficient ideal in general is not surprising.

The RPAA, especially Lewis Mumford, subjected the New York plan to a withering attack:

> The chief difficulty . . . with the Plan . . . [is] with its premises: namely, that continued growth at the present rate in the metropolitan area is inevitable, and that the first duty of the Plan is to facilitate such growth . . . I see no reason whatever for hoping that this growth and vast expenditure will be compatible with a sufficient and timely provision of parks, playgrounds, and housing facilities: so long as growth and the maintenance of land values are the ends in view, it is rather safe to say that these vital facilities will remain in "embellishments"—scamped and squeezed in order to accommodate the budget.[15]

Mumford went on to award the New York plan a "Booby Prize for 1929" for its "admirable demonstration that by providing for a population of 20,000,000 in the New York area, the problems of transportation which are now insoluble would become less so, and park areas and playgrounds, which are now nonexistent or impossible to reach, would then be more numerous and easier to reach." He concluded by charging that the planners were too "eager to fasten . . . a solution acceptable to their committee full of illustrious names in financial and civic affairs."[16]

Thomas Adams, returning the fire, branded Mumford an "esthete-sociologist."[17] Adams declared that the major difference between Mumford's ideas and the proposals advanced by the regional plan was that the plan was workable, the ideas were not. On this point, Adams had the better argument. Over the next two decades New York undertook to reshape itself along the lines suggested by the regional plan. The major architect of the spatial ordering was Robert Moses, who, as New York City Park Commissioner and head of both the Long Island State Park Commission and the Triborough Bridge Authority, implemented many of the plan's transportation proposals. As early as 1938, Moses had begun or completed more than 40 percent of the highway and park proposals, and work was underway on a regional airport and sewer, garbage, and waterfront improvements. It was not surprising that a large model of the regional plan was prominently displayed at another Moses creation, the 1939 New York World's Fair.

Though both the RPAA and the New York Regional Plan shared a metropolitan vision, their perspectives were strikingly different. Mumford and his colleagues sought a balanced region characterized by planned, humane communities, whereas the New York plan was a blueprint for the continued dominance of the central city. A third metropolitan vision emerged in the early 1930s positing a region without a city at all, or at least a city in the traditional sense. This was Frank Lloyd Wright's Broadacre City.

Wright, America's leading architect by 1930, shared the concern of other regionalists that the current metropolitan configuration was unacceptable: that the suburb was merely an extension of the central city into the countryside. Wright correctly perceived the potentially revolutionary impact of the automobile and the road systems that supported it. Broadacre City was thus a dispersed settlement held together by superhighways. All land uses, from industrial to recreational to residential, were strung out along the road. The basic unit of Broadacre was not the neighborhood but the individual residence from which families set out in their automobiles to reach the various destinations for work, shopping, and school along the superhighway. Broadacre City called for no concentration, central business district, or government center. In addition, residents of Broadacre were closer to the land and its inspirational influence. The architecture of their homes was organic, built low to the landscape and with new materials such as steel and stressed concrete to make them affordable.

For those regionalists who emphasized the concept of community, Broadacre City was a nightmare, the completion of the atomization process begun by the large industrial city. But Wright believed that the renewed emphasis on family and the home as well as the freedom that technology now allowed would compensate for any reduction in personal interaction. Unlike the planners behind either the RPAA or the New York Regional Plan, Wright understood that the era of urban concentration had passed and that technology was already reordering urban space. He viewed Broadacre City not as a visionary conception but rather as the logical conclusion of an inexorable process that had already begun.

The three metropolitan visions represented by the RPAA, the Regional Plan of New York, and Broadacre City were important far beyond their immediate time frames of the 1920s and early 1930s. Though these visions conflicted in many aspects, they shared certain assumptions that filtered, almost unquestioned, into urban policy over the next generation. All these plans assumed, some grudgingly, others with delight, that the automobile would play a major role in reordering metropolitan space. All also agreed that the central city was in bad shape, though they differed on solutions as well as on the question of whether it should be saved at all. Finally, all assumed that outward movement, whether to suburbs, planned communities, or highway settlements, was both inevitable and desirable.

Although the three visions correctly gauged the significant attractions of the automobile and the suburb, their projections for the city fell wide of the mark. The city may have been in economic, physical, and moral decline. It was also, however, a place of economic vitality, new and even inspirational physical forms, and vibrant cultural life. For many planners and policy makers, the standard by which they judged the city of the 1920s was a vanished community of a different time and decidedly different scale. Lewis Mumford was a great admirer of the tenth-century Old World city, and many of his cohorts sought to recreate in some form the preindustrial village. Even Frank Lloyd Wright's visionary Broadacre City looked backward to a time when family and home were the essential units of civilization. But nostalgia is a weak policy tool, and when the federal government with its massive resources entered the picture in the 1930s the weakness of this sentiment would become even more evident. In the meantime, had these visionaries looked up from their drawing boards, they would have discovered that the metropolis of the future had already materialized.

Los Angeles: The Present as Future

If two words could describe the centrifugal direction of American metropolitan life in the 1920s, they would be "Los Angeles." In the early nineteenth century, New York was the golden city embodying the mix of activities, people, and space that would dominate a national urban system and serve as a model, for good or ill, for all other major metropolises. By the late nineteenth century, another city had appeared that reflected the raw, brash dynamism of an international power—militarily and corporately—a broad-shouldered city, blasting out into the prairie, that did everything in wide, hard strokes, whether butchering hogs or building skyscrapers. That was Chicago, the great commercial hub of a great nation. But within a single generation—thanks to technology, mobility, immigrant offspring, greater affluence, and the persistence of the American dream for space and still more space—Los Angeles burst on the scene, a prototype for the country's urban destiny.

In 1931, California Real Estate Commissioner Stephen Bornson peered into the future and saw his state "as a deluxe subdivision—a hundred million acre project."[18] By that date, Los Angeles had become the vanguard city of that vision, a seemingly endless tract of single-family homes where city and suburb knew no sharp boundaries. The popular myth, handed down to the present day, was that the automobile shaped the City of the Angels. In fact, the single-family home was preeminent here long before the 1920s, and it was the world's largest mass transit system, not cars, that linked these far-flung homes with the city center.

Before the 1880s, Los Angeles was a sleepy market town catering to a handful of cattlemen and truck farmers eking out a meager living from the arid coastal plain. But the coming of the transcontinental railroad and the application of artesian well technology broke both the city's isolation and its relative poverty as citrus crops were planted and thrived in the rejuvenated soil. These developments, coupled with the discovery of oil and the construction of an artificial harbor at San Pedro, generated a land boom in the 1880s. Southern Pacific Railroad founder Collis P. Huntington became the fledgling city's most prominent promoter and developer, coupling extensive land purchases with an electric rail system, Pacific Electric, that penetrated the as-yet uninhabited canyons and foothills of southern California. By 1920, the light rail system carried 250,000 passengers daily into the city. The major difference from eastern trolley systems was the fact that the area from which Pacific Electric drew its ridership was considerably greater and much less dense—the built-up portions of the city were relatively small compared with their eastern counterparts.

The city's economic boom continued during the 1920s as the oil industry expanded, agriculture prospered, and new activities such as motion pictures added to the diverse economic base. Despite the extensive public transit system, a major road-building program after World War I encouraged residents to convert to automobile use. By 1925, Los Angeles had the highest ratio of cars to people in the world. And as the radial road and rail system converged on downtown in the typical pattern of the radial center era, congestion became intolerable, even moreso than in other cities.

Pacific Electric's solution was to suggest the construction of elevated lines along major routes connecting with a subway in the immediate downtown area. Civic leaders associated with the Automobile Club of Southern California offered a different plan—the construction of six-lane highways extending north-south and east-west. The plans would have radically different impacts on the spatial organization of the urban area, and both had negative features. Based on the experience of older cities, the construction of elevated lines would raise property values along the routes, freezing out the single-family home; Los Angeles would take on the appearance of eastern cities as apartment houses clustered along the elevated tracks. The highway proposal, on the other hand, would break the radial pattern in favor of a grid system with no particular center point, thereby threatening both the vitality of the downtown and the public transit system.

The Automobile Club won its case, primarily because real-estate development was the city's prime economic activity, overshadowing the interests of downtown entrepreneurs. Because the single-family home subdivision was the major engine driving real-estate business, any transportation alternative that raised land prices to restrict the supply of land for single-family home development threatened the financial and mortgage network that had formed to service and promote such development. Civic leaders, moreover, envisioned Los Angeles as a city of single-family homes and small businesses linked together by a vast network of highways. They associated mass transit with congestion and the automobile with space and speed. As the influential City Club noted in a 1926 report, the "city of the future will be a harmoniously developed community of local centers and garden cities."[19] This vision comported well with prevailing regional theory that emphasized the evils of congestion and the benefits of decentralization and reconcentration, though Lewis Mumford and his colleagues would have been horrified to learn that in this case real-estate speculation rather than humanistic concerns was the prime motivation.

After nearly a decade of implementing the road plan, the Automobile Club assessed the new lifestyle patterns of metropolitan Los Angeles in the mid-1930s:

> The day for the X family, automotively speaking, starts at 7 AM with the arrival of the Mexican gardener from Belvedere. At 7:30 AM the milkman arrives on his daily round from Culver City. Breakfast over, at 8 AM the son departs for classes at USC, and the daughter for a fashionable Pasadena school. At 8:30 the husband sets forth for his office in the Central Manufacturing District at Ventnor. At 11 o'clock the wife leaves for a shopping tour [of the Miracle Mile at Wilshire Boulevard]. . . . By 6 o'clock husband, son and daughter are back home. By 7 Mr. and Mrs. X have left again for dinner at the California Club, and an evening at the Hollywood Bowl. After dinner the son dashes over to consult a school mate in Hollywood, and the daughter scurries to Long Beach for a dance.[20]

What had emerged was a suburban city, the logical outcome of the decentralization process that began to take precedence during the 1920s. Most metropolitan areas would not begin to replicate the Los Angeles pattern until the 1960s and 1970s. The unique combination of climate, history, preference, technology, and economy had thrust Los Angeles precociously into the urban future. Civic leaders had exchanged centralized congestion for decentralized congestion (despite its sprawling image, Los Angeles today is among the three densest cities in the United States) and had adopted a simple solution for the latter problem—more roads. It was not surprising that Los Angeles pioneered the limited access highway or freeway in 1939. The solution, of course, became part of the problem and the vicious circle continues today.

Los Angeles embodied the delightful range of experience the new twentieth-century American city could offer. The lifestyle in that California metropolis differed markedly from that of older northeastern and midwestern cities. Yet the trends that were shaping the older cities in the 1920s—the movement to the suburbs and the development of a metropolitan economy—also shaped Los Angeles. A third event during the decade—the emergence of a single countrywide urban culture—also transcended city type. In fact, New York and Los Angeles, two very different cities, played leading roles in promoting that culture.

Creating a National Urban Culture

The emergence of a national urban culture owed a great deal to two trends from the radial center era of urbanization: middle-class reform and immigration. The middle-class drive to order the city through planning and policy extended to the creation of formal institutions to educate the diverse urban population. The development of public school systems was one obvious manifestation of this objective, but reformers also understood that education was a lifetime experience. Adult education classes appeared after 1900, as did numerous museums and libraries. Large cities boasted symphony orchestras comprised of professional musicians, conducted by such international luminaries as Bruno Walter, Fritz Kreisler, and Arturo Toscanini. After 1920, few cities lacked a choral society or an amateur orchestra or chamber music group. Educators sought to incorporate cultural institutions into the curriculum. Scarcely any child could go through a school year without a visit to the local museum or a concert.

These examples of "high culture," largely supported by the middle class, were not merely for the benefit of newcomers and immigrants. They helped to define and separate the urban middle classes.

Mass, or popular, urban culture was more inclusive. Though the middle classes supported this culture as well, its origins were often plebeian. Specifi-

cally, immigrants and their sons and daughters were most responsible for na-
tionalizing urban culture in the years after World War I. The separation of leisure activities by social class and ethnic groups, epitomized by the Bowery and
Broadway a century earlier, became less distinct. This is not to say that neighborhood taverns, churches, fraternal organizations, and amusement parks such
as Coney Island in Brooklyn did not reflect ethnic and social divisions. But
newer institutions that transcended these categories were emerging.

The role of the immigrant in bringing the divided city together was ironic
since many observers in earlier eras had believed the flood of foreigners after
1880 was most responsible for fragmented and disorderly cities. But European
immigration slowed with World War I and came to a virtual halt in the 1920s
when Congress, prompted by fears of subversion and a resurgence of nativism,
severely restricted migration to the United States.

There were exceptions to the decline in immigration, notable because of their
future impact on urban America. For example, few restrictions were imposed
on immigration from south of the border; the number of Mexican migrants
increased significantly during the 1920s in response to industrial and agricultural expansion in the North and West, respectively. By 1928, there were 15,000
Mexicans both in Detroit and Chicago, where they moved into dwellings formerly occupied by Italians and Greeks. The largest migration occurred in the
Southwest, to cities like San Antonio, where Mexican-born citizens comprised
more than one-third of the city's population by 1930. There were 167,000 Mexicans living in Los Angeles County at the same time, so many concentrating in
East Los Angeles that the residents both within and outside the area began to
call it "el Barrio." Los Angeles was also home to an increasing Japanese population. By the late 1920s, Japanese immigrants were involved in numerous small
business enterprises in and about the city, ranging from truck farming to fruit
stands and flower shops.

But in the European ethnic neighborhoods of the major cities, the constant
shifting about that had resulted from wave upon wave of newcomers subsided.
Immigrants, and especially their American-born sons and daughters, settled in
and began to make important contributions to American society, including contributions to the development of urban culture.

Vaudeville, variety programs consisting of "ballads, minstrel acts, comic
songs, gymnastics, jugglery, fancy dancing and short sketches," appeared as early
as the 1850s.[21] The first theater erected primarily to house such performances
was probably the Vaudeville Theater in San Antonio in the early 1880s. But
vaudeville did not emerge as a popular entertainment form until the 1890s.
Productions became lavish by World War I, with New York performers and
repertoires becoming nationally known.

Genuine vaudeville "stars" appeared by this time. Many of these stars were
second-generation immigrants. During the 1920s, Fanny Brice, a product of

Japanese "Picture Brides," 1931
One of the few legal ways for Asian women to enter the United States was to marry someone living there. These women had exchanged photographs with Japanese men (most likely living in California) and were on their way to join their husbands-to-be.

New York's ethnic cauldron, the Lower East Side, entertained millions of New Yorkers with her songs and comedy sketches; she also took her act on the road. Brice's numbers, which included such standards as "Second-Hand Rose," became part of vaudeville shows across the country, even down to the heavy Yiddish accent Brice affected. It is impossible to estimate how many vaudeville performers sang from one knee in blackface, but Al Jolson, son of immigrant Jewish parents from Washington, D.C., was probably the most imitated performer of his day. In such lyrics as "My heart strings are tangled around Alabammy," Jolson sang about the sunny South as if he were a displaced native longing for home, but the vaudeville audiences in New York, Boston, and Chicago had about as much familiarity with the region as Jolson did. To the audience, the South was exotic, warm, mannerly, and traditional, whereas the urban

North was often cold, indifferent, and insensitive to tradition. The blackface
and the alternately upbeat and sentimental styles affected by those who wore
blackface conformed to prevailing racial stereotypes and comforted northern
urban whites anxious about the increasing numbers of blacks in their midst.

The urban vaudevillians enjoyed laughing. Indeed, a sense of humor was one
of the major self-help devices in the immigrant neighborhoods. In vaudeville,
the laughs were typically on the performers themselves. Stories about how lowly
immigrants or other "little people" outsmarted "the authorities" were especially
enjoyable to audiences. The comedy teams of Weber and Fields and Clayton,
Jackson, and Durante were probably best at this pointed social commentary
veiled in humor. The motion picture industry flowered in Hollywood during
the 1920s, where Charlie Chaplin, Harold Lloyd, and Buster Keaton borrowed
freely from vaudeville's comedy routines to make a hero out of the common
urban man. Mack Sennett's Keystone Cops were probably the most popular
representations of inept and stupid authorities. Although the entire country enjoyed these and similar films, urban audiences particularly could identify with
the downtrodden, often abused, but usually triumphantly vindicated characters.
In the 1930s, the legacy of social comedy passed on to the Marx Brothers—
products of urban immigrant neighborhoods.

When Americans were not laughing at the movies, they were being shocked
by them. The lurid urban penny dreadfuls that had enthralled readers in the
1850s now came alive on the silver screen for everyone. *Alimony,* a movie that
boasted "brilliant men, beautiful jazz babies, champagne baths, midnight revels,
petting parties in the purple dawn, all ending in one terrific smashing climax
that makes you gasp," captured urban audiences—composed primarily of
women and children, incidentally.[22] Audiences viewing such pictures as *Sinners
in Silk* and *Women Who Give* could be titillated by scenes of wicked big city
sophistication.

The recording industry was another mass cultural creation of the 1920s in
which black and ethnic influence was evident. When urban Americans were not
dancing to the Charleston or to the music of vocalists like Bing Crosby and
Eddie Cantor, they were listening to a variety of popular or "Tin Pan Alley"
music with a decidedly urban flavor. Jazz, one of the few distinctively American
music forms, derived from the blues of the rural South and the jam sessions of
black musicians in turn-of-the-century New Orleans; it traveled first to Memphis, then to St. Louis, Chicago, and New York to become the musical craze of
the 1920s. When the first important commercial recording was made in 1917
by New Orleans native Nick La Rocca and his Original Dixieland Jass Band,
the music was denounced as immoral because of the freewheeling beat and its
alleged ancestry in bawdy houses. By the early 1920s, however, Dixieland had
gone "uptown" and such legitimate orchestras as Paul Whiteman's performed

jazz to rapt urban audiences. Jazz also inspired another urban immigrant son, George Gershwin, whose *Rhapsody in Blue* mixed jazz with classical and romantic styles.

The fact that jazz's greatest early commercial successes were due, in part, to white musicians and composers should not obscure the black urban origins of jazz. Indeed, jazz and urban audiences provided blacks with their first major entrées to commercial musical success. Lionel Hampton and Louis Armstrong, for example, began their great careers in the 1920s. The queen of the blues, the more soulful, sorrowful side of jazz, was undoubtedly Bessie Smith. Her mid-1920s rendition of "Yellow Dog Blues" evoked all the personal heartache and loneliness of the black experience. Listeners could recognize the sense of fatalism and dejection in her rich, deep tones.

Blacks also participated in the urban cultural outpouring of the Twenties. The Harlem Renaissance (a misnomer because this movement did not represent the rebirth of black culture so much as its flowering, and Harlem was only one of several big city black districts participating) was one important example of how the metropolitan city nurtured a diversity of cultures. The formation of racial ghettos following World War I provided a critical mass to support creative activities among urban blacks to counter urban cultural trends that devalued and stereotyped blacks.

And the new black ghettos of the North throbbed with creative activity. By then, the best jazz was no longer heard in the Quarter in New Orleans or on Beale Street in Memphis, but on the South Side of Chicago. For musical reviews, poetry, and fiction, Harlem surpassed Broadway in originality and its writers matched the great white literati of the decade.

One of the leading poets of the Harlem Renaissance was Claude McKay. McKay arrived in the United States from Jamaica in 1912 at the age of twenty-three. After a brief stint as an agricultural student at Booker T. Washington's famous Tuskegee Institute in Alabama, he migrated to Harlem, where he published his first poem in 1917. McKay joined a small group of West Indians in the diverse Harlem black community. As with other blacks from the West Indies, McKay found it difficult to adjust to what he perceived as a servile attitude among American blacks. Poetry became his vehicle of protest, as his 1919 poem "If We Must Die," written in response to the race riots of that year, attests:

> If we must die, let it not be like hogs
> Hunted and penned in an inglorious spot,
> While round us bark the mad and hungry dogs,
> Making their mock at our accursed lot.
> If we must die, I say let us nobly die,
> So that our precious blood may not be shed in vain; then even the
> monsters we defy

Bessie Smith

During the 1920s, black urban artists began to attract a national audience. Bessie Smith, "the queen of the blues," was one of the most acclaimed singers of the decade.

Shall be constrained to honor us though dead!
What though before us lies the open grave?
Like men we'll face the murderous, cowardly pack,
Pressed to the wall, dying, but fighting back![23]

White visitors to Harlem, to the Cotton Club and the Apollo Theater, rarely saw this side of the Renaissance. To them, Harlem in the 1920s was an exotic place, an Africa-on-the-Hudson, free from the constraints of modern urban life, captured well in Carl Van Vechten's 1927 novel, *Nigger Heaven,* which served as a guidebook for white visitors to "the barbaric rhythms of Negro jazz, the intoxicating dances, and the wild abandon of cabaret life after midnight."[24] In fact, Harlem was a neighborhood seething in revolt and race pride. It was a hospitable incubator for Marcus Garvey (another West Indian) and his Universal Negro Improvement Association (UNIA), which sought to transport blacks to a new and better life in Africa. It was the home of what Renaissance writer Alain Locke termed "the New Negro," a person infused with "a spirit to seize, even in the face of an extortionate and heavy toll, a chance for the improvement of conditions."[25] The spirit persisted through the Twenties, compounded by the desire to emulate and enter the white world. Mary Love, an exponent of the New Negro philosophy in *Nigger Heaven*, said dejectedly that "her race spent more money on hair-straightening and skin-lightening preparations than they did on food and clothing."[26] The tension between race pride and assimilation, what black leader W. E. B. Du Bois called the "twoness" of black life in America, became a source of frustration, conflict, and violence often directed by and at blacks themselves.

The cultural flowering of immigrant sons and daughters in the 1920s was less confrontational and, therefore, ultimately more acceptable to the urban and national public. The ethnic entertainers preserved their cultural identities while at the same time drawing the diverse city together to share common experiences in vaudeville halls, movie theaters, and jazz clubs.

Few institutions developed a more devoted and diverse following in cities and, eventually, in the nation, than organized sports. It was no coincidence that the 1920s witnessed the emergence of the first great sports heroes. Baseball became the proverbial "national pastime." Urban rivalry, so long a concern of rival elites, now reached the hearts and voices of the general public. Metropolitan citizens, fragmented into city and suburb, poor and wealthy, black and white and ethnic, could identify collectively with their city through their baseball teams. The backgrounds or places of residence and work of all those who thronged to the new Yankee Stadium, completed in 1923, were immaterial. They were all Yankees and New Yorkers. Of all the spaces in the city, the sports arena was common ground, and the sports heroes were common heroes, reflecting the free-wheeling spirit of the age.

Babe Ruth typified the new sports hero. Rising from poverty and neglect in Baltimore, he became the king of the home-run hitters, the Sultan of Swat, for the New York Yankees. Anchoring the famed Murderers' Row batting order, Ruth slugged an incredible sixty home runs during the 1927 baseball season. His lifestyle earned him as much publicity as his hitting. Brash, generous, swaggering, fond of eating and drinking (recall that this was the era of Prohibition), Ruth fit easily into the lifestyle of the 1920s. When a reporter asked him in Depression-ridden 1930 if he felt concerned that as a baseball player he was making more than President Hoover, Ruth retorted, "Why not? I had a better year."[27]

The cheers for new sports heroes rolled over cities throughout the country. They cheered for Gene Tunney—145,000 of them in Chicago's Soldier Field— as he knocked out Jack Dempsey. They cheered for Red Grange as he galloped like a ghost across the football fields of the Midwest. They cheered for Knute Rockne and for Notre Dame's Four Horsemen. They cheered for Bill Tilden as he sent another forehand careening down the line. The collective roar of the crowd gave a sense of belonging to those urban residents no longer anchored by a distinctive and exclusive ethnic culture or unsure of the new metropolis forming around them and their own place in it. For these and other reasons, the new urban culture offered membership in a mass community, even as that community was being redefined.

Americans tuned into cities, not only for sports, fashion, music, and film, but for radio broadcasts as well. Clear-channel stations beamed news and music from the metropolis to the hinterlands. The major radio networks such as the National Broadcasting Company and the Columbia Broadcasting System packaged news, information, and entertainment from their headquarters in New York. Remote hamlets and small towns now no longer waited days for reports of national and international events. Even country music came from the city as rural residents gathered around crystal sets picking up signals from Charlotte and Nashville.

The national urban culture, then, performed at least three important functions. First, through vaudeville, movies, and radio, members of ethnic groups found opportunities to preserve and share their traditions and talents. Second, the urban standard of culture became the national standard. Traveling vaudeville shows, movies, and radio reached even the most remote communities. More than the Sears catalogue in an earlier era, these media put Americans in touch with life in the major cities. Americans listened to songs written and recorded in New York and Chicago; they watched films produced in New York and Los Angeles; they listened to radio programs emanating from New York, Nashville, Atlanta, and Los Angeles. Daily contact with the songs and programs of the metropolis provided outlanders with insights (often stereotypical) into urban life. Finally, the national urban culture improved city life; the ball park and the movie theater offered the opportunity to bridge the gap, however briefly, between disparate elements of urban society.

Organized Crime Incorporates

The corporate metropolis set standards in other areas besides culture. Prohibition became law in 1919, but urban residents generally preferred to imbibe rather than abide. Alcohol, with its association in the urban middle-class mind with poverty and immigrants, had been a reform target since the early nineteenth century. By the time Prohibition became the law of the land, however, moralistic concerns about poverty and immigrants had faded. The ill-timed and ill-fated measure turned generally honest citizens into lawbreakers and bred a general disrespect for the law. Many movie audiences doubtless equated the high jinks of the Keystone Cops with the futile efforts of their local police to enforce Prohibition. It is little wonder that local law enforcement during this period ranged from lax to nonexistent. In a large sense, the cities of America nullified a federal law. In the process, the urban flouting of Prohibition put a great deal of the roar in the Roaring Twenties. And, much as other corporations benefited from the profitable decade by growing and consolidating, organized crime used Prohibition to develop an international network controlled from the major cities.

Aside from its central role in providing urban residents with a valued commodity—spirits—organized crime fit in well with two themes of the 1920s: the upward mobility of immigrants and the suburban trend. Like politics and small business, organized crime was an avenue of upward mobility, and usually quicker—though obviously riskier. Many of the emerging bosses were second-generation immigrants, such as Jewish mobsters Arnold Rothstein, reputed kingpin of organized crime in New York, Waxey Gordon, a prominent bootlegger in that city, and "hit man" Big Jack Zelig.

But it was Chicago rather than New York that earned a reputation as America's capital of organized crime. Assisted by a willing local government under the dominance of Republican William Hale "Big Bill" Thompson, accompanied by crooked police and bought judges, Chicago's crime czars established wide-ranging vice, gambling, and bootlegging operations that were unopposed by law enforcement officials. Though Prohibition provided an enormous cash flow for other criminal activities, organized crime in Chicago had surfaced before 1920 under the leadership of Big Jim Colosimo, who made his millions primarily from prostitution. On his untimely death in 1920, aide Johnny Torrio succeeded Colosimo and added bootlegging to the organization's activities.

A Raid on Illegal Alcohol, Long Island, 1930
Police destroyed thousands of bottles of bootleg liquor worth more than $20,000 in
this suburban home, which had doubled as a bottling and distribution center.
Organized crime entrepreneurs frequently used suburban locations for their ventures.

Torrio was a pioneering thug. Just as many urban-based activities sought suburban locations, once auto and truck transport became widely available, organized crime mechanized and suburbanized as well. The truck replaced the train
as the primary bootlegging conveyance. Torrio also located most of his gambling and prostitution enterprises in Chicago's suburbs, sites that were now
easily accessible thanks to the advent of the automobile. In addition, the working-class suburbs were small enough and sufficiently hungry for capital that
their governments would provide the necessary protection for these activities.
Torrio virtually subjugated the suburb of Burnham, south of Chicago, because
it conveniently bordered on Indiana, enabling the denizens of the various gambling and prostitution houses to give Illinois authorities the slip and make a
quick getaway across the state line if they needed to. He soon added the suburb
of Stickney, where he erected his largest brothel, the sixty-woman Stockade.
Torrio's proudest acquisition was Cicero, a working-class suburb of 50,000 residents west of Chicago. On election day 1924, Torrio's lieutenant Al Capone

led a motorcade into town, ensuring the election of a favorable slate of candidates. Within a year, Cicero was home to 160 speakeasies and gambling houses. The automobile made it possible for pleasure seekers from such posh and staid suburban havens as Lake Forest to arrive in bustling Cicero in half an hour.

The Torrio-Capone organization was not the only group doing business in Chicago. Dion O'Banion and his successor, Hymie Weiss, reaped an annual income of more than a million dollars from the illicit liquor trade, though the Torrio-Capone group was grossing $300 million a year by the late 1920s. By the end of the decade, consolidation had taken over organized crime in Chicago much as in the rest of the corporate world. Literally cut-throat competition resulted in O'Banion's and Weiss's deaths and Torrio's retirement, leaving Al Capone as Chicago's leading crime entrepreneur.

The link between crime and politics was not unique, of course. Corruption had been the bane of American city government since the late nineteenth century, though the Thompson administration in Chicago probably set a record for chicanery. Although Thompson himself managed to escape the weight of the law, authorities caught his Republican colleague "Swede" Lundin dipping into the treasury of the city's public school system for over one million dollars. Lundin may have been a sacrifice to the reformers to enable Thompson to continue his subsidization of organized crime. Al Capone's bulletproof office had three portraits—George Washington, Abraham Lincoln, and "Big Bill."

This is not to imply that the influence of the new urban mass culture in all its forms caused Americans in small midwestern towns to shoot up the local police station or engage in "petting parties in the purple dawn." What it *did* mean was that the statistical confirmation of America as an urban nation in 1920 had its cultural counterpart. Though observers, foreign and domestic, could wax eloquent about America's rural heritage, they acknowledged, for better or for worse, that "America" and "urban" were becoming more synonymous. That alleged repository of American virtue the small town fared poorly in the Twenties. Novelists such as Sinclair Lewis, Sherwood Anderson, and Thomas Wolfe wrote about the "murderous entrenchment against new life" and "the starved meagerness of . . . lives" in small towns. If the city seemed shocking and brutal at times, at least it was also alive, creative, and open.[28]

The vast majority of urban residents manifested no special concern about the city's loose image. They *enjoyed* the urban milieu. Their general affluence supported a vital, heterodox culture that formed a community of common interests amid the diversity of the city. The new mass culture and morals, whatever their reflection of deeper values and needs, touched and indeed emanated from all segments of urban life. A Ruthian clout clearing the right-field fence, Jolson belting out a Dixie melody, all the sights and sounds of Harlem and Broadway were shared by a broad spectrum of the urban population—and, through the technology of communications and transportation, by a good many other Americans as well.

Ethnic Mobility: The Jewish Example

The major ethnic role in shaping urban culture (and organized crime) reflected the immigrants' continuing adaptation to the American city, mixing Old World and American culture to form a distinctive new mass urban sensibility. The musical contributions of the Gershwins and Irving Berlin, for example, were not specifically identifiable as "Jewish," though their backgrounds informed their work and helped, in turn, to transform American music. Place of residence was another marker of the changing ethnic identity among Jews. By the 1920s, second-generation Jews and Italians alike were moving out of the immigrant districts of lower Manhattan to middle-class neighborhoods in the Bronx and Brooklyn. Jewish realtors and builders helped to create some of these neighborhoods, and they employed Jewish craftsmen and laborers as well. The Art Deco apartment buildings that lie in disrepair today along the Grand Concourse in the Bronx were once proud reflections of middle-class emergence and enterprise among New York's Jewish community.

Ironically, and perhaps purposefully, despite the move out of the ghetto and the increasing contact of second-generation Jews with Gentiles, these newer neighborhoods were even more segregated than the lower East Side. In 1920, 54 percent of the city's Jews resided in segregated neighborhoods. By 1930, 72 percent of Jewish New Yorkers did so. At that date, New York's second-generation Jews had acquired many of the trappings of the American urban middle class—a home or apartment in a "nice" neighborhood, a white-collar professional position (eventually, better than three out of four teachers in the New York City school system were Jewish), and a college education at one of the municipal colleges. The sons and daughters of immigrants were also involved in local Democratic politics; eventually they would make their mark in the New Deal administration of Franklin D. Roosevelt. Yet their entrée into the American mainstream did not signify an exit from ethnicity as the neighborhood and its institutions, such as the synagogue, the Young Men's Hebrew Association (inspired by the Young Men's Christian Association, a Protestant-oriented reform institution of the late nineteenth century), and a new creation of the 1920s, the Jewish Center, which combined secular and religious activities ("a *shul* [synagogue] with a school and a pool"), reflected a persistent yet changing ethnic identity.[29]

Other ethnic groups besides the Jews experienced this second-generation transition as well. During the 1920s, second-generation Italians surfaced as an influential political group in New York and other major cities, yet another example of the blend between American ideals and ethnic culture. Once Italian neighborhoods had evolved a social organization growing out of their kinship and personal loyalties, middle-class Italians who emerged as community leaders during the first two decades of the twentieth century used the social network to forge political power. In New York, they joined the Irish as bulwarks in the ruling Democratic Tammany Hall political machine. Where Jewish political ideology tended to be liberal (even socialist at times) and anti–political machine, the Italians were much less concerned with philosophy than with the rewards of power. Consequently, Jews were prominent from the 1920s through the 1960s in anti-Tammany reform efforts and Italians generally were not. Again, ethnicity blended with local politics in a way that both reinforced and transformed both the groups and the institutions they joined.

The first suburban decade capped a remarkable generation of change in the urban environment just as it simultaneously inaugurated a new era. Think of the altered experience of those urban residents who, in 1930, had lived in the city for little more than a generation. In 1890, the average American city was relatively small, limited by the range of the horse-drawn railway; immigrant populations from Europe and the South had not yet begun to make themselves noticeable in large numbers; and the metropolis presented a fairly modest skyline. By 1930, electric trolleys were skimming out to the suburbs as automobiles jammed every urban street; foreign-born and black residents were the majority population in a dozen major cities, creating new cultural forms and influencing urban life in myriad ways; and towering skyscrapers loomed over everything. Change, of course, is the essence of urbanization, the prime factor each generation must cope with and respond to. But 1930 must have been an especially difficult year for some oldtimers, for the change had been rapid and extensive beyond imagining.

Particularly appropriate was the fact that a suburban city—Los Angeles—had emerged to epitomize the first suburban decade—its automobility, the scattering of work and residence and shopping, and the dominance of the single-family home. It would be a mistake, however, to assume that the new spatial order meant a random scattering of uses and people across the metropolitan landscape. The *barrio* of East Los Angeles, the emerging black ghetto of Watts, and the mansions of Bel Air reflected the rigid spatial and social divisions of the new suburban city. In the years after 1930, both the suburb and the metropolitan fragmentation it reflected would become even more marked patterns. A major new actor in the Balkanization of the twentieth-century American city would be the federal government.

Notes

1. Quoted in Kenneth Fox, *Metropolitan America: Urban Life and Urban Policy in the United States, 1940–1980* (Jackson, Miss.: University Press of Mississippi, 1986), pp. 28–29.

2. Quoted in *ibid.*, p. 29.
3. Quoted in Carl Abbott, *Urban America in the Modern Age: 1920 to the Present* (Arlington Heights, Ill.: Harlan Davidson, 1987), p. 41.
4. Quoted in *ibid.*, p. 43.
5. Quoted in James J. Flink, "The Metropolis in the Horseless Age," *Annals of the New York Academy of Sciences* 424 (May 1984): 297.
6. Quoted in Jon C. Teaford, *The Twentieth-Century American City: Problem, Promise, and Reality* (Baltimore: Johns Hopkins University Press, 1986), p. 64.
7. Quoted in Howard L. Preston, *Automobile Age Atlanta: The Making of a Southern Metropolis, 1900–1935* (Athens, Ga.: University of Georgia Press, 1979), p. 113.
8. Quoted in David R. Goldfield, *Cotton Fields and Skyscrapers: Southern City and Region, 1607–1980* (Baton Rouge: Louisiana State University Press, 1982), p. 154.
9. Quoted in *ibid.*, pp. 154–155.
10. Theda Shapiro, "New York–Paris–Berlin: A Tale of Three Cities in Art, 1890–1945," presented at Second International Conference on the History of Urban and Regional Planning, Brighton, England, August, 1980, p. 30.
11. Both quotes from Bayrd Still, ed., *Urban America: A History with Documents* (Boston: Little, Brown, 1974), pp. 367, 368.
12. Benton MacKaye, "End or Peak of Civilization?" *The Survey* 68 (October 1932): 443.
13. Quoted in David R. Goldfield, "Neighborhood Preservation and Community Values in Historical Perspective," in Irwin Altman and Abraham Wandersman, eds., *Neighborhood and Community Environments: Human Behavior and Environments, Advances in Theory and Research* (New York: Plenum, 1987), p. 231.
14. Quoted in William H. Wilson, "Moles and Skylarks," in Donald A. Krueckeberg, ed., *Introduction to Planning History in the United States* (New Brunswick, N.J.: Center for Urban Policy Research, Rutgers University, 1983), p. 100.
15. Quoted in David A. Johnson, "Regional Planning for the Great American Metropolis: New York Between the World Wars," in Daniel Schaffer, ed., *Two Centuries of American Planning* (London: Mansell, 1988) p. 180.
16. Quoted in *ibid.*, p. 179.
17. Quoted in *ibid.*, p. 184.
18. Quoted in Robert Fishman, *Bourgeois Utopias: The Rise and Fall of Suburbia* (New York: Basic Books, 1987), p. 155.
19. Quoted in *ibid.*, pp. 155–156.
20. Quoted in *ibid.*, pp. 171–172.
21. Quoted in Gunther Barth, *City People: The Rise of Modern City Culture in Nineteenth-Century America* (New York: Oxford University Press, 1980), p. 198.
22. Quoted in Gilman M. Ostrander, "The Revolution in Morals," in Joan Hoff Wilson, ed., *The Twenties: The Critical Issues* (Boston: Little, Brown, 1972), p. 139.
23. Quoted in Wayne Cooper, "Claude McKay and the New Negro of the 1920s," *Phylon* 25 (Fall 1964): 297–306.
24. Quoted in Eugene Arden, "The Early Harlem," *Phylon* 20 (Spring 1959): 27.
25. Quoted in August Meier, *Negro Thought in America, 1880–1915* (Ann Arbor: University of Michigan Press, 1966), p. 259.
26. Quoted in Arden, "Early Harlem," p. 27.
27. Quoted in Robert W. Creamer, "Colossus of the Game," *Sports Illustrated* 40 (April 1, 1974): 47.
28. Quotes are from Thomas Wolfe, *Look Homeward, Angel* (New York: Scribners, 1929), p. 155; and Wolfe, *You Can't Go Home Again* (New York: Harper & Bros,. 1934), p. 143.
29. Quoted in Robert A. Rockaway, "World of Their Children: Second-Generation New York Jews," *Journal of Urban History* 12 (February 1986): 194.

CHAPTER 10

The Federal Connection: Urban America in Depression and War

Federal policies did not shape modern metropolitan America any more than the automobile did. Beginning with Franklin D. Roosevelt's New Deal legislation in the 1930s, however, the federal government has subsidized, reinforced, and encouraged the suburban trend. Ironically, no such animal as an explicit urban policy emerged from the array of "alphabet agencies" created during the New Deal era. And these agencies, with a few minor exceptions, had no desire to reorient metropolitan space. Yet the rapidly expanding federal bureaucracy, billions of dollars in grants and loans, and supporting legislation designed to return the nation to economic prosperity all had a significant impact on cities and regions as the federal government took on the role, willingly or not, of partner in metropolitan development.

The Great Depression and the American City

The first step in understanding this unintended but significant relationship between the federal government and the American city is to learn how the Great Depression crippled the capacity of cities to deal with mounting social and economic problems. By the spring of 1932, the human casualties of the Depression had overwhelmed the nation's cities. Unemployment varied widely, from 90 percent in one-industry towns such as Gary, Indiana (steel) to less than 10 percent in oil-rich Houston. Perhaps the best barometer of the Depression's impact on employment were those cities that boasted diversified economies: in Chicago, for example, 40 percent of the workforce was out of work by 1932. Similar rates prevailed in Philadelphia and Baltimore.

These statistics paint a bloodless picture of the Depression's toll. Contemporary reports and observations, in contrast, offer a more vivid glimpse of the human misery generated by the fallen economy. In early 1932, one observer reported the following scene from Chicago: "You can ride across the lovely Michigan Avenue bridge at midnight [with] the lights all about making a dream city of incomparable beauty, while twenty feet below you, on the lower level of the same bridge, are 2,000 homeless, decrepit, shivering and starving men, wrapping themselves in old newspapers to keep from freezing, and lying down in the manure dust to sleep." Writer Edmund Wilson reported in the *New Republic* that "there is not a garbage-dump in Chicago which is not diligently haunted by the hungry." There, bereft of pride and sensibility, they would scavenge for and devour scraps of food. Wilson noticed a woman who, before eating discarded meat, "would always take off her glasses so that she couldn't see the maggots."[1]

The situation was equally bad in Philadelphia. In July 1932, the governor estimated that nearly a quarter of a million of the city's residents "faced actual starvation."[2] A woman in that city reported that she and a friend subsisted mostly on stale bread, purchased for 3½ cents a loaf, for eleven days. Several families reported to the city's Committee for Unemployment Relief (a private agency) that they had routinely gone without food for a day or more to stretch their limited funds. The husband of one of those families gathered dandelions in empty lots for his family to eat in the interim.

Conditions in southern cities were equally miserable and possibly worse. Men who could find work in Birmingham's U.S. Steel colony received 10 to 15 cents per hour, and loan sharks preyed on those who could not. Workers in the steel mills received script for salary, redeemable only at the company store. The murder rate soared, and in 1931 Birmingham led the nation in murders. In Atlanta, half the businesses on famed Peachtree Street lay vacant; the situation was so desperate that some local leaders concocted a "back-to-the-farm" movement in 1931. In reality, the movement was going the other way: hundreds of cotton farmers from rural Georgia roamed the city streets looking for employment because they could not sell their crops.

The depth of urban misery arose in great part from the inability of local governments to fulfill their social service obligations. The cycle of the economic downturn was tragic and seemingly unbreakable. As businesses sank, workers were laid off or fired. Bankrupt businesses and unemployed workers paid no taxes, and the coffers of city treasuries and local charity drives quickly emptied. In most cities real property assessments plummeted, tax revenues fell by anywhere from 25 to 50 percent (and even more in some places), and the debt service on municipal bonds—many floated during the prosperous Twenties—ate up increasingly large proportions of city budgets, rising as high as 70 percent or more in some cities. With little market for new bonds, state limits on bonding authority, and an already burdensome bonded debt, municipalities had pitifully few choices. As cities and school boards ran out of money, they too were forced to lay off or dismiss many police, firefighters, teachers, sanitation workers, clerks, and other public employees. City payrolls were slashed by 50 percent and more, and many programs—especially city planning and public works—were virtually eliminated. And all the unemployed joined the ranks of the sick, the elderly, and the disabled in making tremendous demands on public agencies just as those agencies were becoming less and less able to offer help than ever before. In Cincinnati, where the unemployment rate was 50 percent in 1932, city officials were forced to reduce welfare payments to $5 per week per family to stretch the diminishing treasury. Denver authorities ran out of money entirely in 1931 and formed a private committee that raised $452,700. By the spring of 1932, the committee was over $100,000 in debt.

The situation was worse in the South, where cities had traditionally spent little if anything on public welfare. Birmingham's local government quickly went broke and in 1933 attempted to sell the city parks to raise money. New Orleans authorities did not provide funds for family relief during the 1920s and were unable to generate sufficient revenues to begin doing so during the Depression. The city's major relief effort went into encouraging the unemployed to purchase boxes of oranges and sell them on street corners. At the same time, the city council voted to give $10,000 to the Chamber of Commerce to advertise the city as the "home of cheap and docile labor."[3] Little Rock's government succeeded in securing an emergency appropriation of $20,000 in January 1931, combined with $25,000 raised privately, but the entire sum evaporated three months later.

Even when southern localities were able to establish modest relief appropriations, they invariably discriminated against blacks. In 1931, an article in *Survey Graphic* about the welfare system in Richmond noted that "there was flagrant discrimination in the dispensing of relief to Negroes by both public and private agencies."[4] The city of Norfolk reduced the daily relief allocation to blacks from $2 to $1.25 in early 1933 while retaining the $2 for whites. Houston refused to accept relief applications from Mexicans or blacks.

Municipalities had turned early to state governments for aid. But politically sensitive governors and rural-dominated state legislatures were not very sympathetic, often blaming the cities for spending themselves into bankruptcy.

Banks were of even less help. Because their first priority was to protect their investments, they made loans conditional on balanced municipal budgets or exacted a high price for the renegotiation of existing notes. So local officials looked to a new source for assistance and sought in Washington what they had failed to find elsewhere.

The federal government was aware of the mounting seriousness of the situation but responded with great hesitancy at first in hopes that the downturn would eventually bottom out. Indeed, some government economists looked upon the crisis as an inevitable and necessary adjustment of the business cycle. President Herbert Hoover was a capable man with a record for efficiency and humanitarianism. He also had a proven interest in urban affairs, especially in the areas of planning and zoning. But Hoover and many other Republicans and conservative Democrats were opposed to federal intervention of any kind in local affairs, and especially to large-scale government relief programs that would, they reasoned, only foster dependence and lethargy among the recipients. There was equally no way, they reasoned, to ensure that monies distributed directly to needy citizens would be spent wisely in accomplishing economic recovery.

Consequently, the Hoover administration's programs, devised mainly to assist corporations and banks rather than the mass of citizens, were limited and largely ineffective. The Emergency Relief and Construction Act of 1932 provided a mere $1.5 billion to deal with the economic crisis, and only $300 million of that sum was allocated for emergency relief loans. Detroit alone was spending up to $2 million a month for relief. Projects funded under the act had to be self-liquidating and, even more important, required the approval of state governors, which was often not forthcoming. The Reconstruction Finance Corporation (RFC) established by the act was an inadequate response, and very few of its benefits reached the huge numbers of individual citizens who had been thrown into the maw of poverty and economic uncertainty. As the year 1933 approached, the nation was drifting ever deeper into depression and municipal officials were growing desperate.

By the time the Roosevelt administration took office in March 1933, the conditions in the nation's cities were shocking but not surprising to the new president. Franklin Roosevelt shared some of the assumptions about cities promoted by theorists such as Clarence Perry and Lewis Mumford, including the premise that contemporary urban life was unnatural and debilitating. The men sleeping beneath the Michigan Avenue Bridge or the widow scouring the garbage heaps for food in Philadelphia were tragic but logical results of a civilization that fostered impersonality and isolation. Roosevelt felt great compassion for the victims of this environment, and he was equally aware that urban votes were becoming more important in the Democratic coalition. The advance of trade union membership and the enfranchisement of second-generation immi-

A "Hooverville" in Seattle, 1933

During the Depression, massive unemployment and meager welfare services resulted in countless foreclosures and evictions. In cities across the country, homeless people established makeshift communities on vacant land and derisively named them after the president who was opposed to large-scale federal relief programs.

gránts and blacks significantly expanded the urban electorate. The Roosevelt administration was not especially interested in saving cities, but it was concerned with saving their residents. Philosophical preferences aside, in the end the New Deal transformed the cities and their citizens in equal measure.

Putting the Cities Back to Work

Specifically, four New Deal measures passed between 1933 and 1937 had a major impact on cities and their inhabitants: the Public Works Administration (PWA), established in 1933; the Works Progress Administration (WPA), passed in 1935; the Federal Housing Administration (FHA) in 1934; and the U.S.

Housing Act in 1937. Taken together, these programs pumped more than $8 billion into the nation's cities and metropolitan areas. They reflected a primary objective of the New Deal: to get people and business back to work while minimizing the disruption to basic principles and structures of the economic and political systems.

The PWA spent nearly $2.5 billion between 1933 and 1939 on such urban projects as bridges, airports, public buildings, and water and sewer facilities. Some of these funds were in the form of matching grants and loans that required localities to set up separate agencies or "authorities" with the power to tax and distribute revenues. New York's Robert Moses became that city's most powerful nonelected official by virtue of his management of the Triborough Bridge Authority, the New York Bridge Authority, the Jones Beach State Parkway Authority, the Henry Hudson Parkway Authority, and, eventually, twenty other authorities. Moses controlled millions of federal dollars and was responsible for employing thousands of workers. The impact of the PWA was especially significant in the urban South, where expenditures for infrastructure before the New Deal era had been minimal. In Virginia, for example, the PWA funded a $3 million hydroelectric plant in Danville, a sewage treatment complex in Arlington costing $2.5 million; a public housing project in Richmond for $663,000; and a waterworks for Lynchburg costing $600,000. Perhaps more noteworthy was the assistance granted to small towns, because these communities lacked the resources for most infrastructural improvements at any time. In fact, three out of four projects funded by the PWA in the South were located in towns of less than 1,000 inhabitants, such as Tyronza, Arkansas and Goose Creek, Texas, which both received public water systems.

The WPA was more strictly an urban employment program and employed workers directly at $50 per month to work on labor-intensive projects. The largest percentage (40 percent) of WPA funds went to constructing roadways, including 67,000 miles of urban streets. The WPA also built and designed 25,000 urban parks, athletic fields, and playgrounds, including New York's Central Park Zoo and Grant Park in San Francisco. Again, the impact on southern cities was significant, for many of these localities had exhausted public and private sources of unemployment relief. Though critics claimed "WPA" stood for "We Poke Along" (workers knew that once they finished a project they returned to the unemployment rolls), it paid cash wages that not only sustained the workers and their families but businesses as well, for the latter benefited from the increased consumer purchasing power.

The New Deal also initiated a federal housing program. The housing construction industry was traditionally an economic barometer: if housing starts rose, the thinking went, so would the rest of the economy. And housing was intimately connected to the nation's weakened financial institutions. The pre-

WPA Workers Outside Memphis, 1936

Aside from providing means of employment, the Works Progress Administration built roads, bridges, public buildings, and other essential structures for many cities, especially in the South. These men are working on a farm-to-market highway.

vailing mortgage system required the borrower to pay interest on the loan until the end of five or ten years, when the full value of the loan was due. Most borrowers merely refinanced at that time, but when the Depression struck banks had no capital to support refinancing. Unemployed homeowners could not pay up, and the nation attained a rate of 1,000 foreclosures a day by 1932. The banks had plenty of properties but no capital; erstwhile middle-class families had no homes and, in some cases, no place to live. Though officials did not keep figures on the homeless, an estimated more than 5 million urban residents were homeless at any particular time between 1933 and 1937. New Deal housing policy sought to address all these concerns, but it was most successful in restoring the financial security of mortgage loans for borrower and lender alike and in supporting the middle-class home buyer in fulfilling his dream of a single-family home, preferably in the suburbs.

The Home Owners Loan Corporation (HOLC) was the Roosevelt administration's first attempt to stem foreclosures and lay a sound financial foundation for both lender and borrower. Signed in June 1933, the HOLC refinanced over 1 million short-term mortgages, replacing them with long-term (twenty to thirty years) notes whose payments included both principal and interest. The HOLC also devised a uniform appraisal system that divided urban neighborhoods into four categories. Generally, increasing age of properties and growing numbers of ethnic or black residents guaranteed a less favorable rating. HOLC bureaucrats subscribed to prevailing theories of urbanization that viewed age and diversity of uses and residents as liabilities. Though HOLC did not usually discriminate in its loan procedures, private institutions and HOLC's successor, the FHA, took up the categories and proceeded to condemn scores of urban neighborhoods to decay as a result of disinvestment. This practice became known as "redlining" after the agencies' practice of color-coding neighborhoods by category, with those least desirable outlined in red.

The adverse results of this urban form of triage would not become evident until the 1950s and 1960s. In the meantime, the FHA improved on the support tendered to home buyers under the HOLC by guaranteeing loans for private lending institutions so that defaults would not hurt banks. An immediate result of this guarantee was a drop in interest rates by 2 to 3 percentage points (prior to the establishment of the FHA, mortgage rates had averaged between 6 and 8 percent), which increased the affordability of home loans. The long-term result was a sharp increase in home ownership, from 44 percent in 1934 to 63 percent by 1972. Builders were also eligible for long-term loans, which reduced their risk and encouraged larger-scale projects while at the same time ensuring that their customers would also have access to long-term guaranteed loans. The FHA further assisted builders by listing new suburban homes in their top loan guarantee category. Finally, the Internal Revenue Service allowed borrowers to deduct mortgage interest (and property taxes) on their tax returns. By the early 1950s, this tax subsidy amounted to several billion dollars annually, more than for any other federal housing program.

The federal government also constructed its own housing for families that could not afford market-rate dwellings. The Federal Emergency Housing Corporation (FEHC), created as a division within the PWA in December 1933, erected some fifty housing projects in thirty-six cities until the program ended in 1937. Prospective residents had to be employed and earn a monthly family income six times the monthly rent. These were clearly not units for the poor, though working-class families could and did qualify. And the units were open to all ethnic and racial groups, though the PWA maintained segregation within respective projects.

The FEHC's activities came to an abrupt halt in July 1935, as the U.S. Circuit Court of Appeals ruled in *U.S.* v. *Certain Lands in the City of Louisville* that the federal government had no constitutional authority to build housing and to condemn land for that purpose (except on federal property). The government could, however, provide funds for *local* authorities to erect public housing. By the end of 1936, moreover, no less than thirty states had passed enabling legislation for local public development authorities. The following year, Congress passed the U.S. Housing Act (also known as the Wagner-Steagall Act) to direct federal funding to these local authorities. By 1941, local authorities had constructed 130,000 new units in 300 projects across the country under USHA auspices. The housing, generally of low-rise design, was built in brick with no architectural frills. Though uninspired, it was considerably better than what it replaced—rotting, wood-frame, rat-infested dwellings lacking toilets and hot running water. In addition, every room in public housing had a window, and residents looked out on well-landscaped grounds where children could play without fear of traffic.

Creating an environment rather than merely putting up housing was a basic goal of the USHA program. The inclusion of this objective came in great part from the effective lobbying of such housing reformers as Catherine Bauer and Edith Wood, who admired the European public housing developments of the 1930s characterized by low-rise, light and airy structures sited among landscaped grounds with play areas and communal facilities designed to create a neighborhood that would buffer residents from the harsher features of the urban environment. The new environment, theorists believed, would reconstruct the sense of community shattered by contemporary urban life and help to rebuild and improve the lives of the residents. As housing reformer Abraham Goldfield explained in 1938, "The very purpose of the public project is to eliminate as many as possible of the grave social evils of the slum and none is more deadly than the state of unorganized isolation of families and of individuals which the slum makes inevitable."[5]

The Roosevelt administration "sold" Congress on USHA by promoting it both as an employment package and as a way to protect threatened center city property values. In turn, cities countered the charges of creeping socialism by touting the housing program as a boon for free enterprise. As Atlanta's housing chief Charles F. Palmer (himself a real-estate developer) explained to his colleagues, "wiping out the slum area would enhance the value of our central business properties."[6] This is the primary reason that cities did not construct public housing on the urban periphery as European cities did. The periphery was to be the location for private, single-family homes; the center city was the candidate for radical surgery and reconstruction in order to boost property values in decayed areas and protect them in adjacent commercial districts. The authorities granted the design preferences of the housing reformers but otherwise ignored their counsel. As one discouraged housing reformer summarized the USHA experience in New York: "Sovereignty over geographical allocation, quantity, quality, and the relation of units to families is exercised under the rights of ownership in the interests of shortage, price, and profit."[7]

The arguments of federal officials and local housing reformers were not always persuasive, especially in the South, where some urban and state leaders regarded federal intrusions of any kind with suspicion. New Deal relief efforts reduced the dependence of blacks on whites, and federally funded housing would further that process. Some state administrations threw as many obstacles as possible in front of federal programs, especially those concerned with housing. As Georgia Governor Eugene Talmadge offered, "Slums don't hurt nobody. In fact, slums are good for people. It takes strong people to survive 'em."

By 1939, Congress was in a conservative mood and alarmed at skyrocketing federal expenditures. Real-estate developers became concerned that too much public housing would reduce the need for private housing. Congress cut off USHA funding except for those projects already planned or underway.

The USHA episode is instructive primarily because it foreshadowed nearly a generation of federal housing policy after World War II. First, it demonstrated the important role played by real-estate interests in formulating and implementing federal housing legislation. Second, it reflected the growing concern over center city decline and the need for drastic solutions to reverse this process. Third, it indicated that employment rather than housing provision was the primary focus of federal housing policy. Finally, it demonstrated that local governments, more vulnerable to local pressures than the federal bureaucracy, could undermine attempts to set national standards and policy for urban America. The Roosevelt administration had openly challenged neither the segregationist local governments in the South nor the big city bosses elsewhere.

This is not to suggest that cities took New Deal money and ran. The federal-city relationship that developed during this era was complex and worked in both directions. Mayors from across the country formed the U.S. Conference of Mayors in 1933 as a lobbying group for federal urban programs. This conference, which marked the first time that the nation's mayors had acted in concert to identify common issues, continues today as the prime conduit for urban interests.

At the federal level, the National Planning Board (later renamed the National Resources Planning Board) reflected the administration's understanding that urban problems required regional solutions. By 1938, the NRPB had helped create planning authorities in 500 regions and counties throughout the country; it produced 370 major reports on such topics as housing, welfare, and public works designed to assist local and regional bodies in planning for future development; and, in 1937, its Urbanism Committee produced the first major analysis of urban problems in both metropolitan and national contexts, titled *Our Cities—Their Role in the National Economy.*

Our Cities examined thirty-two metropolitan problems from poverty to the lack of regional cooperation and recommended an array of federal policies and programs, many of which the government has implemented in the ensuing half century. Contrary to the impression of many theorists and some popular perceptions at the time, the tone of the report was generally optimistic. The authors' major concern was that decentralization would sap the vitality of urban life, and they framed that concern in language the civic leadership could understand: "What is to become of our great cities? Is 'suburbanitis' a kind of disease with everyone rushing to the fringes of the urban area, or is it a healthy growth? What is to become of the property values downtown?" Unlike the real-estate community, however, the report did not recommend radical surgery for the center. Using the organic metaphor, it asserted that urban problems "are but blemishes or infections which an otherwise healthy organism can check . . . [through] judicious reshaping of the urban community and region by systematic development and redevelopment in accordance with forward-looking and intelligent plans." Although the authors urged policy makers to take a metropolitan perspective and draw plans in concert for both urban and suburban development, the clear objective of *Our Cities* was to reclaim the city and extend its influence, a sentiment more in line with the Regional Plan of New York than with Lewis Mumford's conception of regional balance. The report's suggestions, once implemented, would increase "the benefits of modern civilization which the great city has brought to an ever-increasing proportion of our people."[8]

Our Cities highlighted the metropolitan spatial implications of the Roosevelt administration's urban policy. New Deal housing policy as reflected in FHA and USHA either sought to develop a building program for the suburbs (FHA) or to reclaim the city center through slum clearance and reconstruction (USHA). One policy would obviously reserve the suburbs for residence, draining the city of its middle class; the other would restructure the center as a corporate concentration surrounded by poor people. Metropolitan spatial development was moving in this direction anyway by the 1920s, but federal policy sharpened the divisions. The driving perception behind these policies was that city and suburb represented two different environments that demanded very different policy approaches. Where European planners perceived the metropolitan area as a single entity, *Our Cities,* for all of its devotion to metropolitan notions, framed its discussion in city versus suburb rhetoric, with the suburbs generally cast in the role of villain.

On the other hand, another New Deal program developed by the Resettlement Administration (RA) took up the opposite side's cause, though that program also viewed city and suburbs as distinctive and separate parts of the metropolitan environment. RA director Rexford Guy Tugwell believed that the metropolitan future belonged to the suburbs. He felt that slum clearance and center city rebuilding efforts would neither halt urban decline nor improve living conditions for urban residents. Rather than merely monitoring or reinforcing contemporary decentralization trends, Tugwell proposed, the federal government should assume an active role in the suburban process. To that end, he proposed satellite cities outside of major urban centers. "My idea," he explained, "is to go just outside centers of population, pick up cheap land, build a whole community and entice people into it."[9] Tugwell's idea was not new—Lewis Mumford and his RPAA colleagues had advanced similar proposals more than a decade earlier. The major difference, however, was that Tugwell did not assume that his satellite cities would create a corresponding revival of the city. Tugwell believed he was merely organizing the inevitable—the decline of the city and the rise of the suburb.

The greenbelt towns program, as Tugwell called his experiment, adopted several of the Radburn planning notions even if they did not follow that project's philosophy. Superblocks comprised the basic units of these communities, which also had a careful separation of automobiles and pedestrians, open spaces for play areas, and small shopping centers to service the superblock neighborhood. Tugwell hoped that, unlike Radburn, his greenbelt towns would attract low- to moderate-income families. To hold down costs and fulfill this objective, the RA built large numbers of multiple-unit dwellings.

Between September 1937 and June 1938, families moved into three greenbelt towns—Greenbelt, Maryland (near Washington, D.C.); Greenhills, Ohio (outside Cincinnati); and Greendale, Wisconsin (near Milwaukee). Tugwell hoped to build twenty-five of these towns that would eventually house over 200,000 people who would enjoy a quick commute to work, community center facilities, and abundant opportunities for organized recreational and social activities. The sense of community that had allegedly been sundered by the city would be restored in this new environment.

Tugwell never realized his vision. The conservative wave that drowned the USHA program killed the RA as well. Opponents claimed that the three towns were "socialistic" and adversely affected nearby land values by virtue of their building densities and the type of people they attracted. Even if Congress had not scuttled the program, however, it is unlikely that the greenbelt program would have advanced much further. Land and construction costs ran far ahead of estimates and the communities failed to attract businesses and light industry, making the towns little more than planned middle-class bedroom suburbs. By 1954, the federal government had sold off its remaining holdings in the towns.

The New Deal Legacy

The failure of the greenbelt program as well as the abortive attempts to provide low-cost housing should not obscure the very real urban advances that arose out of the New Deal. New infrastructure, relief assistance, and encouragement for formalizing the city and regional planning bureaucracies were important elements in urban recovery. As New York's mayor Fiorello La Guardia, said, "If it weren't for the federal aid, I don't know what any of us could have done."[10]

La Guardia exemplified the new leadership that emerged in some cities in response to New Deal initiatives. Their objectives centered on channeling federal funds into a variety of city-building projects and planning systematically for future development. The Depression convinced civic leaders as never before that growth was not inevitable and that decline, especially given the suburban trend during the 1920s, was a distinct possibility. The New Deal presented these leaders with an opportunity to adopt aggressive strategies to reorder the space of the industrial city into a form more compatible with the realities of the metropolitan era. The various public works projects undertaken with federal assistance were much more than "make-work" for the urban unemployed; they were investments in future economic development. In Dallas, for example, a group of bankers, builders, and retailers formed the Citizens Council in 1937 to set a development agenda for the city's government. In Atlanta, the new administration of Mayor William B. Hartsfield in 1937 streamlined budgeting procedures, adopted long-range planning techniques and, most important, resolved to build a major new airport that would transform Atlanta from a regional distribution hub to one of the nation's major commercial centers. In some respects, these programs represented a revival of the business progressivism of the 1920s. But unlike the earlier efforts, these new developments were accompanied by expanding bureaucracies, the hiring of experts, the willingness to use planning for more than merely zoning or traffic control, and federal support.

A new sense of urgency obtained as well in instituting these measures. The Depression was in part responsible for the more sober outlook. But there was also an increasing pessimism among Americans about cities and their possibilities. Although voices of doom had been audible in the previous decade, the artists, filmmakers, and novelists whose business it was to interpret American life frequently made strong positive statements about the urban environment even while acknowledging its shortcomings. These affirmations of the city became less common during the 1930s. This was hardly surprising in view of the fact that most cities scarcely presented a majestic aspect amid the human and structural debris of the Depression. Artists Raphael Soyer and Reginald Marsh chose the homeless and breadlines for subjects. Ben Shahn depicted the isolation and loneliness of urban life—a favorite theme of academic theorists—in his cityscapes of monotonous façades and empty lots. And Edward Hopper's simple scenes of diners and theaters evoked the sense of alienation that urban life had fostered.

The film industry, which remained one of the few prosperous business activities during the 1930s, frequently helped moviegoers drown their woes in frothy musicals. But when Hollywood tried realism, the city often fared badly, as in

Angels with Dirty Faces (1937), which hammered home the moral that the degradation of slum life led inevitably to crime. *Dead End* (1937) carried a similar message, adding the menace of class struggle. But it was a documentary, *The City,* produced by noted filmmaker Pare Lorentz with a grant from the Carnegie Foundation, that most effectively embodied the informed perspective on urban America in the 1930s. Lewis Mumford served as script consultant and Aaron Copland helped with the score of this movie, which opened in 1938 and became a mainstay at Robert Moses's New York World's Fair the following year. *The City* opens with scenes of a bucolic New England village, then moves to a slum-scarred Pennsylvania mill town and, eventually, to New York City during the lunch hour with its attendant congestion and pollution. The weekend offers no escape from the crowd, as city dwellers jam roads for the beaches barely able to make their way around overheated cars. Babies wail and tempers flare; the respite from the tensions of the week evaporates. Finally, deliverance comes in a form of a squeaky-clean suburb where life proceeds at a human pace and the countryside waits just outside the front door. This idyllic vision was a fitting introduction to the postwar era.

Cities at War

World War II itself did not so much alter the spatial arrangements in metropolitan America as it accelerated them. This is surprising considering the great amount of mobility that took place during the war: the migration from depressed rural areas to cities bursting with war industries; the movement of young men and women to training bases around the country and then overseas; and the entrance of middle-class women into the urban workforce in record numbers. A good deal of this mobility, however, reinforced the suburban tendencies already visible in metropolitan America.

Decentralization in fact occurred at two levels during the war. The technological demands of modern warfare gave significant boosts to the infant electronics and aircraft industries. These industries required spacious facilities that could be built with a minimum of delay. From a strategic point of view, the location of war industries in the midst of large urban populations made little sense. The high-tech bastions of today—Route 128 around Boston, and the Silicon Valley south of San Francisco—originated during World War II. The federal War Production Board spent over $100 million each to construct the massive Willow Run bomber plant 17 miles outside Detroit and the Kaiser Steel Plant in Fontana, 35 miles outside Los Angeles. The government also furnished defense facilities with roads and housing.

The location of these and other defense establishments highlighted a second focus of industrial decentralization. If strategic considerations demanded sub-

Riveting at a Nashville Defense Plant, 1942
World War II provided a big economic boost to southern cities and their residents. Although the labor shortage did not erase discrimination, it did allow some blacks to work at well-paid occupations for the first time in their lives.

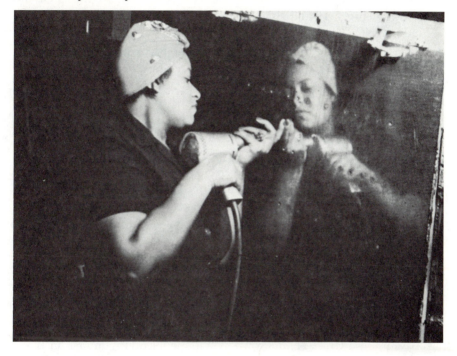

urban sites, they also suggested a policy of dispersion throughout the country. The nation's sudden plunge into global war required the rapid training of troops that was best accomplished in the milder climates of the South and Southwest. The dispersal of bases and defense contracts also addressed the economic needs of the South, a region that had been dubbed the nation's "Number One economic problem" in 1938. Not so coincidentally, southern Democrats occupied key committee chairmanships in the Congress. Naval facilities at Charleston and Norfolk as well as major shipbuilding operations at Pascagoula, Mississippi and Mobile were some examples of the dovetailing of strategic necessity and politics. Atlanta benefited from the expansion of Fort McPherson and the location of a B-29 plant in nearby Marietta. In the Southwest, perpetual sunshine led military planners to locate two major aircraft plants in Tucson and Phoenix, respectively. By 1943, southern California was the aircraft capital of the world, with Douglas, North American, Lockheed, Hughes, and Northrop scattered about the Los Angeles metropolitan area.

The sudden burst of economic activity overtaxed the capacities of many urban governments. The tendency to locate facilities in the smaller cities of the South and Southwest as well as in suburban areas meant that local administrations that had previously carried minimal responsibilities now confronted unprecedented health, housing, and service problems. Mobile was the fastest-growing city in the country between 1940 and 1943; Norfolk placed second. The population crush overwhelmed Mobile; with two major shipyards in addition to an Alcoa plant, the city turned into a dense makeshift campground almost overnight. Rooming-house boarders slept in shifts and any multiple-unit structure became a tightly packed dormitory. When author John Dos Passos visited the city in 1943, the scene shocked even this veteran observer of disorder. Mobile, he said, looked "trampled and battered like a city that's been taken by storm. Sidewalks are crowded. Gutters are stacked with litter. . . . Garbage cans are overflowing. Framehouses on treeshaded streets bulge with men. . . . Cues [sic] wait outside of movies and lunchrooms."[11] The nineteen-member police force was inadequate to challenge the street gangs, vandalism, and looting that accompanied the frontier conditions. City services disintegrated, with refuse collection and water supply disappearing altogether at too-frequent intervals. By 1944, the federal government had assumed the task of providing housing and services to residents.

If Mobile, a city of over 100,000 inhabitants in 1940, was unable to cope with its newfound reality as a boom town, smaller southern cities and towns experienced even more chaotic upheavals. In 1940, Pascagoula was a quiet fishing and farming town on the Mississippi Gulf Coast. As the site of the sprawling Ingalls shipyard after 1941, the town saw its population quintuple in three years. Most of the newcomers arrived from the Mississippi countryside and were unfamiliar with urban densities and lifestyles that soon characterized the town. "In the grocery stores they are lost," one observer wrote, "because they do not know what to buy, cannot make up their minds quickly in the crowd, and get jostled around by the others." They crowded into trailers and tents in areas of inadequate or absent services, sewage facilities, and roads. Overworked medical and social service personnel provided sporadic assistance when possible, but frequently it was not. A young mother whose husband worked at Ingalls expressed the human costs of this situation in a resigned country drawl, as if her story were not extraordinary. Her two-year-old son, she explained, "was sleeping and he waked up and began crying, so I carried him in the living room, and his hands began drawing, and his feet, and I thought he was going into convulsions. . . . My husband . . . went to call the doctor . . . and told him the baby was going into convulsions, and the doctor told him to give him the medicine . . . and he thought the baby would be all right. And my husband told him he was vomiting it up just as fast as we gave it to him, and the doctor said he was tired and had to go to bed and get some sleep, and he didn't come."[12] The baby died.

The sudden intrusion of newcomers created tensions. As one observer noted of the population explosion in Connecticut's river valleys, "New England fears, justly, that the emigrations will distend and misshape beyond prospect of future repair the coastal towns and valley cities which are their objectives." At the huge suburban Willow Run bomber plant, one long-time resident complained, "Before the bomber plant was built, everything was perfect here. Everybody knew everybody else and all were happy and contented. Then came that bomber plant and this influx of riffraff, mostly Southerners. You can't be sure of these people."[13] Many of the newcomers were single and unaccustomed to living in congested settings.

Generally, however, the war had a favorable long-term impact on the urban South. Ellington Air Force Base in Houston eventually became NASA's Johnson Space Flight Center. The federal government spent over $1.5 billion in Florida from 1941 to 1945—the largest sum appropriated to any state in the nation; almost one-half of this expenditure went to shipbuilding operations at Jacksonville, Miami, Tampa, and Panama City. Military spending, in turn, encouraged the development of electronics research and manufacturing firms, scientific equipment companies, and aeronautics machinery plants. The growth of high-technology industry in the South had a positive impact on a region traditionally burdened with low-technology, low-wage rural industries. Between 1940 and 1960, the high-wage industrial sector increased by 180 percent in the South, compared with a national rate of 92 percent.

In the short run, however, the overcrowding in the urban South and elsewhere, and the competition for jobs, housing, and recreational facilities generated tensions that occasionally exploded into violence. Wartime opportunities and labor shortages encouraged blacks to migrate from southern rural areas to cities across the country. Between 1940 and 1943, roughly 600,000 blacks left the rural and small-town South for cities, more than half of that number migrating to cities of the North and Midwest, with Detroit experiencing the largest absolute increase—65,000 blacks. When large numbers of blacks had migrated during World War I, race riots occurred in several cities. A similar scenario unfolded during the years of World War II, though with one crucial difference.

In 1943, trouble flared at an amusement park in Detroit when a gang of black youths attacked whites. Whites retaliated and the riot spread to the city itself, accompanied by burning, looting, and the deaths of twenty-five blacks and nine whites. Whereas blacks were primarily victims in the riots during and following World War I, the Detroit riot, along with a similar disturbance in New York's Harlem, offered a new and—to urban whites— more threatening prospect— blacks either initiated the violence or retaliated when whites attacked them. This pattern foreshadowed the racial violence of the 1960s.

In southern cities, federal objectives to end discrimination in hiring at defense plants clashed with local customs relegating blacks to the most menial positions regardless of skill levels. Black leaders argued that discrimination was both contrary to the fight for freedom and to efficiency in war production. At the Charleston Navy Yard, for example, blacks trained whites for skilled positions yet did not receive promotions to those positions for themselves. And when a few blacks entered skilled positions, their wage rates were usually lower than the rates for white workers. But when the Alabama Dry Dock and Shipbuilding Company in Mobile upgraded some black workers to skilled jobs, white workers rioted.

Blacks were not the only targets of racial violence during the war. In 1943, the same summer as the Detroit riot, restless sailors in Los Angeles, avenging an attack by a Mexican youth gang on one of their own, roamed for several nights through the Chicano *barrio,* attacking every Mexican boy they could find, while the police stood idly by. The targets were different, but this fact merely underscored the continued drift of urban society into separate racial entities.

The federal government sought to alleviate at least one source of conflict by providing housing for workers in defense plants where private builders were unable to meet the demand. Most of these structures, however, by agreement with real-estate interests, were temporary. The government thus missed an opportunity to supplement the nation's metropolitan housing stock at a time of housing shortages. Congress also provided strapped cities with assistance for nursery schools, child-care centers, elementary and secondary school expansion, and recreational facilities through the Community Facilities Act, passed in 1941, which enabled married women with children to work in defense plants and offered nutritional and parenting advice as well.

For those who were concerned that the war would further disintegrate the sense of community and the family in metropolitan areas, these communal facilities were reassuring. But they proved to be as temporary as government housing. Retrenchment and elimination of federal programs were top priorities of the first postwar Congress. The business community was concerned that the precedent of government intrusion into private spheres of activity would spread. These sentiments stood in marked contrast to European perceptions of how their national governments might relate to cities after the war. In Great Britain, for example, the national government brought all land development under national control to direct the postwar distribution of industry and population, especially into new, planned communities on the periphery of major metropolitan areas. The ultimate objective was to end the "disastrous harvest of slums, sickness, stunted population, and human misery."[14] No such comprehensive planning program emerged in the United States, though the National Resources Planning Board recommended such an effort. Centralized planning ran counter to the real-estate free-for-all that had traditionally characterized metropolitan development. Then, too, the urgency for a comprehensive document was not present—the United States had experienced none of the wartime destruction suffered by the British. After the war, therefore, federal urban policy continued to emerge in a piecemeal and often contradictory fashion. And private development interests continued to exert a significant influence on both policy formulation and implementation.

Notes

1. Both quotes from Jon C. Teaford, *The Twentieth-Century American City: Problem, Promise, and Reality* (Baltimore: Johns Hopkins University Press, 1986), pp. 77, 78.
2. Quoted in Bayrd Still, ed., *Urban America: A History with Documents* (Boston: Little, Brown, 1974), p. 421.
3. Quoted in Roger Biles, "The Urban South in the Great Depression," unpublished manuscript, p. 90.
4. Quoted in Ronald L. Heinemann, *Depression and New Deal in Virginia: The Enduring Dominion* (Charlottesville, Va.: University Press of Virginia, 1983), p. 39.
5. Quoted in Gail Radford, "Reform Housing in the Twentieth Century: The New Community Ideal Takes Shape," presented at the Organization of American Historians Convention, New York, April 1986, p. 34.
6. Quoted in Biles, "Urban South in the Great Depression," pp. 140–141.
7. Quoted in Rosalie Genevro, "Site Selection and the New York City Housing Authority, 1934–1939," *Journal of Urban History* 12 (August 1986): 343.
8. Quoted in Carl Abbott, *Urban America in the Modern Age: 1920 to the Present* (Arlington Heights, Ill.: Harlan Davidson, 1987), p. 54.
9. Quoted in John Hancock, "The New Deal and American Planning: the 1930s," in Daniel Schaffer, ed., *Two Centuries of American Planning* (London: Mansell, 1988), p. 215.
10. Quoted in Mark I. Gelfand, *A Nation of Cities: The Federal Government and Urban America, 1933–1965* (New York: Oxford University Press, 1975), p. 46.
11. Quoted in David R. Goldfield, *Cotton Fields and Skyscrapers: Southern City and Region, 1607–1980* (Baton Rouge: Louisiana State University Press, 1982), pp. 183–184.
12. Both quotes from David R. Goldfield, *Promised Land: The South since 1945* (Arlington Heights, Ill.: Harlan Davidson, 1987), pp. 9, 10.
13. Quoted in Phillip J. Funigiello, *The Challenge to Urban Liberalism: Federal-City Relations During World War II* (Knoxville: University of Tennessee Press, 1978), p. 34.
14. Quoted in *ibid.*, p. 191.

Divided Metropolis: City and Suburb in the Postwar Era, 1945–1970

The greatest domestic concern among postwar public officials was the potential of a relapse into economic depression once the war machinery was dismantled. For returning GIs and their young families, the most important issues were finding a job and a place to live. Through the Depression and World War II, jobs and housing had stayed in short supply. The means to obtain that housing were equally scarce: one source estimated that by 1945, new housing—even if it had been available—would have been beyond the means of 75 percent of American families. In addition, many consumer items, from automobiles to washing machines, had not been accessible in terms of price and quantity since the early 1930s. For more than a decade the American Dream had been on hold. Now at last it was possible to dream again.

Buoyed by massive federal spending, the urban economy experienced a new wave of corporate consolidations that, in turn, generated new demands for accounting, legal, banking, advertising, and management consultant activities. At the same time, industries maintained the labor-saving technology developed or purchased during the war while they converted to peacetime production. The result was a significant increase in white-collar jobs for both men and women after the war—an increase that coincided with the preferences of returning GIs as well. Factory work, especially for women, did not enjoy high status or income. Moreover, the second and emerging third generations of immigrants perceived the factory as the bottom rung on the success ladder, something their fathers and mothers or grandfathers and grandmothers put up with in order to subsist in the New World. Finally, the generous GI Bill enabled returning veterans to obtain free college educations to train for the growing numbers of white-collar positions. Because office jobs paid higher wages than factory occupations, consumer demand increased and so, consequently, did production.

The changing economy also revived the moribund home building industry with a significant boost from the federal government. Over 2.5 million families lived with relatives in 1946, an arrangement that created strains on both people and housing stock, limited family size, and reduced job-hunting mobility. The problem was to create enough housing units at affordable prices to satisfy, at least in part, the burgeoning demand for private residential space. Constructing affordable housing depended in part on cheap and abundant land. Building many houses lowered the per unit cost of each dwelling, and cheap land reduced the selling price as well. Because few builders could finance large-scale production and land assemblage costs, it was reasoned, the FHA (with its categories of eligible neighborhoods) would need to play a mediating role. The government agreed to supply large builders (those who built more than a hundred houses per year and employed over a hundred people) with billions of dollars in credit and insured loans up to 95 percent of the value of the house. In turn, builders were able to offer financing to prospective buyers. The combined result of pent-up demand and subsidized supply was a suburban land and housing boom that fixed the suburb as the residential location of choice among Americans. By 1970, we had become a suburban nation.

The Apotheosis of the Suburban Dream

William J. Levitt was fond of saying, "No man who owns his own house and lot can be a Communist. He has too much to do."[1] Levitt's homily doubtless struck home in the Cold War era, but his was more than a political statement. For if home ownership was an antidote to Communism, then Levitt must rank as one of the greatest anti-Communists who ever lived. In 1947, Levitt's father and business partner, Abraham, purchased 1,400 acres of Long Island potato farms 30 miles from New York City. Utilizing prefabrication, employing his own workforce, manufacturing and supplying his own materials (lumber, for example, came from Levitt's own company and was cut from his own timber with his own equipment to his own specifications), and coordinating work-

Levittown, Long Island
From above, this post–World War II suburban housing development looks terribly
boring. But it was an affordable dream come true for working-class city dwellers. Over
time and with ingenuity, homeowners were able to transform their cookie-cutter
houses into distinctive residences.

forces and materials with precision, Levitt was producing 35 houses per day and
150 houses per week by 1948.

The houses in the several Levittowns constructed in the Northeast by the
early 1950s sold initially for $7,990, or more than $1,500 less than the nearest
competitor's houses. All of Levitt's houses were small, detached, single-family
homes, Cape Cod in style and centrally located on a small lot. It became fashionable to refer to these structures as "ticky-tacky," but they were well constructed, and variety in any case had never been a characteristic of suburban
architecture, whether there were 9,000 builders or just one. A visit to any Levittown today reveals neat, tree-lined streets with small but solid houses that have

been lent some individuality by owners' additions to the original house or variations in the façade. Most important, the Levittowns enabled thousands of families to fulfill their dreams of home and land ownership—dreams that previously
had been primarily confined to upper-income groups and portions of the middle
class. For $56 a month, with no down payment, a GI could move into a house
equipped with a fireplace, electric range and refrigerator, washer, and even a
television—at no extra cost. It was cheaper than renting an apartment in the
city, and cheaper still with federal and state tax incentives. Eager buyers camped
out overnight before a Levitt opening.

America's transformation into a suburban nation turned it into a nation of
homeowners at the same time. By 1970, nearly two out of every three American
families owned their own home, compared with Sweden's rate of home ownership—the highest in Europe—of 35 percent. The FHA helped to introduce
equity into the estates of more than 35 million families between 1933 and 1978.
The suburban housing demand generated record building years that, in turn,
supported a national economy oriented toward continued suburban growth.
Builders constructed 14 million single-family homes between 1946 and 1960,
compared with 2 million new apartment units during that time period. The
building boom spawned an economy of its own that supported the appliance,
automobile, and furniture industries, among others. The building process itself
required steel, lumber, glass and textiles, and the construction of infrastructure
and schools providing work from laborers to teachers. Not surprisingly, the
suburban population of the nation's twenty largest metropolitan areas grew by
45 percent during the 1950s, whereas their center cities added only 0.1 percent.

The American suburb was no longer the posh and spiritually barren playground for decadent urban wealth, as Fitzgerald portrayed it, nor was it, as
Mumford suggested, "merely a halting place."[2] After the postwar economy
democratized it, the suburb became a place for the average American family to plant its roots, to fulfill its dreams and spin new ones. Jay Gatsby pursued his dream to suburbia and never reached it. But millions of other urban
Americans did.

Not everyone welcomed the rise of postwar suburbia. Just as an earlier generation of urban theorists and planners had expended considerable energy dis-
secting the alleged pathologies of urban life, a new generation of experts offered
equally dire diagnoses of the suburbs. Sociologist David Riesman complained
about low suburban densities in the 1950s with the same fervor as earlier sociologists had condemned high urban densities. Low densities, Riesman claimed,
destroyed diversity and rendered the suburb sterile. Picking up that theme, William Whyte's analysis of Park Forest, a Chicago suburb, in his book *The Organization Man* found a stifling conformity, from the designs of the homes to the
people within them—"organization men"— trained to work within large cor-

porations. Their wives functioned primarily to establish a comfortable home environment for their husbands, with few outside interests except their childrens' recreational and school activities. Other works on suburban life in the 1950s, bearing titles such as *The Split Level Trap* and *The Crack in the Picture Window,* stressed similar themes.

The interior and exterior spatial arrangements of the new suburbs seemed to lend credence to some of the critiques. Earlier in the century, Frank Lloyd Wright, among others, had introduced the concept of separating the home from its surroundings, emphasizing the family rather than the community; this ideal became a common feature of suburban architecture after World War II. The two-car attached garage dominated the front view of many suburban homes. Residents frequently entered through a side door. Porches were gone from the front; they had crept around to the back of the house and were now called a "deck" or a "patio." Front entrances were no longer special or even obvious entrées to the home. This was a *private* residence turned in on itself and its occupants. Beyond its borders lay an alien, or at least a sharply demarcated, space, a judgment reflected in the lack of sidewalks in most communities. Single-family home zoning, lot size minimums, and "Caucasian only" covenant restrictions ensured further protection. This was not the protection of ethnicity but rather of class and race. If "melting pot" was a poor metaphor for the ethnically segregated neighborhoods of the city, it was a bit more descriptive at least in the suburbs. But the bow to diversity ended there.

The uniformity of the suburban population extended to age and family composition. The suburb was the habitat of the young family with small children. The suburban school was thus a major institution, and open spaces, friendships among residents, conversation, and support services (pediatricians, retail stores, and scouting and athletic organizations) revolved around the needs of children. Almost all of the 12,000 inhabitants of Levittown, New Jersey, in the mid-1950s consisted of husband and wife families with an average of two young children. Only 4 percent of the women with children under the age of six worked outside the home. The range of generations typical of urban neighborhoods was missing, and some felt that this was a mark in the suburb's favor. The suburban childrearing bible, Dr. Benjamin Spock's *Baby and Child Care,* assumed the husband-wife-two-children household as a given and suggested that the permanent presence of adults other than the mother and father interfered with the child's psychological development.

The interior space of the suburban home similarly reflected the isolation and uniformity that critics charged were primary elements of suburban life. Separate bedrooms, bathrooms, and closets for family members became absolute requirements in suburban design. The formal dining room entered a design twilight zone, sometimes merging with a larger living or "family" room. Many of the family meals took place in an "eat-in" kitchen reflecting the busy schedules of family members, or in front of the television. The TV dinner, popularized in the 1950s, reduced the time needed to prepare food while combining eating with the leisure of watching television. On the television screen itself, which often became the focus of family gatherings, new suburban residents could see themselves, or at least their ideal, in shows such as *Ozzie and Harriet, I Love Lucy,* and *Father Knows Best.* Commentators singled out these programs as proof of the vacuity of suburban life.

But these experts were misreading both the context of the mass movement to the suburbs and the people who joined it. If interior and exterior suburban spaces seemed uniform and dull, perhaps that was understandable, given nearly two decades of uncertainty. Besides, homes and lots soon bore the marks of their individual owners. The popular image of the bored housewife, anesthetized by alcohol and idleness, was a wild extrapolation. Although careers outside the home were rare for these young mothers, it is incorrect to assume that no fulfillment was present within the home. It may be stretching the concept to talk about a suburban sisterhood, but women got together daily and provided mutual support. If anything, the housewife's tasks in suburbia—with a home, a garden, and an array of children's activities to administer—were more varied than in the city. Above all, suburban men and women derived a great deal of satisfaction from the fact that they had attained an ideal of American life. Regardless of their backgrounds or even of their occupations, suburbanites perceived themselves and others as solidly middle class. Indeed, the lifestyles they pursued defined the national middle-class culture in America by the 1950s.

The racial and class segregation that observers attributed to suburban life was merely an extension of an urban phenomenon. Cities were, of course, more diverse—spatially, visually, and socially. But this diversity owed more to history and density than it did to preference. Whenever and wherever possible, and at least since the early nineteenth century, urban residents had sought refuge from diversity.

Finally, observers were guilty of overdrawing the suburban image of the neat lawn, two-car garage, and husband dashing off to work in his gray flannel suit while his wife stands in the doorway dressed in her housecoat waving goodbye with 2.3 children clinging to her legs. The vast majority of suburbs were not Levittowns, though they may have shared many of the characteristics of these pioneering towns. They ranged from Cambridge, Massachusetts (older than most American cities), through heavily industrialized Hoboken in New Jersey, to fashionable Shaker Heights in Ohio, Larchmont in New York, and Beverly Hills in California. Some suburbs were populated predominantly by blacks, but most were lily-white, or close to it. Some—like Pullman in Illinois and Fairfield in Alabama—had arisen as small towns or industrial centers that only later found themselves close to the city's edge. Others were planned as exclusive enclaves, with houses set on estate-sized lots and all but small, acceptable businesses prohibited entirely.

The experts' dismay over the suburban environment had its corollary in their anxiety over urban decline. The perception of urban crisis was nothing new, of course. But the magnitude of postwar migrations, not only of middle-class families to the suburbs but of poorer families to the cities, rendered these concerns more imminent and shaped policy.

Urban Renewal: Towers and Tombs

New leadership emerged in postwar cities as an acceleration of the trend begun during the 1930s. Returning GIs became impatient with old-style political arrangements, and challenges emerged even in those cities with strong political machines. Charter revision was an early mechanism to introduce efficiency into urban government; the appointment of city managers and the establishment of at-large electoral systems further removed policy from the capricious hands of interest groups and neighborhoods. The hope was that coalition and consensus, not fragmentation and discord, would characterize urban government, which would, in turn, become an efficient engine for the economic salvation of the city.

In many respects, these were dressed-up themes from the progressive era. But the decade after the war witnessed renewed confidence that the objectives of political reform would not prove illusory this time around. New management techniques, a generation of professionally trained managers and planners, and, above all, a close relationship with the federal government and its treasury augured well for the emergence of effective growth coalitions that would build cities out of their problems in much the same way as the suburban building boom forestalled a return to the economic doldrums of the 1930s.

In New Orleans, a young returning veteran, de Lesseps Morrison, was elected mayor in 1946. Morrison introduced budgetary reform, established recreation and housing departments to serve both races, and launched public works projects that extended streets and sewers into new neighborhoods. Once a political cesspool, New Orleans became a national model, with Morrison symbolizing, as *Time* magazine put it, "as well as anyone . . . the postwar energy of the nation's cities."[3]

The combination of businesslike efficiency in government and major building projects proved to be an elixir for postwar cities. The impact was especially noticeable downtown, where streamlined urban administrations and their private-sector partners focused most of their efforts. Evoking the organic image of cities then popular among academics, civic leaders conjured up images of clogged arteries, congestive heart failure, and cancerous blight to describe their city centers. These images translated into policies designed to remove slums, erect clean, efficient public housing and commercial properties in their place, and open up the road system. Pittsburgh became a prototype of what could be done through the combination of political coalitions and economic development objectives.

On the face of it, Pittsburgh was not the most likely candidate to be a national role model for urban revitalization. A grimy, gritty metropolis struck hard by the Depression, it had been revived to some extent by the war but faced an uncertain future. Millionaire Richard King Mellon and Mayor David Lawrence joined forces to shape that future in a positive manner. First, they undertook to clean up the environment long before ecological issues became popular elsewhere. Despite opposition from powerful U.S. Steel, they devised programs for smoke abatement, flood control, and stream pollution. Second, in 1945, Lawrence and Mellon together with several of Mellon's colleagues in the business community devised a major redevelopment program for downtown Pittsburgh, the so-called "Golden Triangle" district at the confluence of the Allegheny, Monongahela, and Ohio rivers—at that time an unsightly jumble of rail yards, warehouses, and dilapidated residences. The coalition, using state, local, and private funds from such businesses as the Equitable Life Assurance Society, cleared the district and created a park and eventually six twenty- to thirty-story office buildings, a hotel, and an underground parking garage. By 1960, the Pittsburgh Renaissance was complete, and within two decades at least one magazine poll listed the erstwhile "hell's kitchen" as America's most livable city.

Pittsburgh's rags-to-riches story did not go unnoticed, and soon other cities sought to duplicate it. The main difference, however, was that federal funds were becoming available to prime redevelopment efforts by the 1950s. Initially, the federal government had not intended to become involved with such comprehensive redevelopment projects. After the war, in fact, Congress was in such a conservative mood that urban programs of any sort were unlikely to be implemented. In 1949, however, concern about maintaining full employment and reviving the construction industry, pressure from cities anxious over suburban population and economic growth and eager to participate in a building boom of their own, and worry over festering slum areas convinced Congress to pass a housing act.

The 1949 Housing Act authorized local redevelopment authorities to assemble and clear land and then sell the vacant area to private developers. The federal government would reimburse the city for most of the money they lost in the transaction and developers were relieved of the costs of purchasing slum buildings and tearing them down. The developers would then erect suitable housing for the area's poor residents. The removal of blight, the thinking ran, would not only stem its cancerous spread but would help to stimulate other redevelopment programs in and about the area.

Though Congress authorized the construction of 800,000 housing units over the next six years, only a fraction of that number was built. The type of urban redevelopment the urban growth coalition had in mind included little or no public housing. They were more interested in revenue-generating projects that would benefit both city government and private enterprise. Accordingly, the Eisenhower administration and an obliging Congress passed the 1954 Housing Act, which was more in line with growth coalition interests. In fact, it may be stretching the language to refer to this act as one that promoted the construction of housing. Congress slashed the number of authorized dwelling units to 10,000 per year and increased the appropriation for redevelopment from $500 million over five years ($400 million of which had not been spent) to $400 million over the next two years. The act also encouraged cities to develop city-wide comprehensive plans demonstrating how renewal projects would fit in the new scheme. In addition, the federal Urban Renewal Administration could grant up to 10 percent of the appropriation for nonresidential projects (later changed to 35 percent).

The 1954 act, with subsequent minor alterations, touched off a nationwide downtown redevelopment bonanza. It stimulated public-private partnerships where those had not already existed. In Boston, a group of business and government leaders organized the "Vault" (so named because they met in the board room of a bank) in 1959 to support development-oriented political candidates and to draft plans for downtown renewal. The Vault helped to hire Edward Logue to head the Boston Redevelopment Authority and implement plans that included the Prudential Center at a cost of $202 million; the Government Center for $217 million; and the Waterfront for $131 million. The residential components of these projects included a gain of roughly 2,700 luxury units and a loss of 989 low-rent units. Logue also directed renewal projects outside downtown, often with a similar imbalance of public housing. In a black Roxbury neighborhood, he demolished 2,570 low-income units and replaced them with 1,550 low-income units. In Charlestown and South End low-income districts, Logue cleared more than 6,000 low-rent units and built nearly the same amount of units, but these rented at market rates.

Southern cities, though generally not experiencing the same extent of urban blight as in the North and Midwest, warmed to the urban renewal program as well. Growth coalitions were nothing new in the urban South, though the groups in power after World War II were less interested in racial politics than they were in using federal dollars to enhance their cities' economic position within the region. Norfolk launched downtown redevelopment efforts in the late 1950s with the promise that it would soon be the "Manhattan of the South."[4] Charlotte leaders hoped that wiping out an unsightly black neighborhood on the edge of downtown would serve as a catalyst for new development that would transform the city into the Atlanta of the Carolinas.

Of all the southern cities, Atlanta was the most prepared to take advantage of federal urban renewal legislation. In 1947, the Chamber of Commerce, the Greater Atlanta Association, and the Central Atlanta Improvement Association joined to coordinate government structures in the metropolitan area. Though they were only partially successful, the combined groups succeeded in establishing a metropolitan planning district and identifying potential renewal projects in the downtown area. By the late 1950s, the city began to recreate the old downtown and build a new one. The city's original downtown was clogged with abandoned railroad tracks and warehouses until developers transformed it into Underground Atlanta (much of modern Atlanta is actually built on top of the old downtown area), a glamorous new venue that opened with fanfare and offered restaurants, ice cream parlors, and shops dressed in Victorian decor. Unfortunately, the only thing the city and its private entrepreneurial partners proved was that, given enough capital, they could transform an old deteriorating area into a new deteriorating area. The poorly policed location, still frequented by derelicts after its facelift, eventually became a security problem in the evening. As the quality of shops and clientele declined, the city finally closed the area (a lavish new version opened in 1989).

Atlanta had better fortune starting from scratch. Architect John Portman was the major figure behind the Peachtree Center, highlighted by the dazzling twenty-one story Hyatt-Regency hotel, which featured spaceship elevators, a lobby as high as the hotel, and a revolving dome from which tourists and conventiongoers could sip their peach daiquiris as they surveyed the urban prospect. The center also included shops and restaurants sealed away in a secure, climate-controlled environment. The Peachtree complex was among the earliest downtown development projects that consciously imitated suburban space, though Portman would hotly deny the connection. Other urban complexes such as the Crown Center in Kansas City and the Embarcadero Center in San Francisco, initiated during the urban renewal era between 1954 and 1965, expanded on the idea to include more shops, restaurants, and hotels, as well as ready access to another new downtown feature, the convention or civic center. Soon sports stadiums were added to the mixture, including Three Rivers in Pittsburgh and Riverfront in Cincinnati.

But where was the housing? As these accounts imply, the growth coalitions were interested in public housing primarily as a lever for federal funds. This was especially so in southern cities, where blacks, who were the typical residents of slum neighborhoods, had little political clout during the two decades after

World War II. In Atlanta between 1957 and 1967, the city demolished 21,000 housing units, most occupied by blacks, and constructed only 5,000 new units. In Charlotte, the city tore down an average of 1,100 black-occupied housing units per year from 1965 to 1968 but erected only 425 new units during that whole time. And when cities actually built public housing, it was invariably in the worst locations, usually neighborhoods that were already black, thereby reinforcing existing patterns of racial residential segregation.

The public housing structures themselves were scarcely improvements over the dwellings they replaced. Low-rise detached structures with some open spaces had characterized an earlier generation of public housing. But new philosophies emerged by the late 1940s that favored more concentrated, high-rise developments. In 1943, New York's Robert Moses and the Metropolitan Life Insurance Company erected a mammoth eighteen-block complex housing 25,000 people, known as Stuyvesant Town. *Fortune* magazine called it "a self-contained new community, a virtual suburb within the city," but both the density of the development and the pedestrian access to shops and services were hardly suburban staples.[5] Apparently, the planners' great bugaboo, the congested city, became its great salvation, a way to create "community," an island in the urban maelstrom. The success of Stuyvesant Town as a middle-class development gave high-rise, high-density, multipurpose developments a good name. And a decade later, when cities undertook their urban renewal programs, the public housing skyscrapers seemed to be the economic and practical solution to housing for the poor.

In 1954, the Pruitt-Igoe public housing complex opened in St. Louis to national attention. Thirty-three eleven-story apartment buildings, based on the ideals of the noted Swiss architect Le Corbusier and designed by Detroit architect Minoru Yamasaki, were set in a parklike area, linked together by "a river of trees." The buildings featured open galleries on every third floor that served as communal porches, laundries, and play areas. The galleries would become the focal points of "vertical neighborhoods." The development won numerous design awards and *Architectural Forum,* which rarely commented on public housing, devoted a lengthy article to Pruitt-Igoe. A decade later, however, the *Forum* returned to the complex and discovered a wasteland of "scrubby grass, broken glass and litter." The vaunted "vertical neighborhoods" were "anything but cheerful social enclaves."[6] The elevators were inviting settings for muggings and rapes and receptacles for garbage and urine. Outside the buildings youth gangs often terrorized the residents. Had the *Forum* returned in yet another decade, its reporter would have found an empty field. In 1972 the city demolished its model public housing development.

Whereas high-rise apartment dwelling may have been appropriate for wealthy or middle-class urban residents, it proved disastrous for the poor. Surveillance

Pruitt-Igoe Complex, St. Louis, 1964
Despite its award-winning design, this $21 million public housing project epitomized all that was wrong with post–World War II federal urban renewal policy. Planners misjudged the difficulties low-income families living in a dense complex of high-rise buildings would face. And the city underestimated the management and maintenance problems associated with such a large development.

of children was difficult from the upper floors, and the concentration of families with criminal records, even if only a minority of the tenants, invited chaos. Though Pruitt-Igoe represented a genuine, if ill-advised, commitment to decent housing for the poor, it also symbolized a shift in perspective that transcended the design element. Urban renewal and the migration of mostly poor blacks to northern and western cities (5 million, mainly from the South, between 1950 and 1970) created a major housing shortage for the poor. As whites left for the suburbs, black political power increased, and the carefully prescribed guidelines for admission to public housing from an earlier era passed with it. By 1963, 50 percent of the families moving into St. Louis's public housing were on welfare, and a majority of those families were headed by women. Public housing, initially perceived as a temporary stop on the way to middle-class respectability, now became a permanent warehouse for the urban poor. As one resident of Chicago's Robert Taylor Homes put it in 1965, "We live stacked on top of one another with no elbow room. Danger is all around. There is little privacy or peace and no quiet. And the world looks on all of us as project rats, living on a reservation, like untouchables."[7]

The rapid decline of public housing both as a priority and as a favored vehicle of social reform mirrored the growing preference for using downtown revitalization as an urban panacea. In political terms, the flashy projects and the jobs and revenues they created paid significant dividends for local government officials. Public housing projects appealed only to a small constituency and bred an array of problems that could scarcely enhance the popularity of officeholders. In economic terms, polishing up the downtown instead offered city administrations an opportunity to recoup the staggering financial losses suffered by losing the middle class and gaining the poor. Some observers have blamed the federal government for encouraging such calculated neglect of the poor. As with the suburban movement, however, the federal support of downtown revitalization in fact reinforced rather than initiated a trend.

Downtown development occurred in cycles. One burst of building activity in the major cities occurred during the 1890s and another at the turn of the century. A third boom followed in the 1920s. Depression and war, however, sharply curtailed the usual recycling of downtown space. Pittsburgh's Golden Triangle redevelopment was the first major urban project in the nation since New York's Rockefeller Center in the early 1930s. By the 1950s, economic recovery was secure and the changing nature of the national economy—away from industry and toward services—generated new office demands. The relatively long building hiatus and the delay of maintenance led to physical decay that made new construction even more imperative. Finally, the rapid expansion of suburban development that drew investments and people away from the city alarmed downtown civic leaders and their political allies. Federal policies dovetailed with all these factors, but in the main they were not, as commonly assumed, responsible for the results of downtown revitalization across America.

Downtown revitalization reflected changing functions and land uses for the city center. Downtown was becoming less a place of shopping and more exclusively a place of work. Between 1948 and 1958, retail sales in downtown Pittsburgh declined by 9 percent, whereas sales in suburban shopping centers jumped by 51 percent. Predictably, three major department stores closed in downtown Pittsburgh between 1958 and 1960, and smaller retail establishments failed or moved. Cut-rate stores and novelty shops sometimes replaced the more traditional retailers, but the heart of downtown retail business was gone by the mid-1960s. There was little to attract suburban shoppers: parking was difficult and selections were equal if not greater at suburban shopping centers. Mass transit might have provided an alternative to the parking dilemma, but it had been in decline in most cities since the 1920s; neglect and increasing automobile use were crippling public transportation systems.

Other portions of downtown, however, were thriving. Atlanta's Peachtree Center helped to generate a major downtown building boom in that city, including a convention center, additional hotels, and a sports stadium that attracted major-league football and baseball teams. The complement of uses oriented toward visitors catapulted Atlanta to a position among the nation's top five convention cities by the mid-1960s. Atlanta mayor Ivan Allen, Jr., summarized the impact of the 1960s building boom on his city: "In 1959 we were known for Coca-Cola, Georgia Tech, dogwoods, the Atlanta Crackers, and easy southern living; by 1969 we were known for gleaming skyscrapers, expressways, the Atlanta Braves, and . . . traffic jams." Though growth had eroded some of the city's southern charm, Allen felt that the overall result was beneficial to Atlanta and its citizens. The city had moved "from being a somewhat sluggish regional distribution center to a position as one of the dozen or so truly 'national cities.'"[8]

Other cities followed Atlanta's downtown formula in the 1960s: high-rise luxury hotels, shopping malls, convention centers, and sports complexes. Journalist Calvin Trillin, looking back on the decade, commented: "It seemed for a while that boosters . . . were following a kind of checklist of what was required for true major-league status."[9] But even cities whose major-league status was never in question, such as New York and Chicago, embarked on extensive construction of hotels, shopping malls, and concert halls (New York's Lincoln Center complex, for example). Many of these new features catered to the visitor, the conventioneer. Cities liked conventiongoers because they came for a few days, dropped their money, and left, requiring very few services. Even retail resurfaced in the form of boutiques selling specialty and designer items directed more to free-spending visitors than to urban residents.

Occasionally, some cities sought to salvage their major retail stores by enhancing their façades, building skyways, eliminating or reducing vehicular traffic along the major downtown thoroughfares, and establishing a zone for foot traffic often referred to, revealingly, as a pedestrian "mall." Minneapolis pioneered this strategy in 1955 with its Nicollet Avenue Mall, excluding all vehicles except for buses, widening sidewalks and installing sidewalk furniture, and curving the road to change the monotonous vistas created by the old gridiron street pattern. In addition, a series of enclosed skyways connecting the second stories of downtown buildings kept the shopper or visitor protected from the harsh Minnesota winters. The mall has been successful, much less because it saved traditional retail establishments—they are still struggling—but because of the exciting architecture along the avenue, including the Crystal Court, the IDS Center, hotels, and a Federal Reserve building—in other words, the same types of buildings that have changed and revitalized downtowns elsewhere. Nicollet also has the unique advantage of a substantial and affluent residential population nearby.

Elsewhere, the areas adjacent to downtown have become much less places of residence. Urban renewal eliminated much of the low-income housing near city centers. Occasionally, as in Chicago and Denver, luxury apartments and condominiums appeared along with the offices and hotels. But these units were insufficient to create a significant residential presence near the city center. The poor residents displaced by urban renewal crowded into adjacent neighborhoods, frequently creating slum conditions that cities addressed through further demolition.

The passage of the National Interstate and Defense Highway Act in 1956 facilitated additional destruction of slum properties and even of neighborhoods that were merely old. The Eisenhower administration did not design the act as an adjunct to the urban renewal program; in political terms, it rewarded state governments and suburban jurisdictions that had supported Republican candidates. The federal government put up 90 percent of highway construction costs. For a mere 10 percent, state officials could reap the political benefits of more jobs, enhanced economic opportunities, and an expanding constituency as erstwhile urban residents could push further into the metropolitan countryside with better roads.

Urban growth coalitions, however, looked on the interstate highway as another downtown redevelopment project. They had long blamed many of the center city's problems on congestion, and here was an opportunity to open up downtown streets more suited to the horse-car era than to the automobile. Driving downtown would be a matter of getting on and off the interstate. To divert traffic that wanted to bypass the city, civic leaders supported beltway systems to take travelers around the city rather through it. These systems, they believed, would further alleviate downtown congestion.

The scenario did not unfold the way civic leaders had hoped. The highways increased the volume of traffic going into downtown, but it also dumped more traffic on downtown streets. The highways themselves often became elongated parking lots during the rush hour. The Long Island Expressway, an interstate highway connecting suburban Long Island with New York City, became notorious for its traffic jams by the mid-1960s. Radio traffic reporters developed a convenient shorthand to describe the situation for stranded motorists: "The LIE is LOL (Lots of Luck) this morning."

The beltways also disappointed civic leaders' expectations. They diverted traffic, to be sure, but they also became development magnets, accelerating the loss of population and economic base within the city. The Capital Beltway around Washington, D.C., for example, has become a circular city attracting office and industrial parks, shopping centers, educational and government facilities, and recreational areas. The beltway has reoriented space in the Washington metropolitan area to the extent that residents and publications give directions based on locations within or outside it. If the nation's capital has a main street, the Capital Beltway is it.

The interstates did attain one of the growth coalition's subsidiary objectives by clearing additional low-income properties. But the interstate also bisected viable neighborhoods where the housing stock was aging but generally sound. It further weakened the residential fabric of the center city and worsened the housing situation for the poor. Though by the early 1960s new federal guidelines required cities to provide relocation assistance, how could they replace friendship networks, churches, and businesses torn up by the bulldozers?

Springtime for Urban America: Images from the Fifties and Sixties

As America's cities swung into a full-fledged building boom by the late 1950s, few leaders were concerned about the housing problems of politically-impotent constituents. The gloom of the 1930s and the fears of the immediate postwar years had dissipated, and public perception of the city soared with the office and hotel towers. Now that suburbs were generating the negative press, the popular image of the city once again became relatively wholesome and unthreatening, as in the 1952 Hollywood production of *My Sister Eileen,* which follows the adventures of two young women from the Midwest who manage to conquer Manhattan while getting into only minor mischief. The diversity of the city, once viewed as a serious drawback to human development, now seemed exciting. E. B. White's characterization of New York in the 1950s reflected the changing perspective:

> New York will bestow the gift of loneliness and the gift of privacy. . . . New York is peculiarly constructed to absorb almost anything that comes along without inflicting the event on its inhabitants, so that every event is, in a sense, optional, and the inhabitant is in the happy position of being able to choose his spectacle and so conserve his soul.[10]

The choices never seemed so great as they were in the 1950s. The cultural innovations that marked the beginning of the metropolitan era in the 1920s had their counterparts in the 1950s. As in that earlier decade, urban culture broke the bounds of conformity and even of propriety, and some of its innovations during this decade became synonymous with American culture. New York artist Jackson Pollock led the Abstract Expressionist movement. Abandoning the traditional artist's easel, Pollock spread his canvas on the floor so that he could walk around it and become part of the work. Martha Graham, working in abstract movements and blending different musical forms in her repertoire, changed the form of the American dance. In literature, the "beat generation" emerged from the coffee houses of San Francisco and New York's Greenwich Village. Jack Kerouac's *On the Road* (1957) delivered a strong dissent to the metropolitan materialism evident in the new office towers and spacious suburban homes. It seemed to Kerouac and other beat writers that the metropolitan generation in their flight from depression and war had lost their way. But the "beats" were lonely dissenters in what was generally an upbeat decade. Economist John Kenneth Galbraith summarized the attitude best in *The Affluent Society* (1958) where he predicted that the city's dynamic postwar economic development would eventually dissolve economic inequality and reduce, if not eliminate, poverty.

By the late 1950s, urban youths were listening to another beat, a musical phenomenon as far-reaching as the emergence of jazz in the 1920s: rock and roll. The music's origins were not especially urban, combining black rhythm and blues with white mountain music. But once New York and other major cities adopted it, rock and roll was here to stay. Allan Freed, a disc jockey in Cleveland, coined the phrase in 1954 and, by the end of the decade theaters across urban America rocked to live performances of the new youth heroes.

The revised metropolitan culture of the 1950s reflected the persisting role of the city as a creative environment. Along with scholarly perceptions of the suburb, the new cultural forms helped to rehabilitate the image of the American city. Generally, the refurbished image highlighted the city's diversity. In 1970, writer Norman Hill wrote an essay for the *New York Times* entitled "Ah, For Those Walks in the Bronx." Hill, like millions of other urban Americans, had moved to the suburbs in the 1950s. There, he felt, he could indulge his penchant for walking amid the green and open spaces. Initially his hopes were realized. But after a few years, he reported, "I grew weary of the sameness. All the houses . . . were alike. . . . All the streets looked alike. There were no surprises. . . . By ten in the evening, when dinner was over and the children in bed, and I was ready to go out for a walk, there was not a living being to be seen. There was only the eerie, bluish flickering glow in every house signifying that someone inside was alive, presumably well and watching t.v." Hill began to look with nostalgia on the Bronx streets of his 1940s boyhood: "I remember as a young boy walking in the Bronx. I loved the limitless variety of colorful sights, sounds, smells, and most important, people. . . . There were fascinating store windows in every block. . . . There were children's games to watch. . . . At night the Bronx streets teemed with life." In the 1950s, when he married and moved to Manhattan, he reveled in the "even greater variety of neighborhoods, people and foods."[11]

What Hill felt intuitively had already become accepted theory among academics and planners by 1970. Two books in particular shattered traditional assumptions about the city in general and about federal urban policy in particular. Unlike many academic works, both had significant influence on policy makers and planners. Jane Jacobs's *Death and Life of Great American Cities* (1961) was a searing rebuke of planners and policies that developed city centers in the suburban image and plastered the landscape with high-rises and highways. She relished the heterogeneity and spontaneity of urban life that planners sought to circumscribe. Renewal projects, she predicted, would not restore urban vitality but, on the contrary, would turn the city into a paler, denser copy of the suburb.

Sociologist Herbert Gans followed Jacobs's attack with a more specific critique of urban renewal in *Urban Villagers* (1962). Although he disagreed with Jacobs's interpretation of the center city neighborhood as heterogeneous and cosmopolitan—such districts were rare in American cities—Gans shared her outrage at contemporary renewal policies that sought to eviscerate areas such as Boston's West End, the major focus of his study. The West End was dowdy and decaying, to be sure. But beneath the physical plainness lay a rich mosaic of cultural and pscyhological attachments, "social and cultural moorings that shielded it fairly effectively from the suggested consequences of number, density, and heterogeneity." He found it curious that urban renewal proponents held the quality of the urban physical environment in such high regard after nearly a century of experience had demonstrated its modest influence at best. "People's lives are not significantly influenced by the physical environment," he argued. "To a poverty-stricken family, the separation of car and pedestrian traffic or the availability of park and playground within walking distance are not very crucial; their needs are much more basic."[12]

Subsequent events were to prove Gans correct in his assessment. The design features of the urban renewal housing projects were less impressive to residents than the fact that official policies had effectively eliminated their ability to choose where to live and left them with little hope to learn how to make a living. The shame expressed earlier by the St. Louis project resident had a flip side: rage. As black writer James Baldwin explained, "The projects . . . are hated. They are hated almost as much as policemen, and this is saying a great deal. And they are hated for the same reason: both reveal, unbearably, the real attitude of the white world."[13] The projects underscored the powerlessness of their residents, that no one listened or cared. "It gradually penetrates the minds of the prisoners," black leader W. E. B. Du Bois had written in *Dusk of Dawn* early in this century, "that the people passing do not hear; that some thick sheet of invisible but horribly tangible plate glass is between them and the world."[14] Eventually, they would make themselves visible.

The Long, Hot Summers: The Inner City Explodes

From July 18, 1964, when violence erupted in Harlem, through the aftermath of the Martin Luther King, Jr., assassination in the spring of 1968, 75 major urban riots occurred in all sections of the country, but primarily in the ghettos of the Northeast and Midwest. There were 83 deaths, all but 10 percent of which were blacks. Almost all the looting and property damage occurred within the ghetto, the majority being to white-owned businesses, though some black businesses and many black residences were burnt out by the rioters. The most immediate effect was to increase insurance rates, accelerate commercial disinvestment that left these neighborhoods even more poorly served by retail than before the riots, and to worsen an already bad low-income housing problem. For many whites, the riots merely confirmed their wisdom in leaving the city for the safety of the suburbs. For those whites who remained, fear became an increasing accompaniment of daily urban life, as security systems, homemade and store bought, became an integral part of household furniture. The streets through which Norman Hill had enjoyed walking now became alien avenues of fear. If blacks perceived themselves as prisoners in their projects, increasing numbers of urban residents, especially the elderly black and white, became de facto prisoners themselves.

In attempting to account for this drastic turn of urban events—from the expansive optimism of the 1950s to the violence and pervasive fear of the mid-1960s—President Lyndon B. Johnson appointed a special commission to investigate the riots. With former Illinois governor Otto Kerner at its head, the commission placed the blame for the disturbances on white racism. Specifically, the Kerner Commission noted "pervasive discrimination and segregation in employment, education, and housing, which have resulted in the continuing exclusion of great numbers of Negroes from the benefits of economic progress."[15]

It was a curious, if politically expedient, conclusion. By focusing on white racism, the commission blamed everyone and, therefore, no one. Also, racism had not suddenly appeared in a particularly virulent form in the 1960s. In fact, the argument could be made that the Sixties were years when institutional racism, at least, was disappearing. The Civil Rights Act of 1964 and the Voting Rights Act of 1965, as well as the establishment of the federal Office of Economic Opportunity, President Johnson's War on Poverty launched in 1964, and the emergence of a black middle class in cities throughout the country seemed to auger well for race relations. Finally, racism was presumably more pervasive in the South than elsewhere. Yet very few disturbances occurred in southern cities.

The urban South, in fact, represented an interesting counterpoint to what was happening in other American cities. And its experience can offer a more appropriate explanation for the timing and extent of the riots of the 1960s. Whereas blacks in cities in other parts of the country perceived themselves as prisoners, southern urban blacks perceived their cities as arenas of hope. This had been so since slavery times, but restrictions and discrimination had limited black migration until the Depression era. Federal agricultural policies made black tenants and sharecroppers expendable, and war-related industries soon made urban residence desirable. In 1940, roughly one out of three blacks in the South lived in the region's cities. By 1960, better than one out of two blacks had an urban address. In the cities, the newcomers found supportive institutions such as churches, schools, and political groups that would shield them from the more oppressive aspects of a segregated society, nurture their sense of self-worth, and provide training in leadership for some. Southern cities offered a critical mass for protest, educational institutions, and access to the media.

Urbanization and the civil rights movement worked together. The leaders were urban middle-class blacks—ministers, attorneys, and college students—who used the built-in organizational networks and chose urban venues—parks, lunch counters, courthouses, and the streets—to forge a movement. In an era of visual media, cities provided the opportunity for the massing of large numbers of people in discrete areas to maximize the impact of a demonstration. Protests that occurred in rural areas, even the Mississippi Freedom Summer of 1964, rarely moved national public opinion or Congress. The key locales of the civil rights movement were not the farms of the Mississippi delta but the cities and towns of the South—Little Rock, Albany, Birmingham, Selma, Montgomery. The scenes etched into the public mind were the screaming mob at Central High in Little Rock, Bull Connor's dogs and hoses in Birmingham, and Sheriff Jim Clark's posse poised by Edmund Pettus Bridge in Selma.

The changing political climate in the urban South facilitated the civil rights advances. The new generation of urban political leaders were just as dedicated to economic development as their predecessors, but they were also aware that racial moderation and increased service levels were essential to sustained development. Although southern businessmen were not in the forefront of the civil rights movement, their eventual support was important in gathering a community consensus for racial change. They had reached the conclusion that racial turmoil was bad for business and that racial harmony was profitable. Atlanta, for example, received much favorable national publicity after its peaceful desegregation of schools and public accommodations in 1961. Atlanta promoted itself as "the city too busy to hate."[16]

The point is that even though southern urban growth coalitions eventually recognized the existence of racism in their midst and joined blacks in an attempt to remedy or at least modify its effects, northern urban growth coalitions as-

A Lunch Counter Sit-In, Charlotte, North Carolina, 1960
Inspired by the sit-ins in Greensboro, North Carolina, black college students across the
urban South protested the barriers of racial segregation. The widespread movement of
blacks into southern cities after World War II, combined with the leadership provided
by black churches and educational institutions, worked to initiate and sustain the civil
rights movement.

sumed no problems existed and therefore neither accounted for nor understood
the needs of their black constituents. And the numbers of those constituents
were growing. As white families left for the suburbs, blacks moved into the
cities. Though Washington, D.C., was the only city in the nation with a majority black population by the mid-1960s, black populations formed substantial
minorities in Detroit, Chicago, Newark, and St. Louis. Their political power,
however, was significantly less than their numbers implied. Urban renewal most
directly affected black neighborhoods and residents. Only on rare occasions did
growth coalitions consult with these residents, and then usually only to offer
relocation assistance. Moreover, the deterioration of "model" public housing
projects such as Pruitt-Igoe by the 1960s convinced city housing authorities
that any design, landscaping, and service amenities would be wasted on such a
profligate group of tenants. More broadly, the major institutions of northern
cities that had political influence—labor unions, religious groups, civil service
bureaucracies—were overwhelmingly white and very powerful. Schools, jobs,

housing, and welfare were in the hands of a relatively narrow group of whites who blocked or limited black access. Southern cities generally lacked this bureaucratic overlay, and especially after 1964 race relations there were very fluid compared with the sense of stagnation common in northern urban black communities. The urban South could show tangible results in civil rights: integrated schools, restaurants, hotels, and theaters; voting rights; and jobs. All this stood in sharp contrast to the dull monotony of poverty in the urban North.

The riots, then, were more about empowerment than about racism. They were political protests more than they were attacks against whites and white property. In a few of the disturbances, whites participated along with blacks, and the sign "Soul Brother" in shop windows offered little protection from the rioters. Only rarely were whites the target of black rioters, and never did rioting blacks extend their protests to white neighborhoods.

The summer explosions brought few if any short-term gains for urban blacks. In the long run, the riots helped to accelerate a trend in federal urban policy that had emerged before the disturbances. Calls for change in federal policy from planners and theorists, if not urban residents themselves, had begun to reach Capitol Hill by the early 1960s. And President Johnson, committed to a broad-based attack against poverty, especially black poverty, provided the leadership, assisted by the election of a liberal, urban-oriented Democratic Congress in 1964.

Federal Urban Initiatives: From Renewal to Conservation

The Johnson administration's War on Poverty evolved from several assumptions. First, the nation rediscovered poverty during the early 1960s, in part because of the civil rights movement and in part because of a book by social activist Michael Harrington, *The Other America* (1962). Harrington placed the problem of poverty, hardly a novelty, into a metropolitan context, arguing that the evolution of the metropolitan area allowed poverty to retreat from the national consciousness. "The very development of the American city has removed poverty from the living, emotional experience of millions upon millions of Americans. Living out in the suburbs, it is easy to assume that ours is, indeed, an affluent society."[17] Harrington's purpose was to demonstrate that affluence characterized only a portion of metropolitan society.

A second assumption that laid the groundwork for the War on Poverty related to the genesis and persistence of poverty. Johnson and his advisors believed that the disintegration of the black family was in great part responsible for black poverty. The President's Assistant Secretary of Labor, Daniel Patrick Moynihan, provided scholarly support for that perception in *The Negro Family: The Case for National Action* (1965), where he noted that the family was "the fundamental source of weakness of the Negro community at the present time."[18] Nearly one out of four black births occurred out of wedlock, a figure that would have a significant negative impact not only on the current generation of blacks but on the future one as well. One way to break the generational cycle of poverty was to provide blacks with equal access to jobs, that is, equality of opportunity. Critics charged that Moynihan had gotten his scenario backward, that poverty was responsible for the disintegration of the black family and that the implications of the book tended to reinforce a "blame-the-victim" mentality evident in urban policy since the nineteenth century.

Steering a middle course by addressing both family and economic issues, the administration secured passage of the 1964 Civil Rights Act, which established the Equal Employment Opportunity Commission (EEOC) and introduced the concept of affirmative action in hiring—the conscious attempt to recruit and hire black employees. To prepare and train blacks to take advantage of equal opportunity, the administration established the Job Corps. And to strike against the generational persistence of poverty and the perceived weakness of the black family, Congress authorized Project Headstart, an enriched day-care program for preschool youngsters.

But the Johnson administration believed that the attack on urban poverty should be much broader and, not incidentally, should redound to the benefit of the Democratic party, which already had an extensive urban constituency. The Community Action Program (1964) pumped nearly $2 billion into central city "target area" neighborhoods, the majority of which were black. The idea of the program was to invest black residents with the power to preserve and improve their own districts. Each neighborhood would form a Community Action Agency (CAA) through which federal funds would be funneled for various programs and services. In the impoverished Brownsville section of Brooklyn, for example, the CAA provided consumer education programs, recreational facilities, and health services.

Local political leaders, however, reacted strongly against the CAAs, which they viewed as potential rivals. By 1969, the average CAA had a budget of $5.2 million and a staff of 230, essentially independent of local government. As an irate Mayor Richard Daley of Chicago informed Congress, "any project of this kind . . . must be administered by the duly constituted elected officials." Syracuse mayor William Walsh charged that CAAs in his city were organized to "train agitators" and to teach "Marxist doctrines of class conflict." To support his view, he pulled out a prospectus from a CAA training center which urged applicants to "have a controlled but intense anger about continued injustices."[19]

The administration relented and steered the CAAs toward service provision and away from political action. In addition, the administration launched a new federal urban initiative in 1966, the Model Cities program. The idea was to concentrate huge funds on the worst neighborhoods in a few target cities. Model Cities projects would combine physical and social redevelopment through the construction of low-income housing, the provision of health and educational services, and job training. Neighborhood residents were to play an active, though not an independent, role in devising their program. The new Department of Housing and Urban Development (HUD), established the previous year, would administer the program—though, as Assistant HUD Secretary Ralph Taylor noted, Model Cities would be "a mayor's program."[20] The ultimate objective of Model Cities was to create self-sufficient neighborhoods and residents. In addition, in a novel recognition of the metropolitan scope of the poverty issue, Model Cities legislation required the formation of metropolitan planning agencies to review the applications for most federal programs from *all* of the area's jurisdictions in order to ensure that the request (e.g., to build a hospital, to construct low-income housing, to lay water and sewer systems) was in keeping with metropolitan planning objectives. The hope was to encourage suburban jurisdictions to build facilities at federal expense—housing, training centers, industrial parks—that would attract blacks away from central cities.

President Johnson did not win his war on poverty, in part because of his engagement in another war, but also because of shortcomings within the programs themselves. The President had initially envisaged a handful of Model Cities. Congress, however, expanded the program to 150 cities, a move that helped the bill's passage but also spread appropriations too thinly for them to have a significant impact. The funds authorized for Model Cities were never sufficient to sustain long-term changes in the target neighborhoods. Most neighborhoods did not begin programs until 1968, and in less than three years from its passage President Nixon terminated the Model Cities program, declaring that the urban crisis was over. In addition, the A-95 metropolitan review process (so called because the document that spelled out the review procedures was Circular A-95 from the Office of Management and Budget) helped to establish regional Councils of Governments (COGs). With no enforcement power, these councils could not formulate a metropolitan strategy for dealing with poverty. The COGs did, however, become centers of planning expertise that they shared with smaller jurisdictions in the area, as well as collectors of data that would assist those communities in formulating comprehensive plans.

By the time Richard M. Nixon took office in 1969, federal urban policy was in a state of bloated disarray. In 1960, 44 federal programs provided $3.9 billion to urban America. Nine years later, over 500 programs were doling out more than $14 billion. These programs were generally uncoordinated and at times contradictory. At the local level, accountability was difficult to discern in many cases. In addition, the Johnson administration never seemed quite sure whether it wanted to follow the ghetto enrichment strategy or the integrationist approach. Many of its programs sought to sustain and improve black neighborhoods; others, such as A-95 review, looked for a metropolitan integration. The latter goal was clearly unrealistic. Most suburban jurisdictions had adopted veiled but legal zoning codes designed to restrict status and thereby to restrict race. And it was incorrect to assume that most blacks longed for suburban residences, especially if that meant leaving behind kin and institutions. The basic spatial and economic arrangements of the metropolitan area, in any case, reflected deep racial and class divisions in American society. Unless federal policy challenged those arrangements, a highly unlikely prospect, programs would inevitably fall short of objectives and could create more problems than they would solve, including raising expectations to an unrealistic level.

Despite these shortcomings, perhaps inherent, in federal policy, the War on Poverty generated some positive accomplishments. Atlanta was the first city in the nation to receive a Model Cities grant. The target neighborhood included a population of 45,000 people, indicating that the program allowed cities to define "neighborhood" very loosely. The city used the funds to provide a shuttle bus service in the area, a day-care program, the construction of an educational complex, and the resurfacing of streets. How do we measure the success of this program in Atlanta? Statistics are not kept on how many people, if any, improved their condition, left the area, and began new lives. A decade later, figures might indicate that the poverty level of the neighborhood remained the same. But it might mask the fact that some of the residents who lived there during the 1960s have been able to leave because of Model Cities, and other less fortunate residents have moved in. The physical improvements remain, though the services are gone because of the lapse in federal funding.

The accomplishments of the CAAs are no easier to assess. The most positive aspect of the program was that it provided blacks with training in leadership and citizen participation. Charges were made that the program coopted the local activists and deflected their energies toward acceptable and traditional political activities and that the programs merely benefited the black middle class. But it is also true that almost a quarter of all blacks elected to city executive or council positions as well as to the lower houses of state legislatures between 1964 and 1976 gained their initial political experience working in the community action programs.

Above all, the War on Poverty, especially Model Cities, marked an important transition point in federal urban policy away from the demolition derby of urban renewal toward a conservationist approach to urban policy that would become more evident in the 1970s. An assumption behind Model Cities was that the physical environment was no longer the starting point of federal urban policy. Each community, no matter how old or decaying on the outside, held unique and irreplaceable cultural and social values. It was unlikely that the federal government would much longer continue directly to underwrite the construction of freeways and high-rise office developments at the expense of existing neighborhoods.

The War on Poverty, in conjunction with the riots and the reaction to urban renewal, changed the equation of urban politics by increasing black and Hispanic power. Much of this power would not be evident until a new era of American urban development emerged during the 1970s, but the outlines were becoming clear by the late 1960s. In Boston, for example, Kevin White, a staunch opponent of renewal policies, won the mayoral election in 1967. Though the downtown orientation remained in Boston, there was a new sensitivity at City Hall for the integrity of poor neighborhoods.

On the other hand, some of this newfound citizens' power proved counterproductive. It tended to fragment the city further at a time when that entity was already bleeding from wounds to its population and economic base. New York City provided one example of democracy run amok. By 1968, the city's welfare department had established a "war room" to keep track of demonstrations at neighborhood welfare offices. One group staged a sit-in at the welfare commissioner's office, a siege lifted only when the city forked over $135,000 in additional grants. The bitterest conflict, however, occurred in the Ocean Hill–Brownsville neighborhood in Brooklyn.

Responding to demands of "cultural genocide," city officials had given control of three neighborhood school districts (including Ocean Hill–Brownsville) to neighborhood residents to ensure that curricula would be sensitive to black and Hispanic culture. By the spring of 1968, only months after an all-black school board took control of the neighborhood schools, board members and many of the white teachers were in open conflict over policy and curriculum. The neighborhood board voted to fire thirteen teachers and six assistant principals. The predominantly white teachers' union retaliated by pulling all teachers out of the neighborhood's schools, prompting the school board to dismiss them unilaterally. The city's superintendent of schools overruled the board and the white teachers returned under police escort. But after several days of verbal and sometimes physical harassment of the white teachers, the union called a citywide strike. Eventually, city officials stepped in to resolve the situation, but in the aftermath a lingering bitterness prevailed throughout the city's school system. The teachers' union—predominantly white and Jewish—and the school system—increasingly black and Hispanic—remained at odds. One school board leaflet warned the teachers, "Get Out, Stay Out . . . Shut Up, Get Off Our Backs, Or Your Relatives in The Middle East Will Find Themselves Giving Benefits To Raise Money To Help You Get Out from Under The Terrible Weight Of An Enraged Black Community."[21]

The Widening Gap: The City Splits in Two

So the very policies directed at ameliorating urban race relations often laid bare the simmering distinctions within the city, already brought to the surface by the riots. Cities at the end of the 1960s were more divided than ever before in American history. The issue of black control not only divided blacks from whites and blacks from each other but did not serve the black poor. As black sociologist Orlando Patterson explained, black ethnicity and calls for black control in the late 1960s became "a form of mystification, diverting attention from the correct kinds of solutions to the terrible economic condition of the group."[22] A greater problem, perhaps, was that no one could formulate—let alone implement—the "correct kinds of solutions."

Ethnicity and ethnic divisions were traditionally a distinctive feature of the urban spatial landscape and its politics as well. That landscape was eroding in the 1960s as many ethnics other than blacks left for the suburbs. Those who remained behind in the city found their influence declining. Though the foreign born and their descendants had generally wholeheartedly adopted American symbols and lifestyles (the American flag and the hard hat became prominent ethnic icons during this era), they had also retained their ethnic culture. If anything, the civil rights movement had made them more conscious of their own traditions and less likely to countenance the erosion of either their territory or their political power. The bitter confrontations in Chicago over housing and in Boston over schools reflected the growing and sharpening divisions in American urban society, especially between blacks and white ethnics. Their residential worlds had traditionally been measured in distinct spaces, but by the late 1960s these spaces had taken on a sacred quality, almost inseparable from their culture itself. Neighborhood defense was metropolitan in scope by the late Sixties as pressures mounted on inner suburbs where white ethnics cherished their distance from the city and its problems.

In 1971, when New York City began a low-income housing project in white middle-class Forest Hills in the residential borough of Queens, angry residents successfully halted the project. Although they objected partly because the proposed housing was clumsily designed and would have thrown additional burdens on an already tax-weary community, the incident revealed something of the inner psychology of the fortress residents. A reporter observed the protesters and noted that the main reason behind their objections was "fear—perhaps even justifiable fear. They have moved out of two, three, four or more neighborhoods before coming to Forest Hills. They have watched blacks, Puerto Ricans, and welfare families move in and have seen their neighborhoods deteriorate."[23] Though there were good reasons for this deterioration quite apart from any inherent faults in the minorities themselves, the Forest Hills residents were not about to launch sociological studies to determine why their neighborhoods declined when the reason already seemed obvious to them.

In Rosedale, New York, another community on the fringe between city and suburb, residents confronted the changing scene with various forms of the flight-or-fight response. The Rosedale experience was typical of inner suburban communities in marking the coming together of diverse white ethnic groups for a common purpose of preserving and protecting the neighborhood as it was. As one resident noted, "We've got Jews, we've got Italians, we've got Slovaks. You know, a melting pot." Their fierce pride and protectiveness was evident in a comment by one resident: "It took me eight years to save money to buy a house. . . . And I'm not gonna just say, 'Here, it's yours.' I'm not givin' in to anybody and I'm not gonna run 'cause there's no where to run today." Fatigued by "running," the residents of Rosedale and similar communities were determined to make their stand: "I'm gonna stay and fight because I can't be pushed anymore. They pushed me outta East New York; I'm not gonna be pushed again. I'm too old to move right now, I'm gonna make my stand. I'm stayin'."[24] It was not surprising that subsequent headlines of racial strife in the 1970s and even into the 1980s would come from metropolitan Chicago and New York, not from Birmingham and Little Rock.

The stratification and fragmentation of urban space and groups may not have been the most serious problem cities faced by the late 1960s. The racial turmoil of that decade accelerated the suburban exodus of population and economic base as the city absorbed a smaller number of poor blacks and Hispanics. The new urban residents did not add to the tax base and contributed to increasing disinvestment and rising service costs. Between 1950 and 1970, America's cities grew by 10 million people, the majority of them in the low-income category; suburbs, in contrast, grew by 85 million people, almost all middle class. Loss of jobs reflected loss of people. This was so even in the relatively prosperous cities of the South and Southwest. Between 1960 and 1975, Atlanta experienced an absolute loss of 2,000 jobs as the city's share of metropolitan employment fell from 20 percent to 12 percent. In 1960, central Atlanta contained 90 percent of the metropolitan area's office space. By 1980, that proportion had declined to 42 percent as nearly 100 industrial parks ringed the city.

The demographic and economic patterns working against the city turned vast areas into unclaimed wastelands. Landlords unwilling or unable to make repairs or collect rents allowed their buildings to deteriorate. Burned-out shells of buildings loomed over the landscape in places such as the South Bronx and downtown St. Louis, where, by 1970, nearly 25 percent of the land was vacant. Bricks from the stripped carcasses of buildings in St. Louis and Chicago were shipped to Houston or Los Angeles to build patios and town houses. Winos, prostitutes, and assorted thugs littered areas in and around the downtown, in

clear sight of the gleaming towers and space-age hotels. Detroit offered perhaps
the most striking contrast, with its massive Renaissance Center complex rising
like a fortress above downtown replete with luxury hotels, trendy restaurants,
and chic shops, and surrounded by a sea of decay. Hotel managers placed
printed cards on beds warning visitors against leaving the center premises after
dark. It was scarcely safe for the natives. A baby born in Detroit in 1970 had a
one in thirty-five chance of being murdered during his or her life. Drug abuse
fueled the crime rate. In 1963, Atlanta authorities counted about 500 heroin
addicts in the city. By 1970, that number had increased to 5,000. When Hollywood depicted the American city of 1970, it was no longer the happy-go-
lucky metropolis of opportunity it had seemed in the 1950s. Drugs, prostitution, and violence became stock images in movies such as *The French Connection*
(1971) and *Klute* (1971).

White urban residents attributed much of the American city's problems to the
black and Hispanic newcomers. They were not interested in complicated sociological explanations that seemed to excuse the poverty, crime, and decay they
read about in the urban press and saw on the 6 o'clock news. They remembered
how their city and neighborhood used to be, an earlier time of unlocked doors,
pleasant walks, decent schools, and good services. In their view, whites had been
forced to evacuate transitional neighborhoods since the beginning of the century. So intense was the fear of blacks among whites that the entrance of a black
family into a previously all-white neighborhood frequently caused panic selling
among residents. Real-estate agents often helped speed up the process of neighborhood turnover for their own purposes by entering an area and offering a few
white families at or near market value for their homes, selling them to black
families and then encouraging the panic among remaining white householders,
who would sell at considerably below market rates. The agent would make a
tidy profit by offering these homes to black families above the market price.
This process, known as blockbusting, though not the major cause of neighborhood transition or movement to the suburbs, was symptomatic of a divided and
fearful city.

The suburbs acted as metropolitan filters. They happily accepted middle-class
families, businesses, and light industries but made sure that the poor would not
slip through. The bad press of theorists notwithstanding, suburban residents
contrasted the virtues of their ordered world most favorably with the perceived
chaos of the city, which they wanted none of. By 1970, the metropolitan area
was really two distinct areas: the city and the suburbs.

For a time during the 1960s it seemed as if some city-suburb accommodation
might occur. As early as 1957, the city of Miami and Dade County formed a
two-tier government. The county became responsible for the physical operation
of the metropolitan area—traffic, water, and other public services. More sensi-

tive or lifestyle functions such as public education and residential location remained with the local governments. In 1962, the city of Nashville and Davidson County took the concept of metropolitan cooperation a step further by consolidating all functions within one government. The most comprehensive metropolitan government appeared in the Minneapolis–St. Paul region with the establishment of the Twin Cities Metropolitan Council in 1967, which included more than 300 governments. The council's major responsibility was to establish the guidelines within which development in each of the jurisdictions must occur. It reviewed the development plans of local governments as well as their federal grant applications to ensure compliance with regionwide development objectives.

Despite initial optimism and good results, these experiments did not generate a trend toward formal metropolitan cooperation. It may have been that the specific situations that prevailed in the Nashville and Minneapolis–St. Paul regions were not duplicated elsewhere. In the Nashville case, a service crisis appeared in the area's fast-growing suburbs: septic tanks threatened the water supply, and police and fire services were so deficient that insurance rates shot up drastically. Within the city, residents were angry at an unresponsive government that had annexed considerable land and population without submitting the annexation to a referendum. In the Twin Cities area, a similar service crisis, coupled with a legislative reapportionment that gave the region more power within state government, led to the formation of the council.

Though a few city-county consolidations occurred after Nashville-Davidson (including Jacksonville, Indianapolis, and Baton Rouge), enthusiasm for such maneuvers died quickly. In many instances, de facto metropolitan cooperation emerged through the creation of airport authorities, mosquito control districts, and waste treatment facilities. The Twin Cities Metropolitan Council stands alone, however, in the breadth of its membership. A key factor here was the regional perception that both Minneapolis and St. Paul were not places of decay and crime. In addition, the population of the region remains relatively homogeneous in terms of race and class. Blacks today comprise only 4 percent of Minneapolis's population and the region is among the most affluent and most educated of the thirty major metropolitan areas in the country. Elsewhere, whether in those few cases of formal cooperation or in de facto joint activities, the difficult issues of housing and employment remain matters for individual jurisdictions even if their impact is metropolitan-wide.

By 1970, the dynamics of the metropolitan era had produced two spatial phenomena that reflected severe social and racial divisions. First, city and suburb were sharply divided along race and class lines. Though low-income and black as well as middle-income and wealthy suburbs existed in the major cities, city and suburb were two distinctly separate environments in both image and reality.

The physical city itself mirrored the city-suburb division: urban spaces had become territories and fortresses. The contrasts between the soaring towers and the squalid tenements told only part of the story. Outside the center, in working- and middle-class neighborhoods, white and black, fear filtered into the playgrounds, crept up stoops or boarded elevators, and gripped residents. Cities had always housed the best and worst of American civilization. The contrasts, in fact, were even more noticeable in the horse-car era than in the expanded metropolis of the mid-twentieth century. The city seemed to thrive despite, and in some cases because of, these disparities. By 1970, however, in the aftermath of riots, confrontations, and the wholesale exodus of people and economic base, the historic resiliency of the city was open to question. The ministrations of the federal government, for all its good intentions, seemed to confirm rather than counter these trends. If the FHA appeared to be much more efficient than HUD in fulfilling its objectives, its relative success reflected the fact that the FHA sought to create a reality from a dream, whereas HUD struggled to wrest a dream from a reality. Who could believe the confident statement of the federal report, *Our Cities* (1938), a generation later: "The faults of our cities are not those of decadence and impending decline, but of exuberant vitality crowding its way forward under tremendous pressure—the flood rather than the drought"?[25]

Yet there had been earlier eras of perceived urban crises—the 1930s and the 1890s, for example. Seemingly, the city had weathered those times and had prospered. Even as we became a suburban nation in 1970, the configuration of metropolitan America, the relation of space within cities, between cities, and between cities and suburbs was changing, responding as always to developments in the national economy. A new era was emerging that would justify the confidence of *Our Cities*—in appearance, at least, if not in reality.

Notes

1. Quoted in Kenneth T. Jackson, *Crabgrass Frontier: The Suburbanization of the United States* (New York: Oxford University Press, 1985), p. 236.
2. Quoted in Bayrd Still, ed., *Urban America: A History with Documents* (Boston: Little, Brown, 1974), p. 368.
3. Quoted in David R. Goldfield, *Promised Land: The South since 1945* (Arlington Heights, Ill.: Harlan Davidson, 1987), p. 36.
4. Quoted in Carl Abbott, *The New Urban America: Growth and Politics in Sunbelt Cities* (Chapel Hill: University of North Carolina Press, 1981), p. 145.
5. Quoted in Howard Gillette, Jr., "The Evolution of Neighborhood Planning: From the Progressive Era to the 1949 Housing Act," *Journal of Urban History* 9 (August 1983): 436.
6. Quoted in Teaford, *Twentieth-Century American City*, p. 125.
7. Quoted in *ibid.*, p. 124.
8. Quoted in Bradley R. Rice, "Atlanta: If Dixie were Atlanta," in Richard M. Bernard and Bradley R. Rice, eds., *Sunbelt Cities: Politics and Growth since World War II* (Austin, Tex.: University of Texas Press, 1983), p. 37.

9. Quoted in Carl Abbott, *Urban America in the Modern Age: 1920 to Present* (Arlington Heights, Ill.: Harlan Davidson, 1987), p. 135.

10. Quoted in Kenneth T. Jackson, "The Capital of Capitalism: The New York Metropolitan Region, 1890–1940," presented at the Second International Conference on the History of Urban and Regional Planning, Brighton, England, August 1980, p. 27.

11. Quoted in Still, ed., *Urban America,* pp. 377–378.

12. Quoted in David R. Goldfield, "Neighborhood Preservation and Community Values in Historical Perspective," in Irwin Altman and Abraham Wandersman, eds., *Neighborhood and Community Environments: Human Behavior and Environment, Advances in Theory and Research* (New York: Plenum, 1987), p. 239.

13. Quoted in David R. Goldfield and James B. Lane, eds., *The Enduring Ghetto: Sources and Readings* (Philadelphia: J. B. Lippincott, 1973), p. 120.

14. Quoted in Kenneth Clark, *Dark Ghetto: Dilemmas of Social Power* (New York: Harper & Row, 1965), p. 27.

15. Quoted in Still, ed., *Urban America,* p. 414.

16. See Virginia H. Hein, "The Image of a 'City Too Busy to Hate': Atlanta in the 1960s," *Phylon* 30 (Fall 1972): 205–221.

17. Quoted in Abbott, *Urban America in the Modern Age,* p. 119.

18. Quoted in Kenneth Fox, *Metropolitan America: Urban Life and Urban Policy in the United States, 1940–1980* (Jackson, Miss.: University Press of Mississippi, 1986), p. 130.

19. Both quotes from Jon C. Teaford, *The Twentieth-Century American City: Problem, Promise, and Reality* (Baltimore: Johns Hopkins University Press, 1986), p. 139.

20. Quoted in Fox, *Metropolitan America,* p. 201.

21. Quoted in Teaford, *Twentieth-Century American City,* pp. 133–134.

22. Quoted in William Julius Wilson, "The Urban Underclass in Advanced Industrial Society," in Paul E. Peterson, ed., *The New Urban Reality* (Washington, D.C.: The Brookings Institution, 1985), pp. 132–133.

23. Quoted in Still, ed., *Urban America,* p. 439.

24. Quoted in "Rosedale: The Way It Is," *Bill Moyer's Journal,* transcription of PBS television show aired January 18, 1976.

25. Quoted in Abbott, *Urban America in the Modern Age,* p. 8.

PART 5

The Multicentered Metropolis

1970 TO THE PRESENT

A new era of urbanization emerged after 1970, though few Americans noticed it at the time. Culminating a trend begun in 1920, the 1970 census announced that we had become a suburban nation. Cities across the country, especially in the Northeast and Midwest—the urban core—continued to lose population and economic base. But the rising suburb and the declining city—the two stock elements of twentieth-century urbanization—were overshadowed by new developments. During the 1970s, nonmetropolitan growth outpaced suburban growth, the Sunbelt (generally, the South and Southwest) offered a new regional challenge to the old urban core, and the urban core itself changed. In the process a new urban form emerged—the multicentered metropolis—characterized by self-contained communities often located on the edges of metropolitan areas, a new, more specialized role for the central city, and the geographic expansion of the metropolitan area.

As with previous urban forms, the multicentered metropolis evolved in the context of a changing national economy. Beginning in the late 1960s and accelerating in the succeeding decade, population migration and economic development favored the South and Southwest at the expense of the Northeast and the Midwest. The regional shift was less a new economic ordering than a more balanced arrangement. After nearly two centuries of dominance, the old urban core now shared economic and political power with the southern regions.

The media described the regional shift as the rise of the Sunbelt and the decline of the Frostbelt. Although that description captured some of the economic realities of the 1970s and 1980s, it was overdrawn. The old urban core retained its vitality, even its leadership, in some areas of the national economy. And the Sunbelt was not a smooth canvas of blue sky and sunshine. "Equilibrium" more accurately described the regional relationship by the late 1980s.

Within metropolitan areas, another shift was underway. The familiar central city–suburb division evolved into a metropolitan area that consisted of several centers, one of which was the old central city. Suburbs did not disappear, of course, though some changed into more comprehensive communities that included many functions once reserved for the central city. And new communities emerged on the periphery of metropolitan areas—out-towns, some called them: small cities containing a variety of commercial, employment, entertainment, and residential land uses. Many of these new cities benefited from the "uncoupling" of certain corporate services (for instance, clerical work, insurance claims handling, check clearing operations, and credit card processing) from corporate headquarters in the central city, a development facilitated by electronic technologies.

In the meantime, the central city solidified its function as a headquarters location and also played a leading role as the site for *knowledge functions*—the gathering, processing, analysis, and distribution of information and services, especially in the banking, legal, insurance, and education fields.

Metropolitan areas monopolized national growth in the 1980s; 86 percent of the nation's population growth occurred there. New Jersey became the first state to be entirely metropolitan; that is, every citizen resided in one of several metropolitan areas that covered the state. All farmland in the state was also within metropolitan boundaries.

As in previous eras of urbanization, the changing regional and metropolitan configurations had significant social and, especially, racial consequences. The transformation to a service-oriented economy, the expansion of metropolitan areas, and the concentration of functions in specific communities within those areas sharpened and deepened social divisions. Physical and cultural separation was great, and the optimistic middle-class reform spirit of earlier eras had ebbed away. Moreover, governments at all levels seemed to be occupying the role James Joyce had reserved for God in his novel *Portrait of the Artist as a Young Man:* ". . . within or behind or beyond his handiwork, invisible, refined out of existence, indifferent, paring his fingernails."[1] The federal government increasingly withdrew from urban policymaking during the 1980s, and local governments, faced with fewer state and federal revenues, emphasized economic development projects and policies. Assessments of the health of urban America depended on which city one looked at: the city of the "haves" or the city of the "have-nots."

Note

1. Quoted in David R. Goldfield, *Black, White, and Southern: Race Relations and Southern Culture, 1940 to the Present* (Baton Rouge: Louisiana State University Press, 1990), p. 162.

CHAPTER 12

Frostbelt and Sunbelt: The Regional Shift

During the 1970s, the direction of the American urban core seemed only too obvious. It was heading down: down in population, down in economic base, and down south. A vicious circle had turned cities inside out; businesses followed the middle-class population to the suburbs, public revenues fell, services declined, infrastructure decayed, and more people and businesses left, further reducing revenues, which resulted in poorer services, and so the process began again. At the same time, those better-off residents who left were replaced in part by poorer newcomers. The poor offered little for the public treasury but required a great many services. Budgets tightened further, leading a few cities to the precipice of bankruptcy. Federal policies continued to pump millions into urban economies, but the impact of these funds was mixed for the older core cities.

In the meantime, national demographic and economic trends seemed on the surface to be dealing another blow to the northeastern and midwestern core cities. The population and economic shift of the 1970s was less city-to-suburb than it was region-to-region. The Sunbelt, that area of the United States below the 37th parallel stretching from the Carolinas to southern California, recorded substantial growth during the Seventies at the expense of its counterpart on the other side of the parallel, the Frostbelt. The very terms, *Sunbelt* and *Frostbelt* were emotionally loaded to favor the former over the latter, unless one happened to find long periods of snow, ice, and darkness attractive. By the early

1980s, however, it became evident that *Sunbelt* and *Frostbelt* were not a useful set of terms to describe new urban and regional relationships.

The High Costs of Urban Decline

It was indisputably true, however, that the great industrial cities had been hemorrhaging during the 1970s. The bleeding began as early as the 1950s in some cases, but the wounds deepened in the Seventies. Cincinnati, for example, lost nearly 10 percent of its population during the 1960s, but 15 percent left the city the following decade. Detroit experienced a 9 percent loss in the Sixties but a 21 percent decline in the Seventies. And St. Louis, which had been losing population by large increments (13 percent in the 1950s and 17 percent in the 1960s), lost a whopping 27 percent of its population during the 1970s. St. Louis's population was the same in 1980 as it had been in 1890.

Losses were general throughout the northeastern and midwestern urban core. Five of the twenty largest cities in the core managed population increases during the 1960s, but only one added residents in the 1970s (Columbus, Ohio, at 5 percent). These cities were not just losing residents; they were losing middle-class residents. Poorer residents from the South and from Latin American countries partially replenished these losses. In the 1970s, for the first time in American history, the median family income in the major cities of the urban core declined. Of the twenty largest cities, only Kansas City and Pittsburgh experienced increases in median family income.

As they lost their middle-class population, the core cities lost their middle-class economy. Middle-income residents had supported stores, cultural events, and institutions; they had helped to maintain neighborhoods and schools. The poor could do none of these things. As businesses folded, tax revenues declined. If a city attempted to make up for the decline by raising taxes, that only encouraged more residents and businesses to leave. The poor concentrated on survival, not esthetics, and cities were reluctant to step up maintenance and services in neighborhoods and schools at a time when their budget deficits were climbing. Although cities felt the economic consequences of the population exchange quite severely, they were slower to recognize the political consequences. The riots captured their attention, but the subsequent round of federal spending merely created new layers of city bureaucracy and added other interest groups in the crowded arena of the already badly fragmented urban political process.

The net result was that American cities began to fall apart, literally. Roads were not repaired, sewers and water systems aged, mass transit declined, and all these marks of decay reinforced the exodus of people and money. In effect, a massive disinvestment in capital facilities occurred. Some of the disintegration was deliberate: arson, abandonment, and demolition. The structure of middle-class life left with the middle class. Too many children, too few parents, too little hope, and too much poverty made up a recipe for trouble. Add a dose of irresponsible if not criminal landlords and a local government that sometimes lacked the will and almost always the means to enforce regulations, and the result was disaster. The destruction of the South Bronx was a much-publicized example of this process: between 1970 and 1975, the once-thriving neighborhood lost 20,000 to 30,000 housing units annually. By 1974, there was an average of thirty-four fires a day. *Fortune* magazine declared that the South Bronx "may be the closest men have yet come to creating hell on earth."[1] But every major city in the United States had areas like this that reminded veteran observers of German cities after saturation Allied bombing. The big difference was that no real war had ever taken place and, what was worse, no Marshall Plan would follow. The parallel was not lost on Arthur Naftalin, mayor of Minneapolis, who offered his surrender to Washington. "We've lost the war," he announced to federal authorities. "Now rebuild us like Germany and Japan."[2]

Of course, cities had looked to Washington to cure many of their problems ever since the New Deal era. But the situation in the 1970s was worse in many ways than even the Depression years because of the leeching of middle-class populations, institutions, and businesses. Historically, the middle class had provided the impetus for urban reform, even if many of those reforms were self-serving. In earlier eras, they had stepped forward to demand and pay for public services, to reorient urban administration, to lobby for parks and esthetic and cultural amenities, and to fuel economic recovery. Now their numbers were significantly diminished.

Some wondered whether cities had become dinosaurs, if they had outlived their usefulness to human society. Centuries earlier, citizens came to the city for safety. In an age of intercontinental nuclear weaponry, cities were now prime targets. But most American urban residents and visitors were more concerned about muggings than missiles as they walked the mean streets of the city. A child born in Detroit in 1974 stood a one in fourteen chance of having his or her life ended in murder. To put it another way, taking the murder rate of the nation's largest cities in 1970, you had a greater chance of dying simply by virtue of living in one of those cities than you would if you had served as an American soldier in World War II.

If murderer and murdered had a face, it was likely to be black or brown. Though only one out of every nine Americans was black in 1980, one out of every two persons arrested for murder was black, most of them young. The vast majority of victims were black as well. Younger people are more likely to commit violent crimes, even more so if they are poor. The median age for the nation's central cities in 1977 was 30.3 for whites, 23.9 for blacks, and 21.8 for Hispan-

Teenagers in Spanish Harlem, New York City
The demographic and economic transitions that occurred during the decades after
World War II were especially painful for the poor; housing and employment
opportunities decreased at the same time government social programs proved
insufficient or misguided. The vast majority of the urban poor are women or children.

ics. The traditional nuclear family, which had historically served as both a buffer
against and a facilitator to urban life, had deserted black neighborhoods. When
Daniel Patrick Moynihan published his controversial book, *The Negro Family:
The Case for National Action* (1965), he pointed out that one out of every four
black births was out of wedlock in 1965 and that females headed one out of
every four black families. By 1980, one out of two black babies was born out
of wedlock and 41 percent of black families were headed by females.

The problems that Moynihan had ascribed to the black family structure—
crime, unemployment, low educational levels, and chronic poverty— had also
worsened. In the mid-1960s, for example, black teenage unemployment was 26
percent, or roughly twice the rate for white teenagers. By 1976, 40 percent of
urban black youths were unemployed compared to a white teenage unemployment rate of 16 percent. By 1983, black-white teenage unemployment was 46.9
percent and 19.8 percent, respectively. Although the connection between the
deterioration of family life and the increase in urban problems needs further
study, the connection between discrimination and these problems is even less

certain. To argue that discrimination is responsible for the startling increase in black crime, unemployment, poverty, and family problems is to make the difficult argument that discrimination is considerably more pervasive today than it was in 1965. And as sociologist William Julius Wilson has noted, the "emphasis on discrimination becomes even more problematic in view of the economic progress of the black middle class during the same period."[3]

But whatever its proportion in the equation of failure, discrimination persisted. Decades of urban renewal, the conversion of rental apartments to expensive condominiums, and the elimination or curtailment of federal housing programs sharply reduced housing options for the poor and accelerated the decay of existing low-income properties. Financial institutions "redlined" black neighborhoods, refusing loans for the repair or purchase of properties, further limiting housing choices. A service economy that emphasized the gathering, processing, analysis, and distribution of information had little use for unskilled, poorly educated employees except in the most menial positions, where salaries maintained rather than eradicated poverty.

And poverty triggered a vicious cycle, exposing the greatest cost of urban decline: the human cost. Poverty was a handicap that permanently disabled. Poor nutrition and unstable home environments affected attendance and performance at school. Poor education doomed indigent youngsters to unemployment or under-employment. Inadequate income limited housing options, produced overcrowding, and contributed to the homeless population. Personal health suffered as grocery chains pulled out of low-income neighborhoods and food costs rose. Public medical services suffered from understaffing, overcrowding, and underfunding. Life expectancy dropped. In Washington, D.C., in 1988, for example, life expectancy for whites was 74.8 years, 67 years for blacks, a decrease since the early Eighties. Infant mortality rose. Ill health affected the abilities of low-income survivors to obtain a decent education, which, in turn, limited job opportunities. And so the cycle continued.

But whites saw only the results of crime and violence, not the underlying causes or sociological explanations. A sharpening of racial antagonism occurred. Although race was a factor in the first decades of postwar suburbanization, most families left the city primarily to fulfill a personal dream of home ownership. By the 1970s, whites were retreating from city neighborhoods and institutions less to fulfill a dream than to avoid a nightmare. Little wonder that nearby white suburban communities sought every means to protect their homesteads from "invasion" and urban whites rearranged their lifestyles, from installing high-tech security systems and carrying weapons to changing neighborhoods and placing their children in private schools. In fact, the white public school population of cities dropped much faster than the white population overall. In New York City, whites comprised 68 percent of the public school population in 1957, 29 percent in 1977, and roughly 14 percent in 1987. During the three-year period 1972–1975, when the city of Atlanta initiated busing to achieve racial integration in its schools, the black share of enrollment jumped from 56 percent to 87 percent.

As the Atlanta case implies, busing was a contributing factor in the white flight from the public schools. After the desultory pace of school desegregation during the 1960s, the U.S. Supreme Court in *Swann* v. *Charlotte-Mecklenburg Schools* (1970) authorized busing as an appropriate remedy to redress racial imbalance in the schools. Theoretically at least, this ruling meant that some white children would be transported to previously black schools in black neighborhoods and some black youngsters would ride the bus to white schools. Though in practice blacks have borne most of the burden of busing, the imminent prospect of school desegregation that busing promised was enough to convince white parents to enroll their children in private schools or to move across the city line. Some white parents believed that black children represented cultural and physical threats to their own youngsters. Between the time when Boston began its busing program in 1973 and 1975, the city's public school system lost one-third of its white pupils. When the U.S. Supreme Court ruled in *Milliken* v. *Bradley* (1974) that the city of Detroit could not compel 52 suburban districts to exchange students with the city, the flight across the city line became an even more attractive alternative. For those white parents who lacked the means to move or to place their children in private schools, busing generated resentment and, in some cases, resistance. In South Boston, a white Irish-American working-class district, violence persisted for four years after the start of busing in 1973, and policemen patrolled the halls of many schools throughout the academic year. Blacks were not the only targets of white animosity in South Boston. The area's white residents nourished a bitter conviction that the city's white leaders had abandoned them. White leaders seemed to be generally unaffected by busing because their homes were safely in upper-middle-class neighborhoods or suburbs, or their children were in private schools.

The white flight from the public schools usually had the same effect as the white abandonment of neighborhoods—decay, decline in quality, and a marked increase in unruliness and violence. The parents of black children were too often preoccupied with the daily struggle for work and food to take much interest in school activities. This was especially so for single-parent households. Some parents were unable to meet with teachers or participate in school programs because they lacked transportation to schools that were often considerable distances from their homes. The weakening of parental support further contributed to the decline in the quality of public education. In these ways the fracturing of the metropolis had become institutionalized by the 1970s. As geographer Brian J. L. Berry wrote in 1977, "The most pervasive feature of the American urban

A Police Escort in South Boston, 1974

During the late 1960s and early 1970s, scenes of racial confrontation became commonplace in some northern cities. Court-ordered busing to achieve racial integration in public schools was an especially volatile issue. Residents of working-class white ethnic neighborhoods were often strongly opposed to busing, and their opposition could take violent forms.

scene today is segregation—of income groups, family types, ethnic and racial minorities, as well as of land uses and activity networks."[4]

Declining services and disorder in the streets and at school fueled the city's economic problems. The movement of business and industry to the suburbs had been going on since earlier in the century, of course. After World War II, urban banks, encouraged by federal loan guarantees, played a major role in financing the rapid growth of suburbia. The trend accelerated after the riots of the 1960s as corporations began to be concerned about the safety of both their urban investments and their employees. New York City lost more than 100 corporate headquarters in the decade after 1965, or double the loss of the previous twenty years. Legal, accounting, and advertising services, primarily city center activities through the 1960s, followed their corporate clients in the 1970s.

These desertions compounded urban fiscal woes, sending tax revenues plummeting still further. The gap between revenues and expenditures grew to alarming proportions. For some cities, the nightmare of public penury seemed about to become reality. New York City was not necessarily typical of cities experiencing financial distress, but as in most things that city presented an exaggerated version of existing trends or set new ones that other cities eventually followed. During the nineteenth century, local government's welfare role was relatively minor compared with private charitable efforts. The public role increased during the twentieth century, especially during and after the Depression, and the scale jumped as well. In some cities welfare was a county or state obligation. New York State, however, required cities to assume most of the financial responsibilities for welfare services. In 1960, New York City spent $67 million for welfare; by 1975, the bill had risen to $911 million. The city also supported the nation's largest municipal university system, in which tuition was a nominal $100 per semester. On top of that, New York funded the nation's most extensive network of public hospitals. The city was also generous to its employees, purchasing harmonious labor relations with the city's financial health, a strategy of mayoral administrations since the 1950s. The administration of John Lindsay during the late 1960s and early 1970s was notable for the absence of labor strife (after an initial period of feuding). Lindsay, a great anomaly in New York politics—a glamorous, wealthy, Protestant Republican—agreed to almost all of the demands put to him by the various municipal labor unions. New York ran— right into a quagmire of red ink. Between 1965 and 1975, the city's operating expenses grew by 260 percent. The affable Lindsay financed some of this expenditure through a broad array of taxes, introducing both business and personal income taxes. He was also successful in coaxing money from Albany and Washington: state and federal funds comprised 36 percent of the city's total revenue in 1965–66, compared with 48 percent in 1973–74. But it was not nearly enough.

Mayor Lindsay resorted to short-term loans in order to meet the city's expanding obligations. As a consequence, New York's short-term debt soared from $467 million in 1966 to $3.4 billion by 1974. As the short-term notes fell due at the end of six months, the city merely refinanced them with additional short-term loans, creating a pyramid of debt.

Abraham "Honest Abe" Beame inherited the financial tangle when he succeeded Lindsay as mayor in 1974. A colorless, diminutive accountant who had moved up through the ranks of the Democratic party, Beame had campaigned on a platform of fiscal conservatism, touting his record as city comptroller. But by November of that year, the city's short-term debt was $5.3 billion, or $1.9 billion more than it had been just five months earlier. By March 1975, the banks announced that they had had enough of this profligacy and refused to finance additional short-term notes until the city embarked on a program of fiscal austerity. At this point the state intervened, creating two institutions—the Municipal Assistance Corporation (MAC) and the Emergency Financial Control

Board (EFCB). Big MAC issued $3 billion in bonds to pay off the city's debt. The seven-member EFCB, comprised of corporate, state, and city officials, supported the bond issue with severe cutbacks in city services and personnel. By 1978, the forced austerity convinced the federal government to grant long-term loans so that the city could meet its financial obligations on schedule. Public employees demonstrated their commitment to the rescue plan by purchasing a large share of MAC securities with their pension fund. Because civil servants now had a stake in the city's fiscal well-being, their unions were unlikely to demand wage and fringe benefits that would disrupt the budget. The strategy worked, and by 1983 Big MAC had paid off the federal loans and released the city's budget from EFCB control.

Though New York's fiscal drama had a happy ending, such was not the case for Cleveland. The situation in Cleveland was symptomatic not so much of good-intentioned municipal generosity as of an economic free-fall that struck the nation's industrial crescent, an area extending from Buffalo through the Great Lakes and the Upper Midwest. By the mid-1970s, this industrial heartland had become the "Rustbelt," strewn with the abandoned carcasses of the Industrial Revolution—silent steel mills, unused railroad sidings, and boarded-up stores. Foreign competition, higher costs, and aging facilities had killed the steel-driving cities. Youngstown's three steel mills stopped production and Akron, the erstwhile rubber capital of the world, no longer produced automobile tires. Infrastructure was not the only casualty. More than 40,000 rubber workers lost their jobs in Akron, and upward of 20,000 steel workers were laid off in Youngstown. But even these figures paled before the massive turnouts in larger cities such as Cleveland and Pittsburgh, where more than half a million industrial jobs disappeared between 1960 and 1975. The Rustbelt states experienced a net outmigration between 1970 and 1975 alone of nearly 1 million people.

The decline of the industrial heartland in the 1970s was part of a major national economic transition to a service-oriented economy. In 1948, manufacturing employment accounted for one-third of the American workforce, whereas service functions (including government, insurance, recreation, and the professions) employed one-half of the workforce. Thirty years later, manufacturing employment had declined to one-quarter, whereas better than two out of every three workers held positions in the service economy.

The fact that the Rustbelt cities were victims of circumstances taking place largely beyond their borders was small consolation. They looked to their futures and saw Cleveland. The city on Lake Erie had never enjoyed a particularly positive reputation. It was one of a group of gritty, grimy, lake cities packed with large numbers of ethnics who wore hard hats, carried lunchpails, and bore last names unpronounceable to most Americans. As a writer once remarked, Cleveland was like Detroit, only without the glitter. Cleveland jokes abounded, and one of the few times the city attained national publicity occurred when the Cuyahoga River caught on fire from the industrial pollutants dumped into it. People dubbed that body of water "Miracle River" because you could walk across it.

As long as everyone worked and the city paid its bills, Clevelanders did not seem to mind this backhanded national attention. They had a fine symphony orchestra, a first-rate university in Case Western Reserve, and major league sports. But the changing national economy and rapidly increasing service costs generated huge municipal debts in short order. By July 1978, the city's banks refused to lend it additional money. So when $15.5 million in previous loans fell due on December 15, Cleveland became the first major American city to default since the Depression. The city's young populist mayor, Dennis Kucinich, was partly responsible for the impasse. His confrontational demeanor toward the banks and their directors, whom he charged with "corporate greed," alienated the money lenders, and their refusal to work with the city was as much a punishment of the mayor as it was a business decision.[5] Kucinich claimed that the bankers had ordered him to sell off the municipal lighting company, an act that would have given the privately owned electric company a monopoly. When he refused, the banks refused as well. Kucinich angrily marched into the Cleveland Trust Company and closed out his personal account of $9,000, declaring, "I don't want my clean money in a dirty bank."[6] But it was a futile gesture. The city averted further defaults when voters turned Kucinich out the following year in favor of George Voinovich, who quickly reached an agreement with the banks to exchange the city's short-term debt for long-term bonds. To pay for the bonds, Cleveland raised its local income tax by 1 percent and cut government expenses.

The New Federalism: Revenue Sharing and Its Consequences

The federal government was not especially eager to bail out the cities of America. New York could make the argument that it was a metropolis of national and international importance, but few other cities dared try that tactic. The federal government was also in a period of pulling back from its domestic obligations, not only to finance its commitments in Vietnam, but also for ideological and political reasons. The declining urban populations of the Northeast and Midwest and the corresponding growth of metropolitan areas in the more conservative South and West were factors in limiting the enthusiasm of the Nixon administration (1968–1974) for underwriting urban bailouts. By 1975, suburbanites held the largest bloc of seats in Congress. Aside from the demographics, poor people—and they were concentrated in those declining cities of the Northeast and Midwest—voted at much lower rates than middle-class voters. So it was not surprising when President Nixon announced in 1972 that the urban crisis was over. If serious urban problems no longer existed, there was no need to formulate policies to deal with them.

In defense of the Nixon administration, it should be noted that the riots of the mid- and late 1960s had passed and few major disturbances had occurred in the early 1970s. Red ink and lengthening unemployment lines were quieter and less visible signs of decay than blocks of burning buildings. Moreover, the Nixon administration did not abandon the cities so much as it attempted to recast or eliminate previous urban initiatives. In fact, federal aid to cities rose from $14 billion in 1968 to $26.8 billion by the time President Nixon resigned in 1974. But the Nixon administration axed Model Cities and the controversial urban renewal, replacing these programs with the "new federalism," an approach whose cornerstone was revenue sharing. Boiled down to its essentials, revenue sharing meant turning back tax revenues to states and localities for whatever uses officials deemed appropriate. In a sense, the new federalism was a no-strings urban policy.

Between 1972, when revenue sharing began, and 1980, the federal government transferred more than $36 billion to local governments. But because jurisdictions as large as New York and as small as a town of 500 were equally eligible, the money was spread thinly across the country. As a consequence, revenue sharing turned out to be primarily a suburban policy. Much of the funding went for infrastructure such as sewer and water systems, which supported suburban development. After 1974, the major vehicle for revenue sharing was the Community Development Block Grant (CDBG), which consolidated seven federal urban programs in a single or "block grant" of $8.4 billion until 1977. Congress renewed the program that year, and again in 1980 and 1983, reducing the funding each time. Though the Nixon administration promoted the CDBG as a primarily central city program, block grant funds also went to "urban counties" with populations of more than 200,000 and to all cities of 50,000 inhabitants or more located within metropolitan areas. Congress included a provision requiring that cities use the block grant "principally [to] benefit people of low and moderate income."[7] But HUD, which administered the block grant program, received no powers to withhold funds from communities that did not conform to this guideline.

The CDBG resembled earlier major federal urban programs in its dispersal of government resources over a wide area with only slight regard to need. Cities did not fare well under the block grant program. Of the 487 communities eligible for block grants, 204 received less money than they had under the old programs. Of these 204, 181 were central cities within metropolitan areas. Small cities and suburbs fared best. Skokie, Illinois, an affluent Chicago suburb that had received no funds under the old categorical grant programs, obtained nearly half a million dollars during the first year of block grants.

When cities did receive their block grant, local officials diluted its impact even further. They obtained the grants directly (as opposed to Model Cities or urban renewal, which funneled money to authorities or citizens' groups) and merged the money with city funds. In the give-and-take of urban politics, civic leaders spread rather than concentrated the benefits of the block grant. Generally, they used the grant in two ways: first, to initiate physical improvements and housing rehabilitation in marginal neighborhoods where results would be visible quickly and, second, to apply the funds to long-term capital improvements such as sewers and roads. The fiscal crunch that had trapped many cities was especially hard on infrastructure maintenance. The block grant relieved some of this pressure.

City officials often adopted a "triage" approach to neighborhood rehabilitation with block grant funds. Triage is a term adapted from military combat, when medics divide the wounded into three categories to make the best use of limited supplies and personnel: those with superficial wounds who do not demand immediate attention; those with more serious injuries requiring prompt attention; and those whose wounds are so severe that even the most heroic efforts probably would not save them. Local officials designated certain neighborhoods in the same manner: stable, marginal, and substandard or deteriorated. Though Congress intended the grants to go toward areas in the third category, city officials perceived these neighborhoods as sucking precious resources from more viable programs and areas. New York housing and development administrator Roger Starr, searching like every other New York official for ways to cut costs, suggested in 1976 (without success) that the city close schools and police and fire stations in poor neighborhoods in order to accelerate the evacuation of these areas. Given this kind of official thinking, these types of districts rarely received block grant funds. City authorities were antagonistic toward them, feeling residual resentment about the disturbances during the 1960s, their role in perpetuating the city's bad image, and the political and economic liability of blasted space and a hopeless population.

The allocation criteria adopted by Memphis officials typified the use of block grants for urban neighborhoods. The city developed a ranking system to determine eligibility for block grant funds. Appropriately, most of those areas eligible were predominantly black. But only those neighborhoods with moderate-income families and a relatively high proportion of homeowners received the funds. The hardening fiscal crisis and the political and economic realities emerging from it had reoriented the perspectives of both urban and federal officials. The "war on poverty" had become the "war against welfare cheaters," and the second battle, which required relatively little financial or political capital, was much the favored of the two.

After 1980, the new Reagan administration cut and eventually ended the block grant program. Despite its problems, however, the CDBG program scored some successes. At the least, it shored up the shaky financial structures of some cities—not enough to stave off chaos in New York or bankruptcy in Cleveland, but enough to soften some of the pains of retrenchment. The program's best achievements occurred in cities such as New Haven, which used the funds to provide low-interest loans to upgrade commercial strips in marginal neighborhoods. When the businesses completed their renovations, the city provided additional CDBG funds to rehabilitate the entire neighborhood, including new sidewalks, street lights, and paint for homes. In the New Haven example and numerous others, the policy emphasis had changed from demolition to rehabilitation and preservation. This turnaround did not necessarily imply that local officials suddenly evinced a consummate pride in the structural heritage of their cities, although the Revolutionary bicentennial celebration in 1976 may have heightened their awareness of history in general. It merely reflected the fact that federal policy had become intimately connected with the nature and survival of the physical city. If the national urban policy, incoherent as it was, funded projects calling for slum clearance and new construction, then cities would demolish low-income housing and erect new structures; when federal urban policy shifted, so did local priorities.

But cities did not slavishly follow the fine print from Washington, just the broad outline. As urban renewal demonstrated, cities attained great expertise in knocking down substandard housing but never quite got the hang of building enough low-income units to replace what they demolished. When federal policy gears shifted in 1974, cities were no more solicitous of their poorest residents than they had been during the previous two decades. Indeed, the feeling was widespread among local officials that they could not afford to be solicitous, given their mounting fiscal problems. So they tailored the block grant program to fit their needs, fill holes in their budget, halt the erosion of neighborhoods and commercial areas as in New Haven, and coax or "leverage" private lenders and entrepreneurs to participate in these rehab programs. As with the urban renewal program, few or no fiscal and political advantages were to be gained from focusing on poor people or their neighborhoods.

The block grant program's easy eligibility requirements led to projects that Congress probably never intended. In Scottsdale, Arizona, an affluent suburb of Phoenix, town officials used CDBG money to install brick crosswalks on the main commercial streets and to erect lights for baseball fields. There was some discussion about using the federal money to build a polo field. Many other well-off communities like Scottsdale used the money on public works rather than raising low tax rates or floating bonds. But even in some of the largest cities, block grant funds found their way into uses hardly imagined by Congress, such as Chicago's $32 million expenditure on snow removal.

The Carter administration, which took office in January 1977, did not alter the basic framework of the "new federalism" initiated by President Nixon in 1972. Jimmy Carter, the first president from the Deep South since Zachary Taylor took office in 1849, hoped for better. He owed his election, in part, to black votes and the support of political and labor organizations in the large cities of the Northeast and Midwest. Carter shifted more block grant funds to cities in these areas, roughly 25 percent more than the preceding Ford administration. He also ordered HUD to require cities to use 75 percent of CDBG funds in low-income areas. If cities used the federal funds for public works projects, 10 percent of those funds had to go to minority contractors. Finally, President Carter established the Urban Development Action Grant (UDAG), a concept that exemplified what he called the "new partnership" to subsidize private investment in the "distressed cities" of the Northeast and Midwest.[8]

It was an impressive package designed to restore the policy emphasis of the Johnson years using the mechanisms established during the Nixon administration. It didn't work. First, as inflation, interest rates, and unemployment rose dangerously after 1978, the economy did not cooperate. Second, the Carter administration proved inexperienced in steering its domestic legislation through the Congress. The growing strength of the South and West precluded a major program reorientation to the Northeast and Midwest. Finally, the UDAG grants, though centered in the older cities, generated projects that differed little from those of the urban renewal era—primarily office, shopping, and hotel complexes. In 1980, for example, Detroit received a $12.8 million award for a downtown department store and office space. The Harborplace development in Baltimore, which included luxury condominiums and shops, also received a $6.4 million UDAG grant. Although these projects produced employment, the trickle-down effect was minimal.

In addition, the translation of Carter's directives to the local level was sometimes garbled. City officials defined the category "low income neighborhood" broadly, and genuine involvement by local residents was minimal. As one observer noted, the CDBG is "a neighborhood program only in the sense that most expenditures attributed to it go to residential areas."[9] Aside from the urban renewal–type projects spawned by the UDAG program, the Carter urban policy had achieved few results by 1979. Questions arose within the administration itself by that time whether the President's emphasis on the distressed cities was either good policy or good politics. President Carter's own Commission for a National Agenda for the Eighties concluded that urban policies should be "locationally neutral" rather than directed at "shoring up an outdated concept of the city."[10] In effect, the commission recommended much the same triage approach to cities that cities themselves had adopted toward neighborhoods.

But the commission may have been more realistic than insensitive. By 1980, the distressed cities of the urban core were making something of a comeback, partially as a result of the accumulation of federal initiatives, but also because of changes in the national economy and some innovative local policies. The problems of distressed cities related to situations that only drastic policies could address—the chronic poverty of minority groups and the exodus of people and economic base to the suburbs. Neither Congress nor the Carter administration had the will, the financing, or the popular support to implement policies that could influence any of these basic factors in American metropolitan life. The plea for a "locationally neutral" policy also had a meaning beyond the spaces of neighborhood and metropolitan areas. The economic and political power bases of the nation had not only shifted from the cities to the suburbs, but also from the traditional centers of power in the Northeast and Midwest to the South and West, the so-called Sunbelt. Whatever the liberal sensibilities of the Carter administration, they could not ignore the basic demographic and economic facts of American life in the 1970s.

But few federal policies since the New Deal era had been "locationally neutral." The Roosevelt administration rewarded the new Democratic party coalition in the northern cities; federal housing policy, especially after World War II and in conjunction with the Interstate Highway Act, favored suburban areas and their middle-class constituents, who had become politically influential. The Nixon administration continued to favor suburban jurisdictions—the "new federalism" was primarily a suburban construct—but the South and West became the most favored regions. Although Jimmy Carter initially sought to redress that bias, political and economic considerations scuttled his designs, leading his commission to lapse into the fiction that federal policy could be formulated in a political and economic vacuum. The Nixon administration at least forthrightly recognized that federal policies have different impacts in different parts of the nation, and there was little government could or should do to alter that situation. In 1972, President Nixon's Domestic Council concluded that

> patterns of growth are influenced by countless decisions made by individuals, families and business . . . aimed at achieving the personal goals of those who make them. . . . Such decisions cannot be dictated. . . . In many nations, the central government has undertaken forceful, comprehensive policies to control the process of growth. Similar policies have not been adopted in the U.S. for several reasons. . . . it is not feasible for the highest level of government to design policies for development that can operate successfully in all parts of the nation.[11]

Though the council was a bit disingenuous in assuming that only the free market was at work in those "countless decisions"—federal policies were boosting both metropolitan expansion and the growth of the Sunbelt—it was accurate in pinpointing a major regional reorientation that affected not only the pattern of urbanization in the United States, but also the metropolitan areas that gained and lost the people and the profits.

The Rise of the Sunbelt, Image and Reality

The timing of the Sunbelt's rise to economic and political prominence was not coincidental. It occurred precisely at the time that racial strife, municipal debt, deindustrialization, and middle-class desertion of the cities peaked—the late 1960s and the early 1970s. The South and, to a lesser extent, the West, were passing from a commercial economy to a postindustrial economy without the burden of adjusting to the human, fiscal, and physical losses incurred by the decline of heavy industry. The obsolete infrastructure, large numbers of blue-collar workers, extensive bureaucracies, and high social service costs that characterized the older cities were less evident in the cities of the South and West. These newer cities had grown up in the automobile age and were, on average, half as dense as cities elsewhere. They were more suited to the transportation technology of the late twentieth century and to the leisurely, family-oriented culture that came with postwar suburban living, including shorter working hours and earlier retirements. These metropolitan areas were located in parts of the country that enjoyed moderate, even semitropical weather. Of the thirteen fastest-growing metropolitan areas between 1970 and 1974, seven were located in Florida, two in Texas, and two in Arizona. What exhilaration to step off a plane in West Palm Beach or Phoenix in January, fresh from Cleveland or Chicago, and have the warm air embrace your dry winter skin!

Most of these newcomers had already left central cities far behind. They were accustomed to suburban living; the metropolitan South and West would enable them to enjoy more of it, for less money, and with none of the residual worries and congestion that increasingly intruded on northern suburbs by the early 1970s. Personal preferences aside, there were other good reasons for the attractiveness of the Sunbelt. Technology had softened the oppressive heat and humidity of places like Houston and Memphis. Taxes were generally lower as well. True, this implied reduced service levels, but considering the problems confronting service-heavy cities of the Northeast and Midwest, this feature of Sunbelt fiscal life might not be so bad. The Sunbelt was also more accessible than it had ever been. The construction of the interstate highway network had advanced considerably by 1970 and more airlines flew more flights to growing Sunbelt cities. By 1970, Atlanta's Hartsfield airport was among the busiest airports in the nation. By the early 1980s, Piedmont Airlines had established a major hub at Charlotte and American Airlines had hubs at Raleigh-Durham, Nashville, and Dallas–Fort Worth.

The accommodation to civil rights that had come about in the South also enhanced that region's reputation as a place to live and work. Southern political and business leaders who had diverted their energies to race relations since the end of World War II were now free to pursue the economic main chance. Their pitches, which stressed hospitality and wholesome living along with such standards as cheap, nonunion labor and low taxes, would no longer have a hollow ring. Birmingham's slogan, plastered on license plates and stuck on shop windows—"It's Nice to Have You in Birmingham"—had become a derisive chant in the early 1960s. By 1970, the city's infamous police chief, Eugene "Bull" Connor, was gone and a business-oriented local government headed by Republican mayor George Siebels was in place. Civic leaders always took pains to distance themselves and the city from Governor George Wallace, who still held forth down the road in Montgomery, though the worst of his race-baiting days were over. By the late 1970s, Birmingham's attention to its image as well as the reality of reformed race relations helped turn the erstwhile Johannesburg of America into the Deep South's most important medical center. By the 1980s, Birmingham sported hip neighborhoods such as Five Points South, a flourishing gay community, and first-class hotels and restaurants. Though many factors had played a role in Birmingham's reconstruction, it would probably not have occurred without the racial accommodation.

The media also played an important role in keeping the Sunbelt before the public and identifying this area with attributes most Americans valued, including climate, relative safety, relaxed lifestyle, lower cost of living, honest government, and values that supported family, God, and country. These were the "quality of life" issues that competed with and sometimes overshadowed monetary considerations in convincing families to relocate during the 1970s and 1980s.

Though Army Air Force planners were using the phrase "sunshine belt" to describe the area below the 37th parallel as early as the 1940s, the concept of a perpetually pleasant region that the very term conveyed did not touch the popular imagination until a series of articles in the *New York Times* during Feburary 1976, followed by a *Time* magazine cover story in March of that year entitled, "Americans on the Move," reported that the pursuit of the American Dream had taken on a regional cast. These stories were often juxtaposed with pictures and articles from the blustery, decaying, crime-ridden cities of the Northeast and Midwest. In 1979, the *Wall Street Journal* printed an article on Dallas outlining why that city "worked" and, by implication, why northern cities did not:

> Dallas is a contented city because it works. Policemen don't strike in Dallas. The parks and streets are clean. Unemployment is among the lowest in the country, and there is $400 million in construction under way downtown. The city has a balanced budget and a $7 million cash reserve for emergencies. Dallas works so smoothly because,

probably more than any other major city in the country, it is run by businessmen. Its entrepreneurs, bankers, executives and developers are cheerily confident that they know what's best for the 900,000 people who live here.[12]

These cities radiated an air of energy and expectation that many urban residents elsewhere had not felt since the 1950s. They touched the nation's pioneer spirit, the questing after new opportunity. The most common feature on these landscapes—so the popular image ran—was the building crane, and "Help Wanted" was as common a phrase as "Sir" and "Ma'am." Houston's Mayor Fred Hofheinz summarized the feeling for the *New York Times* in 1976: "The South and Southwest are frontiers of the new industrial America, where people can still reach the American dream. This is the new Detroit, the new New York. This is where the action is."[13]

The federal government had played a major role in directing that action to the Sunbelt. Aside from such indirect subsidies as the interstate highway network and a social security system that permitted earlier and more comfortable retirement, the federal government introduced the high-tech economy into the Sunbelt during World War II. The government consciously looked to the South and Southwest for strategic reasons, but also because, as a 1938 report noted, the South was "the nation's Number One economic problem."[14] Defense plants and military bases appeared in and about those cities where "corporate power, capitalist development, and regional economic maturity had not already produced a more modern economy."[15] After the war, many of these installations converted to peacetime production and provided a solid industrial base for other economic activities. Lockheed in Atlanta and General Dynamics in Ft. Worth produce military aircraft today on the sites of World War II factories. Fort Bliss in El Paso, Texas and Kirtland Air Force Base in Albuquerque are among the most sophisticated air defense centers in the world. Aside from generating employment, the existence of such facilities stimulated the growth of public universities, which in turn encouraged other high-tech facilities. By 1976, the South and West were receiving 78 percent of all military payrolls and southern and western companies secured 56 percent of all major defense contracts, more than double their share twenty-five years earlier. Little wonder that envious critics in other parts of the country complained that the Pentagon was "a five-sided building that faces South."[16]

But it would be a mistake to attribute the rapid economic and demographic growth of the Sunbelt to the so-called military-industrial complex. Defense industries were part of a larger complement of economic activities drawn into the region after 1965. Contrary to the popular image of firms picking up lock, stock, and payroll and moving to some low-tax, high-amenity location below the 37th parallel, much of the economic development in Sunbelt metropolitan

areas consisted of the establishment of branch offices and the emergence of lo-
cally based enterprises. Historically, the South in particular had not been an
attractive region for northern corporations considering expansion, franchising,
or "branching." The region's economic base was thin, the pool of trained and
professional workers required in postindustrial economic activities was low, and
the buying power of consumers lagged behind that of the rest of the country.
Southern cities also lagged behind in cultural activities, restaurants, high-quality
education, and upscale shopping—factors that executives who made branching
or relocation decisions would weigh for their families and colleagues. People
were leaving the South, not coming to it. All this changed during the 1960s,
when the factors mentioned earlier operated to attract more residents into the
South, both as retirees and as white-collar workers. Skill levels rose, and so did
wages. Universities expanded, and the quality of curriculum and faculty increased. Cultural activities common in the more established cities began to appear. And branches soon followed, from IBM to McDonald's hamburgers.

North Carolina's Research Triangle Park—located between Raleigh, Durham,
and Chapel Hill, an area with a high concentration of universities, technically
skilled workers, relatively low land costs, and the climate and lifestyle attractions
associated with the Sunbelt—exemplified the Southern economy's new look.
Educators at Chapel Hill and political leaders such as Governor Luther Hodges
had long touted the efficacy of a nonprofit, taxpaying corporation devoted to
research and development apart from, but at times associated with, the three
major universities in the capital area—the University of North Carolina, North
Carolina State University, and Duke University. The park was born in 1958 on
an expanse of land donated by private sources. By 1980, nearly thirty research
and development firms were located there and another research park was blos-
soming in Charlotte near the campus of the University of North Carolina at
Charlotte. Most of these firms were either indigenous creations or branches of
larger companies headquartered elsewhere such as IBM, Verbatim, and the *Wall
Street Journal*.

Still the image persisted of aggressive Southern governors and mayors spir-
iting away industries and companies with promises of free land, almost free
labor, and no taxes. Northern urban leaders cited North Carolina's Governor
Luther Hodges, who had logged 67,000 miles on recruitment trips by 1960
and Atlanta Mayor Ivan Allen, Jr., who boldly established an economic recruitment office in New York City during the 1960s. Though doubtless some states,
such as Mississippi, were prepared to sell off anything to get anything (offering
long-term tax deferments, picking up land and infrastructure costs, and training
prospective employees), after 1965 southern metropolitan areas were not generally offering blank-check incentives to northern firms, nor were those firms
moving in the numbers imagined by northern lawmakers and local officials. The

image was strong enough, nonetheless, to produce a renewal of sectional tensions in the Congress as some northern Congressmen gathered in an informal group to stem the alleged raid on the federal treasury undertaken by Sunbelt jurisdictions. The rise of the Sunbelt was so unexpected, and the decline of northern cities seemed so precipitous by comparison, that specific villains had to be found to take the blame for such phenomena. These efforts were generally futile. As President Nixon's Domestic Council noted, significant numbers of Americans continued to make their individual decisions unencumbered by sectional loyalties, but very much in pursuit of their own happiness.

And, by the mid-1970s, these millions of individual decisions had accumulated into major differences between metropolitan areas in the Sunbelt and the "Frostbelt" ("Sunbelt" required a media antonym). Much as they had abandoned central cities for suburbs in the half-century after 1920, families and businesses left northern metropolitan areas in massive numbers for the South and West after 1970 (see Table 12.1). Between 1970 and 1974, every one of the top eleven metropolitan areas in the Northeast and Midwest lost population; none of the major metropolitan areas in the South and West did. Put another way, the South and West accounted for 62 percent of the nation's metropolitan growth in the 1960s and 96 percent in the 1970s. The impact was especially noticeable on the rank order of American cities. In 1920, nine of the largest ten cities were located in the Northeast and Midwest; the same was true in 1950 (Los Angeles was the only city to break into the top ten); by 1980, however, five of the ten largest cities were located in the Sunbelt: Los Angeles, Houston, Dallas, Phoenix, and San Diego.

The Sunbelt bellwether was Florida. Between 1930 and 1980, the state's population grew by an unprecedented 564 percent, from 1.5 million to nearly 10 million. During the 1970s, Florida accounted for six of the twenty fastest-growing metropolitan areas, with Fort Myers and Ocala leading the way nationally. Many reasons lay behind this boom, but a key element was the "mailbox" economy. Millions of retirees received their social security and pension checks from Frostbelt states, localities, and firms, and deposited and spent them in Florida (or, secondarily, Arizona). This represented several billions of dollars in transfer payments annually, further draining the financial resources of Frostbelt cities and states.

Jobs moved south in the same proportion as population. Employment in northern metropolitan areas grew 12.4 percent during the 1970s, compared with 40.0 percent for the South and 45.4 percent for the West (see Table 12.2). The gap was slightly larger in the so-called "nodal" (basic services) sector of the economy (including transport, communications, wholesale, finance, and business and professional services), where the North grew by only 11.5 percent, compared with 43.9 percent in the South and 41.6 percent in the West. The economy was not only shifting to a service orientation, but the vast majority of

Table 12.1

Percentage Growth of Metropolitan Areas, 1950–1984

Region and Division	1950–1960	1960–1970	1970–1980	1980–1984
Northeast	13.7	9.6	−1.5	1.1
New England	13.0	12.8	2.6	1.6
Mid Atlantic	14.0	8.7	−2.7	0.9
Midwest	23.5	13.0	2.6	0.4
East North Central	23.4	12.7	2.0	−0.3
West North Central	23.8	13.8	5.0	2.7
South	36.2	22.0	21.5	8.0
South Atlantic	39.7	25.9	20.7	7.4
East South Central	22.6	11.6	14.4	2.8
West South Central	38.1	21.3	26.4	11.4
West	48.5	28.5	22.6	8.2
Mountain	63.9	34.6	41.4	11.4
Pacific	45.8	27.3	18.6	7.4
Total	26.5	16.8	10.3	4.4
Average annual rate	2.38	1.57	0.99	1.03

Source: Data for 1950–1980: *County and City Data Books* (prepared by the U.S. Bureau of the Census); Data for 1980–1984: U.S. Bureau of the Census, *Current Population Reports,* Series P-26, no. 84-52-C (Washington, D.C.: Government Printing Office, 1984).

Table 12.2

Employment Growth and Net Migration, 1970–1980

Functional Type	Region			Total
	North	*South*	*West*	
Employment growth (percent)				
Nodal*	11.5	43.9	41.6	27.7
Manufacturing	12.0	24.4	—	13.3
Government/military	—	28.5	46.7	34.8
Medical/educational	30.2	61.0	65.2	47.1
Resort	26.1	88.6	102.8	86.0
Mixed	28.8	34.4	59.7	43.7
Total	12.4	40.0	45.4	26.0
Net migration (per 1,000 population)				
Nodal*	−66.8	109.9	90.1	19.6
Manufacturing	−60.0	14.7	—	−51.9
Government/military	—	−17.0	175.1	50.2
Medical/educational	10.5	221.2	257.0	127.0
Resort	93.0	630.6	558.8	569.5
Mixed	31.5	65.7	258.7	138.4
Total	−60.1	92.1	128.4	16.2

*Includes transportation, wholesale trade, communications, and financial and business services.

Source: U.S. Bureau of the Census, *Censuses of 1970 and 1980, Characteristics of the Population: US Summary* (Washington, D.C.: U.S. Government Printing Office).

positions in that sector were going to the Sunbelt. Though only one out of every five jobs in 1975 was in the manufacturing sector (compared with one out of four in 1960), the South added nearly 1.5 million manufacturing jobs during this period, accounting singlehandedly for American manufacturing growth. The Northeast alone (not counting the depressed industrial cities of the Midwest) lost more than 781,000 manufacturing jobs during these fifteen years. The vast majority of these positions, however, did not move south; they simply disappeared.

Much as the artisan vanished from the nineteenth-century American city, the industrial worker was becoming a relic of the past in the late twentieth century. Fathers could no longer expect to hand down jobs to their sons. And the working-class culture that had grown up around taverns, restaurants, union halls, and ball fields receded with those institutions. The revival of ethnic identity in the 1960s coincided with the decline of a working-class identity. As grandsons and granddaughters of immigrants moved into white-collar occupations and scattered across the country, the workplace no longer identified a cultural or ethnic group. Some of the old ethnic neighborhoods such as the "Hill" in St. Louis, Little Italy in New York, and Chinatown in San Francisco lingered on, but a younger generation left these areas behind as well. Though the spatial anchors of work and residence mattered much less, family and ethnicity persisted. And by the 1970s, the story of the immigrant in urban America had a sequel, and one with a regional dimension as well.

The Newest Immigrants: Hispanics and Asians

During the late nineteenth century, when northern and midwestern metropolises entered the Industrial Revolution, immigrants drawn by the promise of employment provided much of the manpower to maintain and extend the growth of American industry. By the 1970s, though deindustrialization was well underway, the growing service economy drew a similar response from overseas. In sheer numbers, immigration into the United States during the 1970s and 1980s resembled the migration of the earlier era, though the latter-day newcomers came from different parts of the world. The destinations of these immigrants were primarily the cities of the Sunbelt. Whatever else the media or census figures might say about regional redistribution, this fact alone underscored a new era in American regional and urban development.

As with many other factors relating to Sunbelt urbanization, the federal government played a role in stimulating the new wave of immigration. When Congress restricted immigration in 1924, it assigned a quota to every country. Congress abolished that system in 1965, substituting overall limits of 170,000 immigrants annually from the Eastern Hemisphere and 120,000 from the Western Hemisphere. The result was that legal immigration increased from 1.8 million during the 1966–1970 period to 2.9 million between 1976 and 1980. The majority (80 percent, divided equally) came from Latin America and Asia, with Mexico the single largest source, accounting for more than half a million legal immigrants during the 1970s. In 1970, only fourteen metropolitan areas contained a foreign-born population exceeding 10 percent; by 1980, there were thirty-two such metropolitan areas. The New York region maintained its historic lead as the most preferred destination of immigrants, but Miami and Los Angeles were close behind.

By 1980, in fact, Miami had become an extension of Latin America. It was not unusual to see signs in shop windows announcing, "English Spoken Here." Miami's transformation began in the early 1960s, when more than 200,000 Cubans fled the Castro revolution and its aftermath in Cuba. By the late 1980s, nearly 1 million Hispanics resided in the Miami metropolitan area, comprising 60 percent of the city's population. Their neighborhoods have become discrete communities, more exclusive in fact than the ethnic districts at the turn of the century. "Little Havana" is well known, though it is more a city within a city than a neighborhood—a thriving re-creation of the shops, recreational activities, religious institutions, and family patterns of the Cuban capital's pre-Castro days. More than 25,000 businesses of various sizes are located in the area. Other, smaller districts include "Little Haiti" and "Little Managua." Miami's Hispanic flavor, superimposed on its mélange of ethnic refugees, especially Jews, from the urban North, have given that city a unique character. At some hotels, it is possible to get *huevos rancheros* with lox. *Rolling Stone* magazine summarized the city as "afterlife for Ohio, surrogate for Cuba, landing strip for Colombia, laundromat for the mob, beach for Brooklyn."[17]

Los Angeles is now the second largest Mexican city in the world. It is also the new home of more than a half million Filipinos, Koreans, Japanese, Chinese, Pacific Islanders, and Southeast Asian immigrants. The city's varied immigrant population is similar to New York's mix; next to New York, in fact, Los Angeles is the nation's second largest point of entry, a western Ellis Island.

Texas cities such as El Paso, San Antonio, and Houston continued to increase their Hispanic populations during the 1970s and 1980s. In 1980, the Atlanta metropolitan area contained 50,000 Hispanics and a number of Koreans, Chinese, Indians, and Vietnamese. Every major southern city now includes these groups. For confirmation, just look at the supermarket shelves and the restaurants.

The influence of these immigrants on Sunbelt cities extends, of course, beyond the supermarket and the restaurants. The newcomers' large numbers also imply an impact on urban politics previously unknown in most Sunbelt cities.

A Proclamation in Los Angeles

Although their points of origin have changed, recent immigrants share the same dreams and objectives as early-twentieth-century immigrants. Hispanic residents have begun to wield significant political and economic power in Los Angeles and other cities in California, Florida, and Texas.

Even in places such as San Antonio and Miami with a history of bi- or multi-ethnic politics, the new wave of immigration altered the political landscape. The 1965 Voting Rights Act, passed primarily as a measure to secure the right of southern blacks to vote, has proved helpful to Hispanics in several Texas cities, where they have used the act to end at-large elections and gerrymandered districting. Henry Cisneros became the first Hispanic mayor of a major city when he assumed the office in San Antonio in 1981. The Cuban-dominated City Council in Miami as well as Cuban-born mayor Xavier Suarez attest to the political clout of that community.

The Hispanic and Asian presence in California, Texas, and Florida metropolitan areas has generated the type of ethnic pluralism in politics familiar to the major northern cities. Hispanics, Asians, and blacks have their own political organizations, make endorsements, financially support candidates, and serve as voter registration agencies. The dominance of Cubans in Miami, however, has enabled that group to operate without brokering the power of the numerous other, but considerably smaller, ethnic groups. Miami's Cubans, in fact, have presented historians with a new model for immigration. They have adjusted well to their new environment, and have prospered, without assimilating. The keys to the Cubans' distinction are the general affluence and skill levels they brought with them and the large size of their community. The Cubans are further unique among America's immigrants in perceiving an economic value in maintaining their own language: merchants, professionals, and politicians have discovered that Spanish is an essential common denominator for transacting business.

The ethnic diversity of Sunbelt cities coupled with the Voting Rights Act, which monitored electoral procedures that affected minority representation, ushered in a new political era in the United States. New groups challenged business-oriented local government, fracturing the consensus of postwar Sunbelt urban administrations. Traditionally, that consensus had relied on a relatively narrow base of white males who controlled the major economic institutions, belonged to the same clubs and churches, and generally agreed on low taxes, minimal social services, and economic development. Blacks challenged that consensus in the 1960s, especially in the urban South, and Hispanics and other immigrant groups clamored for a role in city government during the 1970s.

In addition, the neighborhood emerged as another powerful interest group. This was true not only in Sunbelt cities, but around the nation as well. Buffeted by urban renewal and the decline of services or, in the Sunbelt, by the voracious land appetite of cities that gobbled up territory at breakneck rates while neglecting older, more established areas, the neighborhoods struck back. Often joining forces in response to a specific crisis such as the construction of a freeway or the threatened development of adjacent nonconforming uses, and sometimes organizing as part of federal requirements for citizen participation, neighborhood groups plunged into the political process in the late 1960s (the Ocean Hill–Brownsville school controversy was a more extreme example of this neighborhood activism). By the early 1970s, Sunbelt urban neighborhoods joined the trend. While neighborhood groups in northern cities were following in the well-worn path of a lengthy tradition of pluralist politics, groups in the Sunbelt cities entered a much less cluttered political arena. Their impact, along with that of energized ethnic groups, was immediate and significant.

The potency of the neighborhood as a political force was illustrated in Atlanta when a group of predominantly white neighborhoods banded together in 1973 to block the construction of highway I-485 in the city, a project advocated by downtown businesses and the development community. At roughly the same time, several eastside Atlanta neighborhoods—Inman Park and Ansley Park among them—were being rediscovered by young middle-class urbanites, who demanded an upgrading in urban services, a chronic complaint of the city's black neighborhoods. The neighborhood and racial coalition helped to elect the city's first black mayor, Maynard Jackson, thus ending for the time being the domination of urban government by a narrow elite with ties to the financial-mercantile interests and northside residential areas. Once in office, Jackson threatened to delay several major projects, including the expansion of Hartsfield airport, unless minority firms received a portion of the contracts. In addition, Jackson warned local banks that he would counter discriminatory lending practices by withdrawing city funds and moving them to banks in Birmingham, of all places.

Similar, though less dramatic, political changes unfolded in other parts of the Sunbelt. Houston accountant Kathy Whitmire built a coalition of blacks, gays (a new Sunbelt political interest group), and inner city residential areas concerned about the drain of funds to annexed districts and won the mayoral election in 1981. In San Antonio, concern about water and flood control coupled with a change to district elections mandated by the Voting Rights Act led to a black-Hispanic majority on the city council and the election of Henry Cisneros as mayor in 1981.

The new Sunbelt governments were generally more skeptical about growth than their predecessors. Just as the industrial cities at the turn of the century bartered health and esthetics for prosperity, Sunbelt cities have encountered some environmental problems. The automobile-generated pollution of Los Angeles is well known, but cities such as Charlotte, Atlanta, and Houston choke in exhaust fumes when certain weather conditions prevail. In the metropolitan Southwest, the great issue is water. Both the quantity and quality of the water supply are major concerns as cities such as Phoenix spread outward and as chemicals continue to be a major part of agriculture in the surrounding countryside. The new governments have sought to address these issues by limiting and redirecting growth. Phoenix, for example, has pushed infrastructure costs onto developers whose projects create traffic congestion and require new water and sewer lines. Developers pay impact fees to support these services. In urban Palm Beach County, Florida, developers contribute $10 million annually for roads. In conservative Orange County, California, officials adopted tough growth control policies in 1988, compelling developers to provide impact statements for their projects and restricting their right to build if the development impedes the flow of traffic. Many Sunbelt residents shared the sentiment expressed on a San Diego airport billboard: "Leaving San Diego? Take a Friend." By the 1980s, limited-growth forces became another element in pluralistic Sunbelt governments. These are significant trends if for no other reason than the fact that the abundance of land and its private distribution and development have been major themes of American urbanization for three centuries.

The transition to a pluralist political process has not been entirely smooth in some Sunbelt cities. The revival of the Ku Klux Klan; the growing visibility of right-wing paramilitary fringe groups; the residual racism that persists in clubs, boardrooms, banks, and neighborhoods; and the popularity of anti-bilingual legislation reflect not so much an epidemic as an incremental escalation of racial and ethnic tensions that could, ultimately, flare into violence. These phenomena are by no means confined to the Sunbelt. The assault on two black youths in the predominantly white New York suburb of Howard Beach in 1986 attests to the national problem of bigotry. But many Sunbelt cities are confronting, for the first time, a wide array of ethnic groups. Traditionally conservative and—in the South, at least—accustomed to dealing with differences in terms of black and white, Sunbelt citizens are entering a new era of heterogeneity in both their political and social institutions.

Shadows on the Sunbelt

The increasing combativeness of Sunbelt urban politics reflects the ethnic, racial, and spatial divisions within those cities. Prosperity has not penetrated into all social groups or to all urban settlements in the Sunbelt. And, in fact, the transition to a service-oriented economy has created new divisions in urban society. Much as observers dwelled on the downside of urbanization in the North, they played up the positive elements of urban development in the Sunbelt. Both characterizations were incomplete and misleading. In 1980, economist Bernard Weinstein extolled the broad prosperity of the Sunbelt. Five years later, in a *Wall Street Journal* editorial, he announced that the Sunbelt had "collapsed into only a few 'sunspots.'"[18] The major transformation he and others had predicted had not occurred in the interim. What did happen was the replication of a familiar pattern. The American city had been at least two cities since the colonial era, and the urban Sunbelt proved not to be immune to that tradition.

The movement to the Sunbelt was a migration primarily from the suburbs of the North to the suburbs of the South and Southwest. The impressive gains registered by many Sunbelt cities during the 1970s reflected the easy procedures of urban spatial annexation in Sunbelt states rather than the accretions of newcomers to central cities. Dallas grew from 42 square miles in 1942 to 266 square miles thirty years later. In 1945, Houston comprised a modest 73 square miles; by 1975, it had burgeoned to 556 square miles, with an option on annexing an additional 2,000 square miles. The centrifugal tendencies were just as common in these urban areas as up north, with the important exception that many Sunbelt cities were able to go out and capture their fleeing residential and economic base. Boston expanded by only 3 square miles between 1870 and 1970, and San Francisco increased its territory only 9 square miles between 1890 and 1970. For those Sunbelt cities not blessed with accommodating annexation laws, statistics told a familiar tale. Atlanta, for example, declined in population at a faster rate than both Newark and Detroit between 1970 and 1975. New Orleans and Norfolk lost population faster than New York City and Detroit. During the 1960s, Atlanta's population increased by 1.9 percent while its metropolitan area was growing at a rate of 36.7 percent. More ominous, 80 percent of new jobs in metropolitan Atlanta between 1975 and 1984 were located in the suburbs.

A walk through some of the major southern urban downtowns in the 1970s confirmed the figures. A Memphis resident described his downtown perspective in 1978: "You can stand on Main Street now and see to where the city limits were fifty years ago and it's all vacant land."[19] Retail establishments were closing and moving to the suburban shopping malls. Downtown Memphis accounted for only 5 percent of the metropolitan area's retail sales.

By the 1980s, the types of social and racial divisions common in northern metropolitan areas were becoming evident in the Sunbelt. The service and high-tech economy has created a two-tiered workforce of high-skilled, well-educated, white-collar personnel and poorly educated, low-skilled workers with little hope of upward mobility in salary and responsibility. The majority of low-skill level jobs (and they comprise most of service employment) appeared on the metropolitan periphery, where few of the lower-income people live, and so the inadequacy of public transit in the metropolitan South worsened the gap between work and residence.

Just as industrialization depressed the condition of most artisans in the nineteenth-century American city, the service economy has not offered the wages and fringe benefits earned by most industrial workers. Even the positive employment statistics are misleading because jobs, in fact, are a major source of urban poverty in the southern portion of the Sunbelt, as service wages often rise little above the minimum wage. Residents of southern urban slums are poorer, based on per capita income, than slum dwellers in northeastern cities, yet almost one-half of the northeastern poor are unemployed, compared with only one-quarter jobless in poor southern urban neighborhoods. The situation lowers the economic incentive in southern cities to establish comprehensive social service programs, because the poor, rather than being an economic burden, are often a resource in the form of cheap labor.

Subemployment rates—figures for those working below a government-defined living wage—were significantly higher in southern inner cities than in the North. In Memphis in 1980, for example, 21.5 percent of the inner city workforce earned less than two dollars an hour, compared with 8.6 percent for workers in Newark, one of the most economically crippled cities of the Frostbelt. In fact, no southern inner city subemployment rate was lower than any northern city's rate.

The sharply varied economic landscape of Sunbelt metropolitan areas may become a terrain as dangerous as that in the older cities. Crime statistics do not indicate that Sunbelt cities are safer than any other metropolitan areas in the United States, and perhaps they are even less so. Gangs roam at will in Los Angeles. Downtown Atlanta and New Orleans are as murderous as central Detroit. And the cities of southern Florida are among the nation's prime conduits for illicit drugs. Though civil disturbances on the scale of the 1960s are rare, the two major uprisings between August 1988 and February 1989 occurred in Shreveport, Louisiana, and Miami, respectively. Citizens who live outside central cities in the Sunbelt region doubtless feel the same about them, especially after dark, as their counterparts who live in Detroit or Philadelphia suburbs.

Move beyond the metropolitan areas of the Sunbelt, and the scenes often resemble those from Larry McMurtry's *The Last Picture Show,* a novel and later a movie about a dying West Texas town whose younger residents try to come to terms with a future that will be vastly different from that of their parents. The small town, long the characteristic urban settlement in the Sunbelt South, often shows few signs of the prosperity of its metropolitan neighbors. Up and down the Carolina Piedmont textile region, for example, in places such as China Grove, Ware Shoals, and Pelzer, the movie theaters are closing, too. These are the one-industry towns, rescued from penury by textiles in the late nineteenth and early twentieth centuries only to be thrust back to the brink of bankruptcy when foreign competition, mechanization, and corporate mergers cut workforces and spurred "restructuring," that is, plant closings.

And when the mills shut down, the towns shut down, too. The Riegel Textile Corporation created Ware Shoals, South Carolina, on the banks of the Saluda River in 1906. The company closed its plant at the end of 1984, throwing 900 people out of work. Riegel provided 60 percent of the tax base and 20 percent of the school budget. Young people moved to find work elsewhere. Sixty percent of the population is retired. Mayor Hugh Frederick tried to put a brave face on the situation: "Riegel built the town. They built all the homes around the mill. They provided the water, electricity and the company store. It looks bad, but we've got a lot of assets. . . . We're pretty gritty people."[20]

In other Piedmont communities, urban death did not come so suddenly, but the long decline has set in. Vacant storefronts dot downtown Chester, South Carolina. In Whitmire, South Carolina, as the textile giant J. P. Stevens cut its workforce, a department store, a drugstore, and a clothing store have left the downtown.

The small towns face a difficult prospect. Many, like Woodville, Mississippi, list welfare as their major industry. Their populations are dependent, highly skewed toward the elderly, and offer little attraction for outside investment and little inspiration for indigenous entrepreneurship. Though they may have once hosted prosperous industries, they are now competing against the low wages and low operating costs offered by Third World nations. These are the places of high dropout rates, high infant mortality, and high unemployment—37 percent higher than in the larger cities of the South. The resources that have fueled the postindustrial metropolitan economy—the expertise and financial support of government, business, and higher education—are considerably beyond the reach of these communities. They are, in effect, microcosms of the great industrial cities of the Northeast and Midwest, tucked away in the corner of the urban hierarchy, much less publicized but, in the end, much worse off. The Clevelands and the Detroits, for all of their problems in the 1970s, had built a network of support institutions, from social services to symphonies to universities, that would help with the transition. The one-industry towns, lacking these institutions, had nothing to make a transition to. Not only in the Sunbelt but all over America, the closing of industries, the construction of the bypass or interstate, and the absence of educational and occupational opportunities compelled the next generation to move away. This was not a new phenomenon, for thousands of Americans had left farms for cities in the nineteenth century. But one result of the latter movement was a more efficient farm economy; today the exodus represents the loss of another vital sign for small towns.

If there were a shorthand to summarize the changing nature of urbanization after 1970, *Sunbelt/Frostbelt* would not be it. Prosperous as they were in the new service economy, Sunbelt cities were experiencing social and environmental problems connected with that very prosperity. In addition, urban growth was uneven in the Sunbelt, favoring suburban areas and newer cities such as Phoenix and Charlotte while it bypassed many small towns and barely touched older larger cities such as New Orleans and Mobile. At the same time, those dinosaur cities of the North were not endangered species after all. Although it is true that in some parts they resembled the aftermath of a major meteor shower, other parts glistened with wealth and confidence. During the 1970s, the media told a cautionary tale of two cities—the prosperous Sunbelt city and the down-at-the-heels metropolis of the Frostbelt. In the 1980s, more and more observers wrote about "sunspots" and "shadows" to describe southern and western cities, and "recovery" to characterize the erstwhile dead cities of the Frostbelt. As usual, the more accurate picture lay somewhere between the two extremes of this misleading polarity.

Notes

1. Quoted in Jon C. Teaford, *The Twentieth-Century American City: Problem, Promise, and Reality* (Baltimore: Johns Hopkins University Press, 1986), p. 143.
2. Quoted in Bayrd Still, ed., *Urban America: A History with Documents* (Boston: Little, Brown, 1974), p. 483.
3. William Julius Wilson, "The Urban Underclass and Advanced Industrial Society," in Paul E. Peterson, ed., *The New Urban Reality* (Washington, D.C.: The Brookings Institution, 1985), p. 142.
4. Brian J. L. Berry and John D. Kasarda, *Contemporary Urban Ecology* (New York: Macmillan, 1977), p. 82.

5. Quoted in *New York Times,* December 16, 1988.
6. Quoted in Teaford, *Twentieth-Century American City,* p. 145.
7. Quoted in Neal Peirce, "Community Development: An Anniversary Review," *Washington Post,* December 29, 1984.
8. Quoted in John H. Mollenkopf, *The Contested City* (Princeton, N.J.: Princeton University Press, 1983), p. 274.
9. Quoted in Mollenkopf, *Contested City,* p. 278.
10. Quoted in Peter K. Eisinger, "The Search for a National Urban Policy, 1968–1980," *Journal of Urban History* 12 (November 1985): 10–11.
11. Quoted in Brian J. L. Berry, *The Human Consequences of Urbanization* (New York: St. Martin's Press, 1973), p. 71.
12. Quoted in Martin V. Melosi, "Dallas–Fort Worth: Marketing the Metroplex," in Richard M. Bernard and Bradley R. Rice, eds., *Sunbelt Cities: Politics and Growth since World War II* (Austin, Tex.: University of Texas Press, 1983), p. 177.
13. Quoted in Richard M. Bernard and Bradley R. Rice, introduction, in Bernard and Rice, eds., *Sunbelt Cities,* p. 26.
14. See President's Emergency Council, *Report on the Economic Conditions of the South* (Washington, D.C.: Government Printing Office, 1938).
15. Roger W. Lotchin, "Conclusion: The Martial Metropolis," in Lotchin, ed., *The Martial Metropolis: U.S. Cities in War and Peace* (New York: Praeger, 1984), p. 229.
16. Quoted in Bernard and Rice, eds., *Sunbelt Cities,* p. 13.
17. Quoted in Raymond Arsenault and Gary R. Mormino, "From Dixie to Dreamland: Demographic and Cultural Change in Florida, 1880–1980," in Randall M. Miller and George E. Pozzetta, eds., *Shades of the Sunbelt: Essays on Ethnicity, Race, and the Urban South* (Westport, Ct.: Greenwood Press, 1988), p. 161.
18. Quoted in Stuart Rosenfeld, "A Divided South," *Southern Exposure* 14 (November-December, 1986): 10.
19. Quoted in Roger Biles, "Epitaph for Downtown: The Failure of City Planning in Post–World War II Memphis," *Tennessee Historical Quarterly* 44 (Fall 1985): 267.
20. Quoted in *Charlotte Observer,* November 4, 1984.

CHAPTER 13

Central City and Out-Town: The Metropolitan Shift

In the late 1970s, as the Sunbelt/Frostbelt distinctions became less accurate, the media began to revise their perceptions of northern cities. Though few observers realized it at the time, they were chronicling much more than an urban recovery; they were describing a new metropolitan form.

Older central cities passed from shunned to chic. "America Falls in Love with Its Cities—Again," the *Saturday Review* enthused in 1978. That same year, *Harper's* proclaimed, "The Urban Crisis Leaves Town." Images in magazines chronicled the revival: hard hats erecting new skyscrapers, young couples renovating row houses, trendy restaurants salvaged from warehouse shells, brick walkways and gas lamps brightening dingy side streets, rivers and bays suddenly open to pedestrians and lined with boutiques, hotels, and restaurants. Media lists touted the likes of Baltimore and Pittsburgh as "most livable" cities. Newark went from bust to boomtown, and Cleveland received accolades from the *New York Times,* which announced in December 1988 that the perennial "mistake on the Lake" was "now in a building boom" and had recovered from its fiscal nightmare.[1]

The early 1980s were "feel-good" years; from televangelists to the President, the accent was on the positive. The media, caught up in the euphoria, found many positive things to say about northern cities. Toward the end of the decade, however, it was clear that both the American public and the media had suffered a saccharine overdose. News reports focused on the drug epidemic and home-

410

lessness, implying that the lifestyle of the early 1980s, now transformed in hindsight from prosperous to profligate, inevitably produced the problems of the late 1980s. Rather than following national trends in prophecy, therefore, it is more useful to trace the actual trends in the cities themselves. Doing so, it becomes apparent that northern cities neither died nor ascended to heaven during the Eighties. They merely changed. And depending on which changes you monitored, the city was one of two very different places.

The transition to a service economy that had provided a substantial boost to Sunbelt urbanization during the 1970s contributed to northern urban prosperity as well. Downtown, which had been evolving in form and function since the early nineteenth century, divested itself of some functions in the process and took on others. Once a retail center, the new downtown now specialized in so-called "knowledge functions"—the acquisition and delivery of information and services. And, as with previous economic transitions, the move to the service economy resulted in the exclusion of one portion of the population from the affluence generated by the new economy. Experts termed these excluded people the "underclass," a term that aptly described their position in urban America.

Similar effects during earlier economic transitions had usually evoked a middle-class call for urban reform. This was especially so during the late nineteenth and early twentieth centuries. But the cities of the 1980s generally lacked the large middle-class population from which previous reform efforts had arisen. In addition, the priorities of city government and the changing patterns of urban administration reduced the likelihood of reform at the local level. The underclass could expect little assistance from Washington, for Reagan-era budgets had cut urban programs sharply. It was not surprising, then, that by the end of the decade the relatively few discussions of urban reform stressed self-help and voluntarism as the most appropriate approaches.

Though the social and economic fragmentation of the urban population was visible even during the colonial era and these divisions increased during the nineteenth century, the fractures of the late twentieth century seem deeper and wider than ever. The nature of the urban economy may be one reason, but another is the emergence of a new urban form—the multicentered metropolis. This form has three characteristics. First, people, work, and institutions are concentrated in new or former suburbs, usually located on the periphery of metropolitan areas. Second, the central cities within these metropolitan areas retain their importance as cultural and economic centers, though they have less relevance for, and contact with, the people who live in these new outlying concentrations than ever before. Third, the metropolis itself, as a result of these outlying concentrations, has expanded its boundaries. By the year 2000, in fact, it is entirely possible that very few Americans will be living outside metropolitan areas.

The multicentered metropolis is a segregated metropolis, by race and especially by class. In other words, it offers considerably fewer opportunities than cities in the past for contact and interaction between classes and especially with the underclass, given the spatial realities of the late-twentieth-century metropolis. Nor is there any compulsion to change this situation. At least one lesson from three centuries of American urbanization is this: not only can misery and prosperity exist side by side, they can even complement one another.

Urban Recovery: The Story of Two Cities

During the 1970s, Pittsburgh and Newark would have been unlikely candidates for success stories. Both cities were hard hit by deindustrialization accompanied by the usual catalogue of ills: loss of population and economic base, high unemployment, physical decay, racial unrest, and bad image. Pittsburgh lost almost one-fourth of its residents between 1970 and 1983 and one-half of its industrial jobs between 1979 and 1984. By the late 1970s, however, Pittsburgh was poised to take advantage of the changing national economy. Though losing 45,000 blue-collar positions between 1979 and 1984, the city gained 40,000 jobs in high-tech fields. Its retail base, eviscerated by suburban shopping malls and depopulation, has revived in the form of the restored Pittsburgh and Lake Erie Railroad Terminal, which offers such boutiques as Crabtree & Evelyn for English soaps and Maison de Campagne for French pottery, suitable for the affluent white-collar clientele newly attracted back to the city. Convention bureau ads now tout Pittsburgh as the San Francisco of the East. According to a *New York Times* article in May 1987, in the city's chic French restaurants, "white wine spritzers are ordered nearly as often as 'an Imp and an Arn'—Imperial whisky and Iron City beer."[2] The city had managed to maintain its solid economic and cultural foundation through the difficult years of the Seventies, mainly because symphonies, museums, universities, and large corporate headquarters are not as mobile as people and smaller businesses. Now Pittsburgh has the largest concentration of Fortune 500 companies in the United States after New York and Chicago, as well as topnotch universities and medical institutions. These assets provided the basis for recovery in the 1980s.

The case of Newark reflects perhaps a more amazing turnaround. During the long hot summer of 1967, central Newark was the scene of a brutal race riot. The disturbances left twenty-three people dead—two whites and twenty-one blacks—and a swath of destruction where only weeds grow today. Since the early 1980s, however, Newark has experienced a $250 million office construction boom, a spillover effect from super-hot Manhattan, by virtue of offering more reasonable rents than its neighbor to the north. The city and private developers have restored Pennsylvania Station and established an enclosed street market. As with Pittsburgh, though on a lesser scale, Newark built on its position as corporate headquarters for such major insurance companies as Prudential and Mutual Benefit Life as well as home of a state university campus. Black mayor Sharpe James, who took office in 1986, has streamlined city administration and established an economic development and land use office. By 1987, Newark, with a population of 314,000, was drawing nearly 1 million workers to its downtown daily.

The economic and physical changes in the city centers of Pittsburgh and Newark were common throughout urban America. There were fewer general retail stores, such as department stores, and more specialized high-priced boutiques catering to affluent visitors and office workers. Industry declined, and service employment increased. In Boston and San Francisco between 1950 and 1980, for example, central-city industrial employment declined by more than half, comprising less than 15 percent of the total central city workforce; professional, managerial, and clerical positions accounted for more than 50 percent of the workforce. City centers became strongly identified as corporate headquarters; striking postmodern buildings often became corporate symbols. And clerical and other labor-intensive activities moved to suburbs or to locations entirely out of metropolitan areas.

The uncoupling of some services from corporate headquarters became especially evident during the 1980s. New York's Citibank has its credit card operations in North Dakota, clears its checks in upstate New York and Delaware, and is locating its data processing activities in suburban New Jersey. Clerical staffs are increasingly hired and managed by outside firms, often in suburban locations. Taking advantage of the computer technology, facsimile machines, and advanced telecommunications that can link outlying locations to central city headquarters, these corporate activities joined the high-tech and research and development functions that had gravitated to peripheral locations since the 1950s. A major research and development boom occurred on the metropolitan fringe in the 1980s. Firms pushed beyond Boston's circumferential Route 128 as far as Nashua, New Hampshire, and Washington, D.C.'s highway magnet, the Beltway, was outpaced by high-tech industrial development in the Maryland and Virginia countryside. These developments helped northern metropolitan areas reverse the population decline of the 1970s. The New York metropolitan area experienced a population loss of 6.5 percent in the 1970s but, through 1985, has managed a growth rate of nearly 2 percent. Boston area population declined by 1.3 percent in the Seventies but experienced a 1 percent increase during the first half of the 1980s.

Downtowns: The New Hub of the Knowledge Economy

Meanwhile, downtown became more than ever the corporate center, despite the defections of two decades ago. Crucial to the new economy were *knowledge functions*, activities that create and manage technology and information. They include product design; advertising; the setting of production schedules and inventory controls; marketing; and legal, financial, accounting, public relations, travel, and communications services. These knowledge functions require considerable interaction, or what experts refer to as "high-density contact," with peers and colleagues. In turn, knowledge functionaries are connected through communications systems ranging from facsimile machines to computers with their colleagues in cities in other parts of the country and the world. These knowledge workers must frequently upgrade their skills to analyze and process new information. They must learn about changes in political and economic systems not only in the United States, but abroad as well. In this field the rule of thumb is: the more specialized a specific knowledge function becomes, the greater the need for access to more generalized knowledge. Accordingly, knowledge workers form linkages with nearby universities and training centers.

The interconnection of knowledge functions with personal interaction favors central city locations, though not exclusively. Major institutions in knowledge functions, especially banks and government, have traditionally held prominent central city addresses. The city center also possesses the sophisticated communications infrastructure to support rapid knowledge transfers. It is true that someone with a computer terminal and access to a mainframe computer could live in the middle of a forest and keep abreast of major economic trends throughout the world—and, in fact, numerous predictions in the 1970s held that the computer revolution would make central cities even more obsolete. The preference for human interaction, however, as well as the necessity for multiple contacts at various times during a given day, rendered those predictions inaccurate.

And just as the major corporate headquarters find it advantageous to locate or remain close to large banks, insurance companies, and legal firms, they have also continued the postwar trend of attracting other services, including retail stores, restaurants, theaters, and universities. The variety and quality of these auxiliary services are rarely duplicated outside the central city. When traveling executives visit, they expect and look forward to central city night life. This expectation accounts to a large extent for the downtown hotel building boom of the 1980s and the renovation of grand hotels such as the Plaza in New York, the Seelbach in Louisville, the Brown Palace in Denver, the Palmer House in Chicago, and perhaps the most spectacular example, the venerable Willard Hotel in Washington, D.C., saved from the wrecker's ball to become an anchor for Pennsylvania Avenue revitalization.

The survival of the stately Willard illustrates two important elements of central city strength that were not as evident in the 1970s as they became in the 1980s. First, the knowledge economy generally pays a premium salary to its functionaries. These are highly educated and highly paid workers who are likely to expect the amenities a central city can offer and be able to afford them as well. If they are married, there is a better than 50–50 chance that their spouses work, too. Though the United States has not approached the Swedish example, where more than three out of four married women work, the figures for women's employment have risen steadily since the 1960s; in the mid-1980s, more than 60 percent of married women worked. Although they tend to work more in clerical jobs—where shortages exist—women are found increasingly in managerial positions. With greater disposable income, they can afford the expense of central city luxury. A renewed emphasis on the work ethic has carried with it the feeling for these privileged workers, that they deserve the service and opulence offered up by a Willard Hotel or a five-star restaurant such as New York's Lafayette.

The American metropolitan center remains a synonym for prestige. It is important to have an address on Fifth Avenue, or La Salle Street, or Union Square that is instantly recognized not only by other firms around the country, but by companies worldwide. A status address draws customers and employees; it suggests excitement, creativity, success. During the allegedly dark days of the late 1960s and early 1970s, business firms were making decisions that solidified the economic base of the city center even as observers were writing off the American city as a dead loss. By 1967, the prominent New York publishing house McGraw-Hill had farmed out numerous operations, including clerical, circulation, and distribution services, to suburban Highstown, New Jersey. The company also erected major book distribution centers in suburban St. Louis and San Francisco. Speculation followed on the heels of this dispersal that the corporate headquarters itself would join the suburban exodus. But as McGraw-Hill president Shelton Fisher explained, "the more we explored the possibilities for our headquarters building, the more our thoughts seemed to turn to the advantages of remaining in New York City." What were those advantages? According to Fisher, the city offered incomparable support services. It was a financial, communications, and advertising center. These factors, however, were "the smallest part of the story in making our decision. McGraw-Hill's principal assets are . . . talented, creative, imaginative people. . . . New York pulls these creative people to its core like a magnet. . . . And these are the kinds of people McGraw-Hill needs to be successful."[3] In much the same way as the early-nineteenth-century cities of New York, Philadelphia, and Boston became focal points for innovation, for organizing and presenting technology, and for exchanging ideas, today the American central city remains a crucible of creativity for the interaction it generates and the people it attracts.

Renovating the Central Cities

The example of Washington's Willard Hotel also underscores the growing public awareness of historical tradition as a factor in promoting downtown revival. At some point during the 1970s, the city discovered its own history. In the past, American cities had proven poor custodians of their built environment. Changing functions of central cities in the nineteenth century prompted changing land uses; old structures gave way to new, open spaces disappeared, roads appeared where buildings had once stood, rivers changed courses, swamps were drained, streets were buried, and skylines were altered dramatically. The nineteenth-century city was a real estate free-for-all, and this pattern scarcely changed during the twentieth century. Land use regulations and various measures designed to minimize social costs did not so much restrict speculation and development as they imposed order on these spiraling trends. If anything, the cycle of demolition and construction accelerated, responding to changes in technology—the skyscraper, for example—and changes in funding patterns—the availability of federal funds. For a quarter century after World War II, urban renewal and highway construction policies fueled development patterns, cutting wide swaths through the city and transforming residential and industrial uses into commercial and/or recreational land.

But the cycle slowed considerably during the 1970s. Neighborhood groups rebeled against freeways and encroaching commercial uses. With the passage of the Housing and Community Development Act in 1974, federal policy no longer subsidized urban renewal. On the contrary, the act encouraged rehabilitation. The Arab oil embargo helped to focus public attention on the concept of nonrenewable resources and the importance of conservation. The approaching bicentennial celebration turned attention to our nation's heritage: any city with eighteenth-century structures was automatically linked to the birthday theme. Cities with no such claims either created ersatz connections or fastened on some particularly ancient building as a surrogate. Finally, the publicity surrounding the rise of the Sunbelt highlighted the effective uses to which southern cities in particular had put history.

Charleston and Savannah had built their civic reputations on historic preservation, and experts touted the ambience of sites like the Battery in Charleston and the Victorian District in Savannah. The Vieux Carré in New Orleans was among the nation's first historic districts and became a major tourist attraction. Cynics pointed out that the extent of the urban South's physical heritage was less a product of reverence for the past than a marker of the slow rate of growth and chronically depressed economy that had traditionally discouraged development. To the credit of these cities, however, when development pressures did appear after the 1920s, they were quick to devise innovative means to protect their treasures from destruction or alteration. Perhaps the most impressive aspect of southern urban historic preservation, as far as northern observers were concerned, was its profitability. Simply put, history paid dividends in the form of tourists and other visitors, and federal tax breaks. On that basis, northern urban developers could similarly display a civic conscience and make money in the bargain. In the process, the American downtown and its surrounding area took on a "new-old" look that represented a conscious attempt to mimic, as well as preserve, the past.

Several innovative examples of historical consciousness altered the urban landscape during the late 1970s and 1980s. One was the attempt to revive the central city's sagging retail trade. Frequently, the strategy involved renovating the original central business district, such as Larimer Square in Denver and the Quincy Market area in Boston. Quincy Market, along with historic Faneuil Hall, opened in 1976, the first of numerous urban "festival marketplaces" that included shops, restaurants, and, in a few cases, hotels. In a sense, the idea duplicated the variety of the suburban shopping mall, with a stronger dose of history and ambience. In several cities, half-abandoned railroad stations such as Union Station in St. Louis and the similarly named facility in Washington, D.C., were transformed into indoor shopping centers featuring specialty shops and restaurants. In other cities, the river or bay rather than the railroad became the new-old retail focal point—the French Market complex in New Orleans, Laclede Landing in St. Louis, and Harborplace in Baltimore—provided examples of cities rescuing their watery heritage from the clutter of warehouses and railroad tracks.

These projects, though important in themselves, helped to stimulate adjacent development. Most of the festival marketplaces were built and renovated with a combination of public and private funds. The public portion occasionally came from the federal government, but more often from the city in the form of bond issues, tax revenues, or in-kind payments involving land donations, low-interest loans to private developers, and tax deferments. Adjacent development was usually private and often included the renovation of an old hotel in keeping with the historic theme. By these means a city redevelopment authority could leverage a small amount of money into a major retail project that, in turn, spurred further development. In many cities, this has proven to be an excellent investment: St. Louis, for example, has increased its property tax valuation by 7 per-

Quincy Market, Boston

This festival marketplace epitomizes the upscale recycling of historic centers (note Faneuil Hall, pictured background, right). Located in Boston's financial district, Quincy Market attracts an affluent working crowd as well as conventioneers and tourists from nearby hotels. Not all developments that combine history and shopping have been as successful as this one.

cent annually between 1984 and 1988, a significant accomplishment for a city that lost 27 percent of its population during the 1970s alone.

Though many observers credit the festival marketplace for serving as a catalyst for additional downtown revitalization, the concept is not a sure-fire success, especially in smaller cities lacking a tourist or convention trade. Festival marketplaces in Richmond, Flint (Michigan), and Toledo have lost millions of dollars. In these places, according to journalist Neal Peirce, "there just aren't enough customers for expensive boutiques, stuffed animals, cutesy food stands, chocolate-chip cookies and left-handed scissors." The problems of Toledo's Portside marketplace elicited the following comment from Toledo Chamber of Commerce director Michael Porter: "Who the hell in their right mind was going to go down there in the middle of winter and buy a kite?"[4]

Central city farmers' markets have enjoyed more general success than festival marketplaces because they appeal to a broader spectrum of the urban population and do not rely on convention or tourist support. Many of these markets, moreover, represent more genuine examples of urban history than the festival marketplaces. Seattle's eighty-year-old Pike Place Market includes 350 farmers, fishmongers, bakers, butchers, artists, and craftsmen; more than 70,000 people per week frequent Philadelphia's ninety-five-year-old Reading Terminal Market. As concerns increase about the safety and cost of supermarket produce, these markets offer the shopper fresh, unadulterated produce at reasonable prices. They also reunite the consumer with the producer, a union commonplace in cities a century and a half ago.

The spotty performance of the festival marketplaces indicates that downtown will have a difficult time recovering its retail function. Very few new downtown department stores were opening in the 1980s; many more were closing. Sakowitz, a mainstay of Houston's downtown retail trade, closed its doors in 1986. Belk's, the retail anchor for Charlotte's downtown for a century, abandoned its store in 1989. True, a Macy's hangs on and upscale stores such as Saks, Bloomingdales, and Neiman-Marcus thrive, but only certain cities can attract the clientele that will keep their expensive retail establishments profitable. For the majority of metropolitan area residents, retail shopping is synonymous with the suburban shopping center, which has become larger and more diverse than ever.

Neighborhood Preservation

The changing philosophy on downtown revival began to emphasize preservation and re-creation more than demolition and the construction of new glass and steel skyscrapers; even postmodern architecture blended historic designs (like Art Deco and Victorian) with new materials. This trend paralleled a similar trend in central city neighborhoods.

In a few instances, the historic impetus spread through entire neighborhoods, such as the Victorian District in Savannah. The forty-five-block district of distinctive wood-frame, gingerbread-style houses erected between 1870 and 1900 stands just south of the city's revitalizing downtown. Once a fashionable area, the district had fallen into disrepair by the early 1970s, with the old homes subdivided into rental properties. As part of Savannah's renewed interest in its rich history, it was likely that the general "rehab fever" in the city would eventually touch this neighborhood. The residents were predominantly black, poor, and elderly renters who would be unable to withstand a wave of speculative buying and selling. In 1977, investment banker Leopold Adler II brought together an interracial group of neighborhood leaders, bankers, architects, and preservation specialists to form a nonprofit development corporation, the Savannah Landmark Rehabilitation Project. The firm's objective was to rehabilitate roughly one-third of the 800-odd homes in the district without displacing their low-income residents. Financed initially by federal subsidies and more recently by private syndicates taking advantage of tax benefits geared to historical structures, Savannah Landmark attained its goal in 1984. In addition, it constructed forty-four infill units. The renaissance has stimulated middle- and upper-income rehabs in other parts of the Victorian District, providing a unique mix of race and income in this inner city neighborhood.

Most residential preservation efforts were not so comprehensive. Usually they involved the individual purchase of run-down properties in which the new owners would put a considerable amount of "sweat equity," renovating much of the premises themselves. These were the young professional couples, usually without children, or affluent singles who felt isolated in suburban communities and wanted to be near the excitement of the city center at a time when the center was reviving and becoming more diverse. This trend did not begin in the 1970s; in fact, it had been underway in some cities rather unobtrusively for several decades. Washington, D.C.'s fashionable Georgetown neighborhood, for example, was a black slum as late as the 1930s. But the movement seemed to catch fire in the 1970s as young couples were priced out of the suburban housing market and lifestyle preferences altered to favor urban locations. Aside from existing urban housing stock, creative adaptive reuses such as turning old mills or warehouses into condominiums or infill developments increased densities but made central city housing more affordable.

Such residential activity prompted some observers to claim a "back-to-the-city" movement by the mid-1970s. Actually, the vast majority of new residents in these districts had simply moved from other parts of the city; relatively few had come from suburbs. Nevertheless, the spectacle of young couples with their sleeves rolled up transforming a previously decaying neighborhood became a popular metaphor for urban revival. It even generated a new term, "gentrification," to denote the socioeconomic upgrading of the neighborhood as a result of the rehabilitation process. City officials were especially delighted with this trend because affluent newcomers were rehabilitating marginal properties and therefore adding to the city's tax base. Officials also assumed that the new residents cost the city less in terms of services. They did not require social services and, because most did not have any children, they did not burden the schools.

Some cities such as Pittsburgh and Baltimore hoped to accelerate the gentrification process by offering an urban version of homesteading. During the 1960s, cities of the Northeast and Midwest became the reluctant owners of numerous properties as a result of tax defaults by landlords. Proprietors simply walked away from their buildings in deteriorating neighborhoods, unable or unwilling to pay their property taxes or repair code violations. Baltimore mayor (now governor of Maryland) Don Schaefer devised a plan to sell these derelict properties by lottery to interested buyers for one dollar provided they renovated and lived in the dwelling for a specified amount of time. The program had numerous takers at first, but by the early 1980s both the supply of suitable properties and the demand had fallen.

There was also rising concern about the gentrification process, especially as conducted in the private market. Critics assumed that the process displaced large numbers of poor black renters who were subsequently unable to find comparable housing nearby, a pattern reminiscent of the early days of urban renewal, when black tenants were forced on a tight housing market with little preparation or resources. Adjustments to the urban renewal law in the 1950s required cities to assist displaced residents in finding new housing. No such requirements applied to displacement by private transaction. Although a few landlords voluntarily assisted their former tenants, most did not. Some cities such as Washington, D.C., where such previously black areas as Capitol Hill and Adams-Morgan were rapidly transformed into affluent enclaves, considered legislation requiring displacement assistance as well as measures to tax the speculative profits from the sale of gentrified properties. A 1978 HUD survey of gentrification around the country revealed, however, that displacement was not a significant by-product of the upgrading process and occurred in less than 15 percent of the cases. Most upgrading took place on vacant properties or where tenants were planning to move. Also, the image of long-established communities suddenly disrupted by affluent young professionals was generally inaccurate. Most of the neighborhoods were unstable and residents' tenures were short, often less than one year. The HUD survey also indicated that observers had overestimated the extent of gentrification. The Washington case was unusual, a factor of the government's rapid growth during the late 1960s and 1970s.

By the early 1980s, the rush for central city properties subsided, though neighborhoods in New York City along Columbus Avenue from 60th to 80th streets, in the Church Hill district in Richmond, and in Dilworth in Charlotte still attracted young professionals. Landlords continued to convert rental properties into upscale condominiums, and new infill developments emerged, often in combination with offices and other zoning variances designed to inject more diversity into the central city. But by this time it had become obvious that gentrification was less a trend than a transient phenomenon of a single stage in the city's life cycle. The demand for central city housing grew as the central city attracted more young, white-collar, professional, service-oriented workers during the 1970s. As urbanist Louis H. Masotti asked, "If you're 25, MBA, trying to make it, single, aggressive, why in the world would you want to live in Bolingbrook where the streets are rolled up at 6 pm?" These so-called "yuppies" (young upwardly mobile professionals), however, have aged. The baby boom (reflecting the high birth rate between 1946 and 1964) has turned to bust, and the supply of twenty- to thirty-five-year-olds that fueled the central city residential movement in the 1970s is decreasing. Paul Grogan, an urban redevelopment specialist, predicted in 1986, "We may be on the verge of a new exodus to the suburbs." Grogan argued that the city continues to pose significant problems for families: "The schools are still a mess. There are not enough housing options."[5]

But it is unlikely that central cities will be subject to a new era of mass exodus to the suburbs. For one thing, the numbers for such a movement are not there. Also, as the service economy expands, even if the twenty- to thirty-five-year-old age group contracts, the market for inner city housing will remain strong in some city neighborhoods. Finally, cities are responding to the changing demographics by erecting luxury or near-luxury apartments for "empty nesters"— middle-aged couples and the elderly whose children have left and who now find themselves in a large suburban house. City residence can offer shopping, restaurants, and museums, often within walking distance.

By the late 1980s, the central city presented a considerably different aspect than it did twenty years earlier, and public perceptions had changed accordingly. In 1986, columnist Neal Peirce announced, "The American City Scores a Spectacular Comeback." Peirce based his headline on a Gallup Poll in which 82 percent of the respondents were optimistic about their city's future. He contrasted this optimism with a statement by a prominent urbanist in 1971 that cities were "physically obsolete, financially unworkable, crime-ridden, garbage-strewn, polluted, torn by racial conflict, wallowing in welfare, unemployment and despair." In the ensuing decade, however, the suburban exodus slowed and central city populations by the 1980s were stable, with some cities such as New York, which had lost people in the 1970s, registering small gains. The poll also indicated that only 4 percent of the respondents liked the idea of telecommunicating their work from a "placid rural spot." Most of those polled preferred to interact with colleagues and participate in the city's amenities.[6]

Juxtaposing the urbanist's statement in 1971 with the Gallup Poll of 1986, it appears that the city has undergone a remarkable transformation in a relatively short amount of time. But urban images have historically operated in cycles. The images are not so much inaccurate as they are selective. Even the enthusiastic respondents to the Gallup Poll had some reservations. A significant 81 percent of those surveyed stated that they would not consider living in or near the downtown or city center. The problems catalogued in 1971, especially crime, services, and unemployment, persisted in the late 1980s. But the city center's attraction as a workplace, a location to meet with colleagues and conduct business, and a place of excitement and culture made it an excellent temporary destination. The city today is less a place to live than a place to visit—as the old adage about Manhattan runs. Physical spaces are increasingly oriented to the visitor—the daily commuter or the even more temporary conventiongoer. Hotels, restaurants, trendy boutiques in historic marketplaces, new theaters and concert halls from Spirit Square in Charlotte to Lincoln Center in New York, and major new convention center complexes in Cincinnati and Kansas City, among many other places, reflect the visitor-oriented landscape of the city center. Though some cities, such as Minneapolis, continue to make efforts to build new city center housing, most cities prefer to see valuable central plots developed differently.

The visitor-oriented city has several distinct advantages. From the perspective of civic leaders, visitors are less likely to demand a high level of services and more likely to spend their money than permanent residents. Expensive hotel and office projects can equally be justified not only in esthetic and practical terms, that is, in the need for additional rooms and office space, but also by the additional development they will generate. In the same manner, mass transit, whose obituaries were as numerous as the city's in the early 1970s, made a comeback to serve both the new downtown landscape and the new postindustrial workforce. Portland, Charlotte, and Denver constructed bus malls downtown to ease transfers and inaugurated express service from the suburbs to the center. More ambitious plans involved so-called "light rail" facilities, such as the electric trolley, which returned to the streets of San Diego and Pittsburgh.

Still more extensive commitments to radial mass transit were the subway-rail systems built in the 1970s, supported by funding from the Urban Mass Transit Administration. Most of these systems failed to win new recruits or interest former patrons. The automobile, the suburbanization of work, and the negative images of mass transit held by white commuters overruled promotional campaigns and high technology features. The Bay Area Rapid Transit system (BART) in San Francisco, completed in 1972, was the first major attempt at a new generation of subway systems. Though it has stimulated real estate development (following the precedent of earlier mass transit systems), it has been neither a financial nor a technological success. In the early years, computer-controlled doors opened while trains whizzed along at 70 miles per hour, and those same computers "forgot" to stop a train until it plunged from its elevated tracks. Even the rise of gasoline prices above $1 a gallon after 1973 did not significantly increase BART ridership. Subsequent rail systems in Atlanta and Miami were not financially successful, either; the Miami system lost $1 million a week on average in 1988. On the other hand, the radial Metro system in Washington, D.C., has proven to be a successful, efficient, and safe subway/rail system. But again, the unique nature of Washington's employment base makes that situation exceptional. The spotty record of the new mass transit systems reflect the fact that even though the city's image has improved, commuters are reluctant to abandon much of their suburban lifestyle, especially the automobile. In addition, perceptions of mass transit as a lower-income and, more specifically, a black mode of transportation persist.

The Second City: Separate and Unequal

Visitors are selective in the way they choose to experience the central city. Commuters come in private automobiles, park in underground garages, and work in hermetically sealed office buildings. They may eat lunch in trendy alfalfa bars or staid restaurants downtown; occasionally they may take in a museum or a concert. But they are not really *of* the city. Their positive perceptions of the urban environment reflect the fact that they are typically sealed off from it, or at least from its less attractive features. It is easier to be optimistic about the city when one's surroundings are climate-controlled, earth-toned, mahogany-filled office towers, restaurants with crisp white table cloths and modern art, and spacious and acoustically sophisticated concert halls and theaters where Brahms or Brecht can transport you anywhere.

Anywhere, that is, except to the other city, the city different from the one depicted in *Harper's* or the *Washingtonian*. Beyond Newark's new Gateway Center, New Jersey's largest office complex, is a city where one-third of the population is on welfare and where drug abuse and teenage pregnancy rates are among the highest in the nation. Despite management efficiencies, Mayor James faces periodic budget crises relieved only by skyrocketing property taxes that tend to dampen development. The school system is so bad that the state of New Jersey has contemplated taking it over.

It may seem unfair to pick on Newark, but that city is symptomatic of the fact that most American cities in the last decade of the twentieth century are really two cities. This has been the case at least since the early nineteenth century, but seldom has the gap between the two cities been wider in reality and less visible from a policy viewpoint. The structural paeans to history and the gleaming office/restaurant/retail/hotel/convention center complexes describe relatively small portions of urban land use, though they loom large in the city's tax base and revitalized image. Decay of infrastructure and neighborhoods outpaces the budgets of most cities. Race continues to polarize, as Chicago politics, Miami riots, and New York vigilantes attest. The black urban underclass has grown during the 1980s even as the black middle class has expanded. Drugs have conquered entire neighborhoods and generated a separate economy, an economy that is also service oriented, in which fortunes are quickly made and lives easily lost. Drugs mean access to the trappings of a consumer-oriented culture: successful dealers drive the flashiest cars and wear expensive clothes. Youngsters in these neighborhoods learn early the equation of drugs and success, and some eagerly act as messengers and lookouts for their older heroes. Police attempts to deal with this situation are holding actions at best. Moreover, the dealing and the violence rarely spill over into the other city, the city of tall towers, affluent neighborhoods, and chic restaurants. Not surprisingly, the rhetoric and publicity of the war on drugs has not been matched in public funding.

Two news stories in 1989 underscored the deep divisions that scar contemporary urban society. The first was a well-publicized attack in New York's Central Park. A gang of eight teenagers from East Harlem roamed the park on the evening of April 19, attacking people who happened across their path. Their vicitms included a twenty-eight-year-old female jogger, whom they raped and beat into a coma. Some media sources portrayed the attack as a symbol of the senseless violence and brutality in the modern drug-infested city. But four of the youths lived in a middle-class community in East Harlem. They were not drug addicts or products of broken families. Apparently, however, these young men had succumbed to the prevailing culture of violence that permeates East Harlem.

East Harlem ranks higher than any other U.S. neighborhood in underclass indicators: households headed by women, school dropouts, and households on public assistance. The standard of behavior expected of teenage males in this environment centers on violent expression. As one analyst noted, "If you're going to be successful, you have to show you're violent."[7] Much of this violence revolves around the buying and selling of "crack," a highly addictive derivative of cocaine. Crack dealers assume de facto control of housing projects, setting curfews for residents, punishing those they see as unfriendly, taking over playgrounds, and preventing maintenance work. Occasionally, police root them out, but overworked courts and understaffed police forces mean that such sweeps are temporary lulls in the daily war.

Immediately to the south of East Harlem is the Upper East Side. If East Harlem is the worst neighborhood in the country, the Upper East Side, according to one researcher, "represents the greatest concentration of wealth that we have found anywhere in the United States."[8] Despite its proximity, the Upper East Side has been relatively immune from the terrorism that pervades its northern neighbor. As public law enforcement proves unequal to the task of breaking the culture of violence, homeowners who can afford to resort to extensive private security measures. This strategy is not limited to the large cities of the Northeast. In 1988, neighborhoods in Fort Lauderdale, Florida, began to barricade streets and hire private security guards to check entering motorists. Cities are not only divided in a social sense, they are becoming war zones. The unfortunate residents of poor neighborhoods, virtually unprotected by public or private security, are the victims of the escalating violence.

Yet their victimization goes largely unreported. At the heart of the furor over the Central Park assault was the fact that the female jogger was affluent and white. Stories of the poor attacking each other rarely become news; but when the culture of violence penetrates the security of affluence, the public's interest and temper become aroused.

The second news story centered around the announcement that the nation's capital had become the nation's murder capital. As in New York, crack was a leading cause of the violence in Washington, D.C. And, as in New York, much of the violence was confined to poor neighborhoods. Despite the high crime rate, the city's tourism and convention business continued to thrive. Again, the poles of poverty and affluence seemed very far apart.

High crime rates are not new to Washington, of course; they caused whites to leave in droves decades ago. Now the city is experiencing black flight. In fact, a majority of the metropolitan area's blacks—52 percent—reside in the suburbs. Abandoned by the middle class, both black and white, the city has become the enclave of the wealthy and the poor. The wealthy enjoy the benefits of the private city—private schools, private security, and private residences—while the poor endure the breakdown of the public city—police and fire protection, housing, and educational services. As one political scientist observed of Washington, "There's no buffer in terms of a middle class that helps to maintain the schools, the values of a community, the entrepreneurial businesses. It leaves the stark contrasts that you see, the relatively affluent and the very, very poor."[9]

The future configuration of the service economy is not likely to improve the prospects of the underclass. Better than 80 percent of the service jobs that will be created in the 1990s are in the lower tier. In addition, high-tech industries do not mean high-quality employment. Two out of three workers in high tech are in low-paying production, clerical, and technical jobs. The average semiconductor production worker receives an hourly wage that is 57 percent of the rate paid to typical unionized steel or auto workers. Those statistics that show the impressive number of new high-tech jobs to balance the blue-collar positions lost often do not include salary and benefit figures because the new jobs rarely pay as much as those lost to technology or to other countries.

Take SCI Systems, Inc., in Huntsville, Alabama, as an example. They employ 1,100 engineers and scientists and 3,300 production workers. According to a former official of the firm, the two groups have "no interaction, they're even in different buildings." He added that the production part of SCI is "just like a poultry plant. You pay them as little as you can, give them a benefit package that's competitive in the community, and you hope—hope they don't vote in a union." Most of these production workers are women. Plant manager J. R. Bell commented, "Most of our workers are off farms, chicken houses, processing plants, sewing factories, places like that. . . . You can train a worker in one hour. . . . They're doing real well within one week."[10]

If increasing numbers of urban residents have been pushed to the margins of the new economy, increasing numbers have also fallen off entirely. There were more homeless people in the nation's cities by the end of the 1980s than at any other time since the Great Depression. Private agencies and churches that have traditionally coped with the homeless have been overwhelmed, even in the most prosperous cities. In Denver, the homeless sleep in church pews, on the floor,

59th Street and Fifth Avenue, New York City
This view of New York, near the Plaza Hotel, pointedly illustrates the "two cities"
concept of modern urban America; wealth and extreme poverty coexist in most
American cities.

and around the altars of churches participating in a homeless program. In New
York, the church-based Partnership for the Homeless has opened more than 100
homeless shelters since 1981, but these facilities fall far short of the demand.

There seems little likelihood that the homeless problem will subside much in
the 1990s, even if the urban economy continues to prosper as it did during
much of the 1980s. The housing situation in most cities is frightful. Conver-
sions of rent-controlled or moderate rental properties to condominiums con-

tinue in the major cities. Public housing construction and rent subsidies have virtually come to a halt as the federal government has sharply reduced its support. The few units of public housing under construction receive funding from the city and state and from banking consortiums. Usually, these are small, scatter-site projects that scarcely make a dent in the low-income housing demand. Some cities such as Memphis and Chattanooga have made major financial commitments to public housing, though it is too early to tell whether those commitments will be translated into significant numbers of dwelling units. There have been well-publicized private efforts at public housing construction, most notably former President Jimmy Carter's Habitat for Humanity, where work crews and local volunteers construct moderately priced single-family housing in low-income neighborhoods. Though the goal of home ownership is a laudable one, the project is appropriate for only a small segment of the urban underclass, and the number of units constructed in a particular city during a given year—rarely more than thirty—makes only a minor contribution to the affordable housing shortage. More promising in the long run, perhaps, has been the proliferation of neighborhood development corporations that typically leverage a small amount of public money to attract private lenders to renovate and, in some cases, to build new housing and businesses. The strategy has the advantage of involving local residents in their own redevelopment efforts, and it possesses the flexibility necessary to address the specific needs of different neighborhoods.

Charlotte Gardens in the ravaged South Bronx is only one example of how these neighborhood corporations operate. If you found yourself in the middle of this development, you could mistake it for suburbia anywhere: the neat, ranch-style homes surrounded by white picket fences, doors bedecked in wreaths heralding the Christmas season, the toys of summer—a boat, a bicycle, a grill—huddled in corners of backyards. But this is the South Bronx and a ninety-home development completed in 1985 that represents the fulfillment of the American dream of a single-family home to its residents, even if Times Square is only a 20-minute subway ride away. The three-bedroom homes that sell for a modest $52,000 have a long waiting list of hopeful buyers. "I always dreamed of having my own private house," Deloris Deleston confessed. Her neighbor Julio Cruz remarked, "It's not like living in an apartment where you don't know your next-door neighbor." And twelve-year-old Melody Sellers noted, "In the summertime, it's like the country."[11] The neighborhood-based South Bronx Development Organization was responsible for Charlotte Gardens. It coordinated a consortium of banks, foundations, businesses, and local and federal agencies that provided financing for the project.

The vast majority of under- and unemployed urban residents, however, would never qualify for single-family home ownership. In some respects, these projects reflect a neighborhood-level version of an assumption that evolved at local and federal policy levels during the early 1970s. This assumption, which wrote off numerous people and neighborhoods as beyond the pale of policy ministrations, still prevails at city hall, in the state house, and in Washington. It accounts, in part, for the absence of policies that would address the housing requirements of the neediest.

Urban Administration: The Management Metaphor

The notion that certain neighborhoods and people are impervious to correction is only a partial explanation for the policy neglect of urban housing needs. The solution to the housing problem involves more than housing per se. Jobs, education, services, and day care (especially when the vast majority of urban poverty consists of women and children) must be part of the housing equation. Urban resources are insufficient to undertake such a comprehensive program, so local government attempts little or none of it. In addition, the nature of late-twentieth-century urban administration makes such comprehensive policies less likely. The key word in current urban administration is management. Mayors and council members are "managers," even when a city manager is present. James Peterson of the Council for Urban Economic Development has noted this transition: "The old mayor divide[d] up the pie by special-interest groups and going to the state and local government for help. The new mayor is the manager." Because urban political leaders still live with the fiscal nightmares of the 1970s, the management metaphor stresses financial responsibility, reliance on computers, and "work management systems" borrowed from private industry. As one example of the "new" mayor, Tampa's Bob Martinez (later the governor of Florida) boasted in 1985, "When our parks personnel go out in the morning, a computer tells them where to go."[12] The result is a streamlined administration, with fewer, better-paid workers, higher technology, and marketing and service innovations. In Harrisburg, Pennsylvania, Mayor Stephen Reed devised a system of burning trash and sludge from neighboring towns and selling the steam to industries. Other cities are beginning to contract out services, hike user fees, and engage in long-range budget planning. These processes, useful as they are, preclude expensive and extensive social programs that would disrupt budgets and add bureaucratic layers. At the same time, the nationwide tax revolt that began in California in the late 1970s made raising taxes a political anathema. The privatization of services reflects the limited tax bases and service capabilities of local governments.

The business orientation of contemporary local government extends from process to policy. With the recovery of many northeastern and midwestern cities, the competition for economic development became fierce. In the 1960s and early 1970s, Sunbelt cities offered liberal tax incentives, land subsidies, and creative financing to potential investors. By the 1980s, such policies were common everywhere. Civic leaders learned that economic development offered relatively painless and quick personal and political gratification. With the increasing fragmentation of urban politics, the economy was one area that could generate a rough consensus.

City officials also became traveling salesmen, visiting not only different parts of the country but cities around the globe. During the 1980s, Atlanta's mayor Andrew Young logged over a million miles selling his city. One journalist termed his approach to urban policy "Andynomics."[13] Civic leaders actively participate in regional and statewide economic recruitment consortia. And the partnership between banking institutions and city hall has never been closer. The decline in federal funding, the uncertainty of state assistance, and persistent local budgetary problems have spurred this intimate relationship between business and city government. As a consequence, social priorities become secondary.

Current local officials are more limited in their policy options than their predecessors in several other respects as well. First, there is the memory of bad times and the accompanying political and fiscal disruptions. Northern urban officials are not likely to tolerate the lackadaisical accounting procedures or the generous expenditures of the 1960s; in the Sunbelt, the crises of the 1970s merely confirmed the wisdom of low-tax, low-service traditions. Second, city budgets are less flexible today than they were a decade or two ago, when federal funds accounted for significant portions of urban revenues. Roughly 75 percent of a typical city budget goes for infrastructure maintenance or traditional services such as fire and police protection and for utilities such as water and sewer systems. City officials are reluctant to raise taxes and fees because of their potential to dampen economic development.

A third problem limiting local government's ability and willingness to engage in social reform has been the erosion of executive authority, or at least the dispersal of functions typically associated with the powers of elected officials. Political scientist John J. Harrigan offered an extreme example of such fragmentation in St. Paul, Minnesota, where the mayor and city council have become merely two of the many "governments" that affect decision making in the city. Ramsey County is responsible for welfare and health policies. The Board of Education is responsible for education, and the Port Authority makes policy on commercial development along the Mississippi River and at several other locations throughout the city. The Civic Center Authority constructed and manages the sports and exhibition arena. A group of highway planners decides on the location of freeways, and the Metropolitan Transit Commission runs the buses. The Metropolitan Airport Commission operates the airports, and the Metropolitan Waste Control Commission takes care of the city's sewerage service. The

Metropolitan Health Board can veto decisions on the construction or expansion of public or private medical facilities. The Capitol Center Commission devises plans for the area around the state capitol. And the Metropolitan Council can veto the city's development plans if they conflict with metropolitan objectives. Such "functional fiefdoms" are becoming more common, especially because they are associated with good management concepts. The result is usually that no one government body has exclusive authority over a major problem.[14]

There was some hope in the 1970s, when black mayors and council members were elected in increasing numbers in cities across the nation, that local administrations would assume more social responsibilities. The changes were most dramatic in the South where, prior to the 1965 Voting Rights Act, less than 20 percent of the region's black population was registered to vote and only a handful of officeholders were black. The act not only provided federal registrars to guarantee black registration, it guarded against attempts to dilute black votes through such subterfuges as redistricting, changing the location and operating times of polling places, or purging registration lists. As a result, by the mid-1980s, better than 3,500 of the approximately 5,600 black elected officials in the United States (a fivefold increase since 1970) were in the South.

Although more than 70 percent of black elected officials serve communities of less than 5,000 people, black politicans had made notable gains as big-city mayors by the mid-1980s, holding office in cities such as Charlotte, Atlanta, New Orleans, Birmingham, Detroit, Chicago, Philadelphia, Los Angeles, Dayton, and Washington, D.C.

These political advances reflect not so much a new era in urban race relations as a change in black population demographics (Charlotte was an exception in 1985, with better than 40 percent of the white electorate supporting black mayor Harvey Gantt's reelection bid). In 1977, Ernest N. ("Dutch") Morial received only 19 percent of the white vote but 95 percent of the black vote to become the first black mayor of New Orleans. Birmingham's Richard Arrington has won three mayoral terms, never receiving more than 15 percent of the white vote.

The growing Hispanic presence in some cities has generally not helped black candidates, though the late Chicago mayor Harold Washington was successful in forging a Hispanic-black coalition in 1983. Hispanics in Detroit, for example, have been vigorous opponents of Coleman Young's administration; a similar division exists in Miami.

Black mayors often find themselves in difficult and unique political straits. If their policy orientation is perceived as too "black"—i.e., if whites think an emphasis on social services overshadows infrastructural and economic concerns—then they risk losing the support of white business leaders or middle-class residents. When Cleveland's Carl Stokes became the first black mayor of a major

American city in 1967, he doubled the number of public housing units and sought to raise taxes to improve city services, especially to black neighborhoods. As a result, during his two terms as mayor he faced a hostile white-dominated city council and received very little support from the white electorate. In some places, whites have withdrawn from local politics. One observer explained the defection of whites from politics in Petersburg, Virginia, after the mid-1970s: whites "just don't get involved in Petersburg. They have their golf games and their bridge games and that's the extent of their civic involvement. Their children are in private schools. . . . So long as they get their garbage picked up, they don't have a stake."[15]

Few cities in the wake of rising black political power have been as racially polarized as Chicago. Although city government had been tightly controlled by the Daley machine for over a generation, Harold Washington won the mayoral race in 1983, garnering 99 percent of the black vote and less than 18 percent of the white vote. In office, Washington angered white politicians and constituents by engaging in an old Chicago tradition, dispensing patronage to political allies. His response to his critics was direct: "We try to push our own and everybody asks for an explanation: 'Why would you push your own? Are you racist or something?' Any politician will stress his base. Is there something wrong with a black base?"[16] After decades of waiting in the wings, Chicago's black residents now play a major role in city politics. It remains to be seen, however, whether this influence can translate into effective policies, given the open hostility of a white-dominated city council and business community.

Perhaps one of the most controversial, yet potentially beneficial, policies of black urban political leaders has been the establishment of set-aside programs, where black contractors receive a certain percentage of city or federal public-works contracts. Atlanta mayor Andrew Young, for example, allotted 38 percent of city contracts to minority firms during his first term (1981–1985). In 1986, he sought to create a similar policy to "see that Hispanics get a fair share of the [city] contracts."[17] Newark mayor Kenneth Gibson set aside 25 percent of federal construction work for minority firms during the late 1970s and early 1980s.

But set-aside programs have encountered internal and external problems. There have been complaints of shoddy workmanship, bid-fixing, and of allegedly black-owned firms that were actually controlled by white entrepreneurs. Some minority firms have been plagued by poor management and lack of capital, problems compounded by the absence of management training programs and the unwillingness of banks to loan money to minority contractors. But the biggest blow came from the U.S. Supreme Court in January 1989, when, in a 6-to-3 ruling, the justices struck down Richmond's set-aside program.

Under the direction of Mayor Roy West and his allies on the city council, Richmond had instituted an aggressive affirmative action program that required public contractors to set aside 30 percent of their subcontracts for minority firms. Prior to 1983, when the city initiated the program, 0.67 percent of Richmond's contracts went to minority-owned businesses. By 1986, that figure had jumped to nearly 40 percent. The Court ruled, however, that Richmond's quota was too rigid and that the city had not proven discrimination existed prior to 1983. After the ruling, the share of minority contracts plummeted to 2.7 percent. Since blacks occupy key positions in Richmond's city government, it is not clear whether the drop is primarily due to discrimination or the internal problems of minority firms.

The success of black administrations in broadening black participation in city bureaucracy has been more straightforward. In Detroit, for example, the percentage of black men and women in administrative positions doubled between 1973 and 1977, from 12 percent to 24 percent. The percentage of blacks on the police force jumped from 5 percent in 1967 to 30 percent in 1978. During Maynard Jackson's first term as mayor of Atlanta (1973–1977), the percentage of professional and administrative positions in city government held by blacks jumped from 19 percent to 42 percent. Black bureaucracy became a symbol of urban political power in the 1970s and 1980s.

But black participants in city government have been primarily drawn from the middle class. Black political power has played an important role in expanding the black middle class. Successful mayors like Coleman Young and Andrew Young have been able to connect the black middle class and the city to the white business community. Though both mayors vigorously pursued affirmative action programs, economic development was the top priority of their administrations. They believed that the cooperation of the business community and economic growth were necessary to ensure contracts for minority firms and jobs for black citizens. Both mayors were strong boosters of their cities and worked to build positive images. Andrew Young, for example, won a regressive sales tax to hold the line on property taxes. (Similarly, his predecessor, Maynard Jackson, crushed the strike of Atlanta's predominantly black garbage collectors' union by firing the workers.)

Black urban political power is real and growing. But the limits of black economic power mean that the policies of black administrations rarely have a direct effect on the underclass. The effectiveness of the trickle-down theory of urban development remains to be seen.

Reagan and the Federal Retreat from Urban Assistance

At the national level, Ronald Reagan firmly believed that a thriving national economy would eventually redound to the benefit of cities and their people.

The Omnibus Budget Reconciliation Act (OBRA) of 1981, introduced by then-Representative (now U.S. Senator) Phil Gramm of Texas, reduced the rate of federal spending and controlled transfer payments to individuals and grants to state and local governments while authorizing an increase of $52 billion in military spending between fiscal year 1982 and fiscal year 1984. In the meantime, OBRA cut $14 billion from grants to cities and $11 billion in social service grants to individuals, including food stamps, unemployment insurance, and social security.

OBRA was only the beginning of the federal budget ax. The Reagan administration cut the number of subsidized housing units in half and halted new construction while increasing rents to public housing tenants by 25 percent. The administration cut job training and youth employment programs entirely along with drastic reductions in urban waste water projects. Gone, too, were HUD's neighborhood self-help fund and VISTA. President Reagan banked on tax cuts to stimulate the urban economy, which would, in turn, provide jobs. But the tax and budget changes between 1982 and 1985 actually reduced by more than $20 billion the income of those urban households with incomes under $10,000. In contrast, those households with incomes above $80,000 received a windfall of $64 billion. The older cities of the Northeast and Midwest had been more dependent than Sunbelt cities on federal assistance and therefore suffered more from the cuts. In 1983, for example, Detroit and St. Louis financed over 25 percent of their basic services, including public works, sanitation, and police and fire protection, from federal funds. In Los Angeles and Houston, in contrast, federal funds accounted for less than 5 percent of expenditures for those services.

The Reagan administration's version of "new federalism" included removing certain categorical grant programs from cities and neighborhoods and funneling them instead toward the more Republican-oriented state governments. The infant nutrition program that previously went directly to cities was merged into a broad health and community development block grant that now went to the states. The states, in turn, had the discretion to distribute the funds to urban, suburban, or rural communities. Studies have indicated that states have tended to favor rural jurisdictions and that the states in the Southwest and Rocky Mountain areas—solid Republican regions—have received a disproportionate share of these grants.

The Reagan administration was not entirely opposed to direct urban assistance. The Urban Development Action Grant was replaced, in large measure, by the urban enterprise zone concept. The enterprise zone was an area in a low-income neighborhood where new businesses were eligible for tax concessions; the federal government additionally waived minimum-wage and environmental and occupational safety standards. Relatively few takers emerged, however, and the primary entrepreneurial activities in inner city neighborhoods remain fencing and drug trafficking. Employers were concerned about the reliability and quality of the labor pool as well as the safety of themselves and their employees. The support services represented by transportation, communications, and knowledge functions were usually missing or in poor repair in these areas.

Some observers have referred to a "back-door" urban policy during President Reagan's first term, when tax breaks substituted for traditional grant programs. In 1984, for example, tax credits stimulated $2.1 billion in private investment for 2,100 urban rehab projects generating 70,050 jobs. In Philadelphia alone, the tax credits produced $350 million in private investment, 10,000 jobs, and $11 million in property-tax revenue. The 1986 tax reform, however, eliminated many of these credits.

The Reagan administration's budget cuts seemed to contradict its philosophy of ending welfare dependency and increasing self-sufficiency. The programs hardest hit—education and training, public service employment, nutrition programs, Medicaid, and other social services—were precisely those programs designed to fulfill the administration's stated objectives.

There is little indication that Reagan's successor, George Bush, will significantly alter the federal retreat from urban policy. His first statement on cities, early in 1989, touted the enterprise zones. He has also stressed voluntarism in his image of "a thousand points of light." Even though private agencies have indeed picked up some of the slack, the problems of poverty and homelessness are too great to be addressed by strictly private efforts. Bush's proposal for a day-care tax credit is more promising because it recognizes the link between poverty and inadequate child-care facilities. It seems likely, however, that cities and states will continue to scramble for creative partnerships with private institutions, hustling outside investment to carry on basic social policies. A comprehensive approach to the divided metropolis seems more remote than ever.

The Multicentered Urban Chain: Out-Towns, Mall-Towns, and Conurbations

The administrative and economic transformations of the central city during the 1970s and 1980s occurred within a metropolitan area that was also undergoing change. The traditionally voracious land appetite of Americans continued to push metropolitan settlement outward. At the same time, concentrations formed outside the central city that came to rival it in functions and amenities. Although the central city retained its importance as a cultural and economic center, it was, as one historian noted, "no longer central to the lives of most metropolitan Americans." Except in the newer cities of the Southwest or in locations where annexations have masked demographic trends, the majority of jobs, shopping space, and even office space is concentrated outside the central city. A 1978 *New York Times* survey of suburban New Yorkers revealed that only 21 percent of the household heads worked in the city, 53 percent visited the city less than five times a year, and 25 percent never went there at all. The *Times* concluded that "the suburbs have become a multicentered urban chain with surprisingly limited ties to the metropolitan core. . . . suburban residents have established their own institutions and go about their lives in an increasingly separate world."[18] The suburbs, in other words, have become urban.

The phrase "multicentered urban chain" implies a string of relatively equal nodes held together by ribbons of highway. High-tech industrial-residential areas such as the Silicon Valley south of San Francisco and Boston's Route 128 are examples of this chain. The central cities—San Francisco and Boston, respectively—may perform knowledge functions (finance, and legal and accounting services, for example) for the concentrations on their metropolitan periphery, but the people who live and work in the chain have only occasional direct contact with the central city. These out-towns or minicities (the names for these concentrations are legion) have attained a sufficient residential density to support, for example, major league sports franchises: the sports teams probably still bear the city name, even though they play in one of the out-towns, such as the New York Giants and New York Jets (who play at the Meadowlands in New Jersey) or the Detroit Lions (who play in Pontiac). When there is more than one central city, or when a metropolitan area is so large that identification with the central city is especially weak, the teams adopt the state name, such as the Texas Rangers in Irving, Texas, between Dallas and Fort Worth, or the California Angels (based in Anaheim but technically within the Los Angeles region).

Out-towns, those components of the multicentered urban chain, can either be former suburbs, as Pontiac and Irving, or new communities that have grown up around regional airports, such as Atlanta's Hartsfield International Airport and Chicago's O'Hare Airport, which has more office space than any place in Illinois outside downtown Chicago. Out-towns can also take shape around a regional shopping mall that functions as the Main Street of the new city. The Cumberland/Galleria complex on the periphery of the Atlanta region, Las Colinas outside Dallas, and Tyson's Corner, Virginia, in the Washington, D.C., metropolitan area are examples of mall-towns.

The mall-towns are strikingly different from the postwar suburbs that first featured the enclosed shopping mall: these newer communities are immense and varied by comparison. Tyson's Corner, little more than a gas station and general store a generation ago, now hosts a daytime population of 60,000 working in 16 million square feet of office space. Las Colinas, a former ranch occupying 19 square miles and including tenants such as Xerox, IBM, and AT&T, is surrounded by canals, a 125-acre lake, and expensive homes. More than 500 firms do business here. And City Post Oak in Houston, where the first of the Galleria shopping complexes opened in the late 1970s, became the nation's tenth largest downtown in 1985.

Whether emerging from new industries, airports, or megamalls, the out-town reflects the geographic expansion of the metropolitan area since the 1970s. By 1985, the New York metropolitan area sprawled over 3,600 square miles and the Los Angeles region extended over 2,200. In 1970, the Atlanta metropolitan area consisted of five counties with a population of 1.4 million; by 1980, it covered fifteen counties with a population of 2.1 million. Even these figures are rough estimates because the extent of contemporary metropolitan areas is so vast that some are growing together to form "conurbations"—giant, multicentered urban chains connected by interstate highways. The most extensive and populous conurbation is the area extending from northern New England to south of Washington, D.C., identified as an emerging "megalopolis" as far back as 1961. More recent conurbations include one along the California coast from San Francisco to San Diego; one extending up both the Atlantic and Gulf coasts of Florida from Miami; a thin line along the Gulf Coast from Pensacola to New Orleans; and a Great Lakes conurbation stretching in a crescent from Buffalo to Chicago. In a generation or so, perhaps, it will be possible to talk of a national conurbation system.

The out-towns reflect the lifestyle preferences of the 1980s. They are as much a revolt against the old suburb as they are against some of the negative aspects of the old central city. These are new forms where "people can work, live, shop and play in close proximity, thereby enjoying many advantages of urban density but avoiding its high costs and problems."[19] In some respects, the out-towns are reminiscent of the visions of Lewis Mumford and the Garden City advocates, minus the social content. They also resemble in concept, though the form is more dense and varied, the "new towns" of the 1960s such as Columbia, Maryland, developed by James Rouse, and Reston, Virginia, created by Robert E. Simon. Rouse and Simon presented their towns as urban alternatives to both city and suburban life that would feature a sense of community, organized activities, employment, schools, and abundant open spaces. But today's households, usually with both spouses working, have considerably less time for "community." The family is the basic unit, and the town or suburb where they live is likely to be only one of numerous physical locations they are committed to during the course of a given day.

This splintering of "spatial loyalties" is a widespread feature of the expanded metropolitan areas. In Orange County, outside Los Angeles, one resident describes her various life spaces as follows: "I live in Garden Grove, work in Irvine, shop in Santa Ana, go to the dentist in Anaheim, my husband works in Long

Cherry Hill, New Jersey: An Out-Town

Cherry Hill is not just another Philadelphia suburb. It is a city in itself, containing residential dwellings in many shapes and sizes (including high-rise apartment buildings), shopping malls, workplaces, and recreational facilities. It is linked to the central city and other out-towns in the Philadelphia region by a network of highways.

Beach, and I used to be the president of the League of Women Voters in Fullerton."[20] Among other things, this statement reflects the fact that women are becoming fuller participants in metropolitan patterns than they have ever been before. It also echoes the commuting oscillations in Los Angeles of fifty years earlier. Two differences, however, are that Orange County residents feel little or no identification with Los Angeles, and the current pattern is becoming much more prevalent than it was a half century ago. By the mid-1980s, commutes from the suburb to the central city in the Boston region accounted for only 3.4 percent of the total volume, whereas 61.4 percent of the commuting trips were lateral, suburb-to-suburb movements.

Precedents and Prefigurations

It is important, however, to keep these changes in perspective. The rise of the multicentered metropolis and its various components may have taken some observers by surprise, but its spatial and social character reflect the same basic

American traditions that have shaped urbanization for the past two centuries. More than two hundred years ago, Hector St. John de Crevecoeur asked the question, "Who, then is this new man, the American?" His answer included several traits that have persisted since that time, including a love of newness, a desire to be near nature, and individualism. These characteristics account, in part, for the high degree of mobility in American society. The average American moves fourteen times in his or her lifetime, compared with a move rate of eight for the British and six for the French, which is why foreigners find this wanderlust among the most curious elements of American culture. As one observer noted in 1974, "The typical American's life might be characterized as a prolonged odyssey."[21] Though mobility has declined slightly in the 1980s, the compulsion and the necessity to move still distinguish Americans from members of other cultures. It accounts for the fact that as soon as Americans built and lived in cities, they wanted to leave them. And many had the means to do so. Moreover, it is incorrect to identify this exodus as a uniquely American custom. Given the opportunity and the affluence, western Europeans have sought out single-family homes and nonurban residential environments just as eagerly as their New World counterparts.

But the compulsion to move does not necessarily imply outward movement. That other cultural standard—the desire for a single-family home—has loomed large in American expectations. And as the fulfillment of that dream became less likely in the city, the suburb and much later the reconstituted city on the periphery became desirable destinations. The move outward also represented a desire for homogeneity, what geographer, Brian J. L. Berry has summed up as "a predictable life style, a territory free from status competition . . . a safe area . . . a haven from complexity."[22] This proclivity manifested itself in the early-nineteenth-century cities as middle-class merchants sought to distance themselves from laborers and, later, immigrants. Technology, affluence, and ideals propelled the American middle class ever outward in its search. The search has not necessarily been antiurban, though cities have gone through image cycles. Rather, each successive form has represented an attempt to purge the city of its negative qualities while retaining the more positive features. The newest urban forms reflect the fact that even as families still seek social homogeneity, they are also interested in physical diversity. They prefer the variety of downtown without the parking and security problems, hence the regional shopping mall. They enjoy the entertainment offerings of the central city and have sought to duplicate some of them on the periphery, from athletic teams to opera and ballet companies. The central city is both a model for, and a single cog in the wheel of, numerous metropolitan centers. Its history and physical traditions as well as its economic importance and array of cultural activities, however, ensure the prominence of the central city.

Given the trends of American urban history and culture, the multicentered metropolis is not a great surprise. In fact, predictions have been made as far back as the turn of the century that the current form would eventually evolve from the industrial city. In 1902, H. G. Wells discerned the same "passion for nature . . . and that craving for a little private imperium" that Crevecoeur had noticed more than a century earlier. Based on that "passion," Wells predicted that the industrial city "will diffuse itself until it has taken up considerable areas and many of the characteristics of what is now country. . . . The country will take itself many of the qualities of the city. . . . We may call . . . these coming town provinces 'urban regions.'"[23] In a similar way, Frank Lloyd Wright's visionary Broadacre City of the 1930s, an urban center spread over the countryside and held together by the superhighway, prefigured the Silicon Valleys of the 1980s. At critical intersections, Wright posited, there would be "great spacious roadside pleasure places . . . markets, rising high and handsome . . . not only of commodities but of cultural facilities"—something like the modern megamalls and their adjoining environments.[24] Wright also predicted that schools, churches, and entertainment centers would probably appear around these areas as well. The great architect missed badly, however, when he concluded that these functions and the spatial character of Broadacre would result in the disappearance of the central city.

Controlling the Leviathan

Much as Lewis Mumford, Frank Lloyd Wright, and New York's regional planners responded to the implications of suburbanization for city and countryside in the 1920s, a new group of observers has gathered to lobby for controlling the multicentered metropolis. They point to the same problems of density and chaos that have perennially faced the American city, and they offer the same solution—regional planning. A new out-town is growing up outside Princeton, New Jersey, for example. It is likely that by the year 2000 this area will become the state's largest city. Exxon, Merrill Lynch, and Siemens, A.G., line U.S. 1, and projects such as Princeton-park, Princeton Corporate Center, and Office Center at Princeton Meadows are in various stages of construction. All these corporate enclaves share one feature: none are located in Princeton. Princeton's mayor, Barbara Boggs Sigmund, calls the development "a soulless, congested, harassing anti-city," as traffic becomes clogged and Princeton loses its village atmosphere.[25] At the same time, the nearby cities of Trenton and New Brunswick continue to decay and benefit little from the new development.

From an esthetic standpoint, with the possible exception of carefully planned urban villages such as Las Colinas, the reviews of the multicentered metropolis are similar to the notices the suburb received after World War II. Architecture critic Ada Louise Huxtable has complained that life in the peripheral city is "no voyage of discovery or private exploration of the world's wonders, natural and man-made; it is cliché conformity as far as the eye can see."[26] Critics cite the absence of public spaces and the lack of scale in the commercial sectors.

The new developments also display a certain jarring disorder—they spring up very quickly, at relatively high densities. Along with supporting infrastructure, the offices, megamalls, and housing developments are often disruptive to the countryside and to adjacent communities. In other parts of the country, especially the South, where rural areas as recently as the 1970s were considered happily well beyond the boundaries of expanding metropolitan areas, the sudden thrust into postindustrial urbanization can be traumatic. Journalist Mary Hood recounted a 1987 visit to her home in Cherokee County, Georgia, nearly 50 miles outside Atlanta. Hood relates that the county has become three distinctive places, each defined by a Wal-Mart. In the traditional portion of the county, where residents still drink well water and pay cash, the Wal-Mart has clerks named Delma, Edna, or Bud, Jr., and the shoppers are mostly nuclear families. The radio is tuned to the local country station and the booths at the snack bar are the major media centers. Nine miles to the southeast are a four-lane highway, shopping plazas, and water towers. The ball fields, speedway, and churches of the old community remain, but the Wal-Mart in this part of the county does not have a snack bar, and few people loiter. As Hood notes, "There are busy people, involved in PTA and soccer and tennis camp. They shop in their crisp realtor's blazer, nurse's or policeman's uniform; everyone has somewhere else to be, and soon." The radio is tuned to 96ROCK, and the customers' names are Brandon, Angie, Kim, Scott, and Dawn.

Driving (always driving) toward the interstate, finally, she finds that apartments and homes replace the horse barns and oak trees. "The road names and mall stores," Hood writes, "make no claim on native loyalties and sympathy." At this Wal-Mart "we are all newcomers, all strangers, and I shop in the same anxiety and alienation as everyone else. . . . I shop here in that anonymity attained more often in large cities." The clerks "are chic, worldly." Yet despite the very real physical and lifestyle changes she witnessed in traveling across her county, Hood concludes that the important things have not been lost: "the purest things, and the everlasting springs, run deep."[27] But for how long?

As development overruns the outer edges of the metropolitan area and engulfs long-established communities, tensions between oldtimers and newcomers appear in politics and policies. The refugees, often affluent and engaged in professional or managerial occupations, want water and sewer systems and improved public schools. Long-time residents, typically less affluent, are content with existing infrastructure and worry about rising taxes. But the transformation of old towns into new communities is a process that has gone on for two centuries. The major difference today is that connections to the central city are considerably more tenuous, if they exist at all.

The problems generated by overheated out-towns have aroused increasing interest in metropolitanwide solutions. These communities obviously have regional impacts—on traffic, on the environment, on employment patterns, and on infrastructure—especially because of their extent and concentration. The flurry of activity that occurred during the 1960s in places like Minneapolis, Jacksonville, and Miami toward regional government and city-county consolidation passed quickly and is unlikely to reemerge in the near future. Since that time, special districts and authorities have assumed some regional functions, but attempts at comprehensive coordination of services have been rare. At the least, however, more central cities today are beginning to think in regional terms. Sometimes it is a modest first step, such as forming a regional study group under the auspices of a university for the purposes of collecting data, identifying mutual issues, and eventually lobbying the state legislature. Such efforts are already underway in the Philadelphia region, under the leadership of Ted Hershberg and the University of Pennsylvania, and in the Charlotte region, sponsored by Bill McCoy and the University of North Carolina at Charlotte. These efforts highlight both the new roles of urban universities acting as regional facilitators as well as the extent of regions that have grown far beyond the comprehension and capabilities of their respective units to grasp.

Other expanded metropolitan areas are beginning to market themselves as single entities for the purpose of economic development. The Denver region formed the "Metro Denver Network" in 1987, a regionwide information system for business recruitment. Its purpose is to track every new business lead and all available sites as well as provide a unified national advertising campaign. Prospects receive regionwide data in 3.6 seconds and see where their businesses best fit in various regional locations.

Even more ambitious is the LA 2000 group, formed in 1988 to devise regional solutions to pollution, crime, traffic, and development. The group's members, who represent a wide spectrum of constituencies and professions, have recommended two regionwide agencies encompassing 157 local governments. The first would be a growth management agency to guide regional land use decisions. There is concern, for example, that even though most of the jobs in the region are being created in Los Angeles and Orange counties, the new housing subdivisions are going up in the eastern Riverside and San Bernardino counties. If trends persist, commuter trip hours will increase by 300 percent, with region residents spending five times as much time in traffic as they do now. The proposed growth management agency would redirect some of the new housing and job locations to shorten journeys-to-work. A second regional agency would control environmental quality, including air and water pollution and the regulation of toxic and solid waste dumps. Conventional wisdom in the 1970s stated that energy costs, commuting times, and development costs all made further significant expansion of metropolitan areas unlikely. The rapid growth of the multicentered metropolis in the 1980s demonstrated otherwise, and only now are the environmental costs being assessed and addressed.

Social Implications of the Multicentered Metropolis

Critics also point out that, like their suburban predecessors, the new communities are relatively homogeneous places and tend to reinforce the racial and socioeconomic Balkanization of the metropolitan area. Again, this homogenizing process is a traditional pattern of American urbanization, but given the distances that now separate disparate groups as well as the segmented lifestyles that avoid, by design or happenstance, any but the most superficial contacts with the urban underclass, it seems likely that these problems will not be addressed. The resurgence in regional cooperation focuses mainly on service and environmental issues. And the central city, which continues to house a disproportionate number of the poor and minorities, is less able to confront the web of problems associated with this underclass. We have, in political scientist John J. Harrigan's words, entered the "postreform era" of urban policy.[28]

In terms of social equity, the 1990s present us with the anomalous metropolis. Gleaming downtowns compete successfully with peripheral office parks while hope-lost people crouch in the shadows of decaying neighborhoods. It is a Dickensian setting for the future—the best of times and the worst of times—what Brian J. L. Berry has called a "*mosaic culture,* a society with a number of parallel and distinctively different lifestyles." As for the incendiary potential of this mosaic culture, Berry is rather sanguine: "While one result is divisive tendencies for the society as a whole, at another level, mutual harmony is produced by mutual withdrawal into homogeneous communities, exclusion and isolation from groups with different lifestyles and values."[29] Lewis Mumford and others would cringe at this privatized metropolis, but the devolution of government and the growth of private services and enclaves encourage this perspective.

We are obviously no closer to solving the social fallout from American urbanization than we were when cities were mere clusters huddled around the waterfront. The rising tide of voluntarism and self-help are encouraging, just as such movements were in the nineteenth century. Though these efforts usually lack the resources and scope of government programs, they are successful in raising awareness, no small feat in the fragmented metropolis. As heartwarming as such stories as Charlotte Gardens and successful tenant management programs are, however, they reach only a very small portion of the needy. Observers insist that without major government support, any attempt to solve these social problems will be patchwork. But even here, it is not clear that significant change can occur without revolutionary changes in policies and institutions. At least, we should be able to answer correctly the question posed by Lewis Mumford a half-century ago: "Does a city exist to promote the life of its citizens? Or do the citizens exist in order to increase the size, importance, and the commercial turnover of the city?"[30]

The American response has generally been, "Both": The economic prosperity of the city, this thinking runs, will ultimately promote the lives of its residents. There is good historical support for this view. The United States is unique among western nations in terms of the generous distribution of real estate and home ownership. The historic shaping of the metropolitan area—the emergence of discrete residential neighborhoods within cities, the suburbs, and then the out-town—attests to the success and pervasiveness of this drive for land and home. The creation of a national urban economy, industrial development, and, most recently, the service economy generated dreams and the profits and jobs to fulfill them. Cities not only survived these changes and the ceaseless coming and going of people and work, but thrived—not all the time, but with enough steady momentum to continue to manufacture the profits and jobs to fulfill the dreams.

This should be the happy ending to the story of urban America. But the history of urban America has not all been happy, and it has no end. We have noted the divisions of class, ethnicity, gender, and race that have accompanied the profits, jobs, and dreams of the city. These divisions, traditionally expressed in spatial and cultural terms, are possibly wider now in space and culture than they have ever been in our history for black and white, middle-class and poor. Will future metropolitan residents be willing and able to close this gap? Concerted efforts to eradicate epidemic disease in the nineteenth century were not made until sickness and death spilled over easily permeable neighborhood boundaries into middle-class areas. In today's multicentered metropolis, the distances separating groups are much greater and the opportunities for contact much less. The institutions that once drew disparate urban residents together—the department stores, theaters, sports teams, and newspapers—are scattered over various parts of the metropolitan landscape as well. We have not yet demonstrated that we are willing to divert the historic role of urban America as a speculative enterprise to the role of social reformer. The penchant for land and the single-family home is hardly a prescription for collective concern. Nor is it clear that the modern city or metropolitan area has the resources and administrative structures to address fundamental social issues. If living in the United States in the year 2000 means living in a metropolitan area, then perhaps national (i.e., federal) solutions are most appropriate.

If it is difficult to foretell urban policies of the future, what about the evolving shape of cities? More than a half-century ago, Los Angeles offered a preview of the multicentered metropolis. Does any one city or metropolitan area today portend yet another reorganization of space for urban America? If suburbs have become cities, will central cities assume the spatial dimensions of suburbs? Medium-sized cities such as Charlotte and Austin have identifiable downtown concentrations along with the usual knowledge functions associated with larger cities. Beyond downtown, however, they are collections of residential neighborhoods and shopping centers; they are, in effect, suburban cities. The larger cities have demonstrated that functions, not residents, account for prosperity. Will these cities continue to lose population and become the home for only the very rich and the very poor? Finally, technology has played a major, albeit not a decisive, role in shaping urban America. Transportation and communications innovations, building construction advances, and infrastructure technologies have influenced land uses and reinforced economic transitions. How will new energy sources, computer technologies, and transportation innovations alter the nature of work and the way we live—and hence the shape and function of the city?

These questions have no immediate answers. But the history of urban America so far makes two things clear. First, the experts who have the answers to these questions will invariably be mistaken as often as they are correct. Second, the city will keep changing, and it will keep surviving. We opened this book by noting that the first European settlements in this country were not beginnings but rather continuations of urban life, both in Europe and in America. "Continuation" describes the dynamic process of urbanization well, and that is the easiest prediction of all: the process will continue.

Notes

1. "Cleveland Recovers Financially," *New York Times,* December 18, 1988.
2. Lindsey Gruson, "Pittsburgh's Revival Breath of Fresh Air," *New York Times,* May 31, 1987.
3. Quoted in Bayrd Still, ed., *Urban America: A History with Documents* (Boston: Little, Brown, 1974), p. 384.
4. Quoted in Neal Peirce, "Bubble Has Burst for Some Big-City Festival Marketplaces," *Charlotte Observer,* September 3, 1988.
5. Both quotes from Neal Peirce, "Will Yuppies Abandon Inner Cities for the Suburbs?" *Charlotte Observer,* July 19, 1986.
6. Neal Peirce, "The American City Scores a Spectacular Comeback," *Charlotte Observer,* May 10, 1986.
7. Quoted in Gina Kolata, "Experts: Air of Lawlessness Invites Senseless Violence," *New York Times,* May 1, 1989.

8. Quoted in *ibid*.
9. Quoted in Matthew Purdy, "Blocks Away, A Muffled Horror," *Charlotte Observer*, May 7, 1989.
10. All quotes from Marc Miller, "The Low Down on High Tech," *Southern Exposure* 14 (November-December 1986): 37.
11. Quoted in "Community of Delight Rises from Rubble of South Bronx Ghetto," *Los Angeles Times*, December 22, 1984.
12. All quotes from Neal Peirce, "'New' Mayors Slash Staff, Act Like Corporate Boss," *Washington Post*, May 4, 1985.
13. Art Harris, "Atlanta, Georgia: Too Busy to Hate," *Esquire* 103 (June 1985): 129.
14. John J. Harrigan, *Political Change in the Metropolis* (Boston: Little, Brown, 1985), p. 195.
15. Quoted in David R. Goldfield, *Black, White, and Southern: Race Relations and Southern Culture, 1940 to the Present* (Baton Rouge: Louisiana State University Press, 1990), p. 272.
16. Quoted in Clarence Stone, Robert K. Whelan, and William J. Murin, *Urban Policy and Politics in a Bureaucratic Age* (Englewood Cliffs, N.J.: Prentice-Hall, 1986), p. 164.
17. Quoted in Ronald H. Bayor, "Models of Ethnic and Racial Politics in the Urban Sunbelt South," in Raymond A. Mohl, ed., *Searching for the Sunbelt* (Knoxville, Tenn.: University of Tennessee Press, 1989), p. 136.
18. Both quotes from Jon C. Teaford, *The Twentieth-Century American City: Problem, Promise, and Reality* (Baltimore: Johns Hopkins University Press, 1986), pp. 153, 154.
19. Neal Peirce, "Can Urban Villages Become Real People Places?" *Washington Post*, August 17, 1985.
20. Quoted in Carl Abbott, *Urban America in the Modern Age: 1920 to the Present* (Arlington Heights, Ill.: Harlan Davidson, 1987), p. 115.
21. Peter Morrison, quoted in Brian J. L. Berry, "The Counterurbanization Process: Urban America since 1970," in Berry, ed., *Urbanization and Counterurbanization* (Beverly Hills, Calif.: Sage, 1976), p. 26.
22. Brian J. L. Berry, *The Human Consequences of Urbanization* (New York: St. Martin's Press, 1973), p. 51.
23. Quoted in Berry, "Counterurbanization Process," p. 26.
24. Quoted in Robert Fishman, *Bourgeois Utopias: The Rise and Fall of Suburbia* (New York: Basic Books, 1987), p. 189.
25. Quoted in Neal Peirce, "Gridlock: Will it be Suburban Plague of 1990s?" *Washington Post*, August 24, 1985.
26. Quoted in Fishman, *Bourgeois Utopias*, p. 203.
27. Mary Hood, "Of Water and Wal-Mart: The Demographics of Progress in a Georgia Community," *Southern Magazine* 1 (January 1987): 22.
28. Harrigan, *Political Change in the Metropolis*, p. 341.
29. Berry, *Human Consequences of Urbanization*, p. 64.
30. Quoted in Daniel Schaffer, *Garden Cities for America: The Radburn Experience* (Philadelphia: Temple University Press, 1982), p. 62.

Population and Rank of Largest U.S. Cities, 1790–1986

Table 1

Twenty Largest U.S. Cities, 1790

Rank	City	Population (Thousands)	Rank	City	Population (Thousands)
1	New York	33.1	11	Portsmouth, N.H.	4.7
2	Philadelphia	28.5	12	Brooklyn, N.Y.	4.4
3	Boston	18.3	13	New Haven, Ct.	4.4
4	Charleston, S.C.	16.3	14	Taunton, Mass.	3.8
5	Baltimore	13.5	15	Richmond, Va.	3.7
6	Salem, Mass.	7.9	16	Albany, N.Y.	3.4
7	Newport, R.I.	6.7	17	New Bedford, Mass.	3.3
8	Providence, R.I.	6.3	18	Beverly, Mass.	3.2
9	Gloucester, Mass.	5.3	19	Norfolk, Va.	2.9
10	Newburyport, Mass.	4.8	20	Petersburg, Va.	2.8

Source: Most figures are from James Vance, Jr., "Cities in the Shaping of the American Nation," *Journal of Geography* 17 (January 1976), 43. Population figure for Philadelphia is from Sam Bass Warner, Jr., *Private City: Philadelphia in Three Periods of Its Growth* (Philadelphia: University of Pennsylvania Press, 1968), p. 3.

Table 2

Twenty Largest U.S. Cities, 1830

Rank	Previous Rank	City	Population (Thousands)
1	1	New York	202.5
2	5	Baltimore	80.6
3	2	Philadelphia	80.4
4	3	Boston	61.3
5	—	New Orleans	46.0

Table 2 *(continued)*

Rank	Previous Rank	City	Population (Thousands)
6	4	Charleston, S.C.	30.2
7	—	Cincinnati	24.8
8	16	Albany	24.2
9	13	Brooklyn	20.5
10	—	Washington, D.C.	18.8
11	8	Providence	16.8
12	15	Richmond	16.0
13	—	Pittsburgh	15.3
14	6	Salem	13.8
15	—	Portland, Me.	12.5
16	—	Troy, N.Y.	11.5
17	—	Newark, N.J.	10.9
18	—	Louisville, Ky.	10.3
19	13	New Haven	10.1
20	19	Norfolk	9.8

Source: Compiled from U.S. Bureau of the Census, *Sixteenth Census, 1940, Population*, I: *Number of Inhabitants* (Washington, D.C.: Government Printing Office, 1942), pp. 32–33.

Table 3

Twenty Largest U.S. Cities, 1870

Rank	Previous Rank	City	Population (Thousands)
1	1	New York	942.3
2	3	Philadelphia	674.0
3	13	Brooklyn	420.0
4	—	St. Louis	310.9
5	—	Chicago	299.0
6	2	Baltimore	267.4
7	4	Boston	250.5
8	7	Cincinnati	216.2
9	5	New Orleans	191.4
10	—	San Francisco	149.5
11	13	Pittsburgh	139.3

Table 3 *(continued)*

Rank	Previous Rank	City	Population (Thousands)
12	—	Buffalo	117.7
13	10	Washington, D.C.	109.2
14	17	Newark	105.1
15	18	Louisville	100.8
16	—	Cleveland	92.8
17	—	Detroit	79.6
18	—	Milwaukee	71.4
19	11	Providence	68.9
20	12	Richmond	51.0

Source: Compiled from U.S. Bureau of the Census, *Sixteenth Census, 1940, Population,* I: *Number of Inhabitants* (Washington, D.C.: Government Printing Office, 1942), pp. 32–33.

Table 4

Twenty Largest U.S. Cities, 1920

Rank	Previous Rank	City	Population (Thousands)
1	1	New York[a]	5,620.0
2	5	Chicago	2,701.7
3	2	Philadelphia	1,823.8
4	17	Detroit	993.7
5	16	Cleveland	796.8
6	4	St. Louis	772.9
7	7	Boston	748.0
8	6	Baltimore	733.8
9	11	Pittsburgh	588.3
10	—	Los Angeles	576.7
11	12	Buffalo	506.8
12	10	San Francisco	506.7
13	18	Milwaukee	457.1
14	13	Washington, D.C.	437.6
15	14	Newark	414.5
16	8	Cincinnati	401.2
17	9	New Orleans	387.2

Table 4 *(continued)*

Rank	Previous Rank	City	Population (Thousands)
18	—	Minneapolis	380.6
19	—	Kansas City, Mo.	324.4
20	—	Jersey City, N.J.	298.1

ªIncluded Brooklyn after 1898.

Source: Compiled from U.S. Bureau of the Census, *Sixteenth Census, 1940, Population,* I: *Number of Inhabitants* (Washington, D.C.: Government Printing Office, 1942), pp. 32–33.

Table 5

Twenty Largest U.S. Cities, 1970

Rank	Previous Rank	City	Population (Thousands)
1	1	New York	7,894.8
2	2	Chicago	3,366.9
3	10	Los Angeles	2,816.0
4	3	Philadelphia	1,948.6
5	4	Detroit	1,511.4
6	—	Houston	1,232.8
7	8	Baltimore	905.7
8	—	Dallas	844.4
9	14	Washington, D.C.	756.5
10	5	Cleveland	750.9
11	—	Indianapolis	744.6
12	13	Milwaukee	717.6
13	12	San Francisco	715.6
14	—	San Diego	696.7
15	—	San Antonio	654.1
16	7	Boston	641.0
17	—	Memphis	623.5
18	6	St. Louis	622.2
19	17	New Orleans	593.4
20	—	Phoenix	582.0

Source: Compiled from U.S. Bureau of the Census, *Nineteenth Census, 1970, Number of Inhabitants,* Table 13 of reports for individual states.

Table 6

Twenty Largest U.S. Cities, 1980

Rank	Previous Rank	City	Population (Thousands)
1	1	New York	7,071.6
2	2	Chicago	3,005.1
3	3	Los Angeles	2,968.5
4	4	Philadelphia	1,688.2
5	6	Houston	1,611.4
6	5	Detroit	1,203.4
7	8	Dallas	904.6
8	14	San Diego	875.5
9	15	San Antonio	810.4
10	20	Phoenix	790.2
11	7	Baltimore	786.7
12	11	Indianapolis	700.8
13	13	San Francisco	679.0
14	17	Memphis	646.2
15	9	Washington, D.C.	638.4
16	12	Milwaukee	636.3
17	—	San Jose	629.4
18	10	Cleveland	573.8
19	—	Columbus, Ohio	565.0
20	16	Boston	563.0

Source: U.S. Bureau of the Census, *County and City Data Book, 1988* (Washington, D.C.: Government Printing Office, 1988).

Table 7

Twenty Largest U.S. Cities, 1986

Rank	Previous Rank	City	Population (Thousands)
1	1	New York	7,262.8
2	3	Los Angeles	3,259.3
3	2	Chicago	3,009.5
4	5	Houston	1,728.9
5	4	Philadelphia	1,642.9

Table 7 *(continued)*

Rank	Previous Rank	City	Population (Thousands)
6	6	Detroit	1,086.2
7	8	San Diego	1,015.2
8	7	Dallas	1,003.5
9	9	San Antonio	914.4
10	10	Phoenix	894.1
11	11	Baltimore	752.8
12	13	San Francisco	749.0
13	12	Indianapolis	719.8
14	17	San Jose	712.1
15	14	Memphis	652.6
16	15	Washington, D.C.	626.1
17	22	Jacksonville	609.9
18	16	Milwaukee	605.1
19	20	Boston	573.6
20	19	Columbus, Ohio	566.0

Source: U.S. Bureau of the Census, *County and City Data Book, 1988* (Washington, D.C.: Government Printing Office, 1988).

Suggestions for Further Reading

Introduction

Starting points for the study of American urbanization are offered by two books that discuss cities worldwide, providing important comparative perspectives: Lewis Mumford, *The City in History: Its Origins, Its Transformations, and Its Prospects* (New York: Harcourt, Brace & World, 1961), which relates the impact of technology on the urban form and the urban resident from ancient times to the twentieth century; and Adna F. Weber, *The Growth of Cities in the Nineteenth Century: A Study in Statistics* (New York: Macmillan, 1899), probably the first major study to point to space, technology, and population trends as foundations of urban growth analysis.

General historical surveys of the American city include Howard P. Chudacoff and Judith E. Smith, *The Evolution of American Urban Society*, 3rd ed. (Englewood Cliffs, N.J.: Prentice Hall, 1988); Charles N. Glaab and A. Theodore Brown, *A History of Urban America*, 3rd ed. (New York: Macmillan, 1983); and a more idiosyncratic work that includes excellent discussions of urban services and local government, Eric H. Monkkonen, *America Becomes Urban: The Development of U.S. Cities and Towns, 1780–1980* (Berkeley: University of California Press, 1988). Daniel Schaffer, ed., *Two Centuries of American Planning* (London: Mansell, 1988), provides a history of American urban planning, broadly defined to include most aspects of the physical development of cities. A less comprehensive but valuable history of planning is John W. Reps, *The Making of Urban America: A History of City Planning in the United States* (Princeton, N.J.: Princeton University Press, 1965), a survey of early plans for America's cities from the colonial period to World War I. For a more specialized perspective on the physical aspects of American urban history, see Wayne Andrews, *Architecture, Ambition, and Americans: A Social History of American Architecture* (New York: Free Press, 1964); and Vincent Scully's *American Architecture and Urbanism* (New York: Praeger, 1969), both of which provide an easily understood survey of the city's constructions, their spatial relationship, and how they reflect and affect urban society. Sam Bass Warner, Jr., *Private City: Philadelphia in Three Periods of Its Growth* (Philadelphia: University of Pennsylvania Press, 1968); and Warner, *The Urban Wilderness: A History of the American City* (New York: Harper & Row, 1972), discuss the relationship among economics, technology, and the internal structure of the city. Also, the *Journal of Urban History* is an excellent source of contemporary research, and its review essays place that research in a broad context.

There are three excellent surveys of urban historiography and urban history as a field of inquiry. The most comprehensive is Michael H. Ebner, "Urban History: Retrospect and Prospect," *Journal of American History* 68 (June 1981): 69–84. Two more specialized views of urban historiography are Michael Frisch, "American Urban History as an Example of Recent Historiography," *History and Theory* XVIII (no. 3, 1979): 350–377; and Kathleen Conzen, "Community Studies, Urban History, and American Local History," in Michael Kammen, ed., *The Past Before Us: Contemporary Historical Writing in the United States* (Ithaca, N.Y.: Cornell University Press, 1980), 270–291.

Part 1
Seedtime for Urban America: The Colonial Town

Because of fragmentary evidence, there is no work on Indian urbanization in North America. We know, however, that Indians in the South tended to live less nomadic lives than northern Indians. So it is not far-fetched to state that an urban South existed before the Europeans came, although they quickly turned it into a rural South. The best discussion of southern Indian civilization is J. Leitch Wright, Jr., *The Only Land They Knew: The Tragic Story of the American Indians of the Old South* (New York: Free Press, 1981). For a high-quality perspective on New England Indians, see William Cronon, *Changes in the Land: Indians, Colonists, and the Ecology of New England* (New York: Hill and Wang, 1983). For comments on early Spanish and French encounters with Native Americans and a discussion of Spanish concepts of town planning, see John R. Stilgoe, *Common Landscape of America, 1580 to 1845* (New Haven: Yale University Press, 1982).

A decade or so ago, there were no comprehensive treatments of colonial towns except for Carl Bridenbaugh's two studies, *Cities in the Wilderness: The First Century of Urban Life in America, 1625–1742* (New York: Ronald Press, 1938); and *Cities in Revolt: Urban Life in America, 1743–1776* (New York: Capricorn, 1955). These books still provide excellent material for students seeking an introduction to colonial urban life, although the absence of substantive discussions of blacks and women reflects the era in which Bridenbaugh wrote. A number of books by John W. Reps— especially *Town Planning in Frontier America* (Princeton, N.J.: Princeton University Press, 1969)—provide detailed analyses of the design and physical structure of colonial cities and indicate their indebtedness to European patterns, as does Sylvia Doughty Fries, *The Urban Idea in Colonial America* (Philadelphia: Temple University Press, 1977).

In recent years, two general works have provided keen insight into the evolution of colonial urban life and its connections to the Atlantic world. Geographer D. W. Meinig's *The Shaping of America: A Geographical Perspective on 500 Years of History: Volume I, Atlantic America, 1492–1800* (New Haven: Yale University Press, 1988) notes the increasing divergence of northern and southern colonies; and Gary B.

Nash, *The Urban Crucible: Social Change, Political Consciousness, and the Origins of the American Revolution* (Cambridge, Mass.: Harvard University Press, 1979), though it concentrates on Boston, New York and Philadelphia, evokes the dynamic nature of urban life in the eighteenth century through a study of class structure and electoral politics.

Community studies remain a staple of colonial urban historiography. The list of New England studies continues to grow, though the emphasis has changed from the consensus perspectives of Michael Zuckerman, *Peaceable Kingdoms: New England Towns in the Eighteenth Century* (New York: Knopf, 1970); Kenneth A. Lockridge, *A New England Town, The First Hundred Years: Dedham, Massachusetts, 1636–1736* (New York: W. W. Norton, 1970); and Philip T. Greven, Jr., *Four Generations: Population, Land, and Family in Colonial Andover, Massachusetts* (Ithaca, N.Y.: Cornell University Press, 1970). Christine Leigh Heyrman, *Commerce and Culture: The Maritime Communities of Colonial Massachusetts, 1690–1750* (New York: W. W. Norton, 1984), challenges the earlier studies by noting that in Gloucester and Marblehead, community consensus and institutions formed *after* initial economic development. Stephen Innes also diverges from the pioneer works by noting the materialist base and social divisions of another New England community, Springfield, in *Labor in a New Land: Economy and Society in Seventeenth-Century Massachusetts, 1690–1750* (Princeton, N.J.: Princeton University Press, 1983). A forerunner of these dissents, Darrett B. Rutman, *Winthrop's Boston: Portrait of a Puritan Town, 1630–1649* (New York: W. W. Norton, 1965), demonstrates that the Puritan fabric was rending within the first few years of Boston's settlement. Sumner Chilton Powell, *Puritan Village: The Formation of New England Towns* (Garden City, N.Y.: Doubleday, 1965), has helpful material on the physical development of New England communities. Sam Bass Warner, Jr.'s *Private City: Philadelphia in Three Periods of Its Growth* (Philadelphia: University of Pennsylvania Press, 1968) contains a section on the eighteenth century as well as useful general information on colonial cities. Stephanie Grauman Wolf, *Urban Village: Population, Community, and Family Structure in Germantown, Pa., 1683–1800* (Princeton, N.J.: Princeton University Press, 1976), is the first community study of a village that became a colonial suburb. Wolf's work and James T. Lemon's *The Best Poor Man's Country: A Geographical Study of Early Southeastern Pennsylvania* (Baltimore: Johns Hopkins University Press, 1972) note the lack of community spirit and strong desire for profit that Innes documented for Springfield.

The dynamics of town development in the South are explored in Carville Earle and Ronald Hoffman, "The Urban South: The First Two Centuries," in Blaine A. Brownell and David R. Goldfield, eds., *The City in Southern History: The Growth of Urban Civilization in the South* (Port Washington, N.Y.: Kennikat Press, 1977). Although John C. Rainbolt's "The Absence of Towns in Seventeenth-Century Virginia," *Journal of Southern History* 35 (August 1969): 343–360, presents strong arguments to support the case summarized by his title, more recent work has emphasized the existence of urban life in Virginia. Darrett B. Rutman and Anita H. Rutman apply the community study methodology in *A Place in Time: Middlesex*

County, Virginia, 1650–1750 (New York: W. W. Norton, 1984); a more descriptive work is James O'Mara, *An Historical Geography of Urban System Development: Tidewater Virginia in the Eighteenth Century* (Toronto: York University Geographical Monographs, 1983). Darrett B. Rutman provides a survey of community studies in "Assessing the Little Communities of Early America," *William and Mary Quarterly* 43 (April 1986): 63–78.

Charles Town, the major southern seaport, has been the subject of several good studies recently, though none is a comprehensive treatment. Peter A. Coclanis, "The Sociology of Architecture in Colonial Charleston: Pattern and Process in an Eighteenth-Century Southern City," *Journal of Social History* 18 (Summer 1985): 607–623; Richard Waterhouse, "The Development of Elite Culture in the Colonial American South: A Study of Charles Town, 1670–1770," *Australian Journal of Politics and History* 28 (no. 3, 1982): 391–404; and Walter J. Fraser, Jr., "The City Elite, 'Disorder,' and the Poor Children of Pre-Revolutionary Charleston," *South Carolina Historical Magazine* 84 (July 1983): 167–179, are among the better interdisciplinary analyses of the South Carolina port.

The colonial seaports were tied to an Atlantic commercial world. The architecture, social structure, and physical layout of the towns reflected this dependence. For an understanding of the relationship between colonial urban society and commerce, there are a number of works on particular seaports, including Bernard Bailyn, *The New England Merchants in the Seventeenth Century* (Cambridge, Mass.: MIT Press, 1955); Edward C. Papenfuse, *In Pursuit of Profit: The Annapolis Merchants in the American Revolution, 1763–1805* (Baltimore: Johns Hopkins University Press, 1975); and perhaps the boldest analysis to date, Thomas M. Doerflinger, *A Vigorous Spirit of Enterprise: Merchants and Economic Development in Revolutionary Philadelphia* (Chapel Hill: University of North Carolina Press, 1984), which relates economic development in Philadelphia to the emerging northeastern commercial region and the growing commercial dependence of the urban South.

Aside from Gary B. Nash's comprehensive treatment, the best single volume on late colonial urban society is Jackson Turner Main's *The Social Structure of Revolutionary America* (Princeton, N.J.: Princeton University Press, 1965), even though it does not focus solely on cities. Also important are James A. Henretta, "Economic Development and Social Structure in Colonial Boston," *William and Mary Quarterly* 22, 3rd series (January 1965): 75–92; John Demos, *A Little Commonwealth: Family Life in Plymouth Colony* (New York: Oxford University Press, 1970); Elizabeth A. Dexter, *Colonial Women of Affairs: Women in Business and Professions in America Before 1776* (Boston: Houghton Mifflin, 1931); and Raymond A. Mohl, "Poverty in Early America, a Reappraisal: The Case of Eighteenth-Century New York City," *New York History* 50 (January 1969): 5–27.

Nash also tied socioeconomic patterns to political developments. More specialized attempts at studying this connection are Edward M. Cook, Jr., *The Fathers of the Towns: Leadership and Community Structure in Eighteenth-Century New England* (Baltimore: Johns Hopkins Press, 1976); and Thomas J. Archdeacon, *New York City, 1664–1710: Conquest and Change* (Ithaca, N.Y.: Cornell University Press, 1976).

Jon C. Teaford's brief but informative book *The Municipal Revolution in America: Origins of Modern Urban Government, 1650–1825* (Chicago: University of Chicago Press, 1975) contains much interesting material on the period before the Revolution.

Part 2
The Market Place, 1790–1870

There is no comprehensive treatment of the pre-industrial city. There are, however, several studies of individual communities that explore the changes in social, economic, and political life that resulted from urbanization. Small-area studies include Richard D. Brown, "The Emergence of Urban Society in Rural Massachusetts, 1760–1820," *Journal of American History* 61 (June 1974): 29–51; and Michael P. Conzen's *Frontier Farming in an Urban Shadow: The Influence of Madison's Proximity on the Agricultural Development of Blooming Grove, Wisconsin* (Madison: State Historical Society of Wisconsin, 1971). Studies of individual cities or groups of cities that analyze the transition process are Stuart M. Blumin, *The Urban Threshold: Growth and Change in a Nineteenth-Century American Community* (Chicago: University of Chicago Press, 1976); Michael H. Frisch, *Town Into City: Springfield, Massachusetts, and the Meaning of Community, 1840–1880* (Cambridge, Mass.: Harvard University Press, 1972), probably the best single-city urbanization analysis; Roger W. Lotchin, *San Francisco, 1846–1856: From Hamlet to City* (New York: Oxford University Press, 1974); and Richard C. Wade, *The Urban Frontier: Pioneer Life in Early Pittsburgh, Cincinnati, Lexington, Louisville, and St. Louis* (Chicago: University of Chicago Press, 1964).

The development of a national urban economy, initiated by the growth of urban regions in the Northeast and the West (today's Midwest), was one of the major features of urbanization during the first half of the nineteenth century. Diane Lindstrom is the scholar most closely associated with the theory that national economic integration depended first upon the emergence of city-hinterland commercial connections, then upon trade between cities within a larger geographic region, such as the Northeast. Her major work, *Economic Development in the Philadelphia Region, 1810–1850* (New York: Columbia University Press, 1978), is a clear analysis of this two-stage process. Other works detailing the importance of city-hinterland connections in the developing northeastern region include Robert Balstad Miller, *City and Hinterland: A Case Study of Urban Growth and Regional Development* (Westport, Conn.: Greenwood Press, 1979); Francis X. Blouin, Jr., *The Boston Region, 1810–1850: A Study of Urbanization* (Ann Arbor: UMI Research Press, 1978); and Gary Lawson Browne, *Baltimore in the Nation, 1789–1861* (Chapel Hill: University of North Carolina Press, 1980).

The emergence of a western urban region has received less attention from urban scholars, but the existing literature demonstrates that the processes that worked in the Northeast functioned in a similar way in newer western cities. Timothy R. Mahoney, "Urban History in a Regional Context: River Towns on the Upper Mississippi, 1840–1860," *Journal of American History* 72 (September 1985): 318–339, is the best analysis of urban development in the West. Wyatt W. Belcher, *The Economic Rivalry Between St. Louis and Chicago, 1850–1880* (New York: Columbia University Press, 1947), details the conflict between the two major cities in the western urban region.

The urban South did not develop as an urban region. For a discussion of the limits on antebellum southern urbanization (and its consequences), see David R. Goldfield, *Urban Growth in the Age of Sectionalism: Virginia, 1847–1861* (Baton Rouge: Louisiana State University Press, 1977); Harriet Amos, *Cotton City: Urban Development in Antebellum Mobile* (University, Ala.: University of Alabama Press, 1985); and Frederick F. Siegel, *The Roots of Southern Distinctiveness: Tobacco and Society in Danville, Virginia, 1780–1865* (Chapel Hill: University of North Carolina Press, 1987). William H. Pease and Jane H. Pease, *The Web of Progress: Private Values and Public Styles in Boston and Charleston, 1828–1843* (New York: Oxford University Press, 1984), demonstrate clearly the conflicting cultures of urban North and South.

Allan Pred has attempted to relate the regions to each other in *Urban Growth and City-Systems in the United States, 1840–1860* (Cambridge, Mass.: Harvard University Press, 1980), and the result is an effective, if turgid, overview. Pred especially notes how the national urban economy has benefited the Northeast. A narrower, but helpful perspective that focuses on the role of canals and railroads in defining interregional trade patterns is Louis B. Schmidt, "Internal Commerce and the Development of the National Economy Before 1860," *Journal of Political Economy* 47 (December 1939): 798–822.

In addition to transportation, at least two other factors aided urban development in the Northeast and the Midwest: the nature of agriculture and the development of industry. The cultivation of staple crops—grains, primarily—and early mechanization reduced farm labor, providing workers for growing cities. On this point, see Carville Earle and Ronald Hoffman, "The Foundation of the Modern Economy: Agriculture and the Costs of Labor in the United States and England, 1800–1860," *American Historical Review* 85 (December 1980): 1055–1094. The literature on industrialization prior to the Civil War has become extensive, with much of the historiography emphasizing the changing nature of work rather than urbanization. Anthony F. C. Wallace's study *Rockdale: The Growth of an American Village in the Early Industrial Revolution* (New York: Knopf, 1978) is a first-rate exception, detailing the emergence of industries and population centers in the rural Delaware Valley. Jonathan Prude offers another rural-to-urban perspective in *The Coming of Industrial Order: Town and Factory Life in Rural Massachusetts, 1810–1860* (Cambridge, England: Cambridge University Press, 1983). See also Daniel J. Walkowitz, *Worker City, Company Town: Iron- and Cotton-Worker Protest in Troy and Cohoes, New York, 1855–84* (Urbana: University of Illinois Press, 1978); Alan Dawley, *Class and Community: The Industrial Revolution in Lynn* (Cambridge, England: Cambridge University Press, 1976); Susan E. Hirsch, *Roots of the American Working Class: The Industrialization of Crafts in Newark, 1800–1860* (Philadelphia: Temple University Press,

1978); and Bruce Laurie, *Working People of Philadelphia, 1800–1850* (Philadelphia: Temple University Press, 1980). Technological inventions in towns and cities fueled industrial development, which, in turn, spurred other inventions. The Northeast became a leader in technology because of the mechanics, artisans, and financiers concentrated in its cities; Thomas C. Cochran chronicles this process in *Frontiers of Change: Early Industrialism in America* (New York: Oxford University Press, 1981).

The emergence of a national urban economy generated great inequalities between wealthy and poor. The city became increasingly divided by occupation, race, and ethnicity. Among the more significant developments in urban historiography over the past decade has been the recognition and delineation of working-class culture. New York was the nation's most industrial city by the time of the Civil War, yet most of the city's industry was tucked away in garrets, rooms, and shops. The impact of this form of work on family life, child rearing, and urban space is expertly chronicled in two works: Sean Wilentz, *Chants Democratic: New York City and the Rise of the American Working Class, 1788–1850* (New York: Oxford University Press, 1984); and Christine Stansell, *City of Women: Sex and Class in New York, 1789–1860* (New York: Knopf, 1986). Wilentz's study is the broader of the two, relating the emergence of a working-class culture to changes in politics and reform efforts.

The studies of Wilentz and Stansell are more sophisticated analyses of social class than the much heralded, now neglected studies of social mobility. Nevertheless, some valuable studies from the social mobility literature of the late 1960s and early 1970s pointed to the increasing rigidity of social status in the antebellum city. These studies include Peter R. Knights, *The Plain People of Boston, 1830–1860: A Study in City Growth* (New York: Oxford University Press, 1971); Edward Pessen, "The Social Configuration of the Antebellum City: An Historical and Theoretical Inquiry," *Journal of Urban History* 2 (May 1976): 267–306; and Stephan Thernstrom, *Poverty and Progress: Social Mobility in a Nineteenth-Century City* (Cambridge, Mass.: Harvard University Press, 1964).

While the working class crowded into central-city neighborhoods, middle-class and wealthy residents moved out, some to the suburbs. The movement resulted from improvements in transportation, affluence, and changing preferences regarding residential amenities. On the spatial manifestations of this movement, see especially Charles Lockwood, *Manhattan Moves Uptown: An Illustrated History* (Boston: Houghton Mifflin, 1976); George R. Taylor, "The Beginnings of Mass Transportation in Urban America," *Smithsonian Journal of History* 1 (Summer 1966): 35–50, and (Autumn 1966): 31–54; and David Ward, *Cities and Immigrants: A Geography of Change in Nineteenth-Century America* (New York: Oxford University Press, 1971).

Two major works on suburbanization have appeared recently, one noting the European connections of American suburbanization: Robert Fishman, *Bourgeois Utopias: The Rise and Fall of Suburbia* (New York: Basic Books, 1987); the other emphasizing suburbanization's unique character: Kenneth T. Jackson, *Crabgrass Frontier: The Suburbanization of the United States* (New York: Oxford University

Press, 1985). For a more specialized work, see Henry C. Binford, *The First Suburbs: Residential Communities on the Boston Periphery, 1815–1860* (Chicago: University of Chicago Press, 1985).

The growing diversity and division in urban society resulted in part from the rise in European immigration, especially from the German states and Ireland, and the growth of an urban black population. John Bodnar's *The Transplanted: A History of Immigrants in Urban America* (Bloomington: Indiana University Press, 1985) has become the standard survey of immigration, though most of his material relates to the post–Civil War era. Works covering the antebellum era more specifically include Kathleen Neils Conzen, *Immigrant Milwaukee, 1836–1860: Accommodation and Community in a Frontier City* (Cambridge, Mass.: Harvard University Press, 1976); and Robert Ernst, *Immigrant Life in New York City, 1825–1863* (New York: King's Crown Press, 1949). Studies dealing with the black experience include Ira Berlin, *Slaves Without Masters: The Free Negro in the Antebellum South* (New York: Pantheon, 1974); Claudia D. Goldin, *Urban Slavery in the American South, 1820–1860: A Quantitative History* (Chicago: University of Chicago Press, 1976); Leon F. Litwack, *North of Slavery: The Negro in the Free States, 1790–1860* (Chicago: University of Chicago Press, 1961); Robert S. Starobin, *Industrial Slavery in the Old South* (New York: Oxford University Press, 1969); Richard C. Wade, *Slavery in the Cities: The South, 1820–1860* (New York: Oxford University Press, 1964); and Leonard P. Curry, *The Free Black in Urban America, 1800–1850: The Shadow of a Dream* (Chicago: University of Chicago Press, 1981).

The growing divisions in urban society stimulated a reform movement led by the middle class. The standard works on poverty and its relief are Robert H. Bremner, *From the Depths: The Discovery of Poverty in the United States* (New York: New York University Press, 1956); and Raymond A. Mohl, *Poverty in New York, 1783–1825* (New York: Oxford University Press, 1971). Reform efforts eventually found their way into local government; new services (offered by fire, police, and health departments) reflected the growing complexity of urban life and increasing efforts by government to protect citizens and property. The 1830s and 1840s were especially tumultuous for urban residents. The ethnic, religious, and racial violence of the time is covered in Michael Feldberg, *The Philadelphia Riots of 1844: A Study in Ethnic Conflict* (Westport, Conn.: Greenwood Press, 1975); David Grimsted, "Rioting in its Jacksonian Setting," *American Historical Review* 77 (April 1972): 361–397; and Theodore M. Hammett, "Two Mobs of Jacksonian Boston: Ideology and Interest," *Journal of American History* 62 (March 1976): 845–868. The public response to the police service is analyzed by Roger C. Lane, *Policing the City: Boston, 1822–1885* (Cambridge, Mass.: Harvard University Press, 1967); and James F. Richardson, *The New York Police: Colonial Times to 1901* (New York: Oxford University Press, 1970). For information on government's adoption of responsibility for health services, see John Duffy, *A History of Public Health in New York City, 1625–1866* (New York: Russell Sage Foundation, 1968); David R. Goldfield, "The Business of Health Planning: Disease Prevention in the Old South," *Journal of Southern History* 42 (November 1976): 557–570; and Charles E. Rosenberg, *The Cholera Years: The United*

States in 1832, 1849, and 1866 (Chicago: University of Chicago Press, 1987). For information on a related topic, water service, see Nelson M. Blake, *Water for Cities: A History of the Urban Water Supply Problem in the United States* (Syracuse: Syracuse University Press, 1958). For information on social services, see M. J. Heale, "From City Fathers to Social Critics: Humanitarianism and Government in New York, 1790–1860," *Journal of American History* 63 (June 1976): 21–41. Finally, for information on the growth of local government in general, see Robert A. McCaughey, "From Town to City: Boston in the 1820s," *Political Science Quarterly* 87 (June 1973): 191–213; Edward Pessen, "Who Governed the Nation's Cities in the 'Era of the Common Man'?" *Political Science Quarterly* 87 (December 1972): 591–614; and Jon C. Teaford, *The Municipal Revolution in America: Origins of Modern Urban Government, 1650–1825* (Chicago: University of Chicago Press, 1975).

One of the ideals espoused by middle-class reformers was the benefit derived from open spaces. Frederick Law Olmsted executed this ideal in parks and planned communities. See Albert Fein, *Frederick Law Olmsted and the American Environmental Tradition* (New York: Braziller, 1972); and David Schuyler, *The New Urban Landscape: The Redefinition of City Form in Nineteenth-Century America* (Baltimore: Johns Hopkins University Press, 1986).

How Americans saw the nineteenth-century city is the theme of several books, including Thomas Bender, *Toward an Urban Vision: Ideas and Institutions in Nineteenth-Century America* (Lexington: University Press of Kentucky, 1975); Kevin Lynch, *The Image of the City* (Cambridge, Mass.: MIT Press, 1960); Anselm Strauss, *Images of the American City* (Glencoe, Ill.: Free Press, 1961); and Morton White and Lucia White, *The Intellectual Versus the City: From Thomas Jefferson to Frank Lloyd Wright* (Cambridge, Mass.: Harvard University Press, 1962). See also Leo Marx, *The Machine in the Garden: Technology and the Pastoral Ideal in America* (New York: Oxford University Press, 1964).

Part 3
The Radial Center, 1870–1920

For a general survey of urbanization during this period, see Raymond A. Mohl, *The New City: Urban America in the Industrial Age, 1860–1920* (Arlington Heights, Ill.: Harlan Davidson, 1985). An excellent single-city survey is Francis G. Couvares, *The Remaking of Pittsburgh: Class and Culture in an Industrializing City, 1877–1919* (Albany: State University Press of New York, 1984).

For information on the period's economic expansion (especially in the industrial sphere), see Gunther Barth, *Instant Cities: Urbanization and the Rise of San Francisco and Denver* (New York: Oxford University Press, 1975), which deals with entrepreneurial activity on the urban frontier; Charles N. Glaab, *Kansas City and the Railroads: Community Policy in the Growth of a Regional Metropolis* (Madison: State Historical Society of Wisconsin, 1962); Peter G. Goheen, "Industrialization and the Growth of Cities in Nineteenth-Century America," *American Studies* 14 (Spring 1973): 49–65; Carol E. Hoffecker, *Wilmington, Delaware: Portrait of an Industrial*

City, 1830–1910 (Charlottesville: University Press of Virginia, 1974); and Robert H. Wiebe, *The Search for Order, 1877–1920* (New York: Hill and Wang, 1967). Recently, historians have begun to discuss the urban South in the context of the post–Civil War national economy. See especially James Michael Russell, *Atlanta, 1847–1890: City Building in the Old South and the New* (Baton Rouge: Louisiana State University Press, 1988); and Don H. Doyle, *New Men, New Cities, New South: Atlanta, Nashville, Charleston, Mobile, 1860–1910* (Chapel Hill: University of North Carolina Press, 1989).

The transformation of urban labor generated by the new economic order was the subject of numerous contemporary novels, including Edward Bellamy, *Looking Backward* (New York: Amsco, 1888); and Upton Sinclair, *The Jungle,* rev. ed. (New York: Signet, 1973; originally published 1906). The best general account of labor during this period is David Montgomery, *The Fall of the House of Labor: The Workplace, the State, and American Labor Activism, 1865–1925* (Cambridge, England: Cambridge University Press, 1987). For a discussion of urban labor in a broad context and time frame, see Herbert G. Gutman, "Work, Culture, and Society in Industrializing America, 1815–1919," *American Historical Review* 78 (June 1973): 531–588. See also Daniel Nelson, *Managers and Workers: Origins of the New Factory System in the United States, 1880–1929* (Madison: University of Wisconsin Press, 1975). Other helpful works are Samuel P. Hays, *The Response to Industrialism: 1885–1914* (Chicago: University Chicago Press, 1957); and Neil L. Shumsky, "San Francisco's Workingmen Respond to the Modern City," *California Historical Quarterly* 52 (Spring 1976): 46–57. Stanley Buder, *Pullman: An Experiment in Industrial Order and Community Planning, 1880–1930* (New York: Oxford University Press, 1967), contains excellent material on how workers responded to an "ideal" industrial community. For information on one response by corporate America to labor activism, see Stuart D. Brandes, *American Welfare Capitalism, 1880–1949* (Chicago: University of Chicago Press, 1976).

Industrial development and the accompanying emergence of a service economy opened up numerous employment opportunities for women. The best general survey is Alice Kessler-Harris, *Out To Work: A History of Wage-Earning Women in the United States* (New York: Oxford University Press, 1982). A good review essay of working women in the city during this era is Julia Kirk Blackwelder, "Working-Class Women and Urban Culture," *Journal of Urban History* 14 (August 1988): 503–510. Department stores offered new, if low-paying, occupational alternatives for women. See Susan Porter Benson, *Counter Cultures: Saleswomen, Managers, and Customers in American Department Stores, 1890–1940* (Urbana: University of Illinois Press, 1988). To find out what working women did with their meager wages and limited leisure time, see Kathy Peiss, *Cheap Amusements: Working Women and Leisure in Turn-of-the-Century New York* (Philadelphia: Temple University Press, 1986). For information on working women in specific cities, see Susan J. Kleinberg, "Technology and Women's Work: The Lives of Working-Class Women in Pittsburgh, 1870–1900," *Labor History* 17 (Winter 1976): 58–72; and Gerd Korman, *Indus-*

trialization, Immigrants, and Americanizers: The View from Milwaukee, 1866–1921 (Madison: State Historical Society of Wisconsin, 1967).

Whether there was social mobility in the post–Civil War urban working classes used to be a prominent historiographical issue. Research studies did not answer the question any more clearly than similar studies of antebellum cities. Nevertheless, as in the antebellum period, important insights can be found in the old social mobility studies, especially Howard P. Chudacoff, *Mobile Americans: Residential and Social Mobility in Omaha, 1880–1920* (New York: Oxford University Press, 1973); and Stephan Thernstrom, *The Other Bostonians: Poverty and Progress in the American Metropolis, 1880–1970* (Cambridge, Mass.: Harvard University Press, 1973).

The literature on immigrant life in urban America is extensive. John Bodnar, *The Transplanted: A History of Immigrants in Urban America* (Bloomington: Indiana University Press, 1985), has replaced Oscar Handlin, *The Uprooted* (Boston: Little, Brown, 1951), as the standard general treatment. John Higham, *Strangers in the Land: Patterns of American Nativism, 1860–1925* (New York: Atheneum, 1963), recounts the organization of anti-immigrant sentiment.

Immigration studies concerned with particular ethnic groups or specific cities include Abraham Cahan, *The Rise of David Levinsky* (New York: Harper & Brothers, 1917); Dennis Clark, *The Irish in Philadelphia: Ten Generations of Urban Experience* (Philadelphia: Temple University Press, 1973); Dean R. Esslinger, *Immigrants and the City: Ethnicity and Mobility in a Nineteenth-Century Midwestern Community* (Port Washington, N.Y.: Kennikat Press, 1975); Irving Howe, *World of Our Fathers* (New York: Harcourt Brace Jovanovich, 1976); Thomas Kessner, *The Golden Door: Italian and Jewish Immigrant Mobility in New York City, 1880–1915* (New York: Oxford University Press, 1977); Humbert S. Nelli, *The Italians in Chicago, 1860–1920: A Study in Ethnic Mobility* (New York: Oxford University Press, 1970); Moses Rischin, *The Promised City: New York's Jews, 1870–1914* (Cambridge, Mass.: Harvard University Press, 1962); Betty Smith, *A Tree Grows in Brooklyn* (New York: Harper & Row, 1943); and Olivier Zunz, *The Changing Face of Inequality: Urbanization, Industrial Development, and Immigrants in Detroit, 1880–1920* (Chicago: University of Chicago Press, 1982).

More recent studies have stressed the dynamic interaction between Old World and New World cultures in the formation of new immigrant cultures. See Donna R. Gabaccia, *From Sicily to Elizabeth Street: Housing and Social Change among Italian Immigrants, 1880–1930* (Albany: State University of New York Press, 1984); and John W. Briggs, "Fertility and Cultural Change Among Families in Italy and America," *American Historical Review* 91 (December 1986): 1129–1145. Recent studies of a few southern and western cities reveal distinctive patterns of immigrant adjustment. See Dino Cinel, *From Italy to San Francisco: The Immigrant Experience* (Stanford, Calif.: Stanford University Press, 1982); John Modell, *The Economics and Politics of Racial Accommodation: The Japanese of Los Angeles, 1900–1942* (Urbana: University of Illinois Press, 1977); and Gary R. Mormino and George E. Pozzetta, *The Immigrant World of Ybor City: Italians and Their Latin Neighbors in Tampa,*

1885–1985 (Urbana: University of Illinois Press, 1987). Studies focusing on the residential dimensions of the ethnic experience include Jeffrey S. Gurock, *When Harlem Was Jewish, 1870–1930* (New York: Columbia University Press, 1979); and several essays in Theodore Hershberg, ed., *Philadelphia: Work, Space, Family and Group Experience in the Nineteenth Century: Essays Toward an Interdisciplinary History of the City* (New York: Oxford University Press, 1981).

The material on urban blacks is also voluminous and has increased in recent years. The student should begin with August Meier and Elliott Rudwick, *From Plantation to Ghetto* (New York: Hill and Wang, 1966); and Gilbert Osofsky, "The Enduring Ghetto," *Journal of American History* 55 (September 1968): 243–255. More specific studies include Nathan I. Huggins, *Harlem Renaissance* (New York: Oxford University Press, 1971); David M. Katzman, *Before the Ghetto: Black Detroit in the Nineteenth Century* (Urbana: University of Illinois Press, 1973); Kenneth L. Kusmer, *A Ghetto Takes Shape: Black Cleveland, 1870–1930* (Urbana: University of Illinois Press, 1976); Gilbert Osofsky, *Harlem: The Making of a Ghetto: Negro New York, 1890–1930* (New York: Harper & Row, 1966). Peter Gottlieb, *Making Their Own Way: Southern Blacks' Migration to Pittsburgh, 1916–1930* (Urbana: University of Illinois Press, 1987), follows the outlines of most immigrant studies by looking at the impact of pre-migration culture on Pittsburgh's black community. William Tuttle, Jr., *Race Riot: Chicago in the Red Summer of 1919* (New York: Atheneum, 1970), looks at one of the consequences of black migration. Howard N. Rabinowitz, *Race Relations in the Urban South, 1865–1890* (New York: Oxford University Press, 1978), is the standard work on blacks in the urban South during this period. See also George C. Wright, *Life Behind a Veil: Blacks in Louisville, Kentucky, 1865–1930* (Baton Rouge: Louisiana State University Press, 1985). For a contemporary account, see W. E. B. Du Bois, *The Black Flame, Book Two: Mansart Builds a School* (New York: Mainstream Publishers, 1959), which includes a discussion of education for blacks in Atlanta.

Although there is no general survey of the age of urban reform, Michael H. Ebner and Eugene M. Tobin, eds., *The Age of Urban Reform: New Perspectives on the Progressive Era* (Port Washington, N.Y.: Kennikat Press, 1977), provides a good introduction to the subject. Dewey W. Grantham, *Southern Progressivism: The Reconciliation of Progress and Tradition* (Knoxville: University of Tennessee Press, 1983), includes helpful material on urban reform in the South.

Two legendary adversaries—bosses and reformers—have mellowed in historians' perceptions. Recent studies indicate that their respective importance may have been overrated and their differences exaggerated. Nevertheless, some of the earlier, more traditional literature provides insight into the politics of the era and the rise of the service city. See, for example, Melvin G. Holli, *Reform in Detroit: Hazen S. Pingree and Urban Politics* (New York: Oxford University Press, 1969); Joy J. Jackson, *New Orleans in the Gilded Age: Politics and Urban Progress, 1860–1896* (Baton Rouge: Louisiana State University Press, 1969); Seymour Mandelbaum, *Boss Tweed's New York* (New York: Wiley, 1965); Zane Miller, *Boss Cox's Cincinnati: Urban Politics in the Progressive Era* (New York: Oxford University Press, 1968); Jerome Mushkat,

Tammany: The Evolution of a Political Machine, 1789–1865 (Syracuse: Syracuse University Press, 1971); and William L. Riordan, *Plunkitt of Tammany Hall* (New York: McClure, Philipps & Co., 1905).

The most persuasive case for a new view of political structure in the age of urban reform is Jon C. Teaford, *The Unheralded Triumph: City Government in America, 1870–1900* (Baltimore: Johns Hopkins University Press, 1984). Two exceptional earlier case studies had begun to cast doubt on the bosses–reformers dichotomy: Carl V. Harris, *Political Power in Birmingham, 1871–1921* (Knoxville: University of Tennessee Press, 1977); and David C. Hammack, *Power and Society: Greater New York at the Turn of the Century* (New York: Russell Sage Foundation, 1982). See also Terrence J. McDonald, *The Parameters of Urban Fiscal Policy: Socioeconomic Change and Political Culture in San Francisco, 1860–1906* (Berkeley: University of California Press, 1986); and William Issel and Robert W. Cherny, *San Francisco, 1865–1932: Politics, Power, and Urban Development* (Berkeley: University of California Press, 1986). The rise of the service city and its impact on the political process are expertly highlighted in Harold L. Platt, *City Building in the New South: The Growth of Public Services in Houston, Texas, 1830–1910* (Philadelphia: Temple University Press, 1983). Stanley K. Schultz and Clay McShane, "To Engineer the Metropolis: Sewers, Sanitation, and City Planning in Late-Nineteenth-Century America," *Journal of American History* 65 (September 1978): 389–411, stresses the importance of professional engineers in the shaping of the industrial city.

The increasing historiographical emphasis on technology and technocrats in the industrial city is not an entirely new interpretive focus. Carl W. Condit pioneered the study of technology in urban society in *Chicago, 1910–29: Building, Planning, and Urban Technology* (Chicago: University of Chicago Press, 1973). Transportation and the infrastructure that supports it are key issues in Condit's work. Two fine single-city studies of transportation technology and urban reform are Clay McShane, *Technology and Reform: Street Railways and the Growth of Milwaukee, 1887–1900* (Madison: State Historical Society of Wisconsin, 1974); and Joel A. Tarr, *Transportation Innovation and Changing Spatial Patterns: Pittsburgh, 1850–1910* (Pittsburgh: Carnegie Mellon University, 1972). An excellent case study of a particular system is Olivier Zunz, "Technology and Society in an Urban Environment: The Case of the Third Avenue El," *Journal of Interdisciplinary History* 3 (Summer 1972): 89–101.

But expansion of infrastructure did not necessarily alter the direction of urban growth. The impact of expansion was generally conservative, even when unforeseen disasters enabled cities to alter their structure dramatically, as Christine Meisner Rosen demonstrates in *The Limits of Power: Great Fires and the Process of City Growth in America* (Cambridge, England: Cambridge University Press, 1986). For a model study of a particular service, see Martin V. Melosi, *Garbage in the Cities: Refuse, Reform, and the Environment, 1880–1980* (Chicago: Dorsey Press, 1981). Frequently, the pressure for services came not only from middle-class reformers, but from residents of older neighborhoods who felt neglected by a government that favored the rapid geographic expansion of the city and the servicing of new areas; see Joseph L. Arnold, "The Neighborhood and City Hall: The Origins of Neighborhood Associations in Baltimore, 1880–1911," *Journal of Urban History* 6 (November 1979): 3–30. For an effective summary of the new urban technocracy, see Jon A. Peterson, "Environment and Technology in the Great City Era of American History," *Journal of Urban History* 8 (May 1982): 343–354.

The reformers' greatest challenge was the urban poor. The classic work on the settlement house is Allen F. Davis, *Spearheads for Reform: The Social Settlements and the Progressive Movement, 1890–1914* (New York: Oxford University Press, 1967). For information on impoverished children, see Joseph M. Hawes, *Children in Urban Society: Juvenile Delinquency in Nineteenth-Century America* (New York: Oxford University Press, 1971). Nathan I. Huggins, *Protestants Against Poverty: Boston's Charities, 1870–1900* (Westport, Conn.: Greenwood Press, 1970), is a fine case study of the rationale behind Progressive-era poor relief. And the definitive work on the leading exposer of urban poverty, Jacob Riis, is James B. Lane, *Jacob A. Riis and the American City* (Port Washington, N.Y.: Kennikat Press, 1975).

Housing reform—a key issue for many Progressive-era urban reformers—has inspired an extensive literature. The standard work, even though it limits its focus to one city, is Roy Lubove, *The Progressives and the Slums: Tenement House Reform in New York City, 1890–1917* (Pittsburgh: University of Pittsburgh Press, 1962). A fine comparative study is Martin J. Daunton, "Cities of Homes and Cities of Tenements: British and American Comparisons, 1870–1914," *Journal of Urban History* 14 (May 1988): 283–319. An excellent review of one popular housing reform is Eugenie Ladner Birch and Deborah S. Gardner, "The Seven-Percent Solution: A Review of Philanthropic Housing, 1870–1910," *Journal of Urban History* 7 (August 1981): 408–438.

Historians have often been critical of another social reform—public education—but views have softened in recent years. A fine overview of the early literature is Ronald D. Cohen, "Urban Schooling in the Gilded Age and After," *Journal of Urban History* 2 (August 1976): 499–506. See also Maxine Seller, "The Education of Immigrant Children in Buffalo, New York, 1890–1916," *New York History* 57 (April 1976): 183–199; and Selwyn K. Troen, *The Public and the Schools: Shaping the St. Louis System, 1838–1920* (Columbia: University of Missouri Press, 1975). For a summary of the critical literature, see Selma Berrol, "Urban Schools: The Historian as Critic," *Journal of Urban History* 8 (February 1982): 206–216. For information on the growing diversity of assessments of urban education, see Harvey Kantor and Theodore Mitchell, "Class, Politics, and Urban School Reform," *Journal of Urban History* 14 (February 1986): 269–276.

The urge for reform extended to suburban development. No longer an elite preserve, the suburb in the late nineteenth century became accessible to growing numbers of urban residents, thanks to transportation technology and the burgeoning middle class. The key work on suburban development during this era remains Sam Bass Warner, Jr., *Streetcar Suburbs: The Process of Growth in Boston, 1870–1900* (New York: Atheneum, 1974). The more general surveys—Kenneth T. Jackson, *Crabgrass Frontier: The Suburbanization of the United States* (New York: Oxford University Press, 1985); and Robert Fishman, *Bourgeois Utopias: The Rise and Fall of Suburbia* (New York: Basic Books, 1987)—are helpful as well. Michael H. Ebner, *Creating*

Chicago's North Shore: A Suburban History (Chicago: University of Chicago Press, 1988), offers a convincing account of the development of suburban consciousness in a group of affluent suburbs outside Chicago. For information on the suburban ideal in the South (which incorporated the region's particular racial and class customs), see Catherine W. Bishir and Lawrence S. Early, eds., *Early Twentieth-Century Suburbs in North Carolina* (Raleigh: North Carolina Department of Cultural Resources, 1986). For an imaginative perspective on the relationship between the suburban ideal and family life, see Margaret Marsh, "Suburban Men and Masculine Domesticity, 1870–1915," *American Quarterly* 40 (June 1988): 165–186. The single-family home was a key attraction of suburban living; see Gwendolyn Wright, *Building the Dream: A Social History of Housing in America* (New York: Pantheon, 1981). Mary Corbin Sies, "The City Transformed: Nature, Technology, and the Suburban Ideal, 1877–1917," *Journal of Urban History* 14 (November 1987): 81–111, offers a useful synthesis of recent scholarship and connects the suburban movement to developments within the city.

The essence of the radial center era was suburban expansion *and* central-city vitality and diversity. For a view of how the downtown in the industrial city served to tie the disparate parts of the city together through shopping, entertainment, recreation, and journalism, see Gunther Barth, *City People: The Rise of Modern City Culture in Nineteenth-Century America* (New York: Oxford University Press, 1980). On the meaning of the skyscraper at the beginning of the tall-building boom, see Mona Domosh, "The Symbolism of the Skyscraper: Case Studies of New York's First Tall Buildings," *Journal of Urban History* 14 (May 1988): 321–345.

City planning emerged as a profession during the Progressive era. For a comparative perspective, see Anthony Sutcliffe, *Towards the Planned City: Germany, Britain, the United States and France, 1780–1914* (Oxford, England: Basil Blackwell, 1981). The 1893 Columbian Exposition in Chicago was a pivotal event in focusing public attention on how architecture and planning could reshape a city and improve the lives of its residents. The story of the fair is told in David F. Burg, *Chicago's White City of 1893* (Lexington: University Press of Kentucky, 1976). For a summary of the City Beautiful movement and its impact on urban planning, see Jon A. Peterson, "The City Beautiful Movement: Forgotten Origins and Lost Meanings," *Journal of Urban History* 2 (August 1976): 415–434.

Part 4
The Vital Fringe, 1920–1970

General surveys of this period include Carl Abbott, *Urban America in the Modern Age: 1920 to the Present* (Arlington Heights, Ill.: Harlan Davidson, 1987); and Jon C. Teaford, *The Twentieth-Century American City: Problem, Promise, and Reality* (Baltimore: Johns Hopkins University Press, 1986). Kenneth Fox, *Metropolitan America: Urban Life and Urban Policy in the United States, 1940–1980* (Jackson: University Press of Mississippi, 1986), provides a helpful, if idiosyncratic, overview on the relationship between urban theorists and public policy.

The impact of the automobile on metropolitan space became evident by the

1920s. Good surveys of that impact include John B. Rae, *The Road and the Car in American Life* (Cambridge, Mass.: MIT Press, 1971); James J. Flink, *The Car Culture* (Cambridge, Mass.: MIT Press, 1975); and Blaine A. Brownell, "A Symbol of Modernity: Attitudes Toward the Automobile in Southern Cities in the 1920s," *American Quarterly* 24 (March 1972): 20–44. Three fine case studies are Carl W. Condit, *Chicago, 1930–70: Building, Planning, and Urban Technology* (Chicago: University of Chicago Press, 1974); Howard L. Preston, *Automobile Age Atlanta: The Making of a Southern Metropolis, 1900–1935* (Athens: University of Georgia Press, 1979); and Paul Barrett, *The Automobile and Urban Transit: The Formation of Public Policy in Chicago, 1900–1930* (Philadelphia: Temple University Press, 1983). A study of the interactions among urban expansion, technology, and popular attitudes toward urban life is Blaine A. Brownell, *The Urban Ethos in the South, 1920–1930* (Baton Rouge: Louisiana State University Press, 1975). Robert Fishman, *Bourgeois Utopias: The Rise and Fall of Suburbia* (New York: Basic Books, 1987), offers an excellent discussion of the automobile's conquest of Los Angeles. Mark S. Foster places the automobile against the backdrop of other transportation forms and public policy in *From Streetcar to Superhighway: American City Planners and Urban Transportation, 1900–1940* (Philadelphia: Temple University Press, 1981).

Most works on the automobile also emphasize the decentralization of the urban economy. As Paul Barrett demonstrates in "Cities and Their Airports: Policy Formation, 1926–1952," *Journal of Urban History* 14 (November 1987): 112–137, the newest transportation technology aided suburbanization as well. For a statistical profile of these spatial changes, see A. H. Hawley, *The Changing Shape of Metropolitan America: Deconcentration Since 1920* (Glencoe, Ill.: Free Press, 1956).

Urban theorists attempted to devise policies to manage the outward movement of metropolitan America in the 1920s and 1930s. For discussions of these varying views, see Daniel Schaffer, *Garden Cities for America: The Radburn Experience* (Philadelphia: Temple University Press, 1982); William H. Wilson, "Moles and Skylarks," in Donald A. Krueckeberg, ed., *Introduction to Planning History in the United States* (New Brunswick, N.J.: Center for Urban Policy Research, 1983), 88–121; David R. Goldfield, "Neighborhood Preservation and Community Values in Historical Perspective," in Irwin Altman and Abraham Wandersman, eds., *Neighborhood and Community Environments* (New York: Plenum, 1987), 223–256; David A. Johnson, "Regional Planning for the Great American Metropolis: New York Between the World Wars," in Daniel Schaffer, ed., *Two Centuries of American Planning* (London: Mansell, 1988), 167–196; and Stephen Grabow, "Frank Lloyd Wright and the American City: The Broadacres Debate," *Journal of the American Institute of Planners* 43 (April 1977): 115–135.

The Great Depression significantly increased the role of the federal government in urban life. The best single study of the growing involvement of the federal government in urban affairs is Mark I. Gelfand's *A Nation of Cities: The Federal Government and Urban America, 1933–1965* (New York: Oxford University Press, 1975). Also see Joseph L. Arnold, *The New Deal in the Suburbs: A History of the Greenbelt Town Program, 1935–1954* (Columbus: Ohio State University Press, 1971); Paul

K. Conklin, *Tomorrow a New World: The New Deal Community Program* (Ithaca, N.Y.: Cornell University Press, 1959); and the Urbanism Committee to the National Resources Committee, *Our Cities: Their Role in the National Economy* (Washington, D.C.: Government Printing Office, 1937). Three useful case studies of the impact of the New Deal on local politics are Arthur Mann, *La Guardia Comes to Power: 1933* (Chicago: University of Chicago Press, 1965); Bruce M. Stave, *The New Deal and the Last Hurrah: Pittsburgh Machine Politics* (Pittsburgh: University of Pittsburgh Press, 1970); and Roger Biles, *Memphis in the Great Depression* (Knoxville: University of Tennessee Press, 1983). Recent scholarship on working women during the Depression has highlighted the changing nature of the workforce and the persistence of racial and ethnic discrimination. See Winifred D. Wandersee Bolin, "The Economics of Middle-Income Family Life: Working Women During the Great Depression," *Journal of American History* 65 (June 1978): 60–84; and Julia Kirk Blackwelder, *Women of the Depression: Caste and Culture in San Antonio, 1920–1939* (College Station: Texas A&M University Press, 1984). The New Deal helped many cities launch major building campaigns. Few individuals used these programs to establish their power over a metropolitan infrastructure to the extent that New York's Robert Moses did. See Robert A. Caro, *The Power Broker: Robert Moses and the Fall of New York* (New York: Random House, 1974).

The city during World War II has enjoyed much less scholarly attention than the city during the Depression and the New Deal. Yet federal outlays to the city were more than three times as great as Depression-era expenditures. See Philip Funigiello, *The Challenge to Urban Liberalism: Federal-City Relations During World War II* (Knoxville: University of Tennessee Press, 1978). A fine regional study is Gerald D. Nash, *The American West Transformed: The Impact of the Second World War* (Bloomington: Indiana University Press, 1985). For information on the increase in racial tensions during the war years, see Dominic J. Capeci, Jr., *Race Relations in Wartime Detroit: The Sojourner Truth Housing Controversy, 1937–1942* (Philadelphia: Temple University Press, 1984). For an excellent discussion of how the impact of depression and war on the South eventually fueled urbanization, see Jack Temple Kirby, *Rural Worlds Lost: The American South, 1920–1960* (Baton Rouge: Louisiana State University Press, 1987).

Both the federal government and private industry jumped in to satisfy pent-up demand for housing after World War II, and a suburban boom that would last through the 1960s was underway. The best account of this boom is Kenneth T. Jackson, *Crabgrass Frontier: The Suburbanization of the United States* (New York: Oxford University Press, 1985). Also see Herbert J. Gans, *The Levittowners* (New York: Pantheon, 1967); and Scott Donaldson, *The Suburban Myth* (New York: Columbia University Press, 1969).

Urban renewal complemented and stimulated suburban growth. Though renewal policy scored some notable successes in downtown revitalization, it also had a devastating impact on some poor neighborhoods. The most thorough account of the rise of the growth coalitions and their implementation of urban renewal policies is John H. Mollenkopf, *The Contested City* (Princeton, N.J.: Princeton University

Press, 1983), which focused on urban renewal in San Francisco and Boston. Howard Gillette, Jr., "The Evolution of Neighborhood Planning: From the Progressive Era to the 1949 Housing Act," *Journal of Urban History* 9 (August 1983): 421–444, demonstrates that urban renewal was the logical conclusion of a series of decisions that began in the 1920s. Two excellent single-city analyses of urban renewal are Arnold R. Hirsch, *Making the Second Ghetto: Race and Housing in Chicago, 1940 to 1960* (Cambridge, England: Cambridge University Press, 1983); and John F. Bauman, *Public Housing, Race, and Renewal: Urban Planning in Philadelphia, 1920–1974* (Philadelphia: Temple University Press, 1987). Urban renewal was not only a problem for poor blacks, but white ethnics as well, as shown in Gary Ross Mormino's *Immigrants on the Hill: Italian-Americans in St. Louis, 1882–1982* (Urbana: University of Illinois Press, 1986). Two searing but exaggerated critiques of federal urban policy during the 1960s are Jane Jacobs, *The Death and Life of Great American Cities* (New York: Vintage, 1963); and Herbert Gans, *Urban Villagers* (New York: Free Press, 1962). A conservative critique is offered by Edward C. Banfield, *The Unheavenly City: The Nature and Future of Our Urban Crisis* (Boston: Little, Brown, 1968). An equally withering analysis of the planning profession's role in the dismantling of urban America is M. Christine Boyer, *Dreaming the Rational City: The Myth of American City Planning* (Cambridge, England: Cambridge University Press, 1983).

The racial violence of the middle and late 1960s underscored the policy failures of postwar urban America. Kenneth Fox, *Metropolitan America: Urban Life and Urban Policy in the United States, 1940–1980* (Jackson: University of Mississippi Press, 1986), discusses the political dimensions of the civil disturbances. For background discussions of postwar ghetto life, see Kenneth B. Clark, *Dark Ghetto: Dilemmas of Social Power* (New York: Harper & Row, 1965); St. Clair Drake and Horace R. Cayton, *Black Metropolis: A Study of Negro Life in a Northern City*, 2 vols. (New York: Harper & Row, 1962); Leo Grebler et al., *The Mexican-American People* (New York: Free Press, 1970); and Lee Rainwater, *Behind Ghetto Walls: Black Families in a Federal Slum* (Chicago: Aldine, 1970). *The Report of the National Advisory Commission on Civil Disorders* (New York: Bantam Books, 1968) blamed the violence on racism, a charge both prescient and simplistic.

Part 5
The Multicentered Metropolis, 1970 to the Present

There is no general account of the rise of the multicentered metropolis, though several works have discussed this phenomenon in part. Some of the best discussions are in Robert Fishman, *Bourgeois Utopias: The Rise and Fall of Suburbia* (New York: Basic Books, 1987); Brian J. L. Berry, ed., *Urbanization and Counterurbanization* (Beverly Hills, Calif.: Sage, 1976); and Jack Meltzer, *Metropolis to Metroplex: The Social and Spatial Planning of Cities* (Baltimore: Johns Hopkins University Press, 1984). An early description of the multicentered future of the metropolitan area was provided in Jean Gottmann, *Megalopolis: The Urbanized Northeastern Seaboard of the*

United States (Cambridge, Mass.: MIT Press, 1961). See also Raymond A. Mohl, "The Transformation of Urban America Since the Second World War," *Amerika-studien/American Studies* 33 (1988): 53–71. In addition, articles in the *New York Times* and columns by Neal Peirce have chronicled the emergence of the multicentered metropolis over the past two decades. See especially Paul Goldberger, "When Suburban Sprawl Meets Upward Mobility," *The New York Times,* July 26, 1987. For an excellent policy overview, see Peter K. Eisinger, "The Search for a National Urban Policy, 1968–1980," *Journal of Urban History* 12 (November 1985): 3–23.

Los Angeles was probably an early manifestation of the multicentered metropolis, and the northeastern megalopolis is a vast (and often menacing) version. The Sunbelt was especially hospitable to this form of development, and the wide open spaces of the metropolises there are often contrasted with the cramped and decaying metropolitan areas of the North. Carl Abbott, *The New Urban America: Growth and Politics in Sunbelt Cities* (Chapel Hill: University of North Carolina Press, 1981), provides a sober overview of the Sunbelt phenomenon. And the Advisory Commission on Intergovernmental Relations, *Trends in Metropolitan America* (Washington, D.C.: ACIR, 1977), supplies statistical support for the Sunbelt trend. Growth coalitions were particularly noticeable in the Sunbelt, according to most of the selections in Richard M. Bernard and Bradley R. Rice, eds., *Sunbelt Cities: Politics and Growth Since World War II* (Austin: University of Texas Press, 1983). Roger W. Lotchin, ed., *The Martial Metropolis: U.S. Cities in War and Peace* (New York: Praeger, 1984), demonstrates that the Sunbelt benefited from postwar defense expenditures. Perhaps the best example of scholarly overstatement, though it does contain some useful discussions, is Bernard L. Weinstein and Robert E. Firestine, *Regional Growth and Decline in the United States: The Rise of the Sunbelt and the Decline of the Northeast* (New York: Praeger, 1978).

By the late 1970s, challenges to analyses that emphasized the Sunbelt/Frostbelt dichotomy were appearing. David C. Perry and Alfred J. Watkins, *The Rise of the Sunbelt Cities* (Beverly Hills, Calif.: Sage, 1977), was among the earliest. James C. Cobb, *The Selling of the South: The Southern Crusade for Industrial Development* (Baton Rouge: Louisiana State University Press, 1982); and David R. Goldfield, *Cotton Fields and Skyscrapers: Southern City and Region, 1607–1980* (Baton Rouge: Louisiana State University Press, 1982), indicated that, for the southern portion of the Sunbelt at least, media hype may have overshadowed but did not remove the burden of regional history. The investigations of *Southern Exposure* magazine, published at Duke University's Institute for Southern Studies, have underscored the findings of Cobb and Goldfield. Many essays in Raymond A. Mohl, ed., *Searching for the Sunbelt* (Knoxville: University of Tennessee Press, 1989), question whether the Sunbelt concept was ever valid. The Sunbelt concept may provide some value as a framework for research, as discussed in Randall M. Miller and George E. Pozzetta, eds., *Shades of the Sunbelt: Essays on Ethnicity, Race, and the Urban South* (Westport, Conn.: Greenwood Press, 1988). Nonetheless, even official Sunbelt agencies are beginning to question their own publicity; see two reports issued in 1986 by the Commission on the Future of the South: "Equity: The Critical Link in Southern

Economic Development" and "Rural Flight/Urban Might: Economic Development Challenges for the 1990s," both published by the Commission, which is located in the Research Triangle Park, North Carolina.

The much-heralded death of the city did not occur in the 1980s. A new knowledge-oriented economy revived the city if not its residents. See especially Timothy K. Kinsella, "Traditional Manufacturing Cities in Transition to Human-Centered Cities," *Journal of Urban History* 13 (November 1986): 31–53. Neighborhood revitalization complemented downtown revival. See Rogert S. Ahlbrandt, Jr., and Paul C. Brophy, *Neighborhood Revitalization* (Lexington, Mass.: D. C. Heath, 1975); and Irwin Altman and Abraham Wandersman, eds., *Neighborhood and Community Environments* (New York: Plenum, 1987). The federal policies that spurred downtown revivals are analyzed in Victor Bach, "The New Federalism in Community Development," *Social Policy* 7 (January/February 1977): 32–38. And the corresponding transformation of suburbia is discussed in David R. Goldfield, "The Limits of Suburban Growth," *Urban Affairs Quarterly* 12 (September 1976): 83–102; Louis H. Masotti and Jeffrey K. Hadden, eds., *The Urbanization of the Suburbs* (Beverly Hills, Calif.: Sage, 1973); and Peter O. Muller, *The Outer City: Geographical Consequences of the Urbanization of the Suburbs* (Washington, D.C.: Association of American Geographers, 1976).

Three works published in the 1980s offer a comprehensive view of urban policy, the changing urban economy, and the social impact of both: John J. Harrigan, *Political Change in the Metropolis*, 3rd ed. (Boston: Little, Brown, 1985); Paul E. Peterson, ed., *The New Urban Reality* (Washington, D.C.: The Brookings Institution, 1985); and Clarence N. Stone et al., *Urban Policy and Politics in a Bureaucratic Age*, 2nd ed. (Englewood Cliffs, N.J.: Prentice Hall, 1986).

INDEX

Abbott, Robert, 230
Abilene, Kansas, 266
Abolitionists, 151, 159–160
Adams, Henry, 183
Adams, John, 59
Adams, Samuel, 70
Adams, Thomas, 303–305
Addams, Jane, 197, 240, 255–256, 271
Adler, Felix, 251
Adler, Leopold, II, 419
Afro-American Realty Company, 227
Agriculture
    and American character, 58–59
    cotton and tobacco, in developing South,
        104–109
    in early settlements, 22, 26
    rice, 30–32
    southerners' reliance upon, 73
Akron, Ohio, 387
Alabama, 107, 293, 313. *See also individual
    cities.*
Albany, New York, 62, 361
Albuquerque, New Mexico, 396
Alcoholism
    temperance movement, 163–164
    and working class, 144–145
    see also Social problems
Alexandria, Virginia, 24, 73, 109
Algonquin Indians, 14
Allen, Ivan, 355
Allen, Ivan, Jr., 397
Allen, William, 50
Allis, E.P., Company, 207
Almshouses, 51–52. *See also* Housing
American City Planning Institute, 279
American Federation of Labor, 205
American Institute of Planners, 279
American Revolution, 35
    effect of, on urbanization, 77
    role of colonial towns in, 70–72
American Society of Civil Engineers, 246
American Society for the Encouragement of
    Domestic Manufacturers, 88
American Society for Municipal
    Improvements, 246
American Woman's Home, 260
Anaheim, California, 437

Anderson, Sherwood, 319
Annapolis, Maryland, 41, 69
Architectural Forum, 352
Architecture
    in Boston suburbs, 262
    in Broadacre City, 305–306
    in Charleston, 31
    in colonial period, 74
    Columbian Exposition, 275
    in eighteenth-century cities, 46
    English villa style, 131
    in New Orleans, 20
    and preservation, 419–420
    residential, 274, 297
    row houses in Philadelphia and Baltimore,
        132
    single-family home, in 1920s, 291
    skyscraper, 268, 272–273
    suburban, 344–345, 346
    in Williamsburg town plan, 22–23
Arizona, 394, 398
Arlington, Virginia, 328
Armour, Philip, 231
Armstrong, Louis, 313
Army Corps of Engineers, 109
Arrington, Richard, 431
Artisans
    in colonial America, 22, 25, 39, 49
    decline of, 143, 191
    influence of, on local government, 70
    organizations of, 143
    and urban market place, 91
"Ash Can School," 300
Asylum for Lying-In Women, 161
Atlanta, Georgia, 268, 294, 331, 396, 403–
    404, 407
    auto dealers in, 293–294
    black elected officials in, 431
    and blacks in city administration, 433
    and building boom, in 1960s, 354–355
    and desegregation, 361
    downtown as financial center, 269
    drug abuse in, 370
    Druid Hills, 289
    economic development efforts in, 430
    geographical expansion in, 297–298, 437
    during Great Depression, 324

Atlanta, Georgia (*cont.*)
   Hartsfield International Airport, 436
   immigrants in, 401
   and Model Cities grant, 366
   population decline in, 405–406
   public works in, 335
   and railroads, 180–181, 423
   residential segregation in, 226
   school systems in, 258
   set-aside programs in, 432
   suburban exodus in, 369
   and urban renewal legislation, 351, 352
   and War on Poverty, 366
   and World War II, 337
Augusta, Georgia, 83
Austin, Texas, 445
Automobile, *see* Transportation
Automobile Club of Southern California,
   308
Avilés, Pedro Menéndez de, 18

Baldwin, James, 359
Baltimore, 38, 94, 278, 392, 410
   character of, 173
   and clothing industry, 186, 188
   gentrification in, 420
   Harborplace, 417
   industrial waste in, 191
   railroad strike in, 206
   row house architecture in, 132
   and unemployment, during Depression,
      324
Balzekas, Stanley P., 219 (illus.)
Bank of the United States, 109
Barbados, 31
Bassett, Edward M., 279
Baton Rouge, Louisiana, 371
Bauer, Catherine, 331
Beam, Abraham, 387
Beard, Mary, 244
Beecher, Catherine, 128, 260
Beecher, Lyman, 128
Behrman, Martin, 242
Bell, J.R., 426
Bellamy, Edward, 252–253
Bellows, George, 300
Bender, Thomas, 183
Berlin, Irving, 320
Berry, Brian J.L., 439, 443
Bessemer, Henry, 186
Beverley, Robert, 21
Beverly Hills, California, 347
Big Lick, Virginia, 267
Bigelow, Jacob, 166
Biloxi, Mississippi, 20
Birmingham, Alabama, 297, 361, 369, 395,
   404
   black elected officials in, 431

   during Depression, 324–325
   industrial development in, 186, 190
Black Ball Line, 102
Blacks
   in business, 230–231
   churches of, 140–141, 232
   civil rights of, 364, 395
   covenants against, 68, 299
   discrimination against, 224, 325, 339,
      340, 382–383
   family disintegration of, 363–364
   in ghettos, 229–230, 232
   immigrants and, 141
   institutions of, 140, 229, 231
   migrations of, 224–225, 339
   and music, 312–313
   occupational/social mobility of, 139, 141,
      225–226, 382–383
   in politics, 403, 431, 433
   population of, in cities, 221, 222–223
      (table)
   and poverty, 363–364, 367, 382–383
   and public schools, 258
   racial stereotypes about, 312
   residential patterns of, 137–140
   segregation of (*see* Segregation)
   and social order, 64–65
   in southern cities, 360–361
   and suffrage, 138–139
   and Underground Railroad, 141
   unions and, 226
   and violence, 159–160, 360, 381
   and War on Poverty, 367
Bornson, Stephen, 307
Bosses (political), 237–243, 247–248
Boston, Massachusetts, 29, 254, 278, 311,
      336, 359, 413
   during American Revolution, 72, 77
   and annexation, 405
   black residential areas in, 139–140
   boot and shoe industry in, 93–95
   central business district expansion in, 270
      (illus.)
   clothing industry in, 186
   commuting in, 438
   as corporate center, 416
   cultural life in, 59–60
   disease control in, 67
   ethnic communities in, 217
   Faneuil Hall, 417
   immigrants in, 218
   "New Guinea," 139
   "Nigger Hill," 139
   Old State House, 47 (illus.)
   and omnibus, 120
   prostitution in, 64
   Quincy Market, 417, 418 (illus.)
   and redevelopment, in 1950s, 350

revival meetings in, 54
school busing in, 368, 384, 385 (illus.)
slave code in, 68
social structure in, 146
during Stamp Act crisis, 70–71
and suburbs, 259, 262, 289
taverns in, 55, 56
and trade, during colonial period, 38, 43
urban renewal in, 367
violence in, 158, 159
waterfront settlement in, 39
and wealth, during colonial period, 49
Boston Manufacturing Company, 88
Boston Redevelopment Authority, 350
Bowery, 144–145
Bowery B'Hoys, 144
Bowery Girls, 145
Bowery Theatre, 144
Brace, Charles Loring, 163, 171, 253–254
Bradford, William, 28
Bradstreet, Anne, 59
Brice, Fanny, 310–311
Bristol, England, 38
Broadacre City, 440
Bronx, New York, 320
Brooklyn, New York, 320, 364
    growth of, in 1800s, 123
    separation of workplace and residence in,
        124
    suburbs in, 289
    teachers' union strike in, 367
Brooklyn Eagle, 169
Brown, Moses, 87
Bryant, William Cullen, 168
Bryce, James, 238
Buffalo, New York, 186, 206, 252, 437
Bureau of Public Roads, 292
Burley, Maria, 161
Burnaby, Andrew, 53
Burnham, Daniel H., 275, 276
Burnham, Illinois, 318
Burnham Plan, 304
Bush, George, 435
Business
    farmer's markets in city center, 418–419
    "festival marketplaces," 417, 418
    first shopping center, 297
    retail trade in city center, 270–271, 354,
        417
    see also Industry; Trade
Byrd, William, II, 23

Cahan, Abraham, 216
Cahokia, 16
Cairo, Illinois, 99
California, 267, 402, 404, 437, 438
    tax revolt in, 429
    see also individual cities

Cambridge, Massachusetts, 39, 58, 166, 347
Camden, South Carolina, 32
Canals, *see* Transportation
Cantor, Eddie, 312
Capone, Al, 318–319
Carnegie Foundation, 336
Carnegie Steel Works, 192
Carolinas, The
    early settlements in, 30–32
    see also individual cities
Carter, Jimmy, 428
    administration of, 392–393
Case Western Reserve University, 388
Cash, W.J., 268
Catholicism, 214
    and anti-Catholic violence, 158–160
    in colonial America, 54
    and evangelism, 150
    of immigrants, 211, 216
    and Indians in the Southwest, 16
    and schools, 216
    and social class, 146
Cemeteries, 166–168
Central city, *see* Downtown
Central Park (New York), 169–171, 179
    (illus.)
Central place theory, 3
Central Railroad, 101
Chadwick, Edwin, 153, 155
Chapel Hill, North Carolina, 397
Chaplin, Charlie, 312
Charity Organization Societies (COS), 254
Charleston, South Carolina, 30–32, 35, 59,
        337, 340
    American Revolution and, 70–72
    blacks in, 140–141
    character of, 165–166, 173
    cultural life in, 60
    Exchange Building, 31
    government in, 63
    harbor of, 57 (illus.)
    historic preservation in, 416
    immigrants in, 108
    land and urban design in, 31
    merchants in, 44–45
    St. Michael's Church, 31
    "single house" in, 31
    slave code in, 68
    and trade, in colonial period, 38, 43
    and wealth, in colonial period, 49
Charlestown, Massachusetts, 350
Charlotte, North Carolina, 268, 316, 394,
        397, 404, 408
    blacks in, 431
    gentrification in, 421
    and lunch counter sit-in, 362 (illus.)
    mass transit in, 423
    redevelopment in, 351–352

Charlotte, North Carolina (*cont.*)
  and regional study group, 442
  retail trade in, 419
  Spirit Square, 423
  as suburban city, 445
Charlotte Gardens, South Bronx, 428, 444
Chattanooga, Tennessee, 428
Chawanoac, 14
Cheek, Joel O., 268
Cherokee County, Georgia, 441
Cherry Hill, New Jersey, 438 (illus.)
Chester, South Carolina, 32, 407
Chestnut Hill, Pennsylvania, 261
Chicago, Illinois, 109, 295, 307, 311, 355,
    362, 391, 412, 414
  blacks in, 225, 231, 368, 369, 431, 432
  Daniel Burnham's plan for, 276
  city government in, 243
  fire in, 179
  geographic expansion of, 437
  during Great Depression, 324
  and gridiron plan, 85
  housing in, 252, 353, 356
  immigrants in, 210–211, 218, 310
  industry in, 185, 192–193, 194
  jazz in, 312, 313
  land values in, 83
  O'Hare Airport, 436
  organized crime in, 317–319
  politics in, 238–239, 242, 424
  and population growth, in 1800s, 98
  and railroad line, 99–101
  railstrikes in, 206
  real estate prices in, 272–273
  road building in, 292, 293
  social mobility in, 146
  and suburbs, 259, 289
  Union Stock Yards, 187 (illus.)
  and urban-industrial core, 180
  violence in, 229
Chicago School of Architecture, 273
Chicago Times, 220
Chicago World's Fair, 274–275, 299
Chicago Vice Commission, 197
Children's Aid Society, 163
China Grove, North Carolina, 407
Chopin, Kate, 198
Christaller, Walter, 3
Chrysler, Walter, 300–301
Cicero, Illinois, 318–319
Cincinnati, Ohio, 83, 84, 99, 351
  blacks in, 139
  convention center in, 423
  and fire protection, 157
  during Great Depression, 325
  population in, 97, 380
  railroads and, 101–102
  as reproduction of Philadelphia's gridiron
    plan, 84–85

  social mobility in, 146
  violence in, 146
Cisneros, Henry, 402, 404
City(ies)
  as cultural centers, 56–60
  as depicted in films, 370
  disorder and violence in, 158
  images of, 319, 326, 335–336, 358, 422
  and Industrial Revolution, 87–88
  in mid-nineteenth century, 124
  as reflected in colonial literature, 58
  see also Urbanization/urban growth; Urban
    planning
"City Beautiful" movement, 274–279
City center, *see* Downtown
"City Efficient" movement, 278–279, 304
City planning, *see* Urbanization/urban
    growth; Urban planning
City Post Oak, Texas, 437
City-suburb accommodation efforts, 370–
    371
Civil War, 179–180
Clark, Dennis, 217
Clark, George Rogers, 83
Clark, Jim, 361
Cleveland, Ohio, 185, 259, 387, 388, 391,
    410
  blacks in, 225, 227
  and industrial waste, 191
  and population growth, in 1800s, 97
  Stokes administration in, 431–432
Clinton, DeWitt, 95
Clothing industry, 186, 194, 278. *See also*
    Industry
Cluster (urban form), 6–7, 36, 72
Cofitachiqui, 16
College of William and Mary, 22, 58
Colonial towns
  and American Revolution, 70–72
  economics and, 27
  European influence on, 11
  evolution of, 11
  government in, 24
Colonial trading patterns, 42 (illus.). *See also*
    Trade
Colosimo, "Big Jim," 317
Columbia, Maryland, 437
Columbia Broadcasting System, 316
Columbian Exposition, 274–275
Columbus, Ohio, 380
Commerce
  in colonial world, 22, 38–46
  conditions for, 86
  and housing, 133
  and quarantine, 156
  and street cleaning, 154–155
  see also Business; Trade
Commerce, Georgia, 267
Commercial Club of Chicago, 276

Commission on Industrial Relations, 200
Commission for a National Agenda for the
    Eighties, 392
Commons, John R., 199
Communications, *see* Technology
Community Action Agency (CAA), 364, 366
Community Action Program, 364
Community Development Block Grant
    (CDBG), 389, 391, 392
Connecticut, 339. *See also individual cities*
Connolly, Richard "Slippery Dick," 243
Connor, Eugene "Bull," 361, 395
Constitution, U. S., 73
"Conurbations," defined, 437
Cook, Fields, 141
Cook, Fields, Jr., 141
Cook, Mary, 141
Copland, Aaron, 336
Corn trade, 24
Corporate economy, *see* Economy
Cotton trade, 99, 102, 104–109
Coughlin, "Bathhouse John," 238–239
Council for Urban Economic Development,
    429
Councils of Government (COGs), 365
County courthouse towns, 24
Coxe, Sally, 51
Crafts and craftsmen, *see* Artisans
Crane, Stephen, 196, 250
Crevecoeur, Hector de, 439, 440
Crime, *see* Social problems
Croker, Richard "Boss," 239
Crosby, Bing, 312
Crump, Edward H., 242
Cruz, Julio, 428
Cuba, 401
Cultural institutions, 286
Cultural life, in colonial America, 56–60
Cultural transmission, in Indian settlements,
    16–17
Culture, mass, 310–312, 347. *See also*
    Entertainment
Cutler, Timothy, 54

Daley, Richard J., 364, 432
Dallas, 395–396, 398, 436
    and annexation, 405
    black elected officials in, 431
    public works in, 335
Dallas-Fort Worth, 394
Danville, Virginia, 328
Davenport, Iowa, 99
Davis, Alexander Jackson, 126
Defender, 224, 230
De Lancey, Margaret Lawrence, 51
Delano, Frederic A., 303, 304
Delaware, 413
Delaware River, 29, 39
Deleston, Doris, 428

Democratic Party, 110, 137, 144, 326, 363
Dempsey, Jack, 316
Denver, 84, 180, 356, 414
    crime in, 158
    during Great Depression, 325
    homeless in, 426–427
    Larimer Square, 417
    mass transit in, 423
    "Metro Denver Network," 442
    town lot speculation in, 83
Department stores, 144, 266
    in 1850s, 115
    as entrée into middle-class world, 117
    in radial center (urban form), 270–271
    see also Trade
Depression, Great, *see* Great Depression
Detroit, 19, 362, 392, 406, 407
    blacks in, 339, 431, 433
    crime in, 381
    and federal financing of services, 434
    during Great Depression, 326
    immigrants in, 212–213, 310
    industry in, 186, 292–293, 336
    population in, 380
    and residential segregation, 226
    school busing in, 384
    violence in, 159, 339
Dickens, Charles, 5
Dinwiddy, Emily, 212, 252
Disease, *see* Social problems
Dodge City, Kansas, 267
Dorchester, Massachusetts, 120
Dos Passos, John, 338
Downing, Andrew Jackson, 128, 131,
    168–169
Downtown
    as city center, 113–118
    as economic center, 113–118
    and multicentered metropolis, 375–376,
        439
Drayton, William Henry, 70
Dreiser, Theodore, 179, 198
Drunkenness, *see* Social problems
Du Bois, W.E.B., 233, 315, 359
Dubuque, Iowa, 99
Duke University, 397
Dun and Company, 137
Durgin, Samuel H., 245
Durham, North Carolina, 397
Dutch West India Company, 45

Ebenezer, South Carolina, 32
Economy
    and advantages in Northeast, 86–87
    in colonial towns, 27
    corporate, 285–286, 299–300, 376
    development of national urban economy,
        78
    "downtown" as economic center, 113–118

Economy (*cont.*)
　and federal government, 109 (*see also*
　　Government, federal)
　during Great Depression, 323–327
　service-oriented, 245, 376, 411
　urbanization and specialization in, 114
　and World War II, 337
　see also Business; Commerce; Industry;
　　Trade; Wealth
Education
　in colonial America, 58
　and environmental reform, 257
　G.I. Bill and, 343
　among immigrants, 215–216
　Project Headstart, 364
　public, 257–258, 309, 383–384
　urban universities, 442
Eisenhower, Dwight, administration of, 350,
　356
El Paso, Texas, 396, 401
Electricity, *see* Technology
Eliot, William G., Jr., 128
Elizabeth I, 14
Ellsworth, Kansas, 267
Emerson, Ralph Waldo, 129, 172
Employment, *see* Labor
England
　architecture in, 46
　charities in, 254
　colonial settlements of, 20–25
　and directives regarding towns, 21–22
　garden cities in, 280, 304
　merchants in, 38
　and model of municipal incorporation, 63
　planning in, contrasted with U.S., 340–
　　341
　trade with, 55, 106
English mercantile law, 42–43
English mercantile system, 40
Entertainment
　jazz, 312
　motion picture industry, 312, 335–336
　recording industry, 312
　sports, 436
　television, 347
　vaudeville, 310–312
Environment
　and industrial development, 39, 190–191
　in Pittsburgh, clean-up efforts, 349
　and poverty, 249–252, 254
　and regional planning, 443
　and social problems, 331
　in Sunbelt cities, 404
　and urban planning, 129–130
Equal Employment Opportunity
　Commission (EEOC), 364
Erie Canal, 103
Europe, trade with, 44

Fairfield, Alabama, 347
Falmouth, Massachusetts, 24
Family, in colonial America, 53–54
Federal Emergency Housing Corporation
　(FEHC), 330
Federal Housing Administration (FHA),
　327, 330, 343, 345, 372
Federal Road Acts of 1916 and 1921, 292
Film industry, 312, 335–336
Fire(s)
　in Boston, 65–67
　in Charleston, 65
　in New York, 67
　in Philadelphia, 67
Fish trade, 42
Fisher, Shelton, 415
Fisher, Sidney George, 127–128
Fitzgerald, F. Scott, 292, 345
Five Points, New York City, 162 (illus.)
Flint, Michigan, 418
Florida, 394, 402, 404, 437
　illegal drugs in, 407
　population growth in, 398
　see also individual cities
Ford, Gerald, administration of, 392
Ford, Henry, 292, 295, 297
Ford Motor Company, 292
Forest Hills Garden, Queens, New York,
　280–281
Forsyth, John, 110
Fort Duquesne, 19
Fort Lauderdale, Florida, 425
Fort Myers, Florida, 398
Fort Worth, Texas, 394, 396, 436
Fortune magazine, 352, 381
Foster, George G., 144
Francises, The (Philadelphia family), 50–51
Franklin, Benjamin, 39, 54, 58, 59, 60, 66
Franklin Institute, The, 94
Frederick, Hugh, 407
Freed, Allan, 358
French settlements, 18–20
"Frostbelt," 375, 379–380, 398
Fullerton, California, 438
Fur trade, 40–41, 44, 62

Galbraith, John Kenneth, 358
Gallup Poll (1986), 422
Gans, Herbert, 359
Gantt, Harvey, 431
Garden cities, 279–280, 304, 437
Garden Grove, California, 437
Garment industry, 186, 194, 278
Garvey, Marcus, 315
Gary, Elbert, 189
Gary, Indiana, 189, 296, 324
Gaston County, North Carolina, 187
Gentrification, 420–421

Geographic mobility
 in American society, 439
 of colonial population, 49
 in urban America, 258–259
 and women, in eighteenth century, 52
 during World War II, 336
Georgia, 32. *See also individual cities*
Georgia Central Railroad, 105
German immigrants, 32, 43, 215
Germantown, Pennsylvania, 39
Gershwin, George, 313, 320
Ghetto, *see* Blacks; Housing; Immigrants;
 Social problems
Gibson, Kenneth, 432
Gitlow, Benjamin, 200
Glasgow, Ellen, 297
Gloucester, Massachusetts, 27
Goldfield, Abraham, 331
Gompers, Samuel, 205
Gooch, William, 23
Goodyear, Charles, 90
Goodyear Company, The, 191
Goose Creek, Texas, 328
Gordon, Waxey, 317
Government, colonial, 11, 23, 26–28, 62–75
Government, federal
 and housing, 428–429,
 and immigration, 400–401
 and national economy, 109
 and "new federalism," 434–435
 Office of Economic Opportunity, 360
 relief efforts by, 326–334, 340
 and rise of Sunbelt, 396
 and urban development, 286, 323, 417
 and urban policy, 9, 365–366, 377, 388–
 393, 416, 444–445
Government, local, 63
 administrative structure of, 152
 and aid to poor, 157, 161, 164, 324
 business orientation of, 429–430
 and city-county consolidation, 371, 442
 city management form, 429
 and economic development, 62, 151, 377,
 429–430
 and public health, 155, 156–157
 and public services, 154–155, 157, 237
 and set-aside programs, 432–433
 and social reform, 151, 429–430
 and social services, 324–325
 and triage approach to neighborhood
 redevelopment, 390
 voting and, 69
 wealthy in leadership positions in, 69
Government, state
 and "new federalism," 434
 relief efforts, during Depression, 325
Graham, Martha, 357
Gramm, Phil, 434

Grange, Red, 316
"Great Awakening," 34–35. *See also* Religion
Great Depression, 323–327, 335, 342
Greenbelt, Maryland, 334
"Greenbelt" towns, 302, 334
Greendale, Wisconsin, 334
Greenhills, Ohio, 334
Greensboro, North Carolina, 190, 268
Green-Wood Cemetery, 168
Gregg, William, 110
Gridiron pattern
 in *bastide* towns of southern France, 19
 monotony of, 85
 in New Orleans, 20
 in New York, 28–30
 in Philadelphia, 28–30, 84–86
 as predominant urban form in West, 84–86
 in Richmond, 23
 in Savannah, 34
 in streetcar suburbs, 262
Griffith, David W., 228, 232
Griscom, John C., 153, 155, 157, 161
Grogan, Paul, 421–422
Gunston Hall, 25

Habitat for Humanity, 428
Hamilton, Elizabeth Lawrence, 50
Hamilton, James, 50
Hampton, Lionel, 313
Hancock, Thomas, 44, 50
Harlem, 227
 Hispanics in, 382 (illus.)
 and omnibus, 120
 violence in, 339, 360, 425
Harlem Renaissance, 313–315
Harmony Grove, Georgia, 267
Harper's, 410, 424
Harper's Monthly, 119
Harper's New Monthly Magazine, 275
Harper's Weekly, 240–241
Harrigan, John J., 430, 443
Harrington, Michael, 363
Harris, Lillian, 233
Harrisburg, Pennsylvania, 429
Harrison, Peter, 46
Hartsfield, William B., 335
Harvard, John, 58
Harvard University, 58, 88, 146
Haskell, Llewellyn, 125–127
Haussmann, Baron, 171
Haymarket Square, 206
Henretta, James, 48, 50
Henry, O., 196–197, 198
Hershberg, Ted, 442
Hightown, New Jersey, 415
Highways, *see* Transportation
Hill, Norman, 358–359, 360
Hine, Louis, 300

Hinterlands
  and central place theory, 3
  and developing urban South, 107
  and rural-urban relationship, 109
  and trade, 72 (*see also* Trade)
Hispanics, *see* Immigrants
Hoboken, New Jersey, 347
Hodges, Luther, 397
Hofheinz, Fred, 396
Holme, Thomas, 29
Holyoke, Massachusetts, 90
Home Insurance Company, 273
Home Owners Loan Corporation (HOLC),
  329–330
Hood, Mary, 441
Hoover, Herbert, 291, 316, 326
Hopper, Edward, 335
Horowitz, Louis J., 274
Hotels, 272
House of Burgesses, 23–24
Housing
  and building codes, 252
  Charlotte Gardens, South Bronx, 428
  "dumbbell" tenement, 249, 250 (illus.)
  and Eisenhower administration, 350
  federal housing acts, 328, 333, 349–350
  Federal Housing Administration (FHA),
    327, 333
  and gentrification, 420–421
  ghetto, 226, 232
  Habitat for Humanity, 428
  Indian dwellings, 13–18
  and need for comprehensive program,
    427–429
  New York Tenement House Law of 1901,
    251
  policy in colonial towns, 68
  and poor, 51–52, 161, 248–253, 383
  public, 331–332, 350, 351–354, 428
  and Reagan administration, 434
  "redlining," 330
  reform, 134
  and restrictive legislation, 251–252
  settlement houses, 255–257
  shortages in, 53, 132–134
  single-family home, 290–291, 439
  slum, 134, 203–204
  for workers in defense plants, 340
Housing and Community Development Act,
  416
Housing and Urban Development (HUD),
  Department of, 365, 372, 389, 392,
  421, 434
Housing industry, 345
Houston, Texas, 339, 369, 398, 404
  and annexation, 405
  crime in, 158
  and discrimination in relief allocations, 325
  federal financing in, 434

  retail trade in, 419
  unemployment in, 324
Howard, Ebenezer, 279–280, 304
Howe, Frederic C., 240, 287
Hull House, 255–256
Huntsville, Alabama, 426
Huxtable, Ada Louise, 441

Illinois, 19. *See also individual cities*
Immigrants
  Asian, 278, 401–402
  Chinese, 278
  and concentration in cities, 5, 134–137
  covenants against, 299
  Czech, 213
  discrimination against, 136–137, 299
  and education, 215
  German, 69, 135–137, 210–211
  in ghettos, 212–214
  Greek, 218
  Hispanic, 367, 381–382, 400–404, 431
  and industrial expansion, 207–208
  Irish, 89, 135–137, 146, 218
  Italian, 210–212, 214, 217–218, 255, 320
  Japanese, 218, 220–221, 401
  Jewish, 211, 215, 216
  Mexican, 310
  and movement to suburbs, 263
  nativism movement and, 136–137
  occupational preferences of, 217–218
  Polish, 211, 212, 218
  and politics, 401–405
  Russian, 213, 214
  Scotch-Irish, 69
  and settlement houses, 255–257
  as social problem, 240, 242
  in Sunbelt, 400
  urban settlements of, 212–214
Indentured servants, 48
Indian villages
  and influence on colonial towns, 11
  and influence on Spanish settlements,
    18–19
  spatial organization of, 14, 15 (illus.)
Indianapolis, Indiana, 206, 278, 371
Indians
  and agriculture, 13–16
  codes against, 68
  dwellings of, 13–18
  as first urban dwellers, 13
  and influence on colonial settlements, 17
  patterns of migration of, 14–16
  patterns of settlement of, 16–17
  and trade, 42, 44
Indigo trade, 72
Industrial Revolution, 87–88, 187
Industry
  and the artisan, 143, 191 (*see also* Artisans)
  automobile, 294 (*see also* Transportation)

clothing, 186, 194
decentralization of, 336–337, 385
development of, in early U.S., 46, 86, 87–
  90
meat, 187–188
shipbuilding, 46
steel, 186, 189, 190, 297, 349
in suburbs, 385
textile, 87–89, 90, 187, 407
and transportation technology, 86
and working conditions, 91–93
  see also Business; Commerce; Labor; Trade
Internal Revenue Service, 330
International Harvester Company, 193
Irvine, California, 437
Irving, Texas, 436
Isaacs, Rhys, 70
Izard, Ralph, 51
Izard, Susannah De Lancey, 51

Jackson, Andrew, 159
Jackson, Maynard, 404, 433
Jackson Square, New Orleans, 20
Jacksonville, Florida, 339, 371, 442
Jacobs, Jane, 359
James, Sharpe, 413, 424
Jamestown, Virginia, 14, 20–25
Jefferson, Thomas, 49, 59
Jenney, William L., 273
Jews, 211, 213, 214, 320–321
  in colonial America, 54
  and education, 215–216
  and Jewish Center, 320
  and social class, 146
Job Corps, 364
Johnson, Lyndon B., 360, 363
  administration of, 364, 366–367
Johnson, Tom L., 248
Jolson, Al, 311, 319
Jones, George, 242
Jones, Rev. Hugh, 21
Jones, Samuel "Golden Rule," 248
Josselyn, John, 16
Joyce, James, 376

Kansas, 83, 266–267
Kansas City, 238, 297, 351, 380, 423
Kaskaskia, 19
Keaton, Buster, 312
Keith, Sir William, 69
Keithians, 69
Kenna, Michael "Hinky Dink," 238–239,
  242
Kentucky, 84
Keokuk, Iowa, 99
Kerner Commission, 360
Kerner, Otto, 360
Kerouac, Jack, 358
Keystone Cops, 312, 317

King, Martin Luther, Jr., 360
Kingsland, Ambrose, 155
Knights of Labor, 205
Know Nothings, 137
"Knowledge functions," 376, 411
Kreisler, Fritz, 309
Ku Klux Klan, 228, 404
Kucinich, Dennis, 388

Labor
  and apprenticeship, 91
  black, 139, 141, 224, 225, 230–231, 339–
    340, 363–364, 382
  child, 92–93, 194–196, 258
  in colonial towns, 48–49, 52–53
  family, 195
  and Great Depression, 323–327
  immigrant, 92–93, 108, 118, 136, 217–
    218, 220
  in industrial cities, 133, 191
  protective legislation and, 199
  and proximity to work, 118–119, 190
  in service economy, 426
  shortage of, 48, 108
  strikes, 189
  in Sunbelt, 398–400, 406
  and wages and hours, 192
  and women, 88–89, 92–93, 118, 196–
    200, 426
  and working conditions, 91–93, 153, 192–
    196, 204
  Works Progress Administration (WPA),
    327–328, 329 (illus.)
  after World War II, 342
  see also Artisans; Business; Commerce;
    Economy; Industry
Lafayette Restaurant, New York City, 415
La Guardia, Fiorello, 335
Lake Forest, Illinois, 289, 319
Lancaster, Pennsylvania, 32
Lancaster, South Carolina, 32
Land
  abundance of, as influence on
    development, 11, 17–18, 21, 33, 73–74,
    124
  and development of colonial settlements,
    11, 17–18, 21, 26–27, 29
  division, 28
  grants, 19, 33
  and growth of suburbs, 124
  ownership, 48–49
  use, in Philadelphia, 39
  see also Housing; Suburb(s); Spatial
    organization; Urban planning; Urban
    renewal; Urbanization/urban growth
Larchmont, New York, 347
La Rocca, Nick, 312
Las Colinas, Texas, 436, 440
Latrobe, Ferdinand C., 244

Laurel Hill Cemetery, 168
Laurens, Henry, 50, 70
Lawrence, Andrew, 51
Lawrence, David, 349
Lawrence, John, 50, 51
Lawrence, Mary Johnston, 51
Laws and legislation
    and civil rights, 228, 232, 360, 431
    and community facilities, 340
    economic, 326, 340
    enforcement of, 67–68, 157–160
    and highways, 292, 356
    and housing, 251, 340, 416
    mercantile, 42–43
    and rivers and harbors, 109
Le Corbusier, 352
L'Enfant, Pierre, 22, 276–277
Letchworth, England, 280, 304
Levinsky, David, 217, 233
Levitt, Abraham, 343
Levitt, William J., 343–344
Levittown, New Jersey, 343–346
Lewis, Sinclair, 294, 319
Lima, Peru, 35
Lincoln, Abraham, 110
Lind, Jenny, 110
Lindsay, John, 386
Literary Digest, 295
Little Rock, Arkansas, 325, 361, 369
Liverpool, England, 55, 106
Llewellyn Park, New Jersey, 125–127, 131
Lloyd, Harold, 312
Locke, Alain, 315
Logue, Edward, 350
Lomasny, Martin, 237
London, England, 11, 46, 254, 38
London Town, Maryland, 41
Long Beach, California, 437–448
Long Island State Park Commission, 305
Lorentz, Pare, 336
Los Angeles, California, 180, 267, 369, 398,
        407, 436
    blacks in, 431
    commuting in, 437–438
    as corporate center, 299
    environmental problems in, 404
    federal financing in, 434
    geographical expansion of, 437
    immigrants in, 218, 221, 401, 402 (illus.)
    industry in, 296, 336
    and LA 2000 group, 442
    as multicentered metropolis, 445
    as suburban city, 306–309, 321
Louisiana, 20, 293
Louisville, Kentucky, 83, 84, 99, 41
    mob violence in, 158
    and population growth, in 1800s, 97
Lowell, Francis Cabot, 88
Lowell, Massachusetts, 88–90, 97

Lubove, Roy, 1, 281
Lumber trade, 42
Lundin, "Swede," 319
Lynchburg, Virginia, 328

Mackaye, Benton, 302
McCoy, Bill, 442
McGraw-Hill Publishing Company, 415
McKay, Claude, 313
McLaren, John, 245
McMillan, James, 276
McMurtry, Larry, 407
Mabila, 16
Madison, James, 73
Maine, 16
"Mall towns," 436–437
Marblehead, Massachusetts, 27
Marietta, Georgia, 337
Market place (urban form), 7, 36, 72, 77–80
Marshall Plan, 381
Martha Washington Societies, 163
Martinsville, West Virginia, 206
Marsh, Reginald, 335
Martinez, Bob, 429
Marx Brothers, 312
Maryland, 413. *See also individual cities*
Mason, George, 25
Masotti, Louis H., 421
Massachusetts Bay, 16, 26
Massachusetts Bureau of the Statistics of
        Labor, 192
Mather, Cotton, 51
Mellon, Richard King, 349
Memphis, Tennessee, 99, 259, 298, 390, 406
    and jazz, 312, 313
    public housing in, 428
Merchants
    in Charleston, 32
    in colonial period, 7, 41–46, 48
    and department stores, 419
    lifestyle of, in colonial America, 46
    in New Haven, 40–41
    in Philadelphia, 44
Merchants Association of San Francisco, 290
Metropolitan Life Insurance Company, 181
Mexicans, 325, 340
Mexico, 401
Mexico City, 35
Miami, Florida, 293, 339, 407, 437
    city-county government in, 370–371, 442
    Cubans in, 402–403
    Hispanics in, 401, 402
    rail system in, 423
    riots in, 424
Middlesex County, Virginia, 23
Mifflin, Thomas, 51
Milwaukee, Wisconsin, 136, 185, 207
Minneapolis, Minnesota, 381
    center-city housing in, 423

city-county government in, 442
retail trade in, 355
Minneapolis-St. Paul, 371
Missions, 18
Mississippi, 293, 397
Mitchell, Thomas, 298
Mobile, Alabama, 20, 108, 337, 338, 408
Mobile Register, 110
Model Cities program, 365, 366, 389, 390
Modesto, California, 278
Molasses trade, 42–44
Monkkonen, Eric, 183
Montgomery, Alabama, 361, 395
Montreal, Canada, 19
Morial, Ernest N. ("Dutch"), 431
Morrisson, de Lesseps, 348
Moses, Robert, 245, 305, 328, 336, 352
Moskowitz, Henry, 232
Motor Magazine, 295
Mount Auburn Cemetery, 166–168
Moynihan, Daniel Patrick, 363–364, 382
Multicentered metropolis (urban form), 8–9,
   375, 411–412, 444
Multicentered urban chain, 436
Mumford, Lewis, 302, 304–306, 326, 333,
   334, 336, 345, 437, 440, 443, 444
Municipal Affairs (1897), 247
Municipal Art Society of New York, 275
Municipal corporations, 63
Municipal ordinances, 68
Municipal Review, The (1911), 247

Naftalin, Arthur, 381
Nashua, New Hampshire, 413
Nashville, Tennessee, 268, 297, 316, 337,
   394
   city-county government in, 371
   gridiron pattern in, 85
Nashville Coffee and Manufacturing
   Company, 268
Nast, Thomas, 240–241
Natchez, Mississippi, 99, 173
National Aeronautics and Space
   Administration (NASA), 339
National Association for the Advancement of
   Colored People (NAACP), 231–232,
   256
National Broadcasting Company (NBC), 316
National Housing Association, 252
National League of Improvement
   Associations, 275
National Municipal League, 247
National Resources Planning Board (NRPB),
   332, 340
National Urban League, 231
Nativism, 136–137
Native Americans, *see* Indians
Nature of man, views on, in 1700s, 63–64

Naugatuck, Massachusetts, 90
Negro Convention Movement, 140
Neighborhood Guild, 255
New Amsterdam, 28. *See also* New York City
"New Athens," 82
New Brunswick, New Jersey, 440
New Deal, 320, 327–336
New England (early)
   blacks in, 68
   church in, 25–28
   commerce and industry in, 46, 87–90
   culture in, 56–60
   family in, 53–54
   first settlements in, 25–28
New Haven, Connecticut, 40, 254, 391
New Jersey, 63, 302, 303, 413
New Mexico, 16, 19
New Orleans, 20, 406, 407, 408, 427
   blacks in, 431
   character of, 173
   and effect of railroads on trade, in 1800s,
      101–102
   as export center, 99
   French Market, 417
   during Great Depression, 325
   historic preservation in, 416–417
   jazz in, 312, 313
   police in, 160
   after World War II, 348
   yellow fever in, 152, 154
New Republic, 302, 324
"New towns," 437
New York Bureau of Municipal Research,
   247
New York City, 354, 383, 391, 397, 406,
   412, 413
   during American Revolution, 71, 72, 73,
      77
   and central position in national economy,
      102–104
   character of, 113, 173, 357
   cholera epidemic in, 153, 156
   clothing industry in, 186
   in colonial America, 35, 38, 56, 60
   and corporate economy, 299, 385–387,
      415–416
   cultural life in, 56, 60, 311, 313–316, 358
   disease control in, 67
   and entertainment, 311, 313–316, 414,
      415
   first settlements, 28–29
   gentrification in, 421
   geographical expansion of, 437
   ghettos in, 226
   government in, 62–63
   Harlem, 120, 227, 313, 315, 339, 360,
      382, 425
   homeless in, 427
   and housing, 251, 368

New York City (*cont.*)
    immigrants in, 210, 400, 401 (*see also*
       Immigrants)
    Lincoln Center, 423
    Long Island Expressway, 356
    manufacturing in, 94
    park design in, 168–171
    police in, 160
    politics in, 320–321
    population in, 11, 91, 180, 304
    poverty in, 164, 201, 254, 367, 427
    redevelopment in, 355
    regional planning in, 440
    skyscrapers in, 300–301
    slowing of suburban exodus in, 422
    social structure in, 146
    South Street (1828), 103 (illus.)
    taverns in, 55
    and trade, 43, 87, 99, 106
    "Tweed Ring" scandals in, 240
    "two cities" concept, 427 (illus.)
    union rally in, 110
    and urban-industrial core, 180
    violence in, 158, 369, 424, 425
    Wall Street, 28
    wealthy in, 143–144
    zoning in, 278
New York Post, 168
New York Society Library, 58
New York State, 386–387. *See also individual
    cities*
New York Tenement House Law of 1901,
    251
New York Times, 91, 115, 220, 242, 272,
    358, 395, 396, 410, 412, 436
New York Tribune, 91, 127
New York World's Fair, 336
New York Yankees, 315–316
Newark, New Jersey, 362, 406, 410
    Gateway Center, 424
    recovery of, in 1980s, 412–413
    set-aside programs in, 432
    social and educational problems in, 424
Newburyport, Massachusetts, 49
Newport, Rhode Island, 35, 38, 46, 58
Nichols, J.C., 297
Nixon, Richard, 365
    administration of, 388–389, 392, 393, 398
Nolen, John C., 278, 279, 298
Norfolk Association for the Improvement of
    the Condition of the Poor, 164
Norfolk, Virginia, 23–24, 72–73, 337, 338,
    406
    during American Revolution, 77
    and discrimination in relief allocations, 325
    Dismal Swamp Canal, 109
    redevelopment efforts in, 350–351
    yellow fever in, 152

North Carolina, 14, 224, 257, 397
North Carolina State University, 397
North Dakota, 413
Norton, Charles Dyer, 303, 304

Oakland, California, 290
O'Banion, Dion, 319
Ocala, Florida, 398
Office of Management and Budget (OMB),
    365
Ogden, William B., 100
Oglethorpe, James, 32–34, 166
O'Keeffe, Georgia, 300
Oklahoma, 266–267
Olmsted, Frederick Law, 124–127, 129, 131,
    169–171, 175, 276
Olmsted, John, 129
Omaha, Nebraska, 212–213, 227, 259
Omnibus, 119, 120
Omnibus Budget Reconciliation Act
    (OBRA), 434
Orangeburg, South Carolina, 32
Osofsky, Gilbert, 228
Otis, James, 70
"Out-towns," 376, 436, 438 (illus.), 442
Ovington, Mary White, 231–232

Palmer, Charles F., 331
Panama City, Florida, 339
Panic of 1837, 83
Paris Health Council, 153
Park Forest, Illinois, 345–346
Park, Robert E., 4, 231
Parks, 29, 166, 168–171, 305
Pascagoula, Mississippi, 337, 338
Patterson, Orlando, 368
Pawtucket, Rhode Island, 87
Payton, Philip A., Jr., 227
Peirce, Neal, 418, 422
Pelzer, North Carolina, 407
Pendergast, James and Tom, 238
Penn, Ann Allen Lawrence, 51
Penn, John, 51
Penn, William, 29, 33, 35, 38–39, 43, 74,
    84–85
Pennsylvania, 63, 101. *See also individual
    cities*
Pennsylvania Gazette, 60
Pensacola, Florida, 437
Perry, Clarence, 303, 326
Petersburg, Virginia, 432
Peterson, James, 429
Philadelphia, 96, 407
    during American Revolution, 35, 71,
       72–73, 77
    architecture in, 132
    artisans in, 91
    black elected officials in, 431

character of, 173
charity groups in, 254
coffeehouses and taverns in, 55
Committee for Unemployment Relief, 324
as corporate center, 416
cultural life in, 58, 60
disease control in, 67
expansion in (1854), 147
federal tax credits in, 435
first settlement, 28–30
during Great Depression, 324
Irish communities in, 217
manufacturing in, 90, 94
Market Street, 39
merchants in, 121 (illus.), 122
as model for western cities, 84–86
and municipal incorporation, 63
pattern of development in, 33, 39
police in, 160
population in, 11, 35
Populist Party in, 69
as publishing center, 56, 58
Reading Terminal Market, 4
and regional study group, 442
tenement housing in, 252, 253 (illus.)
trade in, 38–39, 43, 87
violence in, 158, 159
wealth in, during colonial period, 49
yellow fever in, 152
Phoenix, Arizona, 337, 391, 398, 404, 408
Physicians, in colonial America, 48, 59
Pingree, Hazen, 248
Pitts, Thomas H., 297
Pittsburgh, Pennsylvania, 351, 354, 380,
     387, 410
   described, in 1880s, 185, 190–191
   first settlement, 19, 83
   gentrification in, 420
   immigrants in, 218
   Philadelphia plan as model for, 85
   railstrike in, 206
   recovery of, in 1980s, 412–413
   return of electric trolley in, 423
   workers in, 192
   after World War II, 349
Place d'Armes, 20
Plan of New Orleans, 20
Plan of Philadelphia, 30 (illus.)
Plan of Savannah, 33, 34 (illus.)
Plan of Washington, D.C., 277 (illus.)
Plunkitt, George Washington, 239
Poe, Edgar Allan, 113
Polish immigrants, *see* Immigrants
Politics
   in England and America, contrasted, 68
   and parties and factions, 69 (*see also*
     individual parties)
   and political machines, 237–243

progressivism, 240
   in radial center, 236–237
   and reform efforts, 247–248
Pollock, Johnson, 357
Pontiac, Michigan, 436
Population
   change in urban areas, 285
   growth, 36 (table), 179–180, 376, 447–
     452 (tables)
   immigrant migrations and, 208
   reversal of decline in central cities, 413
   of suburbs, after World War II, 345
   of U.S. cities, in 1890, 209 (table)
   see also Urbanization/urban growth
Populist Party, 69
Porter, Michael, 418
Portland, Oregon, 423
Portman, John, 351
Portsmouth, New Hampshire, 49
Portugal, 42–43
Poverty
   attitudes toward, 161
   race and class division and, 5
   in Sunbelt, 406
   see also Social problems
Powderly, Terence V., 205
Powhatan, 14
"Praying towns," 16
Presidios, 18
Princeton, New Jersey, 440
Prisons, in eighteenth-century America,
     51–52
Prohibition, 316–317. *See also* Social
     problems
Project Headstart, 364
Prospect Park, 171
Protestantism
   and anti-Catholicism, 158–160
   in colonial America, 54–55
   and social class, 146
   see also Religion
Providence, Rhode Island, 97
Pruitt-Igoe public housing complex, 352–
     353
Public health, 152–157
Public housing developments, 353, 362
Public services
   data on, 246–247
   and local government, 62 (*see also*
     Government)
   in market place (urban form), 79
   and new technology, 244–245
Public Works Administration (PWA), 327
Pueblos, 16, 18
Pullman, Florence, 231
Pullman, George, 189
Pullman, Illinois, 189 (illus.), 205, 296, 347
Puritans, 25, 64, 84

Quakers, 29, 43–44
Quebec, Canada, 19

Radburn, New Jersey, 302, 334
Radial center (urban form), 7–8, 182
Radio Corporation of America (RCA), 300
Railroads
    Baltimore and Ohio, 97, 107
    Boston and Lowell, 136
    Chicago, Burlington and Quincy, 125
    corporate management and, 101
    effect on western urbanization, 100–101
    Penn Station, 271–272
    Pennsylvania, 107, 261, 271
    Southern, 181
    Southern Pacific, 307
    strikes, 205–206
    Union Pacific, 207
    and urban South, 104–105, 267
    westward extension of, 267
Raleigh, North Carolina, 397
Raleigh, Sir Walter, 14
Raleigh-Durham, 394
Ramsey, David, 172
Reagan, Ronald, 433
    administration of, 391, 411, 434–435
Reconstruction Finance Corporation (RFC),
    326
Reed, Stephen, 429
Reform movements, *see* Social reform
Regional Plan of New York (1929), 303–
    306, 333
Regional Planning Association of America
    (RPAA), 302–306, 334
Religion
    blacks and, 140, 232
    in colonial America, 18, 23, 25–28, 54–56
    immigrants and, 213–214 (*see also*
        Immigrants)
    Indians and, 16
    Mormons and, 84
    and nativist violence, 137
    Puritans and, 25, 64, 84
    and role of home in Christian morality,
        128
    and social class, 145–146
    and temperance movement, 163
    and urban reform, 172
    see also Catholicism; Protestantism; Jews
Republican Party, 110, 228, 326
Resettlement Administration (RA), 333, 334
Reston, Virginia, 437
Revenue sharing, 389. *See also* Taxation
Reynall, John, 43, 44
Rice planters, 30–32
Rice trade, 42, 45, 72–73
Richmond, Virginia, 23, 259, 328
    festival marketplace in, 418
    gentrification in, 421

immigrants in, 108, 136
life in, during 1860s, 110–111
set-aside programs in, 432–433
trolley in, 263
Riesman, David, 345
Riis, Jacob A., 195, 201–204 *passim,* 240,
    256–258 *passim*
Riordan, William L., 239
Rivers and Harbors Act (1826), 109
Riverside, Illinois, 125, 126 (illus.), 169
Roanoke Island, 14
Roanoke, Virginia, 267
Robb, James, 110
Rochester, New York, 221
Rockefeller, John D., 300
Rockne, Knute, 316
Rolling Stone magazine, 401
Roosevelt, Franklin D., 320, 323, 326–327,
    393
Roosevelt, Theodore, 239, 268
Rosenwald, Julius, 136, 231
Rossiter, Clinton, 74
Rothstein, Arnold, 317
Rouse, James, 437
Roxbury, Massachusetts, 39, 120, 350
Rum trade, 42–43, 72
Russell Sage Foundation, 280, 303
Russell, William and Ella Gibson, 260–261
"Rustbelt," 387
Ruth, Babe, 316, 319

St. Augustine, Florida, 18
Saint Domingue, 20
St. Louis, 16, 83, 99, 109, 415
    autos in, 293 (illus.)
    blacks in, 363
    cholera epidemic in, 152
    deterioration of downtown in, 369
    federal financing in, 434
    French settlement in, 19
    immigrants in, 400
    jazz in, 312
    Laclede Landing, 417
    as modeled after New Orleans, 85
    police in, 160
    population growth, in 1800s, 97–98
    population loss in, 380
    property tax in, 417–418
    Pruitt-Igoe public housing complex, 352–
        353
    and steamboat trade, 100
    Union Station transformation, 417
St. Louis Cathedral, New Orleans, 20
St. Paul, Minnesota, 430–431
Sainte Genevíéve, 19
Salem, North Carolina, 32
Salina, New York, 96
Salt Lake City, Utah, 84
Salt trade, 44

San Antonio, Texas, 310, 401, 402, 404
San Diego, California, 293, 398, 404, 423, 437
San Francisco, 180, 358, 415, 437
  annexation in, 290, 405
  Bay Area Rapid Transit (BART), 423
  character of, 173
  crime in, 158
  gridiron pattern in, 85
  immigrants in, 146, 400
  industry in, 336, 413, 436
  land use in, 83, 147
  population growth in, 147, 259
  Silicon Valley, 336, 436
  urban renewal in, 351
Santa Ana, California, 437
Santa Elena, 18
Santa Fe, New Mexico, 16, 18, 19, 33
Saturday Review, 410
Savannah, Georgia, 30, 32–35, 38, 72
  civility in, 173
  and cotton trade, 105
  historic preservation in, 416
  Landmark Rehabilitation Project, 419–420
  parks in, 166
  plan of, 33–35
  and railroad building, 101
  revival meetings in, 54
  taverns in, 55
  Victorian District, 419–420
Saxe Gotha, South Carolina, 32
Schaefer, Don, 420
Schlesinger, Arthur M., Sr., 179
Schuylkill River, 29
Scotch-Irish immigrants, 32, 43. *See also* Immigrants
Scottsdale, Arizona, 391
Sears, Roebuck and Company, 136, 231
Seattle, Washington
  "Hooverville" in, 327 (illus.)
  Pike Place Market, 419
Secoton, 14, 15 (illus.)
Selma, Alabama, 361
Segregation
  occupational and residential, 225–228
  racial and class, 347
  see also Blacks; Housing; Social problems; Spatial organization; Suburb(s)
Sellers, Melody, 428
Sennett, Mack, 312
Sephardic Jewish synagogue, Newport, 46
Settlement houses, 231, 255–257. *See also* Housing; Social reform
Seven Years War, 70
Shahn, Ben, 335
Shaker Heights, Ohio, 347
Shipbuilding, 44
Shippers, The (Philadelphia family), 50
Short Hills, New Jersey, 260, 261

Shreveport, Louisiana, 407
Siebels, George, 395
Siemens, William, 186
Sigmund, Barbara Boggs, 440
Simon, Robert E., 437
Sinclair, Upton, 187–188, 193, 195, 202, 208
Skokie, Illinois, 390
"Skunksburgh," 83
Skyscrapers, 300, 301, 352
Slater, Samuel, 87
Slavery and slave trade, 42, 45, 48–49
  in Charleston, South Carolina, 52, 64, 68
  codes, 68
  in Savannah, Georgia, 33
  in urban South, in 1850s, 108
Sloan, John, 300
Smith, Bessie, 313, 314 (illus.)
Smith, Betty, 197, 215, 216
Smith, John, 14
Social order/patterns
  blacks in, 64–65 (*see also* Blacks)
  church and, 54–55
  and class divisions, 142, 146, 424–425
  in colonial America, 11, 46–51
  and disparities in social structure, 142–143
  family and, 54–55
  and law enforcement, 64, 160
  and leisure and recreational habits, 143
  and social/occupational mobility, 49, 50, 146, 217
  taverns and, 55–56
  "underclass," 411, 412
  violence and, 159, 160 (*see also* Social problems)
  wealth and, 142, 146
Social problems
  alcoholism and drunkenness, 64, 68, 144–145, 202–203, 317–318, 369–370
  attitudes towards poor, 51–52
  among blacks, 382–383 (*see also* Blacks; Segregation)
  in colonial period, 48–53
  crime and vice, 134, 150, 158–160, 317
  discrimination, 220 (*see also* Blacks; Immigrants; Segregation; Social order/patterns)
  disease, 65, 152–157
  drug abuse, 370, 410, 424–425
  federal solutions for, 444–445
  fire, 65 (*see also* Fires)
  gambling, 238, 318
  during Great Depression, 323–327, 335
  homelessness, 335, 410–411, 426–427
  housing, *see* Housing
  and law enforcement, 64, 160
  in market place (urban form), 80
  poverty, 5, 9, 160–165, 200–204, 383

Social problems (*cont.*)
  prostitution, 64, 197–198, 202, 238, 317,
    318, 369–370
  public health, 130, 244
  racial and socioeconomic division, 219,
    224, 368–370, 424–425, 443
  and role of rice planters, in early
    Charleston, 32
  unemployment, *see* Labor
  urban underclass, 443
  and voluntarism, 435, 443
  welfare system, *see* Social services
  working conditions, *see* Labor
Social reform
  abolitionism, 151
  as effort to impose order, 79
  fear and, 253–254
  in garden city plans, 280
  ideals behind, 150
  mechanisms for, 151
  politics and, 143, 238–243, 328–349
  and public housing, 354 (*see also* Housing)
  temperance movement, 151
  see also Urban reform
Social services
  afforded by property tax, 66
  in black church, 232
  government and, 338 (*see also*
    Government)
  settlement houses, 231, 255–257 (*see also*
    Housing)
  social workers and, 254
  welfare system, 325, 386, 424
  see also Public services
Socialist party, 231
Society for the Prevention of Pauperism, 161
Society for the Promotion of Arts,
    Agriculture, and Economy (1765), 46
South Carolina, 18. *See also individual cities*
South Bronx, New York, 369, 381, 482
South End, Boston, Massachusetts, 350
Soyer, Raphael, 335
Spain, 18–20, 44
Spanish-American War, 269
Spatial organization, 1, 4, 9
  and city expansion, 269–270
  of colonial towns, 74
  and crime, 160
  divisions along economic and social lines,
    78–79, 118–119, 134, 371–372
  and federal urban policy of New Deal, 333
  of French colonial settlements, 19–20
  and growth of suburbs, 290
  and immigrant settlements, 212
  of Indian villages, 13–14
  in industrial cities, 202
  industrial rings in cities, 190
  of market place (urban form), 78–79
  of New England settlements, 26

  and ordering of urban space, 276–279
  and police service, 160
  projected, during 1990s, 443
  of Spanish settlements, 18
  and transportation, 119–123, 263–265,
    308
Spock, Benjamin, 346
Sprague, Frank, 263
Springfield, Massachusetts, 27, 90
Springfield, Ohio, 275
Stamp Act crisis, 70, 71 (illus.)
Standard Oil Company, 300
Starr, Roger, 390
Stead, William T., 197
Steel industry, 186, 387
Steffens, Lincoln, 242
Steichen, Edward, 300
Steiner, Edward, 211
Stella, Joseph, 300
Stephens, Uriah, 205
Stewart, A.T., 117, 129
Stickney, Illinois, 318
Stieglitz, Alfred, 300
Stokes, Carl, 431–432
Stone, Amasa, Jr., 132
Street railways, 120. *See also* Transportation
Streets, 154–155
Strong, George Templeton, 113, 119
Stowe, Harriet Beecher, 128, 260, 261
Suarez, Xavier, 402
Suburb(s)
  criticism of, 302, 345–348
  defined, in 1815, 127
  and demographic and economic patterns,
    in 1960s, 369
  first decade of, 289
  government and, 323
  gridiron pattern in, 262
  Grosse Pointe, 299
  growth of, after World War II, 286
  idealized, 124–128
  Llewelyn Park, 125–127
  and migration from North to South, 405
  New York Times survey regarding, 436
  population growth in, 259
  as railroad communities, 289
  as streetcar developments, 262, 289
Sugar trade, 42–43
Sullivan, Louis, 74
Sumner, Charles, 100
Sunbelt, 375, 379–380, 393, 394–400
  environmental problems in, 408
  social problems in, 406–408
  urban politics in, 405
"Superblocks," 334
Supreme Court, U.S., 109, 299
  and Richmond set-aside program, 432–
    433
  and school busing, 384

Survey Graphic, 325
Sweeney, Peter B. "Brains," 243
Syracuse, New York, 96, 364

Tacoma, Washington, 267
Talmadge, Eugene, 332
Tammany Hall, 144, 239–240, 321
Tampa, Florida, 339, 429
Taxation
  assessments, 30
  and central cities, 385
  incentives, 345
  lists, 48
  in New Mexico pueblos, 16
  of property, 66, 151
  reform, 435
Taylor, Frederick W., 192
Taylor, Ralph, 365
Technology
  balloon-frame construction, 130
  building, 130, 272–273
  and change in central city, 413
  communication, 285, 316
  and decline of craftsmen, 191 (*see also*
    Artisans)
  and design of suburban homes, 130
  and development of national urban
    economy, 78
  elevators, 273
  and expanding markets, 191
  and growth in South, 339
  and growth of suburbs, 259
  and household space, 260
  and increase in workforce, 191
  influence of World War II on, 336
  information services, 376
  introduction of electricity, 269
  "knowledge functions," 414
  in market place (urban form), 78–79
  and rise of Sunbelt, 394
  role of, in shaping urban America, 5, 186–
    188, 445
  and sanitation, 244
  sewing machine, 199
  steam engine, 94
  textile, 87
  transportation, 259, 285
  and women in workforce, 198–199
Temperance movement, 151
Terre Haute, Indiana, 179
Texas, 224, 267, 394, 407
  Hispanic population in, 401, 402
  see also individual cities
Textile industry
  first mill in America, 87
  mill closings, 407
  mill towns, 88–89, 90
  in post-war South, 187
  see also Industry; Labor; Technology

Thalhimer, William, 136
Thernstrom, Stephen, 217
Thomas, Evan, 97
Thompson, William Hale "Big Bill," 317,
  319
Thomson, Reginald H., 245
Thoreau, Henry David, 129, 173
Tilden, Bill, 316
Tilden, Samuel, 240
Time magazine, 348, 395
Tobacco, 21, 25, 33, 41, 106–109
Tobacco trade, 24, 42, 72–73
Tocqueville, Alexis de, 129
Toledo, Ohio, 418
Torrio, Johnny, 317–319
Toscanini, Arturo, 309
Town Acts, of 1680 and 1705, 22–23
Town common, 26
Town plan
  in Philadelphia, 29
  in Savannah, 32–35
  as vehicle for establishing order, 84
Trade
  balance of, 40–46
  and Black Ball Line, 102
  in Boston, 27–28
  in colonial world, 38–46
  corn, 24
  cotton, 73, 99, 102, 104–109
  fish, 42
  flour, 72
  fur, 40–41, 44, 62
  horses, 43
  illegal, 42–45
  indigo, 42, 44, 72
  intraregional, 78, 95–97
  lumber, 42
  meat, 72
  molasses, 42
  and national urban economy, 78, 114
  patterns in colonial period, 42 (illus.)
  rice, 31, 42, 45, 72–73
  rum, 42–43, 72
  salt, 42, 44, 45
  with southern Europe, 44
  with Spain, 44
  sugar, 42–43
  tobacco, 24, 41, 42, 72–73
  and towns as collection points, 22
  among urban areas, 72–73
  wheat, 24, 32, 43–44
  wine, 44
  with Wine Islands, 44–45
Train, George Francis, 267
Transportation
  airplane, 298, 436
  automobile, 245, 292–296, 306, 307, 308,
    318–319
  cable car, 263

Transportation (*cont.*)
  canals, 95–96, 98
  in colonial America, 53
  and commerce, 86
  commuter railroad, 121–123
  commuting in Los Angeles, 437–438
  electric trolley/streetcar, 259, 262,
    263–266, 264 (illus.), 265 (illus.)
  and growth of urban West, 98–102
  highways, 293, 305, 356–357
  mass transit, in 1980s, 423
  omnibus, 119
  railroads, 98–102, 307–308
  steam boat, 98–102
  steam ferry, 123
  steam railroad, 97
  and suburban migrations, 263
  subway, 263, 423
  and urban development, 3–4
  and urban markets, 95
  Urban Mass Transit Administration, 423
Transportation break, 83, 99
Transportation technology, 119–123
Treatise on Domestic Economy (1841), 128
Trenton, New Jersey, 440
Triborough Bridge Authority, 305
Trillin, Calvin, 355
Tucson, Arizona, 337
Tugwell, Rexford Guy, 333–334
Tunney, Gene, 316
Tuskegee Institute, 313
Twain, Mark, 120, 173
Tweed, William Marcy, 240
Tyronza, Arkansas, 328
Tyson's Corner, Virginia, 436

Underground railroad, 141
Unemployment, *see* Labor
Union Fire Company of Philadelphia, 66
Unions, 143
  and blacks, 226
  early organization of, 204–207
  and women, 200
  see also Labor
United Company of Philadelphia for
  Promoting American Manufactures, 46
U.S. Census Bureau, 247, 375
U.S. Conference of Mayors, 332
U.S. Department of Commerce, 291
U.S. Department of Labor, 1
U.S. Housing Act of 1937 (USHA),
  331–332, 334
U.S. Patent Office, 191
United States Steel Company, 189, 190, 297,
  349
Universal Negro Improvement Association,
  315
University of North Carolina, 397, 442
University of Pennsylvania, 442

Urban culture, 182, 300, 309–317, 357–359
Urban Development Action Grant (UDAG),
  392, 434
Urban ecology, 4, 124. *See also* Environment;
  Social problems
Urban forms, five basic, 6–9, 438–439. *See
  also individual forms*
Urban-industrial core
  and changes in 1970s, 379, 380, 393
  and international commerce, 268–269
  loss of population and economic base in,
    375, 393
  in 1900, 180
Urban networks, 2–4. *See also* Trade
Urban planning
  and automobile, 295
  engineers as promoters of, 246
  federal efforts in, 332
  garden cities, 304
  and promotion of healthy environment,
    129–130
  in Radburn, New Jersey, 302–303
  regional agencies in, 442–443
  "superblock," 303
  in U.S., contrasted with England,
    340–341
  and zoning, 278–279, 346
Urban policy, 9, 434–435, 443
Urban reform, 5–6, 149–150
  and garden cities, 280
  government and, 151
  as middle-class movement, 78–79
  in Reagan administration, 411
  religion and, 150
  and temperance movement, 163–164
  and urban services, 182–183
  after World War II, 348–349
Urban renewal, 67, 367, 416
  critique of, 359
  and Model Cities program, 365, 366
Urban Renewal Administration (URA), 350
Urbanization/urban growth
  after 1970, 375
  American Revolution and, 77
  attitudes toward, 74, 171–175
  and change in central city, 296–297
  and civil rights movement, 361
  colonial patterns of, 11–12, 21–22, 28, 72
  and cotton in South, 104–109
  cyclical nature of, 41
  and development of national economy,
    77–78
  as distinctive process in U.S., 4–6
  dominant features in, 50
  downtown as corporate center, 414
  downtown revitalization, 416–418
  as dynamic process, 445
  and environmental concerns, 165
  from 1790 to 1870, 77

gentrification of neighborhoods, 420–421
historic preservation, 416–417, 419–420
and industrialization, 87
influence of countryside on, 25
and intraregional trade, 98
land and, 404, 444
poverty and, 164
price-distance relationship and, 3
public policy and, 78–80
and radial center, 179–180, 181–182
regional imbalances and, 73
and rehabilitation, 416
and residential neighborhoods, 118–128,
    131
service economy and, 411
and social tensions, 441–442
in South, 73
and spatial and cultural separation, 78–79,
    424, 427
and spatial and economic division, 160
specialization and segregation of the city,
    181
and suburban exodus, 369
in Sunbelt, 405
technocrats and, 245–247
and urban failure, 40
urban growth coalitions, 361–362
in West, 81–86
Urbanna, Virginia, 23

Van Vechten, Carl, 315
Vaux, Calvert, 169, 171
Veiller, Lawrence, 251–252
Vernon, Samuel, 50
Violence, *see* Social problems
Virginia, 25, 33, 70, 413
    Public Works Administration in, 328
    railroad building in, 101
    see also individual cities
Virginia Company of London, 21
Vital fringe (urban form), 8, 285
Voinovich, George, 388
Volunteers in Service to America (VISTA),
    434
Voting Rights Act, 402–404

Wabash, Indiana, 269
Wall Street Journal, 395, 397, 405
Wallace, George, 395
Walling, William English, 232
Walsh, William, 364
Walter, Bruno, 309
Waltham, Massachusetts, 88
War of 1812, 102
War on Poverty, 360
War Production Board, 336
Ware, James E., 249
Ware Shoals, South Carolina, 407
Warehouse Act of 1730, 24

Warehouse towns, 24
Warner, Sam Bass, Jr., 217, 262
Washington, Booker T., 230, 232, 313
Washington, D.C., 22, 84, 275, 293, 413
    black elected officials in, 431
    and black flight, 426
    black population in, 362
    Capital Beltway, 356–357
    character of, 173
    gentrification in, 421
    Georgetown, 420
    life expectancy in, 383
    Metro system, 423
    residential segregation in, 226
    Union Station transformation, 417
    violence in, 158, 425–426
    Willard Hotel, 414–415, 416
Washington, George, 172
Washington, Harold, 431, 432
Washingtonian, 424
Washingtonians (temperance group), 163
Wealth
    distribution of, in colonial period, 48–51
    and ethnic culture, 218
    and industrial expansion, 192
    in multicentered metropolis, 9
    and poverty in American urban growth,
        5
    and residential distinctions, 131
    and social status, *see* Social order/patterns
Weber, Adna F., 265
Weinstein, Bernard, 405
Weiss, Hymie, 319
Welfare services, *see* Social services
Wells, H.G., 440
Welworth, England, 304
West Indies, 31, 42–43, 45
West, Roy, 432
Wheat trade, 24, 32, 43–44
Wheeling, Virginia, 97
White, Alfred T., 351
White, E.B., 357
White, John, 14
White, Kevin, 367
Whitefield, George, 54
Whiteman, Paul, 312
Whitman, Walt, 12, 168–169, 171–172,
    174
Whitmire, Kathy, 404
Whitmire, South Carolina, 407
Whitney, Eli, 104
Whyte, William, 345
Williams, Daniel Hale, 231
Williams, Fannie Barrier, 225
Williamsburg, Virginia, 41, 69
    coffee houses in, 55
    as colonial capital, 21–23
    town plan of, 22–23
Wilson, Edmund, 324

Wilson, William Julius, 383
Wine Islands, 44–45
Wine trade, 44
Winthrop, John, 16, 26, 64, 221
Wolfe, Thomas, 319
Women
  in colonial America, 51–52
  role of, in nineteenth century, 117
  and social change, 261
  see also Labor; Social problems
Wood, Edith, 331
Wood, Fernando, 110
Woodville, Mississippi, 407
Woolworth, Frank, 274, 300
Worcester, Massachusetts, 97
Workers' associations, 143
Workhouses, 51–52
Working Men's Party, 143
Works Progress Administration (WPA), 327
World War I, 179
World War II, 336, 339, 342
Wright, Carroll, 200, 250, 265

Wright, Frank Lloyd, 261, 305–306, 346, 440

Yamasaki, Minoru, 352
Yonkers, New York, 261
York, South Carolina, 32
Young, Andrew, 430, 432, 433
Young, Brigham, 84, 221
Young, Coleman, 431, 433
Young Men's Christian Association (YMCA), 231, 291, 320
Young Men's Hebrew Association (YMHA), 320
Young Women's Christian Association (YWCA), 231
Youngstown, Ohio, 387
"Yuppies," 421

Zelig, "Big Jack," 317
Ziegfeld, Florenz, 272
Zoning, *see* Urban planning